Mike Meyers' Computer Skills

Survey of Operating Systems

Jane Holcombe and Charles Holcombe

McGraw-Hill/Osborne

New York   Chicago   San Francisco
Lisbon   London   Madrid   Mexico City   Milan
New Delhi   San Juan   Seoul   Singapore   Sydney   Toronto

McGraw-Hill/Osborne
2100 Powell Street, 10th Floor
Emeryville, California 94608
U.S.A.

To arrange bulk purchase discounts for sales promotions, premiums, or fund-raisers, please contact **McGraw-Hill/Osborne** at the above address. For information on translations or book distributors outside the U.S.A., please see the International Contact Information page immediately following the index of this book.

Survey of Operating Systems

234567890 QPD QPD 019876543

ISBN 0-07-222511-4

This book was composed with Corel VENTURA™ Publisher.

Publisher
BRANDON A. NORDIN

Vice President & Associate Publisher
SCOTT ROGERS

Editorial Director
GARETH HANCOCK

Acquisitions Editor
CHRISTOPHER C. JOHNSON

Senior Project Editor
LEEANN PICKRELL

Acquisitions Coordinator
ATHENA HONORE

Peer Reviewers
ROBERT A. ANDREWS, II, ERIC S. ECKLUND, JORGE GARCIA, LEWIS PULSIPHER, KENNETH WALLACE, PATRICIA WHITE

Development Editor
JILL BATISTICK

Copy Editor
JUDY ZIAJKA

Proofreader
STEFANY OTIS

Indexer
DAVID HEIRET

Computer Designers
CARIE ABREW, ELIZABETH JANG

Illustrators
LYSSA WALD, MELINDA MOORE LYTLE, KURT KRAMES, MICHAEL MUELLER

Cover Design
GREG SCOTT

Series Design
JOHN WALKER, PETER F. HANCIK

■ About the Authors

Jane Holcombe (A+, Network+, MCSE, MCT, CTT+, and CNA) is a pioneer in the field of PC support training. In 1983, she installed a LAN for her employer, a financial planning company. Since 1984, she has been an independent trainer, consultant, and course content author, creating and presenting courses on PC operating systems. Through the late 1980s and early 1990s, these courses were taught nationwide. She also co-authored a set of networking courses for the consulting staff of a large network vendor. In the early 1990s, she worked with both Novell and Microsoft server operating systems, finally focusing on the Microsoft operating system and achieving her MCSE certification for Windows NT 3.*x*, Windows NT 4.0, and Windows 2000.

Chuck Holcombe has a high-tech background in the use of computers in the nuclear and aerospace fields. In his 15 years at Control Data Corporation, he was successively a programmer, technical sales analyst, salesman, and sales manager in the field marketing force. He ran the Executive Seminar program and was Control Data's liaison to the worldwide university community, and he was a market development manager for Plato, Control Data's computer-based education system.

For the past 23 years, he has been an independent trainer and consultant. He has authored and delivered many training courses, is a skilled writer and editor, and is used to creating complex written materials. For a while, he claimed he was semi-retired, but writing books like this one is too much work for him to be able to say that any more.

The Holcombes have authored the *MCSE Guide to Designing a Microsoft Windows 2000 Network Infrastructure* (Course Technology) and both the *A+ Certification Press Lab Manual* and the *MCSE Certification Press Windows 2000 Professional Lab Manual* (McGraw-Hill/Osborne). They also contributed to *Windows 2000 Administration* (McGraw-Hill/Osborne).

■ About the Series Editor

Michael Meyers is the industry's leading authority on A+ and Network+ certification. He is the president and co-founder of Total Seminars, LLC, a provider of PC and network repair seminars, books, videos, and courseware for thousands of organizations throughout the world. Mike has been involved in the computer and network repair industry since 1977 as a technician, instructor, author, consultant, and speaker. Author of several popular PC books and A+ and Network+ courseware, Mike is also the series editor for both the highly successful Mike Meyers' Certification Passport series and the new Mike Meyers' Computer Skills series, both published by McGraw-Hill/Osborne. Mike holds multiple industry certifications and considers the moniker "computer nerd" a compliment.

■ About the Contributors

The depth and breadth of today's operating systems makes it almost impossible to be deeply knowledgeable about all of them. We were fortunate to have the help of Lee Cottrell, who assisted with the chapter on Windows XP and wrote the chapter on Linux; Nigel Parry and Ken Harper, who wrote the chapter on Mac OS 9 and OS X; and Brian Underdahl, who assisted with the chapter on Windows 2000. We give our thanks to all four accomplished wordsmiths for their mighty contributions to this book.

Lee M. Cottrell has been teaching networking, hardware, and computer programming at the Bradford School in Pittsburgh for seven years. In addition to his teaching duties, Mr. Cottrell advises students, maintains some of the school's networks and computer equipment, and writes curriculum for 10 Bradford School programs. Lee graduated magna cum laude from the University of Pittsburgh with a B.S. degree in pure mathematics. Most recently, he completed an M.S. degree in information science at the University of Pittsburgh.

Nigel Parry is a journalist who has been a Mac user since the 1980s and is regularly cited in national and international publications on issues relating to the development of the Internet in the Middle East. Today, Nigel develops large informational websites for nonprofit organizations through his company, nigelparry.net.

Ken Harper is a freelance web and graphic designer with a B.A. degree in photojournalism from Western Kentucky University. He most recently worked as a multimedia content developer for MSNBC, creating content for MSNBC.com's Year in Pictures 2001 and its coverage of the Olympics in Salt Lake City. Ken works on a freelance basis through his company, ironcladimages.com.

Brian Underdahl is a well-known author of computer books. He has authored or co-authored over 60 titles for publishers such as McGraw-Hill/Osborne, IDG Books Worldwide, Hungry Minds, Que/Macmillan, and John Wiley & Sons. In addition, Brian has written for magazines such as *PC World*.

■ About the Peer Reviewers

This book was greatly influenced by the dedicated group of teachers and subject-matter experts who reviewed this book and whose suggestions made it so much better. To them we give our heartfelt thanks.

Robert A. Andrews, II (MCP, MCSE, MCT, CCNA, Network+) is a certification training specialist and technical coordinator at the Pittsburgh Technical Institute in Pittsburgh, Pennsylvania. He is also a consultant and trainer at InteliZone Consulting, where he is a dedicated network and computer systems specialist with extensive experience and training in PC and network installation, configuration, support, documentation, and troubleshooting.

Eric S. Ecklund is an instructor in the Management and Computer Applications Department of Cambria-Rowe Business College. Eric earned a B.S. degree and Pennsylvania education certificate from the University of Pittsburgh and an M.B.A. degree from Seton College.

Jorge Garcia is a senior instructor at Heald College in San Francisco, California, and teaches operating systems and microcomputer hardware.

Lewis Pulsipher is an instructor at Central Carolina Community College. He founded a Kaypro (CP/M) computer users group and taught continuing education computer literacy and programming classes full time for five years. Thereafter, he took a job as a database programmer and systems analyst at a large Army medical center. In the course of nearly 10 years there, he became founder and chief of PC and networking support, as well as the organization's first Internet and intranet webmaster. When he is not teaching, he spends his time writing. "In a former life," as he likes to say, he designed several published strategic board games, among them the classic Britannia. He holds a Ph.D. degree from Duke University.

Kenneth Wallace is the director of business programs at Craven Community College in New Bern, North Carolina, where he teaches programming, networking, information systems, and Internet technologies. A charter member of the North Carolina Computer Instructor's Association, he is past president, president-elect, and a member of the leadership team since the association's inception. He is also past president of the Coastal Plains DPMA chapter and a member of IBM Partners in Education.

Patricia White is an associate professor at Livingstone College in North Carolina, where she chairs the Computer Information Systems program. Among her many credentials are a Ph.D. degree in information systems and an Education Specialist degree in computer science from Nova Southeastern University in Ft. Lauderdale, Florida. She also holds an M.B.A. degree from Metropolitan University in Orlando, Florida, and a B.S. degree in marketing from Florida Southern College.

■ Acknowledgments

We once thought writing was lonely work. For this book, that was true only when we sometimes worked through the night to meet deadlines. We were always aware of being part of a remarkable team. Before a single word was written, there were many people involved in creating the concept for this book, including Chris Johnson, Mike Meyers, Athena Honore, and the many instructors who were interviewed to discover just what an effective operating system survey book needed to be. We wrote our first outline for this book based on their feedback, and we continued to rely on many of them as peer reviewers who scrutinized each chapter of the book, giving us invaluable feedback on the relevancy and accuracy of the content. It is hard to imagine a book receiving more attention through its many stages of writing and revision.

This is the first book in a new Mike Meyers series, and we were lucky to have Mike as the series editor. His insights and sometimes pungent comments helped greatly.

Athena filled many roles in addition to acting as dispatcher, time keeper, and cat herder while coordinating the flow of chapter versions and reviews back and forth among the many parties. Her editing suggestions were valuable.

Jill Batistick again performed her magic for us as development editor on this book, nailing our toes to the floor to ensure that we had readable text that carefully followed the pedagogy and making sure that we maintained the correct tone and flow. It also fell to her to consolidate the feedback from the many reviewers into a single document for us to work on. In this way, she shielded us from having to comb through the multiple reviewer feedback forms on our own and allowed us to focus on writing content.

Chris Johnson not only did the market research and convinced Osborne of the need for this book series but he designed the pedagogy, conceived the layout and design and watched over its development through every step. He was always available to answer questions and to offer encouragement. He, more than anyone, worked to understand the needs of instructors and students and directed the book's progress to ensure that it was always aligned with student and instructor needs. In so many ways, this is really his book, and we greatly appreciate the chance to work with him.

LeeAnn Pickrell and her staff were wonderful editors. Her professionalism coupled with her sense of humor (she laughs at our jokes) made her a delight to work with. In particular, we'd like to acknowledge the copy editing skills of Judy Ziajka, who took text that we thought pretty good and made it so much better. We thank you both!

We greatly appreciate the expertise of the production group. Elizabeth Jang and Carie Abrew did the actual layout and Lyssa Wald made sure the photos and screen shots were the best they could possibly be. They all worked hard to make the book look wonderful. Creating and laying out the many elements of this complex book design was a huge task, and they handled it with aplomb.

We truly appreciate all who worked hard to make this book what it is. Thank You!

■ *We joyfully dedicate this book to our grandson Dane Holcombe—who has entered a world of possibility and infinite potential....*

About This Book

■ Important Technology Skills

Information technology (IT) offers many career paths, leading to occupations in such fields as PC repair, network administration, telecommunications, Web development, graphic design, and desktop support. To become competent in any IT field, *however, you need certain basic computer skills. The Mike Meyers' Computer Skills series builds a foundation for success in the IT field by introducing you to fundamental technology concepts and giving you essential computer skills.*

Step-by-Step *exercises put concepts into practice.*

Notes, Tips, *and* **Warnings** *create a road map for success.*

Cross-Check *questions develop reasoning skills: ask, compare, contrast, and explain.*

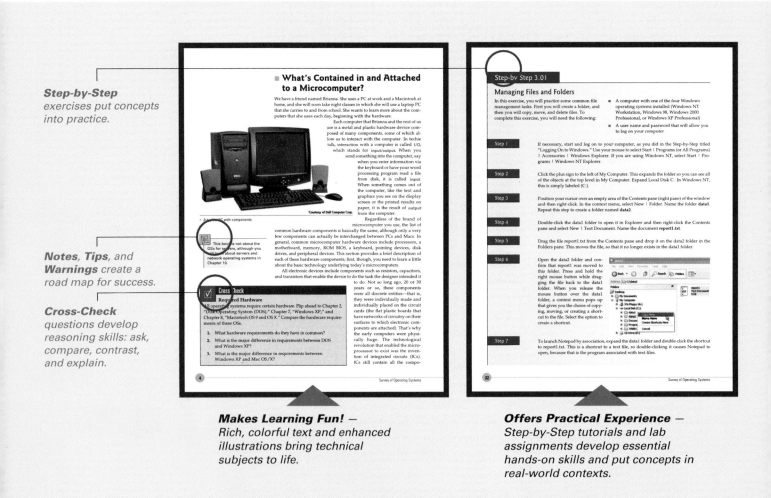

Makes Learning Fun! — *Rich, colorful text and enhanced illustrations bring technical subjects to life.*

Offers Practical Experience — *Step-by-Step tutorials and lab assignments develop essential hands-on skills and put concepts in real-world contexts.*

Proven Learning Method Keeps You on Track

The Mike Meyers' Computer Skills series is structured to give you a practical working knowledge of baseline IT skills and technologies. The series' active learning methodology guides you beyond mere recall and, through thought-provoking activities, labs, and sidebars, helps you develop critical thinking, diagnostic, and communication skills.

Effective Learning Tools

This colorful, pedagogically rich book is designed to make learning easy and enjoyable and to help you develop the skills and critical thinking abilities that will enable you to adapt to different job situations and troubleshoot problems.

Jane Holcombe's and Chuck Holcombe's proven ability to explain concepts in a clear, direct, even humorous way makes these books interesting, motivational, and fun.

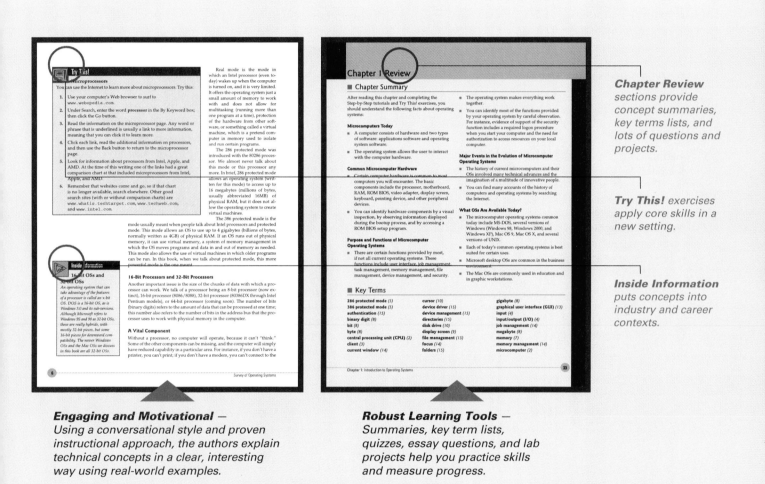

Chapter Review sections provide concept summaries, key terms lists, and lots of questions and projects.

Try This! exercises apply core skills in a new setting.

Inside Information puts concepts into industry and career contexts.

Engaging and Motivational —
Using a conversational style and proven instructional approach, the authors explain technical concepts in a clear, interesting way using real-world examples.

Robust Learning Tools —
Summaries, key term lists, quizzes, essay questions, and lab projects help you practice skills and measure progress.

Each chapter includes:

- **Learning Objectives** that set measurable goals for chapter-by-chapter progress

- **Four-Color Illustrations** that give you a clear picture of the technologies

- **Step-by-Step Tutorials** that teach you to perform essential tasks and procedures hands-on

- **Try This!, Cross-Check,** and **Inside Information** sidebars that encourage you to practice and apply concepts in real-world settings

- **Notes, Tips,** and **Warnings** that guide you through difficult areas

- **Chapter Summaries** and **Key Terms Lists** that provide you with an easy way to review important concepts and vocabulary

- **Challenging End-of-Chapter Tests** that include vocabulary-building exercises, multiple-choice questions, essay questions, and on-the-job lab projects

CONTENTS

FOREWORD FROM MIKE MEYERS

This book, like the other books in this series, is designed for exactly one function: to give you a broad introduction and overview of various aspects of the information technologies (IT) world. If you're new to computers, then welcome! This book is for you. If you're trying to decide where you want to go within the big world of IT, then again welcome—this book will help you sort out the many options and figure out where your interests may or may not lie. Do you want to become a Microsoft Windows expert? Do you want to get into troubleshooting and repair of PCs? What about becoming a network administrator? These books will help you understand the many aspects of IT and the many jobs within the IT world that are available.

So how will this book help you understand what IT is all about? Well, let's start by exploring the text in front of you right now. Like all of the books in this series, it is written in a very relaxed, conversational style that's a pleasure to read. We've tossed the staid, boring technical writing style out the window and instead write as though we're speaking directly to you—because as far as we're concerned, we are. In this and the other books in this series, we aren't afraid of the occasional contraction, nor do we worry about staying in third person. We've pretty much dumped all those other dry, pedantic rules that most technical writing has reduced itself to. I've suffered reading those books, and I swore when it came time to put together this series that we were going to break that mold—and we have! With over a million copies now in print using this series' conversational style, we think a lot of folks agree with what we're doing.

Keep your finger on this page and leaf through this book for a moment. Isn't it beautiful? Sure, there are plenty of exercises and questions for you to use to practice your skills, but let the left side of your brain take a nap and let the right side appreciate just how attractive a book this is. The four-color printing and all of the colorful elements give the book what I describe very scientifically as a "happy feeling"—akin to walking the aisle at a grocery store.

Last—and this is very important—you'll never find yourself lost in any of these books. You'll never get blindsided by a term that hasn't been defined earlier. You won't find yourself reading one topic and suddenly find yourself grinding gears as new, totally unrelated topics smack you in the face. Every topic leads from simple to complex, from broad to detailed, and from old to new, building concept upon concept while you read, making the book hard to put down. This is what I call Flow, and it's the most important aspect of these books.

So enjoy your reading. If you have any questions, feel free to contact me at michaelm@totalsem.com.

Michael D. Meyers

Mike Meyers

INTRODUCTION

■ What Will You Learn?

In this book, you'll learn what operating systems are and why they are necessary—why they are so very important that they are worth studying early in your career. You'll learn about how operating systems work, and perhaps most important for your future peace of mind, you'll learn how to make them behave and do just what you want them to do. You'll learn how different OSs, and different versions of OSs, tackle the same problems. You'll learn where they are similar and where they are different. Best of all, you'll learn to be comfortable with almost any operating system you'll encounter on the job. This book is organized into ten chapters:

- Chapter 1, *Introduction to Operating Systems*, will give you an overview of microcomputer hardware and will introduce you to the basic functions common to all operating systems. This stuff is important because one of the major functions of an operating system is to manage computer hardware.

- Chapter 2, *DOS*, (Disk Operating System) was shipped with the first IBM personal computers in the early 1980s and despite the dominance of the Windows operating systems, DOS still has many relevant applications today. In this chapter, you'll learn how to use DOS to create startup disks, describe the bootup process, use the command-line interface, enter commands, manage files, work with DOS in Windows, and troubleshoot problems.

- Chapter 3, *The Windows Desktop*, will introduce you to the features common to Windows' graphical user interface (GUI). In this chapter, you'll learn how to navigate in Windows, manage files, configure the Windows desktop, run applications in Windows, log off and shut down, and troubleshoot common problems.

- Chapter 4, *Windows NT 4.0 Workstation*, is an exploration of an operating system still popular with many companies and organizations. This chapter will teach you how to install, configure, customize, and manage a Windows NT 4.0 Workstation. You'll also manage security for users, files, and printers as well as do some troubleshooting.

- Chapter 5, *Windows 98*, discusses the first Windows operating system that Microsoft targeted for the consumer. It certainly succeeded on that account, but a lot of business users adopted it, too. So this chapter will teach you how to install and configure Windows 98. It will also teach you how to manage users, files, and printers, and troubleshoot.

- Chapter 6, *Windows 2000 Professional*, covers the Windows operating system that combined the friendly, consumer-oriented versions of Windows with the robust nature of the Windows NT products. This chapter will give you the skills you'll need to install, configure, manage, and troubleshoot Windows 2000.

- Chapter 7, *Windows XP Professional*, is the newest of the Microsoft Windows operating systems. This chapter will give you a basics-and-beyond tutorial of the most stable Windows system released so far.

- Chapter 8, *Macintosh OS 9 and OS X*, is all about the Apple Macintosh OS 9 and Macintosh OS X operating systems (the *X* stands for 10). This chapter will not only teach you about the operating systems found on most Apple computers, it will also give you a chance to compare and contrast these Macintosh operating systems with their Windows rivals. Along the way, you'll learn how to install and configure a Mac OS as well as get to know the Mac workspace.

- Chapter 9, *Linux*, is about an open-source operating system based on UNIX. Because Linux is used to run many large networks and web systems, it's important to know something about this operating system. Linux and UNIX are identical in many ways, so most of the things you'll learn in this chapter you can do in a UNIX environment. Among other things, you'll work with Linux commands, manage files and folders, use the Gnome desktop, configure Linux, and troubleshoot problems. All of the examples in this chapter are based on Red Hat Linux 7.3.

- Chapter 10, *Introduction to Network Server Operating Systems*, provides a good introduction to computer networking and network operating systems. While most of this book teaches you about the client, or user, side of operating systems, this chapter will give you a peek at the network server operating systems—the software that connects us to each other. You'll have to learn this stuff sooner or later: Why not now?

We don't want to simply give you an encyclopedia of information because we don't want you to feel like you're standing in front of an information fire hose! Rather, we're going to present just the key points about operating systems and guide you in your own exploration of the specifics of the technology. This book is designed to teach you skills that you'll need to be successful on the job.

Walk and Talk Like a Pro

Each chapter starts with a list of learning objectives followed by lucid explanations of each topic, supported by real-world, on-the-job scenarios and a liberal use of graphics and tables. To give you hands-on experience and to help you "walk the walk," each chapter contains detailed Step-by-Step tutorials and short Try This! exercises that enable you to practice the concepts. To help you "talk the talk," each chapter contains definitions of computer terms, summarized in a Key Terms list and compiled into a Glossary at the end of the book. Be ready for a Key Term Quiz at the end of each chapter!

Troubleshoot Like a Pro

While there is a ton of good information in this book, one book simply can't give you everything you need to know about operating systems. So in addition to providing you a solid introduction to operating systems, we'll also give you the tools that will help you help yourself, which is a valuable asset when you're on the job. For example, we'll show you how to use the help files found in all operating systems and we'll teach you how to use the Internet to find information that will help you troubleshoot problems.

Think Like a Pro

We've also included Inside Information sidebars, which provide insight into some of the subtleties of life with computers and Cross Checks that help you understand how OSs are similar and how they differ. Notes and Tips are sprinkled throughout the chapters, and Warnings help prevent mishaps (or emotional meltdowns). At the end of each chapter, a Key Term Quiz, Multiple-Choice Quiz, and Essay Quiz help you measure what you've learned and hone your ability to present information on paper. The Lab Projects challenge you to independently complete tasks related to what you've just learned.

■ Resources for Teachers

Teachers are our heroes to whom we give our thanks and for whom we have created a powerful collection of time-saving teaching tools that are available on CD-ROM, including:

- An Instructor's Manual that maps to the organization of the textbook
- Answer key to the quizzes and projects in the textbook
- ExamView® Pro testbank software that generates a wide array of paper or network-based tests, and features automatic grading
- Hundreds of questions, written by experienced IT instructors
- Wide variety of question types and difficulty levels, allowing teachers to customize each test to maximize student progress
- Engaging PowerPoint® slides on the lecture topics

Introduction to Operating Systems

"The future isn't what it used to be."

—Yogi Berra

Understanding microcomputer operating systems (OSs) is critical to your future success in life. Well, it is. Just believe us. You don't? You say you drive a car just fine, but you don't understand the engine, transmission, and other systems? So why can't you just use your computer? Why do you have to even know it has an OS? If you successfully operate a car, you know more about its internals than you admit. You turn on the ignition, take the car out of park, press the accelerator, and drive down the street. You stop it (in time, usually). Maybe you use your car to drive to work, school, shopping, or the lake or beach, making the car your tool, just as your computer is a tool to write a letter, send e-mail, create a report, or create a graphic.

This chapter is an overview of microcomputer operating systems. It begins by defining what a microcomputer is and what types of microcomputers you may encounter. Expanding on this, it describes the physical components you can expect to find in a microcomputer. Then, after a brief definition of OSs and their purpose, this chapter presents an in-depth discussion of OSs and the functions they perform. Next, you'll take a brief journey back in time to learn the history of microcomputer operating systems. Finally, you will be introduced to the microcomputer OSs in common use today, and you'll consider when you would use each of them.

In this chapter, you will learn how to:

- Describe the microcomputers in use today
- Identify common computer hardware components
- Describe the purpose and functions of microcomputer operating systems
- Describe major events in the evolution of microcomputer operating systems
- List and compare the common microcomputer operating systems

■ Microcomputers Today

Before you learn about microcomputer operating systems, you may have a few more general questions: What is a microcomputer? What types of microcomputers are used today? You will find the answers to these questions in this section.

What Is a Microcomputer?

A **microcomputer** is a computer built around a special integrated circuit (IC), or chip (a small electronic component made up of transistors and other miniaturized parts), which performs the calculations, or processing, for the computer. Often referred to as the brain of a computer, this chip is the **central processing unit (CPU)**, but is also called a **microprocessor**, or simply a processor. A microcomputer is small enough, and even cheap enough, to be dedicated to the use of a single person. This was a revolutionary idea in the 1970s when microcomputers first became available.

Courtesy of Dell Computer Corp.

• A typical PC with components

What Types of Microcomputers Are Used Today?

The word *microcomputer* was first widely used in the late 1970s to describe the early forms of these computers. We're now more likely to use the term **personal computer (PC)**, which applies to computers that comply with hardware standards set and supported by Microsoft, Intel (the largest computer chip manufacturer), and to a lesser extent, other companies. We call these the Microsoft/Intel standards (also called Wintel). However, many important microcomputers don't comply with these standards—most notably, computers from Apple and the small handheld computers that are growing in popularity today.

Desktops and Laptops

Today the majority of computers found on desktops in private and public organizations comply with the Microsoft/Intel standard, with Macintosh computers a distant, but significant second. The Macintosh has ardent supporters in the education area and in any line of work requiring high-quality graphical and multimedia support. Most of the portable laptop or notebook computers available today are Microsoft/Intel compatible.

Furthermore, the types of microcomputers can be distinguished based on how they are used. This book is dedicated to the operating systems used by individuals on desktop and portable microcomputers, whether they are PCs or Macs.

Servers

A PC or Mac can also be used as a **server**, which is a computer that plays one of several important roles in a network. In all of these roles, it provides services to other computers, and the computers on the receiving end of these services are referred to as **clients**.

What kind of services does a server provide? A server may be used to store all of the data files of the users in a department or company—this is a file server—and if a server has one or more printers connected to it that it shares with users on the network, it is called a print server; these are often combined into a file and print server. Other servers may offer messaging services (e-mail and fax), web services, and many, many other services. Note that one server can offer multiple services at the same time.

Handheld Devices

There are also many different handheld devices, and they are often proprietary devices that comply with no, or very few, standards in their design. Despite their size, they are still called microcomputers because they are built around microprocessors. They include a wide variety of products ranging from simple handheld computers to multifunction mobile devices. Some handheld computers are dedicated to a single purpose; examples include the handheld devices that employees use in grocery stores to track inventory. Others are wireless phones that not only allow voice communications, but also let you connect to the Internet and view your e-mail on their tiny color screens.

> In this book, we'll use the term *microcomputer* to refer to all small computers as a group, and we'll use the term *PC* when discussing computers that comply with the Microsoft/Intel standards, both desktop and portable. We'll use the term *Mac* to refer to today's Apple computers (which include several models), both desktop and portable.

> This book is not about the OSs for servers, although you will learn about servers and network operating systems in Chapter 10.

▪ What's Contained in and Attached to a Microcomputer?

We have a friend named Brianna. She uses a PC at work and a Macintosh at home, and she will soon take night classes in which she will use a laptop PC that she carries to and from school. She wants to learn more about the computers that she uses each day, beginning with the hardware.

Each computer that Brianna and the rest of us use is a metal and plastic hardware device composed of many components, some of which allow us to interact with the computer. In techie talk, interaction with a computer is called **I/O**, which stands for **input/output**. When you send something into the computer, say when you enter information via the keyboard or have your word processing program read a file from disk, it is called **input**. When something comes out of the computer, like the text and graphics you see on the display screen or the printed results on paper, it is **output** from the computer.

Try This!

More About Handhelds

Although this book will mention handheld devices from time to time, you will not really study these devices in this book. Satisfy your curiosity about this growing area. Try this:

1. Use an Internet search engine, such as www.google.com, and search on the term *handheld*. Browse through the sites you find in the search engine. Results will vary, but some likely sites are www.Microsoft.com/mobile/handheldpc, www.handheldmed.com, and www.hhp.com.

2. What OSs do the handheld devices you discovered use?

3. What industries are using handheld devices?

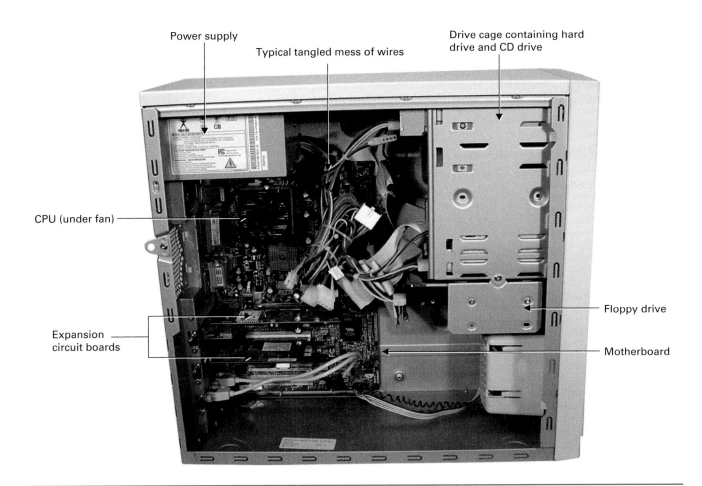

Power supply

Typical tangled mess of wires

Drive cage containing hard drive and CD drive

CPU (under fan)

Expansion circuit boards

Floppy drive

Motherboard

• Open computer showing internal components

Regardless of the brand of microcomputer you use, the list of common hardware components is basically the same, although only a very few components can actually be interchanged between PCs and Macs. In general, common microcomputer hardware devices include processors, a motherboard, memory, ROM BIOS, a keyboard, pointing devices, disk drives, and peripheral devices. This section provides a brief description of each of these hardware components; first, though, you need to learn a little about the basic technology underlying today's microcomputers.

Cross Check

Required Hardware

All operating systems require certain hardware. Flip ahead to Chapter 2, "Disk Operating System (DOS);" Chapter 7, "Windows XP;" and Chapter 8, "Macintosh OS 9 and OS X." Compare the hardware requirements of these OSs.

1. What hardware requirements do they have in common?

2. What is the major difference in requirements between DOS and Windows XP?

3. What is the major difference in requirements between Windows XP and Mac OS/X?

All electronic devices include components such as resistors, capacitors, and transistors that enable the device to do the task the designer intended it to do. Not so long ago, 20 or 30 years or so, these components were all discrete entities—that is, they were individually made and individually placed on the circuit cards (the flat plastic boards that have networks of circuitry on their surfaces to which electronic components are attached). That's why the early computers were physically huge. The technological revolution that enabled the microprocessor to exist was the invention of integrated circuits (ICs). ICs still contain all the components necessary to make the device work, but they are created by special processes that vastly miniaturize all of the individual pieces and place them on a wafer (or chip) of material. Thus, today a computer chip can contain many millions of devices within it and still be only an inch or so in size.

Processor

A microcomputer always has at least one microprocessor, which is also called a central processing unit (CPU), or simply a processor. Like many of the electronic components in a computer, a processor is an integrated circuit (IC), or chip. The processor is the central component of the computer—its brain. Like your own brain, the processor sends and receives commands to and from the computer's hardware and software. For example, when Brianna wants to print a letter she typed on her computer, she chooses the Print command. This seems like a very simple command, but it actually causes many commands to be sent to the processor: commands to transfer the file from memory to the printer, commands to communicate with the printer, and many, many others. The processor doesn't just perform calculations; it is involved in nearly everything that happens in your computer.

Intel® Pentium® 4 Processor on 0.13 Micron. Used with permission.

• Top and bottom views of a processor with many gold pins visible on the bottom

The capabilities of the processor also define the limits and capabilities of the computer, including the speed of the system. In addition, because operating systems must work closely with the processor and other hardware, an operating system is written to work with a certain specific processor and chipset. This limits your choice of OSs that you can run on a computer.

Among the distinguishing features of a processor are operation modes and the size of the chunks of data with which the processor can work.

Processor Modes

We'll use the Intel processors to briefly look at some basic processor features. The Intel 8086 and 8088 processors used in PCs in the early 1980s had a limited bag of tricks, because they had only one mode of operation: real mode. Newer Intel processors beginning with the 386DX have three modes: real mode plus two flavors of protected mode, called 286 protected mode and 386 protected mode.

Real mode is the mode in which an Intel processor (even today) wakes up when the computer is turned on, and it is very limited. It offers the operating system a small amount of memory to work with and doesn't allow for multi-tasking (running more than one program at a time), protection of the hardware from other software, or something called a virtual machine, which is a pretend computer in memory used to isolate and run certain programs.

The **286 protected mode** was introduced with the 80286 processor. We almost never talk about this mode or this processor any more. In brief, 286 protected mode allows an operating system (written for this mode) to access up to 16 megabytes (millions of bytes, usually abbreviated 16MB) of physical RAM, but it does not allow the operating system to create virtual machines.

The **386 protected mode** is the mode usually meant when people talk about Intel processors and protected mode. This mode allows an OS to use up to 4 gigabytes (billions of bytes, normally written as 4GB) of physical RAM. If an OS runs out of physical memory, it can use virtual memory, a system of memory management in which the OS moves programs and data in and out of memory as needed. This mode also allows the use of virtual machines in which older programs can be run. In this book, when we talk about protected mode, this more powerful mode is the one meant.

Inside Information

16-Bit OSs and 32-Bit OSs

An operating system that can take advantage of the features of a processor is called an x-bit OS. DOS is a 16-bit OS, as is Windows 3.0 and its sub-versions. Although Microsoft refers to Windows 95 and 98 as 32-bit OSs, these are really hybrids, with mostly 32-bit pieces, but some 16-bit pieces for downward compatibility. The newer Windows OSs and the Mac OSs we discuss in this book are all 32-bit OSs.

16-Bit Processors and 32-Bit Processors

Another important issue is the size of the chunks of data with which a processor can work. We talk of a processor being an 8-bit processor (now extinct), 16-bit processor (8086/8088), 32-bit processor (80386DX through Intel Pentium models), or 64-bit processor (coming soon). The number of bits (binary digits) refers to the amount of data that can be processed at one time;

this number also refers to the number of bits in the address bus that the processor uses to work with physical memory in the computer.

A Vital Component

Without a processor, no computer will operate, because it can't "think." Some of the other components can be missing, and the computer will simply have reduced capability in a particular area. For instance, if you don't have a printer, you can't print; if you don't have a modem, you can't connect to the Internet over a phone line—but the rest of the computer will work fine. However, without a processor, your computer simply will not work.

Motherboard and Chipset

The **motherboard** is the central circuit board of a computer. All other devices are connected to it in one way or another. It contains one or more CPU slots or sockets into which the processor(s) is plugged, the controlling chipset, some memory slots, the voltage regulator module (VRM), the ROM BIOS, and the expansion bus slots. The chipset consists of several chips that control much of the flow of signals to and from the processor and other components. It is another key element in the overall limits and capabilities of the microcomputer.

Tyan Trinity i845E. Used with permission from Tyan Computer Corporation.

- A typical motherboard with some components installed

Memory

Memory is a huge topic, but we can condense it to the one basic statement: memory *remembers*. Too simple? Let's try again. Computer **memory** involves chips that store programs and data. Got that? Here's the low-tech, but long, explanation. Memory, in a computer, refers to one of several different types. One type of memory, **random-access memory**, or **RAM**, provides the temporary storage for programs and data. RAM consists of one or more special circuit cards that contain memory chips. It is called random-access memory because each of its locations is assigned a discrete address. An address is a pointer to a specific location in memory, used by your OS to organize its use of memory. Programs and data can be stored directly in each of these addresses—thus, each memory location can be directly accessed at random.

DDR SDRAM DIMM PC2100. Copyright Micron Technology. Used with permission.

• Memory module

A Bit About Bytes

If the words *megabyte* and *gigabyte* just sound like jargon, read this. If you learned about megabytes and gigabytes before you ate your first french fries, skip this.

When we talk about storing things in memory or on disk, we use terms like **megabyte** and **gigabyte** to describe amounts of memory or disk space. To understand these terms, first consider the smallest unit of storage (disk or memory), which is a **binary digit** (abbreviated as **bit**). You can think of a single bit as being like a light switch: it is either on or off. When it is on, it represents 1; when it is off, it represents 0. Computers (or the folks who make computers) like binary notation because it can be represented by anything that has two states, like on or off. This is exactly how RAM and ROM works: with the equivalent of on and off switches. Floppy and hard disks have a metallic oxide coating that contains particles that can be magnetized (polarized) by a charge, or left unmagnetized, and can thus represent on and off states.

To put this into context, a relative of ours just called to boast that he had bought a computer with 1 gigabyte of RAM (roughly a billion bytes of RAM) and a hard drive with 120 gigabytes of disk space. (We know that computer memory and hard drives are growing rapidly, so please don't send us e-mail if that sounds like a ridiculously wimpy computer by the time you read this!)

RAM

The most important memory in your computer is the system memory, also called main or physical memory, which active programs use when they're running. System memory is volatile, meaning that when you turn off or reboot your computer, whatever is contained in memory disappears. When an advertisement for a computer states "with 512MB (megabytes) of memory," this is system memory.

```
PhoenixBIOS 4.0 Release 6.0
Copyright 1985-2000 Phoenix Technologies Ltd.
All Rights Reserved
Copyright 2000-2001 VMware, Inc.
VMware BIOS build 212

CPU = AMD Athlon  600 MHz
640K System RAM Passed
15M Extended RAM Passed
Mouse initialized
Fixed Disk 0: VMware Virtual IDE Hard Drive
ATAPI CD-ROM: VMware Virtual IDE CDROM Drive
```

● **Figure 1-1.**   BIOS bootup information

Beyond the system memory, many components in your computer, and the peripherals attached to your computer, also contain memory, but this memory is not included in system memory.

ROM BIOS

Another type of memory is **read-only memory (ROM)**, which is used to store programs more or less permanently. When you turn off your computer, the contents of ROM remain intact. So why did we say "more or less?" Because some ROM can actually be modified, using a special program and sometimes also requiring a temporary change to the hardware, but that is beyond what you need to know right now, so just think of what is contained in ROM as permanent.

The **ROM BIOS** is the chip containing the **read-only memory basic input-output system**. The BIOS is a set of program instructions for starting the computer, as well as for controlling communication between the processor and other components (the input and output). That's why this information is stored in ROM: so that it doesn't vanish when the power is turned off. Also stored in ROM is the system setup program that lets us define the basic configuration information, which is, in turn, stored in another special kind of nonvolatile (doesn't disappear when power is turned off) RAM, called CMOS RAM.

This basic configuration information includes the following:

- The type and capacity of the installed disk drives (both floppy and hard)

- The disk boot order (the order in which the system searches disks for bootup programs)

- The configuration of system memory

- The configuration of the various connectors

- The configuration of power management

- Other system-level configuration options determined by the makers of the motherboard and the creators of the ROM BIOS

ATI RADEON 9700 PRO Video Card.
Copyright ATI.

- Video adapter

Video Adapter and Display

The video adapter is a set of circuitry (either embedded in the motherboard or on a separate circuit board) that receives video control signals from the computer and sends the controlling output signals to the display screen.

A computer will usually have a **display screen**, either a **monitor** or a flat-panel display (FPD), for the visual output from the computer. Traditionally, a display screen was built around a cathode-ray tube (CRT), which is physically bulky and looks like a TV set. However, recent improvements in flat-panel displays, and rapidly falling prices, make these types of displays increasingly common since an FPD has a much smaller footprint on the desktop than a monitor with an equal-sized screen. There are several types of FPDs with varying characteristics.

Keyboard

A keyboard is an input device, usually built around a typewriter-style layout of alphanumeric and punctuation keys (commonly known as the QWERTY key layout after the first six letters in the top letter row) plus additional function, control, arrow, caps lock, and editing keys. Most computer keyboards also have a separate numeric keypad, with the exception of portable computer keyboards, which often have the keypad embedded within the alphanumeric keys (doing double duty).

- Keyboard

Pointing Device

A **pointing device** is required to move a graphical pointer called a **cursor** around a graphical user interface (GUI). A **mouse**, the most common pointing device, is roughly the size of a bar of soap and connects to the computer by a physical cable or through a wireless connection (using infrared or radio signals). When a mouse is moved around on a flat surface, its device driver (the piece of software that tells the computer what a device is doing) translates its movements into similar movements of the cursor on the display screen. Other pointing devices that provide essentially the same function include track balls, joysticks, and light pens.

- Mouse

Disk Drives

Computers today contain one or more **disk drives**, for storing data and programs. A disk drive stores data by putting it onto the surface of small spinning platters using either magnetic or optical technology. Floppy drives and hard disk drives use a magnetic technology in which each disk platter has a metal oxide coating that can be easily magnetized, and data is encoded on this surface magnetically.

A floppy disk has only a single flexible platter, usually made of Mylar, while a hard disk drive will have one or more rigid metal platters. Compact disc (CD) and digital versatile disc (DVD) drives use an optical technology in which a focused light beam generated by a tiny laser is used to read and write information on the disk. CDs and DVDs are made of plastic with a material embedded in the plastic that can be altered by the light beam when information is written to the disk, and which reflects variations in the light beam when the disk is read. Floppy and hard disks are always rewriteable, whereas CDs and DVDs come in both read-only and readable and writeable forms.

IBM Ultrastar 73LZX disk drive.
Courtesy of International Business Machines Corporation. Unauthorized use not permitted.

- A hard disk drive with the cover removed

Peripheral Devices

Peripheral device is a very broad term that pretty much covers all computer components beyond the motherboard components (processor, basic chipset, and memory). Although this term does include a great deal of "under the hood" stuff (that is, devices that are contained within the computer cabinet along with everything else), we most often use the word *peripheral* to refer to nonessential add-on devices such as digital cameras, printers, scanners, pointing devices, and external modems and disk drives.

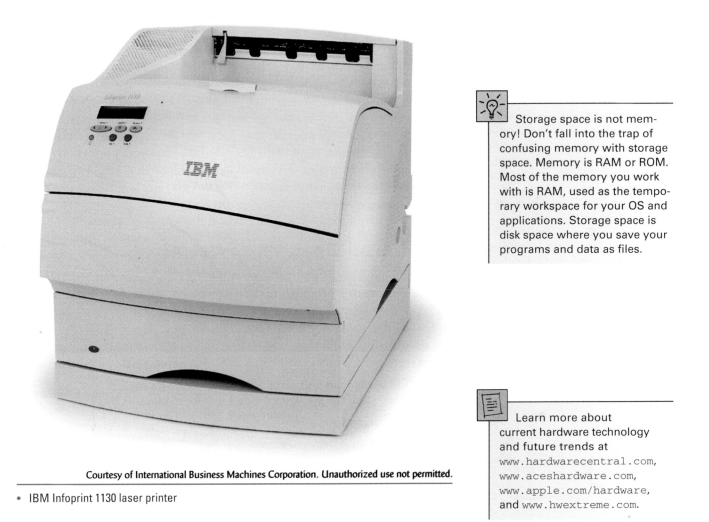

Courtesy of International Business Machines Corporation. Unauthorized use not permitted.

- IBM Infoprint 1130 laser printer

Storage space is not memory! Don't fall into the trap of confusing memory with storage space. Memory is RAM or ROM. Most of the memory you work with is RAM, used as the temporary workspace for your OS and applications. Storage space is disk space where you save your programs and data as files.

Learn more about current hardware technology and future trends at www.hardwarecentral.com, www.aceshardware.com, www.apple.com/hardware, and www.hwextreme.com.

■ Purpose and Functions of Microcomputer Operating Systems

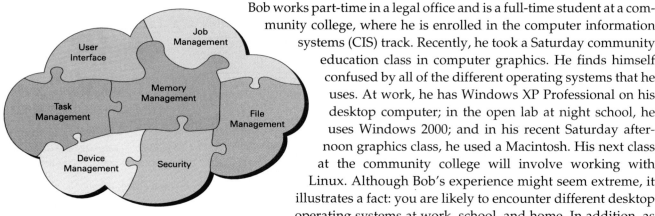

• The functions of an operating system

Bob works part-time in a legal office and is a full-time student at a community college, where he is enrolled in the computer information systems (CIS) track. Recently, he took a Saturday community education class in computer graphics. He finds himself confused by all of the different operating systems that he uses. At work, he has Windows XP Professional on his desktop computer; in the open lab at night school, he uses Windows 2000; and in his recent Saturday afternoon graphics class, he used a Macintosh. His next class at the community college will involve working with Linux. Although Bob's experience might seem extreme, it illustrates a fact: you are likely to encounter different desktop operating systems at work, school, and home. In addition, as computers proliferate, it becomes more important to learn the common characteristics that they share.

Bob spends most of his time on each computer he uses working in one or another specific application, such as a word processor, a graphical drawing program, or an Internet browser. However, he often needs to perform tasks outside of these applications, such as logging on to the computer, launching each application, managing files, and even troubleshooting the occasional problem that may arise with the computer. He has recently gone from not even realizing that such a thing as an operating system existed to wondering how he can learn to perform these common tasks in each of the different operating systems that he encounters. He wants to gain a better understanding of the OSs so that he can both perform better on the job and feel more comfortable while working on the various computers. He has decided to begin by learning what an OS is and what functions it performs, as described in the following sections.

Although a specific operating system can run effectively only on a computer with a specific type of processor and chipset, there are a variety of operating systems that will run on a PC, including MS-DOS, Microsoft Windows (any version), and UNIX (if it is a version created for PCs). Macintosh computers are proprietary and run only Apple operating systems, referred to as Mac OS followed by the version—most recently 9 and X (10).

What Is an Operating System?

An **operating system (OS)** is the program (or group of programs) that acts as the central control program for the computer. As such, it is loaded (or booted up, a derivation of the adage "lifting yourself by your own bootstraps") when the computer is turned on. Its main component (the **kernel**) always remains in memory while the computer is running. The operating system acts as an intermediary between the applications and the hardware. There are several functions performed by the operating system. We'll study them next.

User Interface

The **user interface** is the software layer, sometimes called the shell, through which the user communicates with the OS. The OS, in turn, communicates with the computer. Thus, the user interface includes the command processor, which loads programs into memory, as well as the many visual components of the operating system (what you see when you look at the monitor). On a computer running DOS, this visual component consists of a character-based command line that provides only sparse amounts of information. Figure 1-2 shows the classic DOS prompt: white characters against a screen with a blinking cursor waiting for you to type a command at the keyboard. Only a limited set of characters can appear on the screen, each in its own little equal-sized grid of space.

To become proficient with DOS, you must memorize the somewhat cryptic commands and their modifiers and subcommands. On the other hand, Apple's Mac OSs, and Microsoft's Windows operating systems all provide an information-rich **graphical user interface (GUI)** through which you communicate with the OS and the computer.

The GUI is the grouping of many dots into colorful objects that become elements that you see on the screen. Such a presentation, or interface, offers menus and graphical icons (small graphics) that allow you to use the pointing device to select programs to run and to perform many other tasks, such as opening a word-processed file.

Although you do not have to memorize arcane commands, working within a GUI does require you to learn the meaning of the various graphical pieces that make up the GUI and how to navigate among these pieces to find your programs and data. In addition, you must learn how to make a program become active (to start) so that you can get your work or play done. Figure 1-3 shows a GUI screen. Notice the icons and other graphical components, such as the bar at the bottom containing the button labeled Start.

• **Figure 1-2.** MS-DOS prompt

Although UNIX traditionally had a DOS-like interface, most current versions of UNIX also allow you to use GUIs.

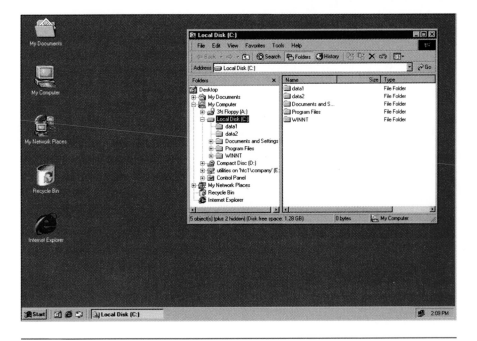

• **Figure 1-3.** A typical GUI screen

Inside Information

Programmers Make It Work!

When programmers (people who create software programs) write an application, they design the application to interact with the operating system and make all requests for hardware services through the operating system. To do this, they must write the program to use the correct commands to request services from the operating system. The operating system, in turn, interacts with the hardware on behalf of the application and fulfills the requests made by the application.

Job Management

Job management is an operating system function that controls the order and time in which programs are run. Two examples of programs that may perform this function are a scheduling program that schedules other programs or batch files to be run on a certain day and time, and a print program that manages and prioritizes multiple print jobs.

Task Management

Task management is an operating system function found in **multitasking** operating systems. Multitasking implies that a computer is simultaneously running two or more programs (tasks) at the same time. In reality, a computer cannot run more tasks simultaneously than the number of processors that exist within the computer. Because most microcomputers only have a single processor, multitasking is accomplished through a scheme that makes order out of chaos by determining which program responds to the keystrokes and mouse movements.

Task management controls the **focus** (where the system's attention is at any given moment). It also allows the user to switch between tasks by giving the focus to the application the user brings to the foreground. In Windows, this application runs in the **current window**. This is the window that is on top of other windows on the screen, and the window that receives input from the keyboard when the user types.

Memory Management

Memory management is an operating system function that manages the placement of programs and data in memory, while keeping track of where it put them. In the case of advanced operating systems, such as Windows NT, Windows 2000, and later similar Windows versions, this involves a scheme for making optimal use of memory. Virtual memory allows more code and data to be active than the actual physical system memory can hold. Using a memory management OS component called the **virtual memory manager**, these operating systems move code and data, as necessary, to a portion of the disk that has been defined as **virtual memory**. This means that this disk space is used as if it were memory, not just disk storage space. This transfer is performed for code and data that is part of any program that currently does not have the user's attention. Reason? This not-needed-right-now information does not need to be kept in RAM memory for immediate use.

The memory management function may not be included in every definition of an operating system, but it is a very important function, especially in Windows, Macintosh, and UNIX operating systems.

File Management

File management, also referred to as data management, is an operating system function that allows the operating system to be used to read, write, and modify data.

Data is organized into entities called files that are saved to storage devices (usually disks). File management also allows users to organize their files, using other special files that act as containers. These special files are called **folders** or **directories**, and they can contain other folders as well as files.

The user works with a specific logical file organization with which he or she is comfortable, while the operating system file management function relates that logical organization to the actual physical location of the file or folder so that it can store and retrieve the data.

Device Management

The **device management** function controls hardware devices through the use of special software called **device drivers**, which must be installed in the operating system. Device drivers are unique to the device and are created by the manufacturer of the device to work with a specific operating system. For instance, a printer or video adapter will come with drivers for several different operating systems. The device driver contains the commands understood by the device and uses these commands to control the device in response to requests it receives from the operating system. You need a component-specific device driver for each unique hardware component with which the operating system interacts.

Security

The **security** function of an operating system provides password-protected authentication of the user before allowing access to the local computer and may restrict what someone can do on a computer. For example, Rachel is the accounting clerk in a small company. She has confidential information on her computer, and she doesn't want just anyone to be able to walk up to her computer and look at the information stored there. What can be done with the OS to help Rachel secure her computer? You could set up her computer so that anyone getting into it must have a user account. A user account includes a name and an associated password stored inside the PC.

After you set up Rachel's account, when she logs on to her computer, she must enter her user name and password. Before giving her access to the computer, her operating system will verify that she used a valid user name and password. The validation of the user account and password is called **authentication**.

A part-time clerk, Kirsten, has just been hired to work at night entering accounts payable information into Rachel's computer. To allow Kirsten to also log on to Rachel's computer, you can create a new user account for Kirsten. Only Rachel and Kirsten can log on to this computer, but Rachel does not want Kirsten to be able to access the payroll information, also stored on Rachel's computer. Now, this is private information, right? What might be done to help Rachel with this problem? One thing you could do (if her operating system supports it) is to set up Rachel's computer so that she can assign special permissions to the files and folders on her hard disk, giving each user account the level of permission needed. For instance, Kirsten needs to be able to add accounting information to the accounts payable files, so you could give Kirsten's account the permission that will allow her to write to the files in the accounts payable folder. You will not give Kirsten's account access to any of the other folders, and you will give Rachel's account full control of all of the folders that Rachel needs to use.

■ Yesterday's Operating Systems

Ever read the book *The Rise and Fall of the Roman Empire*? Even if you haven't, you may know an oft-quoted line from it: "Those who fail to learn about the past are doomed to repeat it." Nothing could be truer in the PC world also—with a small change. Here's the Mike Meyers' amendment to that famous phrase: "Those who fail to understand older PC technology will never understand the current stuff." You would be amazed at how much of the oldest OSs are still alive and well in the newest ones!

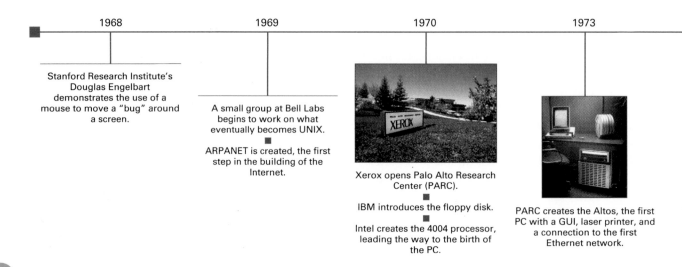

1968 Stanford Research Institute's Douglas Engelbart demonstrates the use of a mouse to move a "bug" around a screen.

1969 A small group at Bell Labs begins to work on what eventually becomes UNIX.

ARPANET is created, the first step in the building of the Internet.

1970 Xerox opens Palo Alto Research Center (PARC).

IBM introduces the floppy disk.

Intel creates the 4004 processor, leading the way to the birth of the PC.

1973 PARC creates the Altos, the first PC with a GUI, laser printer, and a connection to the first Ethernet network.

First the Machines

Computers didn't arrive just yesterday. If you want to, you can argue that they started with the computers that were designed (but never built) by Charles Babbage in the 1820s. Or perhaps you would start with the U.S. military's World War II computers. In general, consumers encountered their first microcomputers in 1977 with the introduction of Apple's Apple II, Radio Shack's TRS-80, or Commodore's PET.

Although computers and microcomputers existed before the Apple II, this computer was the first one to combine a number of critical elements to make what today is considered a microcomputer, including a keyboard, monitor, operating system, desirable and useful applications, and a reasonable price tag.

• Apple II

Then the Operating Systems

The idea for an operating system as complex as what you see on your desktop today didn't just pop into someone's head one day. In fact, an operating system as a separate entity didn't exist in the early years of digital computing (defined roughly as from World War II into the 1950s). Each computer was dedicated to a single purpose, such as performing trajectory calculations for weapons or mathematical analysis for a science lab, in addition to the system I/O functions. Operating systems evolved through many small steps, some in the form of technical advances and others in evolutionary changes in how computers were used.

Operating systems evolved because people saw the need to use computers as multipurpose devices. The "user," who at first was a government agency, research institute, or large business, would define the computer's purpose at any given time by the program chosen to run. Some early "operating systems" were developed in the 1950s to manage data storage on tape for mainframe computers, but it was much more common for application programmers to write system I/O routines (the stuff of today's OSs) right into their programs. By the mid 1960s, as disk systems became more common on large computers, operating systems were needed to manage these disks and to perform other common system-level routines.

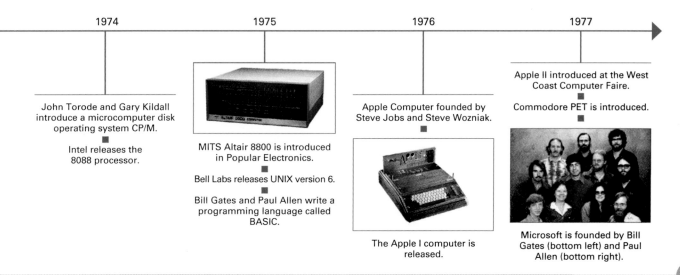

1974

John Torode and Gary Kildall introduce a microcomputer disk operating system CP/M.

Intel releases the 8088 processor.

1975

MITS Altair 8800 is introduced in Popular Electronics.

Bell Labs releases UNIX version 6.

Bill Gates and Paul Allen write a programming language called BASIC.

1976

Apple Computer founded by Steve Jobs and Steve Wozniak.

The Apple I computer is released.

1977

Apple II introduced at the West Coast Computer Faire.

Commodore PET is introduced.

Microsoft is founded by Bill Gates (bottom left) and Paul Allen (bottom right).

The computer enthusiasts who bought the earliest microcomputers of the 1970s, such as the MITS Altair, were infatuated with the technology. Slow CPU speeds, very limited memory, clumsy I/O devices, and lack of software did not deter them. They would network with like-minded people, have informal meetings and discussions, and then gather in self-help groups and form clubs like the Home Brew Computer Club in Silicon Valley. They shared their techniques for creating hardware and programming language software for these computers. Almost every one of these early microcomputers exceeded the expectations of their makers and users, but for a variety of reasons, most of the early entrepreneurial companies and their products disappeared before long.

DOS, CP/M, Apple, and the Killer App

For a microcomputer to truly be a successful, widely accepted product—used in businesses as well as by hobbyists—it had to be a tool that performed an important task; it had to have an application that people needed. That application would be called a Killer App.

One of these tasks was spreadsheet calculations. Before microcomputers, spreadsheets were created manually, on large sheets of paper. People would enter a column of numbers—say, sales for one product in a drugstore on a day-by-day basis for a month. Then the daily columns would be added up to get the total sales for that product for that month. The next column was for the next product, and so on. The process was tedious and error prone, but very valuable to the manager of the drugstore.

Thus, when VisiCalc, an electronic spreadsheet program that ran on early microcomputers, appeared, it became a very successful application. It automated this thankless job, remembering the formulas for the calculations and allowing people to recalculate a column of numbers after a change was made. VisiCalc did more than this, though: it gave people a reason to want a personal computer. Many people were introduced to VisiCalc on the Apple II computer, and this contributed to the success of the Apple II in the late 1970s. However, as the 1980s arrived, Apple failed to come out with a successor to the Apple II in a timely fashion. This strategic error gave IBM the opportunity to bring out the IBM PC.

1978

Apple Computer introduces a 5 ¼ disk drive for the Apple II.
∎
Berkeley Software Distribution (BSD) UNIX is developed at UC Berkeley.
∎
Bell Labs releases UNIX version 7.

1979

Steve Jobs visits Xerox PARC and is given demos of a GUI, icons, and a mouse.
∎
VisiCalc, the first spreadsheet program to run on a personal computer, is released.
∎
MicroPro International introduces WordStar, the first commercially successful word processing program for PCs.

1980

Microsoft announces Microsoft XENIX OS, a UNIX OS for 16-bit microprocessors.
∎
Lotus Development Corporation unveils the Lotus 1-2-3 spreadsheet program.
∎
Sony and Phillips develop first technology standards for compact disc.

1981

Adam Osborne introduces the Osborne 1.
∎
IBM introduces the IBM PC with Microsoft's BASIC in ROM and PC DOS 1.0.
∎
First time *Internet* is used to describe the ARPANET.

Another fateful series of events revolved around the choice of an OS for the IBM PC. IBM came to Microsoft, then a fledgling software company, for the BASIC interpreter, which was being used in other machines at that time. IBM also talked to Bill Gates about providing an OS; but he sent IBM to another company, Digital Research, the creators of the popular CP/M OS. Digital Research, however, refused to sign a contract with IBM, so IBM came back to Bill Gates for the OS.

The IBM PC came with Microsoft's BASIC interpreter installed in ROM, which allowed programs written in the BASIC programming language to be run on the PC. It also came with either PC DOS or a version of CP/M as the operating system for those computers that had the optional floppy drive rather than just the tape drive. IBM, however, priced CP/M far higher than it did PC DOS, which contributed to the demise of CP/M. This computer far exceeded IBM's sales forecast, which was for about a quarter of a million units during the predicted five-year lifetime of the product. According to one account, IBM took orders for half a million computers in the first few days after the IBM PC was introduced. Many who bought it were enthusiasts, who bought it in spite of its roughly $5,000 price tag for a typical configuration, just to see what it could do. However, the "IBM" name behind the product inspired many business users to buy it as well because they could see the potential of the PC.

Want to learn more about the history of PCs? Our favorite book on the subject is *Fire in the Valley: The Making of the Personal Computer* (ISBN 0-07-135892-7). You can read excerpts from the book at www.fireinthevalley.com.

The Second Wave

VisiCalc was the killer app that brought attention, and early success, to microcomputers before the IBM PC was released. And although many say that just having the letters IBM on the box sold that computer, the groundwork that was laid by VisiCalc was enhanced by a second wave of applications. In the fall of 1982, Mitch Kapor of Lotus Corporation introduced Lotus 1-2-3, a DOS spreadsheet application designed to use all of the 640KB of system memory that DOS would allow. Both the 1-2-3 program and the spreadsheet were kept in memory while the user worked. Compared to VisiCalc (written to run on the CP/M OS and designed to use much less memory), it was very fast, and it had additional functionality, such as database functions and a program that would create and print graphs from the spreadsheet data. Lotus 1-2-3 was the "killer app," the software that made the IBM PC and

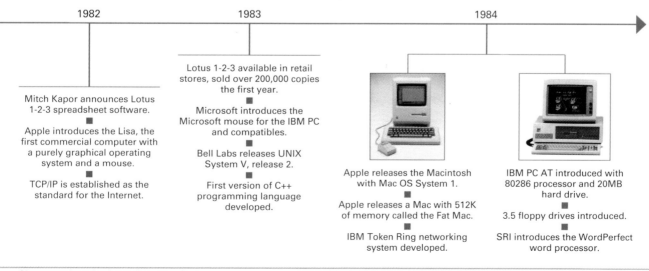

1982

Mitch Kapor announces Lotus 1-2-3 spreadsheet software.
■
Apple introduces the Lisa, the first commercial computer with a purely graphical operating system and a mouse.
■
TCP/IP is established as the standard for the Internet.

1983

Lotus 1-2-3 available in retail stores, sold over 200,000 copies the first year.
■
Microsoft introduces the Microsoft mouse for the IBM PC and compatibles.
■
Bell Labs releases UNIX System V, release 2.
■
First version of C++ programming language developed.

Apple releases the Macintosh with Mac OS System 1.
■
Apple releases a Mac with 512K of memory called the Fat Mac.
■
IBM Token Ring networking system developed.

1984

IBM PC AT introduced with 80286 processor and 20MB hard drive.
■
3.5 floppy drives introduced.
■
SRI introduces the WordPerfect word processor.

PC DOS a must-have combination for people who worked all day crunching numbers and doing what-if calculations. Figure 1-4 shows the Lotus 1-2-3 program with a sample spreadsheet.

OS/2

In 1987, Microsoft and IBM introduced their jointly developed OS/2 (Operating System/2), intended to replace DOS. However, version 1.0 was underpowered in that it was written for the Intel 80286 processor, which had serious memory and mode limits. In spite of the memory limits, it still required much more memory and disk space than DOS (2MB of memory and 8MB of disk space) at a time when 2MB of memory and a 40MB hard drive (considered large in the late 1980s) cost several thousand dollars. Although OS/2 multitasked applications in memory, only one application at a time could be visible on the screen. Also, applications had to be written specifically for OS/2, because it had very limited support for DOS applications.

```
A1:                                                                    MENU
Worksheet  Range  Copy  Move  File  Print  Graph  Data  System  Quit
Global, Insert, Delete, Column, Erase, Titles, Window, Status, Page
          A          B        C        D        E        F        G        H
1
2   Acme Drugs          Monthly Product Sales Report          May
3   Store #84
4              SKU 13   SKU 25   SKU 53   SKU 57   SKU 61   SKU 73
5        1       6        6       54       32       21       31
6        2       3       31       21       12       54       34
7        3       2        0       78        5       14       15
8        4       8        5       31       87       15       24
9        5       9       53       11       14       21       32
10       6      13       12       14       21       24       14
11       7       3       52       87       65       19       18
12       8       7       13       54       54       23       19
13       9       2       25       21       21       26       17
14      10       8       46       11       14       28       24
15
16  Total        61      243      374      325      245      228
17
18
19
20
27-May-2002   09:42 PM                                              NUM
```

• **Figure 1-4.**   Lotus 1-2-3 spreadsheet

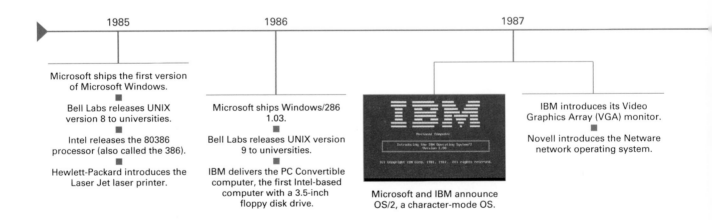

1985
Microsoft ships the first version of Microsoft Windows.
■
Bell Labs releases UNIX version 8 to universities.
■
Intel releases the 80386 processor (also called the 386).
■
Hewlett-Packard introduces the Laser Jet laser printer.

1986
Microsoft ships Windows/286 1.03.
■
Bell Labs releases UNIX version 9 to universities.
■
IBM delivers the PC Convertible computer, the first Intel-based computer with a 3.5-inch floppy disk drive.

Microsoft and IBM announce OS/2, a character-mode OS.

1987
IBM introduces its Video Graphics Array (VGA) monitor.

Novell introduces the Netware network operating system.

In the 1990s, IBM introduced OS/2 Warp, a greatly improved version of OS/2 with a very nice GUI, and pretty much removed itself from the battle for the desktop. IBM now targets the high-end server market. You will find a great deal of information about OS/2 on the Web, where you will discover that it has a very strong following among individual programmer/consultants.

Microsoft Windows

In 1985, when the first version of Windows appeared, it was more smoke than OS. It was a not-very-good GUI balanced precariously on top of DOS. It was very slow and had a very flat look—you couldn't lay one graphic on top of another; the ability to overlap graphical elements, such as windows and icons, did not show up until a later version. However, the GUI gradually improved with each version.

From 1985 to 1990, Microsoft continued to work on both Windows and DOS, but Windows was not much more than a pretty face until 1990 and Windows 3.0, which supported the three Intel processor modes of operation, that Microsoft called Real mode, Standard mode, and 386 Enhanced mode. In Real mode, Windows 3.0 was just a GUI that ran on top of DOS; in the other two modes, it added functionality to DOS to take advantage of the 286 and 386 processor modes.

The most important feature of Windows 3.0 was better support for legacy DOS applications within Windows, which was related to the 386 processor mode. This meant that DOS apps and Windows apps could both be run simultaneously. This version still had its quirks, but for the first time, IT managers saw a potential GUI replacement for DOS as the desktop OS of choice.

In the spring of 1992, Microsoft brought out a minor upgrade, Windows 3.1, which was adopted as the standard desktop OS by many organizations. The fact that Microsoft's entire suite of applications was also available in versions for Windows 3.x helped encourage adoption.

Figure 1-5 shows the Windows 3.1 desktop. Notice that there is no graphical task bar at the bottom of the screen, just the Program Manager window (the main window) with other windows nested in it.

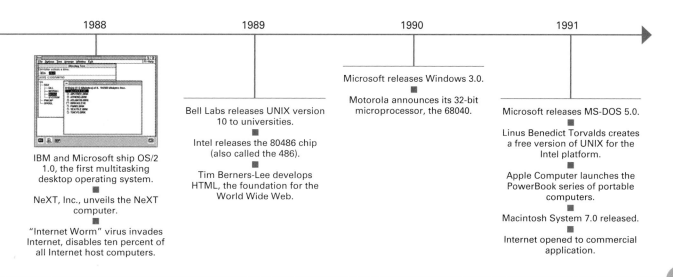

1988 | 1989 | 1990 | 1991

IBM and Microsoft ship OS/2 1.0, the first multitasking desktop operating system.

NeXT, Inc., unveils the NeXT computer.

"Internet Worm" virus invades Internet, disables ten percent of all Internet host computers.

Bell Labs releases UNIX version 10 to universities.

Intel releases the 80486 chip (also called the 486).

Tim Berners-Lee develops HTML, the foundation for the World Wide Web.

Microsoft releases Windows 3.0.

Motorola announces its 32-bit microprocessor, the 68040.

Microsoft releases MS-DOS 5.0.

Linus Benedict Torvalds creates a free version of UNIX for the Intel platform.

Apple Computer launches the PowerBook series of portable computers.

Macintosh System 7.0 released.

Internet opened to commercial application.

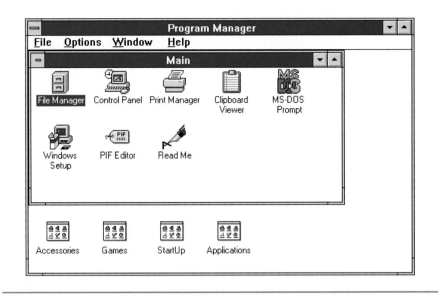

In this book, when discussing versions that share a major number, such as all of the Windows 3 versions, we'll substitute an *x* for the subversion number (Windows 3.*x*). When discussing features common to both Windows 95 and Windows 98, we'll refer to Windows 9*x*.

● **Figure 1-5.** MS Windows 3.1 desktop

Windows for Workgroups

DOS and other OSs through Windows 3.*x* included only the operating system functions. If you wanted to connect to a network, you added a **network operating system (NOS)** on top of your installed OS. This separate network operating system might be from 3COM (yes, 3COM had its own NOS software in the 80s) or Novell, or it might be Microsoft's LAN Manager NOS, developed in the late 1980s.

Novell and LAN Manager were both server network operating systems, providing file and print sharing services to other computers. Network operating systems combined both the operating system functions and the networking functions. A computer needs special client software to connect to each of these servers. The client is the software component that allows users to connect to servers and to request services from them.

Inside Information

Protocols

A protocol is a standard, or a set of standards, that everybody agrees to abide by when they build a piece of software or hardware. Products that adhere to a specific protocol will be able to work together, regardless of who made them.

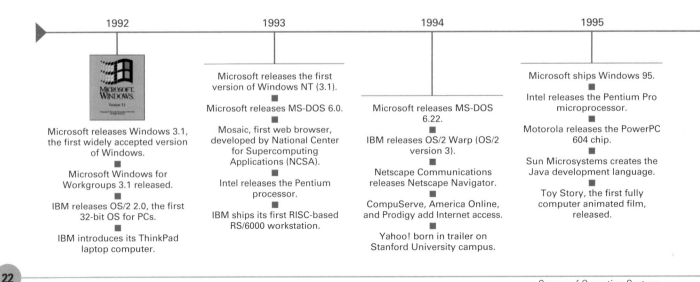

1992	1993	1994	1995
Microsoft releases Windows 3.1, the first widely accepted version of Windows.	Microsoft releases the first version of Windows NT (3.1).	Microsoft releases MS-DOS 6.22.	Microsoft ships Windows 95.
Microsoft Windows for Workgroups 3.1 released.	Microsoft releases MS-DOS 6.0.	IBM releases OS/2 Warp (OS/2 version 3).	Intel releases the Pentium Pro microprocessor.
IBM releases OS/2 2.0, the first 32-bit OS for PCs.	Mosaic, first web browser, developed by National Center for Supercomputing Applications (NCSA).	Netscape Communications releases Netscape Navigator.	Motorola releases the PowerPC 604 chip.
IBM introduces its ThinkPad laptop computer.	Intel releases the Pentium processor.	CompuServe, America Online, and Prodigy add Internet access.	Sun Microsystems creates the Java development language.
	IBM ships its first RISC-based RS/6000 workstation.	Yahoo! born in trailer on Stanford University campus.	Toy Story, the first fully computer animated film, released.

Early client network software, like Novell's client software today, included underlying networking components called drivers and protocols, as well as the component we think of as the client. The network software Microsoft provided for DOS and for Windows 3.1 on top of DOS included only the client component. However, beginning in October 1992 with Windows for Workgroups 3.1, Microsoft included both the client and server software in all of its OS products. This enabled **peer-to-peer networking**, meaning desktop computers could act as servers to their peers. This worked well in a very small workgroup environment of 10 or fewer computers.

Windows for Workgroups 3.1 was followed a year later by Windows for Workgroups 3.11, with the obligatory fixes and improvements. These included faster network and disk I/O operations. However, users were still working with a Windows OS that was running on top of DOS; that is, first DOS was started and then Windows. Windows depended on DOS, which had to be installed on the computer.

What OSs Are Available Today?

The most common microcomputer operating systems in use today include MS-DOS, Windows 98, Windows NT, Windows 2000, Windows XP, the Macintosh OSs, and UNIX (represented in this book by Linux). DOS is very, very rarely still on the desktop, but it survives today in some special devices and is still used by technicians and computer support people. Windows 98 and Windows NT are waning on the desktop as old computers are replaced. This is especially true in corporate settings, where computers are often leased for two or three years and then replaced with new systems with the latest OS under a new lease. At work, you probably won't have a choice, since OS decisions are usually made through the IT department. These OSs are included here because they still have a significant presence.

Table 1.1 summarizes the available OSs, listing the publisher, platform, and types of applications that can be run on each OS.

What follows is a brief description of each of these OSs, including a little history here and there to put things in perspective. You will also discover where you'll be most likely to encounter each operating system.

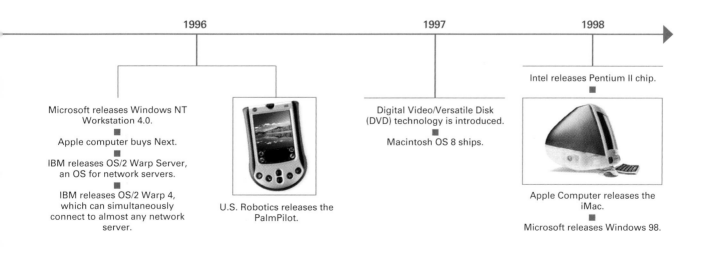

Timeline 1996–1998

1996 — Microsoft releases Windows NT Workstation 4.0.
■ Apple computer buys Next.
■ IBM releases OS/2 Warp Server, an OS for network servers.
■ IBM releases OS/2 Warp 4, which can simultaneously connect to almost any network server.

U.S. Robotics releases the PalmPilot.

1997 — Digital Video/Versatile Disk (DVD) technology is introduced.
■ Macintosh OS 8 ships.

1998 — Intel releases Pentium II chip.
■ Apple Computer releases the iMac.
■ Microsoft releases Windows 98.

Table 1.1	Summary of Current OSs		
OS Version	**Company**	**Platform**	**Applications Supported**
MS-DOS 6.22	Microsoft	Intel/Microsoft	DOS
Windows NT 4.0	Microsoft	Intel/Microsoft	DOS, 16-bit Windows, 32-bit Windows
Windows 98	Microsoft	Intel/Microsoft	DOS, 16-bit Windows, 32-bit Windows
Windows 2000	Microsoft	Intel/Microsoft	DOS, 16-bit Windows, 32-bit Windows
Windows Me	Microsoft	Intel/Microsoft	DOS, 16-bit Windows, 32-bit Windows
Windows XP	Microsoft	Intel/Microsoft	DOS, 16-bit Windows, 32-bit Windows
Mac OS 9	Apple	Apple Mac	Macintosh
Mac OS X	Apple	Apple Mac	Macintosh
UNIX/Linux	Various	Intel/Microsoft	UNIX

Inside Information

MS-DOS vs. PC DOS

In the context of today's micro-computers, DOS usually means Microsoft's DOS (MS-DOS). Microsoft's first version of DOS, called PC DOS, was introduced with the first IBM PC, in 1981. This and subsequent versions of PC DOS were customized specifically for IBM's PC products. Microsoft licensed versions, called MS-DOS, to other manufacturers, such as Compaq, Toshiba, and Dell. PC DOS and MS-DOS, as the names imply, are written to support disks, with minimal I/O support for other hardware.

DOS from Microsoft

DOS, which stands for disk operating system, is an operating system that provides support for interaction, or input and output (I/O), between the memory and disk drives. There have been, and still are, DOS operating systems for computers other than microcomputers. In addition, all of the popular microcomputer operating systems in use include support for disks.

Each major version of DOS was released to support new disk capacities. PC DOS 1.0 supported single-sided 5¼-inch floppies; PC DOS 1.1 added support for double-sided 5¼-inch floppies; and PC DOS 2.0 was released with the IBM PC-XT and included support for the XT's 10MB hard drives. PC DOS 3.0 was released with the IBM PC-AT and included support for the larger AT hard drives. Support for 3.5-inch floppies and the larger hard drives of the IBM PS-2 computers was added in DOS 4.0. MS-DOS 6.22 was the last widely used version of MS-DOS.

The DOS Prompt

DOS has a text-mode, command-line interface that requires users to remember cryptic commands and their subcommands in order to perform

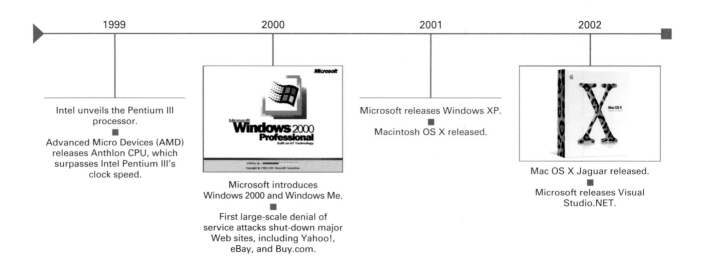

1999 — Intel unveils the Pentium III processor.

Advanced Micro Devices (AMD) releases Anthlon CPU, which surpasses Intel Pentium III's clock speed.

2000 — Microsoft introduces Windows 2000 and Windows Me.

First large-scale denial of service attacks shut-down major Web sites, including Yahoo!, eBay, and Buy.com.

2001 — Microsoft releases Windows XP.

Macintosh OS X released.

2002 — Mac OS X Jaguar released.

Microsoft releases Visual Studio.NET.

file management functions and to launch DOS applications. Figure 1-6 shows a good example of how cryptic DOS can be. The first line is the format command with three parameters: the letter of the drive to be formatted, the /S switch telling the command to transfer the system files to the formatted disk, and the /U switch, which formats unconditionally, meaning that it does not try to save any existing data on the disk so that it can be unformatted later. This is followed by a warning that all data will be lost, and a query asking whether to proceed with the formatting, to which the user must respond by typing Y or N. Then some information is displayed about the progress of formatting, and the user is asked what to use as the volume label (an optional name for the volume); to not use a volume label, the user presses the ENTER key. Finally, some statistics on the formatted disk are displayed, along with the serial number that DOS gave to the disk. As you can see, this assumes knowledge of many, many concepts.

When Would You Use DOS?

Although you would not likely choose it as your main OS on your desktop computer, there are a few exceptions to this rule, as you will see in Chapter 2. Also, you might find DOS as the OS on some handheld devices that do not require a GUI interface, and computer professionals often find DOS handy as a very small OS that fits on a diskette. These will be explored in Chapter 2 as well.

Windows NT

Windows NT was called Windows NT 3.1 when it came out in 1993 because it had the same user interface as Windows 3.1. That was where the similarity ended. To begin with, it was a server operating system, including server protocols in its integrated network support. Furthermore, unlike Windows 3.x, it did not sit on top of DOS.

```
A:\>format c: /s /u

WARNING: ALL DATA ON NON-REMOVABLE DISK
DRIVE C: WILL BE LOST!
Proceed with Format (Y/N)?y


Formatting   502M
Format complete.
System transferred

Volume label (11 characters, ENTER for none)?

  526,106,624 bytes total disk space
      212,992 bytes used by system
  525,893,632 bytes available on disk

        8,192 bytes in each allocation unit.
       64,196 allocation units available on disk.

Volume Serial Number is 3A4E-17DA


A:\>_
```

• **Figure 1-6.** MS-DOS prompt with the format command

What's New in Windows NT?

Windows NT was the first Microsoft OS to take full advantage of the capabilities of the special protected mode that Intel introduced in its processors manufactured after 1986. A major benefit of this was more stability and security in the OS. In fact, NT was so powerful that Microsoft decided to make two versions of NT: one designed mainly for servers, and another geared more toward individual user systems—what some folks call workstations. Thus, the next version of NT (NT 3.5) was also the first Windows OS to have separate products: Windows NT Workstation and Windows NT Server. Both of these used the same kernel (you'll recall that a kernel is the main OS component) and interface, but the Server version had enhancements and components that were needed only on a network server. The Workstation version was configured as a desktop operating system.

In 1996, Microsoft introduced Windows NT 4.0, which had a GUI similar to that of Windows 95 as well as other improvements and enhancements to the OS. Figure 1-7 shows the Windows NT desktop.

When Would You Use Windows NT Workstation?

Windows 95 predated Windows NT 4 and has passed its seventh year in service. It has been replaced by Windows 98 and all other subsequent versions of Windows. We will not discuss Windows 95 in detail in this book, but we'll talk about it from time to time.

Even when it was the latest Microsoft OS, you would not likely have used it at home, if only because of the cost, which was more than twice that of the Windows 3.x OSs that preceded it and of Windows 95, which was considered the upgrade OS for a Windows 3.x OS.

At this writing, you can still buy Windows NT 4.0 Workstation, but it will probably not be available by the time you read this. However, you may run into Windows NT 4.0 Workstation on existing PCs in an organization, and that is the main reason we include it in this book.

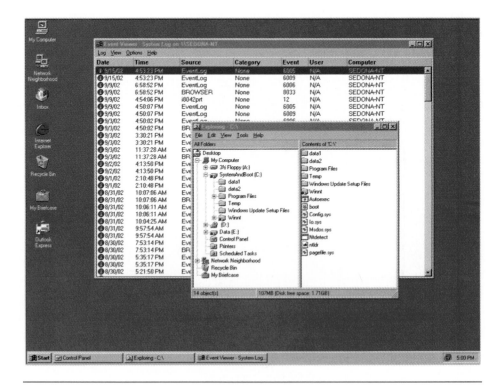

• **Figure 1-7.** MS Windows NT 4.0 desktop with open Windows

Windows 98

Windows 98 was an evolutionary development in the Windows operating system, including improvements in both visible and under-the-hood components. It offered more stability than its immediate predecessor, Windows 95, meaning that it was less likely to stop in its tracks just when you were about to complete that book order on Amazon. Although improved, Windows 98 is not as stable as the newer Windows OSs. We include it in this book only because very large numbers of people still use it. Figure 1-8 shows the Windows 98 desktop.

Cross Check

Compare GUIs

GUIs are not all that different from each other. Flip ahead to Chapter 7, "Windows XP," and Chapter 8, "Macintosh OS 9 and OS X," and compare the GUIs of these two OSs; then answer the following questions:

1. What are the major differences in these two GUIs?
2. How are these two interfaces similar?
3. In your opinion, which interface would be more intuitive to use?

What's New in Windows 98?

Windows 98 offered new options for customizing the GUI, including tighter integration with Microsoft's web browser, Internet Explorer (IE). This feature allows users to configure Windows so that they can, if they wish, always appear to be in an Internet browser, even when they are not browsing the Internet. Windows 98 came with drivers and support for devices, such as DVD drives, that were not included in Windows 95. As usual with an upgrade to an OS, Microsoft cleaned up existing problems and made the OS run faster.

When Would You Use Windows 98?

Well, it is now somewhat "long in the tooth," and there are newer choices from Microsoft. At the time it was introduced, however, the two choices of

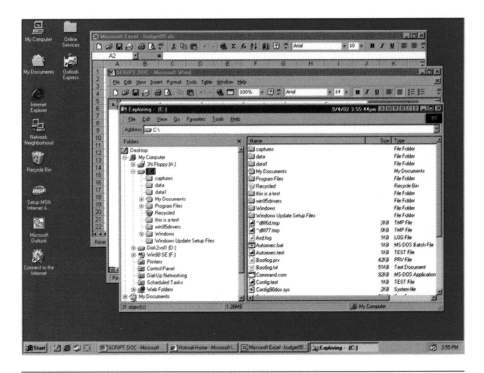

• **Figure 1-8.** MS Windows 98 desktop with open Windows

desktop OSs from Microsoft were Windows 95 and Windows NT Workstation. Windows 98 was an upgrade of Windows 95, and Windows NT had only a limited list of supported hardware. NT also did not support an important technology called plug and play (PnP). Therefore, Windows 98 was the choice for PCs with PnP hardware and/or hardware not supported by Windows NT. It's in use today simply because people haven't yet upgraded to Windows 2000 or Windows XP.

Windows Me (Millennium Edition)

Windows Me (Millennium Edition) was targeted at the home market when introduced in 2000. It is essentially Windows 98 with improved music, video, and home networking support. It included the System Restore utility, which allowed a user to roll back the PC software configuration to a date or time before a bad change was made to the computer. The Windows Movie Maker allowed users to digitally edit, save, and share their home videos, and the Windows Media Player gave users a tool for organizing digital music and video. This was the last Microsoft OS based on the Windows 95 internals (mainly the kernel).

Windows Me is included here only because it was installed on many computers that were sold to individuals, but it is not an OS that was adopted by organizations. You are not likely to encounter it in a work environment.

Windows 2000

In 2000, Microsoft introduced the Windows 2000 family of OS products, which brought together the best of Windows 98 and Windows NT. Microsoft had now united its operating systems in a group of products that all shared the same kernel and covered OS needs from the desktop to the enterprise server. The several versions of Windows 2000 include Windows 2000 Professional (the desktop OS), Windows 2000 Server (for a network server on a small network), Windows 2000 Advanced Server (for a network server in larger networks), and Windows 2000 Enterprise Edition (with lots of features for *really* big servers in *really* big networks).

When Would You Use Windows 2000 Professional?

This is no longer offered as a standard OS when you buy a new desktop computer, but you will find it on existing desktop computers in the workplace for a few more years. Figure 1-9 shows the Windows 2000 desktop. Windows 2000 Professional is included in this book because it is still on many computers.

• **Figure 1-9.** MS Windows 2000 desktop

Windows XP

With its Windows 2000 products, Microsoft brought all of its OSs together, building them on top of the same core internal piece (the *kernel*). Some of us, especially those whose jobs included supporting both desktop and server computers, thought it would simplify our lives. We really liked that idea because we could learn one OS for both the desktop and server. Well, with Windows XP, Microsoft departed from that model. Windows XP is intended only for the desktop, not for the server environment. The new server products come under the umbrella of the Microsoft .NET initiative, which we discuss in Chapter 10.

Cross Check

The Many Windows 2000 Products

What's with these different Windows 2000 products? Skip ahead to the beginning of Chapter 6 and read more about these variations and then answer the following questions:

1. How many processors at one time does each product support?

2. Which product cannot be purchased by itself but is sold only in an OEM version?

3. Which product is appropriate for a small business that needs only a file and print server?

What's New in Windows XP?

There are two XP products: Windows XP Home Edition and Windows XP Professional. Both have the same improved GUI and share many of the same features, but only Windows XP Professional has several network- and security-related features.

The Windows XP default desktop is very different from that of previous versions of Windows in that the Recycle Bin (where deleted files are sent) is the only icon on the desktop. In addition, the Start menu has been redesigned and reorganized, as shown in Figure 1-10.

• **Figure 1-10.** MS Windows XP desktop and Start menu

The Macintosh has a loyal following among people who first encountered it in school. Early in Apple's history, the company strategically targeted schools and universities as places to sell its products, which, over the years, has resulted in large numbers of people who learned computing on a Mac. However, today the largest market share for the desktop, especially in business and government, belongs to Windows-based computers.

When Would You Use Windows XP?

Introduced in 2001, Windows XP is the successor to Windows 2000, although both are available as of this writing. Windows XP Home Edition is the choice for home users who want a computer based on the Microsoft/Intel standards, who want to run a variety of personal use software and even many business applications, and who want to connect to the Internet. Windows XP Professional is the choice for corporate or home users who want a Microsoft/Intel standard computer and need to connect as a client computer to Microsoft Windows NT or Windows 2000 servers. The Professional version is also the choice for users who want to be able to run the enormous variety of software written for Windows and to take advantage of the features that are supported only in this version of Windows XP.

Macintosh OSs

The Macintosh operating systems run only on Apple Macintosh computers. The OSs in common use today are Mac OS 9 and Mac OS X (X is the roman numeral for 10). OS 9 reflects evolutionary changes from the first strictly GUI-based Mac operating systems, while OS X is a revolutionary change, based on NextStep, an OS with a UNIX kernel.

Macintosh hardware and software are proprietary products of the Apple Computer Company, which results in better integration of the OS and the hardware, but at a higher price. Apple computers are based on an entirely different architecture than the Microsoft/Intel personal computers. For the past several years, Macintosh computers have used the PowerPC chip with an architecture that is enhanced for graphics and multimedia.

Until Mac OS X, the Macintosh OSs were strictly GUI environments, with no command-line option (see Figure 1-11). Mac OS X, with its UNIX origins, does give you the option of a character-based interface.

When Would You Use a Macintosh OS?

Well, it is your only choice if you buy a Macintosh computer. Basically, you can do everything with a Mac that you can do with a PC. Many business applications, including Microsoft Office, come in a version for the Macintosh. One area in which the Macintosh traditionally shines is ease of use, although Windows now provides competition in this area. In addition, the Macintosh is often the OS/computer of choice among graphics and video-editing professionals.

UNIX/Linux

UNIX has a longer history than any other popular operating system. It grew out of an operating system developed for an early Digital Equipment Corporation (DEC) computer and went through several generations of changes before it emerged from the Bell Labs Computing Science Research Center (Bell Labs) as UNIX version 6 in 1975. This was a portable operating system for minicomputers and mainframe computers, and it was distributed via government and commercial licenses and inexpensive academic licenses.

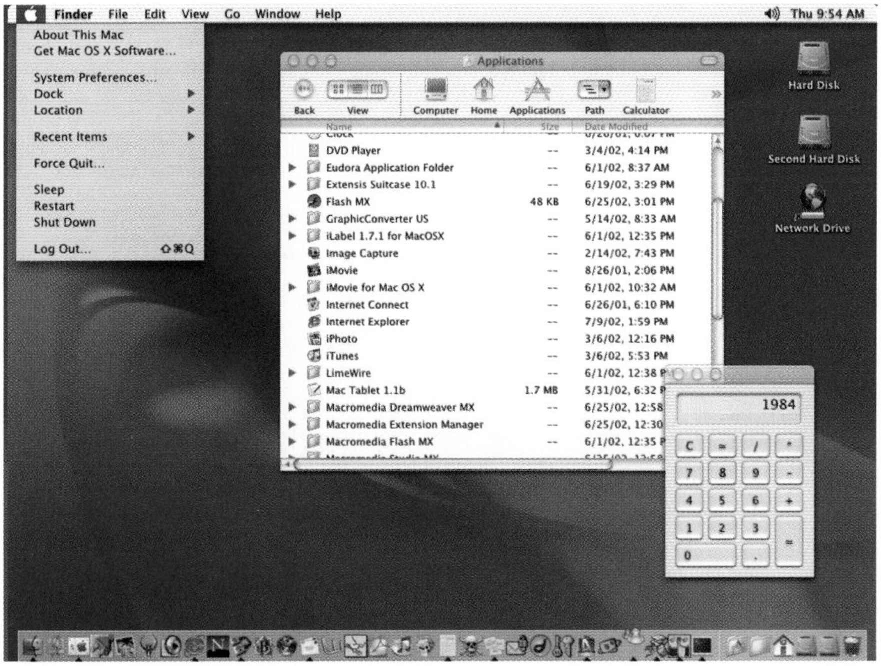

● **Figure 1-11.** Macintosh OS X GUI

The University of California at Berkeley (UCB) licensed UNIX, modified it, and distributed it to other schools as Berkeley Software Distribution (BSD) version 4.2. Later versions have followed. The schools paid licensing fees to Bell Labs. A lot of the development of **TCP/IP**, the Internet standard family of network protocols, occurred at UCB. Students and others improved on and added to UNIX, freely sharing their code with others. This tradition still prevails today.

In addition to portability (the ability to run on different types of computers), UNIX supports timesharing and multiuser systems, and there are versions that run on personal computers.

The Many Faces of UNIX

The current commercial versions of UNIX include Sun Microsystems' Solaris, Hewlett-Packard's HP-UX, IBM's AIX, and Compaq's Tru64 UNIX. These versions are high-end server applications and quite expensive, as are the computers they are intended to run on. There are also many **open source** versions of UNIX, including Linux, FreeBSD, and NetBSD. Even with these free versions available, however, it is worthwhile to buy one of the modestly priced packages from companies that charge small fees just for the value they have added to the OS in the form of additional software, installation and configuration instructions, and documentation. We use the Red Hat 7.3 version of Linux for the UNIX chapter in this book. Figure 1-12 shows an example of a Linux directory.

Inside Information

The User Interface

Most versions of UNIX also offer several different user interfaces. Some use character mode, like the traditional shells, such as the Bourne shell and the C shell. Others use a graphical interface, such as X Window.

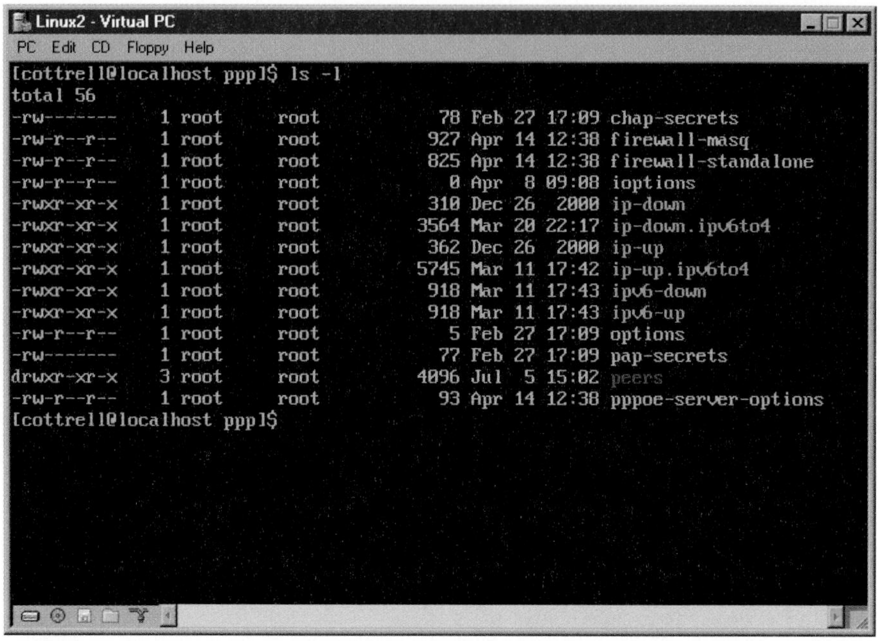
Linux2 - Virtual PC
PC Edit CD Floppy Help
[cottrell@localhost ppp]$ ls -l
total 56
-rw------- 1 root root 78 Feb 27 17:09 chap-secrets
-rw-r--r-- 1 root root 927 Apr 14 12:38 firewall-masq
-rw-r--r-- 1 root root 825 Apr 14 12:38 firewall-standalone
-rw-r--r-- 1 root root 0 Apr 8 09:08 ioptions
-rwxr-xr-x 1 root root 310 Dec 26 2000 ip-down
-rwxr-xr-x 1 root root 3564 Mar 20 22:17 ip-down.ipv6to4
-rwxr-xr-x 1 root root 362 Dec 26 2000 ip-up
-rwxr-xr-x 1 root root 5745 Mar 11 17:42 ip-up.ipv6to4
-rwxr-xr-x 1 root root 918 Mar 11 17:43 ipv6-down
-rwxr-xr-x 1 root root 918 Mar 11 17:43 ipv6-up
-rw-r--r-- 1 root root 5 Feb 27 17:09 options
-rw------- 1 root root 77 Feb 27 17:09 pap-secrets
drwxr-xr-x 3 root root 4096 Jul 5 15:02 peers
-rw-r--r-- 1 root root 93 Apr 14 12:38 pppoe-server-options
[cottrell@localhost ppp]$

• **Figure 1-12.** Red Hat Linux directory listing (ls command)

Why Would You Use UNIX?

> Open source is a certification standard of the Open Source Initiative (OSI) through which a program's source code (the original language in which a program is written) is made available free of charge to the general public. Learn more about open source at `www.opensource.org`.

The Windows family of operating systems presently dominates the desktop, especially in corporate America. Even fierce UNIX advocates do not see UNIX taking over the desktop any time soon. However, it is an excellent server operating system, because it tends to use resources carefully, allowing you to load only the services needed. It is also considered very secure, and versions of UNIX are present on many of the world's web servers.

With several free or inexpensive versions now available for the Microsoft/Intel platform, this is the OS of choice for present-day hobbyist and computer enthusiasts, who use it to develop new UNIX utilities and other software and to run games. If you fit this description, you may be in the market for (or already own) UNIX.

Chapter 1 Review

■ Chapter Summary

After reading this chapter and completing the Try This! exercises, you should understand the following facts about operating systems:

Microcomputers Today

- A computer consists of hardware and two types of software: applications software and operating system software.

- The operating system allows the user to interact with the computer hardware.

Common Computer Hardware

- Certain computer hardware is common to most computers you will encounter. The basic components include the processor, motherboard, RAM, ROM BIOS, video adapter, display screen, keyboard, pointing device, and other peripheral devices.

- You can identify hardware components by a visual inspection, by observing information displayed during the bootup process, and by accessing a ROM BIOS setup program.

Purpose and Functions of Microcomputer Operating Systems

- There are certain functions provided by most, if not all current operating systems. These functions include user interface, job management, task management, memory management, file management, device management, and security.

- The operating system makes everything work together.

- You can identify most of the functions provided by your operating system by careful observation. For instance, evidence of support of the security function includes a required logon procedure when you start your computer and the need for authorization to access resources on your local computer.

Major Events in the Evolution of Microcomputer Operating Systems

- The history of current microcomputers and their OSs involved many technical advances and the imagination of a multitude of innovative people.

- You can find many accounts of the history of computers and operating systems by searching the Internet.

What OSs are Available Today

- The microcomputer operating systems common today include MS-DOS, several versions of Windows (Windows 98, Windows 2000, and Windows XP), Mac OS 9, Mac OS X, and several versions of UNIX.

- Each of today's common operating systems is best suited for certain uses.

- Microsoft desktop OSs are common in the business environment.

- The Mac OSs are commonly used in education and in graphic workstations.

■ Key Terms

286 protected mode *(6)*
386 protected mode *(6)*
authentication *(15)*
binary digit *(8)*
bit *(8)*
byte *(8)*
central processing unit (CPU) *(2)*
client *(3)*
current window *(14)*

cursor *(10)*
device driver *(15)*
device management *(15)*
directory *(15)*
disk drive *(10)*
display screen *(10)*
file management *(14)*
focus *(14)*
folder *(15)*

gigabyte *(8)*
graphical user interface (GUI) *(13)*
input *(3)*
input/output (I/O) *(3)*
job management *(14)*
kernel *(12)*
megabyte *(8)*
memory *(7)*
memory management *(14)*

microcomputer *(2)*	output *(3)*	real mode *(6)*
microprocessor *(2)*	peer-to-peer networking *(23)*	security *(15)*
monitor *(10)*	peripheral device *(11)*	server *(3)*
motherboard *(7)*	personal computer (PC) *(2)*	task management *(14)*
mouse *(10)*	pointing device *(10)*	TCP/IP *(31)*
multitasking *(14)*	random-access memory (RAM) *(8)*	terabyte *(8)*
network operating system (NOS) *(22)*	read-only memory (ROM) *(9)*	user interface *(12)*
open source *(31)*	read-only memory basic	virtual memory *(14)*
operating system (OS) *(12)*	input-output system	virtual memory manager *(14)*
	(ROM BIOS) *(9)*	

■ Key Term Quiz

Use the Key Terms list to complete the sentences that follow. Not all terms will be used.

1. The _____ is the hardware component most central to a computer.

2. If you save confidential data on your local hard drive, you should be using an operating system that includes a/an _____ function, which protects local files and folders from unauthorized access.

3. A/an _____ takes care of the interaction between a program and a computer's hardware, freeing application programmers from the task of including such functions in their programs.

4. An operating system that uses _____ will allow you to simultaneously run more programs than the physical memory of the computer will hold.

5. When you run several applications at once and switch between them, you are experiencing the _____ feature of an operating system.

6. Interaction with a computer involving getting data and commands into it and results out of it is called _____.

7. A/an _____ is an example of a pointing device.

8. Software that allows the operating system to use a hardware component is called a/an _____.

9. The type of memory used as the workspace for the operating system and applications is _____.

10. Your data and programs are stored on a _____.

■ Multiple-Choice Quiz

1. Which of the following operating systems will *not* work on a PC? Select all that apply.

    a. Mac OS 9

    b. Windows 98

    c. Windows NT

    d. Red Hat Linux

    e. Windows XP

2. Select the two general types of software you are likely to use on a computer.

    a. Peripheral

    b. Operating system

    c. I/O

    d. Video

    e. Application

3. In 1983, what "killer app" made the IBM PC a must-have business tool?

    a. Microsoft Word

    b. VisiCalc

    c. BASIC

    d. PC DOS

    e. Lotus 1-2-3

4. Bill has a part-time business as a wedding photographer, taking both still and video pictures of these happy events. Which operating system is best suited for video editing?

   a. Windows 98

   b. Macintosh OS X

   c. Windows NT

   d. Red Hat Linux

   e. Windows for Workgroups 3.11

5. Select all of the input devices in the following list.

   a. Display

   b. Printer

   c. Trackball

   d. Keyboard

   e. Mouse

6. Select the kinds of computers that apply to a single user.

   a. Monitor

   b. Desktop

   c. Laptop

   d. USB

   e. Peer-to-peer

7. What types of components would you expect to be able to exchange between a PC and a Mac? Select all that apply.

   a. Printers

   b. Processors

   c. Mice

   d. Cameras

   e. Internal disk drives

8. Which component, if missing, will keep a PC from functioning?

   a. Scanner

   b. Printer

   c. Camera

   d. Processor

   e. Mouse

9. In the 1950s, the typical computer user would have been (select all that apply):

   a. A small business

   b. Your grandfather

   c. A politician

   d. A government agency

   e. A secretary

10. Which term would best be used in an analogy of an operating system?

    a. Salesman

    b. Intermediary

    c. Steering wheel

    d. Ignition

    e. Spreadsheet

11. What is the generic term for a very tiny computer that fits in your hand?

    a. Mouse

    b. Trackball

    c. Handheld

    d. Macintosh

    e. Laptop

12. Which of the following is not a peripheral device?

    a. Processor

    b. Printer

    c. Scanner

    d. Mouse

    e. Camera

13. What term describes the DOS user interface?

    a. GUI

    b. Dialog box

    c. Message

    d. Character-based command prompt

    e. Menu

14. What term describes both the Windows and Mac user interfaces?

    a. GUI

    b. Dialog box

    c. Message

    d. Character-based command prompt

    e. Menu

15. One important security component in an OS restricts who can work on a computer. What must each user do before working on a secure computer?

a. Back up all data

b. Connect to the Internet

c. Log on

d. Double-click the Start menu

■ Essay Quiz

1. Write a few sentences describing every interaction you have had with computers in the past 24 hours.

2. If you use more than one operating system on a regular basis, describe some of the similarities and differences you have noticed between two of those operating systems. You are not limited to the operating systems described in this chapter. (If you use a handheld computer and use a desktop Windows computer, these are two different operating systems.) If you do not work with more than one operating system, find someone who has (classmate or other) and interview that person to answer this question.

3. Explain why Windows 98 is not a good choice of operating system for a laptop computer holding confidential information being used by a person who works from different locations.

4. Describe virtual memory and list an OS that does not use it.

5. In studying the common operating systems, you have considered the availability of software that runs on each OS and the general reasons one may be chosen over the others. Put yourself in the position of an information technology professional in a new company that will open its doors on day one with 50 employees who will need computers on their desks connected to a corporate network and will need to work with standard business applications. What are some other practical considerations that you can think of that must come into play when making this decision? Your answer does not need to specify a particular OS.

Lab Projects

• Lab Project 1.1

Locate as many of the common components (listed next) in your lab computer as possible. If you're doing this in a class lab, you may use any means permitted by the instructor to find this information. You may need to refer to the documentation, use software, or open up the computer. Then write a brief description of the component. For instance, if you discover that your computer has a Pentium III processor, record that information, and if you can discover the quantity of memory installed, record that information also. If you're quick, you can discover information about your computer as it is booting up.

1 Processor

_____

2 Motherboard

_____

3 Memory

_____

4 ROM BIOS

_____

(5) Video adapter

_____

(8) Disk drives

_____

(6) Keyboard

_____

(9) Peripheral device

_____

(7) Pointing device

_____

• Lab Project 1.2

(1) To understand the relative cost of each of the operating systems you are studying and the availability of each system, use a paper catalog from a software retailer or a website such as www.us.buy.com or www.amazon.com to research the price of each of the operating systems covered in this section. You are not bargain hunting, so you don't need to look for the lowest price; just find the relative cost of the operating systems. You will also find that some are not available as new retail products, although you may find them at other sources. We have listed the full retail versions separately from the upgrade versions. The full versions can be installed on a computer that does not have a previous version of Windows installed. The upgrade versions are cheaper than the full versions, but will not install without a previous version of Windows. In Table 1.2, enter the cost of each product. For those that are unavailable, enter N/A in the cost column.

(2) Once again, using paper catalogs, retail stores, and/or the Internet, research the number of software titles that run in each of these operating systems. This information may be difficult to find. You may have to search other sources. You may find this information at the Microsoft, Apple, and Red Hat websites or at an Electronics Boutique or Wal-Mart. This will give you a rough idea of the amount of software available for each OS, because it takes into account only software sold at retail through the sites you selected and does not include other free or nearly free software distributed elsewhere. Be careful not to count other versions of the operating system, especially when looking for Linux software titles. Only count software that runs on the operating system. At the Buy.com site, we searched on each OS in turn, noticed the total number of titles in the results, and then browsed through them to estimate the total. You're looking only for estimated numbers, because your goal is to gain an understanding of the relative number of software titles available

Table 1.2	Price and Availability Comparison		
Operating System	**Cost**	**Operating System**	**Cost**
MS-DOS (any version)	_____	Red Hat Linux	_____
Windows 98 full	_____	Red Hat Linux Professional	_____
Windows 98 upgrade	_____	Windows XP Professional full	_____
Windows NT 4.0 Workstation full	_____	Windows XP Professional upgrade	_____
Windows NT 4.0 Workstation upgrade	_____	Mac OS 9	_____
Windows XP Home Edition full	_____	Mac OS X	_____
Windows XP Home Edition upgrade	_____		

Table 1.3	Comparison of the Number of Available Software Titles		
Operating System	Estimated Number of Titles	Operating System	Estimated Number of Titles
MS-DOS	N/A	Windows XP	
Windows 98		Mac OS 8/9	
Windows NT Workstation		Linux	

for each OS. While you are at it, notice the type of software available for each OS, which is an indication of the market for that OS. Windows OSs can usually run software written for any of the older versions of Windows, so a low number of titles that name Windows XP in their system

requirements does not indicate that there are few applications that will run on XP. Enter your findings on the number of titles in Table 1.3.

• Lab Project 1.3

Examine the operating system on your class lab computer and answer questions related to the operating system functions described in this section. If you're not familiar with the operating system on your lab computer, you may need to do some research to answer some of these questions. If so, there are several places you can search. First, look for a Help program in the OS or read any documentation that is available to you for this OS. If you cannot find the answers in one of these sources, use a search engine on the Internet to find another source of information for your OS.

For this Lab Project, you will need the following:

■ A computer with a desktop operating system
■ Internet access

① Start your computer and record the name and version number of your operating system here.

_____

② In your own words, describe the user interface.

_____

_____

③ Can you see an indication that this operating system provides a job management function? If so, provide a description.

_____

_____

④ If your operating system supports task management, explain how you can demonstrate the task management functions to someone else.

_____

_____

⑤ Look for tools used to manage files. Then describe how you can copy a file from a location on your hard drive to a diskette.

_____

_____

⑥ Did you see any evidence that this OS provides security? If so, describe why you believe this.

_____

_____

"No one needs more than 640K."
—BILL GATES, 1986

Who cares about DOS? Why should you need to learn about an operating system that first came to light over 20 years ago with the very first PCs? Well, some organizations still have DOS applications lurking somewhere that they can't or won't replace with newer applications, and there actually are devices (specialized computers) that still use DOS. In addition, because Windows OSs still have a command-line DOS-like interface, knowing how to use DOS will allow you to accomplish some tasks faster than you can using the standard interface of your OS.

In this chapter, you will explore DOS in depth. You'll begin with an overview of the presently available choices for a DOS operating system, you'll explore the two primary reasons DOS is still in use today, and you'll look at the features and limits of DOS OSs. You'll install DOS on your lab computer, and you'll practice file management tasks in DOS as you create, copy, move, and delete files and directories. You'll study the DOS bootup process and create a DOS startup disk. Finally, you'll work with DOS in Windows, running a DOS application from the command prompt.

In this chapter, you will learn how to:

- Measure the value, strengths, and weaknesses of DOS
- Install DOS
- Use the FAT file system
- Use DOS commands for file management and other tasks
- Describe the DOS bootup process and create startup disks
- Work with DOS in Windows
- Troubleshoot common DOS problems

■ Finding DOS and Understanding Its Strengths and Weaknesses

Your first step in understanding DOS is knowing where it still lurks in your world. Then you can begin to understand its strengths and weaknesses. We'll discuss these topics in turn.

Versions of DOS, Past and Present

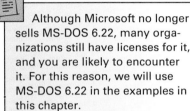

Although Microsoft no longer sells MS-DOS 6.22, many organizations still have licenses for it, and you are likely to encounter it. For this reason, we will use MS-DOS 6.22 in the examples in this chapter.

There have been many versions of DOS in the more than 20 years that PCs have existed. For many years, the most commonly used versions of DOS came from Microsoft, and there were several variants. First there was PC DOS, which Microsoft created for IBM and licensed it for its personal computer (PC) products, beginning with the IBM PC in 1981.

Later Microsoft licensed DOS as MS-DOS to many other PC manufacturers. It was often customized to satisfy the manufacturer's particular needs and then sold under that company's name. In such an arrangement, the product is said to be an original equipment manufacturer (OEM) product. IBM sold an OEM version of DOS as PC DOS, Compaq sold an OEM version as MS-DOS, and many other manufacturers sold versions as well.

DOS 5.0 was the first version available as a separate product from Microsoft. Microsoft's last retail version of MS-DOS was version 6.22. Presently, Microsoft does not offer a DOS product, but IBM continues to offer PC DOS.

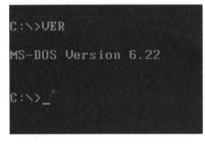

```
C:\>VER

MS-DOS Version 6.22


C:\>_
```

• The VER command

Even though the importance of DOS is greatly diminished in today's computing environment, there is a good chance that you will encounter it in some form on the job. Therefore, you should be familiar with the DOS versions that you might run into.

PC DOS

IBM continues to offer PC DOS, which is no longer designed specifically for IBM PCs. It can be installed on any Microsoft/Intel–compatible computer, or as IBM states, any "IBM or compatible personal computer." The latest version at this writing is PC DOS 2000. At its website, IBM offers three retail products: a download delivery product, a CD-ROM boxed product, and a diskette boxed product. Older versions of PC DOS are not available through IBM, but may be found at other retail sources.

For more information about IBM's latest version of PC DOS, see www-3.ibm.com/software/os/dos.

DR-DOS

Digital Research, the creators of CP/M (the very first real operating system), developed a DOS product, DR-DOS, in the 1980s. Novell bought Digital Research in 1991 and briefly offered DR-DOS. The DR-DOS product has since been acquired by Lineo, who, at this writing, offers an updated DR-DOS product, DR-DOS 7.03 (www.drdos.com), but only in quantities of 50 or more. Lineo no longer supports DR-DOS, which means that you cannot call the company's support staff with questions and problems about DR-DOS. We found DR-DOS frequently asked questions (FAQs) at www.lineo.com/cgi-bin/drdos/faq, and we also found DR-DOS solutions in the solutions database at the `www.lineo.com/cgi-bin/drdos/search` site. An unofficial DR-DOS page is at `www.drdos.org`.

An interesting use of DR-DOS was shown to us by Lou, who works at a large sporting goods retailer. This company uses handheld scanning devices to take inventory. The scanners run DR-DOS version 3.01-01. As you can see in Figure 2-1, it has a keypad to allow users to work in the inventory application and to enter DOS commands.

Try This!

Finding the Version Number of DOS

If you have a computer handy with DOS already installed, you can check out the version number by using a command that is common in most DOS versions. Try this:

1. At the DOS prompt, type **VER** and press ENTER. The version information should appear on the screen.

2. What version are you running? _____

DOS for Free

There are also versions of DOS distributed without charge. One of these is FreeDOS, which is distributed under the GNU GPL license. GNU (pronounced "guh new") is a project that began many years ago at MIT with the goal of distributing free, open software. People may modify the software, as long as they freely share their modifications with others. This is called the GNU General Public License, or GNU GPL. FreeDOS is designed to be 100 percent compatible with MS-DOS. You can learn more about FreeDOS at `www.freedos.org`.

Although Lineo has announced that it does not plan to continue development or support of DR-DOS, the company optionally will sell the source code to those who want to customize and update it.

We have experimented with some of the free OSs and find that they assume a great deal of knowledge of DOS, which makes them a poor choice for someone just learning DOS, even though you can't beat the price!

DOS's Strengths

DOS has lasted for so many years for two reasons: it works with applications written specifically for DOS, and it takes up only a very small amount of memory. We'll discuss both of these strengths in turn.

DOS for Backward Compatibility

Some organizations use DOS because they still use one or more special applications that require it, and they continue to use DOS on some computers for backward compatibility with the legacy application. Take Christine, for instance. She recently bought a small picture framing business that included an old PC that uses DOS along with an application program that computes frame prices. The program takes the dimensions of a picture and calculates the amount of matte and frame needed. Whenever prices for her supplies change, she can go into the program and enter the new prices. She likes the program, and she feels that it works well.

"Working well" should not be the sole reason for using DOS as the operating system for this application, because all versions of Windows can run DOS applications. How well a DOS application runs in Windows depends on how the DOS application was written—and therein lies the problem. If the application program was created to request operating system services in a standard way, then it should run in Windows much as it does under DOS. If the application was written to request services in a nonstandard way, then there are two possible outcomes: it may run much more slowly under Windows, or it may not run at all under Windows. The best practice is to test your DOS application in Windows before giving up your DOS computer.

● **Figure 2-1.**   A handheld inventory scanner

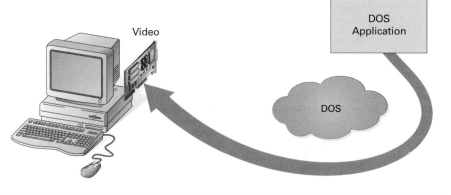

Video

DOS Application

DOS

• An application "reaching around" DOS to access hardware directly

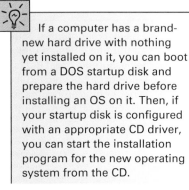

Because DOS was slow at accessing hardware and programmers wanted to make their applications run faster, many, if not most, DOS applications were written to request services from the hardware in nonstandard ways.

If a computer has a brand-new hard drive with nothing yet installed on it, you can boot from a DOS startup disk and prepare the hard drive before installing an OS on it. Then, if your startup disk is configured with an appropriate CD driver, you can start the installation program for the new operating system from the CD.

DOS Startup

1.44MB

High Density

• DOS startup diskette

DOS When You Need a Small OS

Another reason DOS is still hanging around here and there is that it is more compact than the various Windows OSs and therefore is useful when you need a very small operating system for embedded systems or for portability via a floppy disk.

Embedded systems are ROM-based operating systems and applications running on a computer embedded in a device such as a handheld computer or a smart kitchen appliance. Although Microsoft does offer scaled-down versions of Windows for those embedded systems that require a sophisticated GUI interface, DOS is a candidate for embedded systems that do not require such an interface.

The inventory-taking device that Lou uses at work is a good example. It is a scanner/computer that runs DOS as its OS. Both DOS and the application are stored in ROM and loaded into only 640KB of RAM. The device scans the universal product codes (UPCs) on in-store inventory and communicates wirelessly with the store's IBM inventory systems.

Another reason that the small size of DOS makes it attractive to use is that the files required to load DOS into memory (the boot files) fit easily on a 3.5 inch diskette. Because a diskette drive is installed in almost every PC made, a diskette is nearly universally usable. The ability to pack all of this onto a single diskette makes DOS popular as an OS for the software tools used by computer technicians and other computer professionals. Such a diskette, called a **startup disk**, can be used for many tasks, such as booting up a computer that will not boot from its hard drive or running special diagnostic programs to help find a problem. This may be the most important reason to use DOS today.

DOS is so small that a startup disk still has plenty of room for additional files, such as drivers and utilities. A **driver** is a special program that works with an OS to allow use of a particular piece of hardware, such as a mouse or CD-ROM drive, or to connect to a network. A **utility** is a program that allows you to perform handy tasks, usually computer management functions or diagnostics, such as upgrading the program in your computer's ROM BIOS or looking for errors on your disk. A utility is distinguished from an **application** in that an application is software that allows you to perform useful functions that create results you can use in your personal or business life, such as writing a report or calculating a budget.

You can also use a DOS startup disk to help install a new operating system if the contents of the CD for the new operating system are located on a file server computer on the company network. In that case, you need to use a startup disk with special network drivers to boot up the computer and connect it to the file server. Once connected, you can run the installation program for the new operating system over the network and install it on the local hard drive.

Let's talk for a moment about Nigel, who is an information technology (IT) worker in a large corporation. His toolkit carries an array of hardware tools, but the ones he values most are the software tools. He carries several CDs of software utilities, driver files, and patches, but he often surprises his clients when he pulls out a DOS startup disk. In fact, he carries several startup disks that are configured for different purposes. One contains the correct network drivers for his client's computers, and it also contains network client software that allows him to boot up a computer and connect to a network server from which he can start the installation of a new OS. Another disk is configured with the correct drivers and utilities to allow him to update the BIOS on his clients' computers. He never thought the tricks he learned playing on his father's old IBM PC would come in handy so many years later, but customers often are more impressed when he uses these diskettes than when he troubleshoots a very complicated network problem requiring much more sophisticated knowledge!

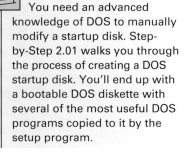

You need an advanced knowledge of DOS to manually modify a startup disk. Step-by-Step 2.01 walks you through the process of creating a DOS startup disk. You'll end up with a bootable DOS diskette with several of the most useful DOS programs copied to it by the setup program.

DOS's Weaknesses

DOS has significant processor mode, memory, multitasking, and hard disk usage limitations. We'll discuss each in turn.

DOS Processor Mode Limitations

DOS's processor mode limitations are actually the cause of the memory and multitasking limitations. This is because DOS was written for the Intel 8088 processor and the computer architecture (design) of the original IBM PC. The 8088 processor had a limited bag of tricks, because it had only one mode of operation: real mode. That means that DOS only understands how to work in real mode.

Newer Intel processors beginning with the 386DX still have real mode. In fact, these processors wake up in real mode; it takes software (the OS) to switch the processor into one of its more powerful protected modes. These processor modes were described in Chapter 1. The Windows OSs discussed in this book are all capable of using the more advanced protected modes of the newer processors.

• An Intel 8088 processor

DOS Memory Limitations

When you run DOS, you see and use only 1MB of memory address space. Further, the architecture of the PC allows only the first 640KB of this RAM to be used as the workspace for the operating system and the application programs and data. This memory is referred to as **conventional memory**. The remaining 384KB of address space

Try This!

Checking Memory Usage

If you already have MS-DOS installed on a computer, you can check out the memory usage with the MEM command. Try this:

1. At the DOS prompt, type **MEM** and press ENTER.

2. How much memory is used and how much is available?

is reserved for the system BIOS and the RAM and ROM on adapters, such as the video adapter and network cards. Figure 2-2 shows the result of using the DOS MEM command to look at memory usage. It shows that the OS is using 65KB of conventional memory, leaving 573KB of conventional memory for an application to use. The 15,360KB of memory shown as being used is the physical memory above 1MB (extended memory), which is not available to DOS as it is configured on this machine.

DOS Multitasking Limitations

DOS can't take advantage of the advanced multitasking capabilities of protected mode in the advanced Intel processors. Although DOS can have several drivers in memory at one time, it can run only one application program at a time. This is called **single-tasking**. The Windows and Mac operating systems discussed in this book allow several programs to run in memory at one time, and users can switch among them. This is called multitasking.

DOS Hard Drive Limitations

Another limitation of DOS is that it does not support hard drives larger than 7.8GB. Further, like most OSs, DOS uses logical drives. A **logical drive** is a portion of a physical hard drive that appears to be a drive with a letter assigned to it. You can have one or more logical drives on a physical drive, but DOS can use only logical drives that are each 2GB or less and within the 7.8GB total disk space limit.

■ Installing DOS

Now that you are familiar with the strengths and weaknesses of DOS, you are ready to install DOS on a PC. In this section, you'll learn the hardware requirements for DOS and the preparation needed before installing it. Then you'll have an opportunity to install DOS on a hard drive.

Remember Christine? She is shopping for a new computer because her old computer has failed. She discovered that her picture framing software

```
C:\>MEM

Memory Type         Total   =   Used    +    Free
--------------      --------    --------     --------
Conventional          638K        65K          573K
Upper                   0K         0K            0K
Reserved                0K         0K            0K
Extended (XMS)     15,360K    15,360K           0K
                   --------    --------     --------
Total memory       15,998K    15,425K          573K

Total under 1 MB      638K        65K          573K

Largest executable program size          573K (587,088 bytes)
Largest free upper memory block            0K       (0 bytes)

C:\>_
```

• **Figure 2-2.** The MEM command shows DOS memory usage.

won't run in any version of Windows, and she's decided that her new computer must have DOS installed so that she can run her picture frame application program—and she's determined to install DOS herself. How will she do this? Well, first she'll check out the hardware requirements of DOS, then she'll prepare to install DOS, and finally, she'll install it.

DOS Hardware Requirements

One of the strong points of DOS is that it can run on the most minimal of PCs—anything from an original 8088-based PC to one of today's lightning-fast Pentium 4 PCs. Therefore, the hardware requirements for DOS are very small. All you need is a personal computer that complies with the old IBM PC standards, or one of its Microsoft/Intel descendents.

Following are general DOS hardware requirements for MS-DOS 6.22 and IBM PC DOS 2000:

- IBM or compatible personal computer
- 6MB of free hard disk space for the DOS utilities, if installing onto a hard disk
- 512KB of memory

Preparing for DOS Installation

To install DOS on a computer hard disk, you must be sure that the computer is physically ready for the installation—that is, that the computer is a complete system, with at least the minimal components (see Chapter 1, "Introduction to Operating Systems") and all necessary connections for the components that are installed. Then, ensure that the computer is plugged into a power outlet.

The computer hard disk does not have to be prepared before the installation, because the MS-DOS 6.22 Setup program can prepare the hard disk. Preparation of a hard disk is a two step process: the first step is to create a partition, and the second step is to format the partition. The storage space on a physical hard disk is either a single logical drive (C:), or it can be subdivided into multiple logical drives (e.g. C:, D:, E:, and so on). A **partition** is an area of a physical hard disk that defines space that will be used for these drives. A logical drive is an area

Try This!

How Minimal Are the DOS Requirements?

Computer hardware and prices have come a long way since we bought our first IBM PC for about $5,000. Check out the cheapest computers you can buy for DOS. Try this:

1. Point your Internet browser to the Google search engine at www.google.com and search on Computer Retailer. In the search results, select a site that compares prices, because that is where you will find the cheapest PCs.

2. Look for the cheapest prices for a desktop PC. Does it meet or exceed the minimum requirements for MS-DOS?

Cross Check

Partitions

Need to know more about disk partition? Flip ahead to Chapter 4 and read the section titled "Creating a New Hard Disk Partition." Then answer these questions:

1. What is a primary partition?

2. What is an extended partition?

3. Which type of partition can be marked as active, and why is a partition marked as active?

within a partition that is viewed by the OS as a disk drive with a letter assigned to it. (Because this drive is not a physical reality, we use the term *logical* to describe the drive.) These logical drives must, in turn, be formatted by the OS before data can be stored on them.

Step-by-Step 2.01

Installing DOS on a Hard Disk

In the following steps, you will use the MS-DOS 6.22 setup diskettes to install DOS on a hard disk. The steps are written assuming that your computer's hard disk is unpartitioned and unformatted. To complete this exercise, you will need the following:

- A Microsoft/Intel standard personal computer (desktop or laptop)
- An unpartitioned hard drive
- The three DOS 6.22 setup disk

Step 1

Insert MS-DOS 6.22 Setup Disk 1 in drive A: and restart the computer. After the computer restarts, you'll briefly see a black screen with a message at the top left, "Starting MS-DOS." A blue Welcome to Setup screen will follow this. Press ENTER to set up MS-DOS.

```
Microsoft MS-DOS 6.22 Setup

    Welcome to Setup.

    The Setup program prepares MS-DOS 6.22 to run on your
    computer.

       • To set up MS-DOS now, press ENTER.

       • To learn more about Setup before continuing, press F1.

       • To exit Setup without installing MS-DOS, press F3.

    Note: If you have not backed up your files recently, you
          might want to do so before installing MS-DOS. To back
          up your files, press F3 to quit Setup now. Then, back
          up your files by using a backup program.

    To continue Setup, press ENTER.



ENTER=Continue   F1=Help   F3=Exit   F5=Remove Color   F7=Install to a Floppy Disk
```

Step 2

If your hard disk is unpartitioned, you will see a message saying that Setup needs to configure the unallocated space on your hard disk. With the highlight on Configure Unallocated Disk Space (Recommended), press ENTER.

```
Microsoft MS-DOS 6.22 Setup

          Setup needs to configure the unallocated space on your
          hard disk for use with MS-DOS. None of your existing
          files will be affected.

          To have Setup configure the space for you, choose the
          recommended option.

         ┌─────────────────────────────────────────────────────┐
         │ Configure unallocated disk space (recommended).      │
         │ Exit Setup.                                          │
         └─────────────────────────────────────────────────────┘

          To accept the selection, press ENTER.
          To change the selection, press the UP or DOWN ARROW key,
          and then press ENTER.

ENTER=Continue  F1=Help  F3=Exit
```

Step 3

You will see a message that Setup needs to restart your computer. Be sure Disk 1 is in drive A: and press ENTER to restart. After the restart, you will see the message "Starting MS-DOS" on a black screen, followed by a blue screen and a message saying that Setup is checking your system configuration. Then Setup will format drive C: (which will take a few minutes).

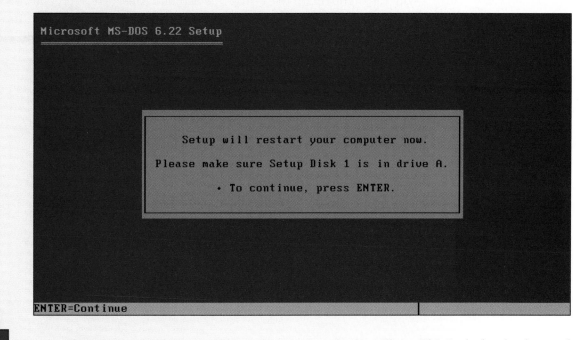
```
Microsoft MS-DOS 6.22 Setup




                ┌─────────────────────────────────────────────┐
                │                                             │
                │      Setup will restart your computer now.  │
                │                                             │
                │  Please make sure Setup Disk 1 is in drive A.│
                │                                             │
                │        • To continue, press ENTER.          │
                │                                             │
                └─────────────────────────────────────────────┘




ENTER=Continue
```

Step 4

The next screen shows you the system settings Setup will use. This includes the date and time, which Setup found by reading your computer's real-time clock, and the disk and directory where it will install the MS-DOS files. Check the date and time and, if they are correct, continue to Step 5.

If the date or time is not correct, use the up arrow key to move the highlight to the Date/ Time line; then press ENTER. Read the instructions on the page that appears and make the needed correction to the date or time; then, with the highlight on System Time, press ENTER to return to the previous screen.

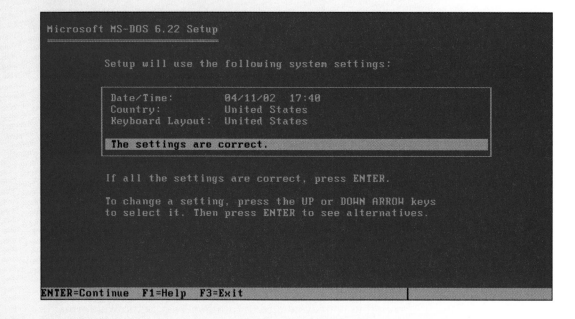

```
Microsoft MS-DOS 6.22 Setup

        Setup will use the following system settings:

        ┌─────────────────────────────────────────────────┐
        │ Date/Time:          04/11/02  17:40             │
        │ Country:            United States               │
        │ Keyboard Layout:    United States               │
        ├─────────────────────────────────────────────────┤
        │ The settings are correct.                       │
        └─────────────────────────────────────────────────┘

        If all the settings are correct, press ENTER.

        To change a setting, press the UP or DOWN ARROW keys
        to select it. Then press ENTER to see alternatives.




ENTER=Continue   F1=Help   F3=Exit
```

Step 5

With the highlight on the words The Settings Are Correct, press ENTER to continue the setup process. The next screen shows you the directory to which Setup will copy your MS-DOS files. The default location is C:\DOS. To accept this default, press ENTER.

```
Microsoft MS-DOS 6.22 Setup

        Setup will place your MS-DOS files in the following
        directory:

        C:\DOS_

        To place MS-DOS files in this directory, press ENTER.

        To place MS-DOS files in a different directory, type its
        path and press ENTER.









ENTER=Continue   F1=Help   F3=Exit
```

Step 6

Setup will now copy files onto your hard disk. While it is copying, you can actually see which files are being copied by looking at the bottom right of the screen, and a yellow bar shows the progress of the copy operation. Copying from diskette is a slow process, but you must still pay attention, because you will be prompted to insert Disk 2 and then Disk 3 at appropriate times as Setup copies files from each of these disks.

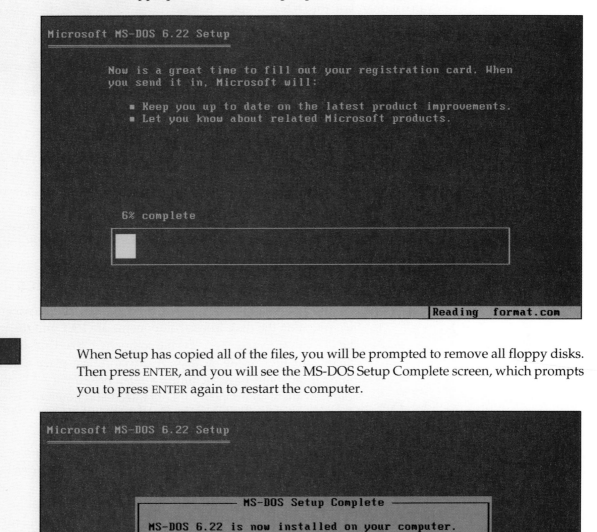

Step 7

When Setup has copied all of the files, you will be prompted to remove all floppy disks. Then press ENTER, and you will see the MS-DOS Setup Complete screen, which prompts you to press ENTER again to restart the computer.

```
Microsoft MS-DOS 6.22 Setup



                    ┌──────────── MS-DOS Setup Complete ────────────┐
                    │                                               │
                    │ MS-DOS 6.22 is now installed on your computer.│
                    │                                               │
                    │  • To restart your computer with MS-DOS 6.22, │
                    │    press ENTER.                               │
                    │                                               │
                    │  • To learn more about new MS-DOS 6.22 features,│
                    │    type HELP WHATSNEW at the command prompt.  │
                    │                                               │
                    └───────────────────────────────────────────────┘



ENTER=Continue
```

Step 8

When the computer restarts, you will see a "Starting MS-DOS" message at the top of the screen. This is usually followed by the results of special DOS commands that run during startup, and they will be followed by a **DOS prompt**, which consists of, at minimum, the drive letter followed by a blinking cursor, indicating that the command interpreter is open for business. This is also called the command prompt. Later in this chapter, you will have an opportunity to learn more about working with DOS, and you will run commands at the DOS prompt. When you use the MS-DOS 6.22 Setup program, you may see output resulting from drivers and programs loaded by DOS from commands read from the CONFIG.SYS and AUTOEXEC.BAT files during bootup.

```
Starting MS-DOS...

HIMEM is testing extended memory...done.

C:\>C:\DOS\SMARTDRV.EXE /X
C:\>_
```

■ How the FAT File System Works

It is important to learn about the FAT system because all of the Microsoft OSs (and some others) can work with this file system—even those OSs that can use more advanced file systems.

Now that you have installed MS-DOS, you should take some time to understand the core components of the FAT file system, including the FAT and the root directory. Learn how DOS uses these components to save and retrieve files and how it lets you manage your files by creating additional directories.

How DOS Uses Files and Directories

When DOS formats a disk, it places the two primary components of the FAT file system on the disk. These components are FAT and the root directory. The **file allocation table (FAT)** is the component that DOS uses to remember where your files reside on disk. A directory is a place where DOS stores information about files, including a reference to the FAT table. Let's consider how these components are organized and how DOS uses them.

FAT Table

The FAT table is a table in which DOS records how the disk space is used. To do this, DOS divides the entire disk space for one volume (A:, C:, and so on) into equal-sized allocation units called clusters. A **cluster** is the minimum space that can be given to a file, even if the file contains only 14 bytes, and the cluster size is 32,768 bytes. The FAT table has a single entry for each cluster. The entry is a status code, showing that a cluster is empty, occupied, or damaged. If it is occupied, the entry indicates whether the file is continued in another cluster. DOS uses the status code to save and retrieve files on disk.

Root Directory and Other Directories

A directory is a special file that can contain listings of files and other directories. The **root directory** is the top-level directory, and the only one that the FORMAT command creates. Other programs and users can create additional directories, which will be stored below the root in a hierarchical structure. A directory that contains other directories is sometimes called a parent directory, and a directory contained within another directory is called a child directory or subdirectory. The information DOS stores in a directory entry for a file includes the file name, extension, date and time of creation or modification, size, attributes, and beginning cluster number. Some of this information is displayed in the directory listing you see when you use the DOS DIR command as shown here.

```
C:\>dir

 Volume in drive C is MS-DOS_6
 Volume Serial Number is 2C98-8B17
 Directory of C:\

DOS          <DIR>         04-24-02    5:24p
COMMAND  COM        54,645 05-31-94    6:22a
CONFIG   SYS            50 07-25-02   10:18a
AUTOEXEC BAT            68 07-25-02   10:21a
XTREE        <DIR>         07-25-02   12:47p
WORD         <DIR>         07-25-02   12:48p
        6 file(s)         54,763 bytes
                   2,136,473,600 bytes free

C:\>_
```

• Directory listing using DIR command

Using FAT and the Directory to Find a File

How does DOS use a directory and FAT to find a file? It uses a directory much like you use a phone directory to find a street address: It searches for the file name in a directory, and when it finds the directory listing for the file, it looks for the starting cluster number (its address on disk). Then DOS uses FAT to locate the file, just as you would use a street map to find out how to get to a street address.

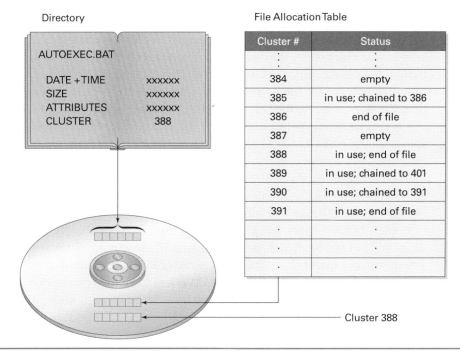

Cluster #	Status
⋮	⋮
384	empty
385	in use; chained to 386
386	end of file
387	empty
388	in use; end of file
389	in use; chained to 401
390	in use; chained to 391
391	in use; end of file
·	·
·	·
·	·

- DOS uses the directory and the file allocation table to find a file.

DOS File-Naming Rules

When working with files in DOS, you must understand the rules for naming files in DOS, and then you must understand the concept of file type. DOS can work only with files with a file name of up to eight characters, followed by a period, followed by an extension of up to three characters. This basic rule of file naming is called the 8.3 (eight-dot-three) naming convention. But wait; there is more to it than that. Aside from the dot, which separates the file name from the extension, within the file name and extension you can use only alphanumeric (A to Z and 1 to 0) characters, no spaces, and only a few special characters. These special characters are:

$ & # @ ! % ' ^ ( ) - _

Other characters, including math symbols and punctuation characters, are illegal or invalid characters in file names. They are:

/ \ [ ] | < > + = ; , * ?

Try This!

Make DOS Look for a File

The DOS TYPE command displays the contents of a text file on the screen. When you use this command, DOS must find the AUTOEXEC.BAT file on disk, using the directory information and the FAT information. Try this:

1. First, verify that the AUTOEXEC.BAT file is in the root of C: by entering **DIR AUTOEXEC.BAT** and pressing ENTER.

2. If the AUTOEXEC.BAT file is present, then enter **TYPE C:\ AUTOEXEC.BAT** and press ENTER.

Make life easier for yourself. Don't try to memorize the valid characters—just avoid using anything but alphanumeric characters.

In two decades of working with DOS, we have used the asterisk wildcard character about a thousand times more than the question mark wildcard character. Don't waste too much brainpower on the question mark character.

Examples of valid DOS 8.3 file names are README.TXT, FORMAT.COM, FDISK.EXE, AUTOEXEC.BAT, MONOUMB.386, and CONFIG.SYS.

Examples of illegal DOS 8.3 file names are READTHOSE.TXT, FORMAT[.COM, and README.FILE. The first file name in this second group is invalid because the file name portion is too long; the second is invalid because it contains an illegal character; and the third is invalid because the extension portion is too long.

In addition to the file name and extension, you may need to tell DOS exactly where a file is, in which case you need to provide the path to the file. The path to a file includes the drive letter (C:) plus a backslash (\). If you stop at that point (C:\), you are pointing to the root directory. If you follow that with a file name (C:\AUTOEXEC.BAT, for instance), DOS looks in the root directory for the file. If the file is in a subdirectory, you need to include that. C:\DOS points to the DOS subdirectory of the root directory, for example. If you want to point to a file in that directory, you add the name: for instance, C:\DOS\EDIT.COM. Directories within directories are separated by the backslash symbol (\).

You can also use the asterisk (*) and question mark (?) as wildcard characters. The asterisk can be used to replace all characters from that point to the end of the file name or all characters to the end of the extension. For example, *.DOC refers to all files with the DOS extension. Similarly, README.* refers to all files with the README file name and any extension. The question mark replaces a single character for each instance of the question mark. For instance DISKCO??.COM refers to all files that match on the provided characters and have any characters in the seventh or eighth place of the file name.

DOS File Types

DOS recognizes several different file types. Some of these file types contain text data, and others contain program code and are referred to as binary files. We usually don't make DOS guess which is which; we identify the file type of a file with a special extension. Following is a list of common file extensions and the file types each identifies to DOS:

.bak	A file containing backup data
.bas	A BASIC program file
.bat	A batch file (a special text file in which each line is treated like a command at the DOS prompt)
.com	An executable binary file
.doc	A word processor data file, usually containing text plus the special codes for formatting the text when printed
.exe	An executable binary file using a more complicated structure than a COM file
.sys	A device driver or operating system file
.txt	A file containing text without special codes for formatting the text

Executable Files

DOS considers three types of files to be executable: COM, EXE, and BAT. COM and EXE files both contain programming code; the difference between these two types of files is not important to us in this chapter. BAT files are batch files, which are not programs, but text files that contain commands that you could type at the command prompt, but which you chose to put in a batch file. When DOS executes a batch file, it uses the command interpreter to interpret each line of the batch file. The batch file acts like a script for the command interpreter. This is called batch processing. Batch processing is a great way to automate tasks you perform frequently. Perhaps you back up the files you are working on every day by copying them to diskette, for instance; you could create a batch file to automate this process.

Step-by-Step 2.02

Creating a Simple Batch File

You can easily create a batch file for copying files from your hard drive to diskette. You would normally do this with data files, but we will do it with some of the files in your DOS directory.

To complete this exercise you will need:

- A computer with MS-DOS 6.22 installed
- A blank formatted diskette

Step 1

At the command prompt, enter **EDIT XBACK.BAT** and press ENTER. This names the batch file you are creating. In the Edit program, type the following.

```
@ECHO OFF
ECHO Data files will be copied to A:
ECHO Please insert a blank formatted diskette. Then...
PAUSE
XCOPY C:\DOS\*.TXT A:
XCOPY C:\DOS\*.INI A:
ECHO All data files have been copied.
ECHO Remove the diskette and store in a safe place.
```

```
 File  Edit  Search  Options                                         Help
                          ┌─────── XBACK.BAT ────────┐
 @ECHO OFF
 ECHO Data files will be copied to A:
 ECHO Please insert a blank formatted diskette. Then...
 PAUSE
 XCOPY C:\DOS\*.TXT A:
 XCOPY C:\DOS\*.INI A:
 ECHO All data files have been copied.
 ECHO Remove the diskette and store in a safe place.




 F1=Help    Enter=Display Menu    Esc=Cancel    Arrow=Next Item      00003:052
```

Step 2

Check your spelling. Case is not significant to DOS. You can enter commands in either uppercase or lowercase. We have used uppercase to distinguish commands and used mixed case for the messages that will be displayed, to make this information more readable here. We don't believe that all uppercase makes text more readable—used in the extreme, it feels like visual shouting! When you are sure that your file is free of typos, save it by pressing the ALT key plus the F key (they do not have to be simultaneously pressed), which will open the File menu. At the File menu, press S for Save. This will save the file in your current directory, which should be the root directory at present, since we have not yet taught you to change the current directory.

Step 3

Leave the Edit program by selecting the File menu and pressing X for Exit. Check for the presence of the file at the DOS prompt by typing **DIR**. Confirm that XBACK.BAT is listed.

Step 4

Test the batch file by typing **XBACK** and pressing ENTER. If your batch file is working correctly, you should see the message you typed on the second and third lines of the batch file without the command ECHO at the beginning of the line. We used the ECHO command in two ways here. First we used it to turn off the echoing of the commands to the screen, with ECHO OFF. We preceded that command with the @ symbol, which turns off echoing of that line to the screen. After that, everything that appears on the screen is the result of the commands. The PAUSE command pauses the execution of the commands in the batch file until you press a key. It's the PAUSE command that sends the message "Press any key to continue . . .".

Step 5

Follow the instructions and press any key. Once more, you do not see the command lines from the batch file, just the results of the commands (the message each command sends to the screen). When the processing is complete, you will see the last two lines of messages. This is a very, very simple batch file. It could be improved in many ways, but it is a great beginning if you have never created a batch file before.

```
C:\>xback
Data files will be copied to A:
Please insert a blank formatted diskette, Then...
Press any key to continue . . .

Reading source file(s)...
C:\DOS\COUNTRY.TXT
C:\DOS\README.TXT
C:\DOS\NETWORKS.TXT
C:\DOS\DRVSPACE.TXT
        4 File(s) copied
Reading source file(s)...
C:\DOS\DOSSETUP.INI
C:\DOS\SCANDISK.INI
        2 File(s) copied
All data files have been copied.
Remove the diskette and store in a safe place.
C:\>_
```

DOS File Attributes

In addition to file types, DOS uses **file attributes** that are saved in each file or directory entry. These attributes determine how DOS handles the file. For instance, if the file attribute for directory is turned on, or *set*, then the file entry is for a directory, and, rather than pointing to the location of a file, it points to another directory listing. The DOS file attributes are as follows:

- **read-only**   An attribute that indicates that a file may not be modified or deleted. DOS automatically puts this attribute on certain files as a small measure of protection. Anyone using a program that ignores this attribute or using a program that lets the user turn off this attribute can delete a read-only file.

- **archive**   An attribute that indicates that a file has been created or modified since the last backup. DOS places this attribute on all new or changed files. Most backup programs can turn off this attribute for each file backed up.

- **system**   A special attribute that DOS gives to the system files, IO.SYS and MSDOS.SYS.

- **hidden**   An attribute that will cause a file or directory to be hidden from programs that pay attention to this attribute, such as the DIR command.

- **volume label**   An attribute used for a special root directory entry, which can be used to give a disk a label or name.

- **directory**   An attribute that indicates that the entry is a directory, not a file.

It is worth learning about these attributes, because they are used in the FAT file system in all OSs, and because later, when you work with newer file systems, you will discover that they also have attributes—and some are identical to the FAT file attributes. How are these attributes used? Well, for example, when you format a disk, as shown in Figure 2-3, you may give the disk a name, which is stored as a special file with the volume label attribute.

If a hard disk drive has a volume label and you attempt to format it again, the MS-DOS FORMAT program asks for the volume label name before it will complete the formatting. This is not actually a security measure, since you can use the VOL command or the DIR command to see the volume label, but it does make you stop and maybe think before formatting a disk. That may be just enough to make you realize that you are trying to format the wrong drive! If you want to add a volume label after formatting a drive, use the LABEL command.

You should never change the directory attribute manually, because it is created by the OS when it creates a directory. This attribute tells the OS that this is not an ordinary file, but a directory. Likewise, you shouldn't mess with the system attribute because it is used by the OS to identify its own very special files, such as IO.SYS and MSDOS.SYS. Also, it's important for a computer professional to understand the read-only and hidden attributes, because the first one may keep you from editing a file someday, and the second one may keep you from seeing a file on disk. You will soon have opportunities to work with each of these attributes.

```
C:\>FORMAT A: /U
Insert new diskette for drive A:
and press ENTER when ready...

Formatting 1.44M
Format complete.

Volume label (11 characters, ENTER for none)? DATADISK1_
```

● **Figure 2-3.**   Adding a volume label with the FORMAT command

Format a disk, adding a volume label during the formatting. Then change the label to a different name. You will need a diskette that is expendable. Try this:

1. Place the diskette in the floppy drive and, at the DOS prompt, type **FORMAT A:** and press ENTER.

2. When prompted for a volume label, enter your first name (up to 11 characters) and press ENTER. When asked if you would like to format another, press N and ENTER.

3. Change the volume label. At the DOS prompt, type **LABEL** and press ENTER. When prompted for a volume label, type **datadisk1** and press ENTER.

One way to display and modify some of these attributes is to use the ATTRIB command, shown in Figure 2-4. The DOS ATTRIB command lets you view and manipulate all but the directory and volume label attributes. This is an important command if you work with DOS and need to modify a file that has the read-only attribute, or if you want to make a file read-only to protect it. The ATTRIB command works in all versions of Windows on both the FAT and the newer NTFS file systems. NTFS stands for NT file system, an advanced file system available only with Windows NT, Windows 2000, and Windows XP desktop OSs.

■ Working with the DOS Command Prompt

At a minimum, you need to know the ins and outs of working at the DOS prompt and with the online Help system. You also need to become proficient with the handful of DOS commands that are the most useful for managing directories and files. We'll discuss each in turn.

Success at the DOS Prompt

The last command line entered is saved in memory. Use shortcut keys to repeat it so you can check for typos. Use the right arrow key to repeat one character at a time, the left arrow key to remove one character at a time, and press F3 to repeat the last line typed.

Up to this point, we have done a few things at the command prompt without much instruction. Were you successful, or did you receive confusing error messages? Success at the DOS prompt is important to you because you will need to use a similar command prompt in almost any OS you encounter as a computer professional—not every day perhaps, but when you want to run small programs that perform a useful administrative or diagnostic task for you. Success at the DOS prompt means correctly entering commands and getting the results you desired. Before you can achieve either of these goals, you need to discover which command will accomplish the task you have in mind, determine the correct syntax for that command, and finally, understand how to correctly enter the command at the command prompt. This requires that you understand how a command is interpreted.

Which Command Will Accomplish the Task?

To discover which command will accomplish the task you have in mind, you must do some detective work. One way to do this is to ask an experienced DOS nerd. Since you probably won't have someone like that handy all the time, a good substitute is the DOS HELP program. Learn to use it!

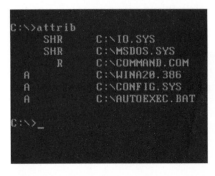

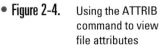

Figure 2-4. Using the ATTRIB command to view file attributes

DOS has a fairly simple help program that does not allow you to conduct the more sophisticated searches you will find in other OS help programs. However, many of the command names are actually related to the task the command performs, unlike some of the UNIX commands you will study later. At the command prompt, simply type **HELP**, and you will get a listing of MS-DOS commands with descriptions. Browse through the list to find the command you need.

> MS-DOS HELP has on-screen instructions, which are helpful, except that they neglect to tell you that you can use the arrow keys to move the selection highlight and the ENTER key to select a highlighted item.

Step-by-Step 2.03

Using the Online Help in DOS

In the following steps, you will learn how to navigate through the DOS HELP program so that, in the future, you can turn to HELP when you are unsure of what command to use and how to use it.

You will also take this opportunity to learn more about the ATTRIB command.

To complete this exercise, you will need a computer with DOS 6.22 installed on the hard disk.

Step 1

At the DOS prompt, type **HELP** and press ENTER. Notice the instructions at the top. If you performed a standard DOS 6.22 installation, you will not have a mouse driver installed and will therefore not be able to use the scroll bars, but you can move around using both the PAGE UP and PAGE DOWN keys and the up and down arrow keys. Press PAGE DOWN to see more of the commands. Press PAGE UP to return to the top of the page.

```
 File  Search                                                          Help
                        MS-DOS Help: Command Reference
 
 Use the scroll bars to see more commands. Or, press the PAGE DOWN key. For
 more information about using MS-DOS Help, choose How to Use MS-DOS Help
 from the Help menu, or press F1. To exit MS-DOS Help, press ALT, F, X.
 
 <What's New in MS-DOS 6.22?>
 
 <ANSI.SYS>                  <EMM386.EXE>                 <Multi-config>
 <Append>                    <Erase>                      <Nlsfunc>
 <Attrib>                    <Exit>                       <Numlock>
 <Batch commands>            <Expand>                     <Path>
 <Break>                     <Fasthelp>                   <Pause>
 <Buffers>                   <Fastopen>                   <Power>
 <Call>                      <Fc>                         <POWER.EXE>
 <Cd>                        <Fcbs>                       <Print>
 <Chcp>                      <Fdisk>                      <Prompt>
 <Chdir>                     <Files>                      <Qbasic>
 <Chkdsk>                    <Find>                       <RAMDRIVE.SYS>
 <CHKSTATE.SYS>              <For>                        <Rd>
 <Choice>                    <Format>                     <Rem>
 <Cls>                       <Goto>                       <Ren>
 <Command>                   <Graphics>                   <Rename>
 F1=Help   Enter=Display Menu   Esc=Cancel   Arrow=Next Item        00006:002
```

Step 2

Press ALT and then H followed by ENTER to access the How to Use MS-DOS Help page. It lists seven topics, each with a green less-than (<) sign to its left. The cursor should be on the first topic, Navigating Through MS-DOS Help; if it is not, use the TAB key to move there, and then press ENTER to select and read the topic.

Step 3	Read through that topic, then press ALT and then B to go back to the topic list. Continue through all seven topics, reading the explanations provided. When you are finished, press ESC (twice, if necessary) to return to the How to Use MS-DOS Help page.
Step 4	Select the ATTRIB command and learn how you can see the file attributes of all of the files in the current directory.
Step 5	When you are finished press ALT, then F, and then X to exit MS-DOS HELP and return to the DOS prompt.
Step 6	Now apply what you learned from the MS-DOS HELP program. At the DOS prompt, use the ATTRIB command to see the file attributes of the files in the root of C:.

What Is the Correct Syntax?

You know how to find the command that will accomplish a task, but you also need to know how to tell the command exactly what to do. This requires that you know the syntax of the command. **Syntax** is a set of rules for correctly entering a specific command at the command line. This includes the command name and the parameters that act as instructions to the command. You can use the DOS HELP program to find the syntax for a command, or you can type the command name followed by the /? parameter. Figure 2-5 shows the result of typing COPY /? at the command prompt.

It should not come as a surprise to you that the MS-DOS syntax is cryptic. Let's look at the syntax of the COPY command together. To correctly enter the COPY command, you must first type **COPY** followed by the optional and required parameters in the order shown. All optional parameters are shown in square brackets, and required parameters are shown without brackets. The brackets, of course, are not to be used in the actual command line. The source is the only required parameter, and it is the file or files to be copied (you can include the path to a file, as in C:\DOS\CHKDSK.EXE). The destination is not required, but if you don't provide it, the directory you're currently in will be assumed.

 Try This!

Check Out the Syntax for DOS Commands

Once you know the name of a DOS command, you can easily discover the correct syntax. Try this:

1. At the DOS command prompt, type **CHKDSK /?** and press ENTER. If you are using MS-DOS 6.22, you may be surprised at the suggestion in the last paragraph of the screen output. It recommends that you use SCANDISK rather then CHKDSK.

2. Check out another command: at the DOS command prompt, type **XCOPY /?** and press ENTER.

How Is a Command Interpreted?

At the command prompt, you might enter a command like DIR, which is only the name of a command. Or you might enter a command that includes both the command name and instructions to the command, as in DIR A: /A. In any case, what you enter at the command prompt is interpreted by a special component of your OS called the command interpreter, which in MS-DOS is COMMAND.COM. This component receives commands, finds the actual

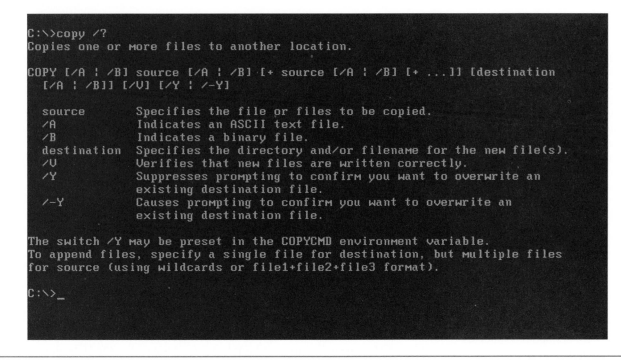

```
C:\>copy /?
Copies one or more files to another location.

COPY [/A | /B] source [/A | /B] [+ source [/A | /B] [+ ...]] [destination
  [/A | /B]] [/V] [/Y | /-Y]

  source        Specifies the file or files to be copied.
  /A            Indicates an ASCII text file.
  /B            Indicates a binary file.
  destination   Specifies the directory and/or filename for the new file(s).
  /V            Verifies that new files are written correctly.
  /Y            Suppresses prompting to confirm you want to overwrite an
                existing destination file.
  /-Y           Causes prompting to confirm you want to overwrite an
                existing destination file.

The switch /Y may be preset in the COPYCMD environment variable.
To append files, specify a single file for destination, but multiple files
for source (using wildcards or file1+file2+file3 format).

C:\>_
```

● **Figure 2-5.** The COPY command syntax

program code for the command, loads the program code into memory, and passes any additional instructions (such as A: /A) to the command.

Some commands have no additional instructions, such as the VER command, which only displays the MS-DOS version and nothing else, but most DOS commands have many instructions you can use. The list of such commands is quite long, but they include DEL, COPY, REN, and XCOPY, just to name a few. In fact, many commands will not work without additional instructions. Figure 2-6 shows the output to the screen after we ran all of the commands listed in the preceding sentence without any command parameters. Notice that only the VER command works successfully without any further instructions.

Let's look at this process more closely. When you type something on the command line and press ENTER, the DOS command interpreter behind the scenes kicks into action. It takes what you entered on the command line and parses it, meaning that it divides the command into its components. DOS's command interpreter parses your entry based on special delimiter characters. The most important delimiter character to remember is the space character (the result of pressing the spacebar). When a command line is parsed, the components are called parameters. For instance, DIR A: /A has three parameters: DIR, A:, and /A. The first parameter must be the command; the other parameters must be valid parameters that the command understands. A parameter that begins with a forward slash (/) is called a switch.

How Is a Program Found and Loaded?

The next job for the DOS command interpreter is to load the command named at the beginning of the command line. DOS looks for the command by searching in some special places. Let's say you entered the command

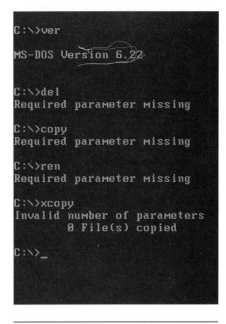

```
C:\>ver

MS-DOS Version 6.22

C:\>del
Required parameter missing

C:\>copy
Required parameter missing

C:\>ren
Required parameter missing

C:\>xcopy
Invalid number of parameters
         0 File(s) copied

C:\>_
```

● **Figure 2-6.** Parameter error messages

Strictly speaking, DOS does not require a space before switches (parameters that begin with a forward slash like /A). But you should get into the habit of always placing a space before each parameter when you type a command, because spaces are required between all parameters when you enter commands from the Start | Run menu in Windows.

There are about 30 internal commands, but you will use only about half of them frequently. They include CD, CLS, COPY, DATE, DIR, MD, PATH, PROMPT, ECHO, REM, RD, SET, TIME, TYPE, VER, and VOL. Use the DOS HELP program to learn more about these commands.

The DOS directory holds 50 DOS commands, but you will normally use only a handful, including ATTRIB.EXE, CHKDSK.EXE, DELTREE.EXE, DISKCOPY.COM, EDIT.COM, FORMAT.COM, MEM.EXE, PRINT.EXE, SCANDISK.EXE, SYS.COM, TREE.COM, XCOPY, and UNDELETE.EXE.

CHKDSK. Because you have not provided a file name extension with the command (which is quite normal), DOS will first check its own list of **internal commands**. This is a list within COMMAND.COM that contains the commands that reside within COMMAND.COM and that are not stored as separate files on disk. If it finds the command name in that list, DOS doesn't search any further and loads the code into memory, passing on any other parameters that were on the command line. Internal commands are fast because they don't need to be searched for.

Well, our example command, CHKDSK, is not an internal command, which DOS will discover after checking the list. Now DOS will look for an external command that matches. An **external command** is a file stored on disk that contains instructions and has one of the following extensions: .com, .exe, or .bat. (Typing CHKDSK.EXE on the command line would have told DOS earlier that this was an external command.) But because we didn't include the file name extension, DOS is still not sure about the exact file. Now DOS will look for a match, using those extensions. But wait! Where does DOS look for external commands? It first looks in the current directory, and then it consults a list called the search path. The search path is controlled by the PATH command, which should be included in the AUTOEXEC.BAT file. If the PATH command looks like PATH=C:\DOS;C:\WORD, then to find the CHKDSK command after it has searched the internal list and the current directory, DOS searches in the C:\DOS directory and then in the C:\WORD directory. In each location, DOS first looks for CHKDSK.COM, then CHKDSK.EXE, and then CHKDSK.BAT, in that order. If it finds a match, it loads the program into memory and doesn't look any further. In the case of CHKDSK, it would stop after finding CHKDSK.EXE in C:\DOS. Since DOS's external commands can be used only when DOS can find them on disk, they may not be available to use if they haven't been installed.

Learning to Manage Files and Directories

DOS has a no-frills file management system which is centered on the abilities and limits of the FAT file system. To manage files in DOS, you need to consider strategies for organizing your data in the FAT file system, and you need to know the commands you will use to do this. This is worth learning, because every Microsoft OS and most UNIX OSs can use the FAT file system. Even OSs that can use more advanced file systems usually can also work with the FAT file system. Therefore, skills you learn here can be applied in OSs other than DOS.

Designing a Directory Structure for File Management

Earlier, you studied how the root directory is used by DOS. Now you will take a different view of the root directory as you decide what directories to create within it to hold your data files. You can even create directories within directories, so your directory design can get pretty fancy.

When it comes to organizing data in your computer, think "office supplies" and imagine that your computer is a filing cabinet and that each logical drive (with its root directory) is a drawer in that cabinet. The directories you create at the root would be the large hanging folders, and the directories created at the next level are the smaller folders placed within the hanging folders.

Of course, individual files can be placed in any of these directories, but you should design a directory structure that works for your own need to save and organize your files. Always reserve the root directory for the files needed by the OS during startup and for your top-level subdirectories.

Figure 2-7 shows the result of using the DOS TREE command to view directories. The DOS Setup program created the DOS directory, but a user created the other directories. The DATA directory is where he stores all of his data files, and the APPS directory is where he installs all of his applications. The directory C:\APPS\EXCEL contains the Microsoft Excel program files, and the directory C:\APPS\WORD contains the Microsoft Word program files.

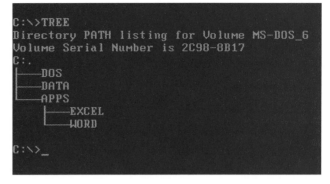

```
C:\>TREE
Directory PATH listing for Volume MS-DOS_6
Volume Serial Number is 2C98-8B17
C:.
├───DOS
├───DATA
└───APPS
    ├───EXCEL
    └───WORD

C:\>_
```

● **Figure 2-7.** Directories viewed with the TREE command

The word processing and spreadsheet files that he creates with these two programs are saved in the DATA directory. The logic behind this design, in which the applications are stored in one directory hierarchy, and the data is saved in another directory structure, has to do with backups.

Regardless of whether this user performs his backups with an actual backup program or simply uses a COPY command, he can start his backup at the top level (DATA or APPS) and back up the contents of all child directories. His data files change more frequently than his application files; so he will want to back up the DATA directory more often than the APPS directory.

Creating and Removing Directories

Let's say you want to create several new directories to organize your data files. Remember that the directory structure is hierarchical: that is, a directory can contain other directories as well as files. The hierarchy is Drive | Directory | File Name. Remember that a directory that contains other directories is a *parent* directory, and a directory inside a parent directory is a *child* directory, or subdirectory.

The DOS command to create a directory is MD (Make Directory). The syntax is MD [*drive:*]*path*.

The DOS command to move between directories has two possible common names: CD and CHDIR. Both stand for Change Directory and are identical in function. You use the Change Directory command to change the current directory. After executing either command, you will be located in the new directory, and any subsequent commands that you issue that operate on a directory will operate on the directory you are currently in.

You should never save data files in the root directory because doing so is like dumping things into a filing cabinet drawer without using folders and dividers to organize them. A technical reason for not saving files in the root directory is that, unlike subdirectories, the root directory can't grow. If everything is saved in the root directory, it will eventually reach that limit, and you will get a "Disk Full" error message, even though the disk isn't full!

Try This!

View Your Directories

If you installed DOS on your lab computer hard disk in Step-by-Step 2.01, you can look at the root directory and a child or subdirectory. Try this:

1. Start your computer. When DOS appears, you will be at the root directory.

2. To see the contents of the root directory, at the command prompt type **DIR** and press ENTER. You will see some files and a single directory, DOS.

3. To view the entire directory structure, at the command prompt type **TREE** and press ENTER.

4. To look at the contents of the DOS directory, at the command prompt type **DIR DOS** and press ENTER.

5. To learn more about the DIR command, at the command prompt type **DIR /?** and press ENTER.

One convenient shortcut when moving between directories is the double dot (..). When you type **CD ..** (or **CHDIR ..**), you move to the parent directory of the directory you are in. Thus, you can easily move up a hierarchy without having to enter the name of each parent directory. Similarly, **CD ** moves you directly to the root.

A number of DOS commands have alternate forms. Use whichever form you can remember most easily.

Use File Management Commands

DOS has several commands you can use for file management tasks. These commands let you copy, move, and delete files, as well as create, move, and delete directories. Remember that some of these commands are internal commands, which are loaded into memory along with DOS, ready to run whenever you need them. These small and fast commands include DIR (Directory), CD (Change Directory), CLS (Clear Screen), COPY, REN (REName), MD (Make Directory), CD (Change Directory), TYPE, and RD (Remove Directory).

Three often-used external commands, XCOPY, DISKCOPY, and DELTREE, are enhancements to internal commands. For instance, XCOPY and DISKCOPY can copy in ways that the internal COPY command can't. XCOPY can copy files and entire directories, while COPY can copy only files—it has no understanding of directories. DISKCOPY can make a diskette-to-diskette copy, creating an exact duplicate of the original diskette. The DELTREE command can delete an entire directory and its contents, while the internal RD (Remove Directory) command can delete only an empty directory.

Another external command is the HELP command (HELP.COM), which is included in the nearly 6MB of files that the DOS Setup program installs in the DOS directory on a hard disk. If you are new to DOS, this command can be the keys to the city for you. While not as fancy as the help programs that come with Windows, the DOS HELP program explains the purpose of each command, defines the syntax (rules for using), and gives examples of each command. We recommend that you practice using it!

Step-by-Step 2.04

Managing Files and Directories

Let's practice. Say you want to create a new directory named testdata in the root of C:, copy several files into it, examine the files to make sure they are there, and then delete those copied files and the testdata directory.

To complete this exercise, you will need a computer with DOS installed on the hard disk.

Step 1

At the DOS prompt, type **DIR** and press ENTER.

A listing of files and directories in the root (C:\) is displayed.

Step 2

To move down one level into the DOS directory, type **CD DOS** and press ENTER.

Your screen display should look like the one shown here.

Step 3

Type **DIR** and press ENTER.

You probably saw only a blur as over 5MB of files contained in C:\ DOS went streaming past. Clearly you need to do something else in order to examine the directories contained in C:\DOS.

```
C:\>dir

 Volume in drive C is MS-DOS_6
 Volume Serial Number is 2C98-8B17
 Directory of C:\

DOS          <DIR>          04-24-02    5:24p
COMMAND  COM         54,645 05-31-94    6:22a
WINA20   386          9,349 05-31-94    6:22a
CONFIG   SYS             71 04-29-02    8:51p
AUTOEXEC BAT             78 04-24-02    6:02p
         5 file(s)         64,143 bytes
                   2,138,013,696 bytes free

C:\>cd dos

C:\DOS>_
```

Step 4

Type **DIR /?** and press ENTER to get a listing of the available syntax for the DIR command: that is, the basic command structure and the available switch settings that provide alternate behaviors of the command. Notice that if you use the /P (for Pause) switch, the listing will pause after each screenful of data. Try it now. Type **DIR /P** and press ENTER. You can now examine the contents of C:\DOS screenful by screenful.

Step 5

To return to the root of C:, type **CD ..** (that's two periods or dots) and press ENTER. You are now back at the root of C:. Test this by typing **DIR**.

Step 6

To create your testdata directory, type **MD TESTDATA** (MD stands for Make Directory) and press ENTER.

Step 7

One of the things you have to get used to with DOS is the lack of feedback when things work correctly. DOS usually will tell you when a command does not work, but when a command does work, there is often no apparent evidence that it did—so you have to check to see whether or not it did work. One common way to check is to type **DIR** again and read the listing to see if your new directory is shown. You also can simply type **MD TESTDATA** again; if you receive the error message that DOS cannot create the directory because it already exists, you know that the command worked. (Checking step-by-step is good.)

Step 8

You will have noticed that the information on the MS-DOS prompt screen simply scrolls up the screen as new lines of text appear, and it is lost when it scrolls off the top; you can't get it back without reentering the command. The screen also becomes very cluttered, and it is often useful to clear it.

Type **CLS** (for CLear Screen) and press ENTER to clear the screen.

Step 9

It's time to copy some information into your testdata directory. Let's find out what the syntax for the COPY command is. Type **COPY /?** and press ENTER.

The syntax for the command is displayed. Complicated, isn't it? This shows how obtuse DOS syntax can be. We'll simplify it for you: the syntax basically is COPY (space) from-location (space) to-location. Be sure to put the space between each entry because that allows the OS to parse the command.

Step 10

Type **COPY C:\DOS*.TXT C:\ TESTDATA** and press ENTER.

You'll notice that we used the wildcard character (*) to copy all files with the .txt extension—and only those files.

Step 11

Check to see if the command worked. Type **CD TESTDATA** and press ENTER to change focus to the testdata directory. Then type **DIR** and press ENTER to display the contents of that directory.

You should see a list of files with .txt extensions in the testdata directory as shown here.

```
C:\>copy c:\dos\*.txt c:\testdata
C:\DOS\COUNTRY.TXT
C:\DOS\README.TXT
C:\DOS\NETWORKS.TXT
C:\DOS\DRVSPACE.TXT
        4 file(s) copied

C:\>cd testdata

C:\TESTDATA>dir

 Volume in drive C is MS-DOS_6
 Volume Serial Number is 2C98-8B17
 Directory of C:\TESTDATA

.            <DIR>         05-01-02   9:52p
..           <DIR>         05-01-02   9:52p
COUNTRY  TXT        15,920 05-31-94   6:22a
README   TXT        60,646 05-31-94   6:22a
NETWORKS TXT        17,465 05-31-94   6:22a
DRVSPACE TXT        41,512 05-31-94   6:22a
        6 file(s)        135,543 bytes
                   2,137,784,320 bytes free

C:\TESTDATA>_
```

Step 12

Let's say you have changed your mind and now you want to get rid of all the files in testdata. You also want to be very sure to delete only the files in testdata.

Type **DEL C:\TESTDATA*.*** and press ENTER to delete all file names with all extensions.

Type **Y** and press ENTER when you see this warning:

```
All files in directory will be deleted!
Are you sure (Y/N)?
```

Notice that we used the wildcard symbol in both the file name and the extension to say that we want to include all files.

Step 13

Again, you need to check what actually happened.

Type **DIR** and press ENTER.

The testdata directory should be empty again, with only the dot (.) and dot-dot (..) files that are part of any subdirectory.

Step 14

We need to get rid of our testdata directory now.

Type **CD ..** and press ENTER to move up to the root of C:.

Step 15

Now we use the RD command to remove a directory. Type **RD TESTDATA** and press ENTER. Confirm that the testdata directory was deleted by typing **DIR** and pressing ENTER again. There should be no sign of testdata.

■ Understanding the DOS Bootup Process and Required Startup Disks

Nigel has found that understanding the boot process has helped him with his job. In this section, you will discover why you should learn the boot process for any OS with which you work. Then you will learn about DOS system files, how the DOS boot process works, and how to create a DOS startup disk.

Why You Should Learn the DOS Bootup Process

Personal computers are multipurpose devices. They become the tools you need them to be only through the installation, first, of hardware components, internal or external to the computer, and then second, through the OS. The OS, in turn, usually has modifications in the form of commands that tell it how to behave and device drivers that add the ability to work with the available hardware. The computer finally becomes the tool you need for the jobs in your personal and business life when application programs are installed. These application programs rely on the OS for services they need.

Nigel has now worked with several different OSs and has found that a significant number of problems with microcomputers occur, or make themselves known, during the bootup (or startup) process. Therefore, understanding the normal startup process for personal computers in general and then for each individual OS helps him to troubleshoot problems that show up during bootup. Careful observation will tell him at what point in the bootup process the failure is occurring. Then he can troubleshoot, using his knowledge of what components must be missing or damaged to cause the problem.

DOS System Files

There are three critical DOS files collectively called the system files. In MS-DOS, they are IO.SYS, MSDOS.SYS, and COMMAND.COM. These files must be present in the root of drive C: to start DOS from your hard disk, and they must be in the root of a floppy disk to start DOS from that floppy. These files make up the bare-bones OS. They are all read-only, and the first two also have both the hidden and system attributes set. IO.SYS handles interaction with hardware and the loading of device drivers during bootup. MSDOS.SYS is the main (or kernel) component of the OS, and COMMAND.COM is the command interpreter that provides you with the famous command prompt and interprets commands.

Figure 2-8 shows the result of running the DIR (Directory) command in the root of drive C: with DOS installed. Notice that we used the /A (All) switch to tell the DIR command to show all files, even those with hidden attributes. You can see the three DOS system files, CONFIG.SYS, and AUTOEXEC.BAT. DOS uses the CONFIG.SYS and AUTOEXEC.BAT files during bootup. These two files are text files, since they contain only text, and they have no special formatting codes. What they have in common is that they can be read using any text editor or word processor. Let's see how they are different by looking at when and how these files are used.

CONFIG.SYS

The CONFIG.SYS file is used to add device drivers to DOS and to modify DOS settings. To work with a CONFIG.SYS file, you use a text editor to create or modify the file, entering special commands. Then you place the file in the root of the **boot disk**, which is drive C: if DOS is installed on your hard drive; or it can be a bootable floppy disk that you insert into your floppy drive. DOS automatically looks for CONFIG.SYS immediately after loading the first two system files and before loading COMMAND.COM. If CONFIG.SYS is present, DOS uses its commands. The most common CONFIG.SYS commands are as follows:

BUFFERS	DOS
DEVICE	FILES
DEVICEHIGH	STACKS

All of these commands are used with an equals sign, as in BUFFERS=30. BUFFERS, DOS, FILES, and STACKS should appear only once in a CONFIG.SYS file, because each of them modifies a single setting for the OS. The DEVICE and DEVICEHIGH commands are used to load device drivers and will be used in a CONFIG.SYS file as many times as there are device drivers to install. The difference between DEVICE and DEVICEHIGH is that DEVICE loads drivers into the first 640KB of memory, whereas DEVICEHIGH loads drivers into special memory above 640KB, which exists only when DOS is installed on

```
C:\>dir /a

Volume in drive C is MS-DOS_6
Volume Serial Number is 2C98-8B17
Directory of C:\

IO       SYS         40,774 05-31-94    6:22a
MSDOS    SYS         38,138 05-31-94    6:22a
DOS         <DIR>           04-24-02    5:24p
COMMAND  COM         54,645 05-31-94    6:22a
WINA20   386          9,349 05-31-94    6:22a
CONFIG   SYS             71 04-29-02    8:51p
AUTOEXEC BAT             86 05-03-02    1:51p
        7 file(s)        143,063 bytes
                  2,138,013,696 bytes free

C:\>_
```

● **Figure 2-8.** A directory listing including the system files

a computer with a 386 processor or greater, and some very special memory management drivers and settings have been loaded. This is a very advanced task, so we suggest that you use the automated method for accomplishing it, using the MEMMAKER program.

AUTOEXEC.BAT

AUTOEXEC.BAT is, first, a batch file, and second, a special batch file, because DOS looks for it immediately after it loads COMMAND.COM. A batch file is a text file containing commands that are run much as if they were typed at the DOS prompt. All of the commands in a batch file require a command processor to run.

The DOS Bootup Process

Every time you turn on your computer, your computer "learns" what hardware it has attached to it and looks for an operating system to start. It learns about the essential hardware components by reading information stored in special nonvolatile RAM. It has a standard way of looking for an operating system and loading it into memory. The OS, in turn, learns how it will behave and how it will interact with the hardware. This section offers a somewhat simplified description of the boot process, from turning on the computer through loading the operating system with all of its configuration settings and device drivers.

The phrase "boot up a computer" comes from the old concept of lifting yourself by your own bootstraps—something that is impossible for humans, but necessary for a computer. The computer starts with basically nothing and then executes little programs, each of which performs a necessary task or adds more capability until the entire computer is up and running.

The Intel and similar processors used in our PCs have a unique characteristic tied to the PC architecture: when your PC is powered up, the processor is designed to load a special ROM-based program called the Power-On Self-Test (POST) into memory. POST runs a series of small diagnostic tests on the hardware. When POST finishes, it passes control to a small program in the ROM-BIOS called the **bootstrap loader**.

You can boot up (or start) DOS in three ways. One way is to turn on the power switch of your PC, which is called a **cold boot**. The other two methods are used after the computer is powered up. One method uses a key combination that reboots DOS without a power-down and power-up cycle. This key combination is CTRL-ALT-DELETE (pressed simultaneously), and this method is called a **warm boot**. A third method, available on many PCs, is to press the Reset button, which (depending on the manufacturer) skips the power-down and power-up cycle and runs POST.

To understand how the bootstrap loader works, you need to understand a little about how a drive is prepared for use. A disk, whether it be a hard disk or a floppy disk, is divided into individual chunks, called sectors, which are each 512 bytes in size. Further, remember that a hard disk can have several areas (partitions) that appear as discrete logical drives (C:, D:,

E:, and so on), with many, many sectors in each. These partitions are defined in a partition table in the first physical sector on the entire hard disk, called the master boot record (MBR).

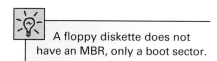
A floppy diskette does not have an MBR, only a boot sector.

The first sector on each logical drive on a hard disk is the boot sector. When you format a disk, (A:, C:, D:, and so on), the OS you are using writes information into the boot sector (not the MBR). This information includes version information about the OS and a small program that calls up the system files for the OS.

The ROM-BIOS bootstrap loader looks for a diskette in drive A:. If it finds one, it loads the boot sector from that diskette into memory, which in turn runs the OS loading program. If the bootstrap loader does not find a diskette in drive A:, it looks for an OS on the hard drive. It first looks in the MBR of the first hard drive and reads the partition table, looking for a special type of partition, called a primary partition, that is also identified as "active." This means that it is the specific partition from which to load the OS. The bootstrap loader reads the first sector of the active partition into memory. Remember that this sector is also special. It is the boot sector and contains a special OS loading program.

On a disk formatted by DOS, the OS loading program looks for IO.SYS and MSDOS.SYS. If it finds them, it loads them into memory. MSDOS.SYS looks for CONFIG.SYS in the root directory of the disk from which it is loaded. If it finds this file, it configures the OS based on the commands in CONFIG.SYS. Then COMMAND.COM is loaded into memory. It looks for AUTOEXEC.BAT. If it finds this file, it executes each command in the file. After this, unless an application was loaded by AUTOEXEC.BAT, the DOS prompt is displayed with its little blinking cursor waiting for you to enter a command.

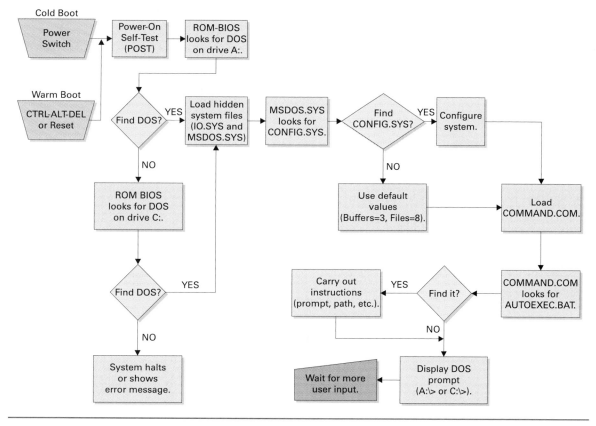

• Flow chart of the DOS bootup process

You can learn what happens when the bootstrap loader fails to find an operating system. If you have a blank, formatted diskette, you can "break" your computer and fix it again! Try this:

1. With your computer turned off, insert a blank, formatted diskette in drive A:.

2. Turn on the computer. After it fails to find an OS, it should display this message:

   ```
   Non-system disk or disk error
   Replace and strike any key when ready
   ```

3. Simply remove the blank disk from drive A: and press a key. The system should restart and load the operating system from your hard disk.

Creating DOS Startup Disks

You have seen the term DOS startup disk, but what is it and how do you create one? It is a diskette that has been prepared with the DOS system files so that it can be used to start DOS on a computer. As simple as DOS is, you cannot create a startup disk simply by copying the three system files onto a formatted diskette with the COPY or DISKCOPY command. You need to use one of the methods you will study next. There are others, but we decided to stop at those that would be most accessible to you.

Using FORMAT to Create a Startup Disk

Pay attention to the listing that begins with a value labeled Bytes Total Disk Space. If FORMAT discovers bad space on your disk, that information will be listed as a number of bytes in bad sectors. Discard the disk. It is a waste of your time to mess with a damaged disk.

If you can boot to the DOS OS from either a floppy disk or hard disk, you can then use the FORMAT command to create a DOS startup disk. Using the FORMAT command requires that you use a special switch (/S) with it. When you use this switch, after the FORMAT command prepares the diskette and places a new root directory and FAT on the disk, it will also place the system files (IO.SYS, MSDOS.SYS, and COMMAND.COM) on the diskette. You will have no other DOS programs on the diskette and will have to manually select and copy the external commands that you want on the diskette. Use this method when you have an unformatted diskette or want to start with a fresh format. You will also have to create the CONFIG.SYS and AUTOEXEC.BAT files appropriate to your computer.

Step-by-Step 2.05

Create a Startup Disk Using FORMAT

You can easily create a simple startup disk using the FORMAT command. To try this, all you need is a computer with a floppy or hard disk that is already started with DOS. You will also need the FORMAT.COM program and a blank diskette.

Step 1

At the DOS prompt, enter the following command:

```
FORMAT A: /S
```

Step 2

Insert a blank diskette in drive A: and press ENTER when you see the following message:

```
Insert new diskette for drive A:
and press ENTER when ready...
```

| Step 3 | You can watch the progress as FORMAT checks the diskette, saves UNFORMAT information, and then continues with the formatting process. Press ENTER when you see the following message: |

```
Volume label (11 characters, ENTER for none)?
```

| Step 4 | Press N and ENTER when you see the following message: |

```
Format another (Y/N)?
```

| Step 5 | Leave the diskette in drive A: and press CTRL-ALT-DELETE to test the startup disk. After a successful test, remove the disk from drive A: and label it Simple Startup Disk. |

```
C:\>format a: /s
Insert new diskette for drive A:
and press ENTER when ready...

Checking existing disk format.
Saving UNFORMAT information.
Verifying 1.44M
Format complete.
System transferred

Volume label (11 characters, ENTER for none)?

    1,457,664 bytes total disk space
      200,704 bytes used by system
    1,256,960 bytes available on disk

        512 bytes in each allocation unit.
      2,455 allocation units available on dis

Volume Serial Number is 0933-1BF4

Format another (Y/N)?n

C:\>_
```

Using SYS to Create a DOS Startup Disk

The SYS command places the DOS system files on a previously formatted diskette. The advantage of this command is that it is nondestructive and works as long as there is room on the diskette for the system files. To do this, you must boot up a computer to DOS and have the SYS.COM program. The actual command you enter to put the DOS system files on a diskette is

```
SYS A:
```

The resulting message (if the command is successful) is

```
System transferred.
```

Try This!
Create a Startup Disk with the SYS Command

You can easily create a simple startup disk using the SYS command. All you need is a computer with a floppy or hard disk that is started in DOS, the SYS.COM file in the search path, and a formatted diskette (it can even have files on it, as long as there is room for the system files). Try this:

1. Place your diskette in drive A: and enter the following command at the DOS prompt:

   ```
   SYS A: /S
   ```

2. After you see the message, "System transferred," remove the disk from drive A: and label it Startup Disk.

Using Setup to Create a DOS Startup Disk

You can use the DOS Setup program to install DOS directly onto a floppy disk. This requires the three DOS Setup disks and a blank disk. The result, when you use the MS-DOS 6.22 Setup program, is a disk that is bootable to DOS and has a few more than a dozen of the external DOS commands. If you want a general-purpose DOS startup disk with a small set of DOS commands, use this method.

In the following steps, you will create a DOS startup disk from the DOS 6.22 setup diskettes. To complete this exercise, you will need the following:

- A Microsoft/Intel standard personal computer (desktop or laptop)
- The three DOS 6.22 setup disk
- A single blank disk

Step 1

With the computer turned off, place disk 1 of the DOS 6.22 setup disks in the floppy drive and power up the computer. At first, you will see information on your screen that is displayed by the ROM-BIOS during startup; then you will briefly see a black screen that has a single line of text at the top that says, "Starting MS-DOS."

Step 2

Next, you will see the blue Welcome to Setup screen. Press the F7 key to select Install to Floppy Disk; the Install to Floppy Disk message box will appear.

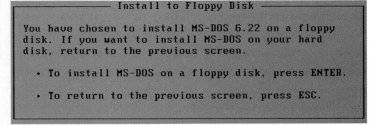

```
─────── Install to Floppy Disk ───────

You have chosen to install MS-DOS 6.22 on a floppy
disk. If you want to install MS-DOS on your hard
disk, return to the previous screen.

 • To install MS-DOS on a floppy disk, press ENTER.

 • To return to the previous screen, press ESC.
```

Step 3

Press ENTER to install MS-DOS on a floppy disk. The resulting screen shows you the system settings that Setup will use. These include the date and time (which Setup found by reading your computer's real-time clock) and the disk and directory where Setup will install the MS-DOS files.

```
Microsoft MS-DOS 6.22 Setup for Floppy Disk


     Setup will use the following system settings:


   ┌──────────────────────────────────────────────────┐
   │ Date/Time:         04/23/02   15:20               │
   │ Install To:        A:\                            │
   ├──────────────────────────────────────────────────┤
   │ The settings are correct.                        │
   └──────────────────────────────────────────────────┘


   If all the settings are correct, press ENTER.

   To change a setting, press the UP or DOWN ARROW keys
   to select it. Then press ENTER to see alternatives.




 ENTER=Continue   F1=Help   F3=Exit
```

Check the date and time. It they are correct, continue to Step 4. If they are not correct, use the up arrow key to move the highlight to the Date/Time line; then press ENTER. Read the instructions on the resulting page and make the needed correction to the time or date; then, with the highlight on System Time, press ENTER to return to the previous screen.

Step 4

With the highlight on the words The Settings Are Correct, press ENTER to continue the setup process. Then follow the instructions on the screen and write **Startup** on the paper label of your blank diskette and set it aside.

```
Microsoft MS-DOS 6.22 Setup for Floppy Disk
═══════════════════════════════════════════════

       Setup will now create a floppy disk that you can use to
       run MS-DOS 6.22.

       Setup copies MS-DOS 6.22 files to the floppy disk that you
       provide. The disk can be either formatted or unformatted.
       Label the disk as follows:

          STARTUP

       When you are ready to continue, press ENTER.
```

Step 5

Press ENTER to continue. Setup will begin copying files. A yellow progress bar will be dis-

played on the screen during the copy process. When prompted, remove the setup disk and place the disk labeled Startup in drive A:.

```
Please label a floppy disk as follows:

            STARTUP

      and insert it in drive A.

  When you are ready to continue,
          press ENTER.

  Caution:  All existing files
  on this disk will be deleted.
```

Step 6

With the startup disk in drive A:, press ENTER to continue. Setup will continue the copying process.

Because the setup program cannot copy all of the files at once, you will be prompted to replace the disk in drive A: with Setup Disk 2. Do this and then press ENTER to continue.

Continue to change disks, as instructed. Two or three passes on each of the three Setup disks will be needed to copy all of the files to your startup disk. Follow the instructions on your screen until the process is complete, at which point you will see the MS-DOS Setup Complete screen.

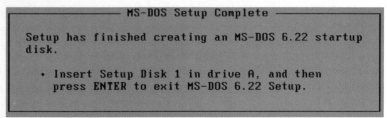

```
────────── MS-DOS Setup Complete ──────────
Setup has finished creating an MS-DOS 6.22 startup
disk.

   • Insert Setup Disk 1 in drive A, and then
     press ENTER to exit MS-DOS 6.22 Setup.
```

Step 7

Insert Setup Disk 1 in drive A; then press ENTER to exit setup. When the DOS prompt appears, remove Setup Disk 1 from drive A: and put your three MS-DOS Setup disks in a safe place or return them to your instructor.

Step 8

To verify that your new startup disk actually works, insert it back into drive A: and restart the computer. When the computer restarts, you will see a "Starting MS-DOS" message at the top of the screen, then the date will appear, and you then will have an opportunity to enter the correct date if it is wrong. If it is wrong, you must enter it in the format shown on your screen. Regardless of whether you correct the date, you must press ENTER.

Step 9

The time now appears on the screen. If necessary, correct the time; then press ENTER. Once you confirm the date and time, the version information and copyright notice appear, followed by a DOS prompt, which is actually the last line displayed on your screen. Notice that it includes the drive letter (A:), followed by a greater than (>) sign and a blinking cursor.

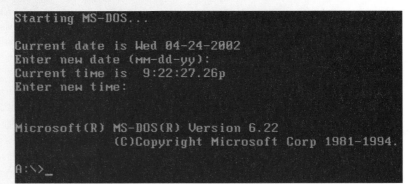

```
Starting MS-DOS...

Current date is Wed 04-24-2002
Enter new date (mm-dd-yy):
Current time is  9:22:27.26p
Enter new time:


Microsoft(R) MS-DOS(R) Version 6.22
            (C)Copyright Microsoft Corp 1981-1994.

A:\>_
```

Step 10

If this operation was successful, remove the disk and set it aside. If it was not successful, you will have to repeat the steps and use a new diskette to create a startup disk.

Using Windows to Create a Startup Disk

You can use Windows to create a DOS startup floppy disk:

 When you use Windows 98 to create a startup disk, let it install CD-ROM drivers and the CD extensions to DOS, which is a nontrivial task for someone unfamiliar with DOS.

- If you have Windows 95 or Windows 98 installed on a computer, you can use the Startup Disk option. This creates a Windows 95 or Windows 98 startup disk, which is really just a bootable DOS diskette using the Windows 98 version of MS-DOS (version 7).

- If you have Windows XP installed on a computer and you format a diskette from within My Computer or Windows Explorer, you will have an option to create an MS-DOS startup disk. This is a very nice feature, since we don't always have access to MS-DOS when we need a startup disk.

■ Working with DOS in Windows

In Windows, you may work with DOS in two ways: you may run DOS applications, and you may use the command prompt. We discuss each in turn.

Running DOS Applications in Windows

Earlier in this chapter, you learned that when a DOS application runs in Windows, it runs in a **virtual machine** that looks and feels to the DOS application like a real DOS machine. Using DOS applications in Windows has at least three disadvantages:

- DOS applications take up quite a bit of memory and also require a lot of processor cycles. To illustrate this, we ran two DOS applications in Windows XP. You can see the memory usage of these two applications in Figure 2-9, which shows the Windows Task Manager, a program that allows you to look at memory usage and other properties of programs that are currently in memory. The highlighted process, NTVDM.EXE, is the primary software component for creating a virtual DOS machine. It appears here twice, because there are two DOS applications running and each one is in its own virtual machine. As you can see in the memory usage column, each instance of NTVDM.EXE is using approximately 2MB of memory. This will vary based on the individual application and its memory needs.

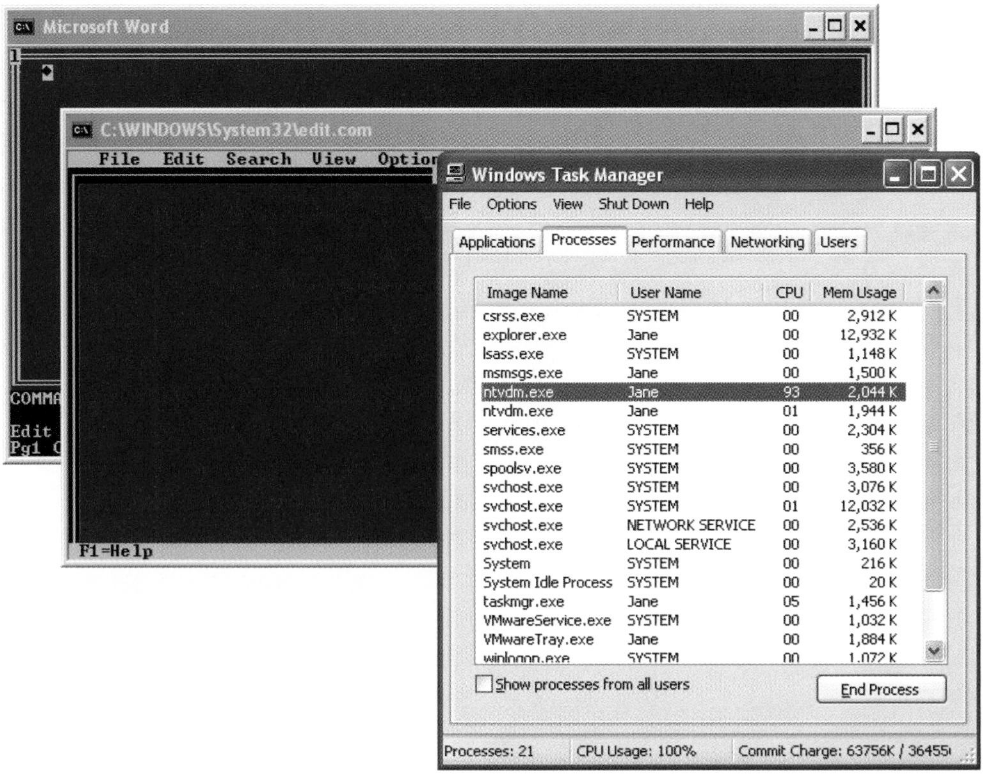

● **Figure 2-9.** Virtual machine memory usage

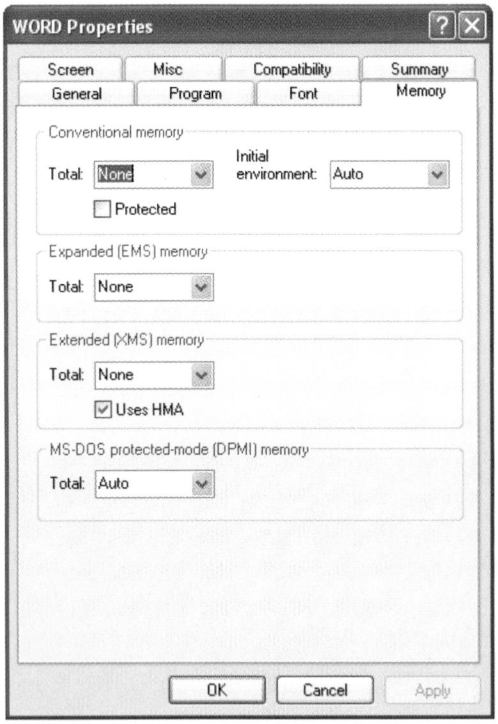

● **Figure 2-10.** Memory page of PIF properties

■ Some DOS applications cannot run in a virtual machine because they need to bypass DOS to directly access the hardware. While Windows 95 and 98 allow this to some extent, Windows NT, Windows 2000, and Windows XP do not. Therefore, these DOS applications will not run in these OSs.

■ DOS applications running in Windows rely on a special file called a program information file (PIF) that tells the OS how to configure the virtual machine with the memory and other options for the application. If you have a DOS application that will not run in Windows, you can try modifying the PIF setting for that application. It may be that the application behaves well enough to run in a virtual machine but has special memory or screen needs. However, you must be familiar with very old DOS technologies and understand how to modify the PIF for the application. Figure 2-10 shows just one page, the memory page, of the PIF properties for Word 5. There are memory terms here that even many experienced IT professionals do not understand, because knowledge of these is not required if you don't support DOS applications.

Windows includes a number of DOS programs: FORMAT, XCOPY, ATTRIB, DISKCOPY, and many more. These programs are all command-line utilities that quickly perform a task and then are gone from memory.

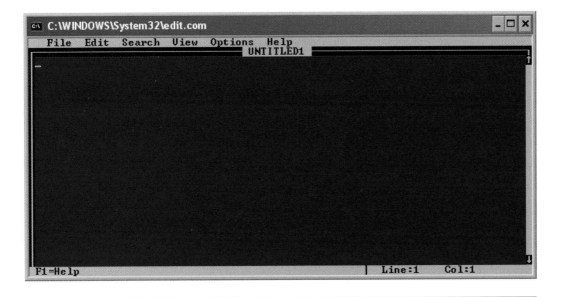

● **Figure 2-11.** The MS-DOS editor—Edit

Programs that we call applications stay in memory and allow us to do work, such as creating and modifying text or word processing documents, or creating, modifying, and manipulating data with a database.

Windows comes with one Windows application and one DOS application that we call text editors, because they can create and edit files using text with only the simplest of formatting codes (like the carriage return, linefeed, and end-of-document codes). The Windows-based text editor is Notepad. It is a typical Windows GUI application and uses the standard Windows commands and mouse actions. There are other applications that can create and edit text files (WordPad and Microsoft Word), but they are primarily word processors, which can create documents with fancy formatting instructions included, but Notepad and Edit create simple text files without the extra formatting.

The DOS editor, Edit, shown in Figure 2-11, has its own simple, nongraphical user interface, with a menu bar and menu commands that you can access with the ALT key plus a key letter from the commands on the menu bar.

Step-by-Step 2.07

Running MS-DOS Editor in Windows

In this step-by-step, you will run MS-DOS Editor in Windows. The instructions are written specifically for Windows XP, but you may use any of the OSs listed here. There may be slight variations in the steps due to differences in the GUI.

To complete this step-by-step, you will need a PC running Windows NT, Windows 2000, or Windows XP.

Step 1

Press CTRL-SHIFT-ESC to start the Windows Task Manager. This application runs on top of all other open windows. To change this behavior, choose the Options menu and remove the check mark from Always on Top.

Step 2

Click the Processes tab and notice that NTVDM.EXE is not listed in the image name column. Click the Minimize button for Windows Task Manager. This is the button labeled "–" at the top right of the window.

Step 3

From the Taskbar, select Start | Run. In the Run box, type **edit** and press ENTER. The DOS Edit applications should open in a Window on your desktop, as shown here.

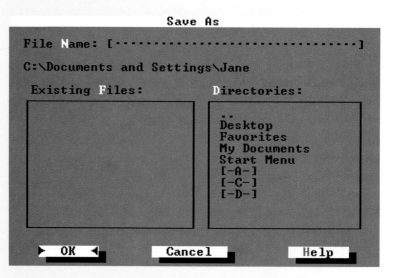

Step 4

Press and hold the ALT key while repeatedly pressing and releasing the TAB key. Do not release the ALT key until Task Manager is selected. In Task Manager, click the Processes tab and locate the file NTVDM.EXE in the Image Name Column. After you have confirmed that NTVDM.EXE is running, close Task Manager by clicking the button with an X in the top right of the Task Manager window.

Step 5

Switch to the Edit program by pressing the ALT-TAB key combination or by clicking inside the Edit window. Type a sentence in the MS-DOS Editor window.

Step 6

Save the file by pressing the ALT-F key combination and then pressing S. The Save As dialog box will appear as shown here.

```
                          Save As
   File Name: [·······································]

   C:\Documents and Settings\Jane

      Existing Files:              Directories:
    ┌─────────────────┐        ┌─────────────────┐
    │                 │        │ ..              │
    │                 │        │ Desktop         │
    │                 │        │ Favorites       │
    │                 │        │ My Documents    │
    │                 │        │ Start Menu      │
    │                 │        │ [-A-]           │
    │                 │        │ [-C-]           │
    │                 │        │ [-D-]           │
    │                 │        │                 │
    └─────────────────┘        └─────────────────┘

    ►   OK   ◄          Cancel            Help
```

Step 7

The blinking cursor should be in the space next to File Name. Press the TAB key twice so that the cursor is in the Directories box. Use the down arrow until My Documents is selected and appears on the File Name line above. Press the TAB key four times until the blinking cursor is after My Documents on the File Name line. Press the right arrow key so that the highlight is removed from My Documents, but the cursor remains in place. Type the name **TEST1.TXT**. Your Save As dialog box should look similar to the one shown here.

```
                        Save As
        File Name: [My Documents\Test1.txt_ · · · · · · · · · ·]

        C:\Documents and Settings\Jane

        Existing Files:              Directories:

                                          ..
                                     Desktop
                                     Favorites
                                     My Documents
                                     Start Menu
                                     [-A-]
                                     [-C-]
                                     [-D-]



            ▶  OK  ◀          Cancel              Help
```

Step 8

To exit from the MS-DOS Editor, type ALT-F to bring up the File menu; then press X to select Exit. The Editor will close, as will the entire window.

If you have never worked in a DOS application but are experienced in working in Windows or with Macintosh computers, the Step-by-Step you just finished should help you understand why most organizations have moved on to applications that run in a GUI, like Windows and the Mac OSs.

Using the Command Prompt in Windows

All versions of Windows allow you to work at a command prompt while the OS is running. However, Windows 95 and 98 have only one way of presenting the command prompt to you while running Windows, whereas the more advanced Windows OSs give you two options for command prompts within Windows.

In addition to these methods of working at the command prompt from within Windows, Windows 9*x*, Windows 2000, and Windows XP have startup options that allow you to start at a command prompt. Accessing the command prompt in this way is useful for troubleshooting startup problems and is addressed in Chapters 4, 6, and 7. In this current chapter, we are concerned with working at the command prompt after Windows has been started normally.

The Command Prompt in Windows 9*x*

In Windows 95 and 98, the command prompt that you can select from Start | Programs runs in a DOS virtual machine. In fact, to start it without going through the menus, you can choose Start | Run and then type **COMMAND** in the Run box. This has the same effect as the Start | Programs method, because both call up the DOS command shell (COMMAND.COM), which in turn causes Windows to launch a DOS virtual machine.

Notice in Figure 2-12 that the choice from the Programs menu in Windows 98 is MS-DOS Prompt. This tells you that the program you launch is MS-DOS running in a virtual machine in Windows 98.

Windows 95 and Windows 98 use MS-DOS 7.

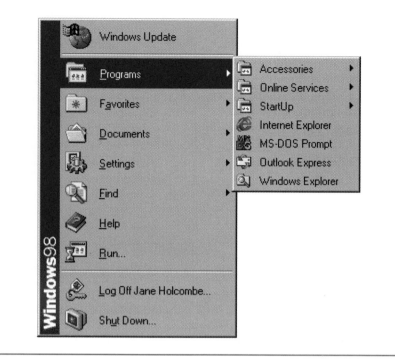

● Figure 2-12. MS Windows 98—Start | Programs | MS-DOS prompt

The Command Prompt in Windows NT, Windows 2000, and Windows XP

In Windows NT, Windows 2000, and Windows XP, the choice you will see when you browse through the Start menu hierarchy is Command Prompt, which reflects a significant difference between these OSs and the Windows 9*x* OSs. The program that is launched when you select the Command Prompt option from the Start menu hierarchy is CMD.EXE. This offers you a full 32-bit, character-mode command prompt that is not a virtual machine with the limits of DOS.

Starting Programs from the MS-DOS Prompt   From the command prompt in these OSs, you can start any program that will run in Windows. If the program is a program written for DOS, a virtual machine will launch to hold the program, but you will still remain in the command prompt window. If the program is a 32-bit GUI program, it will launch in a separate window. If it is a character mode program, it will run within the command-line interface.

Do No Harm!   When working at the command prompt in Windows, the first rule is "Do no harm!" The best way to follow this rule is to never perform file management at the command prompt and to never run third-party disk utilities at the command prompt. The no file management rule is important mainly because, without a GUI, you are in danger of deleting or moving the wrong files. The no third-party disk utility rule is important if you are using Windows 95 or Windows 98, which cannot protect against such programs. The more advanced Windows versions will not allow these programs to run.

Another important reason not to perform file management at the command prompt relates to the issue of 8.3 file names. Beginning with Windows 95,

Now, if you really miss DOS, you can use the Start | Run | Command method to launch a virtual machine!

Windows allows you to create long file names that go beyond the limits of the 8.3 naming convention. It works best when working from the GUI. If you create a file with a long file name, Windows maintains both that long file name and a downward-compatible 8.3 file name for each file. If you create a file with a valid 8.3 file name, that is the only file name associated with the file. You can cause problems with this dual file name system if you copy and modify files from the command prompt using the 8.3 file name. This will cause the file to lose its association with the long file name. Then someone working in Windows may not be able to find their long file name files.

There are some DOS utilities that are included in Windows 9x but not included in other versions of Windows, either because they don't run in these versions or they are considered too harmful to be included. An example of such a program is the FDISK utility. It cannot be run in Windows NT, Windows 2000, or Windows XP, but it is the only disk management tool included with Windows 95 and Windows 98. Fortunately, if you run it at the MS-DOS Prompt in Windows 98, it will not allow you to do any damage, but if you run it after booting up with a startup disk that contains the FDISK program, there is no such safeguard. Therefore, you should use FDISK only after learning how it works. Unless you understand how it works, the best time to partition a hard disk for Windows 9x is when you run the setup program for Windows 9x. It will then run FDISK for you, gathering information from you and guiding you through the process.

Troubleshooting Common DOS Problems

There are some common problems you may encounter if you work with DOS. We'll examine some of these problems, looking at the symptoms, the possible cause, and solutions.

"Non-System Disk" Error Message

In this scenario, DOS is installed on your hard disk, but fails to boot up, and an error message appears that includes the words "Non-system Disk." This indicates that the OS loader program cannot find IO.SYS or MSDOS.SYS, or both. The most likely cause is that a data diskette has been left in drive A:. The OS loader program from the first sector on the disk is loaded into memory and looking for IO.SYS and MSDOS.SYS on drive A:. However, a data diskette is one that is formatted to hold data, but is not a bootable disk, and so it lacks the system files. To solve this problem, check to see if there is a diskette in drive A: and, if so, remove it and press any key. The boot process should continue successfully.

The complete message may vary between DOS versions, but includes the words "Non-system Disk."

If you check drive A: and the drive does not contain a diskette, then you have a bigger problem, because this means that the OS loader was loaded from the first sector on C: and could not find IO.SYS or MSDOS.SYS during bootup. In this case, you should boot with a bootable disk in drive A: that also has the SYS.COM program. Then type the following command to have the system files placed back on your drive C:.

```
SYS C:
```

Next, remove the diskette from the floppy drive and reboot your computer. It should now boot to DOS.

"Bad or Missing Command Interpreter" Error Message

In this scenario, DOS is installed on your hard disk but fails to boot up, and the "Bad or Missing Command Interpreter" error message is displayed. This indicates that the file COMMAND.COM is missing or is a different version than IO.SYS and MSDOS.SYS. To confirm that this is the problem, locate a DOS startup disk of the same version installed on your hard disk, place it in the floppy drive, and boot up again. After the computer boots up, display a directory of the root of C: using the DIR /A command. The /A switch displays all files, including hidden files. First verify that COMMAND.COM is missing. If it is missing, then you have confirmed the problem and can solve it. If COMMAND.COM is present, check the file date and time information in IO.SYS, MSDOS.SYS, and COMMAND.COM. If COMMAND.COM has a different date and time, you need to replace it with a file with the correct date and time.

To solve this problem, verify that the COMMAND.COM file on the floppy disk has the correct date and time (matching that of IO.SYS and MSDOS.SYS on drive C:); then copy COMMAND.COM from A: to C:.

"Bad Command or File Name" Error Message

You have just entered a command at the command prompt and receive the "Bad Command or File Name" message. This means that either the command name or a file name (or a directory name) in one of the parameters is incorrect. For instance, on a computer with DOS 6.22 installed, we wanted to delete a directory called DATA1, and we entered the following with a slight typo:

```
DELTREE DATA
```

In this case, there was no DATA directory, only a DATA1 directory, so the result was the "Bad Command or File Name" message.

Whenever you see this error message, whether you are working in DOS or at a command prompt in Windows, look for a typo in the command line you entered and then reenter the entire line correctly. Typos are the most common cause of this error.

Request to Enter the Current Date and Time

You boot up a computer with DOS, and you are required to enter the current date and time. This means that DOS did not find an AUTOEXEC.BAT file. This problem was mentioned previously in this chapter, but we include it here to discuss it further. If you previously had an AUTOEXEC.BAT file, you may want to investigate how and why it cannot be found now. Perhaps, rather than booting from drive C:, your computer booted from drive A:, because a bootable startup disk was in the drive. If so, the prompt on the screen should show drive A:. If this is the case, remove the diskette and restart the computer.

Another fix for this problem is to use the SYS.COM program, if it is present on the DOS startup disk. To transfer the three system files from the diskette to the hard drive, enter the following command:

sys c:

Inside Information

Once Upon a Date and Time

The original IBM-PC had a real-time clock that could only keep track of the date and time while it was up and running. For this reason, PC DOS and MS-DOS would prompt you for the date and time at every restart. Eventually, battery-supported clocks were added to PCs. Once set, using proprietary programs or the DOS DATE and TIME programs, they continued to keep time—even when the computer was turned off. Each of the earliest battery-supported clocks required a special proprietary program for MS-DOS to read and/or set the clock date and time. This program was usually placed in the AUTOEXEC.BAT file. Therefore, DOS wouldn't prompt for the date and time if an AUTOEXEC.BAT file was present—regardless of whether or not a clock program was in the AUTOEXEC.BAT file. This behavior changed beginning with MS-DOS for Windows 95. This and newer versions won't prompt for the date and time with or without the AUTOEXEC.BAT file.

Chapter 2 Review

■ Chapter Summary

After reading this chapter and completing the Step-by-Step tutorials and Try This! exercises, you should understand the following facts about DOS:

Measure the Value, Strengths, and Weaknesses of DOS

- One reason DOS is still in limited use today is its small size, which makes it a choice for embedded systems.

- Another reason DOS is still in limited use today is that its system files easily fit on a diskette, leaving room for other small programs, which allows technicians to use it to boot up a computer from a diskette. They can then run special diagnostic utilities from the diskette.

- Windows can run DOS in a virtual DOS machine.

- Another reason for using DOS today is that some DOS applications either run too slowly in a virtual machine or do not work at all in a virtual machine. The application then must be run on a computer running DOS.

- DOS can access only the real-mode capabilities of the Intel processors.

- DOS is a single-tasking OS.

- DOS provides limited services for DOS applications.

- DOS applications can use only conventional memory.

- Microsoft no longer supports or sells MS-DOS.

- IBM sells PC DOS 2000.

- Digital Research sold its DR-DOS to Novell many years ago, and DR-DOS is now sold through Lineo, but only in quantities of 50 or more, and Lineo no longer supports it.

- Versions of DOS can also be found for free on the Internet.

Install DOS

- The MS-DOS Setup program will partition and format a hard drive, if needed.

- The hardware requirements for DOS are minimal: an IBM or compatible personal computer, 6MB of free hard disk space for the DOS utilities if you are installing onto a hard disk, and 512KB of memory.

Use the FAT File System

- DOS uses the FAT file system, which is now referred to as FAT16 to distinguish it from the newer FAT32 file system introduced with Windows 95 OEM edition.

- The FAT file system uses a naming convention for files and directories called the 8.3 (eight-dot-three) naming convention. It allows up to eight characters in the file name, followed by a dot (.), followed with an extension of up to three characters.

- It is best to use only alphanumeric characters for 8.3 file names, even though some non-alphanumeric characters are allowed.

- A file's extension can indicate the type of file (executable, text, and so on).

Use DOS Commands for File Management and Other Tasks

- File attributes determine how DOS handles a file or directory. The file attributes are read-only, archive, system, hidden, volume label, and directory.

- The ATTRIB command allows you to view and manipulate the read-only, archive, system, and hidden attributes.

- Internal commands are commands that are part of COMMAND.COM and are always available to use when you are at a DOS command prompt. They are very fast to access.

- CLS, COPY, REN, DEL, MD, RD, CD, and TYPE are internal DOS commands.

- External commands are in individual files, which must be available where DOS can find them on disk if you want to use them.

- XCOPY, DELTREE, FORMAT, FDISK, and DISKCOPY are examples of external DOS commands.

Describe the DOS Bootup Process and Create Startup Disks

- It is important to understand the bootup process of an OS in order to troubleshoot failures that occur during bootup.

- A hard boot of a computer occurs when you turn on the power switch.

- A soft boot of a personal computer occurs when you press the CTRL-ALT-DELETE key combination.

- Many computers have a Reset button, which resets a running computer without a power-down and power-up cycle.

- The order of events during bootup of DOS is cold or warm boot, then POST, and then the bootstrap loader looks on the A: or C: drive and loads the boot record. Then IO.SYS and MSDOS.SYS are loaded, CONFIG.SYS (if it exists) is read and used by MSDOS.SYS, COMMAND.COM is loaded, AUTOEXEC.BAT (if it exists) is read and used by COMMAND.COM, and finally, the DOS prompt is displayed.

- You have many options for creating a DOS startup disk, including use of the DOS Setup program, the SYS or FORMAT command, and the Startup Disk option in Windows 9x.

Work with DOS in Windows

- When you choose Command Prompt in Windows 2000 or XP, you are not using DOS, but CMD.EXE, a 32-bit character-based prompt that allows you to call up any program that can run in that version of Windows.

- When you choose MS-DOS Prompt in Windows 9x, you are running a DOS virtual machine.

Troubleshoot Common DOS Problems

- A failed startup to DOS that results in a "Non-system Disk" error message means that the OS loader program cannot find IO.SYS and/or MSDOS.SYS. The most likely cause of the problem is that a data diskette was left in drive A:. Check for and remove any diskettes in the drive and reboot the computer.

- A failed startup to DOS that results in a "Bad or Missing Command Interpreter" error message means that the file COMMAND.COM is missing or is a different version than IO.SYS and MSDOS.SYS. Boot from a DOS diskette of the correct version and copy the COMMAND.COM file to the root of C:.

- When you enter a command and see the "Bad Command or File Name" error message, check and recheck your spelling and reenter the command.

- If you are required to enter the date and time when you boot up a computer, this most likely means that there is no AUTOEXEC.BAT on the root of the boot disk. Create an AUTOEXEC.BAT file, even if it is empty, and just about any computer built since 1984 will simply use the internal clock to get this information.

■ Key Terms

application (42)	**external command** (60)	**root directory** (50)
boot disk (65)	**FAT16 file system** (52)	**single-tasking** (44)
bootstrap loader (66)	**FAT32 file system** (52)	**startup disk** (42)
cluster (50)	**file allocation table (FAT)** (50)	**syntax** (58)
cold boot (66)	**file attribute** (54)	**utility** (42)
conventional memory (43)	**internal command** (60)	**virtual machine** (73)
DOS prompt (49)	**logical drive** (44)	**warm boot** (66)
driver (42)	**partition** (45)	

Key Term Quiz

Use the Key Terms list to complete the sentences that follow. Not all terms will be used.

1. The DOS file system gets its name from the _____.

2. A _____ is the minimum disk space allocated to a file.

3. An operating system uses special files called _____ to access and control hardware.

4. The 8.3 file naming convention is a feature and a limitation of DOS and the _____.

5. A computer professional may carry a DOS _____ in their toolkit to use in emergencies.

6. The type of memory in which DOS, its drivers, and applications can run is called _____.

7. Saved in each file's directory entry are _____ that determine how DOS handles the file.

8. DOS commands that are part of the COMMAND.COM program and always available when DOS is running are called _____.

9. _____ is a set of rules for correctly entering a specific command at the command line.

10. CHKDSK.EXE is one of many _____ that come with MS-DOS.

Multiple-Choice Quiz

1. Why use DOS today? Select all that apply.
   a. It uses the FAT32 file system.
   b. DOS is small.
   c. DOS can take advantage of Intel protected mode.
   d. It is compatible with old DOS applications.
   e. It has a great GUI.

2. Where can you buy a current version of DOS today?
   a. Microsoft
   b. IBM
   c. Compaq
   d. Hewlett-Packard
   e. Digital Research

3. Which of the following are required when you install MS-DOS 6.22 or IBM DOS 2000 onto the hard drive of a computer? Select all that apply.
   a. 512KB memory
   b. An Intel Pentium chip or higher
   c. An IBM or compatible personal computer
   d. 6MB of free hard disk space
   e. A mouse

4. Which of the following DOS commands can you use to delete a subdirectory? Select all that apply.
   a. DEL
   b. XCOPY
   c. DELTREE
   d. CHKDSK
   e. ATTRIB

5. Which of the following are true when you run DOS applications in Windows XP? Select all that apply.
   a. Each one runs in a virtual machine.
   b. DOS applications can directly access all hardware.
   c. Each virtual machine requires significant memory.
   d. A DOS application may run in a window.
   e. Several DOS applications can run in the same window.

6. Which of the following is true when installing MS-DOS? Select all that apply.
   a. You must have administrator rights to the computer.
   b. You can create a logical drive up to 4GB.

c. You must install from CD.

d. You can't use MS-DOS until you have activated it with Microsoft.

e. You can use the DOS install setup program.

7. What happens when you format a disk with the DOS FORMAT command? Select all that apply.

a. The DOS subdirectory is created on the disk.

b. The FAT table is created.

c. You will be prompted to give the disk a label.

d. You will have to provide an administrator password.

e. A root directory is created.

8. What is tracked in the FAT table?

a. Security information

b. File attributes

c. Disk space allocation

d. User information

e. File names, extensions, size, date and time of creation

9. What do you learn from the syntax of a command? Select all that apply.

a. Where to place the brackets in a command line

b. The rules for entering a command at the command line

c. How to avoid paying a tax on the command

d. The parameters a command will accept

e. How much memory a command uses

10. What command or commands can you use to delete files?

a. FORMAT

b. XCOPY

c. DEL

d. RD

e. DELTREE

11. What BIOS-based program performs diagnostics as a computer is powered up?

a. IO.SYS

b. COMMAND.COM

c. MSDOS.SYS

d. DEBUG.EXE

e. POST

12. Which of the following is a method for creating a DOS startup disk?

a. FORMAT A: /S

b. CHKDSK /F

c. SYS A: /S

d. SETUP A: /S

e. The Startup Disk option in Windows 98

13. If you are unfamiliar with DOS but need to create a DOS startup disk with CD-ROM drivers, which should you choose?

a. FORMAT A: /S

b. CHKDSK /F

c. SYS A: /S

d. SETUP A: /S

e. The Startup Disk option in Windows 98

14. Which command would you use to see the directory hierarchy on a drive?

a. DELTREE

b. CHKDSK

c. SETUP

d. TREE

e. ATTRIB

15. What is the most likely cause of the error message "Bad Command or File name"?

a. Sunspots

b. Typos on the command line

c. A corrupt file

d. You do not have administrator rights

e. Incorrect versions of DOS

■ Essay Quiz

1. Write a few sentences describing why DOS is in use today, contrasting its strengths with its weaknesses.

2. You're a new employee doing computer support in a small manufacturing company that uses DOS on two computers that run an application written in the late 1980s specifically for this company. Your company owns two legal sets of the software; the company that created the software went out of business 10 years ago, and your company has never found an off-the-shelf program to replace this program. For many years, the enterprise has maintained the two computers running the program, but now one of them has completely failed. You have been asked to install DOS on a newly purchased computer that has no OS. Your boss left you with the new computer and a copy of the application software. You have found two original sets of MS-DOS 6.22 on 5¼-inch diskettes, but the new computer has only a 3.5-inch diskette drive. The old computer that failed had a 5¼-inch diskette drive, and the remaining old

computer has only a 3.5-inch drive. One of your co-workers believes that you must now buy a new copy of DOS. Describe what you believe your options for installing DOS on the new computer are, including the issue of whether or not you must buy a new copy of DOS.

3. Christine created a DOS startup disk using the SYS command. Now she wants to copy some of the DOS commands from the DOS directory on drive C: of her computer. There are 6MB of files in the DOS directory, so she knows she can't copy all of them. Suggest several useful commands that you would copy to the diskette and why you selected each command.

4. In a few sentences, describe the DOS bootup process.

5. Nigel likes working at the command prompt in Windows 98. He even likes doing file management at the command prompt. Describe in a few sentences why this is not a good idea.

Lab Projects

● Lab Project 2.1

You have been asked to assist a senior desktop support specialist on a service call. The computer is in the distribution warehouse of a large retailer. He installed DOS on a hard drive, as well as a DOS application that the warehouse uses for tracking received orders within the warehouse. He created a CONFIG.SYS file with commands that configure DOS with the settings and drivers needed. Then he created an AUTOEXEC.BAT file that calls the application so that it starts every time the computer is started. Running this one application is to be the only thing that this computer is used for. However, he has had problems with other users deleting the COMMAND.COM, CONFIG.SYS, and AUTOEXEC.BAT files, causing the system to fail to start properly and requiring that someone replace these files on the hard drive. You have been asked to come up with a solution to this problem and to

test the solution on the lab computer on which you installed DOS.

You will need a lab computer with MS-DOS installed.

Then do the following:

1. Describe your solution to the problem of users deleting the COMMAND.COM, CONFIG.SYS, and AUTOEXEC.BAT files.

2. Determine the location of the COMMAND.COM, CONFIG.SYS, and AUTOEXEC.BAT files on the hard drive.

3. Implement your solution on your lab computer.

4. Test your solution and explain the results.

• Lab Project 2.2

You are a desktop support analyst in a large corporation. You have several versions of Windows available to you, including Windows 95, Windows 98, and Windows 2000. You do not have DOS available to you. You have been asked to go to a customer site and to take a DOS startup disk with CD drivers installed on it.

You will need the following materials:

- A blank diskette

- A lab computer with the OS that you need for the task.

- A data or distribution CD to use in your test of the startup diskette you create

Then do the following:

 Determine how you will prepare the diskette, including the OS you will use and the procedure you will follow in that OS. Your choice of OS depends on which of the available installed operating systems will enable you to create a disk with CD drivers included.

② Prepare the diskette.

③ Test the diskette by booting a PC with it and accessing a CD in the CD-ROM drive.

• Lab Project 2.3

To test your proficiency with DOS, your boss has assigned you the task of creating several directories on 10 computers. You will create the same directory structure on each computer. In the root of C:, you will create a directory called DATA. Below that, you will create two directories: CUSTOMER and SALES. Below CUSTOMER, you will create two directories: WHLSALE and RETAIL. Below SALES, you will create three directories: ADS, PROMOS, and PLANS. You realize that manually entering the DOS commands to create those directories at each computer is going to be boring, and when you do a

boring job, you tend to make mistakes. Therefore, you have decided to automate this task.

① Plan how you will automate this task and write a description of what you will do.

② Test your strategy on your lab computer.

③ Report the outcome, including the amount of time you estimate it will take to run the batch file on a total of 10 computers. Record how much time you estimate it would have taken to do this task manually at each computer.

The Windows Desktop

So, if 50 years ago a computer was as big as our garage, how big was the mouse?

—MINNEAPOLIS STAR TRIBUNE

The interaction of humans with computers has changed in scale and methods since computing's early days. In scale, it has changed from an interaction engaged in by a handful of highly trained experts to one involving millions of people using computers for everyday business and personal tasks. In method, human interaction has also moved from the tedious flipping of switches or feeding of punch cards to the use of graphical user interfaces based on the desktop metaphor. The little boy who made the comment above can't imagine a computer without a mouse, and two generations from now, his grandson may have trouble imagining using something as crude as a mouse!

In this chapter, you will consider this whole idea of how humans interact with computers and how the desktop metaphor describes the graphical user interface (GUI) of Windows and Mac OSs. You will learn concepts and skills common to the GUIs of four versions of Windows (NT, 98, 2000, and XP) while you acquaint yourself with the capabilities of today's Windows desktops. In the process, you will learn skills that will help you in all of your future interactions with OSs.

In this chapter, you will learn how to:

- **Explain the nature and history of the Windows GUI**
- **Navigate the Windows GUI**
- **Manage files in Windows**
- **Configure and customize the Windows desktop**
- **Run applications in Windows**
- **Leave the desktop by logging off and shutting down**
- **Troubleshoot common Windows desktop problems**

You can learn more about the history of Windows. Point your Internet browser to your favorite search engine (ours is www.google.com), and search on "History of Windows." You will find some interesting, and sometimes quite biased, accounts of the history of Microsoft Windows.

■ Who Invented the Desktop?

Remember Douglas Engelbart? He was listed in the timeline in Chapter 1 because in 1968 he gave a demonstration at the Fall Joint Computer Conference in San Francisco that included the use of a mouse to move a "bug" around a screen that contained both text and graphical elements. Even back when the user was most likely to be a highly trained computer or scientific professional, visionaries like Engelbart could see the need to make computers more user friendly.

Years later, in the lab of Xerox's now-famous Palo Alto Research Center (PARC), others continued to work on giving computers a more intuitive (or immediately understandable) user interface. In the late 1970s, some of the pioneers in personal computing visited this lab and were inspired by the technology demonstrated there. You might even say they "borrowed" a few ideas.

Apple's Macintosh computer was the first successful retail product influenced by the work on user interfaces at PARC. Microsoft soon followed suit with its first Windows product.

So what's the big deal about the Windows desktop? It is simply an imaginary workspace where you store objects such as programs and data in **windows**, each of which is a bordered area of the desktop used by a single program. If you were lucky enough to have a Windows-based PC or Macintosh

Try This!

Hear Douglas Engelbart Explain His Work

In 2000, computer/human interface pioneer Douglas Engelbart discussed the ideas behind his 1968 demonstration. If your computer is configured to play sound files, you can connect to `http://www.liquid.org/glossary/68_demo.html` and listen to this interview.

at home as a child, you probably take the desktop metaphor for granted.

Today's Windows and Mac OSs continue to use the metaphor of a desktop for the graphical user interface. This metaphor has endured over decades with the same basic principle, with the mouse and keyboard as the primary input devices to select from objects and menus on the "desktop" display. The graphic display is the primary output device for real-time interaction.

■ Navigating the Windows GUI

The menu-based interface used with DOS was referred to as a shell.

Early microcomputer OSs, such as DOS and CP/M, used a command prompt in a simple character-mode interface. Then **menu**-based interfaces (nongraphical, character-based interfaces offering lists of choices) were added to applications and to DOS. Microsoft Windows offers a **graphical user interface (GUI)** that makes accomplishing tasks easy and fast (well, most of the time). A GUI is a type of user interface that uses graphics or icons for operating and using the computer. Menus are such a good idea that Windows and Mac OSs also have plenty of menus in their GUIs. In this section, we'll go for a spin around the Windows track.

We assume knowledge of Windows GUI and mouse elements. If you need to review GUI and mouse skills, your instructor will help you.

Getting to the Desktop via Logon

You can't navigate in Windows until you get to the Windows user interface. Is that a problem? Not really. You may just have to turn on your computer and wait about a minute for the Windows interface (the desktop) to appear.

However, depending on the version of Windows you're using and how your Windows computer is configured, you may not be able to see the desktop and start working until you log on. That is, you must provide a user name and a password that are verified against a security database, either local or on a server on the network. Let's look at how each of the four Windows versions behaves at startup. If you work with only one of these versions, you may want to skim the information about the other versions and focus on the version of Windows you have on your desktop.

Windows NT 4.0

After Windows NT 4.0 starts, it displays a message instructing you to press the CTRL-ALT-DELETE key combination to log on. This key combination is used for security purposes because it will clear memory of certain types of computer viruses that may be lurking; if not disabled by this action, they would do mischief or damage. For instance, some of these viruses wait to capture the keystrokes you enter for your user name and password.

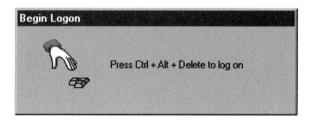

Begin Logon

Press Ctrl + Alt + Delete to log on

- Press CTRL-ALT-DELETE to open the Logon Information dialog box.

When you press these three keys together, you will see the Logon Information dialog box. A dialog box is a form that you fill in; you then either click a special object resembling a button or press the ENTER key to have the computer close the box and process the information you provided. The simple version of the Logon Information box, shown in Figure 3-1, has only the user name and password text boxes. This Logon box will appear only if your computer is not a member of a Microsoft networking domain: that is, if your computer is a stand-alone computer (meaning that it is not on a network), or if it is on a peer-to-peer network as a member of a workgroup.

Logon Information

Enter a user name and password that is valid for this system.

User name:

Password:

OK   Cancel   Help   Shut Down...

- **Figure 3-1.** Windows NT logon screen for a stand-alone or workgroup computer

What Does *Intuitive* Really Mean?

Harry has been an IT professional for over 20 years, working on the front lines in 1983 as PCs were first brought into his company. He now manages the corporate desktop support department, responsible for all end-user computing in the corporation. He believes that the Windows GUI is "intuitive;" he can't imagine anyone not understanding how to perform basic tasks in Windows.

Carl, in contrast, has had a long career with a major airline as an airplane maintenance manager. For many years, his primary use of his office desktop computer was to access a mainframe-based corporate e-mail system. A few years back, the airline switched to a Windows environment. Today, most of Carl's time on his computer is spent reading and sending e-mail, reviewing updates to airplane maintenance bulletins accessed using his web browser (Internet Explorer), and using software that allows him to schedule his team of mechanics. Carl still finds learning new tasks in Windows to be difficult. In spite of the "intuitive" interface, every time Carl needs to perform a new task, someone must show him the steps, and he has to practice them before he feels competent to repeat the task.

As you can see, the definition of intuitive depends on the person and that person's experience with computers. If you pursue a career as an information services or information technology professional, you will encounter people whose experiences fall everywhere within the range between Harry and Carl.

Inside Information

Of Workgroups and Domains

Microsoft defines a **workgroup** *as a grouping of computers on a network for the sake of sharing printers and folders with the group. The only user accounts available in a workgroup exist on member computers that are capable of maintaining a local accounts database (Windows NT, Windows 2000, and Windows XP have this capability). Microsoft has historically stated that a workgroup is practical for up to 10 users in an environment that does not require high security. As more computers are added to a workgroup, the administration of accounts becomes very tedious, since they exist in individual computers. A Microsoft* **domain** *has a centralized security accounts database, maintained on special servers called domain controllers. This centralized database contains accounts for users, groups, and computers participating in the domain. You will revisit workgroups and domains in Chapter 10.*

If a Windows NT 4.0 computer is a member of a domain, as is most likely the case in a corporate environment, the Logon Information dialog box will look like Figure 3-2. Notice the drop-down list box labeled "Domain." This allows you to select between a domain or the local computer. In this case, SEDONA-NT is the name of the local computer. Selecting this will allow you to log on using a local user account. If you have a choice between a local computer or domain logon, you will normally log on to the domain.

Figure 3-3 shows the same dialog box with a domain name, HTC, selected. Logging on with a domain name selected allows you to log on using a domain user account. How can you tell the difference between the computer-based user account and the domain-based user account? You can't tell the difference just by looking at the Logon Information dialog box. Either of these names would be a valid computer or domain name in a Microsoft network. If you are using NT, you simply have to learn the difference between your computer name and the domain name. If you work in an organization that has a Microsoft domain, IT professionals will have configured your computer to log on to the domain and will normally tell users which name to select to do so. This dialog box has been improved in Windows 2000 and Windows XP.

The Logon Information dialog box also has a Shut Down button, which allows someone who has not yet logged on to shut down an NT computer. By default, this button is enabled in Windows NT 4.0 Workstation, but disabled in Windows NT 4.0 Server.

Windows 98

Windows 98 can be used without having to log on, but generally this is done only if you have a stand-alone computer that is not on a network. Even without network access, your Windows 98 computer may be configured to request a logon, in which case you will see the Welcome to Windows dialog box, shown in Figure 3-4. This is not a secure logon, because you can cancel the dialog box and still have access to your Windows 98 computer, though not to the network.

If you need access to network resources, such as files and printers, then a logon is required. In that case, the logon screen appears after the OS is

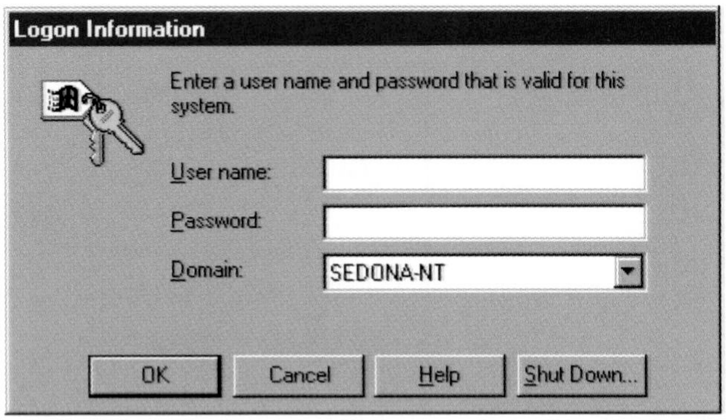

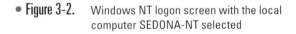

• **Figure 3-2.** Windows NT logon screen with the local computer SEDONA-NT selected

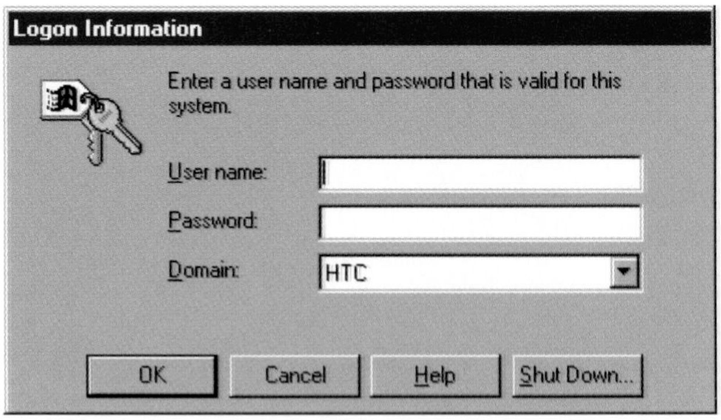

• **Figure 3-3.** Windows NT logon screen with the domain HTC selected

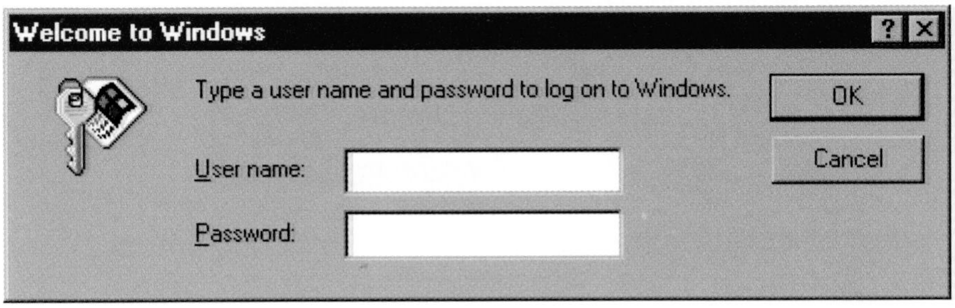

• Figure 3-4. Windows 98 Welcome to Windows logon screen

started. If your computer is in a workgroup, you will see the Enter Network Password dialog box shown in Figure 3-5; if you are logging on to a domain, you will see the dialog box shown in Figure 3-6.

Windows 2000

Windows 2000 combines the ease-of-use features of the Windows 9x OSs and the stability and security of Windows NT. Windows 2000 addresses its ease-of-use mission right after it starts up. If you are required to log on to your Windows 2000 computer but your computer is not part of a Windows workgroup or domain, the Log On to Windows dialog box appears automatically, without your needing to press the CTRL-ALT-DELETE key combination required for Windows NT. In reality, unless Windows 2000 is installed on a stand-alone (non-networked) computer, the CTRL-ALT-DELETE key combination will be required. There are a few ways to remove this requirement, but that would be a foolish thing to do, since it provides some security.

The Windows 2000 Log On to Windows dialog box does not have the Help button that was included in Windows NT (and which was not terribly helpful), but it does give you an Options button, which allows you to simplify the dialog box. If you click the Options button when the Log On to Windows dialog box appears as it does in Figure 3-7, the Log On Using Dial-up Connection check box and its description disappears. Clicking the Options button again causes that choice to reappear. Figure 3-7 shows a logon dialog box on a computer that either is not on a network (stand-alone)

Why is it possible to cancel from a Windows 98 logon, but still access the computer? Security is not the strong point of Windows 98, which was designed to be an easy-to-use desktop OS, with little concern for local security. If you cancel the logon and try to access a network resource, you will be told that the network is not available to you and you will have to log on to get network access.

A computer-based user account is an account that exists in the local account database in Windows NT, Windows 2000, or Windows XP. You may hear people refer to this account database as the SAM. A domain-based user account is an account that exists in a Microsoft domain account database, which exists on special network servers called domain controllers. Domain controllers are central to a domain, which is created to allow administrators to centrally manage the computers, users, printers, files, and other resources in an organization.

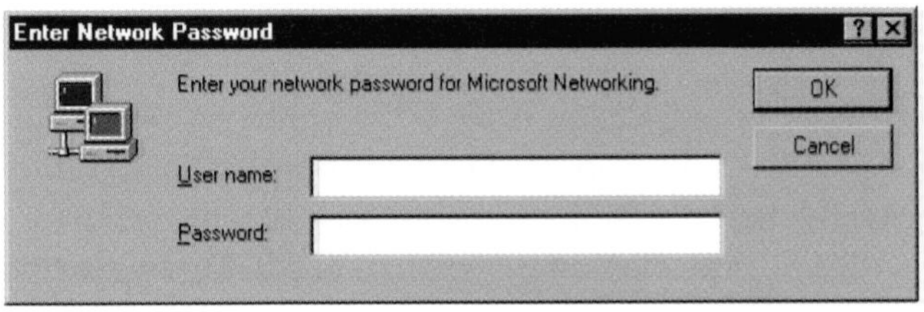

• Figure 3-5. Windows 98 Enter Network Password dialog box for logging on to a workgroup

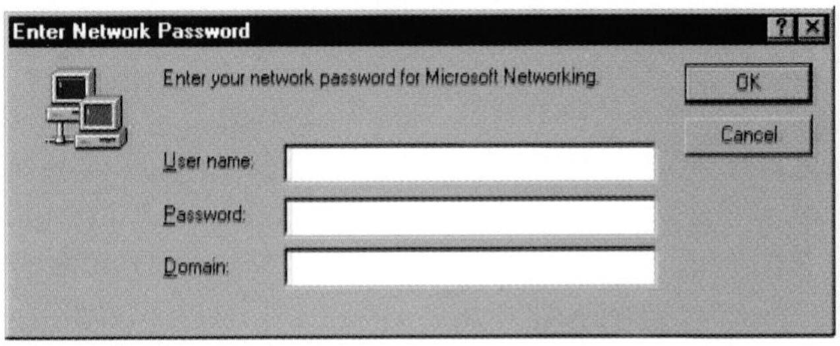

• Figure 3-6. Windows 98 Enter Network Password dialog box for logging on to a domain

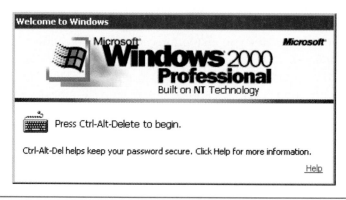

• **Figure 3-7.** Windows 2000 Log On to Windows dialog box for a stand-alone or workgroup computer

or is on a network but not a member of a domain, in which case it is a member of a workgroup.

In addition, Windows 2000 uses the Shut Down button in the same way that Windows NT does, allowing someone who has not yet logged on to shut down a Windows 2000 Professional computer, but disabling this button by default in Windows 2000 Server.

If your Windows 2000 computer is part of a Microsoft Windows workgroup or domain, when you start it you will see the Welcome to Windows box with this message: Press CTRL-ALT-DELETE to Begin.

• Welcome to Windows

After you press the CTRL-ALT-DELETE key combination, the Log On to Windows dialog box appears with a new drop-down list box offering two or more choices. Notice in Figure 3-8 that the Domain field has been replaced by the Log On To field. In the figure, it displays the domain name, HTC, and when the drop-down list button is clicked, it will display the name of the computer and any other domains to which a user is permitted to log on to from this computer, as shown in Figure 3-9. The choice for the local computer is clearly labeled "(this computer)" to avoid confusion. As with NT, there is an Options

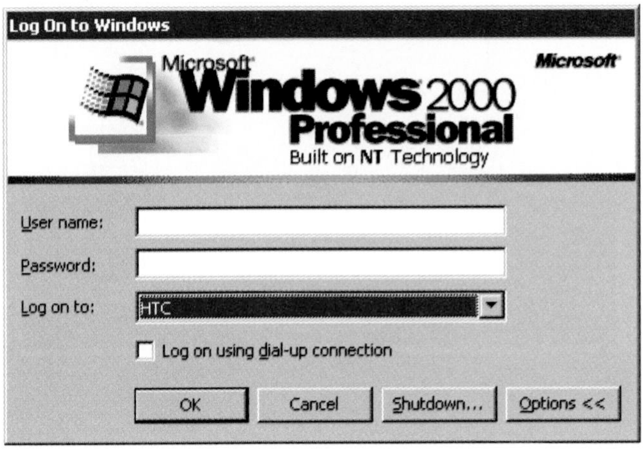

Figure 3-8. Windows 2000 Log On to Windows dialog box with a domain name selected

Figure 3-9. Windows 2000 Log On to Windows dialog box with a local computer selected, as indicated by the label "(this computer)"

button that controls the display of the Log On Using Dial-up Connection check box. Windows 2000 also uses this button to control the display of the Log On To box when the computer is a member of a domain.

Windows XP

In Windows XP, Microsoft made significant changes to the look of the user interface. These changes are apparent before you even reach the desktop, as you can see in Figure 3-10, which is the logon screen you will see the first time you log on to a stand-alone or workgroup member computer.

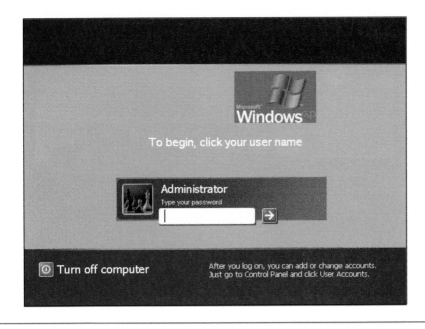

Figure 3-10. Windows XP default logon screen for a stand-alone or workgroup computer

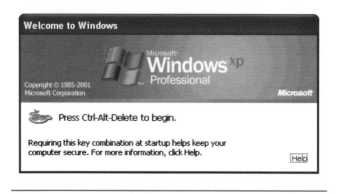

Microsoft
Windows xp
Professional

Copyright © 1985-2001
Microsoft Corporation

Microsoft

Press Ctrl-Alt-Delete to begin.

Requiring this key combination at startup helps keep your
computer secure. For more information, click Help.

Help

Log On to Windows

Microsoft
Windows xp
Professional

Copyright © 1985-2001
Microsoft Corporation

Microsoft

User name: Administrator

Password:

OK   Cancel   Options >>

• **Figure 3-11.**   Windows XP Welcome to Windows screen

• **Figure 3-12.**   Windows XP Log On to Windows screen

If your computer is a member of a domain, you will not see the previously described screen; instead you will see the Welcome to Windows dialog box with a message that tells you to press CTRL-ALT-DELETE (Figure 3-11). Once you press CTRL-ALT-DELETE, you will see the Log On to Windows dialog box, as shown in Figure 3-12.

As in previous Windows versions, the screen has an Options button that will display the choices for logging on to a domain or local computer and for using a dial-up connection to log on, as shown in Figure 3-13.

A Tour of the Desktop

After you have logged on to your computer, you see your desktop—the entire screen area where all of the graphical objects appear. If your desktop hasn't been modified since the OS was installed, you will see a cursor, taskbar, Start menu, and one or more icons, regardless of which of these four

Log On to Windows

Microsoft
Windows xp
Professional

Copyright © 1985-2001
Microsoft Corporation

Microsoft

User name: Administrator

Password:

Log on to: SONORA (this computer)

☐ Log on using dial-up connection

OK   Cancel   Shut Down...   Options <<

• **Figure 3-13.**   Windows XP Log On to Windows screen with Options selected

Logging On to Windows

In this exercise, you will log on to your computer. To complete this exercise, you need the following:

- A computer with one of the four Windows operating systems installed (Windows 98, Windows NT Workstation, Windows 2000 Professional, or Windows XP Professional)

- A user name and password that will allow you to log on to your computer

Step 1   Turn on your computer.

Step 2   If you are prompted, press CTRL-ALT-DELETE.

Step 3   Enter your user name, press TAB or use the mouse to move to the Password box and enter your password, and then press ENTER.

Step 4   Leave the desktop open while you read the next section in the book.

OSs you have. If at all possible, read this section while sitting at a computer running one of the four OSs and locate each object described on your desktop.

Getting Started

The first time you log on to Windows, it offers you a little extra help getting started. This may come in the form of a special dialog box, as you see in NT, Windows 98, and Windows 2000. Or it may be a simple cartoon-style message balloon in Windows XP. They have similar objectives: to help you begin your use of Windows.

> All descriptions of Windows graphical elements are based on a standard uncustomized installation of the retail product. You may see an almost infinite number of variations in your installation.

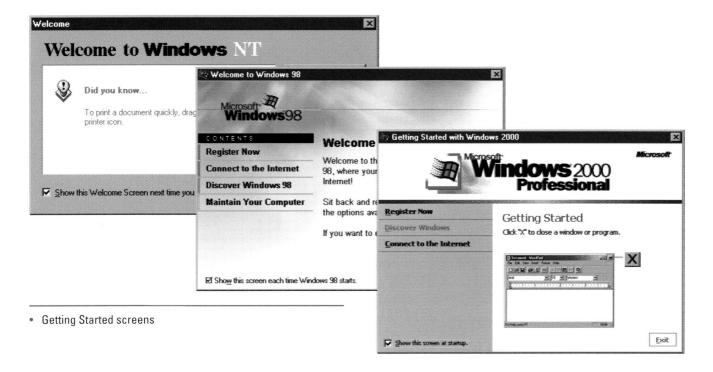

- Getting Started screens

In Windows NT, the Welcome window gives a different tip every time it appears and has buttons that give you access to What's New in Windows NT and Help Contents. The Welcome to Windows screen in Windows 98 has links to Register Now, Connect to the Internet, Discover Windows 98 (a tutorial), and Maintain Your Computer. The Windows 2000 Getting Started window has links to Register Now, Discover Windows, and Connect to the Internet. In all of these, you can remove a check from the Show This Screen at Startup check box so that you will not see the welcome information every time you log on.

After you get past the welcoming efforts of your OS, you can explore the desktop. Let's look at the common elements you may see on the desktop, including the taskbar, icons, and other objects.

Taskbar

All four Windows versions display the **taskbar** across the bottom of the screen, with some variations in the default buttons on the bar. The Windows 2000 taskbar shown in Figure 3-14 includes a Start button, the system tray, the Quick Launch toolbar, and buttons for programs that are running. Most of the taskbar area is used to display buttons for running programs. The newer versions of Windows will include message balloons for events relating to objects in the system tray. You can reposition the taskbar by simply dragging it to the new position, and you can resize it by dragging just an edge of it until it is the desired size. Windows XP has a new taskbar option, Lock Taskbar, which locks the taskbar in place so that it can't be moved until this option is turned off. This is turned on by default, and you can turn it on or off by right-clicking on the taskbar.

Desktop Icons

The biggest variation on the desktop is in the displayed icons. The default desktop icons are as follows:

- Windows NT 4.0, Windows 98, and Windows 2000 all have My Computer, Internet Explorer, and the Recycle Bin as default icons. In addition, if any one of these versions of Windows is on a network, Network Neighborhood (My Network Places in Windows 2000) will also appear.

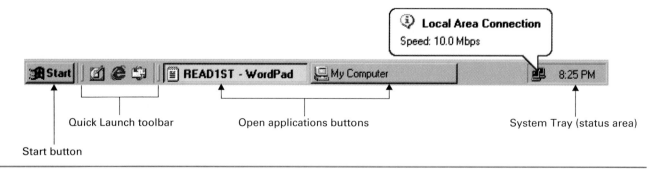

Figure 3-14. Windows 2000 taskbar with components identified

- Inbox appears only on the Windows NT 4.0 desktop. Similarly, Windows 98 has a desktop icon for Outlook Express.

- My Briefcase is on the NT desktop, and My Documents is on the Windows 98 and Windows 2000 desktops.

- Windows 98 also contains several additional icons, including MSN Internet Account, Online Services, and Connect to the Internet.

- The Windows XP desktop is very, very clean, with just the Recycle Bin icon showing.

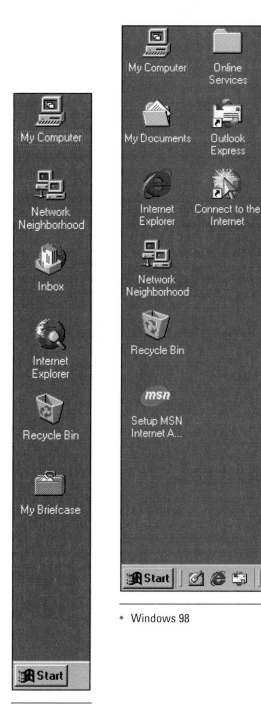

• Windows NT

• Windows 98

• Windows 2000

• Windows XP

Inside Information

Special Folders

*There are certain folders that Windows treats differently than others and are called **special folders**. There are many special folders including the Start Menu, Recycle Bin, Favorites, and Printers. The Start menu folder is the most prominent and is in all versions of Windows studied in this book. This is a disk folder where Windows saves objects you place on the desktop beyond the default objects. It also contains other special folders. In a network environment, an administrator can use a special function called folder redirection to have a user's Programs, Documents, Desktop, and other special folders saved to a network server every time the user logs off. This, plus other settings, allows a user to log on from any computer on the network and still have his or her personal desktop objects. Special folders and their handling varies from version to version of Windows.*

Start Menu

The Start button on the taskbar contains a very important menu, called the Start menu. Click the Start button to open the Start menu. This menu contains several programs and submenus and is the central tool for finding and starting a variety of programs in Windows. Microsoft increased the importance of the Start menu in Windows XP, moving all but one of the default desktop icons off the desktop and onto the Start menu.

As you can see in the illustrations, the Start menu in each of the three older versions of Windows is a simple, one-column menu, but Windows XP has two columns of shortcut icons, because of the space needed for the former desktop icons.

In all four versions, the Start menu contains shortcuts for programs and special folders containing more folders and/or programs. An arrow on a folder icon indicates that the folder item can be expanded to display the contents. In the following sections, you'll look at the menu shortcuts that are common to all or most of these OSs. Some of the shortcut names have been altered slightly between Windows versions, in which case we present the alternative names.

Programs/All Programs   The Programs menu item, in all but Windows XP, has an icon that consists of a folder with an overlapping program icon. This indicates that it is a folder containing links to programs and other folders containing programs. In Windows XP, it does not have an icon and is renamed All Programs. Click this Start menu shortcut to open a menu with a

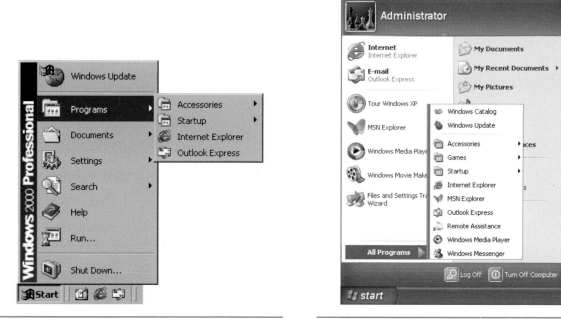

• Windows 2000 Program menu

• Windows XP All Programs menu

list of programs and program categories. When you install a new application in Windows, it will usually add a folder or program icon to this menu.

Documents/My Recent Documents The Documents (Windows NT, Windows 98, and Windows 2000) Start menu icon appears to be an open folder with papers in it. This menu contains shortcuts to recently opened data files. In Windows XP, Documents has been renamed My Recent Documents.

In Windows 98 and Windows 2000, Documents also contains a shortcut to the My Documents folder on the desktop, a folder in which you can save your actual data files. Many Windows applications will default to My Documents for saving and opening files. Each user has a My Documents folder, separate from that of all other users. The menu item My Documents is on the Windows XP Start menu, but not, by default, on the others. This is a link to your personal My Documents folder.

Settings Windows NT, Windows 98, and Windows 2000 have a Settings submenu on the Start menu. This menu contains a group of choices that differs depending on the version of Windows. Control Panel, Printers, and Taskbar icons are common to all three OSs that have the Settings menu. Other items you will find in various versions are Network and Dial-up Connections, Folder Options, Active Desktop, and Windows Update.

While Windows XP does not have the Settings menu, it does have Control Panel and Printers and Faxes as menus

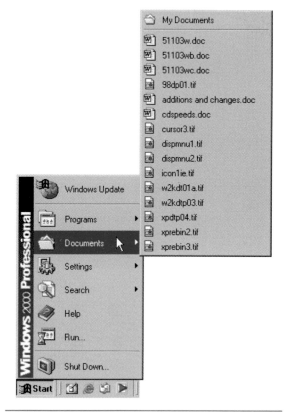

• My Documents menu

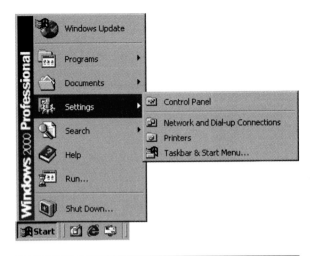

• Settings menu

My Documents is another special folder on which an administrator can use folder redirection to have it automatically saved on a network server. This is very desirable because the data of many users can be redirected to a single network server, which puts this valuable data in one place for easy backup.

directly off the Start menu. All of the items you usually find on the older Settings menus (with the exception of Control Panel) are really links to options within Control Panel. Therefore, we'll now take a look at Control Panel.

Control Panel The Control Panel item on the Settings menu is a link to the Control Panel, which contains a variety of **applets** (mini-application programs) that exist to allow you (or an administrator) to configure your software and hardware. Many of these applets can be accessed elsewhere. For instance, the Control Panel Display applet opens the Properties dialog box for the display, which you can also open by right-clicking an empty area of the desktop and selecting Properties from the context menu.

The Control Panel changed very little through the various versions of Windows, until Windows XP, when it underwent a major reorganization. Compare the classic Control Panel from Windows 2000, shown in Figure 3-15, with the Control Panel from Windows XP, shown in Figure 3-16. In the classic version, you see icons for the individual applets themselves. To use that version, you think about the task you need to do, and then you search for the right tool to do that task. (Let's see. I want to switch the primary and secondary buttons on the mouse for a left-handed user. Because it's a mouse, I'll begin by opening the Mouse applet, and then I'll make the appropriate choice.)

The Windows XP Control Panel, however, is organized by functional category. So, as before, you think of the task you want to perform. Next, however, you must decide what category fits your task. Modifying how the mouse works comes under the category Printers and Other Hardware. It helps that this category happens to have a graphic of a mouse (obviously a huge mouse, since in the graphic it is bigger than the printer). So you click the Printers and Hardware category, and then you have another choice, as

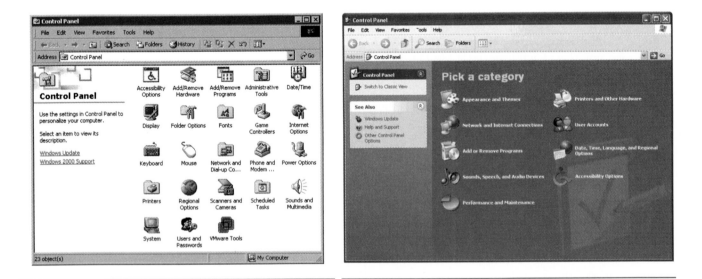

• **Figure 3-15.** Windows 2000 Control Panel

• **Figure 3-16.** Windows XP Control Panel

Survey of Operating Systems

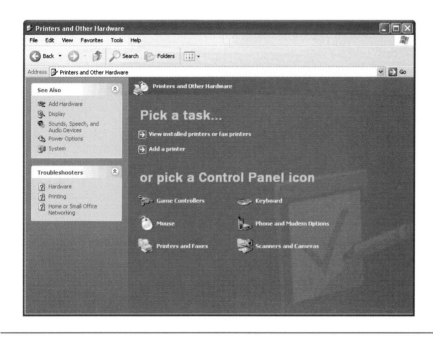

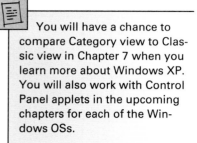
You will have a chance to compare Category view to Classic view in Chapter 7 when you learn more about Windows XP. You will also work with Control Panel applets in the upcoming chapters for each of the Windows OSs.

• **Figure 3-17.** Pick a task…or pick a Control Panel icon

you can see in Figure 3-17. You can select a task, but neither task has anything to do with the mouse, or you can pick a Control Panel icon. Finally, there's the Mouse icon. A single mouse click will bring up the Mouse Properties dialog box, and you can work from there.

It can be argued that Control Panel is easier to use in XP, especially if you are new to Windows or, like our friend Carl, have not found previous versions easy to use. However, experienced Windows users and computer professionals, like Harry, will discover that the more advanced options are somewhat more difficult to find. More experienced users, therefore, may choose to use the Windows XP option for viewing Control Panel in the Classic view.

Find/Search All of the versions of Windows that you are studying here have a Start menu option that opens a Find or Search program (the name change occurred after Windows 98). These programs have increased in capability with each version of Windows, from Windows NT, which allowed you to search only for files, folders, and computers, to Windows XP, which offers a comprehensive search program that allows you to search for almost anything you want on a small or large network—or even on the Internet.

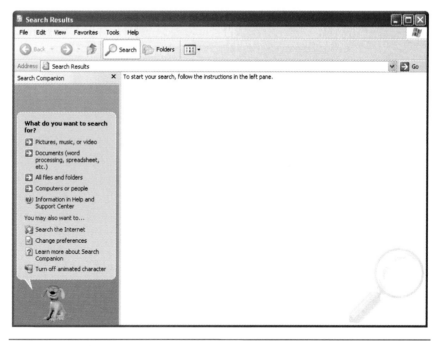

• Windows XP Search menu

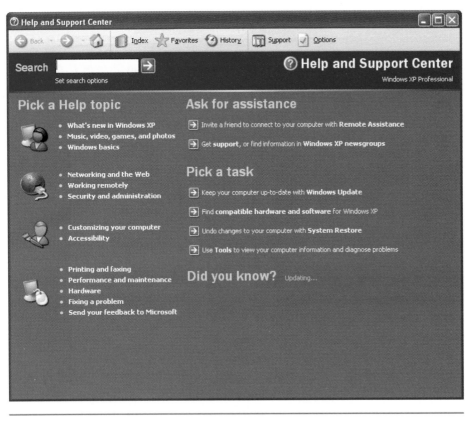

• Windows XP Help menu

Help   All four versions of Windows include a Help option on the Start menu. The help program itself has improved with each version, and with Windows XP the Help and Support option opens up the Help and Support Center window, which gives you links to your local help program, Internet sources, Remote Assistance (see Chapter 7), Microsoft's Windows XP newsgroups, and various programs to help you update your software, restore the system, and diagnose problems. Whatever version of Windows you have, take time to check out Help. You will find answers to most of your questions about Windows in Help. All versions have troubleshooting scripts that walk you through a problem. Don't forget this great resource when you have problems with your computer.

Run   The Run option allows you to launch any program that can run under Windows. When you select Start | Run, a dialog box appears. You can enter the name of the program to be launched or click the Browse button to search for the program on disk (local or network). There are many programs included with Windows that cannot normally be started by an icon or menu entry, but are routinely started from Start | Run. These are generally programs used by intermediate to advanced users. One good example is the RDISK command in Windows NT. This important utility allows an administrator to create a repair disk to use in the emergency repair of the OS.

Run

Type the name of a program, folder, document, or Internet resource, and Windows will open it for you.

Open: wordpad

[OK] [Cancel] [Browse...]

• Run dialog box

Although any program that can run under Windows can be launched from Start | Run, it isn't practical for running most command-line utilities, because the command prompt will not remain open long enough for you to see the result of running the command! For these programs, first launch the command prompt; then run the program.

Shut Down   For years, we have heard users say, "Why can't there be a 'Turn off' switch for a PC?" They really are asking for a single hardware switch that will gracefully shut down their programs and OS. Well, this has not come to the PC world yet, and you should not use the hardware switch before properly shutting down the OS. Windows NT, Windows 98, and Windows 2000 all have a Shut Down option on the Start menu, which leads to other options, including Log Off and (finally) Shut Down. In Windows XP, Start | Shut Down has been replaced by two buttons, Log Off and Turn Off Computer, at the bottom of the Start menu. You will work with your OS's shutdown or turn off option in the section "Logging Off and Shutting Down."

Exploring the Start Menu

In this exercise, you will explore the submenus of the Start menu. To complete this exercise, you will need the following:

- A computer with one of the four Windows operating systems installed (Windows 98,

Windows NT Workstation, Windows 2000 Professional, or Windows XP Professional)

- A user name and password that will allow you to log on to your computer

Step 1

If necessary, start and log on to your computer, as you did in Step-by-Step 3.01.

Step 2

Click the Start button; then move your cursor to the Programs (or All Programs) menu; select Accessories; and then select Notepad. This is a text editor that comes with Windows. It can create and edit only text files that do not have the type of formatting codes that a word processor embeds in a file to control the way that the data is displayed and printed. Text files usually, but not always, have a .txt extension. Create a text file in Notepad just for fun—but you don't need to bother saving it.

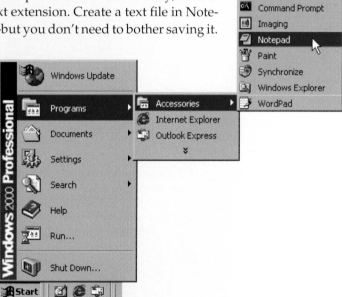

Step 3

Close Notepad by clicking the close button on the Notepad window. Select Start | Programs (or All Programs) | Accessories (in some versions of Windows) | Games | Solitaire. Play exactly one game of Solitaire to enhance your mouse skills. If you do not know how to play, click the Help button (you may even find Strategies and Tips). After you are done, close Solitaire.

Step 4

If you are using Windows 2000 or Windows XP, select Start | Programs (or All Programs) | Accessories | Command Prompt.

If you are using Windows NT or Windows 98, select Start | Programs | Command Prompt (or MS-DOS Prompt).

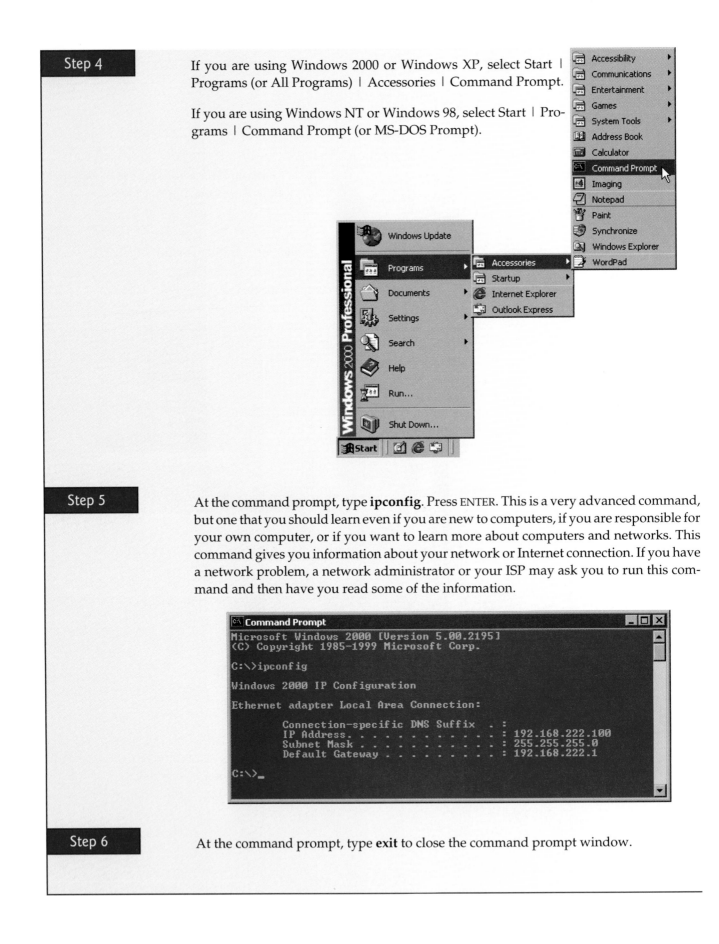

Step 5

At the command prompt, type **ipconfig**. Press ENTER. This is a very advanced command, but one that you should learn even if you are new to computers, if you are responsible for your own computer, or if you want to learn more about computers and networks. This command gives you information about your network or Internet connection. If you have a network problem, a network administrator or your ISP may ask you to run this command and then have you read some of the information.

Step 6

At the command prompt, type **exit** to close the command prompt window.

Managing Files in Windows

A file is information organized as a unit. For instance, the chapter you are reading right now is saved as a single file. We could have chosen to save all of the chapters of this book in a single file, but chose instead to save them in individual files. You have choices like this when you are working with data files. As part of managing your files, you'll perform different actions—such as opening, closing, copying, and moving them. Compared to file management in DOS, file management in Windows is infinitely easier and safer. File management is easier because you don't have to memorize commands that use cryptic syntax. Moreover, you don't have to feel like you are taking a typing test every time you want to create, copy, move, or delete a file or directory (*folder* in Windows-speak). File management is somewhat safer because you can see exactly what files and folders you have selected for a file management operation.

Building on what you learned in Chapter 2, we'll now look at the GUI tools you will use for file management, primarily My Computer and Windows Explorer; then we'll practice basic file management tasks.

> From now on, instructions for selecting a command from a menu will be less detailed. For instance, to have you start Notepad from the Start menu, as you did in Step 2 of Step-by-Step 3.02, we will use the notation: Start | Programs (or All Programs) | Accessories | Notepad.

What Files Should You Manage?

Windows computers use several file types, including, in broad terms, program files and data files. Program files contain programming code (instructions read by the OS or special interpreters). Program files include those that you can directly run, such as files with the .com or .exe extension, and those that are called up by other programs, such as files with the .dll extension. Data files are the files you create with application programs, and there are a large number of data file types. A short list includes text files, which most often have the .txt extension, Word document files (with the .doc extension), graphic files (with a variety of extensions, such as .bmp, .dib, .gif, .jpg, and .tif), database files (Access uses the .mdb extension), and spreadsheet files (Excel uses the .xls extension). When it comes to file management, you should not try to manage program files until you have a great deal of experience with Windows; you should start by managing data files.

✓ Cross Check

File Management

Strange, even as we wrote that part about all of the good information on files and file management in Chapter 2, we could imagine someone (you?) saying, "We don't care about DOS; we skipped that silly chapter on DOS." Well, if so, you missed some helpful information on file systems, file naming, file types, and file attributes. We are assuming that you know all of that stuff, so we won't bother to repeat ourselves here. Look back at Chapter 2 now and read the section titled "How the FAT File System Works." Then answer the following questions:

1. Describe the 8.3 naming convention.

   _____

   _____

2. After reading the description of file attributes in Chapter 2, decide whether you believe that the read-only attribute provides security from unauthorized access to a file. Then write a brief argument describing why you believe setting this attribute does or does not provide security.

   _____

   _____

Which View Do You Prefer?

Decide for yourself which view you prefer. Using any of the four versions of Windows covered in this book, do the following:

1. Right-click My Computer and select Open from the context menu. Double-click to open several objects, including your C: drive. Continue to open folders. Notice the rather flat organization of folders. Click the View menu and select Details. This gives you more information about the objects. Leave folder windows open for comparison.

2. Right-click My Computer (you may have to drag windows to access My Computer) and select Explore. Choose the View menu and select Details. Expand drive C:. Leave the window open.

3. Right-click an empty part of the taskbar and select Tile Windows Horizontally. This allows you to compare the two views and to decide which one you prefer.

Using My Computer to Manage Files

My Computer is an icon on the desktop or Start menu, depending on your version of Windows. It can be opened by double-clicking it if it is a desktop icon, or by single-clicking it on the Start menu. My Computer contains important objects for you, the user. The actual objects vary from version to version and also depend on how the computer is configured.

Explorer View Versus Folder View

Behind the scenes, Windows Explorer is actually used to display many of the objects on your desktop, including My Computer. However, you can also call it up separately when you want to view objects on your computer in a special view called Explorer view. You will find an icon for Windows Explorer at Start | Programs | Accessories (except in Windows NT, which has it on the Programs menu).

When you double-click My Computer in Windows NT, Windows 98, or Windows 2000, it opens by default in Folder view, as shown in Figure 3-18. You can also open My Computer in Explorer view, as seen in Figure 3-19. The main difference between these two views is what is missing in Folder view, which is a second window pane, or bordered area within the window. This is a dual-paned window. The left pane contains a hierarchical view, and the right pane contains the contents of the object that is currently selected in

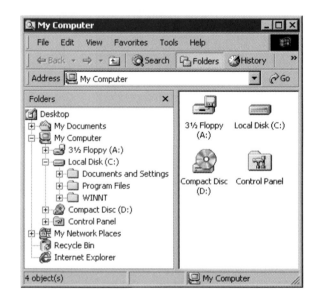

● Figure 3-18.   Windows 2000 My Computer—Folder view

● Figure 3-19.   Windows 2000 My Computer—Explorer view

the left pane. The left pane is the Folders pane, and the right pane is the Contents pane. You can open My Computer in Explorer view by selecting Explore from the context menu.

Step-by-Step 3.03

Managing Files and Folders

In this exercise, you will practice some common file management tasks. First you will create a folder, and then you will copy, move, and delete files. To complete this exercise, you will need the following:

- A computer with one of the four Windows operating systems installed (Windows NT

Workstation, Windows 98, Windows 2000 Professional, or Windows XP Professional)

- A user name and password that will allow you to log on to your computer

| Step 1 | If necessary, start and log on to your computer, as you did in Step-by-Step 3.01. Use your mouse to select Start | Programs (or All Programs) | Accessories | Windows Explorer. If you are using Windows NT, select Start | Programs | Windows NT Explorer. |

| Step 2 | Click the plus sign to the left of My Computer. This expands the folder so you can see all of the objects at the top level in My Computer. Expand Local Disk C:. In Windows NT, this is simply labeled (C:). |

| Step 3 | Position your cursor over an empty area of the Contents pane (right pane) of the window and then right-click. In the context menu, select New | Folder. Name the folder **data1**. Repeat this step to create a folder named **data2**. |

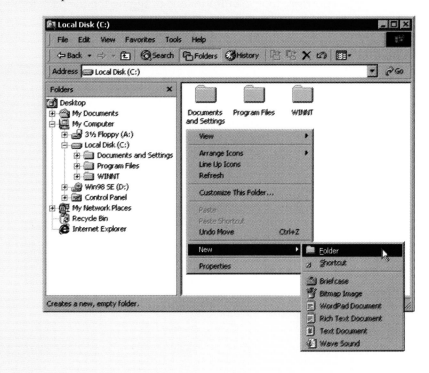

Double-click the data1 folder to open it in Explorer and then right-click the Contents pane and select New | Text Document. Name the document **report1.txt**.

Drag the file report1.txt from the Contents pane and drop it on the data2 folder in the Folders pane. This moves the file, so that it no longer exists in the data1 folder. A drag-and-drop operation between folders on the same drive is a **move** operation, and a drag-and-drop operation between folders on different drives is a **copy** operation.

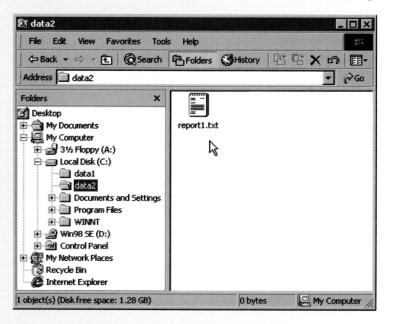

Open the data2 folder and confirm that report1 was moved to this folder. Press and hold the right mouse button while dragging the file back to the data1 folder. When you release the mouse button over the data1 folder, a context menu pops up that gives you the choice of copying, moving, or creating a shortcut to the file. Select the option to create a shortcut.

Step 7

To launch Notepad by association, expand the data1 folder and double-click the shortcut to report1.txt. This is a shortcut to a text file, so double-clicking it causes Notepad to open, because that is the program associated with text files.

Step 8

Type a sentence describing what happens when you drag a file from one folder to another folder on the same drive. Then save the file by selecting File | Save. Exit from Notepad by using the ALT-F4 shortcut key combination.

```
report1.txt - Notepad                                    _ □ X
File  Edit  Format  Help
Assume that "drag" means to point to an object then press and hold the
left mouse button while moving the object. In that case, when you drag
a file from one folder to another folder on the same drive, the file is
 moved to the new folder, and does not exist in the old folder.
```

Step 9

Open the data2 folder and double-click the report1 file. The sentence you typed should be in the file. Exit from Notepad.

■ Configuring and Customizing the Windows Desktop

Windows allows each user to create the desktop environment that suits his or her particular personality and way of working. Some people like icons all over the desktop on a simple background, others like elaborate graphic backgrounds with icons, while yet others like simple, peaceful scenes with few icons. Customizing is easy. In this section, we'll explore some of your options for customizing the Windows desktop: choosing the Classic Desktop or the Active Desktop, changing the background wallpaper or pattern, selecting color schemes, and making video settings.

Classic Desktop versus Active Desktop

Microsoft introduced the concept of the Active Desktop with Internet Explorer (IE) 4.01 and the versions of Windows that came after it. **Active Desktop** is a feature that lets you put web content directly on your Windows desktop. If Active Desktop is installed, you can choose between the classic Windows desktop and Web view. In classic Windows desktop you double-click to open an object on the desktop or in My Computer, while in Web view objects on the desktop behave like links in a web page in that you can open them with a single-click. You can have a combination of the old and the new, with your standard desktop icons requiring a double-click to open, and other objects shown as links with an underline that indicates that they are links and so require only a single-click. Furthermore, you can display web content directly on your desktop, even content that changes, like stock quotes. Figure 3-20 shows web content (from two websites) displayed on the Windows 2000 desktop. While

● **Figure 3-20.** Windows 2000 with Active Desktop

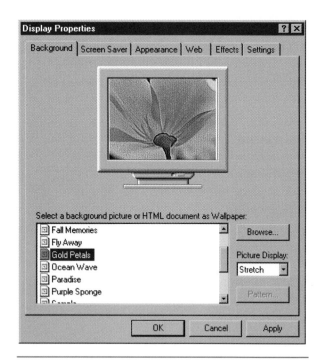

● Windows 2000 Background page

the classic desktop icons on the left require the standard double-click, links in the web content shown on the page only require a single-click.

You use the Display properties applet to enable, customize, or disable Active Desktop. In all but Windows XP, look for the Web tab in the Display Properties dialog box; in Windows XP, you must first select the Desktop tab in Display Properties, then click the Customize Desktop button, and then click the Web tab.

Decorating the Desktop: Background, Color Schemes, and Settings

You have many choices when it comes to how your desktop is decorated. You can have wallpaper or no wallpaper—there are many designs available, and you can also buy designs or get them free from many sources. You can also change the colors of the desktop items. All of this can be done by right-clicking the desktop, selecting Properties, and using the Background and Appearance tabs.

Customizing the Desktop

In this exercise, you will customize the desktop by adding or changing the screen saver and by adding an icon to your Quick Start menu. To complete this exercise, you will need the following:

■ A computer with one of the four Windows operating systems installed (Windows NT Workstation, Windows 98, Windows 2000 Professional, or Windows XP Professional)

■ A user name and password that will allow you to log on to your computer

Step 1

If necessary, start and log on to your computer, right-click an empty area of the desktop, and then select Properties. In the Display Properties dialog box, click the Screen Saver tab.

Step 2

On the Screen Saver page, select a screen saver from the Screen Saver drop-down list. This will cause other buttons and boxes on that page to become active. Keep in mind that although some screen savers, such as those identified as OpenGL, are really cool, they may slow down your computer and interfere with other programs. So, if your computer has more important tasks than displaying a fantastic screen saver, don't choose an OpenGL screen saver.

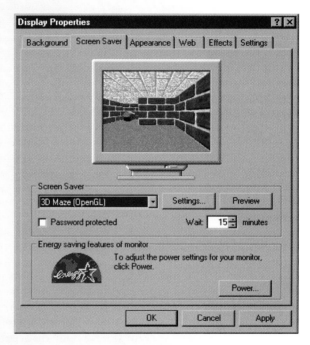

Step 3

Click the Preview button to preview the screen saver on the full screen. Moving the mouse or pressing a key will stop the preview. The value in the Wait box controls how long the computer will have to go without mouse or keyboard activity before the screen saver comes on. Adjust this number to the setting you desire.

Step 4

If you have confidential information on your computer that you do not want others to access when you step away from your computer, one option is to put a password on your screen saver. If you select the Password Protected check box, you will password protect your computer. Password protection on screen savers is available in all four versions of Windows used in this book. It is not available in Windows XP Home Edition, but is in Windows XP Professional. Select Password Protected. Click OK to close the Display Properties dialog box.

Step 5

A better alternative to password-protected screen savers is the ability (in Windows NT, Windows 2000, and Windows XP) to lock your computer, which is probably more secure than using a screen saver (among other things, you can do it immediately). The Lock option is available on the Security menu, accessed from the desktop by pressing CTRL-ALT-DELETE. Press CTRL-ALT-DELETE and select Lock Computer. The Computer Locked message will appear on your screen. Press CTRL-ALT-DELETE and enter your password in the Unlock Computer box.

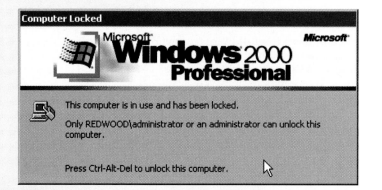

Step 6

If the **Quick Launch toolbar** is not on your taskbar, add it by right-clicking the taskbar, selecting Toolbars, and then clicking Quick Launch. (Note that the Quick Launch toolbar is not available in Windows NT Workstation.)

Step 7

Once the Quick Launch toolbar is enabled, it's easy to add program icons. Try adding WordPad to the toolbar. Use the Find or Search command to find the WordPad program file. Then just drag it to the Quick Launch toolbar. If it ends up where you don't want it, just drag it along the toolbar to where you do want it and release the mouse button.

Step 8

Test Step 7 by single-clicking the WordPad icon on the Quick Launch toolbar. Close WordPad when you are done.

Customizing the Taskbar

One clever thing you can do is to make use of the Quick Launch toolbar. The advantage of the Quick Launch toolbar is that the icons are smaller, thereby taking up less valuable desktop real estate, and can be activated with a single-click. We arrange our icons in the order of frequency of use, putting the ones we use the most on the Quick Launch toolbar, and placing those we use a little less frequently on the desktop.

One of our purposes in writing this book is to help you become comfortable enough with Windows that you are able to figure out how to do things on your own, without needing a step-by-step explanation. Modern computers in general, and Windows OSs in particular, usually have a number of ways to do a particular task or activate a specific function. The procedure you choose is often the first one you find to do the task. People tend not to look for other, perhaps easier, ways to do a task after they have found one that works for them.

Try This!

Moving the Taskbar

While you complete the following tasks, we encourage you to experiment to find other, easier ways to do the tasks. Use the help program to do the following tasks:

1. Reposition the taskbar on your desktop to the left, right, or top edge.

2. The taskbar at the bottom of the window can be set to disappear from the screen and can be made to reappear when the cursor is moved to the bottom of the screen. This frees up more of the screen real estate for applications, while allowing you to get to the taskbar whenever you need it. In the words of Captain Picard of the starship Enterprise, "Make it so!"

Launching Programs in Windows

Someday you may simply have to think about a task, and your computer will load the correct program and lead you through the task—or complete it for you. Until that day, you generally must know what program you need for your task. Then you have to take some action to start the program. The discussion in this section of the chapter will help you become a "champion launcher."

Start Menu

Programs can be launched when they are selected from the Start menu or one of its submenus. For instance, to launch the FreeCell program, we simply use the mouse to select Start | Programs | Accessories | Games | FreeCell.

Program Shortcut

Double-clicking a shortcut to a program will launch the program. Shortcuts can be on the Start menu, as mentioned earlier, on the desktop, on the taskbar, or in a folder.

Start | Run

A program can be launched from Start | Run, which is a handy way to run a program you don't use very frequently. An administrator working on a client's computer might use Start | Run to launch an administrative or diagnostics tool that is available on the user's computer, but is not something she wants the user to easily run. An example of this is a program called Regedit, which is very dangerous in the wrong hands, but, at times, is very necessary

• Run dialog box

You practiced launch by association in Step 7 of Step-by-Step 3.03.

for an administrator to use. (Now don't go running Regedit until you learn more about it!) We also like to use Start | Run to launch applications that are several menu levels down in the Start menu, but for which we don't want to add a shortcut to the taskbar or desktop, when we are familiar with the file name. For instance, Winmsd.exe is the program file that opens System Information. We don't need to run this everyday, but when we sit down at someone's computer and want to get a quick summary of their hardware and software, we simply select Start | Run and type **winmsd** in the Run box.

Launch by Association

When you install an application program, the installation program informs Windows of the file types that it understands and provides Windows with the file name extension of the file type, such as .doc, .rtf, .tif, and so on. The program and the file type are then registered with Windows, and the file type is associated with the program. Then, when you double-click a data file, Windows checks its list of associations, loads the program that can use that type of data file into memory, and hands the file to the program. If you have several programs that can work with the same data file format, Windows will give one of them first priority when it comes to **launch by association**. Changing this priority is an advanced task that we will save for a later chapter.

Command Prompt

Windows has a text-based **command prompt** from which you can launch any program that can be run in Windows. If the program is a Windows program, it will open in a window.

Step-by-Step 3.05

Launch Programs in Windows

Practice launching a program using different methods. While you are performing these steps, consider which methods you would use.
To complete this exercise, you will need the following:

■ A computer with one of the four Windows operating systems installed (Windows NT Workstation, Windows 98, Windows 2000 Professional, or Windows XP Professional)

■ A user name and password that will allow you to log on to your computer

Step 1

If necessary, start and log on to your computer, as you did in Step-by-Step 3.01. Use your mouse to select Start | Programs (or All Programs) | Accessories | WordPad. Then, in WordPad, type a paragraph or two describing your first encounter with a computer.

Step 2

Save the file. Use your mouse to select File | Save As. Next to the Save In box, click the down arrow, click Local Disk C:, and double-click data1 in the Contents pane. In the File Name box, type **First Encounter**; then select Rich Text Format in the Save As Type box and click Save. Select File | Exit to close WordPad.

Save As dialog box

- Save in: My Documents
  - History
  - Desktop
  - My Documents
  - My Computer
    - 3½ Floppy (A:)
    - 3½ Floppy (B:)
    - Local Disk (C:)
    - Local Disk (D:)
    - Local Disk (E:)
    - Local Disk (F:)
    - osborne on 'htc1\company' (G:)
    - company on 'htc1' (H:)
    - Win98 SE (R:)
    - My Network Places

Side icons: History, Desktop, My Documents, My Computer, My Network P...

File name: Document.rtf

Save as type: Rich Text Format (RTF)

☑ Save in this format by default

Buttons: Save, Cancel

Step 3

From the desktop, open the following objects in turn: My Computer, Local Disk C:, and data1. The data1 folder should now contain two objects: First Encounter and a shortcut to report1.

Step 4

Double-click First Encounter. It should open in WordPad because this type of file (RTF) is associated with WordPad by default. If it opens in another word processing program, this indicates that your Windows settings have been modified to associate a different program with RTF. Exit from WordPad.

Step 5

Another way to launch WordPad is to select Start | Run and type **wordpad** in the Run box. After WordPad appears, you can click File or the Open icon to find your document and read it. When you are finished, exit from WordPad.

Run dialog box

Type the name of a program, folder, document, or Internet resource, and Windows will open it for you.

Open: wordpad

Buttons: OK, Cancel, Browse...

Step 6

Now you will test the launching of programs from the command prompt. If you have Windows NT, Windows 2000, or Windows XP, select Start | Run and type **cmd** in the Run box; then press ENTER. If you have Windows 98, type **command** in the Run box.

Step 7

At the command prompt, type **notepad** and press ENTER. This should launch the NotePad program. This approach works only for a program that is in a location where Windows will search for programs. We call that the *search path*, and it is a special setting in Windows.

■ Logging Off and Shutting Down

At the end of the day, you should log off and/or properly shut down your computer. Which you choose to do depends on whose computer it really is and who makes the rules for its use, but never use the on/off switch until you have selected Shut Down from within Windows and you see a message saying that it is okay to turn off the power. If it is your home computer, you will probably log off (if necessary) and shut down each day. If you use a computer at school or work, you will obey the rules of the organization. For instance, some organizations require that all users log off at the end of the day, but leave their computers on. In fact, some organizations even configure Windows so that there is no Shut Down choice (an advanced administrative task). This may be so that a centralized backup of all of the computers, or some other maintenance task, can occur. In this case, you will simply log off at the end of the day.

At work or in your school lab, you are more likely to be required to power down your computer. This actually means that, in most cases, you will both log off and power down. There are two ways that you can initiate these steps.

Start Menu

Selecting Shut Down from the Start menu in Windows NT and Windows 2000 opens the Shut Down Windows dialog box. Selecting Turn Off Computer at the bottom of the Windows XP Start menu leads to a Turn Off Computer dialog box with choices to Standby, Turn Off, or Restart.

Ctrl-Alt-Delete

Pressing CTRL-ALT-DELETE leads to the Security menu in Windows NT and Windows 2000. You can select Log Off and Shut Down from this menu. Selecting Log Off will log off only the current user, but will not shut down the computer. Selecting Shut Down will do both tasks.

Troubleshooting Common Windows Desktop Problems

Some common Windows desktop problems include disappearing dialog boxes, an inability to find something, failure of Windows to start, and failure of Windows when you are working at the desktop or in My Computer or Windows Explorer. Let's look at these problems and how you might solve them yourself.

Disappearing Dialog Box

You have just entered something in a dialog box, but you're not finished and want to move to another field in that same dialog box, but suddenly the dialog box disappears. This most often happens because you have pressed the ENTER key at the wrong time. Within a dialog box, you can move from field to field by pressing the TAB key or clicking the field you want. For each field, you type something or click a button or check box. Only when you are done should you press ENTER. At that point, your entries are accepted, and the box closes. The solution to the disappearing dialog box problem is to be careful not to press ENTER until you have finished working in a dialog box.

> You can even move backward through the fields in a dialog box by holding down the SHIFT key while you press the TAB key.

Inability to Find Something

Maybe the other day you wrote a rough draft of a paper on the life cycle of amoebas that is due next week. Today you want to continue to work on it, but you can't remember where you saved it. You're not even sure of the exact name of the file, except that you used *amoeba* in the name. If you are using any of the versions of Windows you are studying in this book, there is one quick way to find a file or folder: use the Find or Search function from the Start menu. For instance, to find a file with the word *amoeba* in its name, use Start | Find (or Start | Search). Then enter **amoeba** in the Named box. Selecting C: in the Look In box will then start a search of your entire drive C: for any file (or folder) with *amoeba* in its name. The results will look something like Figure 3-21, depending on your version of Windows.

Cross Check

Windows GUI Comparison

Now that you have studied and practiced working with the Windows desktop and practiced skills to navigate, manage files, configure the desktop, and launch programs, answer the following questions:

1. List three differences between the Windows 98 desktop and the Windows XP desktop.

2. Compare the use of My Documents, available in Windows 98, Windows 2000, and Windows XP, with the procedure for managing a user's data files in Windows NT, which does not have My Documents.

3. Discuss methods you can use to make it more convenient for a user to launch programs from the desktop.

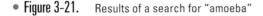

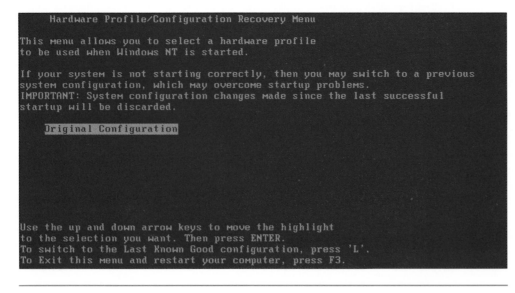

• **Figure 3-21.** Results of a search for "amoeba"

Windows Fails to Start

Strictly speaking, if Windows fails to start, this is not a failure of the desktop but an inability to get to the desktop. There can be many causes of a failure of Windows to start. A common one that is easy to fix is leaving a data disk in your floppy drive; when you start your computer, it tries to boot from the data disk. Unless the diskette drive has been configured in a special way, your computer will not boot to your Windows OS. You may see a message referring to a nonsystem disk or saying that the system could not find NTLDR. In either case, check the floppy drive. If a floppy disk is in the drive, remove it and restart your computer.

Another reason for a failure to start may be a problem with the configuration. Perhaps this is the first restart after installing a new device driver, or after making a significant change to the system, such as modifying the settings for a device. In this case, you can try one of the solutions detailed here.

Last Known Good

Windows NT 4.0, Windows 2000, and Windows XP allow you to go back to the last working configuration. This option has its limits and is not available in Windows 9x. In Windows NT 4.0, you select your OS from the OS Loader screen on startup, and then, before the GUI loads, press the spacebar. The Hardware Profile/Configuration Recovery Menu, appears, as shown in Figure 3-22. From here, press the L key to load the Last Known Good Configuration. In the new OSs, press F8 before the GUI loads during startup. This will bring up the Advanced Options Menu from which you select Last Known Good.

Advanced Options Menu

When Windows 9x, Windows 2000, and Windows XP fail on startup, try working with the choices on the Advanced Options Menu. Figure 3-23 shows the Windows XP version of this menu. There are many options here including Safe Mode, which allows you to start Windows

• **Figure 3-22.** Switch to the Windows NT 4.0 Last Known Good Configuration from this screen.

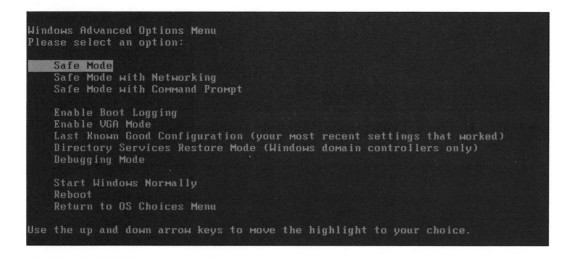

Windows Advanced Options Menu
Please select an option:

Safe Mode
Safe Mode with Networking
Safe Mode with Command Prompt

Enable Boot Logging
Enable VGA Mode
Last Known Good Configuration (your most recent settings that worked)
Directory Services Restore Mode (Windows domain controllers only)
Debugging Mode

Start Windows Normally
Reboot
Return to OS Choices Menu

Use the up and down arrow keys to move the highlight to your choice.

• **Figure 3-23.**   Use the Windows XP Advanced Options Menu to troubleshoot startup problems.

without some of the components that may be causing the startup failure. Then you can remove, replace, or reconfigure the failed driver or other component.

Windows Stalls

Have you ever been working in Windows when it suddenly stops responding? It won't let you close your applications. Maybe the cursor seems to be stuck in busy mode (usually you see the hourglass). If you are using Windows 98, you can press CTRL-ALT-DELETE; you'll then see a message about Explorer not responding. If you are using one of the other three OSs, you can press CTRL-SHIFT-ESC to open the Task Manager; you'll then see the message saying that Explorer is not responding. The best solution is to shut down Windows and restart. Normally, this takes care of the problem, at least for a day, a week, or a month.

> If the system is really locked, you may not be able to shut it down from the GUI. In that case, you'll have to actually turn off the system with the power switch. When you turn it back on, it will probably automatically run CHKDSK or SCANDISK to make sure the hard drive was not damaged during the shut down.

An Application Fails to Start

Harry is working late one night because he is preparing a presentation for a planning meeting in the morning. He is working in Windows 2000 Professional, and he has several applications open. He created a great, complex spreadsheet in Excel, a report in Word, and a slide presentation in PowerPoint. He needs to read a file he found on the Internet during his research on reducing cost of ownership for desktop computers. The file is in PDF format; he double-clicks the file, expecting it to load into the Acrobat Reader program. The hour glass appears briefly, but Acrobat does not start. No error message appears. He opens the Task Manager, which shows current tasks. He expects to see Acrobat listed with a status of "not responding," but it isn't listed. One possible problem is that there is not enough memory to run the additional program. The solution is to close one or more applications, then attempt to open Acrobat.

Chapter 3 Review

■ Chapter Summary

After reading this chapter and completing the Step-by-Step tutorials and Try This! exercises, you should understand the following facts about the Windows desktop:

Explain the Nature and History of the Windows GUI

- The origins of the desktop metaphor go back several decades.

- Many innovative people contributed to the desktop metaphor; the earliest we found was Douglas Engelbart, who demonstrated the use of a mouse with a computer in 1968.

- The mouse and keyboard are your primary input devices.

- The Palo Alto Research Center was a major contributor to the desktop metaphor.

- The Apple Macintosh was the first successful product using a graphical desktop and a mouse.

- Microsoft Windows went through several versions before mainstream businesses and home users adopted it.

Navigate the Windows GUI

- Windows now has a variety of graphical objects, including the cursor, icons, shortcuts, dialog boxes, windows, folders, buttons, toolbars, menus, and the taskbar.

- In most organizations, you will have to log on and be authenticated before you can get to your Windows desktop.

- Windows Help has improved with each version of Windows. Use it!

- The Start button gives you access to menus of programs from which you can launch programs.

Manage Files in Windows

- The Find/Search option has been improved with each version of Windows. In Windows NT, you can search for files, folders, and computers, but in Windows XP this search function has been greatly expanded. If you have an Internet connection, you can search for almost anything in the world that is searchable over the Internet.

- Users can manage files and folders in My Computer and Windows Explorer and from the command prompt. The last is not recommended.

Configure and Customize the Windows Desktop

- Control Panel contains many applets that allow you to configure your hardware and software.

- Right-clicking on the desktop opens a dialog box that allows you to customize many aspects of the desktop.

Run Applications in Windows

- Users can launch programs by using the Start menu.

- Another method for launching programs is with the use of shortcuts on the desktop or other locations.

- Using the file extensions of data files, Windows associates the files with applications that can create and read that file type. When you click on a file that has an extension for which Windows has an association, Windows will start the associated program, and load the file as data for the program.

- Another method for launching a program is to use the Run command from the Start menu. Then you enter a command name in the box to launch a program.

- You can also launch a program from the command prompt. If the program is a GUI program, it will be launched in a window.

Leave the Desktop by Logging Off and Shutting Down

- Your end-of-day procedure depends on the rules for using the computer.

- In some organizations, users are required to log off, but to leave the computer running.

- In other organizations, users are required to log off and shut down the computer.

- You should never just switch off your desktop computer with the on/off switch. You should always do so from within Windows.

Troubleshoot Common Windows Desktop Problems

- Pressing the ENTER key when you intended to select a new field may cause a dialog box to disappear.

- Use the Find or Search function to find lost files.

- Leaving a floppy disk in the drive is a frequent cause of startup failure.

- If Windows stops responding, you may have no other choice but to restart your computer.

■ Key Terms

Active Desktop *(109)*
applet *(100)*
command prompt *(114)*
copy *(108)*
domain *(90)*

graphical user interface (GUI) *(88)*
launch by association *(114)*
menu *(88)*
move *(108)*
Quick Launch toolbar *(112)*

special folder *(97)*
taskbar *(96)*
window *(88)*
workgroup *(90)*

■ Key Term Quiz

Use terms from the Key Terms list to complete the sentences that follow. Not all terms will be used.

1. A/an _____ is a bordered area of the desktop used by a single program.

2. A/an _____ is an object that can contain buttons that let you launch programs with a single-click.

3. It is very easy to select options and programs from a/an _____ in Windows.

4. The Display icon in the classic Control Panel represents a/an _____ that allows you to change configuration settings for your display.

5. The _____ contains the Start menu, buttons for currently open applications, and the system tray, and it may also contain a Quick Launch toolbar.

6. The _____ feature lets you put web content directly on your Windows desktop.

7. The only security accounts available in a/an _____ exist on individual member computers that are capable of maintaining a separate local accounts database.

8. Starting an application by clicking on a document file is an example of _____.

9. A Microsoft _____ has a centralized security accounts database, maintained on special servers called domain controllers.

10. The Start menu is a _____, and as such is treated differently by Windows than an ordinary folder.

■ Multiple-Choice Quiz

1. Which of the following will launch a program? Select all that apply.

   a. Selecting a program icon from the Start menu

   b. Pressing ALT-F4

   c. Double-clicking a program icon

   d. Selecting a program from the Recycle Bin

   e. Clicking the minimize button

2. If you have a problem with Windows that you do not know how to solve, you can begin by:

   a. Calling your brother-in-law

   b. Using the mouse

   c. Using the Windows Help program

   d. Calling the Microsoft toll-free number

   e. Launching FreeCell

3. Who demonstrated the use of a mouse with a user interface at a conference in 1968?

   a. Bill Gates

   b. Steve Wozniak

   c. Bob Metcalfe

   d. Steve Jobs

   e. Douglas Engelbart

4. Which operating systems have a GUI interface for the primary user interface? Select all that apply.

   a. UNIX

   b. CP/M

   c. DOS

   d. Microsoft Windows

   e. Mac OS

5. A user's impression that an OS is intuitive may depend largely on the person's:

   a. Experience with computers

   b. Age

   c. Income level

   d. Job title

   e. Education

6. According to what you learned in this chapter, a shortcut may allow you to do which of the following? Select all that apply.

   a. Open a program

   b. Open a folder

   c. Open a program with a document

   d. Create a new user account

   e. Change the system time

7. You can change the appearance of your Windows desktop using:

   a. Microsoft Word

   b. Outlook Express

   c. The Display applet in Control Panel

   d. The System applet in Control Panel

   e. Windows Explorer

8. Which of the following can be used for managing files and folders? Select all that apply.

   a. Windows Explorer

   b. My Computer

   c. The Display applet in Control Panel

   d. Notepad

   e. MSN Explorer

9. What could cause a dialog box to close before you have completed all the desired changes?

   a. Sun spots

   b. Pressing the ENTER key

   c. Entering invalid information

   d. A poorly tuned aura

   e. You don't have administrator rights

10. What should you do if you are confused about where you saved a file?

    a. Use Windows Help

    b. Record file locations on paper

    c. Use the Search or Find program

    d. Learn memory association tricks

    e. Save all files in the root of C:

11. What is the first task of the day for most Windows users—something they must do before they even see their Windows desktop?

    a. Drink coffee

    b. Play a game of Solitaire

    c. Log on

    d. Call Microsoft

    e. Click Start

12. In most cases, when working in the four versions of Windows studied in this book, what objects will you see on the default desktop? Select all that apply.

    a. One or more icons

    b. A cursor

    c. Start menu

    d. Taskbar

    e. Control Panel folder

13. If you heard a desktop support person talking about your computer's SAM, what would she be referencing?

    a. The name of the last user of your computer

    b. Save All Mice

    c. Start At Microsoft

    d. The local security accounts database

    e. The Start menu

14. What special key combination is used in several versions of Windows to bring up the logon screen?

    a. CTRL-SHIFT-ESCAPE

    b. CTRL-ALT

    c. ALT-F4

    d. CTRL-ALT-DELETE

    e. CTRL-ALT-TAB

15. What standard desktop object can be modified to allow you to launch your programs quickly and to see status information?

    a. Recycle Bin

    b. Cursor

    c. Start menu

    d. Taskbar

    e. Control Panel folder

■ Essay Quiz

1. In your own words, describe why the desktop metaphor, as implemented in Windows, works (or doesn't work) for you. Maybe you like parts of it, but not others. Elaborate.

2. Rosemary is an order processor and office assistant in the small manufacturing company that recently hired you. She has been working in Windows 98, but her present computer will be replaced with a new Windows XP Professional computer and Microsoft Office 2002. Previously, she kept all of her files in a folder named Data on her local hard drive. You have suggested that she now keep her data files in her My Documents folder, and you have arranged to have these files transferred from her present computer to the new computer. She has asked for an explanation of why she should work with the My Computer folder. Write an explanation that you might give Rosemary for this recommendation.

3. Your department is writing a computer-use policy manual. Your boss has asked you to write a paragraph for the manual selling the benefits of taking advantage of the desktop customization capabilities of Windows. The versions currently used in your company are Windows 2000 and Windows XP. Write a paragraph selling the benefits and inviting the users to schedule appointments to have you help them customize their systems to their preferences.

4. You have double-clicked a graphics file that you want to edit. Rather than launch your favorite graphics editor program, Windows started a different program and loaded your data file. You do not know how to use this program, but you want to edit the graphic. You know that the other program is on your computer because you used it earlier today. Explain what is happening and describe what you can do so that you can edit this file with the program you like.

Lab Projects

• Lab Project 3.1

As a desktop support consultant for a real estate brokerage firm, you often help agents with their home office computers. You have been asked to help an agent organize his data files on a new computer with Windows XP. On his previous computer, he saved his data files in a variety of folders in several of the four hard drive volumes, which was awkward when it came time to back up his files. To help him organize his files, you created a table of the applications he uses and the business functions of the data he creates with each application.

Application	Business Function(s)
Microsoft Access	Client list database Contractor list database
Microsoft Word	Introductory letters Proposal presentations Offer presentations
PowerPoint	Listing brochures Self-marketing brochures

① Using this table, design a file management strategy for the agent that will be logical to use and make the backup process easier for him. Write a description and justification of this design to present to the agent.

② Using your lab computer, create the folders that will be required to fulfill your design.

③ Present this plan to a fellow student or to the class in general. You may want to create drawings of your design or use the folders you created in Step 3 to demonstrate it.

• Lab Project 3.2

A small manufacturing company has hired you to be a desktop support person. As such, you must know how to install and configure operating systems on the company's computers and, eventually, learn all the software applications used in the company so that you can train and support the employees in the use of their computers. Your boss has just asked you to help a new user personalize her Windows desktop. You have learned that she will frequently use two applications and less frequently use another three applications. You have noticed that she is a "clean desk" sort of person, and you believe that she may want her Windows desktop to reflect her physical work habits. Since some of the data she will be working with is confidential, she is required to log off whenever she leaves her computer.

You will need a lab computer with any of the four versions of Windows installed.

Then do the following:

① Describe the strategy you will suggest to her for giving her appropriate access to her applications, addressing her clean desk work behavior, and the security issues. All solutions should involve desktop customization.

② Assume that she agreed with your suggestions. Now implement your suggested changes on your lab computer. Remember that two applications should be very quickly available to her, and that three others should be convenient, but don't need to be as quickly available. Use any applications available to you for the five applications in the scenario.

③ Test your solution.

④ Demonstrate your solution for one or more of your fellow students.

• Lab Project 3.3

Loretta is an IT employee at a large company, presently assigned to a group that researches and tests future and alternative computing technology. Her present assignment is to research possible alternatives to the desktop metaphor—in both new OSs and in add-ons to Windows. Give Loretta some help with this project.

① Use an Internet search engine to search on "desktop metaphor." Browse through the results to find two potential metaphors that may replace the desktop metaphor.

② For each alternative you select, write a paragraph or two that describes the new metaphor, gives the author's reason for its superiority to the desktop metaphor, and gives your personal opinion of that metaphor.

③ Present your findings to one or more of your classmates.

Windows NT 4.0 Workstation

"Excuse me," growled Moody,
"you've got strengths if I say
you've got them. Think now.
What are you best at?"

—HARRY POTTER AND THE
GOBLET OF FIRE
BY J. K. ROWLING

From its introduction as version 3.1, Windows NT has been an entirely different operating system than Microsoft's initial Windows desktop OSs. It's simply a better, more secure OS. Windows NT 4.0 Workstation brought an improved user interface and support for more and newer hardware than was previously supported in NT 3.51, and it was offered in parallel with the Windows 9x products. Although Windows NT 4.0 Workstation was a more secure and stable alternative, it came at a price: you couldn't use it with the wide range of hardware supported by Windows 9x.

In this chapter, you'll learn how to install and configure NT 4.0 and then manage users, files, and printers. Of course, no discussion of NT 4.0 is complete without exploration of the bootup process, the startup disks, and troubleshooting; we will cover these in detail later in the chapter.

In this chapter, you will learn how to:

- Describe Windows NT 4.0 Workstation features, limitations, and requirements
- Install and configure Windows NT 4.0 Workstation
- Customize and manage Windows NT 4.0 Workstation
- Manage security for users, files, and printers
- Troubleshoot common Windows NT 4.0 problems

■ NT 4.0 Workstation Overview

What can NT 4.0 do for me? Are there reasons why I shouldn't have NT 4.0 on my desktop? It's been around a while; how much longer will I be able to buy it? We answer these questions and a few others in the following sections.

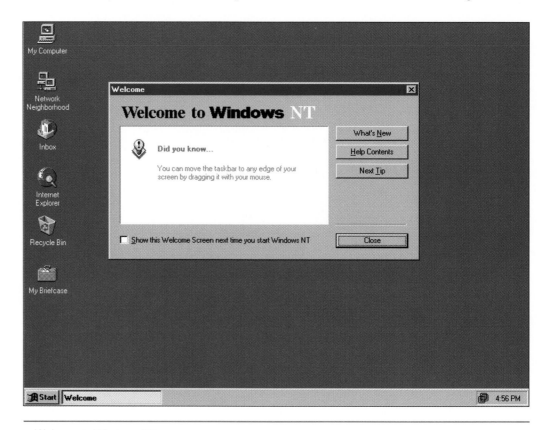

- Welcome to Windows NT

Benefits and Features

What can Windows NT 4.0 do for you? We'll take a look at the features and the benefits, but let's first turn the clock back to 1993, the year the first version, Windows NT 3.1, was introduced. Even then, there was more than met the eye. Although it was an entirely different OS than desktop Windows, Microsoft gave NT a Windows 3.x look and called it Windows NT 3.1, but brought it out strictly as a network server OS. This was followed in the next few years by an upgrade, introduced as two products: Windows NT 3.5 Server and a desktop product, Windows NT 3.5 Workstation. This was in recognition of the need for a desktop operating system with more stability and security than Windows 3.x. The last version of NT with the Windows 3.1 desktop was 3.51.

Windows NT 4.0 also personified the Microsoft Internet strategy of including the software needed to be both an Internet browsing client and an Internet server—even in Windows NT 4.0 Workstation on the desktop.

When Windows NT 4.0 was introduced in the fall of 1996, Windows 3.x and Windows 95 dominated the PC desktop. Whereas the Windows NT 3.x products were stuck in a time warp using the Windows 3.x GUI, Windows NT 4.0 adopted the more pleasant and (dare we say?) more intuitive interface of Windows 95. However, behind the scenes, it was an entirely different OS from Windows 95. Let's look at its features in the following categories: desktop, security, stability, memory, and software compatibility.

Desktop

The Windows NT 4.0 screen area was officially called the desktop, and it included the familiar Windows 95 GUI objects: taskbar, Start button (with its Start menu), right-click context menus, My Computer, and Windows Explorer (called Windows NT Explorer). Microsoft saw this change to the user interface (or shell) to be so important that Windows NT 4.0 was called the Shell Update Release.

After all this time, it's hard to remember working with the Windows 3.*x* program groups, which were simple windows containing program icons. They had shortcomings both visually and organizationally. Our biggest complaint was that you couldn't nest program groups to create a hierarchy of programs. Windows NT 4.0 eliminated this problem because it inherited the new folder and shortcut structure of Windows 95, which allows you to create a hierarchy of folders and shortcuts. Even the menus can be based on this folder structure. The best example of this is the Start menu.

- Windows NT 4.0 Start menu hierarchy

> Quickly open the Start menu by pressing the CTRL+ESC key combination, or simply press the Windows Logo key if it is on your keyboard.

File Systems

Windows NT 4.0 fully supports two file systems: NT file system version 4 (NTFS4) and an implementation of FAT16 (introduced in Windows 95) called the **virtual file allocation table (VFAT)** that supports long file names. NT, however, does not support FAT32, which was introduced in a special release of Windows 95 and is supported in Windows 98, Windows 2000, and Windows XP.

> At the time Windows NT 4.0 was released, it was still common to refer to VFAT as FAT, and NTFS4 as simply **NTFS**. After Windows 2000 came out with version 5 of NTFS, called NTFS5, it became important to use the version-specific name (NTFS4 or NTFS5).

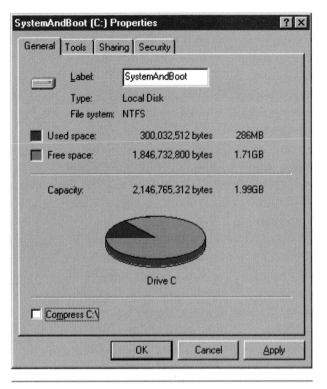

• Disk properties showing NTFS as the file system

Security

Windows NT 4.0 can be made secure on the desktop, meaning that even a stand-alone Windows NT 4.0 has significant security components. This is a claim that can't be made for Windows 95 or Windows 98. Windows NT 4.0 requires a logon, using a user account (either on the local computer or in a network domain). If the user account is local, it is an actual user account in a security accounts database, which the Windows 9*x* products do not have. Moreover, Windows NT 4.0 has file- and folder-level security, if you use Windows NT 4.0's advanced file system, NT File System version 4 (NTFS4) on your local hard drive. With this, you can protect your local folders and files by assigning **permissions** (Read-Only, Full Control, No Access, and so on) to individual users or to groups.

Stability

Windows NT 4.0 is more stable than Windows 3.*x* or 9*x*. What does stability in an OS mean? Mainly, it means that you can work all day in many different applications without risking loss of your data because the system has "hung up"—a term that means that your computer has stopped responding to input from the keyboard and the mouse, and, yes, even to verbal abuse. Back when Windows NT 4.0 was the newest Windows OS, the best reason for installing it on a desktop computer was its stability. It was far more stable than Windows 3.*x* or Windows 9*x*. This appealed to a significant number of users and to IT people who had to support desktop computers.

Hermione is a believer in the stability of NT 4.0 compared to earlier versions of Windows. During the five years that she used Windows NT 4.0 on her desktop computer, her co-worker Neville was using Windows 95 and then Windows 98. As the two worked in adjacent cubicles, Hermione would occasionally hear an anguished cry from Neville: his computer had hung up, had to be restarted, and frequently lost his current work. Hermione might go for months without problems.

Memory

Windows NT 4.0 has a 32-bit address space, which means that it can use up to 4GB of RAM. On top of that, it uses virtual memory, which simply put, means that it can use some of your hard disk storage space as RAM. You can have more programs and data in memory than your physical memory can hold, thanks to the Virtual Memory Manager, which decides what can be safely moved out of RAM and onto a special disk area that the OS uses as memory, sometimes called the swap file.

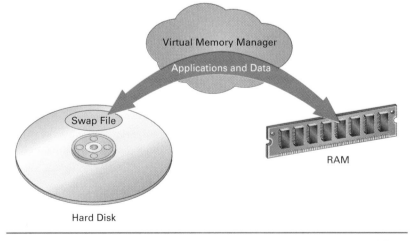

• The Virtual Memory Manager maximizes memory by swapping programs and data between RAM and the hard disk.

Software Compatibility with Legacy Applications

Just because you're running Windows NT 4.0 doesn't mean that all of your software must be written just for Windows NT 4.0. You may not even be able to find updated replacements for your important business applications; Microsoft thought about that problem. Windows NT Workstation 4.0 can run the following types of software:

- MS-DOS applications

- 16-bit Windows-based applications (written for Windows 3.*x*)

- 32-bit Windows-based applications (written for Windows 9*x* and NT 4.0)

- OS/2 version 1.*x* character-based applications

- OS/2 16-bit Presentation Manager applications (with separate add-in product)

- POSIX1-based applications (POSIX is short for portable operating system interface for computing environments)

Windows Applications and DOS Applications Windows NT 4.0 runs applications in environments called *subsystems*. Thirty-two-bit Windows applications are the "native" applications of Windows NT. These applications are written to a specific set of rules, and they run in the Win32 subsystem. DOS applications can run in the Win32 subsystem, with a little help. A DOS application runs within a virtual DOS machine (VDM), as does any 16-bit Windows applications (written for Windows 3.*x*).

OS/2 and POSIX Applications Using subsystems, Windows NT 4.0 provides support for the other types of applications by creating simulated environments that look and feel like the OS for which the application was written. For instance, when an OS/2 application is started, Windows NT 4.0 starts an OS/2 subsystem, but it simulates a very old version of OS/2. Finally, the POSIX1 subsystem emulates POSIX1, a special UNIX environment. When one of these programs is launched, Windows NT 4.0 loads the correct subsystem for it.

The Limitations of Windows NT

Hey, how can an operating system with a name that stands for "new technology" be obsolete? Easy—in the computer world, nothing is new after six months, and a decade is like a geologic age. The Windows NT 4.0 user interface began to show its age when Windows 98 came out two years later with some subtle changes to the GUI. It has really shown its age since Windows 2000 was introduced in 2000 and then Windows XP was introduced in 2001.

Windows NT 4.0 Hard Drive Limits

When you install Windows NT 4.0, the Setup program is able to create a hard disk partition with a maximum size of only 4GB—the partition limit of a FAT partition in Windows NT. Even when you tell the Setup program that you want the new partition to be formatted with NTFS, which has a far larger size limit, the Setup program still can create only a 4GB maximum partition. This is because the Windows NT 4.0 Setup program does not have

The Memory Race

When NT 4.0 came out several years ago, 4GB sounded like a truckload of RAM. But in the context of today's desktop PCs with ever increasing amounts of RAM, 4GB seems generous, but not outlandish. The programs being created today are increasing in size, too. Therefore, the way Windows NT 4.0 handles memory begins to make sense.

The difference between how Windows NT 4.0 handles a DOS application and how it handles a 16-bit Windows application is that NT adds a copy of Windows 3.*x* to the VDM before loading the 16-bit Windows application.

the ability to format a drive as NTFS. Therefore, it formats using FAT and creates a script telling the newly installed OS to perform the NTFS conversion the first time it starts. Once you have Windows NT 4.0 installed and running, you can create additional, larger partitions if you have free space on the same hard disk or on other hard disks in the computer.

Doesn't Work Well with the Latest Hardware

Remember Hermione and Neville? She used Windows NT 4.0 for several years, whereas Neville used first Windows 95 and then Windows 98. Have you wondered why Neville put up with the instability of those OSs? He never considered putting Windows NT 4.0 on his computer because he needs and uses the latest and greatest hardware on his desktop computer, and Windows NT 4.0 doesn't support a great variety of hardware. Its biggest shortcoming in that area is that it doesn't support plug and play. There are many people like Neville, and for them, stodgy old Windows NT is, well, too stodgy. And realistically, this hardware limit has only become worse as more and newer peripherals continue to become available.

Doesn't Work Well with Legacy Software

Although Windows NT 4.0 has built-in support for applications written for several other OSs, some applications, most notoriously some DOS applications and 16-bit Windows applications, won't work in NT's simulated environment. Actually, Windows NT 4.0 can work with some applications, but you need to test each one to see if it will run at all, or if it runs too slowly under Windows NT 4.0 to be useful to you.

Why Is Windows NT 4.0 Still in Use?

Technology does not stand still, and today you're simply not going to select Windows NT 4.0 for your next new desktop PC. However, for the next few years of your career, you are sure to encounter it on the job from time to time. Here are some reasons why.

Windows NT 4.0 for Backward Compatibility

We have heard clients and students say that they're still using Windows NT 4.0 on the desktop because of a vertical market application (one specific to their industry) that was designed to run in Windows NT. Perhaps it would actually run in newer Windows versions, but the vendor will support it only in Windows NT 4.0. Until that application is revised to run on a newer version of Windows, the user will stay with Windows NT. If you work in such an organization, you may have to install Windows NT 4.0 on replacement machines that will run the same application.

Installing Windows NT 4.0 on new machines to use existing licenses is a pretty weak reason for continuing to use it. Because of its limited hardware support, you are likely to run into hardware that Windows NT 4.0 simply can't use.

Windows NT—When That's All You Have!

Many organizations lease their computer systems and therefore use an OS for the length of the lease. A few years ago, a typical computer lease was for three years, but budget cuts have forced many companies to extend current leases, often to five years. This extends the life of old OSs and application suites and also extends the length of time you need to stay knowledgeable about older technologies. Similarly, an organization that owns licenses for Windows NT 4.0 may continue to use those licenses when it replaces old computers with new.

Where Can I Find Windows NT 4.0 Today?

The last time we checked the Microsoft website (about two minutes ago), Windows NT 4.0 Workstation was listed under the Previous Products category, not under Products. Microsoft's published Desktop Product Life-Cycle Guidelines, currently at www.microsoft.com/windows/lifecycle.asp, state that Windows NT 4.0 Workstation will be an unsupported product as of June 30, 2003. Until that date, the software and the licenses can still be purchased through retailers who choose to stock it, and after that date licenses will become available through limited channels. Microsoft will also leave the technical support information for Windows NT 4.0 at its website, but can discontinue this with 12-months notice. Add to that the newer replacements for Windows NT 4.0, and your conclusion must be that Windows NT 4.0 is no longer a viable retail product. However, we still urge you to learn about it because it is still in use in many organizations.

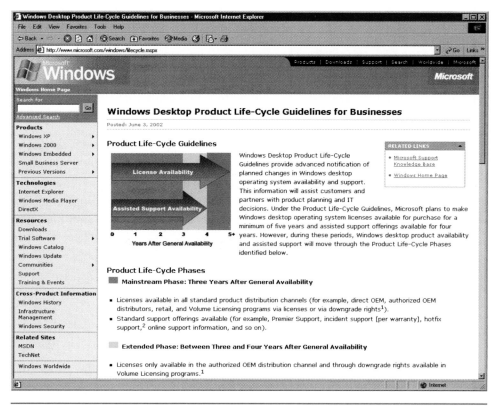

• Windows Desktop Product Life-Cycle Guidelines

Hardware and Windows NT Workstation 4.0

When you prepare to install an operating system, you have three concerns regarding the computer hardware.

- What are the minimum requirements for running the OS? How much "horsepower" is required in the processor, how much RAM and hard disk space, what video capabilities, and what input devices?

- What will support the job you want this computer to do? Do you need a more powerful processor? More RAM or disk space? Fancy video?

- What hardware is compatible with this OS?

Let's take a closer look at these concerns.

> Another reason to learn about Windows NT 4.0 is that Windows 2000 and Windows XP are simply new versions of Windows NT. What you learn here is not completely lost because, although those OSs improved on Windows NT 4.0, they still have many of the same features and characteristics.

Requirements

Windows NT 4.0 Workstation can be installed on a computer that complies with the Intel/Microsoft set of standards. Furthermore, NT Workstation 4.0 supports symmetric multiprocessing (SMP) with two processors.

When Windows NT Workstation 4.0 was introduced in 1996, the published minimums included a 486/33 processor, 110MB of free hard disk space, and 12MB of RAM. However, more recently Microsoft published slightly more realistic minimum requirements on its website, but these still seem laughable when you think of the computers you see advertised in your local paper each week. This shows how far the world has moved since 1996. Even then, these minimums would have left you with a computer with too little disk space and RAM to install an office suite of software.

Ideal Hardware Configuration

In the first two years that Windows NT 4.0 was available, if you made the decision to use this OS over Windows 95, you most likely had a very good reason, such as security and stability. You also were choosing a much more expensive OS than Windows 95. You would not go to the trouble of installing this OS on an underpowered computer.

The ideal hardware configuration varies based on the needs of the applications to be run on the computer, but, for us, the ideal configuration for Windows NT on a desktop computer with a standard set of office applications (word processor, spreadsheet, mail, and so on) installed looks like the following:

- Intel Pentium processor
- 128MB RAM
- 2 to 4GB available hard disk space
- CD-ROM drive
- SVGA or higher-resolution video adapter
- Microsoft mouse

Compatible Products

Microsoft maintains a site where you can search to see if hardware or software has passed Microsoft's compatibility tests. You can check both your computer hardware and the software you hope to install under the OS. Simply connect to Microsoft's Compatible Products page at www.microsoft.com/windows/compatible. Select Windows NT from the Operating System drop-down list and then make selections from the Product Category and Company Name lists.

Microsoft has a certification program for the various versions of Windows that they call their logo program. A manufacturer whose hardware or software product has passed Microsoft's tests for both Windows NT and Windows 98 receives the right to print the "Designed for Microsoft Windows NT/Windows 98" logo on its product. Although this is a convenient indicator for you, you should still double-check with www.microsoft.com/windows/compatible.

If you aren't sure how you would search for compatible hardware or software products, consider Keisha, who is getting ready to install Windows

NT 4.0 on a replacement computer because the previous computer had an application that requires it. The user wants to add a device that requires an Institute for Electrical and Electronic Engineers (IEEE) 1394 controller, and her department is converting from a wired Ethernet network to a wireless network. She has heard that Windows NT doesn't support IEEE 1394 controllers or wireless network adapters and so has decided to learn whether NT does, indeed, support these hardware devices.

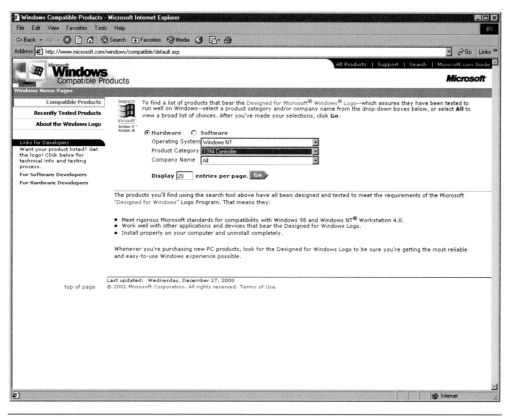

• Microsoft Windows–compatible products

Installing and Configuring Windows NT 4.0 Workstation

You've completed an overview of the features and limits of Windows NT, considered the hardware requirements and recommendations for installing NT, and know where to go to find out if your hardware and software is compatible with Windows NT. Now you need to install Windows NT so you can learn how to work with it.

Preparing for Windows NT 4.0 Workstation Installation

Before you install Windows NT, or any OS, you need to prepare the hardware, determine the method of installation, and gather the materials (disks, drivers, applications, and so on) you'll need to complete the installation.

Prepare the Hardware

To install Windows NT on a computer hard disk, you must be sure that the computer is physically ready for the installation: that is, ensure that the computer is a complete system, with at least the minimal hardware recommendations, and that all of the hardware is compatible with Windows NT 4.0. You also need to ensure that all necessary connections are in place for the installed components and that the computer is plugged into a power outlet. The computer hard disk does not have to be specially prepared for Windows NT installation because the Windows NT Setup program can prepare the hard disk.

Determine the Service Pack and Updates to Use

After any software company releases complex software such as Windows NT, the programming staff continues to work on the software. Programmers receive feedback about problems from customers, and they re-create the problems and come up with software fixes. We may call these **patches** or updates. Those that solve security problems and/or problems that can potentially cause major failures are now called critical updates.

What Do I Need and Where Do I Look? Microsoft releases updates individually, as they are completed, and the company also periodically bundles together a series of accumulated updates into a larger package called a **service pack**. These, in turn, are made available in versions, or levels, such as Service Pack 1 and Service Pack 2. NT 4.0's service packs were numbered through 6a (a post–Service Pack 6 release), which was followed by the Post–SP6a Security Rollup Package (SRP). You can find out more about the updates and service packs for Windows NT 4.0 Professional at www.microsoft.com/ntworkstation.

• Windows NT Workstation home page

Survey of Operating Systems

The service pack level in NT 4.0 is critical; you should never install and use Windows NT 4.0 without planning to add a service pack immediately after the installation.

Although service packs that fix problems are a fact of life with today's very complex OSs, Windows NT 4.0 service packs are also renowned not for just fixing problems with the OS, but for adding new features. However, sometimes the fixes and/or new features actually cause new problems. Therefore, most organizations that exercise any standards and control over their desktop computers mandate that a new service pack can't be installed until it has been thoroughly tested on non-production PCs in a test lab.

If you have reason to install NT 4.0 on a PC at school or at work, be sure to check with an administrator to learn the approved service pack level.

Determine the Method of Installation

To install Windows NT (without using a third-party product), you can choose a manual installation or an automated installation, both of which have variations.

Manual Installation   A manual installation is high maintenance, requiring your attention throughout the entire process to provide information and to respond to messages. You will perform a manual installation in Step-by-Step 4.02. This is the method you would choose for a unique installation, or if the number of computers is too few to warrant the time, effort, and expense that an automated installation requires.

After deciding on a manual installation, you still have choices to make:

The OS you use to boot up the computer and connect to the network can be DOS or another version of Windows. Once you connect to the source location, you run the NT Setup program using WINNT.EXE or WINNT32.EXE.

- Will the source files (those in the i386 directory on the Windows NT 4.0 CD-ROM) be located on the local computer or the network server? If you don't have a CD-ROM drive in the computer, but it is connected to a network, then you'll have to boot up the computer with an operating system that has the network components installed so you can connect to the server where the source files are stored.

- If the computer does have a CD-ROM drive, will it work for the installation—that is, will the Windows NT 4.0 Setup program recognize it and will the computer boot from the CD-ROM drive? If you can boot from the CD-ROM drive, then your manual installation can be completed as shown in Step-by-Step 4.02.

- If a CD-ROM drive is present and is recognized by Windows NT Setup (which you may be able to determine only by trying), but you can't boot from it, you will need the three Windows NT 4.0 Workstation setup disks, as well as the CD-ROM disk. Place the first disk in the drive, restart, and follow the on-screen instructions.

If your computer won't boot from the CD-ROM drive, a change to the computer's system settings may be required. Don't try to change the settings without expert help because the wrong changes to the system settings can disable your computer.

Step-by-Step 4.01

Creating the Windows NT 4.0 Setup Disks from Windows or DOS

To create the Windows NT 4.0 setup disks, you can use any version of Windows or DOS, as long as it recognizes the installed CD-ROM drive. For example, from DOS you can use a Windows 98 startup disk with CD-ROM support, as described here.
  You will need the following:

- A computer running MS-DOS or Windows 3.x or greater

- The Windows NT CD-ROM

- Three formatted, blank high-density 3.5-inch diskettes

Step 1

Place the Windows NT CD in the drive. If your computer supports AutoPlay for CDs, the Windows NT CD window will appear. Close the window.

In Windows 95 or greater, select Start | Run. In the Open box, type the following:

`d:\i386\winnt32 /ox`

Replace *d* with the drive letter of your CD-ROM drive; i386 is the directory where the installation program is located, winnt32 is the 32-bit NT installation program used by Windows 95 or greater, and /ox is a switch used to create a set of installation floppy disks.

In MS-DOS or Windows 3.*x*, enter the following from a command prompt and click OK:

`d:\i386\winnt /ox`

Replace *d* with the drive letter of your CD-ROM drive; i386 is the directory where the installation program is located, winnt is the 16-bit NT installation program used by DOS and Windows 3.*x*, and /ox is a switch used to create a set of installation floppy disks.

Step 2

On the Windows NT 4.00 Upgrade/Installation page, verify that the location of the Windows NT 4.0 files includes the drive letter for your CD-ROM drive and also the i386 directory; then click Continue.

> **Windows NT 4.00 Upgrade/Installation**
>
> MICROSOFT.
> WINDOWS NT.
>
> Location of Windows NT 4.0 Files:
>
> `R:\I386`
>
> Continue   Options...   Exit   Help

Step 3

Follow the instructions in the Installation/Upgrade Information box and label three formatted, blank high-density 3.5-inch diskettes. Insert the one labeled Windows NT Workstation Setup Disk #3 in the floppy drive and click OK or press ENTER.

Step 4

Follow the instructions on the screen; when Disk #3 has been prepared, you'll be prompted to replace it with Disk #2. When Disk #2 has been prepared, you will be prompted to replace it with the disk labeled Windows NT Workstation Setup Boot Disk. When this disk has been prepared, you have your entire set.

> **Windows NT 4.00 Workstation Installation/Upgrade**
>
> ⓘ Setup requires you to provide three formatted, blank high-density floppy disks. Setup will refer to these disks as "Windows NT Workstation Setup Boot Disk," "Windows NT Workstation Setup Disk #2," and "Windows NT Workstation Setup Disk #3."
>
> Please insert one of these disks into drive A:. This disk will become "Windows NT Workstation Setup Disk #3."
>
> Click OK when the disk is in the drive, or click Cancel to exit Setup.
>
> OK   Cancel

If you are installing NT on the same computer, leave the diskette in the drive and restart the computer. However, if you want to install NT on a different computer, remove the diskette and keep all three diskettes together until you are ready to use them in Step-by-Step 4.02.

Automated Installation You perform an automated installation of Windows NT 4.0 using scripts that someone (often a team of people) has prepared ahead of time. This method is used by organizations with large numbers of desktop computers that need identical applications and desktop configurations. This method requires training and planning by one or more people.

The WINNT and WINNT32 Setup Programs Automated installations and some manual installations may require the use of the WINNT.EXE or WINNT32.EXE program.

To learn about the syntax of either the winnt or winnt32 command, open a command prompt and run the command followed by the /? parameter.

- An automated installation using the scripting method for Windows NT 4.0 provided by Microsoft uses either of these programs with appropriate command-line switches to select the scripts.

- A manual installation in which you don't boot from the CD or the setup boot disks requires the use of one of these programs; which one depends on the operating system in control at the time. Did you boot from a DOS disk to install from source files over the network? Then you need to use WINNT.EXE, the version for DOS or Windows 3.*x*. Are you upgrading from Windows 95 to Windows NT? Then you need to boot into Windows 95 and run WINNT32.EXE.

A Windows NT Installation Strategy

Regardless of the method you choose to use for your installation, we strongly suggest a strategy commonly used with Windows NT 4.0—install Windows NT 4.0 using the generic drivers provided with the OS, especially for your video adapter. You will not be able to access all of the capabilities of the adapter right away, but hang in there—we have a reason for this strategy. After you have the OS installed and running with basic drivers, then you should apply service packs. It turns out that some newer drivers do install, but they do not work until you apply service packs. This is because support for such newer technology as the AGP video adapters wasn't included in Windows NT 4.0, but was added in service packs. After applying the appropriate service pack, install the new drivers.

Microsoft Windows NT Upgrade Help

File   Edit   Bookmark   Options   Help

Contents | Search | Back | Print

Winnt32

Performs an installation or upgrade of Windows NT 4.00.

winnt32 [**/s:** *sourcepath*] [**/i:** *inf_file*] [**/t:** *drive_letter*] [**/x**] [**/b**] [**/ox**] [**/u**[**:** *script*] [**/r:** *directory*] [**/e:** *command*]

Parameters

/s: *sourcepath*

Specifies the location of the Windows NT files.

/i: *inf_file*

Specifies the filename (no path) of the setup information file. The default is DOSNET.INF.

/t: *drive_letter*

Forces Setup to place temporary files on the specified drive.

/x

Prevents Setup from creating Setup boot floppies. Use this when you already have Setup boot floppies (from your administrator, for example).

/b

Causes the boot files to be loaded on the system's hard drive rather than on floppy disks, so that floppy disks do not need to be loaded or removed by the user.

/ox

Specifies that Setup create boot floppies for CD-ROM installation.

/u

Upgrades your previous version of Windows NT in unattended mode. All user settings are taken from the previous installation, requiring no user intervention during Setup.

/u: *script*

Similar to previous, but provides a script file for user settings rather than using the settings from the previous installation.

/r: *directory*

Installs an additional directory within the directory tree where the Windows NT files are installed. Use additional **/r** switches to install additional directories.

/e: *command*

Instructs Setup to execute a specific command after installation is complete.

• WINNT32.EXE syntax

Gather the Materials Needed for Installation

If your computer and its components are newer than 1996 (and we hope they are!), Windows NT 4.0 will not have all of the correct drivers for your system. A driver is a special file containing program code that allows an OS to interact with and control a hardware device. You will need the device drivers for your installed hardware. Driver files are supplied by the manufacturer of the device, so if you can't locate the driver disk that came with the device, then contact the manufacturer. Today that's as easy as connecting to the manufacturer's website and downloading the driver.

If you'll be installing Windows NT 4.0 from source files on a network server, you won't need the CD, but you will need to be able to start your computer with an OS configured with the correct drivers and network client software to access the network and the server.

If your computer will boot from a CD-ROM, you need only the Windows NT 4.0 Workstation CD; if your computer has a CD-ROM drive but can't boot from it, you'll also need the three Windows NT Workstation setup disks. If that's the case, and if you don't have the diskettes, you can create a new set. Step-by-Step 4.01 has instructions to do this.

You should also have a 3.5-inch diskette ready so that you can create a recovery disk during the installation.

Begin Installation

If you have selected and prepared the hardware, determined your strategy for installation, checked out the service pack level approved for use at your school or at work, then you are nearly ready to install.

Whenever possible, do a **clean installation** of a new operating system. What is a clean installation? With Windows, it means installing the OS on a perfectly clean hard disk. We even prefer to start with an unpartitioned hard disk. Unless it is a brand-new hard disk, we remove the old partition and allow the Setup program to create a new partition and format it during the installation process.

Step-by-Step 4.02

Installing Windows NT 4.0 Workstation

The steps in this exercise assume a clean install on an unpartitioned hard drive. To complete this exercise, you'll need the following:

- A Microsoft/Intel standard personal computer (desktop or laptop) configured to boot from CD-ROM

- An unpartitioned hard disk (disk 0, the first hard disk)

- The Windows NT 4.0 Workstation CD

- Three Windows NT setup disks, if your computer doesn't boot from CD-ROM

- One 3.5-inch diskette to use as an emergency repair disk

- The CD key code from the envelope of your NT CD

- A 15-character (or less) name for your computer, unique on your network

- The name of the workgroup to be used in the class lab

- A 14-character (or less) password for the Administrator account on your computer

- The TCP/IP configuration information for your computer, or confirmation from your instructor that you should configure Windows NT to get an IP address automatically

Step 1

Insert the Windows NT 4.0 Workstation CD and restart the computer. After the computer restarts, you'll briefly see a black screen with a message at the top left: "Setup is inspecting your computer's hardware configuration..." Then a nearly empty blue screen appears, labeled simply Windows NT Workstation Setup. This is the preparation for text mode of the Setup program. When all of the NT Setup files are loaded into memory, the Setup program's version of the NT kernel will be loaded and initialized (made active).

```
Windows NT Workstation Setup

    Welcome to Setup.

    The Setup program for the Microsoft(R) Windows NT(TM) operating system
    version 4.0 prepares Windows NT to run on your computer.

        •  To learn more about Windows NT Setup before continuing, press F1.
        •  To set up Windows NT now, press ENTER.
        •  To repair a damaged Windows NT version 4.0 installation, press R.
        •  To quit Setup without installing Windows NT, press F3.




    ENTER=Continue   R=Repair   F1=Help   F3=Exit
```

Step 2

For the next several screens, follow the instructions, responding based on the list at the beginning of this step-by-step. In addition, if your hard disk is unpartitioned, have NT Setup create a partition that is greater than 500MB and that leaves unpartitioned space available for use later. Select NTFS as the file system for the new partition. Accept the default location for the Setup program to install the OS. At the conclusion of the text-mode setup, your computer will reboot.

Step 3

After the reboot, NT Setup starts in GUI mode, and the words "Windows NT Setup" appear over blue and black wallpaper. This will be the background for NT Setup until the next reboot. The first message box on this background shows the progress while files are copied. Reinsert your Windows NT 4.0 CD now.

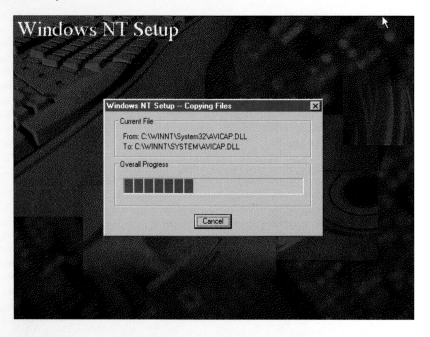

Step 4

The Welcome to the Windows NT Setup wizard message appears, informing you that it will perform three parts: gathering information about the computer, installing Windows NT networking, and finishing setup. Notice that the first step is highlighted. This message will reappear at the beginning of the next two parts of the setup. To continue, press ENTER or click the Next button.

| Step 5 | The wizard will guide you through the information gathering steps. You will have to make choices and provide more information. Select Typical on the Setup Options page, fill in the Name and Organization page, and have NT Setup install the most common components. Provide the Setup program with the information from the list at the beginning of this step-by-step. |

| Step 6 | During the steps for installing Windows NT networking, use the information about your network settings that you prepared at the beginning of this step-by-step. |

| Step 7 | During the steps for finishing setup, select your time zone and test your display settings; then NT Setup will copy the files necessary to complete the installation and configure the components. When it is finished, you will be prompted to restart the computer. A test of a successful installation is a successful reboot, so remove any floppy disks and CDs and then click the Restart Computer button. Log on with the Administrator account, using the password you provided during setup. |

Verify Network Access

You have successfully installed Windows NT Workstation on a user's desktop. If the user requires access to a LAN and the computer was connected to the LAN during installation, it should have all the right stuff to work on the LAN, but you must verify that the computer can connect to the other computers on the network. We're saving the details of networking for Chapter 10, but right now we'll have you do a simple test of network connectivity because this is a task normally done immediately after installing an OS.

The simplest test, although it is not entirely reliable, is to use Network Neighborhood to see other computers on your network. In the example here, the list includes an NT Server named HTC1, a Windows XP computer named LAGUNA, and the computer on which we installed Windows NT 4.0 Workstation, SEDONA-NT. If you encounter problems with your network connection in the class lab, ask your instructor to help you solve the problem.

• Network Neighborhood

Windows NT 4.0 Service Packs

When you install any software, it is important always to check for the latest updates to the software.

Inside Information

What Computers Are Visible in Network Neighborhood?

Computers are visible in Network Neighborhood only if they have a special service called the Server service turned on. This means that a computer is capable of sharing its file folders and printers with others on the network. Windows NT, Windows 2000, and Windows XP have this service turned on by default, and it is available, and often turned on, in Windows 9x. It makes sense that such a service would exist on server operating systems because that is, after all, their reason for being, and those OSs are tuned to support even a high volume of user access. It is available in the desktop operating systems so users can share file folders and printers with a small number of other users. This is called peer-to-peer networking. Enable this option on a desktop computer only if that computer is required to share files or printers with network users.

There are several ways to find the version and service pack information, but using **WINVER** from Start | Run is our favorite because it's fast. This option displays the About Windows NT message box that contains version and licensing information, as well as the amount of memory available. It also shows the service pack level, right after the version information, if a service pack has been installed. This is the same message box you see if you select Help | About from the menu in Windows NT Explorer or My Computer.

Remember that the Windows NT 4.0 service packs include new support for hardware, such as the AGP video standard, which was added in Service Pack 3 but seemed to work even better with Service Pack 6.

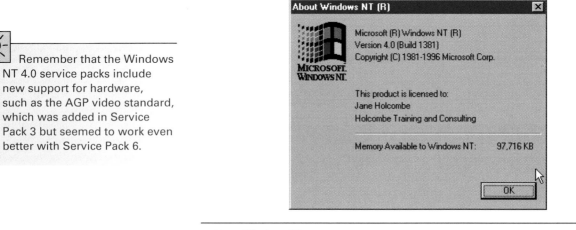

• About Windows NT

Step-by-Step 4.03

Installing Service Packs

In this step-by-step, you will install the latest service pack.

To complete this exercise, you will need the following:

- The computer on which you successfully installed Windows NT in Step-by-Step 4.02, connected to a LAN, with the correct drivers and protocols for your network

- A user name and password for an account that is a member of the Administrators group

- Internet access from your lab computer, or a location on the local network or on your hard drive where the instructor has placed the service pack for you to download

Step 1

Log on as an administrator. Point your Internet browser to www.Microsoft.com/ntworkstation. On the Windows NT Workstation page, look for a link to the latest service pack. Click the link and follow the directions. Select the Intel X86. But wait—we're not done. You also must choose between the standard encryption version and the high-encryption version. Read the restriction on this at `www.Microsoft.com/exporting`. Once you have decided on the version to use, select the link to download it.

Step 2

You will have to specify a language. Once you initiate the download, you should see a Confirm File Open box. You do not want to open (run) the service pack program during the download, but click Save As and save the file to your desktop (or another location, if desired).

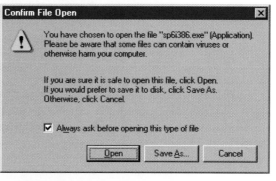

Step 3

After the download is complete (the amount of time it takes depends on the speed of your connection), you should close the browser; then locate the service pack file on the desktop (or other location) and double-click it. Follow the instructions on your screen to complete the service pack installation.

Step 4

Once the service pack is installed, run WINVER.

■ Customizing and Managing Windows NT 4.0 Workstation

Once you've installed an OS, you need to configure and manage it for the person who will use it. This can involve a variety of tasks, including creating a new hard disk partition, installing or removing programs, and customizing the desktop. Take some time now to learn about these tasks.

Creating a New Hard Disk Partition

Creation of a disk partition may seem like an advanced task for a survey class, but if you install Windows NT 4.0 Workstation on a new computer, the probability that you will have unpartitioned disk space after the installation is very high. Therefore, creating a new hard disk partition once in a lab situation is a valuable experience for you.

A partition defines the boundaries on a hard disk that can be used as if it were a separate physical disk. The two standard partition types are primary and extended. A primary partition can have a single drive letter assigned to the entire partition. An extended partition can have multiple logical drive letters. Each area that is defined as a drive letter is a **volume**, so a primary

Inside Information

Create Versus Create Extended

Selecting Create in Disk Administrator will create a new primary partition (of which you may have no more than four per physical disk), and selecting Create Extended will create a new extended partition, of which you can have no more than one per physical disk. Without going into the boring details of what is wrong with extended partitions, simply remember that an extended partition is not a good thing unless you are dual-booting between Windows NT 4.0 and an OS that cannot use more than one primary partition per physical disk.

partition has a single volume, and an extended partition can contain one or more volumes. A PC will start an OS from a primary partition that is also marked as Active. An extended partition cannot be marked as active and therefore cannot be used to start an OS.

A hard disk can have a total of four partitions, but never more than one extended partition. Extended partitions came about to get past limits of the DOS, Windows 3.x, and Windows 9x OSs. You don't need or want an extended partition if you are not using one of these OSs.

When you create a new primary partition, it is automatically assigned a logical drive letter, but you will have to format it before it can be used to store files and folders. When you create a new extended partition, you must define the size and number of logical drives. The tool you use to manage disks in Windows NT is Disk Administrator, which you will use in the following step-by-step.

• Drive letters

Step-by-Step 4.04

Creating a New Partition

In this exercise, you will create a new partition on your hard disk.

To complete this step-by-step, you will need the following:

- The computer on which you successfully installed Windows NT in Step-by-Step 4.02

- Unpartitioned hard disk space

- A user name and password for an account that is a member of the Administrators group

- A blank diskette

Step 1

Log on as an administrator and launch Disk Administrator by selecting Start | Programs | Administrative Tools | Disk Administrator. The first time you run Disk Administrator, you will see a message box stating that it will update system configuration information.

Step 2

Click OK to close the message box, and Disk Administrator will start. On the first startup screen, you'll also see a message stating that Disk Administrator needs to write information (the signature) on the disk. Click OK to allow it to do this and then click Yes in the Confirm box. You don't have any choice, but you won't see this message again.

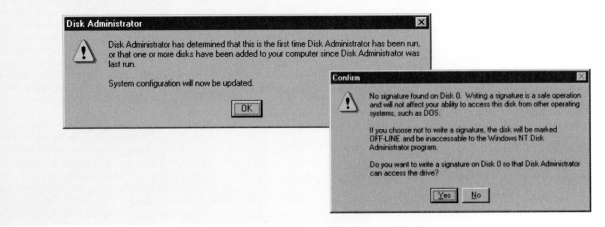

Survey of Operating Systems

Step 3

In Disk Administrator, each physical disk is numbered, beginning with zero. The partitions are defined and labeled in boxes with color-coded bars at the top. The key is in the bottom of the window. If you installed NT according to the instructions in Step-by-Step 4.02, drive C: is a primary partition with the NTFS file system. Drive letters are assigned to hard disk volumes first and then to laser disk drives.

Step 4

To create a new partition in the unpartitioned space, click the area labeled Free Space and then go to the menu bar and select Partition | Create. Read the resulting message in the Confirm box and click Yes to confirm and continue.

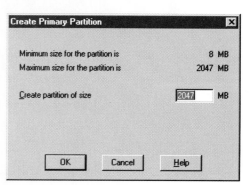

Step 5

In the Create Primary Partition dialog box, enter a size for the new partition in the entry box or accept the maximum size; then click OK. Ask your instructor for guidance if you are not sure what size to create.

Step 6

The new drive will show a drive letter (if you created a new primary partition). Before you can format the new drive, you must commit the changes, which saves the changes in the registry—a huge listing of all of the settings for the OS. To commit the changes, right-click the new partition, select Commit Changes Now, and then click Yes in the Confirm box. An information box labeled Disk Administrator reminding you to update the emergency repair configuration will follow this. Click OK.

Step 7

To format the drive, right-click it and select Format. In the Format box, select the NTFS file system, leave the allocation unit size at the default value, and type **DATA** in the Volume Label box. Do not select either format option; then click Start. In the warning box, click OK. A progress bar will appear in the Formatting box. Click OK when the box pops up with the Format Complete message; then click Close in the Format dialog box.

Step 8

Confirm that you now have drive C: and D:, each of which is a primary partition on your hard disk, and then close Disk Administrator.

Step 9

Update the emergency repair configuration information in the registry and create a new emergency repair disk. Select Start | Run. In the Run box, type **RDISK** and press ENTER. Click Update Repair Info. This updates the Repair folder (C:\WINNT\REPAIR if NT is installed in WINNT) with a copy of portions of the registry, including the system portion, which now contains information about the new drive.

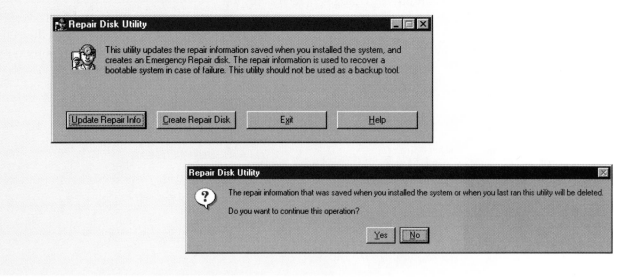

Step 10	When the repair information has been updated, you will be prompted to create an emergency repair disk. Click Yes and follow the instructions. Disk Administrator will format the disk and then copy the contents of the Repair folder to the disk. When this process is complete, remove the disk and place it in a safe location.

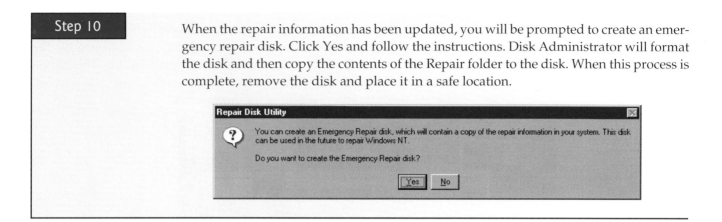

Installing and Removing Applications and Windows Components

After you have installed the OS, you need to install the applications required by the user. Many applications have their own installation programs. In addition, Windows NT has a special Control Panel applet, Add/Remove Programs, that you can use to install and uninstall applications and Windows components.

Step-by-Step 4.05

Using Add/Remove Programs to Install Applications

In this exercise, you will use Add/Remove Programs to verify which programs and Windows components have been installed and to uninstall one of those components. To complete this exercise, you will need the following:

- The computer on which you successfully installed Windows

- A user name and password for an account that is a member of the Administrators group

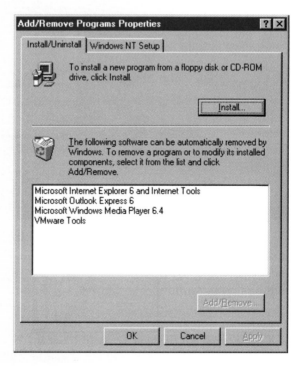

Step 1	Log on as an administrator and select Start	Settings	Control Panel	Add/Remove Programs. Note the programs listed on the Install/Uninstall page.

Step 2

Click the Windows NT Setup tab and note the Windows components listed on that page. Be very careful not to click a check box unless you really want to check or uncheck that component. Click each name (not the check box) and note the Details button. This button becomes active when the listed item includes more than one component. Select Accessories; then click the Details button to see all of the Accessories.

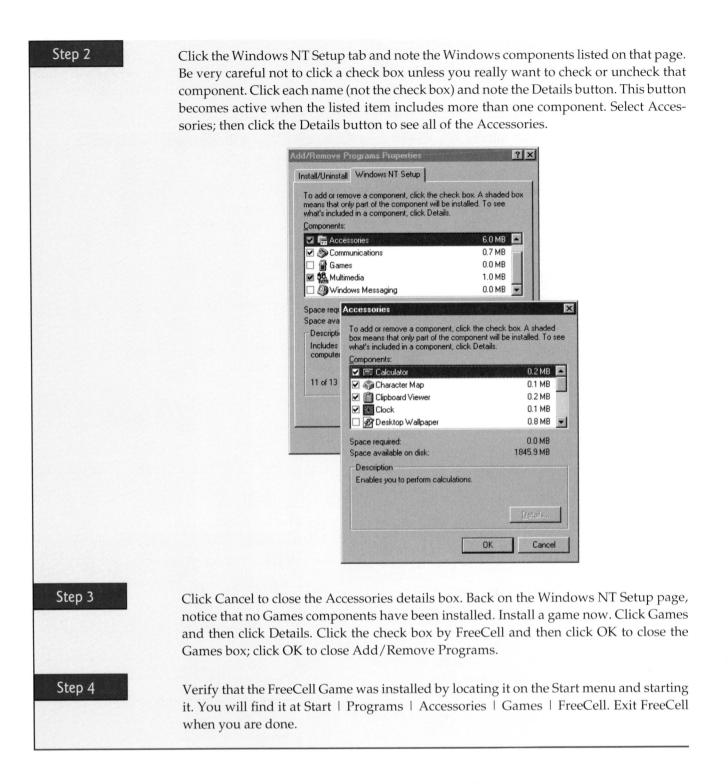

Step 3

Click Cancel to close the Accessories details box. Back on the Windows NT Setup page, notice that no Games components have been installed. Install a game now. Click Games and then click Details. Click the check box by FreeCell and then click OK to close the Games box; click OK to close Add/Remove Programs.

Step 4

Verify that the FreeCell Game was installed by locating it on the Start menu and starting it. You will find it at Start | Programs | Accessories | Games | FreeCell. Exit FreeCell when you are done.

Preparing the Desktop for Users

EXPLORER.EXE works behind the scenes as the program that provides your desktop and opens folders.

After you have installed Windows and tested any required network connectivity, added required service packs, and installed applications, you are ready to customize the desktop. Your goal should be to make the desktop visually pleasant for the user and to make any necessary changes that make using the OS easier.

Novice Users Will Customize the Desktop

One observation many professionals have related to us is that they continue to encounter client users who are new to working with computers and need to be guided through the procedures for turning on the computer, logging on, and performing new tasks. Revisiting the same novice user within a week, they find a customized desktop with a picture of their children or pet poodle as wallpaper. This tells us that they were given a good introduction. Some organizations don't allow such personalization for a variety of reasons, such as corporate image, propriety, and security when computers are in a public area. However, when it is allowed, this type of customization can make the user feel more comfortable with the computer.

Respect the Chair/Keyboard Interface

In 18 years of working with users and teaching desktop and server support skills, Jane has heard thousands of professed true-life stories about human-computer interactions—many of them hilarious, but that's another book. Many of these stories reflect human nature when confronted with a new situation. It's important always to remember what it is like to be introduced to something very new and strange to you and to be told that you have to master its use for school or work. (You may be going through this right now!) A good desktop support person helps the new user feel comfortable with the computer and the required programs. Beyond the training and one-on-one tutoring of the user you may perform, you need to set up the desktop so that it works for the individual. The chair/keyboard interface is a human being!

Inside Information

When to Click Apply

Countless times, when Jane (one of the authors) has demonstrated Windows to a class, students have pointed out that she closes dialog boxes without clicking Apply and, therefore, that the changes won't take effect. This isn't true. The Apply button appears in dialog boxes that have multiple tabbed sheets. If you make changes on one tabbed sheet and want to move to another within the same dialog box, click Apply. This applies the changes from that tabbed sheet without closing the dialog box. When you are done working in a dialog box, you don't have to click both Apply and OK to have changes take effect—OK applies all changes and closes the dialog box.

Step-by-Step 4.06

Customizing the Desktop

Experience will teach you the best methods for customizing the desktop. In this exercise, you will customize the settings for My Computer and Windows NT Explorer and use the Display applet to modify the desktop. Although the particular changes you make in this exercise may not be appropriate for most users, you will have an opportunity to view many of the settings available to you.

To complete this exercise, you will need the following:

- The computer on which you successfully installed Windows

- A user name and password for an account that is a member of the Administrators group

Step 1

Log on as an administrator and right-click My Computer. This brings up the context menu. Notice that one of the options, Open, is in bold. The bold item in a context menu is the default action that occurs when you double-click an object. You are going to change this default behavior. But first, click an empty portion of the desktop to close the context menu without making a choice (the ESCAPE key also closes open menus and dialog boxes).

Step 2

Double-click My Computer. This brings up Folder view. This is what Open means for this object. Leave this window open and go back to the desktop. Right-click My Computer and select Explore to start My Computer in Explorer view. Compare the two views and see which you prefer. Do you like the one-dimensional, single-pane window of Folder view or the double-pane window of Explorer view, with a hierarchy of objects in the left Folder pane and the contents on the right?

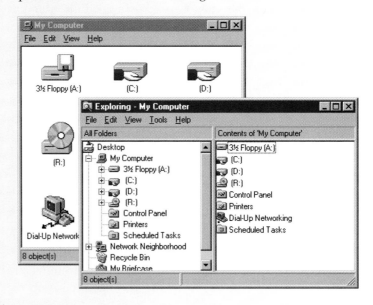

Step 3

We prefer Explorer view. Therefore, one of the first things we do for our own desktops is to make Explorer view the default, as you will do next. (Let's pretend that this is your preference, too!) Click one of the open My Computer windows and select View | Options. In the Options dialog box, click the File Types tab. In the list of registered file types, scroll down and select Folder (*not* File Folder).

Step 4

Notice under File Type Details that Folder opens with Explorer, which opens a folder, whether it is opened in Folder view or Explorer view. With Folder selected, click the Edit button. In the Edit File Type dialog box, the word *Open* in the Actions list is bold. That indicates that it is the default action. To change the default, click Explore and then click the Set Default button.

Step 5

Click OK to close the Edit File Type dialog box. Click the Close button to close the Options dialog box and to make the change take effect. Test the change by right-clicking on My Computer. Explore should now be in bold. Test it further by double-clicking the My Computer icon. It should now open in Explorer view.

Step 6

In Step-by-Step 3.07 in Chapter 3, you configured a screen saver. Make another change to your desktop. Right-click the desktop to open the Display Properties dialog box and click the Appearance tab. Select each of the schemes in the drop-down list box and use the preview box at the top to choose a new scheme. When you find one that suits you, select it; then click OK to close the Display Properties dialog box and to apply the change you made.

■ Managing Windows NT Workstation Security

After you have completed the basic configuration tasks, you have more work to do. Windows NT was the first Microsoft desktop operating system to offer both a local security database for authentication of users and the ability to set permissions on local printers and on local files and folders, provided they are on NTFS volumes. Windows 9x provided no real security on the desktop. Logon rules could be enforced only at the network level. Someone who had access to the local computer had full access to every file, folder, and local printer.

In this section, you will first create local accounts so you can authenticate users and assign permissions to resources, such as files, folders, and printers. Then you will practice file and folder management, including assigning permissions to users. You will also create and manage a local printer.

Managing Users, Groups, Rights, and Permissions

Each Windows NT (all versions), Windows 2000, and Windows XP computer has a local account database in which an administrator can create security accounts. **Security accounts** include individual user accounts and group accounts that can contain multiple users. A skillful administrator can use these accounts to protect sensitive information on a computer. Users and groups can be assigned permissions to printers and to files and folders on an NTFS volume.

In a Microsoft workgroup, the only security accounts are on the individual Windows desktop computers (using Windows NT, Windows 2000, and Windows XP). In a Microsoft domain, security accounts are contained in a centralized accounts database on special servers called domain controllers. A special relationship then exists between the domain security accounts database and the security accounts on individual desktops.

Join us for a brief overview of user and group objects and of how permissions and rights are assigned in Windows NT 4.0.

Users and Groups

Windows NT requires an authenticated logon with a valid user name and password. The user name you use may be from an account that exists either in the local security database on that computer or in the security database on a special network server. When your Windows NT Workstation computer is a stand-alone system (not on a network), or is on a network but is a member of a peer-to-peer group called a workgroup, you can log on only with a local user account. For this chapter, assume that you are logging on using a local account.

In addition to individual user security accounts, NT uses security groups so that administrators can group user accounts to make the granting of permissions and rights easier.

We strongly urge you to create an ordinary user account to use when you are doing ordinary work on your computer and to log on as an administrator only when you need to do things that require a privileged account.

Built-in User Accounts   Windows NT 4.0 Workstation has two built-in user accounts. When you installed Windows NT Workstation on your lab computer, you had to provide the password for the only active user account NT creates automatically: Administrator. The Administrator account is an all-powerful account. If a malicious person gets access to it, that person has full control of your computer. This account cannot be deleted, but it can be renamed, which is a good practice, as long as you remember the new name when you need to log on as a powerful user.

The Power Users group is more limited than the Administrator group, and some administrators assign the primary user of a computer to this group.

Another user account, Guest, is created, but disabled, by default. It is very rare to enable this account on a Windows NT Workstation computer, so we won't waste your time with an explanation.

Built-in Group Accounts   In addition to the built-in user accounts, NT Workstation has several built-in group accounts. They include Administrators, Backup Operators, Guests, Power Users, Replicator, and Users. By default, Administrator is the only member of the Administrators group, Guest is the only member of the Guests group, and all local user accounts are members of the Users group. The other groups are empty until an administrator creates additional local user accounts. All local user accounts automatically become members of the Users group. In other cases, an administrator adds users to the groups.

An administrator creates and manages users and groups with the User Manager program, which you can start from Start | Programs | Administrative Tools | User Manager.

In addition to the groups an administrator can create and administer in User Manager, there are special default groups that you cannot create or modify. Their membership is predefined, and they are available to you only when you assign permissions or rights. The most important of these is the Everyone group, which includes all users on a network, even those who haven't been authenticated.

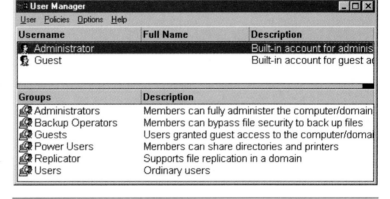

• User Manager

User Rights

In addition to permissions, Windows NT has user **rights**. A right is the privilege to perform a systemwide function, such as access the computer from the network, back up files, change the system time, or load and unload device drivers. You can view the user rights of an NT computer by opening User Manager and selecting User Rights from the Policies menu. NT makes a distinction between basic rights and advanced rights, normally hiding the advanced user rights in the User Rights Policy dialog box. Table 4.1 shows the built-in groups with their default rights. As you can see, rights are what make the Administrators group so powerful.

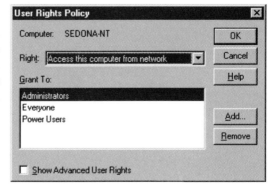

• User Rights

Table 4.1	Windows NT 4.0 Workstation Default Basic User Rights
Group Name	**User Rights**
Administrators	Access this computer from network
	Back up files and directories
	Change the system time
	Force shutdown from a remote system
	Load and unload device drivers
	Log on locally
	Manage auditing and security log
	Restore files and directories
	Shut down the system
	Take ownership of files or other objects
Power Users	Access this computer from network
	Change the system time
	Force shutdown from a remote system
	Log on locally
	Shut down the system
Backup Operators	Back up files and directories
	Log on locally
	Restore files and directories
	Shut down the system
Users	Log on locally
	Shut down the system
Guests	Log on locally
Everyone	Access this computer from network
	Log on locally
	Shut down the system

Permissions

In the NTFS file system, each folder and file has a set of security permissions associated with it. Permissions define what a user or group can do to an object. Table 4.2 lists the standard folder permissions.

Do you have a folder that contains payroll information? You can assign permissions to certain users and groups, and you can keep others out, implicitly or explicitly. You keep users out implicitly simply by not including them in a file or folders list of permissions. You keep users out explicitly by granting them the No Access permission—which is as clear as you can get.

Table 4.2	Standard NT Folder Permissions
Permission	**Description**
No Access	Prevents a user from accessing a folder
List	Allows a user to see the contents of a folder and change to another folder
Read	Permits a user to read and execute a file
Add	Allows a user to add new files or folders to a folder without reading or changing existing files or folders
Add and Read	Allows a combination of the Add and Read permissions
Change	Permits a user to read and add to a folder and to change the contents of existing files and folders
Full Control	Allows a user to read and change a folder, add new files, change permissions on the folder and its contents, and take ownership of the folder

Because permissions are set on individual objects, you view permissions through the Properties dialog box of a file, folder, or printer.

Directory Permissions

Directory: C:\WINNT\system32
Owner: Administrators
☐ Replace Permissions on Subdirectories
☑ Replace Permissions on Existing Files
Name:

Administrators	Full Control (All) (All)
CREATOR OWNER	Full Control (All) (All)
Everyone	Change (RWXD) (RWXD)
SYSTEM	Full Control (All) (All)

Type of Access: Full Control

OK   Cancel   Add...   Remove   Help

- Directory Permissions

Planning for Users, Groups, and Permissions

If a computer is used only by a single user, then you need to create only one additional user account. If an NT Workstation computer is used by more than one local user, you should create additional local accounts. If the computer is a member of a Windows NT or Active Directory domain, you can give access to files, folders, and printers on that computer to the users and groups in the domain. If the computer is a member of a workgroup, then it must have local accounts for granting access to network users.

You must be logged on as a member of the Administrators group to create users or groups, and you must provide certain information for each user you create. To complete the New User dialog box, have this information at hand. We like using planning forms as we prepare to create accounts.

A completed planning form for new users might look like Table 4.3. An asterisk indicates a required field in User Manager's New User dialog box. All users are automatically members of the Users group, but we included it in the planning form. Full Name and Description are optional, but it is good practice to complete these fields. You can add users to groups in the New User dialog box, in the New Group dialog box, or in the properties of the user account. If User Must Change Password at Next Logon is turned on by default, users log on with the password assigned in the New User dialog, but will be prompted to immediately change the password. The default groups are normally sufficient on an NT Workstation computer; therefore, no new groups are included.

Table 4.3	User and Group Planning Form			
User Name*	**Full Name**	**Description**	**Password***	**Groups**
Ssmith	Sue Smith	Manager	Ssmith	Users
				Power Users
Rjones	Ron Jones	Clerk	Rjones	Users

Managing Users and Groups

To complete this exercise, you will need the following:

■ The computer on which you successfully installed Windows

■ A user name and password for an account that is a member of the Administrators group

Step 1

Log on to your lab computer as Administrator. Select Start | Programs | Administrative Tools | User Manager. On the menu bar, select New User.

Step 2

Complete the New User form for Sue Smith, filling in the correct fields from Table 4.3. You must enter the password two times, first in the Password field and again in the Confirm Password field. Leave the check by User Must Change Password at Next Logon; then click Groups.

New User dialog box:

- Username: ssmith
- Full Name: Sue Smith
- Description: Manager
- Password: xxxxxx
- Confirm Password: xxxxxx
- ☑ User Must Change Password at Next Logon
- ☐ User Cannot Change Password
- ☐ Password Never Expires
- ☐ Account Disabled

Buttons: OK, Cancel, Help, Groups, Profile, Dialin

Step 3

In the Group Memberships dialog box, notice that Sue Smith is automatically a member of the Users group. To add her to the Power Users group, click Power Users in the Not Member Of list; then click the Add button. Click OK to add Sue to the Power Users group. Confirm that the information is correct in the New User dialog box; then click OK in the New User dialog box to create the new account.

Group Memberships dialog box:

- User: ssmith (Sue Smith)
- Member of: Power Users, Users
- Not member of: Administrators, Backup Operators, Guests, Replicator
- Buttons: OK, Cancel, Help, <-Add, Remove ->

Step 4

Repeat Steps 2 and 3 to create a user account for Ron Jones. Do not add him to the Power Users group.

Test the new accounts by logging off as Administrator and logging on as a new account. To log off, press CTRL-ALT-DELETE, which brings up the Windows NT Security dialog box. Select Log Off and click OK in the Log Off Windows NT box. When you log on as each user, you will have to change the password.

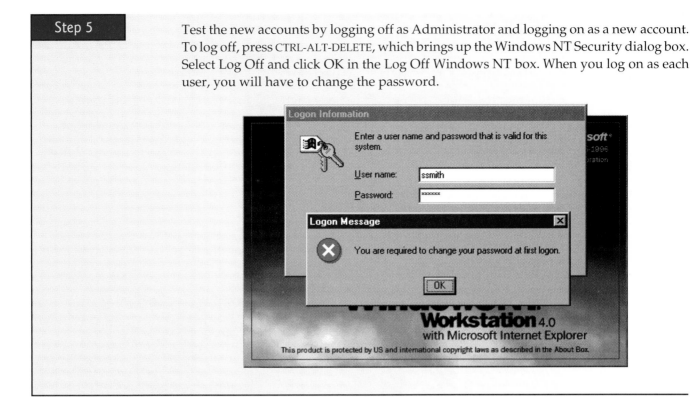

Using and Managing a Local Printer

Before anyone can use a local printer (one connected directly to the PC), an administrator must install the printer driver. After it is installed, users on that computer can print to the printer. Members of the Users, Administrators, and Power Users groups have different rights to the printer for management tasks.

Only the Administrator user or another member of the Administrators group can install a printer driver. NT comes with many printer drivers, but these drivers are of a 1996 vintage. That presents the administrator with two main scenarios: installing a printer driver from the Windows NT CD (only for old printer models), and installing a printer driver that comes with the printer. In Step-by-Step 4.08, you will install a printer driver from the Windows NT CD.

If you need to install a new printer in a Windows NT 4.0 system, you can use the Have Disk button on the Manufacturers page of the Add Printer wizard to point to the location of the drivers for the new printer. Then you continue on through the Add Printer wizard. However, it has been our experience that you almost never need to use the Add Printer Wizard if your printer driver is not on the Add Printer wizard list. Every recently manufactured printer that we have installed has come with its own setup program. Recently, we installed a Samsung laser printer in a windows NT 4.0 system. Following the instructions, we installed the printer driver in five mouse clicks and did not have to enter any information.

> Be sure to read the documentation that comes with the printer. Most manufacturers use the Install Shield installation program, which works very well with Windows.

Installing a Printer Driver from the Windows NT CD

In this exercise you will install a printer driver for a local printer. This is an older printer, and the drivers for it are on the Windows NT CD.

To complete this exercise, you will need the following:

- The computer on which you successfully installed Windows NT

- The Windows NT 4.0 Workstation CD
- A user name and password for an account that is a member of the Administrators group

You do not need a printer connected to your computer.

Step 1

Log on as an administrator and select Start | Settings | Printers. Double-click Add Printer to start the Add Printer wizard.

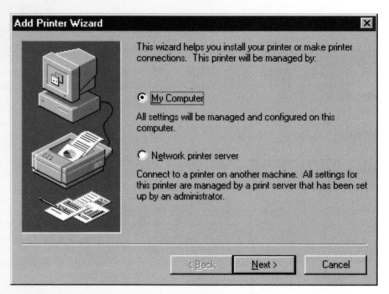

Step 2

Select My Computer and click Next. In the Available Ports list, select LPT1; then click Next. In the Manufacturers list, scroll down and select HP. In the Printers list, select HP LaserJet 5; then click Next. The Printer Name box will default to the model name of the printer, but you can give the printer a friendly name, such as Accounting Printer; then click Next. Leave the printer as unshared because you will share it on your network in Chapter 10. Click Next.

Step 3

Select No on the Printer Test page, unless this specific printer is actually attached. Click Finish. The Add Printer wizard will attempt to find the files it needs. If it doesn't find them, it will prompt you to provide the location. It is looking for the Windows NT CD. Change the drive letter in the Files Needed box if it does not point to your CD drive. Insert the CD and then click OK. A Copying Files box will appear very briefly, and the desktop will be displayed.

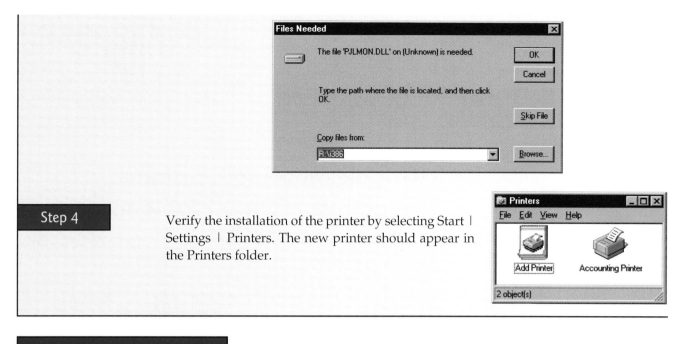

| Step 4 | Verify the installation of the printer by selecting Start | Settings | Printers. The new printer should appear in the Printers folder. |

Managing Files and Directories

To complete this exercise, you will need the following:

- A computer with Windows NT installed on the hard disk

| Step 1 | Log on as **rjones** and open (or explore) My Computer. Browse to C:\WINNT\ PROFILES\ RJONES. The RJONES folder was created when you first logged on as RJONES. If your drive C: is NTFS, then NT assigned permissions to this folder and its subfolders. |

| Step 2 | Right-click the RJONES folder and click the Security tab; then click the Permissions button. Notice that the only accounts that have access to this folder are the Administrators group, rjones, and another special group called System (essentially, the OS). The other user folders listed under Profiles have similar permissions. |

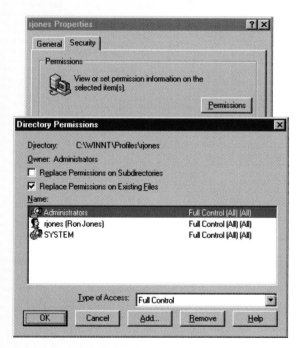

| Step 3 | Click Cancel to exit the Directory Permissions dialog box and click Cancel again to exit the rjones Properties dialog box. Test these permissions. Browse through the RJONES subfolders. Open the Personal folder. Right-click in the contents pane and select New WordPad Document. Name the document **RESUME.DOC**. |

Step 4	In My Computer, browse to the C:\WINNT\ PROFILES\SSMITH folder. You will see an Access Denied message because only Sue Smith, the Administrators group, and the System group have permissions for this folder.	

■ Troubleshooting Common Windows NT 4.0 Problems

Anyone using a computer eventually runs into a situation where something fails or the computer just sort of behaves differently. For those occasions when no one is handy to solve the problem for you, we have some suggestions. In this section, you'll learn where you can find the tools you can use to correct problems. Then you'll practice some simple maintenance tasks, as well as learn some Windows NT 4.0 troubleshooting tips.

The Registry

> ⚠️ Don't edit the registry unless you have expert advice and help or are terribly desperate! You can cause major problems in the OS by entering an incorrect value.

When you're troubleshooting, you'll run into situations in which it is suggested that you edit the Windows NT registry. The registry is a central place where NT stores all configuration settings for the OS. These include settings for drivers, applications, user preferences, and the OS in general. When you run NT Setup, a Control Panel applet, or the setup program for an application or driver, these programs make changes to NT's registry. The registry is actually stored in several files on disk, but you can view and edit the registry as a hierarchical structure using registry editing tools, such as REGEDIT.EXE and REGEDT32.EXE, which come with NT 4.0. The best way to make configuration changes to NT after it is installed is through the Control Panel applets.

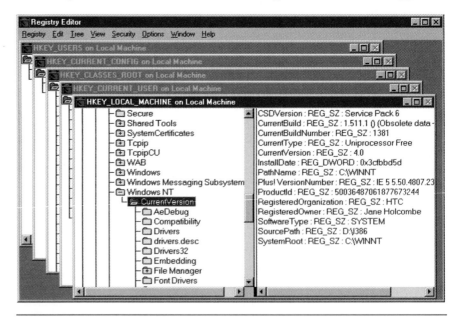

• The Windows NT 4.0 Registry

Event Viewer

When troubleshooting Windows NT 4.0, administrators often wish for De- vice Manager, which exists in Windows 9x, Windows 2000, and Windows XP. However, we also have often wished that Windows 9x had the event logging capabilities of Windows NT. Windows NT 4.0 has three categories of events: system, application, and security. You can view the event log files in Event Viewer, which you can open by selecting Start | Programs | Ad- ministrative Tools | Event Viewer.

> To learn more about Event Viewer, use the help program from within Event Viewer.

System Events

The system log shows events involving the OS system components (drivers, services, and so on). The types of events range from normal events, such as startup and shutdown, to warning of a situation that may lead to an error, to actual error events. The system log is the first place to look when a message indicates a failure of a component, such as a driver or service. Double-click an event to open the Event Detail box, where you can see the actual message that appeared on the desktop in a warning. The message itself may lead you to the solution. Each event also has an ID number. We have had varied suc- cess in searching the Microsoft Web Technet website for a solution using either a portion of the error message or the event ID.

Date	Time	Source	Category	Event	User	Computer
8/30/02	5:21:01 PM	EventLog	None	6005	N/A	SEDONA-NT
8/30/02	5:21:01 PM	EventLog	None	6009	N/A	SEDONA-NT
8/30/02	5:18:51 PM	EventLog	None	6006	N/A	SEDONA-NT
8/30/02	5:18:51 PM	BROWSER	None	8033	N/A	SEDONA-NT
8/29/02	12:51:50 PM	i8042prt	None	35	N/A	SEDONA-NT
8/29/02	12:44:20 PM	EventLog	None	6005	N/A	SEDONA-NT
8/29/02	12:44:20 PM	EventLog	None	6009	N/A	SEDONA-NT
8/16/02	12:51:40 PM	EventLog	None	6006	N/A	SEDONA-NT
8/15/02	10:22:22 AM	EventLog	None	6005	N/A	SEDONA-NT
8/15/02	10:22:22 AM	EventLog	None	6009	N/A	SEDONA-NT
8/15/02	10:20:43 AM	EventLog	None	6006	N/A	SEDONA-NT
8/15/02	10:20:43 AM	BROWSER	None	8033	N/A	SEDONA-NT
8/15/02	10:15:00 AM	NETLOGON	None	5719	N/A	SEDONA-NT
8/15/02	10:00:00 AM	NETLOGON	None	5719	N/A	SEDONA-NT

Event Viewer - System Log on \\SEDONA-NT
Log View Options Help

- System Event Log in Event Viewer

Application Events

The application log shows events involving applications. These applications may be your office suite of applications or Windows components that run in the GUI, such as Windows Explorer. Some application events are recorded in the application log by a special program called Dr. Watson. If you see a Dr. Watson error on your screen, you will find the error in the application log.

Security Events

Security events are not recorded by default. Events are logged after an ad- ministrator turns on auditing by opening User Manager, choosing Policies | Audit, and selecting Audit These Events. Even then, nothing will appear in the security log until events are selected. If the event selected is File and Object Access, the administrator must then select a file or folder and modify its properties so that it is audited. Logging security events comes under the heading of managing security, rather than troubleshooting.

Step-by-Step 4.10

Finding Help in Windows NT

Our two favorite places to find help for problems with Windows are the Microsoft website and Windows NT Help program. The NT Workstation home page is at `www.Microsoft.com/ntworkstation`. From there, you can select Technical Resources and look for a topic.

The Windows NT Help program is available on the Start menu. In a previous step-by-step, you used the help program to find out how to connect to the

Internet. In that case, you searched using the Index tab of the help program, which searches an index of key topics. In this step-by-step, you use the Find tab, which is more powerful because you can search for words and terms within topics.

To complete this exercise, you will need the computer on which you successfully installed Windows.

Step 1

Select Start | Help. In the help program, click the Find tab. If this is the first time you have clicked Find, the Find Setup wizard needs to create a search list. Select Maximize Search Capabilities; and then click Next (twice), and the Find tabbed sheet will appear and the Help Topics window will open. Click the Options button, and under Search for Topics Containing, select The Words You Typed in Exact Order; then click OK.

Step 2

Let's see what Windows NT Help has to say about disk space. Type the words **disk space** in the top box. The second box shows some matching words, and the bottom box shows the topics related to those words.

In the bottom box, locate Disk Space Trouble-shooter and click the check box to select it; then click Display.

Step 3

In the Disk Space Troubleshooter, click Empty the Recycle Bin. You will see instructions on empty-ing the Recycle Bin, which holds files that have been deleted from your local hard disk. Follow these instructions; then click the Back button to re-turn to the last box. Back in the Disk Space Trou-bleshooter, repeat the last two steps for each of the suggested steps shown in the troubleshooter.

In this exercise, you used Windows NT Help to re-search disk space problems. The suggestion you saw for removing temporary files is a little vague, but the next step-by-step will guide you through this process.

Windows NT Help

Help Topics | Back | Options

Disk Space Troubleshooter

This troubleshooter helps you solve problems you might encounter if you run out of disk space. To free up disk space, just click a method you want to try below, and then carry out the suggested steps.

- Empty the Recycle Bin
- Reduce space used by the Recycle Bin
- Back up unneeded files to tape or copy them to a floppy disk and remove them from your hard disk
- Search for and remove temporary files
- Search for and remove files larger than a certain size
- Remove Windows NT components that you don't use
- Create more disk space by using disk compression on NTFS volumes
- Defragment a disk or volume

When Problems Sneak Up on You

Have you ever heard of the term "bit creep"? A friend once said, "Over time, my OS seems to deteriorate through a mysterious process I call bit creep. Therefore, once a year I back up my data, reformat the hard drive, and rein-stall the OS or install a new OS."

We have heard similar stories countless times from computer profes-sionals and savvy users. Our theory was that that this bit creep thing had something to do with unstable OSs. So in 1996, when we installed NT 4.0 on a desktop computer in our office, we decided to use it as a test of that con-cept. This was a more stable OS than Windows 95. As advertised, it stayed fairly stable through daily use for over four years, although that could be be-cause we were conservative about adding new software to the computer, ex-cept the occasional service pack. After that, however, it did get weird, and each time it suffered a hardware failure, we were on the verge of removing the OS and replacing it because of the increased frequency of software hang ups (no response to the mouse or keyboard).

Possible Cause

If your computer seems to have become slower over time, the cause may be a hard drive issue, but not truly a hardware issue. Hard drives save data in a way that can lead to pieces of individual files being saved in wide-ranging areas of the disk. Then when the same files are read into memory, the system takes longer to gather up all the pieces.

Solution

The solution is to run a program on your hard disk that reorganizes, or defragments, the data on your hard disk. This process is called **defragmentation**, or defragging. Windows NT doesn't come with a defrag program, but programs are available from other sources, such as Executive

Software, which publishes Diskeeper. At one time, Microsoft stated that NTFS volumes did not require defragmentation. We used Diskeeper to analyze an NTFS drive on an NT 4.0 computer that we had used for just a few days. It found 203 fragmented files, with a total of 1,642 excess fragments.

Before you defragment your hard drive, you should clean up your hard disk. That includes removing unnecessary or obsolete programs and deleting unnecessary files. The biggest offenders in this second category are temporary files. Many applications save temporary files on your hard disk. When such an application is closed, it should remove the temporary files. Some may not get removed, though, if the application isn't closed properly or it fails to complete the removal process, but other applications purposely don't clean up their temporary files. Your Internet browser may be in this second category.

Temporary files are often stored in a folder named TEMP, and temporary Internet files are stored in a folder named Temporary Internet Files (depending on the version of Internet Explorer). On a regular basis, clean out these locations. You can also check your software to see if it has a setting to manage the temporary files.

Step-by-Step 4.11

Removing Temporary Files

In this exercise, you will look for and delete temporary files and change the settings for temporary Internet files.

To complete this exercise, you will need the following:

- The computer on which you successfully installed Windows NT 4.0 Workstation
- Internet Explorer version 6

Step 1

Log on as Administrator. Close any open applications.

Step 2

Search for the temporary folders. Select Start | Find | Files or Folders. In the Find: All Files dialog box, type **temp** in the Named text box and select Local Hard Drives in the Look In text box. Be sure that Include Subfolders is checked and then click Find Now.

Step 3

You should find a single TEMP directory on drive C:, and perhaps a Temporary Internet Files directory for each user. These folders may have few or no temporary files, depending on what applications you have used since installing NT.

| Step 4 | Double-click the TEMP directory to open it; select the TEMP directory contents, and press DELETE. You can do the same with the Temporary Internet Files directory. |

Loss of Data

It is better to prevent loss of data than to find a "cure" for it after the data is gone. Prevention is at least a twofold process. First you need a plan for organizing your data so that it can be easily backed up, and then you must perform backups at regular intervals.

Any plan for organizing data should make sense to the user so he or she will actually follow it, it should keep data files separate from the application program files, and it should set up a hierarchical structure to make backup easier. A simple hierarchical structure has a folder at the top level and several subfolders stored in that folder, with the subfolders containing files organized by type of data file or by the names of the projects the user works on or by whatever scheme makes sense to the user. With just one folder at the top of the entire hierarchy, you can point a backup or copy program to the top folder and back up all data files at one time.

Back up all valuable files. Windows NT 4.0 Workstation has a backup program, available through Start | Programs | Administrative Tools | Backup. However, this program works only if you have a tape backup system installed, and it must be a tape backup system that is on the list of tested hardware at the Microsoft site. This makes the NT Backup program almost useless for a desktop computer. If your data files are stored on your local computer and you don't have a tape backup system, find another backup method. This is very important. Use a network server, writeable CD-ROM, or other removable media. Third-party backup programs also are available for Windows NT 4.0.

> If you need an alternative to the Windows NT backup program, you might go to www.dantz.com or www.novastor.com to see what they offer.

Troubleshooting Startup Problems

Now you'll learn more about the Windows NT bootup process, including the role of NT Loader (NTLDR) and the other files that enable NT to boot up. This information is important to know so that if a failure occurs due to a missing file during startup, you can identify the missing file. You

Cross Check

DOS Startup

A little voice just told us that you might have skipped Chapter 2 because you believe you will never use DOS. That might be true, but as long as we use operating systems that comply with the Intel/Microsoft standards on PCs, the early bootup process remains the same, no matter which OS you are using. Therefore, it is valuable to you to go back to Chapter 2 and review the section titled "The DOS Bootup Process." After you do that, answer these questions:

1. What is the difference between a cold boot and a warm boot?

   _____

   _____

2. Where is the bootstrap loader found, and what role does it play?

   _____

   _____

3. What is located in the first physical sector of a hard disk?

   _____

   _____

4. What is located in the first sector of each logical drive?

   _____

   _____

will also learn how to create a Windows NT 4.0 startup disk, an important tool for solving Windows NT bootup problems.

Windows NT System Files and Partitions

Windows NT 4.0 is a very large and complicated OS, and for it to start, many files have to be brought into memory while the OS is being put together. These include boot files, which reside in the root of drive C:, and the kernel and many other components that reside in folders below the folder in which you installed Windows NT. The default location is \WINNT, which does not have to reside on the C: drive.

Think back to the description of the DOS bootup in Chapter 2, "DOS." What gets loaded into memory from the boot sector of the active partition (drive C:) on a PC is a program that looks in the root folder of that partition for the file (by name) that begins the loading of the OS. On a Windows NT computer that file is **NTLDR**, the NT operating system loader. It begins the process of bringing all the many OS components into memory.

Beginning with Windows NT, Microsoft calls the active partition (drive C:) the **system partition**, which is confusing because this is where NT's boot files reside. The **boot files** are used to begin (boot) the NT system startup and must reside in the root of this partition. The NT boot files are as follows:

- NTLDR
- NTDETECT.COM
- BOOT.INI
- NTBOOTDD.SYS (present only if a certain type of drive controller is used)

Microsoft also has a special name for the partition that contains the system files: the **boot partition**. The **system files** are important components of the OS and include the operating system kernel, the file that contains the OS settings from the registry, and various driver files. These are installed into the WINNT\SYSTEM32 folder. The NT system files are as follows:

- C:\WINNT\SYSTEM32\NTOSKRNL.EXE
- C:\WINNT\SYSTEM32\CONFIG\SYSTEM
- Many driver files

The backslash (\) after a drive designation (C:) points to the topmost (root) folder (directory in old-speak). A subfolder would be shown after this folder, as in C:\WINNT. And so the path continues with subfolders within subfolders (C:\WINNT\SYSTEM32).

The Windows NT Bootup Process

Windows NT is a very big OS, and its bootup process has several stages: the pre-boot sequence, the boot sequence, and the load sequence.

Pre-boot Sequence   The standard PC bootstrap, up to the loading of NTLDR into memory, is the pre-boot sequence. When NTLDR is loaded into memory and a portion of its instructions is made active (initialized), the next stage, the boot sequence, begins.

Boot Sequence   NTLDR loads, switches the processor to protected mode, and initializes the remainder of itself in memory. It then reads BOOT.INI and displays the OS Selection menu.

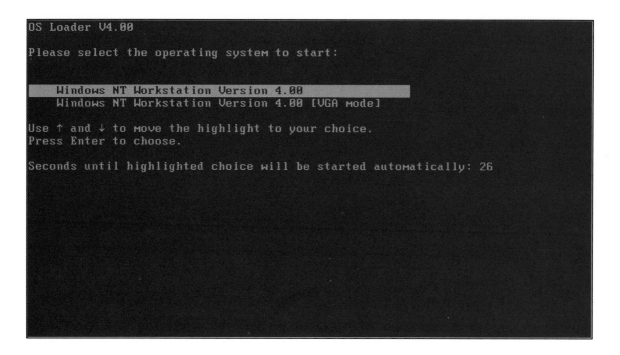

• OS Selection menu

If Windows NT Workstation Version 4.0 is selected, NTLDR loads and starts NTDETECT.COM.

To learn more about Windows NT 4.0 startup, connect to www.microsoft.com/technet and search for the article titled "What Happens When You Start Your Computer." This is Chapter 19 of the *Windows NT Workstation Resource Kit*.

■ NTDETECT.COM scans the hardware in the computer and reports the list to NTLDR for later inclusion in the registry.

■ NTLDR loads NTOSKRNL.EXE (the kernel) and HAL.DLL.

■ NTLDR loads the SYSTEM portion of the registry into RAM.

■ NTLDR loads the drivers that are configured to load at bootup. These drivers are loaded into memory, but not initialized. During this phase, the screen is cleared and progress dots (...) are displayed across the top of the screen.

■ NTLDR passes control to NTOSKRNL.EXE, and the load sequence begins.

Load Sequence   During the NT load sequence, NT is loaded and initialized. This stage also has three phases: the kernel initialization phase, the services load phase, and the Windows system start phase. The components that control the first two of these phases are NTOSKRNL.EXE and SMSS.EXE, respectively. The third phase has many participants, including the Win32 subsystem, which starts the local security authority (LSASS.EXE) and the service controller (SCREG.EXE). The Begin Logon message appears.

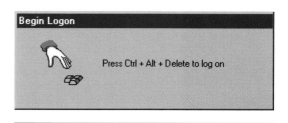

• Begin Logon

Windows NT Startup Diskette

There is one basic fact you can't have missed while installing and working with Windows NT 4.0: it is one very big OS! A large number of files are critical to getting NT up and running. Have you wondered what happens if one of those files is accidentally deleted or maliciously damaged? Not knowing how to solve a problem like this could affect your computing career, or at least ruin your day.

The answer to some bootup problems is to have a Windows NT startup disk handy. NT is far too big to fit onto a diskette the way DOS does, but you can easily fit the NT boot files that must be on the system partition. To create an NT startup disk, first format a diskette in NT; then copy NTLDR, NTDETECT.COM, and BOOT.INI to the diskette.

You can use the diskette to bypass the NT boot files in the root of C:. You will find this capability very handy if, when you try to boot normally from the hard disk, an error message indicates that one of those files was not found.

Step-by-Step 4.12

Creating a Windows NT Startup Disk

In this step-by-step, you will create a Windows NT startup disk. To complete this exercise, you will need the following:

- The computer on which you successfully installed Windows NT 4.0 Workstation

- A single blank diskette

- A user name and password for an account that is a member of the Administrators group

Step 1

Log on as an administrator, insert the diskette into the drive, and double-click My Computer. Right-click the icon for drive A: in My Computer (be careful not to click it before you right-click, or it will not allow you to format). Select Format and click Start in the Format A:\ dialog box. Click OK in the Warning box. The formatting may take a few minutes (diskette drives are very slow).

Step 2

When formatting is complete, close the dialog box and return to My Computer. Expand drive C: and locate the following files in the Contents window: NTLDR, NTDETECT.COM, BOOT.INI, and NTBOOTDD.SYS. Don't be concerned if the last file is not present; it is present only if needed for certain hard disk controllers. CTRL-click to select the boot files; then copy (don't move) them to drive A:.

Step 3

When the files have been copied, leave the diskette in the drive and restart your computer. The restart should work exactly like a normal restart, except it will be slower, and you will hear drive A: work as the boot files are read from there. After a successful restart, remove the diskette, label it "NT 4.0 Startup Disk," and set it aside for later.

Troubleshooting with the Windows NT 4.0 Startup Disk

Now that you're armed with the NT 4.0 startup disk, you need to know when and how to use it. If your computer fails to start and you see any of the following messages, use the startup disk you created for your computer to start NT. Once NT is successfully started from the startup disk, copy the missing file to the root of C:. For startup failures with different messages, check out the use of the emergency repair disk.

NTLDR or NTDETECT.COM Is

Missing   This error message indicates that files in the root of C: may be missing or corrupt. If startup fails and you see a message that NTLDR or NTDETECT.COM is missing when you boot from your hard disk, simply boot with your NT startup disk and copy the missing file from A:\ to C:\.

Bad or Missing NTOSKRNL.EXE   Don't you believe it! This is a misleading message. If startup fails and a message tells you that NTOSKRNL.EXE is missing, the problem more likely is an error in the BOOT.INI file. Try booting from your NT startup disk for that computer. If that is still unsuccessful, you can try to edit the BOOT.INI file on the startup disk. This is an advanced topic, and we urge you to research it on your own if you actually encounter this problem. In brief, the BOOT.INI file points to the location of the kernel (NTOSKRNL.EXE) using a special syntax referred to as the ARC path. The solution to the problem may be as simple as changing a single character in the ARC path in this file.

Using the Emergency Repair Disk

If your Windows NT computer will not boot, but displays a message other than those discussed in the preceding paragraphs, or if it could not be repaired using the startup disk, you can perform an emergency repair. This requires having up-to-date information in the Repair directory (C:\WINNT\REPAIR). You should also have a backup of this information, in the form of a special diskette called an emergency repair disk (ERD). In

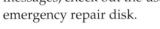

Try This!

Modify View Options

Look at your current view settings and modify them, as necessary, to display the boot files on the root of C:. Try this:

1.   Open My Computer and look at the contents of the root of C:. Are NTLDR and NTDETECT.COM visible? Can you see the file name extensions on the files that are visible? If you can answer yes to both questions, do not make changes to your view settings. If no, go to Step 2.

2.   Select View | Options. On the View page, select Show All Files and deselect Hide File Extensions for Known File Types. Then click OK to close the Options dialog box.

3.   Confirm that you can see NTLDR and NTDETECT.COM and that file extensions are visible. Many other files will also be visible.

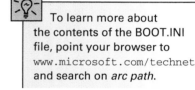

To learn more about the contents of the BOOT.INI file, point your browser to www.microsoft.com/technet and search on *arc path*.

Try This!

Causing A Startup Failure

You can learn what happens when the Windows NT bootstrap loader fails to find NTLDR. You will need a diskette to format. Although you are using a diskette, you will see the same result as when NTLDR is missing from drive C:. Try this:

1.   Format the diskette, as you did in Step-by-Step 4.12, but do not copy the boot files.

2.   Leave the diskette in the drive while you restart your computer.

3.   Restart the computer. After it fails to find an OS, it should display this message:

    NTLDR is missing

    Press any key to restart.

4.   Simply remove the blank disk from drive A: and press a key. The system should restart and load Windows NT 4.0 from your hard disk.

this chapter, you had two opportunities to create an ERD: once during the installation, and once after creating a new partition.

To perform an emergency repair, you need the Windows NT CD, the ERD, and if your computer will not start from CD-ROM, you will need the three setup disks. See Step-by-Step 4.01, "Creating the Windows NT 4.0 Setup Disks from Windows or DOS." The procedure is as follows:

1. Using the CD-ROM or the setup disks, boot to the Windows NT 4.0 setup program.

2. At the Welcome to Setup screen, press R to repair a damaged Windows NT version 4.0 installation.

3. On the following screen, select or deselect the desired actions in the box; then press ENTER to continue.

> Make a habit of updating the repair information and the ERD every time you add a new driver or make other changes, such as when you create or remove a disk partition. See Step-by-Step 4.04, "Creating a New Partition."

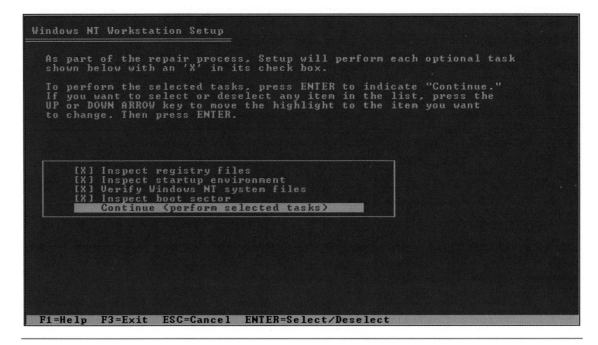

```
Windows NT Workstation Setup

   As part of the repair process, Setup will perform each optional task
   shown below with an 'X' in its check box.

   To perform the selected tasks, press ENTER to indicate "Continue."
   If you want to select or deselect any item in the list, press the
   UP or DOWN ARROW key to move the highlight to the item you want
   to change. Then press ENTER.




        [X] Inspect registry files
        [X] Inspect startup environment
        [X] Verify Windows NT system files
        [X] Inspect boot sector
            Continue (perform selected tasks)






 F1=Help   F3=Exit   ESC=Cancel   ENTER=Select/Deselect
```

- Emergency repair menu

4. On the following screen, press ENTER to continue with detection of mass-storage devices or S to continue after skipping mass-storage device detection. Unless you have tried this and failed previously on this computer, choose the first option.

5. Continue, following the instructions on the screen. When the procedure is complete, remove all disks and restart the computer.

The Blue Screen of Death (BSOD)

The **Blue Screen of Death (BSOD)** strikes horror in the hearts of IT professionals new and old. We actually have yet to hear of someone dying from a blue screen, but it would be fair to say that more than a few important data files have met an untimely demise when a Windows NT computer has crashed

> Perform an emergency repair only if you are unable to boot up, cannot repair with the startup disk, and have kept the repair information up-to-date. You should also first browse the emergency repair topics at the Microsoft Technet site: www.microsoft.com/technet.

and displayed a Stop message on a blue screen. First, we'll answer the question, "What is the BSOD?" and then we'll show you an approach to troubleshooting BSOD problems—and this is well worth learning because both Windows 2000 and Windows XP have similar Stop screens, and the action you take for those OSs is much like what you will learn here.

What Is the BSOD?

The BSOD is actually a feature of Windows NT. It's a blue character-mode screen that displays a message that includes the word *Stop* near the top left of the screen, and seemingly nothing else that makes sense. Stop error screens exist by design. The OS stops everything when it detects that something very bad (also known as a Fatal Error) has happened to make it unstable.

Windows NT 4.0 is not the only OS that is designed to behave like this, although others may not produce the infamous BSOD. When something occurs to make an OS unstable, it is assumed that more damage could be done by allowing things to continue out of control, so the OS stops and displays a blue screen with an error message. Although in-depth study of the handling of stop errors is a more advanced topic for another day, another course, there are several common blue-screen errors that you can learn to decipher just from reading the first few lines of information on the Stop screen.

What Can Cause a BSOD?

Some programs can go bad without causing a BSOD. These are programs, like your application programs, that are isolated from the kernel of the operating system and cannot usually cause harm. With these programs, Windows NT can usually maintain enough control to let you remove an offending program through the Task Manager. Other programs, notoriously drivers, are given the same privileges as the OS kernel and can cause a BSOD. A bad driver can cause the BSOD during installation and during startup.

Solving the Problem by Observation and Research

A BSOD is intimidating because most of the screen is filled with geeky-looking hexadecimal numbers. Ignore them and just concentrate on the first few lines on your screen, which may look something like the following:

```
        DSR CTS
*** STOP:  0x0000000A (0x00000000, 0x0000001A, 0x00000000,
0xFC873D6C
IRQL_NOT_LESS_OR_EQUAL*** Address fc873d6c has base at
fc870000 - i8042prt.sys
CPUID:Geniune Intel 5.1.5 ifq1:1f SYSVER 0xf0000421
```

If you see a Stop screen, observe what you see and either report it to a computer support person or research the cause yourself based on information you gather from the screen. Look for the stop code (the first parameter after the word *Stop*) and then look for the description at the left of the third line. Using just the stop code, search the Microsoft Technet site (www.microsoft.com/technet) for possible causes and solutions (using another computer if this one won't work).

After displaying a Stop screen, the computer may restart on its own. If not, you should restart it. It is possible that the computer will restart and

Inside Information

Stop Error

First, let's have some kind words about this stop error business. The screen appears by design and may keep even worse things from happening. You wouldn't really want to continue driving your car if the oil pan was ruptured and the car was leaking oil by the quart. The oil light shows up on your dash, nice and bright so you can't ignore it. Now if it weren't for the risk of bodily harm to drivers and passengers, we're sure manufacturers would have the car stop itself at the first sign of a major oil leak so that you wouldnot ruin your engine. A desktop OS is not usually involved in propelling humans at freeway speeds, so stopping is considered a good choice if something has happened to make the OS question its own sanity.

function normally, but you should still report the problem or research the cause of the Stop screen.

Preparing for the BSOD

To be prepared for a BSOD, you should decide how you want your computer to behave after a stop error. You do this by modifying the Recovery settings on the Startup/Shutdown tab of the System applet of Control Panel.

- Write an Event to the System Log is, by default, the only Recovery setting selected on an NT 4.0 Workstation machine. We recommend that you leave this selected because it causes NT to write an event to the system log, which is one of several log files that can be viewed using Event Viewer (Start | Programs | Administrative Tools | Event Viewer). This means that even if the computer reboots after a Stop screen, you can read the stop error information that was on the screen in the system log.

- Send an Administrative Alert is a setting that we recommend you select. This sends an alert message to the administrator that will appear on the administrator's screen the next time the administrator logs on.

- Writing Debugging Information To is a setting we don't recommend for a desktop computer.

- Automatically Reboot is a setting we recommend, as long as you have also selected the first option, which preserves the stop error information.

Try This!

Setting Recovery Options

You can set the recovery options on your computer now. To do this, you must be logged on as an administrator. Try this:

1. Right-click My Computer and select Properties. In the Properties dialog box, select the Startup/Shutdown tab.

2. Select Write an Event to the System Log (if it is not already selected), Send an Administrative Alert, and Automatically Reboot. Click OK to close the System Properties dialog box.

3. If the System Control Panel applet message that the Alerter service is not running appears, click OK. Click No when prompted to restart the computer and perform the next step. Otherwise, skip to Step 5.

4. To start the Alerter service, open a command prompt and type **net start alerter** and press ENTER. Then restart your computer and skip Step 5.

5. If you did not receive the Alerter message in Step 3, click Yes to restart your computer.

Chapter 4 Review

■ Chapter Summary

After reading this chapter and completing the Step-by-Step tutorials and Try This! exercises, you should understand the following facts about Windows NT:

Describe Windows NT 4.0 Workstation Features, Limitations, and Requirements

- Windows NT Workstation is a more stable OS than Windows 3.*x* and Windows 9*x*.

- Windows NT Workstation provides local security.

- The Windows NT 4.0 Workstation desktop resembles Windows 95.

- Windows NT 4.0 supports the NTFS4 and FAT16 file systems.

- Windows NT 4.0 can run applications written for MS-DOS, Windows 3.*x*, Windows 9*x*, and Windows NT.

- Some DOS and Windows 3.*x* applications will not work in Windows NT 4.0.

Install and Configure Windows NT 4.0 Workstation

- The Windows NT 4.0 Setup program can create a partition with a maximum size of 4GB.

- NT requires special software drivers for all hardware.

- You can find a list of supported hardware at the Microsoft website on the Hardware Compatibility List (HCL) page at www.Microsoft.com/hcl and on the Windows Compatible Products page at www.microsoft.com/windows/compatible.

- The minimum hardware requirements for NT 4.0 are a Pentium processor, 16MB of RAM, 120MB of available disk space, CD-ROM drive (or other access to the source files), VGA or higher-resolution video adapter, and Microsoft mouse (or compatible pointing device).

- Don't stop at the minimum hardware requirements when you install NT 4.0; you will need more memory, hard disk space, and perhaps more processing power, depending on the applications you install.

- Microsoft's published recommended minimum hardware included an Intel Pentium processor, 32 to 48MB of RAM, 2GB available hard disk space, CD-ROM drive, SVGA or higher-resolution video adapter, and Microsoft mouse.

- Before installing NT, prepare your hardware, determine the installation method, and gather the materials needed to complete the installation.

- The Windows NT setup disks are required when you want to install NT from CD-ROM, but the computer cannot boot from the CD drive.

- You can create a set of NT setup disks by running *d*:\i386\winnt32 /ox.

- You cannot install Windows NT 4.0 without the CD key, a code that appears on the envelope containing your NT CD.

- Service packs are very important for Windows NT 4.0.

- Service packs for Windows NT 4.0 Workstation can be found on the Microsoft NT Workstation page at www.microsoft.com/ntworkstation.

- You can view other computers on the network through Network Neighborhood.

- After installing an OS, check to see what its status is using the WINVER program, which will tell you what (if any) service packs are installed.

- By default, Windows Explorer view options hide hidden files and hide most file extensions.

- If you have an NTFS volume, you can assign permissions to folders and files to protect data from unauthorized users.

Customize and Manage Windows NT 4.0 Workstation

- A Windows NT 4.0 Workstation installation must be configured and managed for the person who will use it. This may include creating a new hard disk partition, installing or removing programs, and customizing the desktop.

- Disk Administrator is the program an administrator uses to create and format partitions and to manage drive letters.

- If there is only one hard drive partition and a CD-ROM drive, NT will assign the hard drive partition drive letter C:, and the CD-ROM drive letter D:. If you create more hard drive partitions, they will get drive letters beginning with letter E:.

Disk Administrator will allow you to assign a different drive letter to the CD-ROM drive.

- Unless you are dual-booting between NT and a less capable OS, such as DOS, Windows 3.*x*, or Windows 9*x* you should not create extended partitions.

- If you are dual-booting between NT and a less capable OS, such as DOS, Windows 3.*x*, or Windows 9*x*, any drive that the second OS needs must use the FAT file system. Also, the drive can be on only the first primary partition or in a logical drive in an extended partition.

- You can remove programs with the Add/Remove Programs Control Panel applet.

- Making the desktop visually pleasant to the user will enhance the user's work experience.

Manage Security for Users, Files, and Printers

- Windows NT Workstation has a local account database containing security accounts.

- Security accounts include individual user accounts and group accounts containing one or more user accounts.

- Groups allow an administrator to group users together to make it easier to administer the accounts.

- Each person using an NT Workstation computer must log on with a valid user name and password.

- You can use User Manager to create local users and groups and to assign user rights.

- The built-in groups include Administrators, Backup Operators, Guests, Power Users, Replicator, and Users.

- By default, Administrator is the only member of the Administrators group, Guest is the only member of the Guests group, and all local user accounts are members of the Users group.

- The built-in Administrator account is all-powerful on a Windows NT 4.0 Workstation computer.

- The built-in Power Users group gives users who are members of that group the right to share directories and printers, change the system time, access the computer from the network, force shutdown from a remote computer, log on locally, and shut down the system.

- The built-in Guest account is disabled by default.

- Create an ordinary user account to use when you are doing ordinary work on your computer; log on as Administrator or a member of the Power Users group only when you need to do things that require a privileged account.

- A right is the privilege to perform a systemwide action, such as access the computer from the network, back up files, change the system time, or load and unload device drivers.

- When a printer is installed, the default permissions allow all users to print to it. An administrator can assign more restrictive permissions if needed.

- Before installing a new printer, read the documentation to see how to install the printer driver.

Troubleshoot Common Windows NT 4.0 Problems

- The Windows NT boot files, used during the boot sequence of NT startup, are NTLDR, NTDETECT .COM, BOOT.INI, and NTBOOTDD.SYS.

- The Windows NT system files, used during the load sequence of NT startup, are NTOSKRNL.EXE, SYSTEM, and many driver files.

- A Windows NT startup disk is created by formatting a diskette and copying the NT boot files from the root of C: to the root of A:.

- A Windows NT startup disk can be used in case of damage to the boot files on an NT computer.

- If you do not know how to perform a task in Windows NT, you can search the help program. It has many tutorials with step-by-step instructions.

- The registry is a central place where NT stores all configuration information. Avoid directly editing the registry because you can cause damage. The Control Panel applets provide a safe way to edit the registry.

- You can view system, application, and security logs in Event Viewer.

- Simple maintenance tasks include removing temporary files, uninstalling unneeded software, and running a disk-defragmenting program.

Key Terms

Blue Screen of Death (BSOD) *(170)*	**NTFS** *(127)*	**service pack** *(134)*
boot files *(166)*	**NTLDR** *(166)*	**system file** *(166)*
boot partition *(166)*	**patches** *(134)*	**system partition** *(166)*
clean installation *(138)*	**permission** *(128)*	**virtual file allocation table (VFAT)** *(127)*
defragmentation *(163)*	**rights** *(153)*	**volume** *(143)*
image *(138)*	**security account** *(152)*	**WINVER** *(142)*

Key Term Quiz

Use the Key Terms list to complete the sentences that follow. Not all the terms will be used.

1. NTLDR, NTDETECT.COM, and BOOT.INI are Windows NT _____.

2. It is important that the most current _____ be installed to fix bugs and add new features.

3. Permissions to access a file, folder, or printer are assigned to _____.

4. An exact duplicate of the entire hard drive contents, including the OS and all installed software, is called a/an _____.

5. NT's system files must reside in the _____.

6. Careful observation may help you discover the cause of a/an _____.

7. A quick way to show the About Windows NT message box that contains version and licensing information, the amount of memory available, and the service pack level is to run the program _____.

8. Each area that is defined as a drive letter in a partition is a/an _____.

9. _____ define what a user or group can do to an object.

10. The _____ file system has a partition size limit of 16 exabytes (one billion billion bytes).

Multiple-Choice Quiz

1. Which of the following is *not* true of Windows NT 4.0? Select all that apply.

   a. The desktop resembles Windows 95.

   b. It is a small OS.

   c. It has security components.

   d. It supports plug and play.

   e. It is the latest Windows desktop OS.

2. Which of the following user rights are normally assigned to the Power Users group?

   a. Change the system time

   b. Backup files and directories

   c. Force shutdown from a remote system

   d. Load and unload device drivers

   e. Restore files and directories

3. Which of the following graphic elements were introduced in Windows 95 and included in Windows NT 4.0?

   a. Taskbar

   b. Menus

   c. My Computer

   d. Windows

   e. Start button

4. In 1996, why would someone choose Windows NT 4.0 Workstation as a desktop OS?

   a. Great screen savers

   b. Stability

   c. Security

   d. Hardware support

   e. Software compatibility

5. Which word or phrase describes something that Windows NT 4.0 and Windows 95 have in common?

   a. NTFS

   b. Common kernel

   c. GUI features

   d. Local user accounts

   e. Administrator

6. Which of the following will not run in Windows NT 4.0?

   a. 64-bit UNIX applications

   b. 16-bit Windows-based applications

   c. MS-DOS applications

   d. OS/2 version 1.*x* applications

   e. 32-bit Windows-based applications

7. The special environments in which NT runs applications are called:

   a. Addresses

   b. Accounts

   c. Quarks

   d. Subsystems

   e. Windows

8. The largest partition size you can create with the NT setup program is:

   a. 7.8GB

   b. 16TB

   c. 2GB

   d. 500MB

   e. 4GB

9. As a new OS in 1996, a major drawback to NT 4.0 Workstation was:

   a. The GUI

   b. Security

   c. Hardware support

   d. Memory

   e. Hard disk limits

10. In 1996, if you needed security on the desktop, which of the following OSs would you choose?

    a. MS-DOS 6.22

    b. Windows 3.1

    c. Windows for Workgroups 3.11

    d. Windows NT 4.0

    e. Windows 95

11. Which of the following statements is true of service packs for Windows NT 4.0? Select all that apply.

    a. Adds features

    b. Fixes file corruption

    c. Installs MS Office

    d. Fixes bugs

    e. Upgrades to a new OS

12. To remove an installed application, you would use the following:

    a. Recycle Bin

    b. My Documents

    c. My Computer

    d. Start | Run

    e. Add/Remove Programs

13. If two or more people log on locally to a Windows NT 4.0 computer, what can you do to protect files in folders on a FAT volume on that computer?

    a. Create local user accounts.

    b. Set folder permissions.

    c. Copy files to My Briefcase.

    d. Save files in the Inbox.

    e. You can't protect files on a FAT volume.

14. Select all statements that are true:

    a. The system partition contains the system files.

    b. The boot partition contains the boot files.

    c. The extended partition contains the boot files.

    d. The boot partition contains the system files.

    e. The system partition contains the boot files.

15. The first NT file to be loaded into memory during bootup is:

    a. NTBOOTDD.SYS

    b. NTLDR

    c. BOOT.INI

    d. NTDETECT.COM

    e. NTBIO.SYS

■ Essay Quiz

1. Write a few sentences describing why Windows NT 4.0 Workstation is in use today. Select the one reason you believe to be the most significant and support your viewpoint.

2. Describe the weaknesses of Windows NT 4.0 Workstation. Select the one weakness you believe to be the most compelling reason not to use it. Support your viewpoint.

3. You work for a small accounting firm that has just purchased a new PC from a local company that builds PCs from standard components. That computer will be running a special application that requires Windows NT 4.0 with Service Pack 5 or greater. Without describing the actual installation, describe the steps you'll take before and after you install Windows NT 4.0 and before the installation of the new application.

4. You're a new employee doing computer support in a small manufacturing company that uses Windows NT in a workgroup on a small network. One of the printers is a sophisticated graphics printer that is expensive to run. It is shared on the network, and your boss has asked you to set it up so that only two people can send print jobs to the printer. Describe what you will do.

5. As you were leaving your office for the day yesterday, a new desktop-support person came in and announced that he had to make some changes to your computer. When you powered up your computer this morning, Windows NT would not start. Instead, you saw the message "NTLDR is missing. Press any key to restart." When you press a key, the computer restarts, but you get the same message. You call the help desk, but no one can talk to you or come to your desk for at least an hour. Describe what you would do in this case.

Lab Projects

• Lab Project 4.1

A virus hit your computer, and many critical files were destroyed. The only data you kept on that computer consisted of some files that luckily were copied to a writeable CD (CD-RW) the day before the virus hit. You have decided it is easier to reinstall Windows NT 4.0 than try to repair the damaged files, and you have decided to repartition and format the hard disk to ensure that all traces of the virus and its damage are gone.

You will need the following:

- Your lab computer on which you previously installed Windows NT

- The Windows NT 4.0 Workstation CD

- The CD key code from the envelope of your NT CD

- The list of configuration information you used for the first installation

Then do the following:

1. Perform the installation.

2. Complete any necessary tasks after the installation.

3. Record your observations on performing an installation of NT for the second time.

• Lab Project 4.2

You and your boss are the entire IT department for a small company with a very limited budget. He has identified 10 computers that should be replaced as slow and obsolete equipment. He has found a nonprofit organization that has agreed to accept the old equipment, with all software removed from the hard drives. The computers presently run Windows NT Workstation 4.0. He plans to build the new computers, with your assistance, out of purchased components. He would like to reinstall NT 4.0 on the new computers and has verified that the components he is purchasing for the new computers are compatible with NT 4.0. He plans to use NT 4.0 on the new machines for three years. He would like you to investigate whether Microsoft has any plans to

discontinue support of NT 4.0 Workstation and, if so, when. Do the following:

1. Determine where you will find the information.

2. Do the research your boss requested and write a report including whether or not Microsoft will discontinue support and what impact this will have on his plans.

• Lab Project 4.3

Your spouse's company is upgrading to all-new computers with new operating systems and has offered to give their existing computers to employees for their personal/family use. The computers will have Windows NT 4.0 Workstation and a full suite of Office products installed on them. They also will include licenses for the OS and application software, but no peripherals will be included. By sheer coincidence, you have also been offered a functioning laser printer for free by the father of a friend. It's an oldie but a goodie—an HP LaserJet IIID. This big old business workhorse is a duplex printer (which means that it can print on both sides of the paper), and it is ideal for a project you have that requires that capability.

You have decided to accept both offers. To ensure that Windows NT 4.0 Workstation will be reliable and stable, you need to research its current status. You also need to verify that the computer and the printer will function together. There are several steps you should take to accomplish these tasks.

Perform the following tasks:

1. Explain how you are going to discover the present status of the OS.

2. Describe how you will eliminate any known problems with the OS.

3. Explain the steps you will take to learn whether the computer and printer can work together. Then perform those steps and describe the results.

Windows 98

"That must be why we're not shipping Windows 98 yet!"

—BILL GATES, AFTER WINDOWS 98 CRASHED DURING A PREVIEW PRESENTATION

When introduced in June of 1998, Windows 98 was the first version of Windows that Microsoft targeted specifically at the consumer market. But Microsoft sort of miscalculated—Windows 98 was indeed accepted by the consumer market, but it was also adopted by corporate users.

In this chapter, you'll get an overview of the strengths of this OS that appealed to both the consumer and corporate markets. Although its considerable strengths led to wide adoption, Windows 98 became a source of frustration for many users because it was notoriously unstable and prone to suddenly locking up. We'll discuss the reasons for this situation, and you'll consider the other limitations of Windows 98. Of course we'll also tell you about the hardware it needs and how to create a startup disk to initiate Windows 98 Setup. You will actually install it and customize the desktop, and in other step-by-steps you will create users and manage files and printers on your lab computer. Finally, you'll explore the tools available for troubleshooting common Windows 98 problems and learn how to solve some of the more common problems you may encounter.

In this chapter, you will learn how to:

- Measure the features, strengths, and weaknesses of Windows 98
- Install and configure Windows 98
- Customize and manage Windows 98
- Manage users, files, and printers
- Troubleshoot common Windows 98 problems

In 1999, just one year after the release of Windows 98, Microsoft brought out an improved, incremental update to Windows 98, called Windows 98 Second Edition, or Windows 98 SE. We used the Second Edition for most screen shots and all step-by-steps in this chapter.

Windows 98 Overview

Although Windows 98 was basically just an upgrade to Windows 95 and targeted at the consumer market, it still made its way into the corporate world. To give you some perspective on these markets, we'll explore the features designed to appeal to home users and **small office/home office (SOHO)** users, and because you'll undoubtedly run into Windows 98 at work, we'll also consider why this OS played so well in the corporate market.

Windows 98 Features and Strengths

If you bought a new PC for home use between the summer of 1998 and the introduction of Windows 2000 in February of 2000, it probably came with Windows 98 preinstalled because you were a member of the target market for this consumer-oriented OS. However, the fact that Windows 98 also found a place on desktops in organizations worldwide surprised many people. After all, Microsoft already offered a desktop operating system, Windows NT 4.0 Workstation, for the business market. Let's explore the features and strengths of Windows 98 that appealed to such a wide range of users, and why Windows 98 was often chosen over Windows NT 4.0 Workstation.

Desktop

The Windows 98 desktop resembles the Windows 95 desktop, with several significant functional modifications.

Internet Explorer Integration   Internet Explorer is intertwined with the Windows 98 OS, meaning that web browsing is integrated into the OS, and that you can connect to the Web from Windows Explorer, other applications, and desktop shortcuts without first consciously starting Internet Explorer.

Inside Information

MS-DOS Command Prompt

Like Windows 3.x, and Windows 95 after it, Windows 98 has MS-DOS as a required component. This is also true of the upgrade to Windows 98, the Millennium Edition (Windows Me), introduced in 2000. These were the last versions of Windows to have such deep ties to MS-DOS. Of the two, only Windows 98 gives you the option of starting up to a true MS-DOS command prompt with full access to the file system. As a networking professional, this feature may be useful to you because it allows you to fix problems such as corrupted system files that you can't fix while the OS is running. However, troubleshooting features that have been added to Windows, such as safe mode in Windows 9x, have given us similar abilities with a friendly GUI.

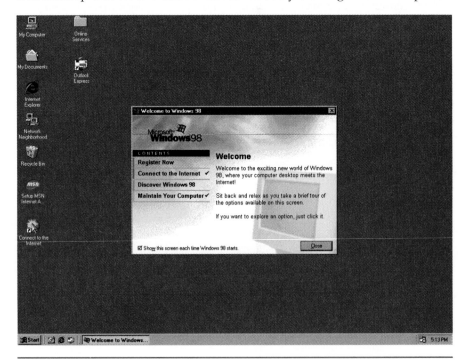

• Windows 98 desktop

This web integration is most apparent visually when you turn on the Active Desktop, as shown in Figure 5-1. The graphic at the upper right of the screen is a hyperlink to www.microsoft.com. A **hyperlink** is an element of a **hypertext markup language (HTML)** document. HTML is the language of the World Wide Web. The pages you view on the Web with your browser are written in this language, which your browser interprets in order to display the pages on the screen. A hyperlink element is a link to a different location or document. That different location can be elsewhere in that same document, or in another

document, or it can be a universal resource locator (URL) that points to a web page, FTP site, or other resource on the Internet.

Another indication of the integration of Internet Explorer is the channel bar. In Windows 98 (First Edition), a channel bar appears on the right side of the desktop. We found this to be as annoying as the pop-up windows that appear when you're browsing the Internet, but there was more to this than met the eye. Each of the services listed maintains an **Active Channel website**, which, by definition, delivers updated information to a subscriber's computer on a regular schedule. You have to initiate the relationship to the sites listed on the default channel bar. This is not a very popular feature.

• Windows 98 (First Edition) channel bar

• **Figure 5-1.** Windows 98 Active Desktop

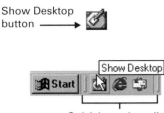

Show Desktop button ⟶

Show Desktop

Quick Launch toolbar

New GUI Navigational Features If you ever worked with Windows 95, did you feel frustrated when you wanted to quickly access an icon on the desktop while one or more windows hid the desktop? You probably first tried the ALT-TAB key combination, but it switched between windows, not between an open window and the desktop. If several windows were open, you likely needed to close or minimize each one to see the desktop. Windows 98 provided a solution with the **Show Desktop button**, included by default on the Quick Launch toolbar. When you click this button, all open windows are minimized so that you can see the desktop.

Navigation from the Start menu has also been improved over Windows 95. The submenus in Windows 98 stay visible long enough for you to make a selection, even if you pause a bit first. You can also customize and add other toolbars to the taskbar. Simply right-click on the taskbar and select the Toolbars menu.

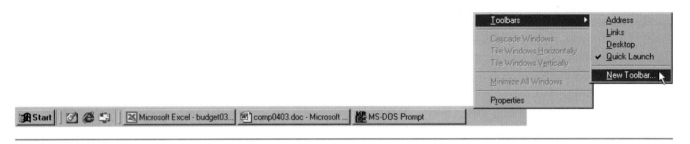

• Windows 98 taskbar

File Systems

Any operating system that uses disk storage must have a method for retrieving information from disks. In the case of writable disks, it must also be able to write and organize the data on disk. Such a method is called a file system, and Windows 98 supports several standard file systems. For CD-ROMs the OS uses Compact Disc File System (CDFS), and it uses the Universal Disk Format (UDF) for digital versatile disks (DVDs). For floppy disks Windows 98 uses the FAT12 file system.

You don't really have to make any decisions about the file systems mentioned so far; the OS uses the appropriate one by default. However, when it comes to hard disk drives, you have two realistic choices—FAT16 or FAT32. The FAT12 file system is only used for incredibly small hard drive partitions (under about 16MB), and FAT16 is used for hard disk partitions up to 2GB in size. However, beginning with Windows 95 and continuing through all subsequent OSs to date, Microsoft added a

---

special driver to the OS called virtual file allocation table (VFAT). VFAT makes disk access faster and also supports the use of long file names on FAT volumes, including a new type of FAT volume, FAT32. Next, we'll compare the FAT16 and FAT32 file systems and then explore the use of long file names.

FAT16   FAT16 was a nice file system for small hard drives. It became something of a liability even as early as 1990 because of its inefficient allocation of disk space and its inability to keep up with the ever-growing hard disk sizes. It also was susceptible to a single point of failure, primarily because it had only one physical location in which it could place the root directory of a volume. FAT16 has a 2GB partition volume size limit.

FAT32   The FAT32 file system addresses the problems with FAT16. It uses space more efficiently because for drives up to 8GB, it uses 4KB clusters, instead of FAT16's 32KB clusters on 2GB drives. A cluster is the minimum space a file system will allocate to a file. The FAT32 file system supports larger drive partition sizes than the 2GB FAT16 limit. But, because FAT32 is much more efficient for large hard drives, Windows 98 will default to the FAT32 file system for partitions larger than 512MB. FAT32 theoretically supports up to 2TB, but in fact operating system, hardware, and BIOS limits can restrict this size to anywhere from 7.8GB to 32GB. However, the root directory location is no longer a single point of failure, because the root directory is not now restricted to the first physical track of the disk, and the OS can also reliably back up the FAT table and use the backup in case the first copy fails.

Converting from FAT16 to FAT32   If you bought a computer with Windows 98 preinstalled and a hard disk larger than 512 MB, FAT32 was usually the file system the manufacturer used, but if your Windows 98 is installed on a FAT16 partition, you can use a Windows 98 utility, Drive Converter, to convert from FAT16 to FAT32. (Drive Converter can be found at Start | Programs | Accessories | System Tools | Drive Converter.) You can also create new FAT16 or FAT32 partitions on free space on a hard disk. Table 5.1 compares the FAT16 and FAT32 file systems as implemented in Windows 98.

Support for Long File Names

You can save files that break the 8.3 naming convention rules with **long file names (LFNs)** up to 255 characters, including spaces. This is a feature supported by the VFAT driver on all implementations of FAT in Windows 98. Adding LFN support to the OS and file systems was forward looking, because people were tired of trying to create meaningful file names under the old 8.3 rules. However, they still had to worry about backward compatibility with applications that understood only 8.3 file names, so Microsoft saved both

Table 5.1	FAT16 to FAT32 Comparison	
Features	**FAT16**	**FAT32**
Maximum Partition Size	2GB	32GB (theoretically 2 terabytes)
Cluster Size	32KB on 2GB partition	4KB on 2GB partition
OS Compatibility	All Microsoft OSs, OS/2, and UNIX	Windows 95 OSR2, Windows 98, Windows Me, Windows 2000, Windows XP

LFNs and 8.3 file names for each file with an LFN. This was not a simple trick, and you'll explore how this was done and you'll work with long file names in the section "Managing Users, Files, and Printers" later in this chapter.

Hardware Support

Like its predecessor, Windows 98 has plug and play support, with added support and drivers for DVD drives, universal serial bus (USB) devices, and IEEE 1394 (similar to Apple's FireWire) devices. It also includes power management features that allow hardware components, such as the disk, monitor, and even PC card modems, to be powered down when not in use—a great feature for laptop users trying to conserve battery power! All of these hardware support features combine to be the most compelling reason why businesses chose Windows 98 for their laptop computers over Windows NT 4.0. Windows 98's enhanced multimedia support, intended to appeal to the home user, also found fans among corporate users. In addition, like Windows 95, Windows 98 allowed users to continue to use older devices with their DOS device drivers, saving them the expense of buying newer devices.

Performance

Each successive edition of Windows has shown performance improvements. Windows 98 continued this tradition with faster bootup, shutdown, and program loading. The **VFAT file system driver** improves performance on both FAT16 and FAT32 volumes. Other performance enhancements, including improved multitasking, exist "under the hood." Experienced Windows 95 users can appreciate the performance difference without having to understand the improvements.

Reliability

Windows 98 did not show a huge improvement in reliability, but there was some due to the evolutionary process of improvements in the underlying program code. Therefore, it was less vulnerable than Windows 95 to problems that caused the system to hang. If you used the FAT32 file system, you also benefited from its improved reliability over FAT16, as described earlier.

Software Compatibility with Legacy Applications

In the area of software compatibility, Windows 98 is generally much more tolerant of older application programs than is Windows NT or the newer OSs. This is by design. Many DOS applications do not need special handling, but some run unacceptably slower on a Windows 95 virtual machine than on a true DOS computer. For those, Windows 98 includes the ability to use **MS-DOS mode** whenever the program is started. In MS-DOS mode Windows 98 removes much of its own program code from memory and loads a real-mode copy of MS-DOS while a DOS program is running. It may even reboot into MS-DOS mode to load special drivers or other programs required by the DOS application. It boots back into Windows 98 when the DOS application is closed. This requires the use of advanced configuration options in the shortcut used to call up the DOS program.

Advanced Program Settings ? X

PIF name: C:\WINDOWS\COMMAND\EDIT.PIF

☐ Prevent MS-DOS-based programs from detecting Windows
☑ Suggest MS-DOS mode as necessary
☑ MS-DOS mode
☑ Warn before entering MS-DOS mode
◉ Use current MS-DOS configuration
○ Specify a new MS-DOS configuration
CONFIG.SYS for MS-DOS mode:

AUTOEXEC.BAT for MS-DOS mode:

Configuration...

OK   Cancel

• Advanced Settings for MS-DOS mode

Limitations of Windows 98

Like any OS, Windows 98 has limitations and troublesome areas. In this section, we'll identify limitations in the following areas: file system, legacy hardware support, and stability.

File System Limitations

Windows 98 has file system limitations in the areas of security and recoverability and file compression.

Security and Recoverability   Although the FAT32 file system is an improvement over FAT16, it still lacks the file-level security of the NT file system (NTFS). Additionally, NTFS was designed to recover data in the event of a system failure, whereas even FAT32 provides only limited recovery of the root directory and FAT table.

File Compression   If your system is low on disk space, Windows 98 has a disk compression function—but we don't recommend that anyone use it. Disk compression in Windows 98 is integrated into the OS, but not into the file system. Windows 98 compresses an entire drive volume (C:, D:, and so on) by compressing all of the files on the drive and storing them in a single file. Then it makes that single file look like your drive C: or D: or other drive, while it hides the underlying "real" drive from the casual user. This smoke and mirrors is clever, but it leaves you with a single point of failure: the file that is storing your compressed files. We have experienced firsthand how easy it is to damage these compressed drives. Don't use this function!

Legacy Hardware Support Limitations

How can legacy hardware support be both a feature and a limitation of Windows 98? If you have an old device that only has Windows 3.1 or MS-DOS device drivers, you can save money by keeping that device and using the old device drivers—something Windows NT, Windows 2000, and Windows XP will not allow. The problem with doing this in Windows 98 is that it will cause Windows to run in **MS-DOS compatibility mode**, which is slower and more prone to failure.

Stability Limitations

Windows 98, like Windows 95 before it, uses a combination of 16-bit and 32-bit code. Yes, they are considered 32-bit OSs, but in reality they are hybrids, and they have instability problems because of this. We have witnessed this in our own computers and in the computers of many clients and students, who experienced frequent crashes of their systems. For this reason alone, when selecting a Windows desktop today for a new computer, you would not even consider Windows 98.

The reason for the instability is tied to the processor modes. The 16-bit code runs in real mode, while the 32-bit code runs in protected mode. The more 16-bit code you have running, the more switching the system has to do between these two modes. If you run only Windows 98 32-bit drivers and also avoid running MS-DOS or 16-bit Windows programs, your computer will perform best and be more stable.

Inside Information

Why Have Both Types of Names?

Why create 8.3 names for files and folders with LFNs? Obviously, if you can create a file or folder with an LFN, you are using software that understands LFNs. However, the theory is that you might also want to access the same file using a program that does not understand LFNs. Therefore, Windows creates an 8.3 file name in addition to the LFN so that older programs can also access the file.

This discussion includes all versions of NTFS. The version in Windows NT 4.0 was version 4, and the version beginning in Windows 2000 was version 5. We now call these NTFS4 and NTFS5, respectively.

To learn how to check for MS-DOS compatibility mode, see "Poor Performance" in the "Troubleshooting Common Windows 98 Problems" section later in this chapter.

Why Would I Use Windows 98 Today?

Why would you choose Windows 98 today? The short answer is that you shouldn't need Windows 98 today, because there are newer and better versions of Windows. It also may simply not be available. The Microsoft website lists Windows 98 in the Previous Products category, not in the Products category. Microsoft's published desktop product lifecycle guidelines, currently at www.microsoft.com/windows/lifecycle.asp, tell us that by the time you read this, Windows 98 will be an unsupported product, which means that licenses will become available only through limited channels. You will still find online support information for Windows 98 at the Microsoft website, but even that service can be discontinued with 12 months notice. Add to all that the newer replacements for Windows 98 (Windows 2000, Windows Me, and Windows XP), and your conclusion must be that Windows 98 is no longer a viable choice if you are shopping for a new desktop OS. However, we urge you to learn about it because it is still in use in homes, schools, and even some businesses.

Newer Windows Does Not Work with Hardware

You may run into situations when newer OSs simply will not work with the existing hardware. Consider our friends Dennis and Jeanette. In the fall of 2001, Dennis surprised Jeanette with a brand-new Windows XP Home upgrade, which he promptly installed on their two-year old Windows 98 computer. A few days later, he called us because his computer hadn't been the same since the upgrade. It was extremely slow, and some of their programs no longer worked. We discovered that Microsoft had scripts that could be used to make some of their programs usable, but that was a moot point once we realized that their computer model was not supported by Windows XP, and that the manufacturer did not intend to create drivers to add support. We uninstalled Windows XP Home, Dennis returned the OS for credit, and they were back to their familiar Windows 98 desktop.

Newer Windows May Lack Features of Windows 98

People also had similar experiences when Windows Me came out in the fall of 2000. While the enhanced multimedia capabilities of Windows Me enticed some users to upgrade from Windows 98, many discovered that they had lost the ability to boot to DOS, run certain DOS applications, and load DOS drivers and resident programs. They returned to their Windows 98 installations.

Hardware and Windows 98

When you prepare to install an operating system, you have three concerns regarding the computer hardware:

- What are the minimum requirements for running the OS? What "horsepower" is required in the processor, how much RAM and hard disk space is needed, what video capabilities and what input devices are required?

Inside Information

Why the Minimums Are Not Practical!

As you can see, the requirements for Windows 98 are pathetically minimal, especially in light of the fact that the minimum computer system you can buy today—for as low as $300—far exceeds the minimum requirements for Windows 98. Even back in 1998, a system meeting only these minimum requirements would not have been acceptable for real-life use. There would be no room on the hard drive to install software, and 16MB of RAM would have caused your software to run very slowly. Many applications would not even install with so little RAM.

- What is the ideal configuration for the job you want this computer to do? Do you need a more powerful processor? More RAM or disk space? Fancy video?

- What other hardware is compatible with this OS?

Let's take a closer look at these concerns.

Minimum Hardware Requirements

Windows 98 can be installed on a computer that complies with the Intel/Microsoft set of standards. The published minimum requirements for Windows 98 include a 486DX/66 or higher processor, 16MB of RAM, 120 to 295MB of free hard disk space depending on the options you install, a CD-ROM or DVD-ROM drive (or access to the Windows 98 source files over a network), a VGA or higher-resolution video adapter, and a Microsoft mouse (or compatible pointing device).

Ideal Hardware Configuration

The minimum hardware configuration just lets you install the OS, look at it, and play around with it. If you need to install a bunch of office applications and expect to work without annoying delays, you need more processing power, memory, and disk space. Here is our recommendation for an ideal Windows 98 computer running standard office applications:

> It's a good idea to check out the compatibility of the hardware and software before attempting to use them with Windows 98.

- Intel Pentium II processor

- 64 to 128MB RAM

- 4GB available hard disk space

- CD-ROM drive

- SVGA or higher-resolution video adapter

- Microsoft mouse

Compatible Products

At present, Microsoft offers a website, www.microsoft.com/windows/compatible/default.asp, where you can search to see if hardware or software has passed Microsoft's compatibility tests for Windows 98.

Consider Bridget, who has decided to install Windows 98 SE on an old Pentium II computer that previously ran Windows 95. She reformatted the hard drive so that she could perform a clean installation of Windows 98. She also wants to buy and install a CD-RW and a wireless LAN PCI card. Before

Try This!

Check Out the Compatible Products

To complete this task, you will need a computer with an Internet connection and a web browser. Try this:

1. Point your web browser to www.microsoft.com/windows/compatible/default.asp. In the Operating System drop-down list box, select Windows 98.

2. In the Product Category drop-down list box, select Storage/CD-Recordable Drive.

3. Leave Company Name set to All and click Go to begin a search.

4. Search results will show you the manufacturer and model name of any DVD-ROM drive that passed the tests for Windows 98 compatibility.

5. Click the Back button in your browser to return to the Compatible Products page. Confirm that Windows 98 is still selected and then select Network/RF in the Product Category list. Leave Company Name set to All and click Go.

6. Search results will show you the manufacturer and model name of any Network/RF products that passed the tests for Windows 98 compatibility.

7. Unless you want to search for more hardware or software, close your web browser.

buying the new components, she wants to check out the devices in these categories that are proven to work with Windows 98. She has decided to use the Microsoft Compatible Products website to decide which components to buy. Do the Try This! on the previous page.

■ Installing and Configuring Windows 98

Now that you understand the strengths and limitations of Windows 98, the hardware requirements, and the ideal configuration, it is time to install it and learn more about working with it, because that's really the only way you'll begin to understand it. You're not just going to walk up to a computer and immediately begin installing a new OS. Well, maybe you will once or twice, but then you'll discover that life is too short to begin such a complicated procedure without some planning, decision making, and preparation.

Preparing for Windows 98 Installation

You'll save time in the long run if you prepare the hardware, determine the method of installation, and decide on and gather the materials (disks, drivers, applications, and so on) you'll need to complete the installation.

Prepare the Hardware

To install Windows 98, you must be sure that the computer is a complete system, with at least the hardware minimums you have earlier decided to use, and that all the hardware is compatible with Windows 98. You also need to ensure that all necessary connections are in place and that the computer is plugged into a power outlet. You can prepare your hard disk ahead of time if you have the know-how, or you can allow Windows 98 to do so during installation.

Determine the Method and Type of Installation

If you are installing Windows 98 on a computer with a previous OS, you will also have to decide whether you want to perform a clean installation or an upgrade or create a dual-boot configuration. In other words, you have to decide what goals you want to achieve. In addition, you can choose **manual installation**, automated installation, or imaging as your Windows 98 installation method; in other words, you also have to decide what to do to achieve your goals.

Clean Installation   When installing a new OS on a computer with a previous OS, we prefer to perform a clean installation, which is one that begins with a completely empty hard disk. We even prefer starting from the very beginning and partitioning and reformatting the hard drive. The advantage to a clean installation is that you don't carry problems from the old OS over to the new one, but the disadvantage of a clean installation is that you have to reinstall all of your applications and reconfigure the desktop to your own preferences. This process is problematic if you have no means of backing up the data on the hard drive. If your computer is on a network, you can back up (or copy) the data files to a network server before repartitioning the hard drive. Then, after the clean installation, you can restore the data files to the computer.

Upgrade Installation   If your computer has a previous version of Windows installed, you can perform an **upgrade installation**, which means that you install the OS into the same directory as the previous OS. This has the advantage of keeping all of your personal preferences and application settings intact, but it may carry over problems from the old installation.

Dual-Boot Configuration   A dual-boot configuration lets you choose during startup between two OSs. We do not recommend that you create a dual-boot computer unless you have, at minimum, intermediate-level knowledge of PCs in general and OSs in particular. However, such a configuration is possible to create, and over the years, we have done so frequently when we needed to work in more than one OS to gain experience or to be able to simultaneously support users of more than one OS. Therefore, we will be brief on this subject.

If the previous OS is MS-DOS or Windows 3.*x*, you can create a dual-boot configuration during installation. To do this, you leave the old OS intact and install Windows 98 in a separate directory. Windows 98 Setup will automatically preserve the files needed to boot the old OS. In the case of MS-DOS or Windows 3.*x*, Windows 98 renames the system files during setup. You can then choose between the two OSs during startup. This type of dual-boot configuration will work only if drive C: uses FAT16. It is also possible to create a dual-boot configuration of Windows 98 and newer OSs, but we won't go there in this chapter!

> When creating a dual-boot configuration, it is best to install the oldest OS first.

Manual Installation   A manual installation requires your attention throughout the entire process to provide information and to respond to messages. You will perform a manual installation in the Step-by-Step 5.01 exercise. This is the method you would choose for a unique installation or if the number of computers is too few to warrant the time, effort, and expense that an automated installation requires.

After deciding to perform a manual installation, you have other choices to make:

- Will the source files (those in the Win98 directory on the Windows 98 CD) be found on the local computer or on the network? If the computer does not have a CD-ROM drive but it is connected to a network, then you'll have to boot up the computer with an operating system that has the network components installed so you can connect to a server where the source files are stored. That OS could be DOS or another version of Windows.

- If the computer does have a CD-ROM drive, will it work for the installation? That is, will the Windows 98 Setup program recognize it?

- If a CD-ROM is present and is recognized by Windows 98 Setup (which you may know only by trying), you will need the Windows 98 boot disk as well as the CD.

Automated Installation You perform an **automated installation** of Windows 98 by using scripts that someone (often a team of people) has prepared ahead of time. An automated installation can run either unattended or with very little input from a user. This method is used by organizations with large numbers of desktop computers that need identical applications and desktop configurations. This method requires training and planning.

Imaged Installation Many organizations that need large numbers of identically configured desktop computers install from images. An image is an exact duplicate of the entire hard drive contents, including the OS and all installed software. You perform this kind of installation by using imaging software, such as Symantec's Ghost (www.ghost.com), to copy the image of the hard drive onto a CD-ROM drive or a network server. From there, the image can be copied to many computers on the network. It can also be copied onto a CD, but it is usually copied to a network server and then distributed from there.

Decide on the Components and Applications to Install

You must plan ahead of time for the optional components that will be installed. These include several categories of options: Accessibility, Accessories, Communications, Desktop Themes, Internet Tools, Multilanguage Support, Microsoft Outlook and/or Outlook Express, Multimedia, Online Services, System Tools, and WebTV for Windows.

Most people don't buy a computer just to look at the OS. They buy it to accomplish some task, whether at home or at work. Therefore, more important than the components available with the OS are the applications you plan to install after the OS is installed. Therefore, if you install an OS, you should also be prepared to install the desired applications on the computer so that the person using the computer has the software tools he or she needs.

Gather the Materials Needed for Installation

The materials you need depend on the choices you made while preparing for the installation. If you are installing on a new computer without an OS, or if you simply want to perform a clean installation, you will need the Windows 98 boot disk that comes with Windows 98. With this disk, you can boot to MS-DOS with CD-ROM support and select Windows 98 Setup from a menu, as described in the following step-by-step exercise. If you do not have this diskette, you can create a similar one from a program on the Windows 98 CD. You can also create this diskette during and after installation, but that doesn't help if you need one before installation, unless you have one from a previous installation. One difference between this diskette and the Windows 98 boot disk that comes with Windows 98 is that the startup menu on the boot disk has a choice that will automatically start the Setup program from the CD-ROM drive. Because this disk does not have an option to start setup, if you use it for setup, you will have to manually start setup by entering this command at the DOS prompt: *d:***win98****setup** (where *d* is the drive letter of your CD-ROM drive). Step-by-Step 5.01 has instructions for doing this.

If you are upgrading from an earlier version of Windows, you will not need to start the computer from a diskette, because you will start the Setup program from the old OS. This is also true if you are creating a dual-boot computer, as long as the existing OS can access the CD-ROM drive or the

To learn about the components available with a Microsoft OS, check out the website for that OS. For instance, the home page of the Windows 98 website is at www.microsoft.com/windows98.

Don't let the use of two names confuse you. Windows 98 boot disks and Windows 98 startup disks are basically the same: diskettes that will boot to MS-DOS 7, the version underlying Windows 95 and Windows 98. We use these two names because that is how the disks are labeled by Microsoft.

network location where the source files are located. In addition, you need a blank diskette (if you choose to create a startup disk during installation).

You should also gather together the driver disks for the components in or attached to your computer. These include driver disks for the network adapter (especially if the adapter is newer than 1998 or so), video adapter, mouse (if non-Microsoft or non-standard), and printer. Some of these you may install during the installation process, but in general we recommend that you let Windows use generic video and mouse drivers during installation and then, after a successful installation, install the correct drivers. We also recommend that you wait to install network adapter drivers until after the installation.

Finally, you will need the installation files for the applications you plan to install after the OS is successfully installed.

 Try This!

Creating a Windows 98 Startup Disk

It is easy to create a startup disk using a computer running MS-DOS or Windows 3.*x* or higher. You'll need the Windows 98 CD and a blank, high-density 3.5-inch diskette. Try this:

1. Place the Windows 98 CD in the drive, and at a command prompt, type the following, replacing *d* with the drive letter of your CD-ROM drive. Press ENTER at the end of each line.

   ```
   d:
   cd \tools\mtsutil\fat32ebd
   fat32ebd
   ```

2. When prompted, insert a floppy disk and press Y to continue.

3. Leave the diskette in the drive and test it by restarting Windows. From the Startup menu, choose Start Computer with CD-ROM Support and press ENTER.

4. Remove the diskette and label it "Windows 98 Startup Disk."

Gather the Information Needed for Installation

The final items needed before you can install Windows 98 is information. This includes a name for your computer, a workgroup name, a password, and net configuration information.

Computer and Workgroup Names Each Windows computer on a Microsoft network must have a name. Use a unique name that contains 15 or fewer alphanumeric characters. A name is unique if no other computer, workgroup, or domain has the same name on your network. A Windows 98 computer must also belong to a workgroup on the network. This name must also contain 15 or fewer alphanumeric characters, and must also be unique on the network, although many computers may belong to this same workgroup.

Password If you've ever installed an OS from the Windows NT family, you may remember having to supply a password for the local Administrator during installation. You don't need to do that for Windows 98, because unlike those more security-conscious OSs, Windows 98 does not have a local security accounts database, and therefore does not have a local Administrator account. However, you do have to be prepared to provide a user name and password during the first logon after installation. This may be a user name and password that you only use to log on to this computer (a Windows logon), or it may be a user name and password that you use to log on to the network (a logon using the Client for Microsoft Networks). In either case, the user name and password you provide are saved in a password list file, which is given an 8.3 file name. The file name portion is the first 8 characters of the user name, and the extension is "pwl." The password should be no more than 14 characters long.

The type of logon (Windows or Network) depends on the questions you answered and how Windows 98 was configured during installation. If the logon dialog box is titled Welcome to Windows, the user name and password you must supply is used to log on to Windows locally. At this point, if you cancel that first logon dialog box, you will not be required to log on in the future, but you will not have network access.

If the logon dialog box is titled Enter Network Password, but only has the User name and Password boxes, your primary logon is to the Client for Microsoft Networks, which will give you network access in a peer-to-peer network (workgroup).

If your logon dialog box is titled Enter Network Password, but has three entry boxes, the first two as before, but with a third box labeled Domain you must provide a domain user name and password. In this case your primary logon is to the Client for Microsoft Networks, with a logon to the domain.

CD Key   Many software installation programs require that you enter a particular string of characters before the software will install. In the case of Windows 98, this key is called a CD key code and you will find it on the envelope of your Windows 98 CD.

Network Configuration Information   If your computer is on a LAN, it probably needs the TCP/IP protocol, which is the one installed by default when the Windows 98 Setup program detects a network. If the school lab computers are on a network, ask your instructor for the network configuration you will need to successfully connect your computer to the network. For TCP/IP this information may be simplified if the network has a special server, called a DHCP server, which gives out IP addresses and other IP configuration settings automatically to each computer. If there is no DHCP server on your network, you will be required to manually enter a static IP address and configuration information. You will need to obtain this information from your instructor before you begin.

> After Windows 98 is installed, you can modify the settings that control the primary logon using the Network Properties dialog box, which you can access by right-clicking Network Places and selecting Properties.

> Whenever you buy software, read the documentation to see if a key code is required. If one is needed, but it is not printed directly on the distribution CD, locate it (on the CD envelope or in the documentation) and use a permanent marker to write the code directly on the CD.

Step-by-Step 5.01

Installing Windows 98

In this step-by-step exercise, you will perform a clean installation of Windows 98, creating a new partition and formatting it during the installation process. To complete this exercise, you'll need the following:

- A Microsoft/Intel standard personal computer (desktop or laptop) with a CD-ROM drive

- A PC connected to a LAN

- An unpartitioned hard disk (disk 0, the first hard disk)

- The Windows 98 CD

- The Windows 98 Setup boot disk or a DOS or Windows 98 startup disk with CD-ROM drivers

- One 3.5-inch diskette to use to create a new Windows 98 startup disk

- The CD key code from the envelope of your Windows 98 CD

- A name for your computer

- The name of the workgroup to be used in the class lab

- A password

- An IP address and other TCP/IP settings for your computer, or confirmation from your instructor that you should configure Windows 98 to get an IP address automatically

Step 1

Insert the Windows 98 CD and the Windows 98 boot disk or startup disk, or DOS boot disk and restart the computer. When the computer restarts, the Microsoft Windows 98 Startup menu appears. Use the up and down arrow keys to move the cursor among the three choices; select Start Windows 98 Setup from CD-ROM. Copyright messages for various drivers appear on the screen while DOS loads; then the screen turns blue and displays the Welcome to Setup message. Press ENTER to begin Windows 98 Setup.

```
Microsoft Windows 98 Setup

   Welcome to Setup.

   The Setup program prepares Windows 98 to run on your
   computer.

       • To set up Windows now, press ENTER.

       • To learn more about Setup before continuing, press F1.

       • To quit Setup without installing Windows, press F3.

   Note: If you have not backed up your files recently, you
         might want to do so before installing Windows. To back
         up your files, press F3 to quit Setup now. Then, back
         up your files by using a backup program.

   To continue with Setup, press ENTER.


ENTER=Continue   F1=Help   F3=Exit   F5=Remove Color
```

Step 2

When the screen with choices for preparing your hard disk appears, select the choice to configure the unallocated disk space and then press ENTER. Another screen will appear if you have a drive over 512MB. If you see this screen, select Yes to enable large-disk support and press ENTER to have Setup continue and partition your disk.

```
Microsoft Windows 98 Setup

   You have a drive over 512MB in size. Would
   you like to enable large disk support?

   This allows more efficient use of disk space
   and larger partitions to be defined.

   ┌─────────────────────────────────────────────┐
   │ No, do not use large disk support           │
   │ Yes, enable large disk support              │
   └─────────────────────────────────────────────┘


   To accept the selection, press ENTER.
   To change the selection, press the UP or DOWN ARROW key,
   and then press ENTER.


ENTER=Continue   F1=Help   F3=Exit
```

Step 3

Follow the instructions on the next screen; then press ENTER. Your computer will reboot, and you'll see a message that Setup is formatting your newly partitioned drive C:. After a minute or two, a message states that Setup is preparing to install Windows. Setup then initializes and checks your system. When prompted, press ENTER to continue. ScanDisk will then run various tests on the disk.

```
Microsoft ScanDisk

ScanDisk is now checking the following areas of drive C:

    √    Media descriptor
    √    File allocation tables
    √    Directory structure
    »    File system
         Free space
         Surface scan



    ◄ Pause ►    ‹ More Info ›    ‹ Exit ›

    1% complete    ▒▒▒▒▒▒▒▒▒▒▒▒▒▒▒▒▒▒▒▒▒▒▒▒▒▒▒▒▒▒▒▒▒▒▒▒▒▒▒
```

Step 4

Setup prepares to start in GUI mode, and the words "Windows 98 Setup" appear over blue and black wallpaper. This will be the background for Setup until the next reboot. The first message box on this background shows the progress while files are copied. Click Continue, and Setup will prepare the Windows 98 Setup wizard.

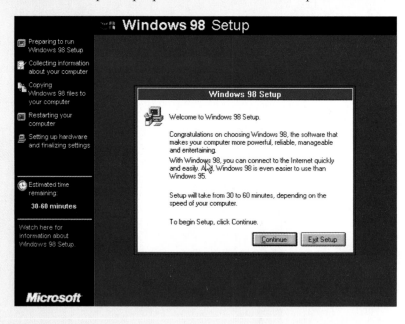

Step 5

The license agreement appears next. Select I Accept the Agreement and click Next. The Select Directory dialog box appears in the Setup wizard. Leave the default (C:\ WINDOWS) and click Next. The Preparing Directory message appears next with a single progress bar while Setup checks for installed components; then a second progress bar appears while Setup checks for available disk space. On the Setup Options page, select Typical and click Next.

Step 6

Enter your name and the name of your school or company on the User Information page. The Company field is optional. Next, the Windows Components page is your opportunity to customize the set of components Setup will install. Since you can also install any of these options after Windows 98 is installed, select Install the Most Common Components and then click Next.

Step 7

In the Identification box, provide the computer name and workgroup name you prepared at the beginning of this exercise. The Computer Description field is entirely optional. When you have completed this page, click Next.

Step 8

In the Location box, select your country or region from the list and click Next. On the Startup Disk screen, click Next. A progress bar will appear, and if you have not yet inserted the disk into the floppy drive, a message box will appear requesting the disk and giving directions for labeling it. Follow the instructions, click OK, and when prompted remove the startup disk; then click OK again and click Next.

Step 9

Click Next on the Start Copying Files screen. When the files have been copied, Setup will continue the installation, and you will see the Welcome to Microsoft Windows 98 message. In spite of the welcome, you're not quite there yet. It will take another 30 minutes, depending on the speed of your computer, and at least one more reboot before Windows 98 is completely installed. When all of the files are copied, Setup will automatically restart your computer.

Step 10

After the reboot, you'll see the Windows 98 splash screen with a message that the system is preparing to start Windows 98 for the first time. The Windows 98 Setup screen will appear again, and you'll see message boxes as it detects and sets up your hardware, both plug and play and non–plug and play. When this process is complete, Setup will restart your computer (again!).

Step 11

After the reboot, the Setting Up Hardware message may appear yet again as Setup continues to detect, configure, and initialize hardware. When this process is done, the Date/Time Properties dialog box will appear. Use the drop-down list box to select your time zone and then adjust the date and time as necessary; then click Close.

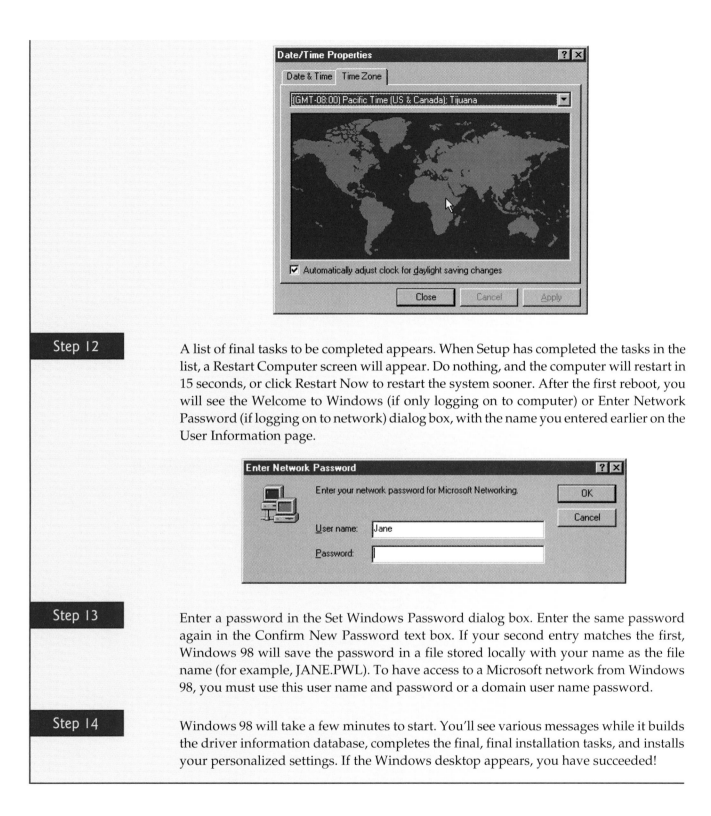

Step 12

A list of final tasks to be completed appears. When Setup has completed the tasks in the list, a Restart Computer screen will appear. Do nothing, and the computer will restart in 15 seconds, or click Restart Now to restart the system sooner. After the first reboot, you will see the Welcome to Windows (if only logging on to computer) or Enter Network Password (if logging on to network) dialog box, with the name you entered earlier on the User Information page.

Step 13

Enter a password in the Set Windows Password dialog box. Enter the same password again in the Confirm New Password text box. If your second entry matches the first, Windows 98 will save the password in a file stored locally with your name as the file name (for example, JANE.PWL). To have access to a Microsoft network from Windows 98, you must use this user name and password or a domain user name password.

Step 14

Windows 98 will take a few minutes to start. You'll see various messages while it builds the driver information database, completes the final, final installation tasks, and installs your personalized settings. If the Windows desktop appears, you have succeeded!

Performing Post-Installation Tasks

Now that you have installed Windows 98, you will want to verify that all devices are working, configure the desktop to your preferences, connect to the network (if necessary), and install the latest service packs.

Device Manager

The Device Manager tool allows you to configure and troubleshoot problems with devices. You can view and change device properties, update device drivers, configure device settings, and uninstall devices. Desktop support people have come to rely on this tool to verify a successful Windows installation by confirming that all of their hardware was recognized and is working properly.

Step-by-Step 5.02

Working with Device Manager

In this step-by-step exercise, we will use Device Manager to verify that your devices are recognized by Windows 98 and functioning normally.

To complete this step-by-step exercise, you will need a computer on which you have successfully installed Windows 98 as described in Step-by-Step 5.01.

Step 1

Right-click My Computer and select Properties. In the Properties dialog box, select the Device Manager tab. You have two options for viewing: View Devices by Type and View Devices by Connection. You will normally use the first view, because it is simpler and more understandable. If Windows 98 recognized all of your hardware, you should see a list of device types under the Computer node.

Step 2

If the OS detects a device and does not know what it is, does not have a device driver for it, or detects a problem with the device, that device type will be expanded and the device in question will have a yellow question mark next to it. If you see this on a device for which you do have a device driver from the manufacturer, you should install the device driver, following the manufacturer's instructions.

Step 3

If you are troubleshooting a problem with a non–plug and play device, you need to know the resources that are in use so you can determine whether there is a resource that your device can use. In this case, you can use Device Manager to view resource use. Do this now: select Computer in the device list, click the Properties button, and look at all four types of resources.

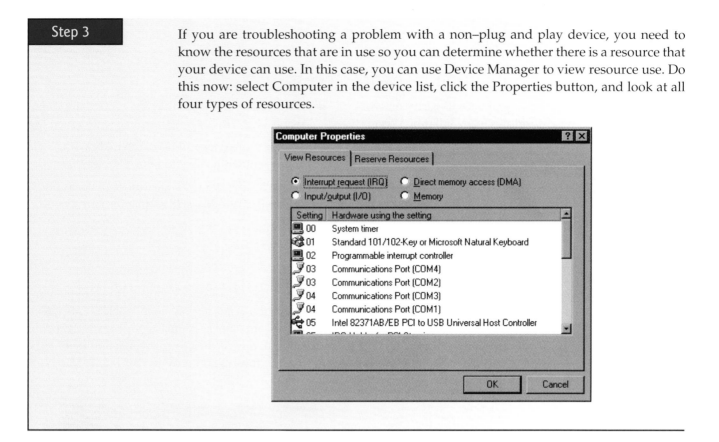

Configuring Network Access

Another common task after installing an OS is verification of connection to a LAN. If the computer was connected during installation, the network drivers should have been installed, but this is one part of the installation that can easily go awry with Windows 98. It is not uncommon to wait until after the installation of base components to install a network card driver or to configure the network protocol.

If the network card driver was successfully installed during setup, you still may not be connected to the network if you are not using the correct network protocol. That usually involves a choice among the protocols supported by Windows 98: NetBEUI, TCP/IP, and NWlink (Novell's IPX/SPX in Microsoft clothing). If your network is using NetBEUI, you just install the protocol and you are done—no configuration needed. If your network is using NWLink or IPX/SPX, you install the Microsoft NWLink protocol and then, in most cases, you are finished.

However, the majority of networks today use TCP/IP, so we will assume that is the protocol you need. That is also the most complicated protocol to work with, but we will do only the absolute basics here. In the following step-by-step exercise, you will verify network connectivity, assuming a TCP/IP network. If you discover a problem with network configuration, you will have to correct that problem. In the class lab, your instructor can guide you through these corrective measures. In the step-by-step exercise, you will open the dialog boxes you would have to use to correct network configuration problems.

Verifying and Configuring Network Access

In this step-by-step exercise, you will verify network access of your new Windows 98 installation. You will also explore a few of the most common scenarios you may encounter.

To complete this step-by-step exercise, you will need the following:

■ A computer on which you have successfully installed Windows 98 as described in Step-by-Step 5.01

■ Connection to a LAN that has other computers using TCP/IP

■ One or more computers on the LAN with shared folders visible to all LAN users

■ The Windows 98 CD or an alternate location where the Windows 98 source files are stored

Step 1

Use Network Neighborhood as a very casual test of network connectivity. Double-click the Network Neighborhood icon now. You should see a globe icon labeled Entire Network and a list of all computers that are in the same workgroup as your computer. In our example, all the computers in the workgroup named Workgroup are listed. But wait; the Windows 98 computer we are using, Cholla, doesn't show up in this list. Why? We'll look at the reason for this next.

Step 2

The only computers that are seen in Network Neighborhood are servers. A service called File and Print Sharing will make a Windows 98 computer act like a server. In our example, the other computers have this service turned on, but Cholla does not. Do not turn on the File and Print Sharing service unless you intend to create folder shares on your computer for others on your network to access. The computer named Charleslee has an optional descriptive comment, "Chuck's New Machine."

Step 3

Right-click a computer in Network Neighborhood and select Properties. You can see the same identifying information shown in Network Neighborhood, plus the workgroup to which the computer belongs and the OS it is running. However, this last item is not entirely accurate because all Windows NT, Windows 2000, and Windows XP computers are identified here as being Microsoft Windows NT. In our example, the computer Charleslee is actually running Windows XP.

Step 4

Sometimes you are not permitted to view the Properties dialog box of a computer in Network Neighborhood. Don't be surprised if this happens, especially if you are trying to see the properties of a server to which you do not have permissions. If it does happen, just close the box and move on.

Step 5

Now check out your network configuration. Close Network Neighborhood; then right-click the Network Neighborhood desktop icon and select Properties. The list of network components should include Client for Microsoft Networks, a network adapter (usually an Ethernet adapter), and TCP/IP for the network adapter. If a modem was detected, you will also see Dial-Up Adapter and a network protocol for the dial-up adapter. Furthermore, the Primary Network Logon field controls which logon dialog box is used (Welcome to Windows or Enter Network Password).

Network `? X`

Configuration | Identification | Access Control

The following network components are installed:

- Client for Microsoft Networks
- AMD PCNET Family Ethernet Adapter (PCI-ISA)
- Dial-Up Adapter
- TCP/IP -> AMD PCNET Family Ethernet Adapter (PCI-ISA)
- TCP/IP -> Dial-Up Adapter

[Add...] [Remove] [Properties]

Primary Network Logon:

[Windows Logon ▾]

[File and Print Sharing...]

Description

[OK] [Cancel]

Step 6

If the network adapter or the protocol is missing, you can add them by clicking the Add button in the Network Properties dialog box, selecting the component type in the Select Network Component Type box, and clicking Add. If the resulting Select Network Adapters dialog box does not contain your network adapter and you have the driver disk that came with the adapter, insert it and click the Have Disk button and provide the path to the driver files (for example, D:\drivers).

Select Network adapters `X`

Click the Network adapter that matches your hardware, and then click OK. If you have an installation disk for this device, click Have Disk.

Manufacturers:
- (detected net drivers)
- (Infrared COM port or do
- 3Com
- Accton
- Adaptec

Network Adapters:
- Existing Ndis2 Driver
- Existing ODI Driver

[Have Disk...]

[OK] [Cancel]

Step 7

When you're finished with the adapter installation (if, indeed, you had to install an adapter at this point), return to the Network Properties dialog box.

Step 8

Select TCP/IP *adapter* (where *adapter* is the name of your network adapter) and click Properties. In most organizations, the desktop computers obtain an IP address automatically from a special server on the network. If this is how you were instructed to configure your computer, it should look like the example shown here.

TCP/IP Properties

Bindings | Advanced | NetBIOS

DNS Configuration | Gateway | WINS Configuration | IP Address

An IP address can be automatically assigned to this computer. If your network does not automatically assign IP addresses, ask your network administrator for an address, and then type it in the space below.

◉ Obtain an IP address automatically

○ Specify an IP address:

IP Address:

Subnet Mask:

OK | Cancel

Step 9

If your instructor gave you a bunch of numbers to enter for your IP address and other settings, you should see those numbers in this dialog box. If you were not able to see other computers on your network, verify that these settings match those you were given and make any necessary corrections.

Step 10

If your computer is configured to obtain an address automatically, but you cannot see any computers on the network (assuming that there are computers to see), you can verify that your computer did obtain an address by using a program that looks at your TCP/IP configuration. To do this, choose Start | Run and type **winipcfg** in the Run box. This will open a small GUI program.

IP Configuration

Ethernet Adapter Information

AMD PCNET Family Ethernet Ada

Adapter Address	00-50-56-40-35-6D
IP Address	10.0.0.13
Subnet Mask	255.255.255.0
Default Gateway	10.0.0.1

OK | Release | Renew

Release All | Renew All | More Info >>

Step 11

If the adapter shown in the box is not your LAN adapter, use the spin arrow to select the adapter. If the IP address and subnet mask show zeros (0.0.0.0), or if the IP address begins with 169.254 (for example, 169.254.182.66) and has a subnet mask of 255.255.0.0, then your computer did not get a response from the server that should have given it an IP address, and, if this is the case, you should notify your instructor.

Step 12

If you and your instructor are satisfied that your computer is working as expected on the network, you can close the IP Configuration dialog box and any others that were opened for this step-by-step exercise. If you have made any changes to your network configuration, you will have to restart Windows to make the changes take effect.

Adding Updates and Service Packs

A Windows operating system is a very complex life form—well, maybe it's not a life form, but people talk to Windows all the time! Like anything so complex, flaws are discovered and solutions found for these flaws. Sometimes the solutions are needed to correct incompatibility with drivers for a class of hardware. Sometimes there are problems with Windows' interaction with an application program. Or maybe hackers have discovered a new way to defeat Windows security. These and many other scenarios cause the Microsoft programmers to work to solve the problems.

> Applications are also updated. Therefore, after installing an application, check out the appropriate website to see if updates need to be applied. There is a link to Microsoft Office Product Updates at the Microsoft Windows Update site.

The software solutions to these problems are called, collectively, updates. Those that solve security problems or problems that can potentially cause major failures are now called **critical updates**. These are made available as programs called patches that solve a single, or more than one closely related problem. A group of patches may be bundled together into one large (several megabyte) installation package and called a service pack.

These updates are available at the Microsoft website, but if you do not have an Internet connection, you can order updates on a CD for a nominal fee. If you do not have an Internet connection, your instructor may provide the updates needed for the next step-by-step exercise on a CD or on a server on the network.

Step-by-Step 5.04

Installing Updates and Service Packs

In this step-by-step exercise, you will connect to the Microsoft website and download and install the latest service pack for Windows 98. Alternatively, if you do not have Internet access or if your Internet access is slow, your instructor may provide the service pack on a CD or on a network server. Service packs and other update files are usually huge—often in the tens of millions of bytes!

To complete this step-by-step exercise, you will need the following:

- A computer on which you have successfully installed Windows 98 as described in Step-by-Step 5.01

- An Internet connection or the service pack on a CD or on a LAN server

Step 1

Choose Start | Windows Update. This should open your Internet browser and connect you to `windowsupdate.microsoft.com`. (If the Windows Update shortcut is not on your Start menu, use your web browser to connect to `windowsupdate.microsoft.com`.) Click Product Updates. If you see a security warning about running Windows Update Control, click Yes (As Long as It Is a Signed File Guaranteed by Microsoft) to allow Update to examine your computer and determine what updates you need. After a short wait, you will see a list of recommended updates.

Step 2

If one or more updates or service packs is checked, download and install just the checked items at first. Look for a Download button on the page and click it. Then follow the instructions on the screen to download. You will have to read and accept a license agreement before the download. At the end of the download, the updates normally will go right into the installation.

Step 3

When prompted to restart your computer, click Yes. After the restart, you will see a Windows 98 Setup message telling you that system settings are being updated. You may also see one or more Windows update messages as some components are updated. Once the desktop is ready, use Start | Windows Update or your browser to return to the Microsoft website to select more updates.

If you see an update for a component that is not installed or that you don't ever use, you can skip it. You may see a warning when you select an update or service pack that must be installed without other updates. At this writing, this is true of the Internet Explorer Service Pack.

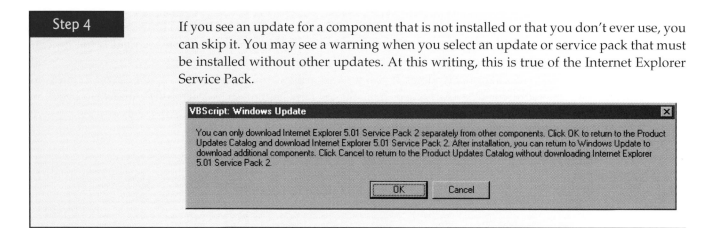

VBScript: Windows Update

You can only download Internet Explorer 5.01 Service Pack 2 separately from other components. Click OK to return to the Product Updates Catalog and download Internet Explorer 5.01 Service Pack 2. After installation, you can return to Windows Update to download additional components. Click Cancel to return to the Product Updates Catalog without downloading Internet Explorer 5.01 Service Pack 2.

OK   Cancel

■ Customizing and Managing Windows 98

After you have verified the success of your OS installation, ensured that the computer is communicating on the network (if necessary), and installed necessary updates, it's time to add the finishing touches that will make the computer the tool you or someone else can use. And there must certainly be applications that need to be installed. In this section, you will install an application using the installation program created for that application. Then you will use the Add/Remove Programs Control Panel applet to add and remove Windows components.

Application Installation Methods

When you install an application in Windows 98 you have two general choices for the method of installation. You can simply run the installation program for the application directly or you can run the installation program from the Add/Remove Programs Control Panel applet. Add/Remove Programs is a Control Panel applet that allows you to install and uninstall applications, add and remove Windows components, and create a startup disk.

Installing Applications from Add/Remove Programs

The Windows 98 Add/Remove Programs Control Panel applet has a page that you can use for installing an application. Our recommendation is that you use this only if you are installing a DOS application or a 16-bit Windows application (written for Windows 3.x). In those cases, running the DOS or 16-bit Windows application from the Install/Uninstall page of the Add/Remove Programs dialog box will ensure that Windows 98 is aware of the installation and can make changes to its configuration information that these older installation programs would not know to do. In that case, you first find out the name and location of the installation program, then you would select the Install button from the Install/Uninstall page, and follow the instructions to enter the path and name of the command needed to run the installation program.

Installing Applications Directly

A program written to run in 32-bit Windows will come with its own installation program. This program will know the "rules" for passing on its configuration requirements to Windows, and you may run this program by starting it without the help and supervision of Add/Remove Programs. In the following step-by-step you will do just that when you install an application using the installation program from the application.

Step-by-Step 5.05

Installing an Application in Windows 98

If you have a standard Office application, such as Microsoft Word, you may substitute that, but you will have to consult the documentation for the exact procedure for installation. In the following steps, we use an application you should have available to you: the Windows 98 Resource Kit Tools Sampler, which can be found on the Windows 98 CD. After installing this application, you will verify that it is installed and that you can open the application.

To complete this step-by-step exercise, you will need the following:

- A computer on which you have successfully installed Windows 98 as described in Step-by-Step 5.01
- The Windows 98 CD or a copy of the \tools\ reskit folder from the CD

Step 1

Insert your Windows 98 CD in the drive. If the Windows 98 CD-ROM window opens, select Browse this CD; otherwise, open Windows Explorer and expand the CD-ROM drive. In either case, expand \tools\reskit. In the reskit folder, double-click (or click, depending on your settings) the Setup.exe program. (If you cannot see the file extensions, the Setup program is the file with the computer icon.)

Step 2

When the software license agreement appears, read it and click Accept. Read the next message and take a minute to close all other open applications. Then click Continue.

Microsoft Windows 98 Resource Kit Tools Sampler Setup

Welcome to the Microsoft Windows 98 Resource Kit Tools Sampler installation program.

Setup cannot install system files or update shared files if the files are in use. Before continuing, close any open applications.

WARNING: This program is protected by copyright law and international treaties.

You may install Microsoft Windows 98 Resource Kit Tools Sampler on a single computer. Some Microsoft products are provided with additional rights, which are stated in the End User License Agreement included with your software.

Please take a moment to read the End User License Agreement now. It contains all of the terms and conditions that pertain to this software product. By choosing to continue, you indicate acceptance of these terms.

[Continue]   [Exit Setup]

Step 3

Enter your name and organization information on the next screen and click OK. A confirmation screen will appear. Verify that your name and organization are correct and then click OK. The next screen displays the destination folder where the tools will be installed. If you want to change this location, use the Change Folder button. Otherwise, click OK.

Step 4

The next screen prompts you to start the installation (finally!). Click the large button to the left of the word Install. Then click OK in the small dialog box announcing that the installation was successful.

Step 5

Confirm that the Windows 98 Resource Kit Tools Sampler has been installed. Choose Start | Programs | Windows 98 Resource Kit. Then select each of the shortcuts on the Windows 98 Resource Kit menu to verify that the Resource Kit Tools Sampler was installed correctly.

Uninstalling Applications

After the installation, you will see programs listed in the Add/Remove Programs dialog box. They also usually come with their own uninstall program, and create a menu shortcut to uninstall when they are installed. For those applications that do not have an uninstall program, you should use the Add/Remove Programs dialog box when you wish to remove them. You simply select the applications from the list, and click the Add/Remove button.

Adding/Removing Windows Components with Add/Remove Programs

Certain programs that come with Windows 98 are considered to be optional components. During installation you can choose which components to install, and after installation you can use the Windows Setup tab of the Add/Remove Programs applet to add or remove components.

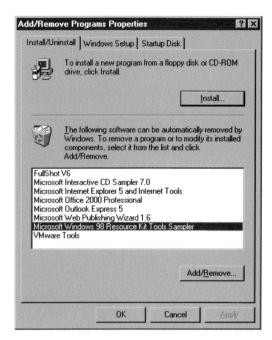

Step-by-Step 5.06

Using Add/Remove Programs

In this step-by-step exercise, you will use the Control Panel applet, Add/Remove Programs, to see the listing of optional Windows components. Then you will install and uninstall Windows components.

   To complete this step-by-step exercise, you will need the following:

- A computer on which you have successfully installed Windows 98 as described in Step-by-Step 5.01

- The Windows 98 CD

Step 1

Choose Start | Settings | Control Panel | Add/Remove Programs. Select the Windows Setup tab. After the list of installed components appears, do not click the check boxes because clearing or checking a box will uninstall or install an entire component category. A category with a check in a gray box has some components installed, a category with a check in a white box has all components installed, and a category with a cleared check box has no components installed.

Step 2

Click the *name* of each of the component categories and notice that when you click a category with multiple components,

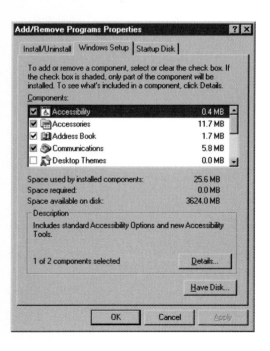

the Details button (bottom right) becomes enabled and the Description box shows the number of components.

Step 3

Now install the mouse pointers and uninstall the Paint program. Click the Accessories Components category name and then click the Details button. Click to place a check in the box by Mouse Pointers. Click to remove the check in the box by Paint (this will cause Paint to be removed). Then click OK. If you removed the Windows 98 CD, you will be asked to reinsert it. When the installation is complete, close Add/Remove Programs but leave Control Panel open.

Accessories

To add a component, select the check box, or click to clear it if you don't want the component. A shaded box means that only part of the component will be installed. To see what's included in a component, click Details.

Components:

☑	📄 Document Templates	0.4 MB
☐	🎮 Games	0.0 MB
☑	🖼 Imaging	4.9 MB
☑	🖱 Mouse Pointers	1.4 MB
☐	🎨 Paint	0.0 MB

Space used by installed components: 26.2 MB
Space freed up: 1.1 MB
Space available on disk: 3620.0 MB

Description
Draws, modifies, or displays pictures.

Details...

OK   Cancel

Step 4

Verify that mouse pointers were installed by opening the Mouse icon in Control Panel. Click the Pointers tab and click the arrow button in the Scheme list box. The default schemes include only Animated Hourglasses and Windows Standard. You now have more schemes.

Step 5

Verify that the Paint shortcut is no longer on the Start | Programs | Accessories menu. Once you have verified that this change worked, if you would like to add the Paint program back, simply return to Add/Remove Programs and place a check in the box by Paint.

■ Managing Users, Files, and Printers

What if two or more people need to share a Windows 98 computer, and they want to keep their files and preferences separate? Are there special issues to be aware of when working with files on a Windows 98 computer? How do you add a printer to Windows 98? In this section, you will learn the answers to these questions, which involve managing users in Windows 98 through user profiles, working with long file names, and installing printers.

Adding a New User

Sometimes a computer is used by more than one person at different times. Perhaps it's a home computer shared by several family members, or maybe it's a computer in an office used by two people working different hours. If you create a new user in Windows 98, you can take advantage of something called **user profiles**. A user profile is a set of folders and desktop settings that are unique for each user.

If your Windows 98 computer is not a member of a Windows domain and is a stand-alone or workgroup computer, then users are managed locally. That's true for Laura and Rebecca, employees of a small import/export company. They share the same Windows 98 computer and desk. This

In the following step-by-step exercise, you will use the F5 key to refresh an open window after making a change that adds or removes one or more objects in an open window. Until you refresh the screen, the object may not appear at all or may appear out of the normal order. Remember to refresh (also an option on the View menu) whenever a window or folder does not look up-to-date.

isn't a big problem, because Laura works days and Rebecca works nights. However, they have different work habits and different ideas of how a computer desktop should be organized, so they need separate user profiles. When Windows 98 was installed, Laura was the only user of the computer and hers was the only profile. Now Rebecca needs a profile added.

Although unlike Windows NT, Windows 2000, and Windows XP, Windows 98 does not truly have a security accounts database, it does allow you to create individual profiles for multiple users of a computer. If you set up this function, as described in the following step-by-step exercise, you can configure the computer for use by more than one user (not simultaneously, of course), and each user will have his or her own personal profile, which includes desktop settings and folders.

> ⚠ All local users will be able to access any file or folder on the local hard drive because Windows 98 and the FAT file systems do not support file- and folder-level security. To avoid conflict, each user should open his or her My Documents folder from the shortcut on the desktop.

Step-by-Step 5.07

Adding a User and Customizing the Desktop

In the following steps, you will add a user profile for a second user on your lab computer to practice the steps necessary to configure the Laura/Rebecca computer. Then you will log on as the new user and customize the desktop for the new user, including installing Desktop Themes from the Windows 98 CD.

To complete this step-by-step exercise, you will need the following:

- A computer on which you have successfully installed Windows 98 as described in Step-by-Step 5.01
- The Windows 98 CD

Step 1

Choose Start | Settings | Control Panel | Users. If the Enable Multi-User Settings box appears, click Next to open the User Settings box. In the User Settings box, click New User. After the Add User wizard starts, click Next. On the next page, enter **Rebecca** in the User Name box and then click Next.

Step 2

Enter a password in each of the Enter New Password boxes (be sure to remember the password!). Then click Next. On the Personalized Items Settings screen, place a check in all five check boxes, click the radio button by Create New Items to Save Disk Space, and click Next. Click Finish on the Ready to Finish screen. Click Close to close the User Settings box.

Log off by choosing Start | Log Off. Click Yes in the Log Off Windows dialog box. The Welcome to Windows or Logon Information dialog box will appear with fields for a user name and password. Enter the user name and password of the new user profile you created and then log on.

While logged on as the new user, use the Desktop applet to modify the desktop so that it looks radically different from the default desktop with which you started as a new user. Then log off and log back on with your old user name. Notice that the desktop settings are preserved for each user. You each also have separate folders for your own use, but you will still be able to access each other's documents—a potential problem when users share a Windows 98 computer!

Each user has a set of profile folders. Use Windows Explorer to look at the profiles stored on your computer. If you installed Windows 98 in C:\Windows, the profile folders are stored in C:\Windows\Profiles. Each user profile is contained in a set of folders bearing the user's name. When you are finished, close Windows Explorer but stay logged on as the new user. Log off and log on again as the new user.

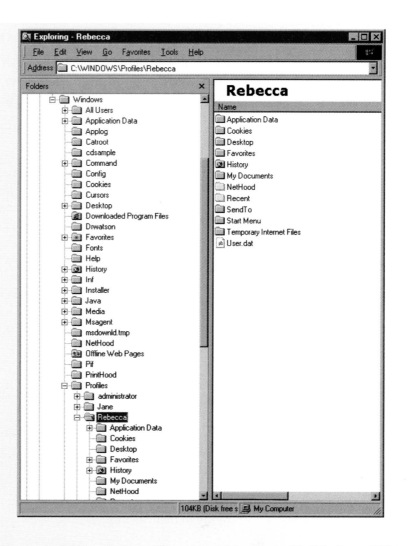

Step 6

Your new user would like Desktop Themes, which come with Windows 98 but are not installed during a Typical installation. To install Desktop Themes, open Control Panel | Add/Remove Programs and select Windows Setup. In the Components list, click the check box by Desktop Themes and then click OK. Insert the Windows 98 CD and click OK. It may take a few minutes for the files to be copied, and then the Add/Remove Programs box will close automatically.

Step 7

You should now have a new Control Panel applet for Desktop Themes. If this does not appear in Control Panel, press F5 to refresh, and it will appear. Double-click the Desktop Themes icon. In the Desktop Themes applet, open the Theme drop-down box and notice that the themes require a minimum of 256 colors and some require high color. Check out your computer's color density on the Settings tab of the Display applet, then select a theme with the correct color density and click OK.

Working with Long File Names in Windows 98

Earlier in this chapter, you learned that Windows 98 includes LFN support for file names up to 255 characters long. Now you will look at how LFNs are stored in a FAT directory and how Windows 98 creates an 8.3 alias for a file with an LFN.

Storing the LFN in a FAT Directory

Each file or folder on a drive must have a directory entry. On a FAT volume, each directory entry is only 32 bytes long—but the file name isn't the only information that has to fit into a directory entry. The size, date, time, file attributes, and beginning cluster information are also stored in those 32 bytes.

Here is how the programmers managed this trick: If you save a file with a standard 8.3 file name, the OS writes the file name and other information as a standard directory entry, just as MS-DOS or Windows 3.x would. But if you save a file with a long file name, where is the OS going to store it in a directory entry that is only 32 bytes long? The answer is that the OS uses multiple directory entries: a primary one to store the standard directory information and additional (secondary) directory entries to store the long file name. Each file has only one **primary directory entry** in which Windows 98 stores an 8.3 version (alias) of the long file name, but the file may have as many **secondary directory entries** as necessary to store the entire LFN, because each secondary directory entry can store only 13 characters of the LFN, in spite of having 32 bytes to work with. Figure 5-2 shows a directory listing of the root of C: in which you can see two 8.3 aliases: MYDOCU~1 and PROGRA~1. The first is the **8.3 alias** of the long file name My Documents, and the second is the 8.3 alias of the long file name Program Files. Both of these happen to be folders, but the same naming rules and methods apply to them as to files.

Windows 98 is not case sensitive when creating file names—you can enter a file name in upper-, lower-, or mixed case, but the OS will convert all alphabetic characters to uppercase in the 8.3 alias while using the exact case you entered in the stored LFN.

Windows 95 and Windows 98 both use this method for creating the 8.3 alias. Windows NT, Windows 2000, and Windows XP use a similar method.

```
Volume in drive C has no label
Volume Serial Number is 1A59-1E06
Directory of C:\

WINDOWS         <DIR>           04-24-02  11:35p
MYDOCU~1        <DIR>           04-27-02  11:37a
PROGRA~1        <DIR>           04-24-02  11:35p
RECYCLED        <DIR>           06-11-02   7:43a
CAPTURES        <DIR>           06-03-02   7:42p
DATA            <DIR>           07-13-02   5:23p
BOOTLOG   TXT        51,478     04-27-02  11:38a
COMMAND   COM        93,890     04-23-99  10:22p
SUHDLOG   DAT         5,166     04-25-02   7:43a
DETLOG    TXT        71,227     04-25-02   8:02a
MSDOS     ---             22     04-24-02  11:31p
SETUPLOG  TXT       118,215     04-26-02   9:31a
NETLOG    TXT         9,971     04-26-02   9:31a
MSDOS     SYS         1,676     04-25-02   8:08a
ASD       LOG           182     04-29-02   9:53p
BOOTLOG   PRV        42,877     04-26-02   9:33a
CONFIG    SYS             0     04-26-02   9:32a
AUTOEXEC  BAT             0     04-26-02   9:32a
SCANDISK  LOG         6,460     08-03-02   5:17p
Press any key to continue . . .
```

● **Figure 5-2.**   8.3 file name for My Documents

Creating the 8.3 Alias

Windows 98 converts long file names to 8.3 file names by first removing all illegal characters (per the 8.3 naming convention discussed in Chapter 2). Then it uses the first six remaining characters and adds a tilde (~) and then a number. If this is the first file in the same directory with these first seven characters, the number will be 1. If a matching file ending with 1 already exists, then it will use 2, and so on until it reaches 99. After that, it uses the first four legal characters, adds a tilde, and than a number, beginning with 100. In addition to using the DOS Prompt, you can view both the LFN and the 8.3 alias with Windows Explorer when you open the Properties dialog box for the file, as shown in Figure 5-3.

Installing Printer Drivers

Installing a new printer in Windows 98 is fairly simple. If it is a plug and play printer, it may be recognized automatically, and if Windows 98 has the correct driver files, it will be installed automatically, if the driver files are available. You may be prompted for the CD even if your computer does have the driver for a device but needs to add support files to go with the manufacturer's driver files you provided.

Always read the manufacturer's installation instructions before connecting a new printer or installing device drivers. They may require you to run the manufacturer's installation program rather than use the Printer applet. In the following step-by-step, you will install the drivers for a printer. You do not need to have a printer physically connected to complete it; you can just pretend that you have a printer connected!

My long file.txt Properties

General

My long file.txt

Type:	Text Document
Location:	C:\My Documents
Size:	0 bytes (0 bytes), 0 bytes used

MS-DOS name:	MYLONG~1.TXT
Created:	Wednesday, August 07, 2002 4:09:10 PM
Modified:	Wednesday, August 07, 2002 4:09:12 PM
Accessed:	Wednesday, August 07, 2002

Attributes: ☐ Read-only   ☐ Hidden
           ☑ Archive   ☐ System

[OK] [Cancel] [Apply]

● **Figure 5-3.** File Properties dialog box

You often need the Windows 98 CD to add components and drivers to Windows 98. Therefore, if you have sufficient disk space, you should copy the contents of the Win98 folder from the Windows 98 CD to a folder on your hard drive.

Try This!

Find a Windows 98 8.3 Alias

If you have a computer running Windows 98, you can create files with LFNs and view the resulting 8.3 alias. Try this:

1. Using Windows Explorer, expand the My Documents folder.

2. Right-click in the contents pane and choose New | Text Document. Name the text document **My long file.txt**.

3. Right-click My long file.txt and select Properties.

4. At the top of the General tab, you can see the long file name, My long file.txt. Further down, you should see the 8.3 alias identified as the MS-DOS name, MYLONG~1.TXT.

Installing a Printer Driver

In this step-by-step exercise, you install a printer driver in Windows 98.

To complete this step-by-step exercise, you will need the following:

- A computer on which you have successfully installed Windows 98 as described in Step-by-Step 5.01
- The Windows 98 CD

Step 1

Choose Start | Setting | Printers and click the Add Printer icon, which starts the Add Printer wizard. Click Next to begin the installation. In the dialog box that asks "How is this printer attached to your computer?" select Local Printer and click Next.

Step 2

There may be a delay while Windows loads the driver information database; then the manufacturer and model page appears. Select HP in the Manufacturers list and HP LaserJet 5Si in the Printers list; then click Next.

Step 3

Select Lpt1 as the port to which the printer is connected and click Next. On the Printer Name page, you can give the printer a name that makes sense to the people using the printer: for instance, "Front Desk" or "Back Office." Replace the printer model name with a more user-friendly name and click Next.

Step 4

In the last dialog box, you can choose to print a test page. This is something you will want to do if you are installing a driver for an actual printer attached to your computer. If you do not have the printer that goes with the driver you just installed, click Finish. If the Windows 98 CD is not in the drive, you will be prompted to insert it; insert the CD and click OK.

Step 5

If you chose to print a printer test page in the preceding step, it will print after the files are copied and the driver is installed. In this case, a dialog box will appear with the name of the printer and ask whether the page printed correctly. Click Yes (if it actually did print correctly) to close this box.

Step 6

Open the Printers folder to verify that an icon for the new printer appears in the Printers folder.

Troubleshooting Common Windows 98 Problems

Troubleshooting is sometimes more art than science. In fact, even if you are new to working with computers, you can solve many problems by carefully observing and recording what you see. Sometimes the problems and solution are obvious—like when you notice that the power cord isn't plugged in. Other times, they aren't so obvious—like when an error message appears on your screen. In this section, we will take a simple approach to troubleshooting the most common Windows 98 problems. First we will list resources you can check when you are looking for a solution; then we will go through some common problems and approaches to solving them.

Resources for Troubleshooting

The resources for troubleshooting Windows 98 problems include components that come with Windows 98, such as Windows Help, Device Manager, and the Registry Editor. Other tools come with the Windows 98 Resource Kit, which can be purchased as a separate product.

Windows Help

Windows 98 has a pretty good help program that includes help topics to get you started using the desktop, connecting to the Internet, using Windows components, configuring hardware and software, and more. It also has troubleshooters that will walk you through many categories of troubleshooting tasks. You can browse for a topic related to your problem on the Contents or Index tab of the help program or use the Search tab to search the contents. Select Troubleshooting on the Contents tab to see an entire list of the Windows 98 troubleshooters listed by topics. Open the one related to your problem, and it may either open a troubleshooter or give you a list of troubleshooter titles if there is more than one related to the topic. Once you find a title that seems to match your problem, click Display and follow the instructions in the troubleshooter.

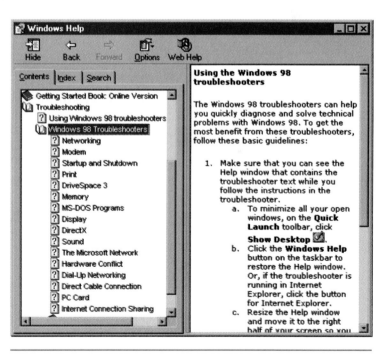

• Windows 98 Help troubleshooters

Device Manager

Device Manager is an important troubleshooting and problem-solving tool. You used it in Step-by-Step 5.02 to verify that there were no hardware detection or configuration problems immediately after installing Windows 98. If your computer or some of its components are not plug and play, you may need to resolve resource conflicts using Device Manager. On a plug and play computer with all plug and play devices, you should never have to bother with resources, because the plug and play BIOS and Windows 98 Configuration Manager work to resolve potential conflicts.

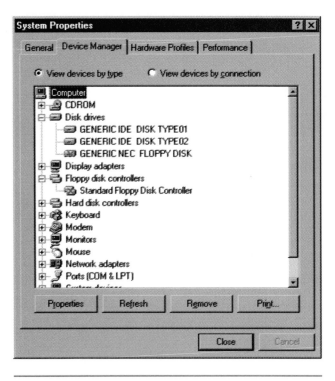

Device Manager also allows you to remove device drivers for physical devices you are removing from a computer. You can also update device drivers through Device Manager. You also may want to disable a device that will remain present when you are troubleshooting a problem. In Figure 5-4, the floppy disk controller and the floppy disk drive are both disabled. If the problem persists when the device is disabled, then the device is not causing the problem, unless just having the device connected to the computer, with or without a device driver, causes problems.

The Registry Editor

The registry is a central place where Windows 98 configuration settings are stored. When you are troubleshooting, you will run into situations in which it is suggested that you edit the Windows NT registry. These suggestions include settings for drivers, applications, user preferences, and the OS in general. When you run Windows 98 Setup, a Control Panel applet, or the Setup program for an application or driver, the program saves its configuration settings in the registry, unless they are older programs, which save their settings in the Windows 3.x configuration files (the ones with an .ini extension). The registry is actually stored in files on disk, but you can view and edit the registry as a hierarchical structure using registry editing tools, such as REGEDIT, which come with Windows 98. The best way to make configuration changes to Windows 98 after it is installed is through the Control Panel applets.

● **Figure 5-4.**   Disabled devices

Editing the registry is a very advanced task that should be done only as a last resort. An incorrect value can make your system unusable.

● Registry Editor

Windows 98 Fails During Startup

Failure during startup indicates a problem with a component required by the OS during startup. A driver file may be missing or corrupt, or you may have the wrong driver. Or perhaps a registry setting intended to configure a device is incorrect. Or a registry file may be corrupt. Failure to start can also be caused by a virus.

Then again, you shouldn't rule out a hardware failure or a conflict between hardware devices. We certainly can't cover all of the possibilities in this chapter, but what we can do is look at a handy feature of Windows 98 that allows you to troubleshoot and pinpoint many of the causes of startup failure in Windows 98. This feature is called **safe mode**.

Try This!

Disable and Enable Devices in Device Manager

Use Windows 98 Help to guide you through disabling and enabling a device in Windows 98. Try this:

1. Open the Windows Help program and click the Index tab.

2. Type the keywords **Device Manager**.

3. Click the Device Manager topic Disabling Devices and then click the Display button.

4. Following the instructions for disabling a device, disable your floppy disk controller. This will also disable your floppy disk drive.

5. View the disabled devices in Device Manager.

6. Place a diskette in the floppy drive and attempt to view it in Windows Explorer.

7. Enable the floppy disk controller and verify that both the controller and the floppy disk drive are enabled by attempting to read the floppy disk again.

Using Safe Mode to Correct Problems

In safe mode, Windows 98 starts without using all of the drivers and components that would normally be loaded. It loads only very basic, nonvendor-specific drivers for the mouse, VGA adapter, keyboard, hard drives, and OS services. If Windows 98 detects a serious problem at startup, it may start in safe mode automatically. You can also initiate safe mode by pressing F8 or the CTRL key while Windows 98 is starting. Then you select Safe Mode from the Startup menu.

Once Windows 98 is in safe mode, you can work to locate and correct the source of the problem using the Control Panel objects, usually Network or System.

Here's just one scenario in which you might use safe mode. Perhaps you just installed a new internal modem, installed the manufacturer's device driver, and restarted your system. At restart, the system fails and is unusable. Restarting the computer in safe mode allows you to disable the device and remove the bad driver or replace it with one that works. You still might have to remove the physical device itself, but give safe mode a try first.

Timing is important. You must wait to press a key until after the BIOS POST test of your keyboard to avoid getting an error message.

Starting in Safe Mode

It's a good idea to practice starting in safe mode and looking at the tools you would use for troubleshooting in safe mode.

To complete this step-by-step exercise, you will need a computer on which you have successfully installed Windows 98 as described in Step-by-Step 5.01.

Step 1

Choose Start | Shutdown | Restart. After Windows shuts down, watch for the black text screen with BIOS startup information. Then press the F8 or CTRL key. When the Windows 98 Startup menu appears, move the cursor to select Safe Mode and then press ENTER.

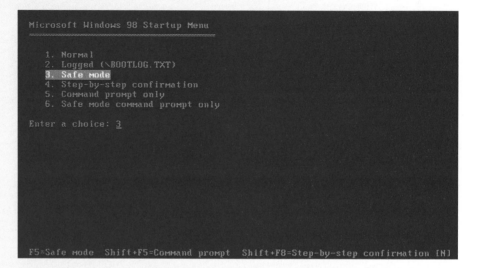

Step 2

Once you have selected Safe Mode from the menu, a dialog box appears that explains safe mode. Click OK to close this box and access the desktop, which displays "Safe Mode" at the four corners as a reminder (as if the poor screen resolution wouldn't remind you). Now you can go into Control Panel and work to solve your problem.

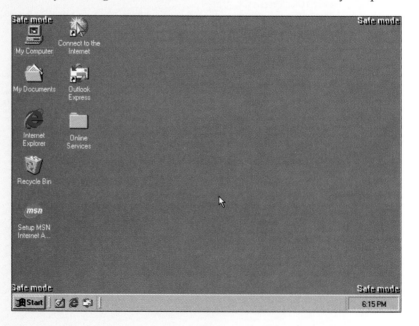

Step 3

Right-click My Computer and select Properties. In the System Properties dialog box, select Device Manager. Notice the radio buttons to change the view are disabled (dimmed). However, you can still browse through all of the devices and look at their properties.

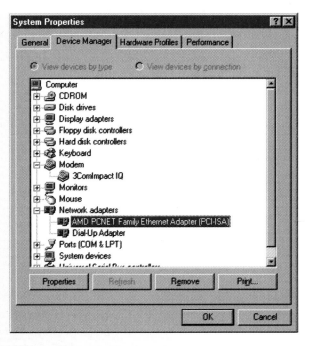

Step 4

Expand a device type node (Modem or Network Adapters, for instance) and open the properties of a device. Look at each page of the Properties dialog box and notice the settings that you can change. If you are not sure which device is causing a problem, you can experiment by disabling suspect device drivers one at a time. Disable one and restart. If Windows 98 restarts normally, then you have found the problem device driver and should contact the manufacturer for a replacement for the driver. You can also view the driver details, update a driver, and manually modify resources (a very advanced task).

Step 5

Cancel the Properties dialog box for the device and return to the System Properties dialog box. Select the Performance tab and notice that safe mode is running in MS-DOS compatibility mode. When you are done, cancel out of the System Properties dialog box.

Step 6

Once you make a change that you hope will solve the problem, restart in normal mode. If Windows 98 starts successfully in normal mode, you are done. If not, you may need to experiment with settings. You should also research your problem at the Microsoft Technet site.

Step 7

If you know that a specific file is corrupted, you can use My Computer to delete and replace the corrupted file. Or if you are unsuccessful in solving the problem so that your computer will start normally, use safe mode to copy your data files from the ailing computer to a safe place.

A Program Stalls in Windows 98

You are happily working at your computer when the "busy" icon attaches itself to your cursor and just remains there. Nothing you do makes a difference. There is no response from mouse movements or keystrokes. Maybe you can't even switch to another program previously opened on your desktop. What should you do?

The first thing you should do is walk away for at least a couple minutes. There is a chance (very slim) that a program has caused the computer to temporarily become very busy, and it may finish soon and let you continue. It's worth trying this first, especially if you've made changes to your data since the last time you saved it. When you come back, if the program is still stalled ("hung up" is another term we use), then you will have to press CTRL-ALT-DELETE. This will open the Close Program dialog box, in which you will see a list of your open programs, as shown in Figure 5-5. Select the program that is currently not responding and then click End Task. You will often see another dialog box, as shown in Figure 5-6. If so, select End Task. If Windows is now responsive, you closed the offending program. If not, one by one select each program (except Windows Explorer) and select End Task. After closing each program, check to see if Windows responds. When it does, you know that you have removed the program that caused the problem. In any case, once you can get back into Windows, you should consider it unstable until the next restart. Therefore, save any unsaved data, close all remaining programs, and restart Windows.

Your program may not be listed as not responding in the Close Program dialog box. If that is the case, select Cancel. If your system is still not responsive, press CTRL-ALT-DELETE again to open the Close Program dialog box. We have often found that the second time it is opened, it will list a program as not responding.

Explorer Performed an Illegal Operation

Once again, you are happily working at your computer when you are rudely interrupted. This time you receive an error message like the one in Figure 5-7 stating that Explorer performed an illegal operation. That doesn't seem like a friendly thing for a Windows program to do, and in this case, it may not be the fault of Explorer. It may actually be another program that is at fault. Click Close to close the message box, and usually all the objects on your desktop disappear temporarily. You may even see the same message

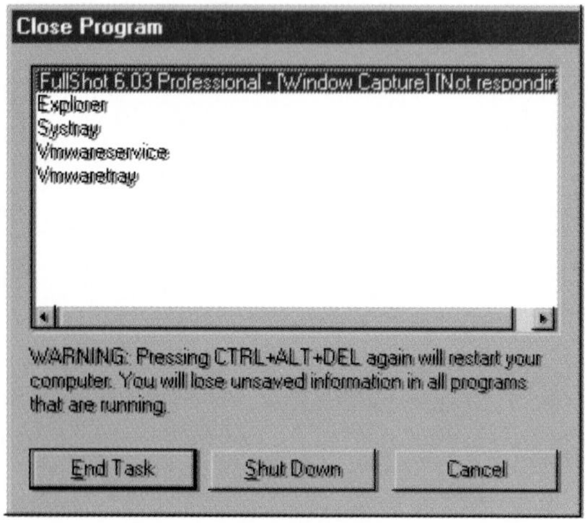

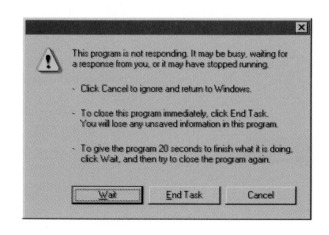

• **Figure 5-5.** Close Program dialog box

• **Figure 5-6.** Program Not Responding message

again, in which case, close it again. If possible, you should save all data, close all applications, and shut down your computer from the Start menu. If this is not possible, meaning that your computer is unresponsive, press CTRL-ALT-DELETE to bring up the Close Program dialog box. This may reveal which program is not responding. Proceed as in the previous section, "A Program Stalls in Windows 98."

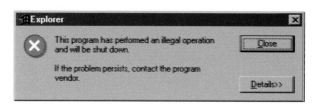

● Figure 5-7.   Explorer Illegal Operation message

Fatal Exception Error: The Windows 98 Blue Screen of Death

And yet again, you are interrupted. This time your application and the Windows desktop disappear entirely, to be replaced by a rude Fatal Exception error message, as shown in Figure 5-8. This is the Windows 98 version of the Blue Screen of Death. Make a note of the information on the top two lines. This information may help you to prevent this from happening again.

Research and Solve the Problem

As the instructions in the Fatal Exception message state, press any key to terminate the offending application. This does not always work, but if it does and you are returned to the desktop, save any data files that are open, close all open applications, and restart Windows 98. After the system successfully starts again, use the information you copied down from the blue screen to research the cause of the problem. In our example, this is the important piece of information: A fatal exception 0E has occurred at 0028:C02402C1 in VXD VMM(0E).

Not all possible fatal exception errors are documented with a solution, but it is worth trying to find the cause.

If You Can't Fix It, Avoid It!

The event that caused the fatal exception may never occur again, and you may be able to continue to work in the application you were previously

> **Inside Information**
>
> **Microsoft Knowledge Base**
> The Microsoft **Knowledge Base** is a database of articles on problems and solutions created by Microsoft Support Services. These articles have traditionally had identifier numbers preceded with a Q. The location of these articles on Microsoft's website has changed and will surely change again by the time you read this. Search for an article by going to the Technet page (www.microsoft.com/technet) and entering the Q number in the Search box. While we cannot guarantee that recommended articles will continue to be available at the Microsoft site, at this time Microsoft maintains a large number of articles on older OSs. As your career progresses, you'll find yourself using the Knowledge Base more and more because it's the one place where the most detailed information about problems and solutions exists. It's in your interest to become an expert on the Knowledge Base!

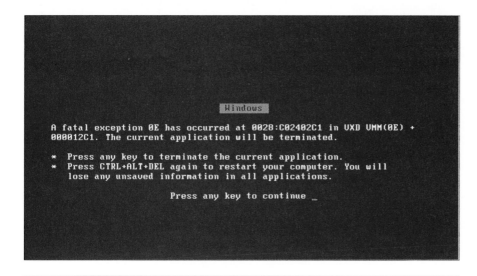

● Figure 5-8.   Fatal Exception message—The Windows 98 Blue Screen of Death!

using at the time of the problem. Our general advice is that after a fatal exception error, if you cannot pinpoint the cause, then modify your work habits slightly to avoid fatal exception errors. You're thinking that you can't avoid what you don't understand, and that is mostly true. However, we have found that having many applications open or even only a few with very large data files can make the system prone to these errors. Therefore, try doing "simple computing" for a while. Keep more than one application open at a time only if you are truly working in both applications at the same time.

Windows 98 Shutdown Problems

It happened to Chuck many, many times. He would choose Shut Down from the Windows 98 Start menu, and his applications would close, but the desktop would remain. He was running Windows 98 Second Edition. When he researched this problem at the Microsoft website, he found that the most common causes of Windows 98 SE shutdown problems had to do with the Advanced Power Management system and the system BIOS on some computers. This was corrected in a patch. To learn more about this, see Microsoft Knowledge Base article Q238096, "Windows 98 Second Edition Shutdown Problems" at http://support.microsoft.com/support/kb/articles/Q238/0/96.asp.

If you experience shutdown problems with Windows 98 (First Edition), check out Knowledge Base Article Q202633, "How to Troubleshoot Windows 98 Shutdown Problems."

To learn more about MS-DOS compatibility mode, check out Microsoft Knowledge Base Article Q130179, "Troubleshooting MS-DOS Compatibility Mode on Hard Disks." You can find other articles by connecting to the Technet site at www.microsoft.com/technet and searching on MS-DOS Compatibility Mode.

Poor Performance

If your Windows 98 system seems slow, here are several things you can check. If you are using an MS-DOS driver for an old hardware component, your computer will run in MS-DOS compatibility mode, because the OS will replace some of its 32-bit code with 16-bit code to support the MS-DOS driver. This happened frequently with CD-ROM drives that did not have Windows 98 drivers. The quick check to see if this is the problem is to look at the Performance tab of the System Properties dialog box and make sure that File System and Virtual Memory both are using 32-bit OS components, as shown in Figure 5-9.

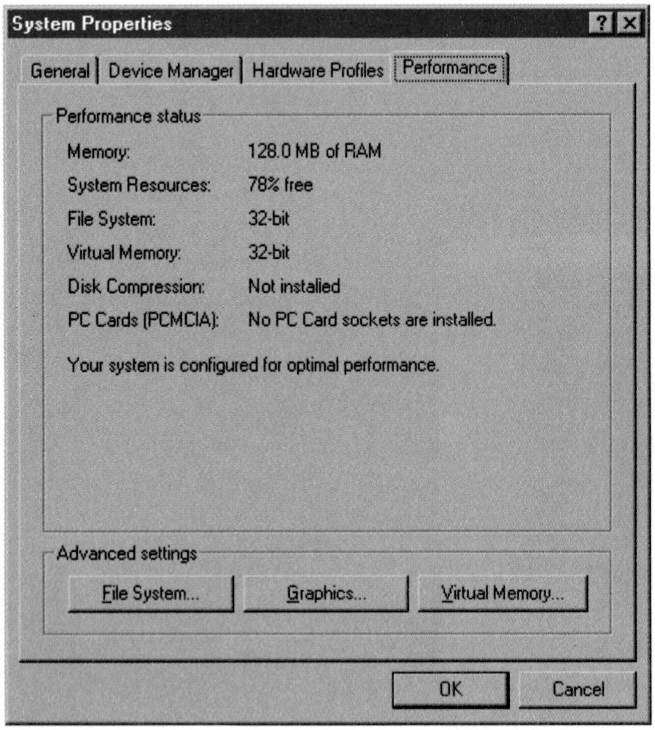

• **Figure 5-9.** The Performance tab

Chapter 5 Review

■ Chapter Summary

After reading this chapter and completing the Step-by-Step tutorials and Try This! exercises, you should understand the following facts about Windows 98:

Measure the Features, Strengths, and Weaknesses of Windows 98

■ Windows 98, an upgrade from Windows 95, was the first Microsoft OS targeted at the consumer market and the last version of Windows to still have ties to the MS-DOS operating system.

■ Windows 98 is available in two editions: the original 1998 release and Windows 98 Second Edition, released a year later.

■ The Windows 98 desktop resembles the Windows 95 desktop, with modifications such as the integration of Internet Explorer, which is apparent if you turn on Active Desktop and add the channel bar.

■ An Active Channel bar contains hyperlinks to services that maintain an Active Channel website, which delivers updated information to the user's computer at scheduled intervals.

■ The Microsoft Knowledge Base is a database of problem-resolution articles maintained by Microsoft. Each article has an identifier number preceded by Q.

■ The Quick Launch toolbar is a small, optional toolbar on the taskbar that can contain icons for programs. Quick Launch toolbar icons launch programs with a single click.

■ Windows 98 has improved GUI navigational features, such as the Show Desktop button on the Quick Launch toolbar (assuming that you enable the Quick Launch toolbar). Show Desktop minimizes all open windows.

■ Windows 98 supports two file systems, FAT16 and FAT32, and it can store long file names in both file systems.

■ Windows 98 supports plug and play, DVD drives, universal serial bus (USB) devices, and IEEE 1394 (similar to Apple's FireWire) devices.

■ Windows 98 has power management features that allow hardware components to be powered down when not in use.

■ The broad hardware and power management support features appeal to laptop users.

■ Windows 98 performs better than its predecessor, with faster bootup, shutdown, and program loading.

■ To support old MS-DOS and Windows 3.x applications, Windows 98 has configuration options and a special mode called MS-DOS mode.

■ The Windows 98 file systems do not provide security, have limited recoverability, and do not provide file compression at the file level. The OS has a file compression capability that is actually disk compression and creates a single point of failure.

■ You can use MS-DOS drivers in Windows 98, but this will cause Windows 98 to run in MS-DOS compatibility mode, which degrades performance and is more prone to failure.

■ The combination of 16-bit and 32-bit code in Windows 98 makes it less stable.

■ Windows 98 is no longer a viable choice for a new OS, because it has been replaced by newer, improved desktop versions of Windows.

■ The minimum hardware requirements are not realistic when you consider that they would not give you enough memory or disk space to install an office suite of software.

■ An ideal hardware configuration, depending on your needs, would include an Intel Pentium II processor, 64 to 128MB of RAM, 4GB of available hard disk space, a CD-ROM drive, an SVGA or higher-resolution video adapter, and a Microsoft mouse.

■ You can research compatible software and hardware products for Windows 98 at www. microsoft.com/windows/compatible/ default.asp.

Install and Configure Windows 98

■ When you prepare for Windows 98 installation, you determine whether the hardware and software you want to install are compatible with the OS.

■ Before installing Windows 98, be sure that your computer hardware and peripherals are connected and ready to use. You must also choose the method and type of installation.

- A manual installation requires your full attention, whereas an automated installation does not require attention during installation but requires time and expertise to create the installation scripts.

- Organizations with a large number of desktop computers that require identical OS installations use images that include installed applications. These images can be created and distributed to the desktop using software such as Symantec's Ghost product.

- A clean installation begins with a completely empty hard disk, whereas an upgrade installation begins with a previously installed OS that can be upgraded to Windows 98.

- A dual-boot configuration allows you to select between two or more OSs during startup. To create a dual-boot configuration, install the oldest OS first. You cannot dual boot between Windows 98 and older versions of Windows if drive C: uses FAT32.

- Select components and applications to install.

- Gather materials needed for installation, based on the decisions you made about the method and type of installation.

- A floppy disk labeled "Windows 98 Boot Disk" comes with Windows 98 and is used to boot up your computer to MS-DOS 7. A similar disk can be created using the FAT32EBD utility on the Windows 98 CD.

- After installation, you should use Device Manager to verify that all devices are working.

- After installation, you should configure the desktop to your preferences and connect to the network and the Internet, if required.

- After you have installed the OS, you should install the latest updates and service packs.

Customize and Manage Windows 98

- Install some applications using the installation program that came with the application.

- Use Add/Remove Programs to install or remove user applications without their own installation programs and to add or remove Windows components.

Manage Users, Files, and Printers

- When you add a new user in Windows 98, you are creating a user profile for that user.

- User profiles allow more than one user to use a computer while preserving each user's desktop preferences and personal folders.

- A user profile is a set of folders and desktop settings unique to each user.

- Press F5 to refresh an open window when it does not show newly added or removed objects.

- All local users of a Windows 98 computer can access any file and folder on the local hard drive.

- Windows 98 can create file names with up to 255 characters, at the same time storing an 8.3 alias for every long file name.

- You can install a new printer driver using the manufacturer's installation program, if provided, or the Add Printer wizard found in the Printers applet.

- You can copy the Windows 98 source files (the Win98 folder) onto your hard drive to make adding components and drivers easier.

Troubleshoot Common Windows 98 Problems

- Use the Windows 98 Help program to find the solution to problems in Windows 98.

- The Windows 98 Help troubleshooters will walk you through steps to resolve common problems.

- The first thing you should do when a program hangs up is give it a few minutes to recover.

- If a program continues to hang, press CTRL-ALT-DELETE, select the offending program in the Close Program dialog box, and click Close. If you still don't get a response in Windows 98, open the Close Program dialog box again and select another program, until you can get back to Windows. Once you are back to Windows 98, attempt to save any open data files; then restart the OS.

- If you receive an error message saying that Explorer performed an illegal operation, close the message box. This will most often cause the desktop to disappear temporarily, and the same message may reappear. If so, close it again. Then, if Windows will respond to keyboard and mouse commands, attempt to save data and close programs. If Windows does not respond, use the Close Program dialog box, as outlined in the previous paragraph.

- If Windows 98 is slow, check the Performance tab of System Properties to see if it is running in MS-DOS compatibility mode.

Key Terms

<div class="columns">

8.3 alias (214)
Active Channel website (181)
automated installation (190)
critical update (204)
hyperlink (181)
hypertext markup language (HTML) (181)

Knowledge Base (223)
long file name (LFN) (183)
manual installation (188)
MS-DOS compatibility mode (185)
MS-DOS mode (184)
primary directory entry (214)
safe mode (219)

secondary directory entry (214)
Show Desktop button (182)
small office/home office (SOHO) (180)
upgrade installation (189)
user profile (210)
VFAT file system driver (184)

</div>

Key Term Quiz

Use the Key Terms list to complete the sentences that follow. Not all the terms will be used.

1. A/an _____ is an element of a hypertext markup language (HTML) document that points to another location.

2. The _____ lets you quickly close all open windows so you can get to the icons on the desktop.

3. A/an _____ can have up to 255 characters, including spaces.

4. The _____ driver improves performance on both FAT16 and FAT32 volumes.

5. _____ is used for DOS applications that will not run well in a Windows 98 virtual machine.

6. When you create a file with an LFN, Windows 98 also saves a/an _____.

7. _____ is the term Microsoft uses to refer to a security-related patch.

8. If you wish to keep all the configuration information from an old version of Windows, install Windows 98 as an _____.

9. _____ allows several people to use a single Windows 98 computer while keeping their unique settings and preferences.

10. _____ is the language of the World Wide Web.

Multiple-Choice Quiz

1. What are the two Windows 98 editions, including the unofficial name for one?
   a. Primo Edition
   b. Gold Code Edition
   c. Active Desktop
   d. Second Edition
   e. First Edition

2. What program is integrated into the Windows 98 desktop interface?
   a. Solitaire
   b. Microsoft Office
   c. Microsoft Exchange
   d. Internet Explorer
   e. Network Neighborhood

3. The Windows 98 desktop most closely resembles that of which other OS?
   a. Mac OS X
   b. Windows 95
   c. Windows 3.1
   d. Linux
   e. Windows XP

4. What is the name of Microsoft's collection of technical articles, each identifying a problem and providing a solution?
   a. .NET
   b. Knowledge Base
   c. Webopedia
   d. Q Base
   e. Microsoft Windows Update

5. How much space would be allocated to a 4KB file on a 2GB FAT16 partition?

   a. 4KB

   b. 80KB

   c. 32KB

   d. 16KB

   e. 512 bytes

6. Using MS-DOS drivers with Windows 98 will cause it to run in which of the following?

   a. Internet Explorer

   b. MS-DOS compatibility mode

   c. Device Manager

   d. MS-DOS mode

   e. Control Panel

7. When installing any operating system, which is most important to consider?

   a. Minimum hardware requirements

   b. Mean time between failures

   c. Prime meridian

   d. Ideal hardware configuration

   e. Speed of the network

8. What should you do if you can see other computers in Network Neighborhood, but not your own computer?

   a. Call the help desk.

   b. Nothing, unless you have file and print sharing turned on.

   c. Restart.

   d. Reinstall.

   e. Refinance.

9. Why should you avoid MS-DOS compatibility mode?

   a. It causes file corruption.

   b. It causes poor performance.

   c. You can't access the Control Panel applets.

   d. You can't shut down.

   e. None of the above.

10. A Windows 98 boot disk or startup disk actually boots up into which OS?

    a. Windows 3.1

    b. PC DOS 6.22

    c. MS-DOS 6.20

    d. MS-DOS 7

    e. Windows 95

11. Why is it important to know how long Microsoft will continue to sell a desktop OS?

    a. To know how long it will be available to purchase

    b. To know how long Microsoft will continue to support it

    c. To plan purchases for desktop computers

    d. All of the above

    e. None of the above

12. Which is the preferred type of installation if you can back up any data saved on the hard drive first?

    a. Dual-boot

    b. Upgrade

    c. Overnight

    d. Clean

    e. Downgrade

13. What type of Internet site is created by an organization to provide updated information, automatically downloaded on a schedule, to a subscriber's desktop?

    a. Search engine

    b. FTP

    c. Newsgroup

    d. Active Channel website

    e. Mail server

14. What should you do if a program hangs up in Windows 98? Select all that apply.

    a. Call the help desk immediately.

    b. Turn off the computer.

    c. Press CTRL-ALT-ENTER.

    d. Press CTRL-ALT-DELETE.

    e. First take a short a break.

15. Where can you find the Windows 98 performance settings?

    a. Start | Settings | Control Panel | System

    b. Start | Programs | Accessories | System Tools

    c. Permon

    d. My Documents

    e. Start | Find | Computer

■ Essay Quiz

1. Write a few sentences describing why, in 1998, Windows 98 appealed to corporate users, even though Microsoft did not intend it for them.

2. Briefly describe the weaknesses of Windows 98. Select the one you believe is the most compelling reason not to use it. Support your statement.

3. Explain the importance of installing critical updates and service packs.

4. Describe the tasks that can be accomplished using the Add/Remove Programs applet.

5. Describe in general terms what happens when you save a file with an LFN in Windows 98 and discuss the issue of case sensitivity as it applies to file names.

Lab Projects

• Lab Project 5.1

You have been asked to install Windows 98 on four computers in a branch office. Each computer will have a slightly different set of Windows components installed and different user applications. The office presently has Windows 95 installed on its computers. The organization has had a lot of problems with Windows (it fails often), and the computers now have unauthorized applications the users have installed themselves. The organization does not want these unauthorized applications in Windows 98, because they believe they are causing some of the problems.

The organization is not installing a newer OS because it owns these four Windows 98 licenses through a purchase someone made a few years ago, and the organization feels that Windows 98 is adequate for the work required on these computers. The computers are in a workgroup, and the network employs a Windows NT Workstation computer that acts as a file and print server. All user data is saved on this server, and it is saved nightly on a tape backup system. The users have been told that any data saved locally will be destroyed during this installation.

Although each computer will be configured with different settings and applications, they will all have the same hardware configuration. A co-worker

researched and confirmed that all of the hardware is compatible with Windows 98 and left you with the list of manufacturers and model names of all components. The current hardware configuration on these machines is as follows:

■ Intel Pentium II processor

■ 96MB RAM

■ 8GB available hard disk space

■ CD-ROM drive

■ A network card that is confirmed as compatible, but is newer than any of the network drivers that came with Windows 98

■ An SVGA video adapter that is confirmed as compatible, but is newer than any of the video adapters that came with Windows 98

■ Microsoft mouse

Describe how you will perform the following:

1 Preinstallation tasks

2 Installation, including the type and means of installation

3 Post-installation tasks that will leave each computer ready for the users

• Lab Project 5.2

You are preparing to visit the sales department in your company to install a new printer. The department assures you that, although the driver is not on the Windows 98 CD, a driver disk that came with the printer is available. Another person has unpacked the printer, connected it to the computer, and left all of the documentation and disks from the printer for you to use. Describe the procedure you will use when you arrive to install the printer. You may go beyond the scope of this course in your answer. Be creative!

• Lab Project 5.3

You have just been assigned to provide desktop support over the phone to a small office. You have a computer running Windows 98 on your desktop to help you support their use of Windows 98. You have not even had a chance to familiarize yourself with the people and the equipment in that office when you receive a call that one of the printers is not working. It is an infrared printer that is used with a laptop. You have told the user that you will call her back in five minutes. You did this to have time to figure out a plan of action, since you have never seen or touched an infrared printer. Now do the following:

1. Describe in a sentence or two a source you will use to find a solution to this problem and why you have picked that source.

2. Using the source described in Step 1, compose a list of questions you will ask the user when you call her back. Follow each question with a description of the action that should be taken.

Windows 2000 Professional

"It seems very pretty, but it's RATHER hard to understand!"

—THROUGH THE LOOKING GLASS
BY LEWIS CARROLL

Windows 2000 Professional was the first Windows version that combined the friendly nature of the consumer-oriented versions of Windows with the robust nature of the Windows NT family. Windows 2000 Professional was familiar enough to legions of Windows 95 and Windows 98 users for them to feel quickly at home when using a Windows 2000 Professional–based PC. This was important because it meant that businesses didn't have to give up the advanced features of a Windows NT–based OS to keep their employees happy with the way their desktop PCs functioned. By combining the best of both worlds, Windows 2000 Professional provides a powerful core and a very usable interface for maximum productivity. It's not an upgrade to Windows 98, however. Switching to Windows 2000 is more like replacing the engine in our old Honda Prelude with that of a Mustang V8.

You'll very likely encounter Windows 2000 Professional in the business world. This chapter will help you prepare so that you will feel comfortable with the essentials of Windows 2000 Professional. You will learn the hardware required to use Windows 2000 Professional as well as how to use the important security features the operating system provides. You will see how to configure Windows 2000 Professional for efficient operation, how to manage files and folders, how to install and use application programs, and how to work with a printer in Windows 2000 Professional. Finally, you'll learn what to do to resolve some of the problems you are likely to encounter.

In this chapter, you will learn how to:

- Describe Windows 2000 Professional benefits, features, and weaknesses
- Install and configure Windows 2000 Professional
- Customize and manage Windows 2000 Professional
- Manage security for users, files, and printers
- Troubleshoot common Windows 2000 Professional problems

■ Windows 2000 Professional Overview

What are the benefits and features of Windows 2000 Professional? What are its weaknesses? Why would anyone want Windows 2000 Professional on the desktop when there are other operating system choices? We'll answer these questions in this section.

• Windows 2000 Professional desktop with several open applications

Benefits and Features

To be successful, an OS must offer benefits for the user. In the case of Windows 2000 Professional, the benefits are in the areas of stability, software compatibility, security, and support for several file systems to suit the performance and security needs of the user. In the following sections, we explore these benefits by exploring the features of Windows 2000 Professional that make them possible.

Desktop

Once again, Microsoft provides a Windows OS with a familiar desktop that shows only subtle changes from previous Windows OSs. The taskbar offers the customizable Quick Launch toolbar with the Show Desktop button, a feature of Windows 98. There are familiar desktop icons (My Documents, My Computer, Recycle Bin, and Internet Explorer) and slightly modified icons, like the Network Places desktop icon, which is now My Network Places (see Figure 6-1).

Security

Since Windows 2000 Professional is a member of the Windows NT family, it is also far more secure than Windows 95 or Windows 98. Not only is a logon to Windows 2000 Professional mandatory, but this logon must be performed from an account that is a member of a security database—either the local security accounts database built into Windows 2000 Professional on the local computer, or a network-based security database, such as in a Windows NT or Active Directory domain. A **Windows NT domain** is one in which all servers maintaining the domain database are running a Windows NT Server OS. An **Active Directory domain** is one in which at least some of the servers maintaining the domain database are running a Windows 2000 Professional Server OS or greater.

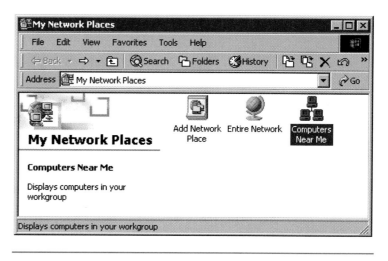

● **Figure 6-1.** My Network Places with added links

In addition, it's possible to restrict access to local resources such as files, folders, and printers to specific user accounts or group accounts, which contain user accounts. This is done through the use of permissions. These features all reflect security as it existed in Windows NT 4.0. However, Windows 2000 Professional offers several improvements to security. A short list of these improvements includes the following:

- New tools are provided for administering security in Windows 2000 Professional, including group policies and new console tools available through the Control Panel.

- The Internet Protocol Security (IPSec) protocols can be used to make network communications more secure.

- Logon authentication from a Windows 2000 Professional computer to a Windows Active Directory domain is more secure with the use of the Kerberos security protocol.

- Files on an NTFS5 volume can be encrypted to further secure them.

Group Policies   Our nomination for the best improvement in security in Windows 2000 Professional is the use of group policies to centrally manage security. Group policy is a very advanced topic, so we'll just give you the abridged version here. Group policy is a grouping of policies for controlling not only the many security settings, but also configuration settings for the OS. This is done to give administrators the ability to centrally manage many hundreds of settings using a single administrative tool.

If a Windows 2000 Professional computer is a stand-alone computer or a member of a workgroup, the administration of these settings must be done at that computer—in which case you are merely setting local policies for that one computer. The real power of group policies comes into play when your Windows 2000 Professional computer is a member of an Active Directory domain. An Active Directory domain is one which has one of the Windows 2000 Professional or newer Microsoft server operating systems in the role of domain controller (the computer that maintains the Active Directory database). Only then can group policies be centrally administered for all member

A Microsoft domain is a collection of accounts representing network computers, users, and groups of users, all maintained in a central security database for ease of administration. These special user and group accounts are often simply referred to as "users" and "groups," even though we are talking about accounts that are stored on disk, not the actual people involved.

The important ingredients for centralized management of group policies are an Active Directory domain and a member computer running Windows 2000 Professional or greater. A computer running Windows NT 4.0 in an Active Directory domain is not affected by group policies!

computers that have Windows 2000 Professional or newer Microsoft operating systems.

The primary tool used for managing group policies is the Group Policy Editor. Using this one tool, an administrator can create a set of group policies to modify settings on a single computer or on hundreds of computers. Figure 6-2 shows the Group Policy Editor with a view of the Local Computer Policy.

> Group policy is an extremely advanced topic, but it is key to successfully managing Windows 2000 Professional. If you want to learn more, connect to `http://support.microsoft.com` and search the Knowledge Base for the topic Group Policy.

More Secure Authentication When you log on, you are proving who you are, which is called authentication. Kerberos is the authentication protocol that Windows 2000 Professional uses when you log on to an Active Directory domain. This is a more secure protocol than the previous Windows authentication protocols, but it is not the only authentication protocol that Windows 2000 Professional can use. There are several others that are used either together with Kerberos or separately, depending on your method of authentication.

File Encryption Encryption is a new feature of NTFS introduced in Windows 2000 Professional. In short, a user can encrypt a folder or individual files. The process is as simple as opening the Properties of a file or folder, clicking the Advanced button, and placing a check in the box by Encrypt Contents to Secure Data, as shown in Figure 6-3. When you turn on encryption for a folder, the folder itself isn't really encrypted; rather, any files already in or added to the folder are encrypted. If an encrypted file is moved or copied, it will retain its encryption. The only person who can unencrypt a file is the person who encrypted it or a member of a special group called recovery agents. By default, only the local administrator is a member of this group.

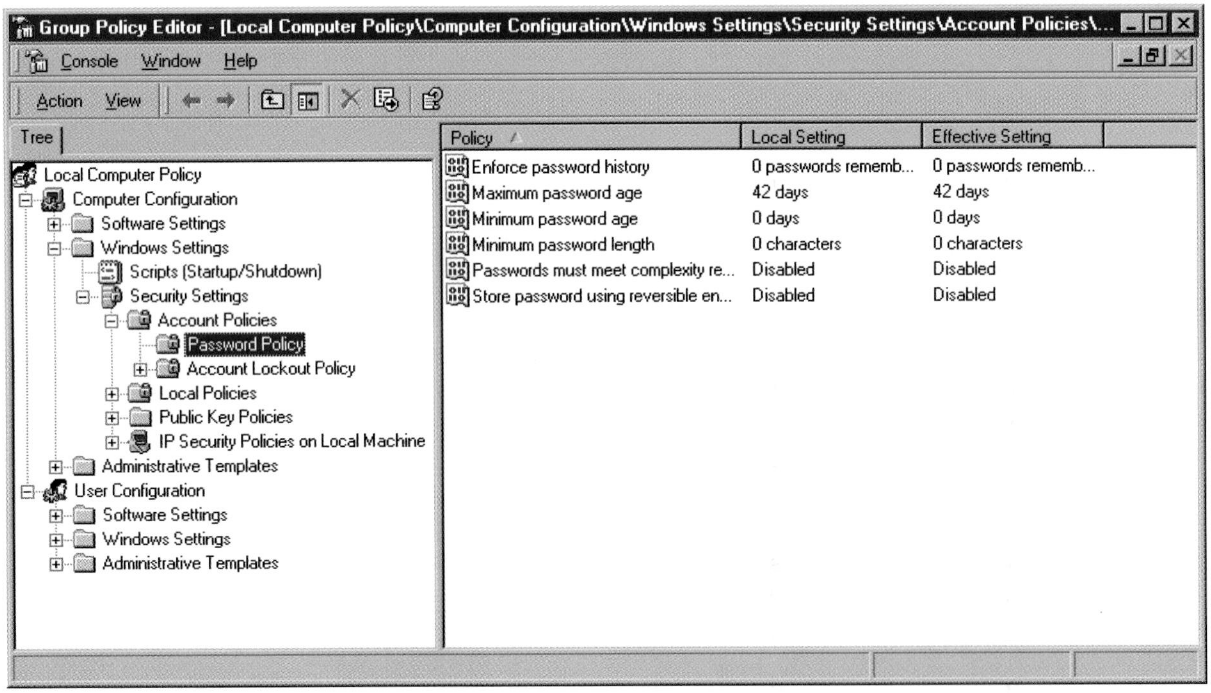

• **Figure 6-2.** Group Policy Editor showing Local Computer Policy

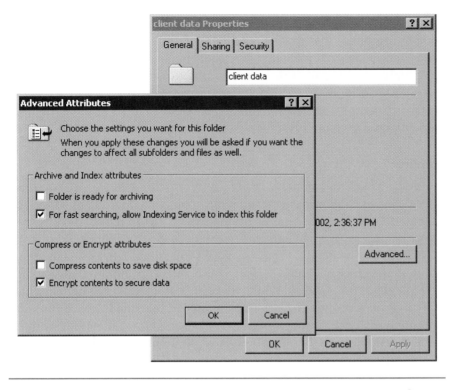

Don't Blink!

The most common method of authentication is the simple logon in which you enter your user name and password using the keyboard and mouse. Other methods may include special devices to authenticate you. One such mechanism is a credit-card-sized device, called a smart card, that provides a token, or password. Other devices allow you to prove who you are through biometrics (measuring a biological characteristic). For example, you might log on to your computer by entering your user name at a keyboard and then placing your thumb on a device that scans your fingerprint. A similar approach is retinal scanning, which confirms your identity by examining the retina of your eye. These are all options if you're logging on to an Active Directory domain from a Windows 2000 Professional computer, but they require special equipment and configuration of all the computers involved.

● **Figure 6-3.** Turn on encryption in the Advanced Attributes dialog box of a file or folder's properties.

Jaime is a financial planner who carries his laptop to meetings with his clients. He has files containing confidential data on each of his clients. He needs to be sure to keep this information secure from prying eyes, and he worries that if his laptop was stolen, this information would fall into the wrong hands. To guard against this, Jaime has four good practices:

■ He encrypts all confidential data files.

■ He makes sure that he always uses a complex password that would be difficult to guess.

■ He changes his password frequently and never reuses old passwords.

■ He always uses the Lock Computer option in the Windows Security dialog box (accessed by pressing CTRL-ALT-DELETE in Windows 2000 Professional) whenever he leaves his computer unattended even briefly.

Jaime has encrypted a folder on his laptop that is called Client Data. All files in this folder are encrypted. This may sound rather high tech and inconvenient, but once Jaime turned on encryption for this folder, he never had to think about it again. As long as he is logged on with the same account that he used when he turned on encryption, he simply opens the encrypted files using his normal applications. The security components of the OS verify that he is authorized to access these files *and* that he is the person who encrypted them. Someone logged on with a different account will not be able to open these files, even if the person uses an account with Full Control permission to the files.

Just a Spoonful of Sugar! Here we go again—introducing several very, very advanced topics and patting you on the head and saying you don't need to know it right now, but it's true that going any further with the security

You cannot use both the Compress and Encrypt attributes on the same file or folder. You may use one or the other. Clicking the Encrypt box will clear the Compress box, and visa versa.

If you use a Windows 2000 Professional computer at school or work, you may discover that encryption isn't available when you look at the Advanced Properties of a file or folder on an NTFS volume. This is because it is possible for a knowledgeable administrator to turn off encryption.

topic at this point would be overwhelming. However, it's important for your future career that you be aware of computer security. In the United States, recent laws mandate that the health care industry and others implement high security standards to protect individual privacy. This applies to the handling of computer-based records as well as paper records. So it's important that you eventually learn more about security options for networked desktop computers.

Stability

Windows 2000 Professional is really just an upgrade version of Windows NT 4.0. It was in development for about four years, and for much of that time Microsoft planned to name it Windows NT 5.0. In the fall of 1998, over a year before the new version was released, Microsoft announced that the new OS would be named Windows 2000 Professional. It still has the same 32-bit architecture of Windows NT, which offers an important advantage over Windows 9x: stability. Windows 2000 Professional runs each application program in its own **protected memory space**. Essentially, this means that a poorly written application program can crash without affecting any other running applications or Windows 2000 Professional itself. This "clean room" approach to applications means that a PC running Windows 2000 Professional can often run for months without ever having to be restarted.

Software Compatibility

Another important benefit of Windows 2000 Professional is the ability to choose from a large selection of application software written to run on Windows computers. Although many application programs are available for Macintosh, Linux, and other OSs, software developers do tend to develop more applications intended for Windows-based PCs than for PCs running any other OS simply because the vast majority of all PCs run some version of Windows.

16-Bit and 32-Bit Windows Applications and DOS Applications   As a member of the Windows family of operating systems, Windows 2000 Professional quite naturally was designed to run a specific group of programs. Although it maintains a limited ability to run many DOS applications as well as older 16-bit Windows programs, Windows 2000 Professional was specifically designed to perform at its best when running 32-bit Windows programs.

Windows 2000 Professional, like Windows NT 4.0, runs applications in environments called subsystems, and as with Windows NT, 32-bit Windows applications are the "native" applications of Windows 2000. These applications are written to a specific set of rules, and they run in the Win32 subsystem. Many programs designed for Windows 95 (or later) or Windows NT 3.51 (or later) are 32-bit Windows programs. This compatibility across both lines of the Windows OS family is one reason why Windows 2000 Professional has been considered by many people to be an excellent solution to the need for an operating system that both runs popular application programs and provides the security required to protect the user's data.

Applications Written for Non-Microsoft OSs   In addition to 16-bit and 32-bit Windows applications, Windows 2000 Professional can run the same types of applications as NT 4.0. For details, review "Software Compatibility with Legacy Applications" in Chapter 4.

Inside Information

Meet the Families!

As with European royalty, there are separate houses, or genealogical lines, of Windows. First there is the House of DOS Windows family, which evolved from the first version of Windows (in 1985) that simply put a graphical interface on top of DOS (16-bit program code). Each version was an improvement over the last, but still depended on DOS as a core component. The last two versions in this line are Windows 98 and Windows Me. They now use primarily 32-bit code, but they still have some 16-bit components and depend on DOS to start.

The other major Windows line is the House of NT, which evolved from the first version of Windows NT (3.1). This is an entirely new and separate line from the House of DOS Windows family. This line includes all versions of Windows NT, Windows 2000 Professional, Windows XP, and .Net Server 2003.

Windows 2000 Professional File Systems

Recall that a file system is the means an operating system uses to organize information on disks. For CD-ROMs, Windows 2000 Professional uses the Compact Disc File System (CDFS), and it uses the Universal Disk Format (UDF) for digital versatile disks (DVDs). A benefit of Windows 2000 Professional is that it supports more file systems than the previous Microsoft OSs. Like all the previous versions of Windows, it supports the FAT file systems, including FAT12 for diskettes and FAT16 for hard disks. Like Windows 98, it also supports the improved FAT32 **file system** for hard disks larger than 512MB. Like Windows NT, it supports NTFS, introducing new features in version 5 (NTFS5). NTFS has always been a more efficient and more secure file system than the FAT file systems, because you can set permissions on each file and folder on an NTFS volume. NTFS also uses a superior method of storing files that guards against file damage or loss, but it now has more features, such as file encryption for better security and a feature that supports indexing to make searches of files and folders faster.

Cross Check

Windows 2000 Professional Versus Windows 98

Compare Windows 2000 Professional to Windows 98, discussed in Chapter 5, and then answer the following questions:

1. Which OS offers the best overall stability?

   _____

2. Which OS offers the best downward compatibility to DOS applications and 16-bit Windows applications?

   _____

Weaknesses of Windows 2000 Professional

Windows 2000 Professional is not a perfect OS—as if there were such a thing anywhere! You may be surprised to learn that some of its benefits appear to also be weaknesses. "What?" you say, "We can't have it both ways?" Just watch! We believe that the enhanced security and support for DOS and 16-bit Windows applications can be seen as weaknesses. We also believe that the more capable an OS is, the more complex it is to work with, especially when you encounter problems. We see this complexity not exactly as a weakness, but as an obstacle to adoption.

> Applications that depend on Windows 9*x* virtual device drivers (VxDs) cannot run under Windows 2000 Professional. A program that uses a V*x*D in Windows 9*x* may be able to work if it is modified to use a service that provides the same functionality in Windows 2000 Professional.

Support for Old DOS and Windows Applications

Windows 2000 does not provide optimal support for all old DOS and Windows applications. The weaknesses in this area are twofold. First, some old applications will not run in Windows 2000 Professional. Second, some applications that do run do so more slowly than in Windows 9*x*.

Some Applications Just Won't Run Backward compatibility issues are not new; there have long been some DOS and 16-bit Windows applications that won't run in newer versions of Windows, but some applications written for Windows 9*x* also won't run in Windows 2000 Professional. An application written for Windows 9*x* should be a 32-bit application, written to comply with certain rules. Problems occur when an application is not carefully created and, while it runs well in Windows 9*x*, simply breaks too many rules to run in Windows 2000 Professional. Even though this incompatibility may not be the fault of Microsoft, if you have an older Windows program that you enjoy or rely on that won't run in Windows 2000 Professional, you will see this as a severe limitation of Windows 2000 Professional.

Some Applications Will Run More Slowly DOS and Windows 3.*x* applications may run more slowly in Windows 2000 Professional than in Windows 9*x*. This slowness has to do with the virtual environment that must be created, and the fact an application may be behaving in a nonstandard way, even for DOS or Windows 3.*x*. Therefore, this problem also depends on the program and how it was written. Because time has diminished the chance that you'll ever need to run DOS or Windows 3.*x* applications, this is a minor weakness of the OS.

The Need to Reboot After Modifying the OS

When Windows 2000 Professional was in development, we heard that Microsoft was working to make the OS behave so that the computer would not need to be restarted every time an OS component is added or removed. Microsoft only partially succeeded, and you will find that although there are fewer event types that require a reboot, there are still plenty. You don't have to reboot when you reconfigure TCP/IP for your network or after installing some OS components and applications, but you still have to reboot after adding some components and applications and after you apply a service pack.

When Is Windows 2000 Professional Needed?

Although Windows 2000 Professional is far more stable and secure than Windows 9*x*, the latter is far more common on the desktop. Quite honestly, this is because when Windows 2000 Professional was introduced, Windows 9*x* was far less expensive for PC manufacturers to install on most systems (less than half the cost of Windows 2000 Professional). General consumers were far more interested in saving a few dollars than in having a more stable and secure OS on their PCs. It is reasonable, therefore, to ask "When is Windows 2000 Professional actually necessary?"

Consider Carlos who runs a business that auctions off historical memorabilia from the days of the California Gold Rush and the Comstock Lode. He has several employees who each work on an individual PC connected to a small network. A substantial part of Carlos's business derives from the extensive research his employees do on the various items contained within each auction. Carlos's company depends on the security and integrity of Windows 2000 Professional to protect his company's research data from loss and to control access to that data so that only authorized people can view or modify information.

Alanna owns a small computer programming company. When she is working on developing an application program, she can't afford to have computer problems that might wipe out days of work. She, too, appreciates the stability that Windows 2000 Professional provides so she can spend her time making sure that her programs run properly and not spend time worrying about losing her work.

These are just two examples of why Windows 2000 Professional is so popular. Compared to an OS like Windows 98, Windows 2000 Professional is a far better choice if you simply want to get work done without constantly worrying about crashes and downtime. Windows 2000 Professional is also a much better choice than operating systems such as Linux or the Macintosh OS for people who want compatibility with the broadest range of fully supported applications at a reasonable price.

Here are some examples of when Windows 2000 Professional would be preferred over Windows 9x as a desktop operating system:

- Although most Windows programs will run under Windows 9x, a few very demanding business-oriented programs (such as certain CAD programs) will run only under a member of the Windows NT family. In this case, Windows 2000 Professional would be an excellent choice.

- If it is vitally important that a PC be reliable (such as in a medical monitoring application), the far greater stability of Windows 2000 Professional may be required.

- A publicly accessible PC (such as one providing Internet access in a business's lobby) likely could benefit from the advanced security features of Windows 2000 Professional to prevent users from performing unauthorized actions.

- In a business environment, it is often very important to maintain precise control over access to resources such as sensitive files. The security features of Windows 2000 Professional make this far easier to accomplish than on a system running Windows 9x.

- A desktop computer that is a member of a Windows Active Directory domain can be managed and administered better if it is a Windows 2000 Professional or Windows XP Professional computer, because these OSs can be centrally managed and secured through the use of group policies.

■ Installing and Configuring Windows 2000 Professional

Now that you understand the benefits and weaknesses of Windows 2000 Professional and when you might consider using this OS, you are ready to install this OS on your lab computer. But first, there are tasks to be completed, such as checking out the hardware requirements for Windows 2000 Professional and the compatibility of your hardware and software, choosing the method of installation, gathering the materials and information needed for installation, and preparing the Windows 2000 Professional setup disks (if necessary).

Hardware and Software for Windows 2000 Professional

Before you install or upgrade a computer to Windows 2000 Professional, you have four concerns regarding the computer hardware and software: the minimum hardware required by the OS, the ideal hardware for the job you hope to do with the computer, the compatibility of your hardware, and the compatibility of the software you want to use. Let's take a closer look at these concerns.

Hardware Requirements

Windows 2000 Professional has more demanding hardware requirements than previous versions of Windows, but these requirements are still very modest considering the way most PCs have been configured for quite a few years. At minimum, Windows 2000 Professional requires a 133 MHz Pentium or higher microprocessor (or equivalent), 64MB of RAM, a 2GB hard disk with 650MB of free space, a VGA or higher-resolution video adapter with a compatible monitor, a keyboard, and a Microsoft mouse or compatible pointing device. Additionally, a CD-ROM drive is required if you want to install from the Windows 2000 Professional CD.

The Ideal Hardware Configuration

If you ask us what the ideal hardware configuration is, we would simply answer, "It all depends." You might recognize that as the consultant's answer to every question. It is, however, the correct answer. The ideal hardware configuration depends on what you hope to do with your Windows 2000 Professional computer. Therefore, here we will suggest a middle-of-the-road configuration that would be overkill for most ordinary tasks, but may not be quite adequate if you are using your computer to play very sophisticated Internet games or run some other type of sophisticated program with high demands on processor, memory, and disk, or a requirement for some exotic piece of hardware. If you are not a computer gamer or other super-high-tech computer user, the following should be ideal:

- Intel Pentium 4 processor
- 256MB RAM
- 30GB of available hard disk space
- Fast CD-ROM drive
- DVD drive
- SVGA or higher-resolution video adapter
- Microsoft mouse

In addition, if this is a clean installation, with no previous OS on the computer, your computer should boot from the CD-ROM drive. This has been a standard feature in PCs for many years, but it must be configured in

Although you can install Windows 2000 Professional on a computer that just meets the minimum hardware requirements, you'll get far better performance with a more generous system configuration. You will get the biggest performance boosts from a faster CPU and increased RAM and disk space.

the system setup program. If your computer will not boot from CD and has no previous OS installed, then a 3.5-inch disk drive is also required. A Windows 2000 Professional–compatible network adapter is also required if your computer is to be on a network.

Checking Hardware and Software Compatibility

Before you install Windows 2000 Professional or add new hardware or software to an existing installation, spend a few minutes to determine whether Windows 2000 Professional will work with the hardware or software you have. If you don't have Internet access, you should check the **Hardware Compatibility List** contained in the HCL.txt file in the Support folder on the Windows 2000 Professional CD. This text file lists all of the system components and peripherals that were tested and shown to be compatible with Windows 2000 Professional at the time Windows 2000 Professional was prepared for release. Note that the HCL.txt file has a date of December 1999, so any products introduced after that time won't be shown.

Inside Information

Use the Web to Check Compatibility
If you have Internet access, find more recent information by connecting to www.microsoft .com/windows2000/ professional/howtobuy/ upgrading/compat/. Our only concern with this site is the very old posting dates shown on the pages, but they're still more recent than the Windows 2000 CD release date of December 1999.

• Windows 2000 Professional hardware and software compatibility

It's important to check out compatibility before installing Windows 2000 Professional and any time you want to add new hardware or software to the computer. Consider Veronica, who last year bought a new computer with

Windows 2000 Professional installed. She's been very happy with this computer and would now like to add an HP Scanjet 7400C scanner. Since she hasn't yet bought the scanner, she is going to check Microsoft's site first.

This is especially important for a device released after Windows 2000 Professional was released, since that means that its device driver is not included on the Windows 2000 Professional CD. If Veronica checks the Microsoft site and finds that the drivers for this scanner are not on the CD and that there is no link at the Microsoft site to download the driver, then she can check out the manufacturer's website to see if the manufacturer has posted a new driver.

Keep in mind, however, that older devices (such as printers) that were available long before the release of Windows 2000 Professional (and which do not appear in the HCL) will probably not have new drivers written for Windows 2000 Professional. In some cases, you can use Windows 2000 Professional drivers for a similar model, but full device functionality may not be available.

> When you search the Microsoft compatibility site, double-check spelling. For instance, when we searched for the Hewlett-Packard 7400C scanner, we left out the hyphen and failed to find the scanner. Repeating the search with the hyphen included worked!

Use the Readiness Analyzer to Check Out Compatibility   The Windows 2000 Professional installation program also performs a hardware compatibility test before beginning the installation. Although you could rely on this test to ensure that your system meets the minimum requirements for Windows 2000 Professional compatibility, we don't advise doing so since if incompatible hardware is found, you'll have to abort the installation and resolve the compatibility issues before proceeding. Generally, this means removing any incompatible hardware and replacing it with compatible hardware.

As an alternative, you may want to use the Readiness Analyzer, a stand-alone hardware and software compatibility test that you can run by running the WINNT32 program with the checkupgradeonly switch. WINNT32 is the program that starts an upgrade installation from Windows 9x. When you run it with the checkupgradeonly switch on, it runs the compatibility test without starting the upgrade installation. The result is an upgrade report on the compatibility of all detected hardware and software. This report can be viewed on the screen or printed, and it is saved in a file called Upgrade.txt, although you can choose a different name from within the Readiness Analyzer. Figure 6-4 shows the upgrade report information after we ran the Readiness Analyzer on a computer with a video adapter unknown to Windows 2000 Professional. In this case, we obtained a Windows 2000 Professional device driver from the vendor.

Determine the Service Packs and Updates to Use

Service packs and updates have become critical for any operating

---

Try This!

Check Out the Compatible Products

Look for the HP Scanjet 4200C device driver that Veronica needs. To complete this task, you will need a computer with an Internet connection and a web browser. Try this:

1. Point your web browser to www.microsoft.com/windows2000/professional/howtobuy/upgrading/compat/. Click the bar labeled Hardware Devices.

2. On the Search for Compatible Hardware Devices page, either enter **Hewlett-Packard** in the Company field or enter **7400C** in the Model field; then select Scanners in the Device Type field and click Find.

3. You may have to scroll the screen to see the results. If you find that the device driver is not available for download, you can connect to the manufacturer's site (www.hp.com) and search for a device driver there.

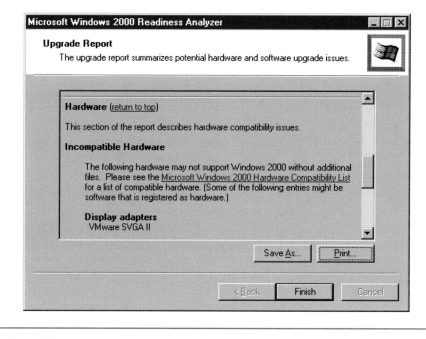

<image src="img_1" />
Microsoft Windows 2000 Readiness Analyzer

Upgrade Report

The upgrade report summarizes potential hardware and software upgrade issues.

Hardware (return to top)

This section of the report describes hardware compatibility issues.

Incompatible Hardware

The following hardware may not support Windows 2000 without additional files. Please see the Microsoft Windows 2000 Hardware Compatibility List for a list of compatible hardware. (Some of the following entries might be software that is registered as hardware.)

Display adapters
VMware SVGA II

Save As...   Print...

< Back   Finish   Cancel

• **Figure 6-4.** Readiness Analyzer upgrade report

system. They often are needed to correct a vulnerability discovered by the growing number of hackers, people who find ways to break into networked computers and wreak havoc. You will most certainly want to apply any necessary service packs or updates immediately after installation. For most of us, that means that we connect to Microsoft's Update site immediately after installation and install the recommended updates and service packs. However, some organizations do not allow service packs or updates to be installed unless they have first been tested by their own IT staff. In this case, you should check out what has been approved and where the appropriate service packs and updates are located. They will probably be somewhere on the local network or on a CD.

Determine the Method of Installation

You can install Windows 2000 Professional manually, or you can use an automated method. There are variations of each of these approaches.

Try This!

Run the Hardware and Software Compatibility Test

You can test the compatibility of the hardware and software on your lab computer. To complete this task, you will need the Windows 2000 Professional CD and a computer running a 32-bit version of Windows. Try this:

1. Insert the Windows 2000 Professional CD. If your computer uses autorun (if it automatically runs a program when a CD is inserted), close any messages or windows that open.

2. Open a command prompt and enter the following commands (where *d*: is your CD-ROM drive; be sure to press ENTER at the end of each line):

   ```
   d:
   cd \i386
   ```

3. Readiness Analyzer will take a few minutes to detect your hardware and software and prepare the upgrade report.

4. When the upgrade report appears, scroll through the summary information and look for any information about incompatible hardware or software.

5. When you have finished, click Save As and save the report as **Upgrade.txt** on your local hard drive. Then click Finish to close the Readiness Analyzer.

Manual Installation   A manual installation requires that someone be present during the entire installation, providing responses to questions asked by the installation program. You may perform a manual installation for an empty hard disk (also called a clean installation) or for an upgrade to an existing Windows computer. An upgrade is an installation that directly replaces an existing Windows operating system, preserving all the configuration information from the previous OS and applications and applying them to the new OS. The following operating systems can be upgraded to Windows 2000 Professional: Windows 95, Windows 98, Windows NT 3.51 Workstation, and Windows NT 4.0 Workstation.

You would usually choose a manual installation for a single computer or if the number of installations is too few to justify spending the time, effort, and expense of an automated installation. Once you decide on a manual installation, you need to make more decisions.

- Where are the source files located? Will you install from the Windows 2000 Professional CD, from the local hard drive, or from a share on a network server? If this will be a clean installation, you must either boot directly from the CD or from the Windows 2000 Professional setup disks, which start the Setup program but require the presence of the CD. If you are upgrading, you will start your old OS, insert the CD, and if autorun is enabled, you will select Install Windows 2000 from the Microsoft Windows 2000 Professional CD window, as shown in Figure 6-5. Otherwise, run WINNT32 (the upgrade program) from the i386 folder on the CD or on a file server.

- If you are planning to perform a clean installation from the CD, test whether the computer will boot from the CD. If your computer will not boot from CD, you will have to create a set of Windows 2000 Professional setup disks. This can be done using the Makeboot program, which is located in the Bootdisk folder on the Windows 2000 Professional CD. Most likely, you will need to run the Makeboot program on another computer (other than the one where you want to install Windows 2000 Professional) since you probably will not be able to access

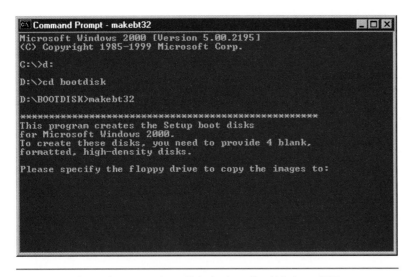

- Makeboot is used to create boot disks for installing Windows 2000 Professional.

the CD drive if no OS is installed. MAKEBOOT.EXE is a character-mode program, not one with a graphical user interface. Note, however, that there are two versions of Makeboot: the 16-bit version for DOS and Windows 3.1 called MAKEBOOT.EXE, and the 32-bit version for 32-bit Windows called MAKEBT32.EXE. The second version is much faster than the first, and therefore should be used whenever the OS will support it.

If you are determined to learn more about setup scripts, check out the Windows 2000 Professional website at www.microsoft.com/windows2000/professional. Search on Deployment. Most of these documents will cure insomnia!

Automated Installation   You can perform an automated installation of Windows 2000 Professional using one of several methods. One method is to use special scripts that are called up using special switches in the WINNT or WINN32 programs that are in the i386 directory of the Windows 2000 Professional CD. The creation of these special scripts and how you prepare the source files for the installation process are very advanced topics.

Many organizations use images as their method of automated installation. An image is a copy of an entire hard disk containing an OS and all applications. This image is copied using special software, and it can then be copied to one or many computers, also using special software. Most medium-sized to large organizations have used this method for many years. The most popular imaging software is Ghost, from Symantec (www.symantec.com/sabu/ghost).

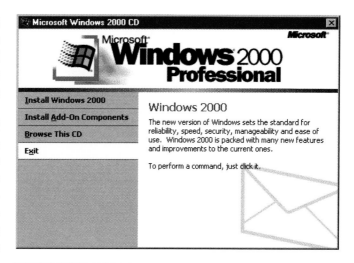

• **Figure 6-5.** Autorun menu on a Windows 2000 Professional CD

Gather the Materials Needed for Installation

The materials you will need for an installation depend on the decisions you have made about the installation and what you have learned about the compatibility of your hardware. You should, at minimum, have the Windows 2000 Professional CD or know a location on the network from which you can run the Windows upgrade program. If you plan to install from the CD but you either do not have an OS installed to access the CD or cannot boot from the CD, then you will need the four Windows 2000 Professional setup disks.

If you did your homework and checked out the compatibility of your hardware, you have gathered any drivers that won't be on the Windows 2000 Professional CD. You can install these drivers when prompted during the installation, or in the case of noncritical devices, such as printers, you can wait until after the installation is complete to install them.

Everything else you will need is listed at the start of Step-by-Step 6.01. Make sure you have all of the items before you begin.

> Whenever possible, perform a clean installation by installing Windows on an empty hard disk. We even prefer to start with an unpartitioned hard disk and have the Setup program create a new partition and format it.

Step-by-Step 6.01

Installing Windows 2000 Professional

The steps in this exercise describe a clean installation on an unpartitioned hard drive. To complete this exercise, you will need the following:

- A Microsoft/Intel standard personal computer (desktop or laptop) compatible with Windows 2000 Professional, with at least the minimum hardware and configured to boot from CD

- An unpartitioned hard disk (disk 0, the first hard disk)

- The Windows 2000 Professional CD

- The four Windows 2000 Professional setup disks, if your computer doesn't boot from a CD-ROM drive

- One 3.5-inch diskette to use as an emergency repair disk

- The **CD key** code from the envelope of your Windows 2000 Professional CD

- A 15-character (or less) name for your computer, unique on your network
- The name of the workgroup to be used in the class lab
- A password for the Administrator account on your computer

- The IP address, subnet mask, and other necessary TCP/IP configuration information, or confirmation from your instructor that you should configure Windows 2000 Professional to get an IP address automatically

Step 1

Insert the Windows 2000 Professional CD and restart the computer. After the restart, a blue character mode screen will appear while the setup files are loaded into memory. This will take several minutes, during which the gray status bar at the bottom of the screen will name the files as they are loaded. Once all of the setup files are loaded, you'll see the message on the status bar that Setup is starting Windows 2000 Professional. Then the Welcome to Setup screen will appear. Press ENTER to continue.

```
Windows 2000 Professional Setup

  Welcome to Setup.

  This portion of the Setup program prepares Microsoft(R)
  Windows 2000(TM) to run on your computer.

    •  To set up Windows 2000 now, press ENTER.

    •  To repair a Windows 2000 installation, press R.

    •  To quit Setup without installing Windows 2000, press F3.




  ENTER=Continue   R=Repair   F3=Quit
```

Step 2

The next screen shows that Setup has detected that the computer startup hard disk is new or has been erased. Press C to continue. Read the license agreement, and then press F8 to accept it. On the next several screens, follow the instructions to create a partition of at least 2GB (2,048MB), select the new partition as the location for Windows 2000 Professional, and format it with NTFS. Setup will then take several minutes to copy files to the new partition (C:), and your computer will reboot.

Step 3

After the reboot, Setup starts in GUI mode, with the message, "Please wait…." Then GUI mode setup begins, and the first screen may flash past before you can read it. Setup will then detect basic hardware, such as the keyboard and mouse, and install device drivers. This will take several minutes, during which time your screen may flicker and flash several times.

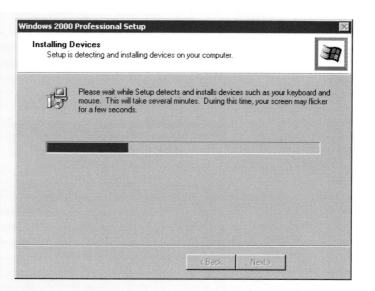

Step 4

On the Regional Setting page, leave the default, unless you need to customize Windows for a different locale. Follow the instructions to continue through the next several pages, providing the necessary responses from the information you gathered before beginning this step-by-step exercise. On the Network Settings page, select Typical Settings unless your instructor has told you otherwise, in which case you should select Custom Settings. That's where you enter TCP/IP configuration information (IP address, subnet mask, and so on). Enter your workgroup name on the Workgroup or Computer Domain page.

Step 5

Setup will take several minutes to copy the files necessary to complete the installation; then the Performing Final Tasks page will appear while Setup installs Start menu items, registers components (with the OS), saves settings, and removes temporary files created during the installation. At the conclusion, the Completing the Windows 2000 Professional Setup wizard page will appear. Follow the instructions and then click Finish. After the reboot, the Network Identification wizard appears.

Step 6

Follow the on-screen instructions to complete the wizard. The default setting on the Users of This Computer page, Windows Always Assumes the Following User Has Logged

On to This Computer, is the least secure. It uses the name you entered on the Name and Organization page. If you choose this option and provide a password, Windows 2000 Professional will create a user account in its security accounts database (the SAM), but Windows will automatically perform the logon for you. Therefore, anyone who can turn on your computer is logged on to the computer using your local account.

Network Identification Wizard

Users of This Computer
Who can log on to this computer?

You can require all users to enter a user name and password to log on, or you can have Windows assume the same user will always log on to this computer.

Which option do you prefer?

○ Users must enter a user name and password to use this computer.

● Windows always assumes the following user has logged on to this computer:

User name:	Jane Holcombe
Password:	
Confirm password:	

[< Back] [Next >] [Cancel]

Step 7

Select Users Must Enter a User Name and Password to Use This Computer. This is a more secure setting. While the previous setting is okay for a computer in a low-risk, low-security environment and, preferably, not on a network, this setting is for computers in most businesses. However, it requires a little more work to create the individual accounts. When you have completed this wizard, the Log On to Windows dialog box will appear, unless you selected the less-secure option.

Step 8

Log on to Windows as Administrator, supplying the password that you gave during the installation. After you log on, you should see the desktop with the Getting Started dialog box. You can use this to learn more about Windows, by clicking Discover Windows (you will need to insert the Windows 2000 Professional CD).

Verify Network Access

If this computer is on a network, you should verify that it can communicate with other computers on the network. A less-than-perfect, but easy, low-tech test is to open My Network Places and see if you can see any computers on the network besides your own.

 Remember that the only computers visible in My Network Places are those with the server service running. Windows 2000 Professional computer has this service installed and enabled by default, so your computer should be visible in My Network Places.

Figure 6-6 shows My Network Places opened in Explorer view (right-click My Network Places and select Explore). With all the icons under Entire Network expanded, you have a pretty good view of the network. There are three domains or workgroups, named Htc, Research, and Workgroup. In fact, Htc is a Windows NT domain, and Research and Workgroup are both workgroups. Then you can see the computers in each of these groups. Finally, Computers Near Me contains all the computers in the workgroup or domain to which the local computer belongs.

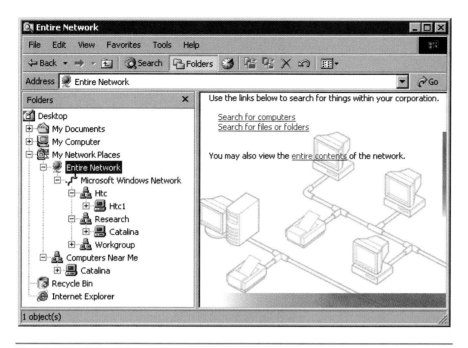

If you install Windows 2000 Professional on a computer at work or at school, be sure to check whether your organization has any restrictions on installing the latest versions of these fixes directly from the Microsoft website, or whether updates and service packs are available on the local network.

● **Figure 6-6.** My Network Places expanded to show workgroups, domains, and computers

Verify Windows 2000 Professional Updates and Service Packs

One reason it's important to verify your network access after installing Windows 2000 Professional is that you may need network access to complete the next important task after installing any software: installing any necessary updates or service packs. Since updates and service packs often fix security problems, it is important to install the latest ones as soon as possible. These are available on the Microsoft website for free download.

If you're permitted to get the very latest from the Microsoft Update site and you have Internet access to your computer, you can use the Windows Update program on the Start menu to connect.

● Windows Update is on the Start menu

Step-by-Step 6.02

Installing Updates and Service Packs

In this step-by-step exercise, you will use Windows Update to connect to the Microsoft Update site; test your computer for installed components, updates, and service packs; and install the recommended updates and service packs. To complete this exercise, you will need the following:

■ A PC with Windows 2000 Professional installed as described in Step-by-Step 6.01

■ Internet access (confirm that you can access the Internet using Internet Explorer)

Step 1

From the Windows 2000 Professional Start menu, select Windows Update. After you connect to the Windows Update page, click the Scan for Updates button. After the scan is complete, Windows Update will display the Pick Updates to Install page. Click Review and Install Updates.

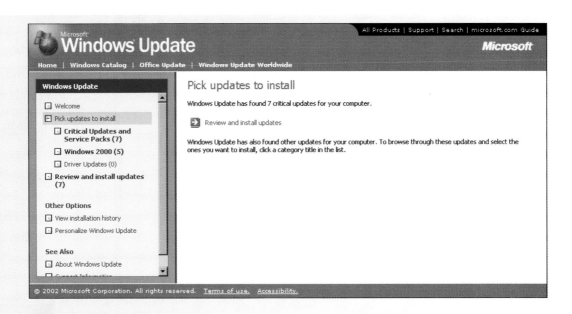

Step 2

You may have to use the scroll bar to view all of the updates. Some can be installed together. Some are described as exclusive and must be installed separately from others. Follow the instructions on the screen and install the updates now. We suggest that you install exclusive updates one at a time.

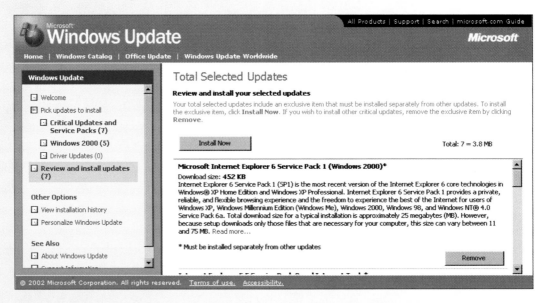

Step 3

The Windows Update wizard will download and install each update. You may be prompted to restart your computer after an update is installed. After the restart, if you have not installed all of the recommended updates, restart Windows Update, rescan your computer, and review the remaining updates. Install the other updates. The smaller updates can often be installed together. Repeat until all of the recommended updates have been installed.

After you have installed all of the Windows Updates to correct any potential problems with the OS, look for any updates for your applications programs. For instance, if you are using Microsoft Office, you can select Office Update from the Windows Update site and go through a process similar to that for installing the Windows updates. If you have applications from other companies, check out their websites for updates.

Customizing and Managing Windows 2000 Professional

Once you have installed Windows 2000 Professional, configured the OS to work with your network, and installed recommended updates and service packs, you can get down to the real fun of customizing the OS for the person who will use it. In addition to being a very stable and robust operating system, Windows 2000 Professional is also quite easy to customize and manage for one user or for hundreds of users.

In this section, we examine several of the tools you can use to customize and manage Windows 2000 Professional. You'll look at the options for making a computer more accessible and the options for customizing display settings. You will practice adding and sharing a printer and customizing the Start menu. Then you'll explore the options for managing files and folders and practice searching the hard drive for a file. You'll also practice other customization tasks, including installing and removing applications.

> Your Control Panel may not look exactly like the Control Panel shown here. Depending on the configuration of your system, your Control Panel may have more or fewer icons.

Using the Control Panel Applets

The Windows 2000 Professional **Control Panel** contains numerous applets that you can use to adjust the configuration of many different aspects of the OS.

As you learned in Chapter 3, each of these applets typically opens a window or a dialog box in which you can make a number of important adjustments. Remember that the Control Panel provides just one of several methods for opening a particular tool.

Although we do not have the room to discuss each of the new Control Panel applets, we'll look closely at a few of them. As will quickly become apparent, you use similar techniques with all of these tools, so you should have no trouble using additional Control Panel tools in the future on your own.

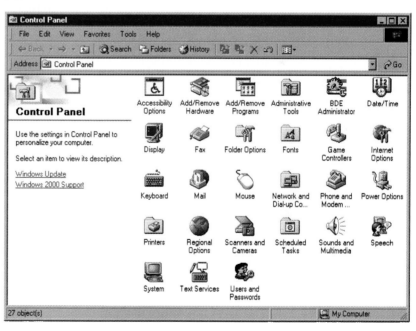

• The Windows 2000 Professional Control Panel

The Accessibility Options

Windows 2000 Professional has a number of built-in features that are designed to make computers more accessible for people with certain common disabilities such as restricted vision, hearing loss, or difficulty with mobility.

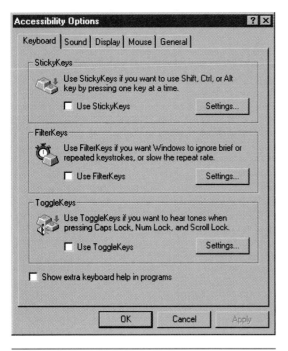

• Accessibility Options

Some of these features can be enabled and configured through the Accessibility Options applet on the Control Panel, and others are in the form of utilities (small, useful programs) that you turn on and configure from Start | Programs | Accessories | Accessibility.

The Accessibility Options dialog box has several tabs that you can use to configure various aspects of the accessibility options. For example, on the Keyboard tab, you can set the StickyKeys option, which is helpful for someone who must use a pointer stick for typing. The CTRL, ALT, and SHIFT keys are often used along with a second key to issue various commands, but holding down multiple keys simultaneously is not possible with a pointer stick. When StickyKeys is enabled, pressing any of those keys and then following that with another key press is considered the equivalent of pressing the two keys simultaneously.

Customizing Display Settings

The Display applet in Windows 2000 is not too different from that in past versions of Windows, and by now you should be able to find your way around this applet to change the background, add a screen saver, and otherwise customize the desktop to your own needs and taste. However, there is one, easy-to-overlook button on the Settings tab that you should take at look at.

The Advanced Button

The Advanced button in the Display Properties dialog box includes an extremely important button that many Windows users seem to miss. The Advanced button displays an additional dialog box that combines the video adapter card and monitor properties so that you can choose settings that are appropriate for the pair.

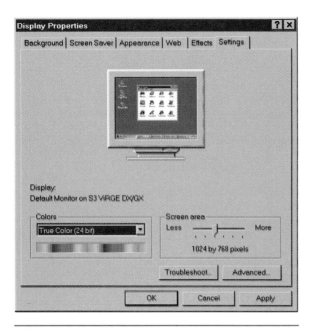

• Press the Advanced button on the Settings tab

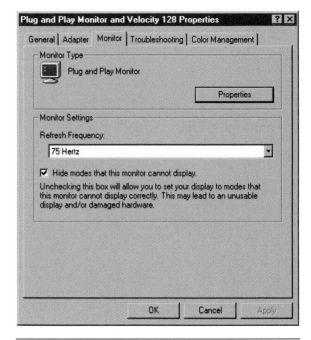

• Select a refresh rate above 60 Hertz

Probably the most important tab in this dialog box is the Monitor tab, where you can choose the **refresh rate** for the display. The refresh rate defines how often the display is refreshed to keep the image flicker free. In every case, this setting must be above 60 Hertz to reduce eyestrain. The reason for this is that at 60 Hertz or below, the monitor flickers—often causing users to develop headaches or other vision-related problems. Depending on the quality of the monitor, you may need to select a lower screen resolution to permit a refresh rate above 60 Hertz.

Adding a Printer

In spite of optimistic predictions heard many times over the years, the "paperless office" is still pretty much a pipe dream. Most computer users still need printers, so we now look at the process of installing a printer in Windows 2000 Professional (which you can do only if you are a member of the Administrators group). Adding a printer in Windows is really adding a printer driver, which you need to do whether the printer is directly connected to your computer or connected elsewhere on the network. When you install a local printer and then share it so that others on your network can use it, your computer plays the role of a print server. Remember that a printer that is directly connected to your computer (local) is still local even if you intend to share it on the network.

Step-by-Step 6.03

Adding a Printer in Windows 2000

Take a few minutes to add a local printer. You will use this printer again in this chapter. To complete this step-by-step exercise, you will need the computer on which you successfully installed Windows 2000 Professional in Step-by-Step 6.01. A physical printer is *not* required.

Step 1

Open the Printers folder by choosing Start | Settings | Printers. Open the Add Printer icon, and the Add Printer wizard will start. At the first screen, click Next to continue. On the Local or Network Printer page, choose Local Printer and clear the check box next to Automatically Detect and Install My Plug and Play Printer, because you don't really have this printer connected. Then click Next.

Add Printer Wizard

Local or Network Printer
Is the printer attached to your computer?

If the printer is directly attached to your computer, click Local printer. If it is attached to another computer, or directly to the network, click Network printer.

⊙ Local printer
    ☐ Automatically detect and install my Plug and Play printer
○ Network printer

< Back   Next >   Cancel

Step 2

On the Select the Printer Port page, ensure that Use the Following Port is selected and then click Next. On the next page, select HP from the list of manufacturers and HP Color Laser-Jet 4500 from the list of printers and then click Next. On the Name Your Printer page (no, it's not a new game), you may enter a name that is friendlier than the model name. This is not mandatory—the illustration shows the model name—but you may want to do this to identify how the printer is being used: for example, Brochure Printer or Accounting Printer.

Add Printer Wizard

Name Your Printer
You must assign a name for this printer.

Supply a name for this printer. Some programs do not support server and printer name combinations of more than 31 characters.

Printer name:

HP Color LaserJet 4500

< Back   Next >   Cancel

Step 3

On the Printer Sharing page, ensure that the Share As option is selected and give the printer yet another name—this time a share name by which it will be known on the network. Leave the default, or enter a short, friendly name; then click Next.

Add Printer Wizard

Printer Sharing
You can share this printer with other network users.

Indicate whether you want this printer to be available to other users. If you share this printer, you must provide a share name.

○ Do not share this printer

● Share as: brochure

< Back   Next >   Cancel

Step 4

On the Location and Comment page, enter a location for the printer and add a description in the Comment box. Then click Next.

Add Printer Wizard

Location and Comment
You have the option of supplying a location and description of this printer.

You can describe the location and capabilities of this printer. This information may be helpful to users.

Location: Marketing Dept, 3rd floor, east

Comment: To be used for printer color brochures

< Back   Next >   Cancel

Step 5

When the Add Printer wizard offers to print a test page, you will normally accept the offer, but in this case, you don't have the printer. To close the wizard, click Finish.

Using the Start Menu Tools

For the final example of Windows 2000 Professional customization, we'll look at the Taskbar and Start Menu Properties dialog box. You display this dialog box by right-clicking a blank space on the taskbar and choosing Properties from the pop-up menu.

The General Tab

As in Windows 98, the General tab of the Taskbar and Start Menu Properties dialog box, shown in Figure 6-7, includes several options. These primarily control the display of the taskbar; however, some affect the Start menu. You can use the Taskbar and Start Menu options to ensure that the taskbar is always visible or to hide it when you want the maximum amount of desktop space for your applications.

The Advanced tab

The Advanced tab of the Taskbar and Start Menu Properties dialog box, shown in Figure 6-8, enables you to further customize the Start menu by adding or removing Start menu items and configuring settings.

Some of the more interesting items on the Advanced tab are located in the Start Menu Settings area near the bottom of this tab. For example, items that begin with the word Expand will create a menu from the items in the respective folder. Thus, if you select the Expand Control Panel option and click Apply, you can then choose the Control Panel objects from a submenu of the Start menu instead of first opening the Control Panel and double-clicking the items.

Inside Information

Headaches and Nausea!

In the early days of motion pictures, people sometimes became nauseated or suffered from headaches when watching a movie. Research showed that the human eye has persistence—that is, the brain retains an image for a fraction of a second after the image is turned off. When about 20 images per second are shown, the human eye can still detect the flickering on and off of the images. Movies are shown in theatres at a rate of at least 32 frames per second so that motion on a screen appears to be continuous. On a CRT monitor, other problems, like the alternating current from an electric wall socket outlet, can cause the flicker to be noticeable if the rate is below about 60 Hz (Hertz—a rate of repetition in cycles per second).

Try This!

Customize the Start Menu

Today you're a desktop support person who's been asked to customize the Start menu for one of your client users. He doesn't like personalized menus, would like a shortcut to the Favorites folder on the Start menu, and would also like the contents of the My Documents folder to appear as a menu when he selects My Documents from the Start menu. Try this:

1. Open Taskbar and Start Menu Properties and clear the check box next to Use Personalized Menus.

2. Select the Advanced tab of Taskbar and Start Menu Properties and place a check in the box next to Display Favorites.

3. Scroll through the list of Start menu settings and place a check in the box next to Expand My Documents.

4. Click OK to close the dialog box and then test for the results of these changes. If you only very recently installed Windows 2000, it may not have truncated (personalized) your menus yet, so you may not yet see a difference. The results of the other two settings are easy to observe.

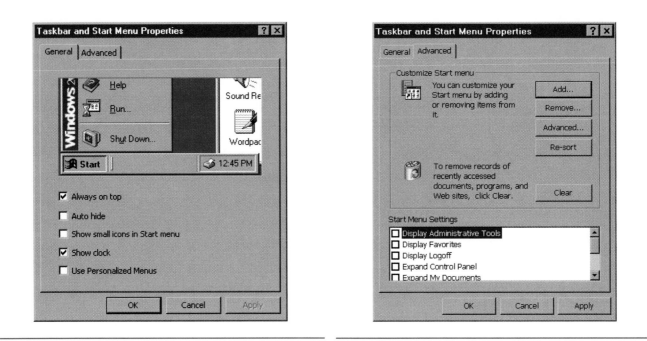

● **Figure 6-7.**　Set the taskbar and Start menu options

● **Figure 6-8.**　Advanced taskbar and Start menu properties

The Use Personalized Menus option, shown in Figure 6-7, is confusing. When this option is first turned on, nothing changes. Then, after the OS watches for a few days to see what options you use and don't use, each menu shows only recently used items—which can be very confusing for users who don't understand where the missing items have gone. To see hidden menu items in a truncated menu, click the chevrons at the bottom of the menu.

You don't have to open the Taskbar and Start Menu Properties dialog box to re-sort the Start menu. Just right-click the Start menu and choose Sort by Name from the pop-up menu to sort the menu in alphabetical order.

Managing Files and Folders in Windows 2000 Professional

All information on a computer is stored in files, and those files are typically organized by separating them into folders containing related files (some operating systems still use the older term *directories* instead of folders, but there is no functional difference between the two). It's important for you to understand how to organize files and folders properly so that you can easily access important files, and so that you know which files should not be touched. And because even the best file organization won't guarantee that you'll always remember the name of that very important file or even where you saved it, you should practice searching for files.

Organizing Files and Folders

All filing systems need a level of organization if they are to be useful. If you use a filing cabinet to hold a number of important documents, most likely you use some sort of alphabetical arrangement of the folders so that you can locate them quickly when you need them. Imagine what a difficult time you would have finding your tax-related documents if all year long you simply threw everything into a large box and then had to sort through each piece of paper to find the few important ones out of thousands.

Windows 2000 Professional provides folders, created by default and arranged in a very logical manner, to place related files in certain common locations. The most important of the default folders include these:

- **My Documents**　This folder is the most common location where application programs store your document files. Each user has his or her own My Documents folder, which is accessed from Start |

Documents and is stored on disk in the Documents and Settings folder. Whenever you open Windows Explorer from the Start menu, the primary focus is on the My Documents folder for the currently logged-on user.

- **My Pictures**   This folder is a subfolder of the My Documents folder and typically is the location where image files are stored.

- **Windows**   This folder, located in the root folder of the boot partition, is where Windows 2000 Professional itself is stored. Note that on dual-boot systems, it's quite common to give the Windows 2000 Professional folder a different (but usually similar) name.

- **Program Files**   This folder is the location of subfolders where your application programs are typically installed.

- **Fonts**   Here you will find the various fonts installed on the PC. This folder is always a subfolder of the Windows folder and is considered a special folder.

- **System** and **System32**   These are subfolders of the Windows folder and are used to store many very important files necessary for the proper operation of Windows 2000 Professional.

- **Temp**   This is a folder used to temporarily store files, such as those used during the installation of new application programs, and those temporary files created by a program while it is working. This folder often contains out-of-date files left over from an installation operation.

> The rule for the Temp folder is that any program writing files to it should delete those files when the program is given the command to close. If a program ends abnormally (you tripped over the power cord or the OS hung up), the program can't do this important chore. Therefore, it is generally considered safe to delete files from the Temp folder that have not been used in over a week. In practice, we delete all temporary files dated before the last restart.

- Windows 2000 installation automatically creates dozens of folders!

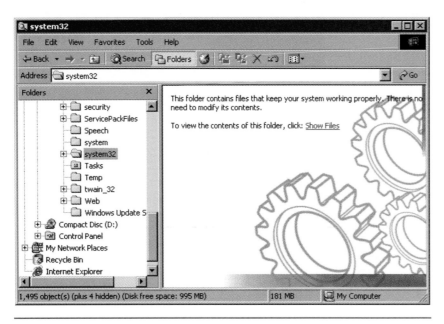

• A warning about system files in the System32 folder

Remember DOS file attributes from Chapter 2? Windows 2000 uses file attributes on all of its file systems; its hidden, archive, and system attributes are employed in the same way as described in Chapter 2. But if you open the properties for a file in Windows Explorer, you'll see additional attributes: index, compress, and encrypt.

Hands Off: System Files

Quite a few files, called system files, are part of the OS and are very important to the proper operation of Windows 2000 Professional. Windows 2000 Professional even warns you if you try to open a folder where system files and other important files are stored.

In addition to this warning, some, but not all, files in these folders have the hidden attribute turned on so that Windows 2000 Professional hides them from view, even when you open the folder. But when you are studying or troubleshooting an OS, you may want to change this default so that you can see the hidden files. You can change these defaults in My Computer or Windows Explorer if you choose Tools | Folder Options and modify the settings on the View tab. Figure 6-9 shows the settings we use when we want to be able to see all files, including file extensions.

Finding Files and Folders

Janelle is the office manager for a small antique furniture appraisal company. She has several appraisers who produce their own files on antique items. When a customer asks for detailed information on a particular item, Janelle must be able to locate the specific file that describes it. To do so, she often turns to the Windows 2000 Professional Search facility. This allows her to search not only her local hard drive, but also any shared folders on the network.

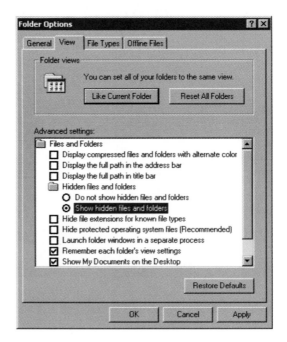

• Figure 6-9. Modified View settings

To open the Windows 2000 Professional search tool, you click the Start button and choose Search | For Files or Folders from the Start menu. Once the Search Results window is open, you use the various options in the window to define your search.

The Search Results window contains text boxes and other controls you use to customize the search. These include the following:

- **Search for Files or Folders Named** This text box enables you to enter the name (or partial name) of the file or folder you want to find. You can use the question mark (?) as a wildcard to replace a single character, or the asterisk (*) as a wildcard to replace any number of characters. To search for a name that includes spaces, enclose the search phrase in quotation marks.

- **Containing Text** This text box allows you to specify text contained in the file you want to find. For example, Janelle is searching for a file containing research she did on an eighteenth-century candlestick table, but she has forgotten the file name she used for it. She remembers that she used the phrase "mahogany candlestick table." Therefore, she enters *.* in the Files or Folders Named box, and the phrase **mahogany candlestick table** in the Containing Text box.

- **Look In** Use this drop-down list to select the locations you want to search. You might want to limit the search to likely locations to speed the search process.

- **Date** Select this check box to display additional date-related search options so that you can find files based on the date they were modified, created, or last accessed. For instance, if Janelle recalls that she modified the mahogany candlestick table file in the past week, she can narrow her search by date to the past seven days.

- **Type** Use this option when you want to locate specific types of files such as Word documents, applications, or image files.

- **Size** This option enables you to specify that the file must be of a certain size.

- **Advanced Options** Select this option to specify that the search should include subfolders or be case sensitive or that you want to search files that will take a long time to search.

- **Indexing Service** Select this option to enable or disable the **Indexing Service**, which will maintain indexes of the files (both properties and contents) on your hard drive. This service watches for changes on the drive and updates the indexes every time changes occur. These indexes speed up searches by any program (such as the Search program) that knows to use them.

Each search condition that you add must be satisfied in addition to all existing search conditions. That is, if you specify that the file must be at least 128KB and that it must contain the text *proposal,* both of those conditions must be met. A file of less than 128KB that contains the text will not be included in the results.

• The Search window

Turn on the Indexing Service only if you do very frequent searches, because you may find the frequent disk activity of index updating annoying, and this service can actually make other programs run more slowly.

Practice Doing a Search

Although the concept of searching for a particular item or group of items is easy to understand, the more options available to help you search, the more complicated the actual search becomes. Searching is a skill that needs practice! Try this:

1. Open the search window from Start | Search | For Files and Folders.

2. Specify that you want to search your hard disk for all application files by using the wildcard *.exe as the name of the file. Search, and note the number of results you get.

3. Next, narrow the search by specifying that you want to see only files created within the past three months. Search, and again note the number of results.

4. Finally, see what happens when you narrow the search so that only those files that are under 25KB are located. Take note of how adding conditions reduces the number of results returned.

Installing and Removing Applications and Windows 2000 Components

Any OS is simply a vehicle for running applications. Therefore, installing the applications a user needs is a necessary task when customizing Windows 2000. In this section, we look briefly at how you install and remove application programs in Windows 2000 Professional.

Installing Applications

Most application programs are distributed on CDs (although some very small programs are still distributed on disks). Luckily, Windows 2000 supports autorun, a feature that enables it to look for and read a special file called **Autorun** immediately after a CD is inserted and to run whatever program is listed in Autorun.inf. Most application programs distributed on CD have an Autorun file that calls up the installation program.

Sometimes, however, it is simply necessary to institute the installation sequence yourself. Perhaps the install CD lacks an autorun installation program, or perhaps your PC is configured so that autorun programs must be started manually. In some cases, a CD may contain more than one program, and you must choose which of them to install. Regardless of the reason, beginning the installation process manually is a simple and straightforward process using the Add/Remove Programs applet in the Control Panel, which will search the CD drive for an installation program.

Before attempting to install an application, check to make certain that the program is actually compatible with Windows 2000 Professional. If the program's requirements do not state that the program is compatible with Windows 2000 Professional, you may have to determine its compatibility through the Microsoft compatibility site at www.microsoft.com/windows2000/professional/howtobuy/upgrading/compat/.

Install an Application

To begin the installation process manually, try this:

1. Open the Add/Remove Programs item in the Control Panel by clicking the Start button and choosing Settings | Control Panel. Then double-click the Add/Remove Programs icon.

2. Click the Add New Programs button along the left side of the Add/Remove Programs dialog box. Be sure you have placed the installation CD in the drive and that you have any registration numbers available.

3. Click the CD or Floppy button to display the Install Program from Floppy Disk or CD-ROM dialog box. When you are ready, click Next and then follow the on-screen directions to complete the installation.

• The Change or Remove Programs page in Add/Remove Programs

Typically, you will have to accept the terms of the software license before you are allowed to install the application. These steps are not optional since the installation simply won't proceed until you accept any terms the software manufacturer provides and enter the correct code. You may also be asked to make several decisions during the installation process. For example, you may be asked where you would like to install the program and if you would like certain optional components installed. Generally speaking, it is best to simply accept the suggested settings.

> You should shut down all other open applications before beginning a software installation. You also may be required to restart Windows 2000 Professional to complete the installation process.

> Most application programs are licensed for use on a single computer. If you want to install the program on another computer, the license typically requires you to remove it from the computer where it was first installed.

Removing Applications

Each application program you have installed takes up space on your computer's hard disk. Programs that you no longer need or use simply waste space that could be used for other purposes, so removing those can be an important piece of housekeeping.

You remove a program from a Windows 2000 Professional PC in much the same manner as you installed it. That is, you begin by opening the Add/Remove Programs dialog box. Next, with the Change or Remove Programs button clicked, you select the program you want to remove and click the Change/Remove button.

You may next see a message similar to the one shown here warning you that the program will be permanently removed from your PC. If you are certain you want to continue, click Yes.

> An application may even be a component of Windows 2000, such as a game, WordPad, or Calculator. In that case, the application can be installed or removed using Add/Remove Programs | Add/Remove Windows Components.

• Confirm that you want to remove the program

Try This!

Remove an Application

Removing an application is quite simple. Try this:

1. Log onto your PC using an account with Administrator rights.

2. Open the Control Panel.

3. Open the Add/Remove Programs icon.

4. Examine the list of installed programs and remove one you no longer use.

Remove Shared File?

The system indicates that the following shared file is no longer used by any programs. If any programs are still using this file and it is removed, those programs may not function. Are you sure you want to remove the shared file?

Leaving this file will not harm your system. If you are not sure what to do, it is suggested that you choose to not remove this shared component.

File name: C:\Program Files\Common Files\Intuit\Internet Client\Certs\ofxb

Located in: C:\Program Files\Common Files\Intuit\Internet Client\Certs

[Yes] [Yes To All] [No] [No To All]

- Shared files that are no longer in use waste disk space

Often you will also see a message telling you that a shared file that appears to no longer be in use is about to be deleted. Generally speaking, it is safe to delete such files. If you don't delete them, they will likely be orphaned and remain unused on your hard disk forever.

In some cases, clicking the Change/Remove button will start the application's install program so that you can modify the features that are installed. This is completely a function of the program you are attempting to remove, however.

◾ Managing Security for Users, Files, and Printers

Windows 2000 Professional contains a large number of security features that are important to maintaining the integrity of your system and data. Because these features are built into Windows 2000 Professional, both local and network security are handled seamlessly. That is, you use the same tools to control both local security and network security.

To help you manage security, Windows 2000 Professional includes the following important security features:

- Auditing
- Encrypted files and folders
- File and folder permissions (on NTFS volumes only)
- Group accounts
- Group policies
- Printer permissions
- Shared folder permissions
- User accounts
- User rights

Managing User Accounts and Groups

The most basic element of Windows 2000 Professional security is the **user** account. Each user must present a valid user name and password of a local or domain user account to log on to a Windows 2000 computer. Each user is also a member of one or more groups of users. **Groups** enable the system administrator to easily assign the same rights and permissions to all members of the group without the need to set those rights and permissions individually.

Using the Users and Passwords Applet

When you installed Windows 2000 Professional, if your computer was not made a member of a domain, you could have chosen to let the OS assume that you are the only user of the computer and that you don't want to see the logon dialog box. You can check this setting after installation (and refresh your memory) by opening the Users and Passwords applet in the Control Panel to see the setting for Users Must Enter a User Name and Password to Use This Computer. Figure 6-10 shows this choice is selected, which means that you will see a logon box every time you restart your computer. If this setting is turned off, anyone with physical access to your computer can use it without entering a user name and password.

There's a second setting in Users and Passwords that's important to enable for the sake of security—the setting on the Advanced tab under Secure Boot Settings. If checked, as shown in Figure 6-11, it requires users to press CTRL-ALT-DELETE before logging on. This setting is a defense against certain viruses that try to capture your user name and password, sometimes by

Try This!

Check Out the Security Basics

The Windows 2000 Help program is a great aid to learning and to on-the-job troubleshooting. You can use Help to learn about the security features listed here. Try this:

1. From the Start menu, select Help.

2. Click the Index tab. If this is the first time you have done this, the system will take a minute or two to index the help data.

3. When the Index page appears, enter the word **security**.

4. Scroll through the list until you see the word Overview. Select it and click Display. In the Topics Found box, select Security Overview and click Display.

5. The Security overview page lists the security features. Click the plus sign next to each one in turn and read the expanded text. When you are done, close the Help program.

Cross Check

Compare Security Features

Security features are very important in an operating system. Compare what you just learned about the Windows 2000 Professional security features with those of Windows NT in Chapter 4 and Windows 98 in Chapter 5. Then answer the following questions:

1. Of these operating systems, which offers the most robust security features?

   _____

2. Which operating systems make it the easiest to protect files using encryption?

   _____

3. Which operating systems enable you to create one or more groups of users to which you can apply permissions to access resources, and rights to perform certain systemwide actions?

   _____

- **Figure 6-10.** Security begins with turning on Users Must Enter a User Name and Password.

- **Figure 6-11.** Make your computer more secure by enabling Secure Boot Settings.

presenting a fake logon prompt. Pressing CTRL-ALT-DELETE will remove a program like that from memory and allow the actual logon dialog box to appear.

Try This!

Turn on Logon Requirements and Secure Boot Settings

Your friend Jordan has a small business with only five computers. He has a stand-alone Windows 2000 Professional computer in his office, on which he does the accounting and payroll. He has told you that when he starts Windows, he doesn't have to enter a user name and password. He would like to change this, because of the confidential data on that computer. You are going to turn on the option to require a log on.

To complete this exercise, you will need a computer running Windows 2000 Professional.

Now try this:

1. Open the Control Panel and open Users and Passwords.

2. If it is unchecked, click to check the box next to Users Must Enter a User Name and Password to Use This Computer.

3. Click the Advanced tab and place a check (if needed) in the box under Secure Boot Settings.

4. Click OK to close the dialog box. The next time anyone logs on to this computer, the user will first have to press CTRL-ALT-DEL to open a logon dialog box and then will be required to provide a user name and password.

Creating a New User

Creating a new user account enables that user to log in with a user name and password. This allows an administrator to set the rights and permissions for the user as well as to audit the user's access to certain network resources. If a Windows 2000 Professional computer is a member of a Windows NT or Active Directory domain, management of users and groups is mainly done at the domain level. But if a computer is a stand-alone computer or a member of a workgroup (as you will often see in very small organizations), users and groups will have to be managed on each computer. For that reason, it is good practice to create users on a desktop computer. You are also working with the same concepts on a small scale that an administrator must work with in a domain.

> ⚠ To create and manage users, you must be logged on as the Administrator or a member of the local Administrators group. Be sure to assign a password to the Administrator account so that only authorized users can access this all-powerful account.

Step-by-Step 6.04

Creating and Configuring a New User Account

Now you'll practice creating a user on your lab computer. To complete this step-by-step exercise, you will need the following:

- The computer on which you successfully installed Windows 2000 Professional in Step-by-Step 6.01

- To be logged on as Administrator or as a member of the local Administrators group

Step 1

Open the Users and Passwords applet in the Control Panel, and click the Add button. This opens the Add New User wizard. Enter the user name that the user will use to log on. Enter the user's first and last names in the Full Name box and, if you wish, enter something that describes this person in the Description box. If this is a work computer, enter a job description in this box. These last two fields are optional.

Step 2

When you have finished entering the user information, click Next to continue. You will be given the opportunity to enter and confirm the initial password for this new user. Do so and click Next to continue.

Step 3

Now you get to decide what groups the new user should belong to. There are two suggested

options—Standard User and Restricted User—or you can select the Other option button and choose a group from the drop-down list. Select Standard User, which on a Windows 2000 Professional desktop makes this person a member of the local Power Users Group, as well as the local Users group. Click the Finish button to close the dialog box.

Add New User

What level of access do you want to grant this user?

○ **Standard user** (Power Users Group)
Users can modify the computer and install programs, but cannot read files that belong to other users.

○ **Restricted user** (Users Group)
Users can operate the computer and save documents, but cannot install programs or make potentially damaging changes to the system files and settings.

○ **Other:** Administrators

< Back   Finish   Cancel

Step 4

You should see your new user listed in the Users and Passwords dialog box. Now suppose you have changed your mind about the password you created and want to change it. Select the new user in the Users for This Computer list on the Users page. Then click the Set Password button on the Users page. Enter and confirm the new password and then click OK to apply the changes.

Users and Passwords

| Users | Advanced |

Use the list below to grant or deny users access to your computer, and to change passwords and other settings.

☑ Users must enter a user name and password to use this computer.

Users for this computer:

User Name	Group
Administrator	Administrators
ahonore	Power Users
Guest	Guests

Add...   Remove   Properties

Set Password

New password: *******

Confirm new password: *******

OK   Cancel

A Word About Passwords

Passwords are a very important part of any security system. Most experts recommend using passwords that are at least eight characters long and contain a mixture of numbers, letters (both uppercase and lowercase), and nonalphanumeric characters. Passwords that use common words—such as the name of a pet—are easily guessed and therefore offer little in the way of real security.

Managing Permissions

In Windows 2000 Professional, you can control who has access to specified system resources such as files, folders, and printers by assigning permissions. These permissions restrict access to local users as well as to those who connect to these resources over the network, but remember (again) that only NTFS volumes allow you to assign permissions to files and folders.

NTFS Permissions

There are important security implications of formatting a hard disk with NTFS in Windows 2000 Professional. When a hard disk is formatted as an NTFS volume, you have far more precise and exacting control over how different users may access data on that drive. The permissions you can set on folders differ slightly from those that you can set on files. In both cases, there are standard permissions, each of which is composed of several special permissions. For example, the standard file permission called Read consists of the following special permissions: Read Data, Read Attributes, Read Extended Attributes, Read Permissions (the permissions on the file), and Synchronize.

Most of the time, standard permissions are all you need.

The standard file permissions are follows:

- Full Control
- Modify
- Read and Execute
- Read
- Write

The standard folder permissions are the same as the standard file permissions with the added permission of List Folder Contents.

Each of the standard permissions and each of the special permissions has three states. Only one box can be checked at a time for any permission. If both the Allow and Deny boxes are clear, that permission is not applied at all—it's implicitly denied. If the Allow box is checked, that permission is allowed, and if the Deny box is checked, that permission is denied—it's explicitly denied.

Groups

Another important part of the Windows 2000 Professional security puzzle is the concept of groups. A group in Windows 2000 Professional is a special security account that can contain local users, domain users, and special domain groups called global groups. Don't be concerned about learning about domain users and groups. That can wait for another course on another day. An administrator adds users to

Try This!

Research Special Permissions

It is important to understand permissions so that you can protect resources from unauthorized access or damage. Don't try to memorize them—remember that help is just a few mouse clicks away. Use the Windows 2000 Help program now to see the list of special permissions that make up each of the standard permissions listed here. Try this:

1. From the Start menu, select Help.

2. Click the Index tab. If this is the first time you have done this, the system will take a minute or two to index the help data.

3. When the Index page appears, enter the words **file permissions**.

4. Under file permissions, select (list) and click Display. The result should be a table of file permissions. Examine this table. When you are done, move to the next step.

5. Now enter a new keyword on the Index tab: **folder permissions**. Under folder permissions, select (list) and click Display. The result should be a table of folder permissions. Examine this table. When you are done, close Help.

You can open each of the group objects to see which users are members, and if you are a member of the Administrators group, you can add users.

a group if they all share the same access needs to one or more resources. Then the administrator can assign permissions for a file, folder, or printer to the group, in effect granting permissions to many users with just a few mouse clicks.

The built-in groups in Windows 2000 Professional are virtually identical to those in Windows NT 4.0 Workstation. These groups include Administrators, Backup Operators, Guests, Power Users, Replicator, and Users. To view these groups, right-click My Computer and select Manage to open the Computer Management console. Then expand Local Users and Groups and then Groups.

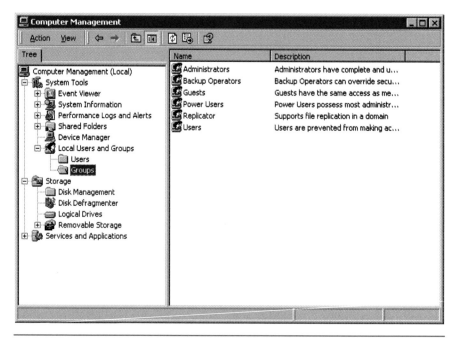

• Windows 2000 built-in local groups

Inside Information

Everyone

Although you won't see a group called Everyone in the Groups folder in the Computer Management window, this is nevertheless an important group. All users automatically belong to the Everyone group, even though an administrator doesn't specifically assign them to this group. When you are assigning permissions, it can be very tempting to grant permissions to the Everyone group since this allows all users to gain those permissions in one simple move. Unfortunately, doing so is generally not a good idea no matter how convenient it may be.

For example, if you were to grant the Everyone group full control to a shared folder, it would not be possible to prevent an otherwise unauthorized user from reading, modifying, or destroying any of the files in that folder. It is best to remove the Everyone group from the permissions list, rather than try to apply restricted permissions to this group, because these restrictions will apply to all users! Some prudent consideration of the implications of your actions will go a long way toward your ultimate success in the business world.

All of these groups are enabled except Guests, which is disabled by default, and the short lecture on Guests is to not use this group, nor should you generally use the Guest account, which is a member of this group and is also disabled.

Controlling File and Folder Access

Ultimately, controlling who can access folders and files and which operations each user is allowed to perform on them is probably the most important part of computer security. If you can prevent unauthorized individuals from reading sensitive documents or from making inappropriate modifications to your files, you've accomplished almost everything necessary to ensure data integrity.

File- and folder-level permissions can be set only on an NTFS volume. A FAT (or FAT32) volume is simply an open door to anyone who is logged on to (as in sitting in front of) your computer. However, when you share a file over the network, you can set permissions that share access to the folder only, thus restricting users who access the folder over the network.

Assigning NTFS Permissions

In this step-by-step exercise, you will explore the NTFS permissions that are assigned. To complete this step-by-step exercise, you will need the following:

- The computer on which you successfully installed Windows 2000 Professional in Step-by-Step 6.01

- The user name and password of the account you created in Step-by-Step 6.04

- Drive C: set up as an NTFS partition

Step 1

Log on using the user name and password of the user you created in Step-by-Step 6.04. Log off again (you'll see why in a moment).

Step 2

Log on as Administrator. Use My Computer or Windows Explorer to browse to C:\Documents and Settings. Notice the folders. There should be one for each user who has logged on, plus one titled All Users. Open the folder with the user name of your new account. These folders make up the user profile for your new user. They were created the first time that user logged on, and they contain the files that hold that user's desktop files, favorites, the Start menu, and several other important folders and files.

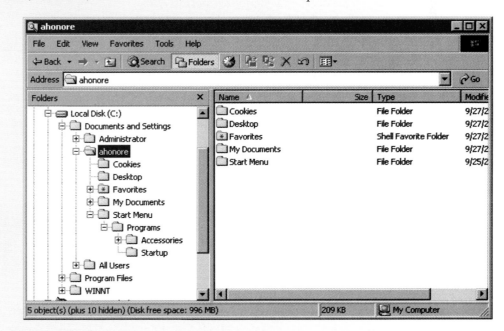

Step 3

When a user logs on to a computer that has NTFS on the boot drive (the drive in which the system files are installed), Windows 2000 Professional sets permissions on those folders and files. Next, you will look at the permissions set for your new user. Right-click the folder with the user's name, select Properties, and then click the Security tab. Click the Permissions button, and you will see the list of users and groups that have permissions to the folder. Notice that the Everyone group is not on the list.

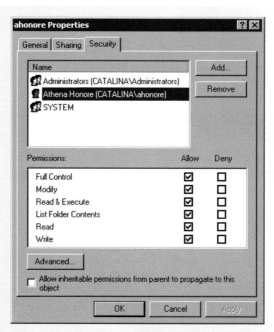

Step 4

The Security tab shows you only the standard permissions and lets you assign only the standard permissions. Notice the check boxes for Allow and Deny for each standard permission. To see the special permissions, click the Advanced button and then click the View/Edit button to see the special permissions assigned to the selected user. You will rarely need these special permissions. Click cancel three times to close the Properties dialog box.

To be safe, change NTFS permissions only for data files and folders that you create to actually hold data. When you install Windows 2000 Professional on an NTFS volume, the Setup program sets default permissions that allow the OS to function, but that keeps ordinary users from harming the OS. You can cause harm to the OS if you change these default settings.

Another Precaution to Keep Local Files Safe

Even though FAT and FAT32 volumes primarily enable you to restrict network access to your PC, you can prevent local access when you leave your desk by pressing CTRL-ALT-DELETE and choosing Lock Computer. When your computer is locked, only you or a system administrator can unlock your PC. (Don't forget your password!)

Combining NTFS and Share Permissions

Anyone sitting at your computer who logs on can access files and folders on an NTFS volume if the permissions allow. You might say that person has to go through two doors: the authorization door (during logon) and the NTFS

Survey of Operating Systems

permissions door. If you share a folder on that same NTFS volume, anyone coming over the network also comes through two doors: the share door and the NTFS permissions door.

Step-by-Step 6.06

Assigning Share Permissions

Serena works as a law clerk in a 10-member law firm. She has a computer on her desk at work, but sometimes she is asked to fill in for the receptionist for short periods of time and must work at the receptionist's computer. At these times, she would like to be able to access some of the files back on her desktop computer. In this step-by-step exercise, you will practice the steps you need to take to help

Serena. You will create a folder, share it, and set share permissions. To complete this step-by-step exercise, you will need the following:

- The computer on which you successfully installed Windows 2000 Professional in Step-by-Step 6.01
- The user name and password of the account you created in Step-by-Step 6.04

Step 1

Log on with the user name and password you created in Step-by-Step 6.04. Open Windows Explorer and navigate to C:\Documents and Settings. Open the folder that matches the user name you are using. Within that folder, create a new folder and name it **shared data**.

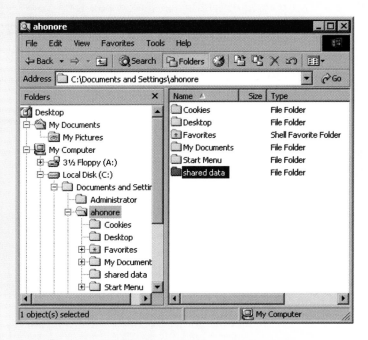

Step 2

Right-click the new folder and select Sharing from the context menu. The Properties dialog box for the folder will open with the Sharing tab already selected. Select the Share This Folder radio button. This activates the settings for sharing. The default share name is identical to the folder name, but you may change it if you wish.

Step 3

Click the Permissions button to display the Permissions dialog box for this folder. You use this dialog box to control who can access the folder over the network as well as the type of access available. Click the Add button and select the user name you used to log on; then click Add and OK. On the Share Permissions page, select the same user name in the Name box and click the Full Control check box under Permissions.

Step 4

There is only one thing wrong—the Everyone group still has permissions to this share. With the Everyone group highlighted, click the Remove button so that the group Everyone is removed. This is a very important step since when the Everyone group has access rights, all users will have whatever permissions have been granted to that group.

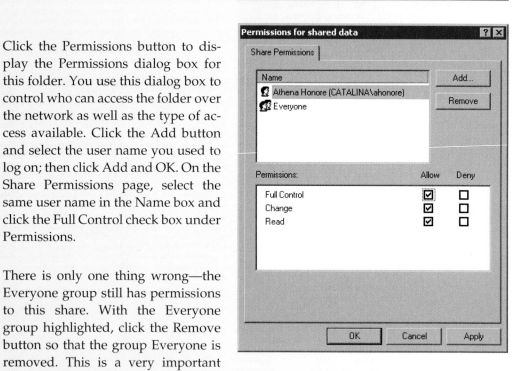

You can add several users or groups at the same time and then assign them different permissions when you return to the Permissions dialog box.

Controlling Printer Access

Another resource that is commonly shared on a network is a printer. In Windows 2000 Professional, you have considerable control over how your printers are accessed. In this section, we'll look briefly at the printer sharing options in Windows 2000 Professional.

A printer has a single set of permissions that affect both the locally logged-on user and users accessing it as a share on the network. Furthermore, the permissions are pretty simple, consisting of Print, Manage Printers, and Manage Documents. In Step-by-Step 6.03, you added a printer to your computer and turned on sharing. Unless you decided to change the permissions yourself, that printer is probably shared with the default permissions, which give full control to both the Administrators and Power Users groups. The special group, Creator Owner, has Manage Documents permissions and nothing else, and the Everyone group has Print permission.

• Properties of a printer named brochure

■ Troubleshooting Common Windows 2000 Professional Problems

Let's face it—any computer can experience problems no matter how stable and secure its operating system. Windows 2000 Professional is certainly one of the most stable and trouble-free operating systems you will find, but you still may encounter difficulties from time to time. In this section, we'll first look at some of the tools used in troubleshooting: Registry Editor, Event Viewer, and Device Manager. Then we will take the proactive approach with best practices to keep the wolves at bay. Finally, we'll look at some common problems and their possible causes and resolutions.

An Approach to Troubleshooting

Our hope is that, with the correct preventative practices (discussed later), you will never suffer a failure or major problem with Windows 2000. However, experience tells us that even smart, savvy people often fail to take even the most basic preventative steps, and even those who do will occasionally be confronted with an OS problem.

When trouble comes calling, your response, depending on your experience, should be to:

1. Carefully observe and record the error messages or other symptoms of a problem.

2. Use the information you gathered to find the cause.

3. Research the solution.

4. Apply the solution.

5. Test the results.

Where to Find Help

Where can you find help in discovering a problem's cause and solution? A great place to begin is the Windows 2000 Professional Help program (assuming that you have access to a working computer). Search on keywords related to the symptoms, and look through the troubleshooters.

- The Windows 2000 Help troubleshooters

We have had a great deal of good luck searching Microsoft's Technet site, at www.microsoft.com/technet. Sometimes a broader search of the Microsoft site, not confined to just the Technet area, yields better results. If you need to cast a larger net, point your web browser to an Internet search engine, such as www.google.com, and enter a few key words from an error message. Believe it or not, this has worked several times for us!

Registry Editor

Windows 2000 has a registry structure very similar to that of its predecessor, Windows NT 4.0. The registry contains all the important settings for the OS. In fact, during bootup, Windows 2000 depends on the registry to tell it what services, drivers, and components to load into memory and how to configure each component. When you install the OS, the registry is created, and it

> If you find that you have absolutely no choice but to modify the registry, back it up first. There are several ways to back up the registry, including using the Backup program (Start | Programs | Accessories | System Tools | Backup) and using the export registry function from within Registry Editor (Registry | Export Registry File in REGEDIT.EXE).

continues to be modified as you configure the OS and add applications and components. It is easy to understand that an error in the registry could cause a serious problem, even a failure of the OS.

Normally, the only methods you should use to modify the registry are indirect, such as by running an installation program or making a change to the OS through Control Panel applets. These usually are safe ways to modify the registry. However, sometimes when you have a problem, the solution you find (after some research) is to modify the registry. The tool you use to do this is the Registry Editor, which comes in two versions: REGEDIT.EXE (our favorite) and REGEDT32.EXE (good editor, but terrible GUI).

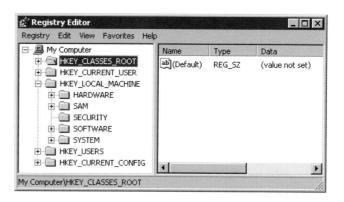

• Registry Editor (REGEDIT.EXE)

Event Viewer

When you see an error message in Windows 2000, the first place to go (if the computer is up and running) is the Event Viewer, to view the log files. You can open Event Viewer by right-clicking My Computer, selecting Manage Computer, and then expanding Event Viewer within Computer Management Console.

Examine the following illustration to see the standard event logs and the types of events each log records. You can call up help from within Event Viewer by clicking the yellow question mark in the menu bar.

• Event Viewer is within Computer Management Console.

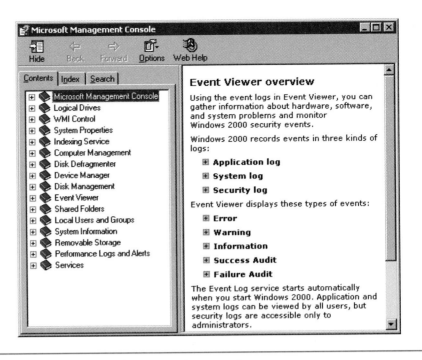

- Use Event Viewer help to learn more about event logs.

Device Manager

For several years, we worked in both Windows NT and Windows 9x. When we had a problem with Windows 9x, we were frustrated that it didn't have Event Viewer (as in Windows NT) to help us pinpoint problems. When we had a problem with a device in Windows NT, we were frustrated that it didn't have Device Manager (as in Windows 9x) to help troubleshoot problems with devices. Hurray! Windows 2000 has both! With Device Manager, you can view and change device properties, update device drivers, configure device settings, and uninstall devices. Desktop support people have come to rely on this tool to verify a successful Windows installation by confirming that all of their hardware was recognized and is working properly.

Of course, Device Manager can't be found in the same location as in Windows 9x, and it looks a little different, and it has a few new features. Learn more about Device Manager in the following step-by-step exercise.

Step-by-Step 6.07

Working with Device Manager

In this step-by-step exercise, you will use Device Manager to verify that your devices are recognized by Windows 2000 and are functioning normally. Then you will make Device Manage reveal more information than usual!

To complete this step-by-step exercise, you will need the following:

- A computer on which you have successfully installed Windows 2000 Professional as described in Step-by-Step 6.01
- To be logged on as an administrator

Step 1

Right-click My Computer and select Properties. In the Properties dialog box, select the Hardware tab and then click the Device Manager button. You have two options for viewing devices and two options for viewing resources, which you can choose from the View menu. You will normally view devices by type, because this approach is simpler and more understandable. The example here shows this view. There is a node for each device type.

Step 2

If the OS detects a device, but detects a problem with the device, that device type will be expanded, and the problem device will have a yellow exclamation mark next to it. If you see this symbol on a device, double-click the device to open its Properties dialog box, which will give you more information. In the example here, the yellow icons on the communications ports indicate that Windows 2000 discovered problems. The General page of the Properties dialog box for one of these devices reports that there are not enough free resources for the device.

Step 3

You may be surprised that we didn't attempt to fix this problem, but we simply have no need to use these devices. If we did need one of these devices, we could begin by following the instructions in the Device Status box and clicking the Troubleshooter button to get help on resolving the problems. Familiarize yourself with the contents of Device Manager by opening the nodes, such as Computer and Disk Drives.

| Step 4 | Click the yellow question mark in the menu bar to open Device Manager Help and browse through the topics to learn more. Read several of the topics and find out how you can print information about a device, because this is a handy thing to know how to do if you need to give information about a problem device to someone helping you. When you are finished, close all open windows. | 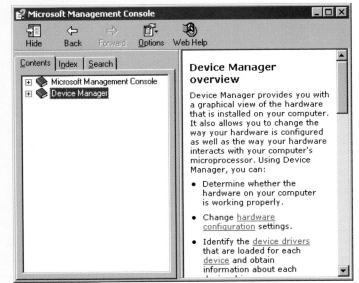 |

An Ounce of Prevention

Someone once said that the best offense is a good defense. Don't wait for problems to occur before you take action. Have a defensive strategy in which you take steps to avoid problems. Your strategy should include installing a good antivirus program, doing periodic housekeeping, backing up data, and disk defragmenting.

Install an Antivirus Program

 You need to be proactive and alert to possible invasions. Don't place a disk or CD into your computer from an unknown source, and never open e-mail that does not look like something you should be receiving. Finally, don't ever open e-mail attachments from unknown sources!

We recommend that you install an antivirus program on your computer, and if you have a connection to the Internet, make sure that the antivirus program is configured to receive automatic updates. To learn more about antivirus programs, check out the following websites: www.symantec.com, www.trendmicro.com, www.drsolomon.com, and www.eicar.org. Make sure that your antivirus software can scan and remove viruses from your existing files, and that it maintains a presence in memory for checking all files that are brought into the computer, including e-mail, which is the number-one vehicle for bringing a virus into your computer. Even the best antivirus programs struggle to keep up with the new methods being used to infect computers. As soon as developers of antivirus software become aware of a new virus, they immediately start working to enable their software to detect and remove it, but new viruses may infect hundreds or thousands of computers before the antivirus companies can get an update to you that will do the job.

Periodic Housekeeping

Keep your computer "lean and mean." If you simply can't resist buying programs that look just a little interesting because they are only $30 or so, you may find trouble in the form of undesirable changes to your system and outright hard drive bloat. Periodically, you should do some serious housecleaning, which should include removing any applications you no longer need, deleting any data files you no longer need, and deleting temporary files. After you have done this, defragment your hard drive, because file fragmentation (even on an NTFS volume) can slow down a computer.

Disk Cleanup   The Disk Cleanup program can simplify your life. Choose Start | Programs | Accessories | System Tools, and it will ask you to select a drive to clean. It then will quickly analyze the disk space it can free up and open the Disk Cleanup dialog box, from which you can select the files to be deleted. This will help you with everything but your data files.

• You decide what to delete, and Disk Cleanup does it for you.

The More Options tab lets you select Windows components and installed programs from Add/Remove Programs. When you have selected all of the files, components, and programs you want removed, click OK and Disk Cleanup gets down to the business of serious cleaning.

Backing Up Data

Yes, we know you've heard it over and over. But you still need to actually back up your data files on removable media or to another computer. It is not possible to overemphasize how important it is to do this! Do it often and do it right. Windows 2000 Professional has a backup program, available through Start | Programs | Accessories | System Tools.

Disk Defragmenter

After deleting a gazillion files from your drives, be sure to defragment the disk. This will reorganize your files so that they are stored contiguously and can be read from disk much faster. A disk defragmenter comes with Windows 2000. Run it from Start | Programs | Accessories | System Tools. First select a volume and click the Analyze button, and the program will perform a quick analysis and give its recommendation—to defragment or not to

You must have at least 15 percent of your disk space available for disk defragmenter to do its work. If you try to proceed with defragmentation with less space, you will see an error message. You have a choice: delete more files to free up enough space, or tell the program to try to run anyway. The wisest thing to do is to open My Computer and delete more files.

Disk Defragmenter working on drive F:

defragment. If you are curious, you can choose to view the analysis report, but you probably have better things to do, so click the Defragment button and let it do its job.

Common Problems and Solutions

There are several common problems that you might encounter with almost any OS. You'll look at five common problems and the actions you might take when you encounter them.

Unable to Access Another Computer on Your Network

If you are unable to access another computer on your network, check the following possibilities:

- Make certain the other PC is turned on, is physically connected to the network, and has shared the folder or printer you want to access.

- Try restarting the other PC. Sometimes computers seem to disappear from the network when a power-saving mode kicks in; restarting the PC makes the computer reappear.

- If this is the first time you have attempted to access the other computer, make certain that you have access rights to that computer. You may also need to check the network settings using the Network icon on the Control Panel to ensure that both systems are using the same networking protocols.

Unable to Print

If you are unable to print, try these solutions:

- Make certain that the printer is on, is connected, has paper, and is not in offline mode.

- Try opening the Properties dialog box for the printer and sending a test page to the printer. If this fails, open the Help program and look in the Index for Troubleshooters, Print. Use the Print Troubleshooter to debug the problem.

- If you are attempting to print to a network printer, make certain that you have the proper permissions and that the printer is currently available.

- Try printing from another application such as Notepad. If this works, make certain the application that cannot print is set to use the correct printer.

Cannot Connect to the Internet

If you are unable to connect to the Internet, here are some things to watch for:

- Make certain that your modem (or other connection device) is on, is properly connected, and that you have established the Internet connection correctly.

- If you are connecting through your network, make certain that the computer or router through which your network connects to the Internet is functioning properly.

- Check your user name and password (if your Internet connection requires these). Remember that these are often case sensitive and that they are usually not the same as your Windows 2000 Professional log on.

Cannot Install a Hardware Device Driver

If you attempt to install a new hardware device and cannot successfully do so, try these options:

- Make certain that the device is on the hardware compatibility list found either on the Windows 2000 Professional CD or at the Microsoft website.

- If Windows 2000 Professional does not offer a native driver for the device, check the disks that came with the device or Microsoft's or the manufacturer's website to locate Windows 2000 Professional–compatible drivers.

Cannot Play Audio, Video, or Other Multimedia Files

If you are unable to play multimedia content on a Windows 2000 Professional PC, consider these possibilities:

- Make certain that the speakers are properly connected and powered on.

- Make certain that the Windows 2000 Professional volume control is not muted. Check this by clicking the speaker icon in the system tray and then clicking the slider. When you do, the speakers should produce a sound.

- If the system was upgraded from Windows 9x, it's possible that Windows 2000 Professional drivers have not been installed for the multimedia devices. Open the Sounds and Multimedia applet in the Control Panel and then click the Hardware tab of the Sounds and Multimedia Properties dialog box to verify that each device is working properly. If a device is not working properly, click the Properties button, and check out the installed driver. You may need to search the manufacturer's website for a new device driver, or replace the device.

Chapter 6 Review

■ Chapter Summary

After reading this chapter and completing the Step-by-Step tutorials and Try This! exercises, you should understand the following facts about Windows 2000 Professional:

Describe Windows 2000 Professional Benefits, Features, and Weaknesses

- Windows 2000 Professional provides benefits through enhanced features in the areas of the desktop, security, stability, compatibility, and file systems.

- Windows 2000 Professional weaknesses are in support for old DOS and Windows applications and in the fact that reboots are still required after some changes to the OS, although reboots are required for fewer reasons than in previous OSs.

- The file systems Windows 2000 supports are FAT12, FAT16, FAT32, and NTFS5, although we usually refer to any of the FAT file systems as FAT, and the versions of NTFS as simply NTFS, unless making explicit statements or comparisons.

- Windows 2000 Professional is needed (rather than Windows 9x) when stability, reliability, and security are required, when a software publisher lists this OS as a requirement for installing an application, and when remote administration of a computer is required.

Install and Configure Windows 2000 Professional

- Before installing Windows 2000, be sure that the hardware you plan to use will be adequate for the work you hope to accomplish on that computer.

- Determine whether Windows 2000 is compatible with the hardware and software you plan to use. You can find out by reading the documentation for the hardware and software items, looking at the compatibility information at www.microsoft.com/windows2000/professional/howtobuy/upgrading/compat/, or contacting the manufacturer. You can also run a compatibility test that comes with Windows 2000, called the Readiness Analyzer.

- You can install Windows as an upgrade on a computer with an earlier version of Windows, or you can install it as a separate OS, in which case, we strongly recommend a clean installation, beginning with an empty hard drive.

- Whether you are performing an upgrade or a clean installation, you can choose to do it manually, which requires your attention and interaction, or automatically, which requires the least amount of hand-holding. The automatic methods involve more work, technical understanding, and even financial investment.

- The four Windows 2000 setup start disks are required if you are installing from the local CD-ROM drive and the computer will not boot from the CD. The Makeboot program will generate these disks. This program comes in two forms: MAKEBOOT.EXE (for DOS and 16-bit Windows) and MAKEBT32.EXE (for 32-bit Windows OSs).

- Install service packs and updates immediately after installing an OS, and after that, periodically check for updates. A shortcut installed on the Start menu, called Windows Update, makes this process easy, provided you have an Internet connection.

- You should check network connectivity after you install Windows 2000 on a computer connected to a network.

Customize and Manage Windows 2000 Professional

- After installing Windows 2000, you will need to customize and manage Windows 2000. The Control Panel applets are your main tools for doing this.

- Make a Windows 2000 computer easier to use for someone with restricted vision, hearing loss, or mobility difficulties. Some built-in accessibility components can be enabled and configured using the Accessibility Options applet, and some accessibility utilities can be enabled from Start | Programs | Accessories | Accessibility.

- The Display applet lets you modify the desktop background, enable or disable a screen saver, and further customize the desktop. In addition, the Settings tab allows you to configure certain video adapter and monitor settings.

- Add a printer using the Add Printer wizard. You can further manage a printer in the properties for an installed printer. This includes assigning permissions to control access to the printer.

- Use the Taskbar and Start Menu Properties dialog box to control the display of the taskbar and Start menu, much as in Windows 98. The new Personalized Menus option is enabled by default, but it may confuse users. If it does, disable it from the Advanced tab.

- Windows 2000 Professional has several default folders that organize files. Some of these folders store files used by the OS, and some, such as My Documents and My Pictures, are created for each user and intended as default locations for data files created by the user. Avoid deleting or modifying system files.

- The Windows 2000 Search option has been expanded with more search options. To enhance the speed of file searches on an NTFS volume, enable the new Indexing Service in the Search Options area of the Search Results window.

Manage Security for Users, Files, and Printers

- Each person who uses a Windows 2000 Professional computer must be logged on using a user name and password of a local or domain security account. This process is called authentication. An administrator can use the Users and Passwords applet to manage local users and groups.

- In a stand-alone or workgroup setting, a Windows 2000 Professional computer will log on a user automatically unless the Users Must Enter a User Name and Password to Use This Computer option is turned on.

- A CTRL-ALT-DELETE key press is not required to display the logon dialog box, unless the Secure Boot Settings option is turned on.

- Only NTFS allows you to set permissions on files and folders. File permissions differ slightly from folder permissions, but each has a set of standard permissions and a set of special permissions. Standard permissions may be all you ever need to use. Each standard permission includes several special permissions.

- An administrator can add users to groups and then apply permissions to groups. Certain groups are built in, and other groups can be created by an administrator. The Everyone group is a special group that includes, literally, all users.

- File and folder permissions control access for both local users and users who access files and folders over the network.

- Share permissions apply only to users who access the files and folders within that share through the network. Share permissions can be applied to shared folders on both FAT and NTFS volumes.

- When you are concerned about security, always use the Lock Computer option before walking away from the computer.

- Check to be sure that an application is compatible with Windows 2000 before installing it.

- Close all open programs before installing an application in Windows 2000.

- You can use Add/Remove Programs to install or uninstall an application or Windows component.

- Most software licenses require that you remove an application from one computer before installing it on another computer.

Troubleshoot Common Windows 2000 Professional Problems

- When a problem occurs, observe and record all symptoms and error messages; then research the cause and solution using Windows 2000 Help, the Internet, or other sources. Once you have found a solution, apply it and test the results.

- Normally, you should not modify the Windows 2000 registry, but if a recommended solution includes editing the registry, use one of the registry editors that comes with Windows 2000, back up the registry, and only then make the recommended change.

- When you see an error message in Windows 2000, use the Event Viewer to see if the error was logged in one of the log files it maintains. The information in the error message may lead you directly to the solution, or you may be able to use the information to search for a solution at Microsoft or elsewhere.

- Use Device Manager when you suspect that a problem is related to a device or device driver. With Device Manager, you can disable or enable a device, update a device driver, or configure a device.

- Take preventative measures to avoid problems. This includes running an antivirus program on your computer, not opening suspicious e-mail messages or attachments from unknown sources, performing periodic housekeeping to remove unneeded files and programs, and defragmenting the disk periodically.

- Be aware of several common problems and their solutions, including the inability to access another computer on the network or the Internet, print, install a hardware device driver, and use multimedia content.

■ Key Terms

Active Directory domain *(233)*
Autorun *(260)*
CD key *(245)*
Control Panel *(251)*
file system *(237)*

group *(262)*
Hardware Compatibility List *(241)*
Indexing Service *(259)*
protected memory space *(236)*
refresh rate *(253)*

user *(262)*
virtual device driver (VxD) *(237)*
Windows NT domain *(233)*

■ Key Term Quiz

Use the Key Terms list to complete the sentences that follow. Not all terms will be used.

1. To make searches faster on an NTFS volume, enable the _____.

2. To determine whether the devices on a PC are compatible with Windows 2000 Professional, you would examine the _____.

3. FAT and NTFS are each examples of a/an _____ that Windows 2000 Professional supports.

4. Tools for configuring Windows 2000 Professional are on the _____.

5. When administrators talk about a/an _____, they are usually referring to an account that represents a person who uses a computer.

6. Programs that rely on Windows 9*x* style _____ cannot run under Windows 2000 Professional.

7. A/an _____ is one in which at least one of the servers maintaining the domain database is running a Windows 2000 Professional Server OS or greater.

8. Because Windows 2000 places each running application program in its own _____, a program can fail without affecting other programs or the OS.

9. The screen _____ must be above 60 Hertz to avoid eyestrain.

10. _____ are accounts that can contain other accounts, and they allow administrators to assign permissions to many users through a single account.

■ Multiple-Choice Quiz

1. Which of the following is *not* a reason to choose Windows 2000 Professional? Select all that apply.
   a. Stability
   b. Compatibility with Windows applications
   c. Low price
   d. Compatibility with Linux programs
   e. Security

2. The minimum amount of memory needed for Windows 2000 Professional is:
   a. 16MB
   b. 24MB

   c. 128MB
   d. 64MB
   e. 4GB

3. Which of the following is *not* one of the Windows 2000 Professional NTFS permission levels?
   a. Full Control
   b. Spindle
   c. Modify
   d. Read and Execute
   e. List Folder Contents

4. When adding a printer that you plan to share on the network, which option do you select in the Add Printer wizard?

   a. Network Printer

   b. FILE

   c. Generic

   d. Automatically Detect and Install My Plug and Play Printer

   e. Local Printer

5. If you want to enable the StickyKeys feature, which Control Panel icon do you use?

   a. Keyboard

   b. Mouse

   c. System

   d. Administrative Tools

   e. Accessibility

6. Which is the preferred file system for Windows 2000 Professional?

   a. FAT32

   b. NTFS

   c. HPFS

   d. Linux32

   e. FAT

7. Which of the following is *not* a part of Windows 2000 Professional security?

   a. Families

   b. Users

   c. Groups

   d. Rights

   e. Permissions

8. To what family of Microsoft OSs does Windows 2000 Professional belong?

   a. House of UNIX

   b. House of LAN Manager

   c. House of DOS Windows

   d. House of NT

   e. Consumer Windows

9. To which group of users must you belong to add new users?

   a. Everyone

   b. Power Users

   c. Guests

   d. Administrators

   e. Backup Operators

10. Which of the following should *not* be part of a standard approach to troubleshooting?

    a. Carefully observe and record the error messages or other symptoms of a problem.

    b. Use the information you gathered to find the cause.

    c. Repartition and format the hard drive.

    d. Research the solution.

    e. Test the results.

11. Which of the following seems out of place in a defensive strategy to prevent problems in Windows 2000?

    a. Antivirus program

    b. Freeware games

    c. Data backup

    d. Disk defragmenter

    e. Deletion of temporary files

12. Which of the following do you use to hide protected operating system files?

    a. Start | Settings | Folders

    b. Tools | Folder Options

    c. Start | Run

    d. Start | Search | For Files or Folders

    e. Start | Programs | Accessories

13. Which of the following won't run under Windows 2000 Professional?

    a. 32-bit Windows programs

    b. DOS programs

    c. Games

    d. Macintosh programs

    e. Windows 98 programs

14. Which of the following can prevent an application from being compatible with Windows 2000 Professional?

    a. Graphical user interface

    b. Virtual device drivers

    c. Drag and drop

    d. Virtual memory

    e. Autorun

15. Why should you defragment your hard drive on a regular basis?

   a. Defragmenting alphabetizes your files, making them easier to find.

   b. Defragmenting may improve the performance of your computer.

   c. Defragmenting makes your files more secure.

   d. Defragmenting cleans out all temporary files.

   e. None of the above.

■ Essay Quiz

1. If you were running a small business with several computers on the network, how would you make certain that everyone could read the company policies document, but that you would be the only person who could make changes to that document?

2. Imagine that your company has an ordinary laser printer and a color laser printer connected to a Windows 2000 Professional workstation. How would you make certain that only certain users could use the more expensive color laser printer?

3. Your old computer is no longer fast enough for your needs, so you've purchased a new computer that runs Windows 2000 Professional. What do you need to do to transfer your application programs to your new PC?

4. You have been assigned the task of setting up a PC that visitors to your company's lobby can use to access certain information about your products on your network. How can you ensure that this PC will not be able to access sensitive accounting data?

5. Your boss wants you to install Windows 2000 Professional on his PC. You go to his office and you discover that he has an old printer and an old scanner that look like they've been sitting around pretty much unused for a long time. How can you be sure that these items will be compatible with Windows 2000 Professional before you begin the installation process?

Lab Projects

• Lab Project 6.1

You have just been given a PC in which the hard disk has failed and been replaced by a new one with no operating system. The system has a CD-ROM drive, but when you try to install Windows 2000 Professional directly from the CD, nothing happens.

   You will need a lab computer with no operating system installed.

Then do the following:

① Describe what you must do to install Windows 2000 Professional on this PC.

② Determine how you can create boot disks.

③ Implement your solution on your lab computer.

④ Test your solution and explain the results.

• Lab Project 6.2

An employee was involved in a serious accident and will be out of the office for the next several months. The employee was working on an important business proposal that you will need to find so that someone else can finish the proposal for a meeting with your customer, Holabird Mining, next week.

   You will need a lab computer with Windows 2000 Professional installed.

Then do the following:

① Describe the process you will need to follow to locate those files without knowing the injured employee's logon password.

② Determine how you can copy the files.

③ Implement your solution on your lab computer.

④ Test your solution and explain the results.

Windows XP Professional

chapter
7

Windows XP Professional is one of several Windows XP products introduced by Microsoft. So far, the Windows XP lineup includes Windows XP Professional for the business and power user and Windows XP Home Edition for the home, very small business, or consumer PC. Although Windows XP Home Edition can work well in a small office depending on its security needs, it's not appropriate for a larger business environment because it does not include many of the security and remote management features of Windows XP Professional.

Other Windows XP products include Windows XP Media Center Edition for users who want to use a TV remote control to view TV listings, and to catalog songs, videos, and pictures; Tablet PC for tablet devices and notebooks; and Windows XP Embedded for other devices.

What you won't find in this list is a server version of Windows XP. With the XP products, Microsoft officially separates their small system OSs from their server system OSs, beginning with Windows .Net Server 2003.

In this chapter, you'll work with Windows XP Professional because this (or its successor) is the desktop OS you'll encounter in most organizations. You'll learn its benefits, features, and weaknesses. You'll install it, configure it, and customize it and you'll learn to manage security for users. Finally, you'll learn to troubleshoot common Windows XP Professional problems.

In this chapter, you will learn how to:

- **Describe Windows XP Professional benefits, features, and weaknesses**
- **Install and configure Windows XP Professional**
- **Customize and manage Windows XP Professional**
- **Manage user security in Windows XP**
- **Troubleshoot common Windows XP Professional problems**

■ Windows XP Overview

Edgar owns a computer consulting business that specializes in small businesses. His company is a Microsoft Solution provider, which means it participates in a special Microsoft program to provide appropriate Microsoft solutions to its customers. In the office, Edger uses Windows 2000 servers and has Windows XP Professional on his desktop and laptop computers. He put together a list of features to present to his customers who are considering purchasing new desktop or laptop computers, or upgrading existing computers. We'll discuss the features he feels are most important.

Benefits and Features

Windows 2000 Professional has benefits in the areas of desktop, speed, security, stability and compatibility, and support for several file systems to suit the performance and security needs of the user. In the following sections, we explore these benefits.

Desktop Beauty and Usability

People will buy visually appealing products. The designers at Microsoft know this. Windows XP fits the bill since it is downright beautiful, and it shows the efforts Microsoft has put into making it more usable.

Visual Appeal   If you are a veteran Windows user, you'll immediately see the changes Microsoft implemented in XP upon booting it up. Gone is the boring, subdued color scheme. In its place is a larger, brighter blue and green scheme. The desktop pictures are all quite appealing. Even the text on the icons has been improved. Until you select the icon, the icon text is now on a transparent background. In prior versions of Windows, a box of color surrounded the text.

Usability   It is an understatement to say that the default desktop is uncluttered, seeing as it contains only the Recycle Bin icon. The former desktop icons have been moved to a reorganized, two-column Start menu that can be customized to suit the needs and experience of the user.

When you make changes through the Display applet, you'll discover the improvements are more than just visual. The desktop seems to learn from you. Your Start menu constantly adjusts itself. Most frequently used programs are listed on the left side of the Start menu, with other programs available on the All Programs submenu. The more you use a program, the higher it is on the list of frequently used programs. Figure 7-1 shows a Start menu on a computer in which Paint is the program used most often.

To learn more about the differences between Windows XP Professional and Windows XP Home, check out Microsoft's official comparison of the two at www.microsoft.com/ windowsxp/home/howtobuy/ choosing2.asp or an unofficial listing at www.winsupersite .com/showcase/windowsxp_ home_pro.asp.

• The Windows XP desktop (with the Bliss wallpaper)

The desktop reorganizes itself as well. If you have used earlier versions of Windows, you are probably familiar with cluttered desktops. Every program you install seems to place its own icon on the desktop. Windows XP solves this problem by periodically moving unused desktop icons into a folder named Unused Desktop Shortcuts. So even if every new program places a shortcut on the desktop, only the shortcuts you actually use stay on the desktop.

Speed

Windows XP is much faster than previous editions of Windows. It boots faster and runs programs better than either Windows 2000 or Windows 98. Faster computers allow you to get more done—and can help lower your stress level. Figures released by Microsoft suggest a boot time 34 percent faster than for Windows 2000. In other words, if your computer used to boot in one minute, it may now boot in under 40 seconds.

How did Microsoft decrease the boot time? By improving the hardware drivers and by employing a special scheme in which XP learns what is needed at bootup in order to create a list of code or data that it can bring into memory before it's needed. This is called prefetching.

Programs also run faster in XP thanks, in part, to prefetching for applications, which works much like prefetching for bootup. Windows XP keeps track of the files an application uses and creates a prefetch list. The next time that application is run, Windows XP uses the appropriate prefetch list, bringing code the program has used in the past into memory before it's requested. Windows XP also rearranges the placement of programs on disk so that they will launch faster.

Microsoft also examined the applications that users work with most often and discovered that CD burning, digital photo manipulation, and Internet messaging (implemented as Windows Messenger in Windows XP) were the three fastest growing applications. Microsoft thus made each easier and faster in XP. CD creation in particular has become much simpler.

Security

As with Windows 2000 and Windows NT, XP's parent and grandparent, Windows XP Professional includes security components, including required logon authentication, and the ability to set file and folder permissions on an NTFS volume.

Required Logon   A logon to Windows XP Professional is mandatory, and this logon must be performed from an account that is a member of a security database—either the local security accounts database built into Windows XP Professional on the local computer, or a network-based security database, such as in a Windows NT or Active Directory domain.

NTFS   In addition to security for files and folders on NTFS volumes, Windows XP Professional also supports a feature introduced in Windows 2000: the encrypting file system (EFS) on an NTFS volume.

As in Windows 2000, NTFS encryption allows you to encrypt files and folders so that only you can read the files, and only a member of the local Administrator's group can recover the file. **Encryption** is very useful for a laptop or in professional settings, where data theft is a real concern.

• **Figure 7-1.**   The Windows XP Start menu

Microsoft claims that XP outperforms Windows 98 by 25 percent and is even with Windows 2000. TechTv (www.techtv.com) ran several tests comparing Windows XP to Windows 2000 and determined that on the ZD Media Creation Winstone 2001 benchmark test, Windows XP ran 20 percent faster than Windows 2000.

The process of setting NTFS permissions on files and folders in Windows XP Professional is identical to that for setting permissions on a Windows 2000 system.

Don't use the file encryption capabilities of Windows XP unless you are an advanced user who has researched it first, or unless you have the support of skilled professionals who can take steps to ensure that your encrypted data can be successfully recovered.

Only the person who encrypts a file can use the file, no matter what permissions anyone else has to the file. By default, members of the local Administrators group can back up, restore, or recover encrypted data, which is not the same as being able to directly access the data. We have done it and it is a very advanced task, described in Windows XP Help.

Stability and Compatibility

Edgar has been using Windows XP Professional on his office desktop for several months. During this time, he has experienced precisely one unrecoverable crash after he installed a bad memory module into the motherboard and booted the computer. Nothing else has caused his computer to crash or stop responding. He routinely runs at least six applications at any given time, each a memory hog. In the rare event that a program has stopped responding, he's been able to stop it without affecting any other application. This is awesome. In contrast, his home computer running Windows 98 crashes frequently (on bad days, hourly!).

Driver signing also verifies that a driver is actually from the vendor and is not a potential computer virus.

Microsoft attacked the stability problem from three angles. They strengthened **driver signing**, originally introduced in Windows 2000, they added the **compatibility mode** for older-program support, and they made **Windows updates** an (optionally) automatic process.

Driver Signing Microsoft must certify XP drivers before the vendor ships the product. A certified driver is called a *signed driver*. Microsoft provides the vendor with a digital signature that is incorporated into the product driver. Signed drivers are supposed to eliminate hardware conflicts and unnecessary delays. Figure 7-2 shows a network card driver with a digital signature.

Compatibility Hardware issues are just part of the stability issue. Older programs, often called legacy applications, exist in both your computer and computers around the globe. In the past, these programs did not run well on newer versions of operating systems. For example, Edgar's most important client is his young daughter, Elizabeth, who has her own computer at home. Her favorite game program was written to take advantage of the way that Windows 9*x* interacted with the video card. When Edgar upgraded her computer to Windows XP, the program didn't run. Elizabeth was not amused. However, Windows XP provides compatibility mode. This allowed Edgar to tell Windows XP to emulate, or pretend, that it is an older operating system. He simply picked the appropriate OS from a list, and XP ran Elizabeth's program using a virtual OS. He forced Windows XP to pretend that it is Windows 95 and forced the required screen resolution and color depth.

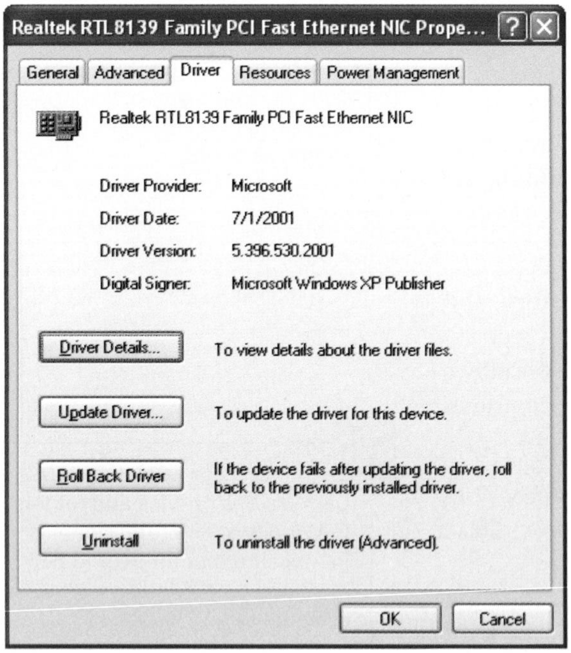
Realtek RTL8139 Family PCI Fast Ethernet NIC Prope...
General
Advanced
Driver
Resources
Power Management
Realtek RTL8139 Family PCI Fast Ethernet NIC
Driver Provider: Microsoft
Driver Date: 7/1/2001
Driver Version: 5.396.530.2001
Digital Signer: Microsoft Windows XP Publisher
Driver Details...
To view details about the driver files.
Update Driver...
To update the driver for this device.
Roll Back Driver
If the device fails after updating the driver, roll back to the previously installed driver.
Uninstall
To uninstall the driver (Advanced).
OK
Cancel

• **Figure 7-2.** Signed network card

Windows Update The final trick Microsoft incorporated into XP is the option to automate Windows updates. Windows updates have been an important, but often neglected, task for computer users. Typically, Microsoft finds and corrects problems with its software in a timely fashion. Earlier versions of Windows let the user decide when, if ever, to update their computers. The net result could be disastrous. The worm

Code Red and the worm-virus Nimda caused thousands of computers across the country to go down. Both viruses exploited flaws in Internet Information Server (IIS) installed on Windows 2000 Server. The flaws had been corrected in a security update released by Microsoft several months earlier. If administrators had updated their computers, the virus-caused damage would not have been so widespread.

Microsoft received a lot of bad press from these incidents. While it's true that Microsoft programming caused the flaw, the company provided the solution well before the incidents. The real fault lies squarely on the shoulders of the administrators who failed to implement the updates. To help avoid this problem in the future, Microsoft has improved their Windows Update web page (`http://v4.windowsupdate.microsoft.com/en/default.asp`).

They also give you the option to automatically update. Actually, they nag you about it! Soon after installing XP (a day or two in our experience), a message balloon will pop up from the taskbar suggesting that you automate updates. If you click this taskbar, the Automatic Updates Setup wizard will run, allowing you to configure the update program. You say you've never seen this message balloon, and would certainly like to automate the update process? No problem—simply right-click My Computer (on the Start menu), select Properties, and then click the Automatic Updates tab and select Automatic Update options. Then, whenever your computer connects to the Web, it checks the Windows Update page. What happens next depends on the setting you choose. Your choices are:

- Notify me before downloading any updates and notify me again before installing them on my computer.

- Download the updates automatically and notify me when they are ready to be installed (this is the default setting when Automatic Updates is turned on).

- Automatically download the updates, and install them on the schedule that I specify.

With the default setting, if a new patch is available it downloads the updates and a balloon message box pops up, as shown in Figure 7-3. If you click anywhere on the balloon (except on the close button) it will display the list of updates available, and you can select which ones you wish to install. Then Windows Update installs it for you. Whichever option you choose, keeping Windows XP up-to-date should reduce the number of viruses that exploit system flaws.

File System Support

As stated previously, Windows XP supports NTFS version 5. It actually has the same file support you learned about in Windows 2000—that is, support for FAT12 for diskettes, and FAT16 and FAT32 for hard disks. The only reason to choose FAT32 is if your computer is going to dual-boot between Windows 98 and XP, and you want the Windows 98 installation to access the files in XP. FAT16 should be your file system of last resort, as it offers neither security nor efficient disk usage.

For a complete list of features and benefits, check out www.microsoft.com/ windowsxp/pro/evaluation/ features.asp.

Only an Administrator can modify update settings, connect to the Microsoft Windows Update web page, or install updates.

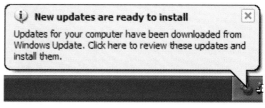

• **Figure 7-3.** Windows Update balloon message

Windows XP Weaknesses

In our view, Windows XP is a very good desktop/laptop OS—it shows the stability of the NT family of OSs, while giving us an improved, attractive GUI. We feel the weaknesses of Windows XP are minor and just in the areas of hardware support and increased hardware requirements.

Hardware Support

If you have an older device that does not have a signed driver, you may be in trouble. Use of a nonsigned driver is frowned on by XP so there's no guarantee that the product will work properly. In addition, using the product may actually slow down boot times. However, in all likelihood the product will work just fine. Experiment on a noncritical system.

We know several network administrators who are choosing to be safe by forcing their XP systems to use only signed drivers. XP's Control Panel allows an administrator to choose the desired level of protection.

Hardware Requirements

Hardware requirements are higher than in previous versions of Windows but quite in line with even a modestly priced computer today.

When to Use Windows XP

Windows XP is a nice product. However, its features are not for everybody. If you're purchasing a new PC, you'll most likely purchase Windows XP. However, if you're upgrading an older computer, you need to answer several questions.

- First, consider the adage, "If it ain't broke, don't fix it." If your computer is doing everything it needs to do, there's no reason to upgrade. If you're happy with your current OS, leave it alone. You're used to it—new is not always better.

- Second, ask yourself if you're ready to deal with the work of upgrading. Even though Windows XP is compatible with most equipment, there are several commonly used pieces of software and hardware that do not work with XP. Edgar's upgrade to XP required the purchase of a new video card. The Voodoo 2000 card he had been running for several years did not support DirectX 8, which XP requires. He also had to uninstall Symantec's Norton Utilities before upgrading to XP and then reinstall it after the upgrade. This process was made more tedious by that program's need to reacquire all the latest virus definitions.

XP Versions

When Edgar's customers consider upgrading or replacing their Windows PCs, how does he decide which version of Windows XP to install? While there are several versions of Windows XP, the two that Edgar considers for desktop or laptop upgrades are XP Home and XP Professional. The Home edition is suited to the average home user, and the Professional Edition is designed to work in an office. However, the distinction is not all that clear. He actually recommends that some of his very small business clients use Home, but for most of his clients he recommends Windows XP Professional as the best OS both for their new PC purchases and their upgrades.

To help choose between the Home and Professional products for his customers, Edgar asks them the following questions.

- Will the user need to connect to the computer remotely?

- Will the computer connect to a Microsoft NT or Active Directory domain-based network?

- Is it important to easily rebuild your machine in the event of a catastrophe?

- Is it important to make individual files secure?

If the customer answers yes to any of these questions, Edgar will recommend Windows XP Professional, but in the case of an upgrade, they need to first compare the existing computer configuration with the hardware requirements for Windows XP.

■ Installing and Configuring Windows XP Professional

The average person may buy a computer with an OS preinstalled and use that computer with the same OS until it fails or becomes obsolete. But you aren't the average person. You're preparing for a technical career, or you may simply wish to be a knowledgeable computer user. In either case, the best way to begin learning a new OS is to successfully install it from scratch. To that end, we'll focus on a clean installation.

You'll prepare for a Windows XP installation just as you did for previous installations of Windows in this book. You'll need to check out hardware requirements and hardware and software compatibility.

> Please keep in mind that IT professionals may use scripted installations or some type of imaged installations, as discussed in previous Windows chapters. These methods are best when you must install an OS onto many computers, using identical configurations.

XP Hardware Requirements

Microsoft XP runs on a wide range of computers but you need to be sure that your computer meets the minimum hardware requirements as shown here. Also shown is our recommended minimum for a system running a typical selection of business productivity software.

Minimum for an XP Computer	Recommended for an XP Computer
Any Intel or AMD 233-MHz or higher processor	Any Intel or AMD 600-MHz or higher processor
64MB of RAM	256MB of RAM
1.5GB of hard drive space	4GB of hard drive space
Video card that supports DirectX 8 with at least 800×600 resolution	Video card that supports DirectX 8 with at least 800×600 resolution
Any CD-ROM or DVD-ROM drive	Any CD-ROM or DVD-ROM drive

Hardware and Software Compatibility

You'll need to check hardware and software compatibility before installing Windows XP Professional—either as an upgrade or a new installation. Of course, if you purchase a computer with Windows XP preinstalled, you're spared this task, but you'll still need to verify that the application software you plan to add to the computer will be compatible.

Luckily, you have two tools for determining whether your hardware is compatible: the Windows Catalog and the Upgrade Advisor on the XP CD.

Windows Catalog   The Windows Catalog is a searchable list of hardware and software that is known to work with Windows XP. The URL for this exact page is so long, it looks like a typing test. Here is another way to get to it through a shorter URL. First, connect to www.microsoft.com/windowsxp/ compatibility/. On the compatibility page, select the link labeled Discover the Windows Catalog.

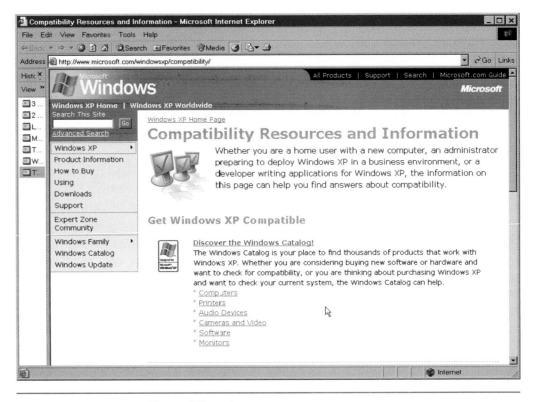

• Windows XP Professional Compatibility web page

Once at the Windows Catalog page, you can search on specific hardware or software products, or browse through the catalog of hardware and software products that will work with Windows XP.

Upgrade Advisor   In our experience, Windows XP has supported a wide range of hardware and software, even some rather old "no name" computers, but we like to be proactive when planning an installation, especially an upgrade. You may not have the luxury of time in upgrading a computer. You may be asked by your boss or client to perform an upgrade *now*. Fortunately, the Upgrade Advisor is the first process that runs on the XP installation CD. It examines your hardware and installed software (in the case of an upgrade) and provides a list of devices and software that are known to have issues with XP. Be sure to follow the suggestions on this list!

The Upgrade Advisor can also be run separately from the Windows XP installation. You can run it from the Windows XP CD, or, if you want to find out about compatibility for an upgrade before purchasing Windows XP, connect to the Windows XP Compatibility web page (www.microsoft.com/windowsxp/compatibly) and select Upgrade Advisor. Follow the instructions on the following page to use the online Upgrade Advisor.

When he was first learning about Windows XP, Edgar ran the advisor on a test computer at the office that was running Windows 98. It produced a report that found only one incompatibility—an antivirus program. The details stated that the program was compatible only if installed after Windows XP was installed. Therefore, it suggested removing the program before installing the OS, then reinstalling it after the OS was installed. Don't ignore the instructions provided by the Upgrade Advisor! On a test computer, like that on which Edgar ran the Upgrade Advisor, you can afford to see what the consequences are of ignoring advice, but you don't always have that luxury or time. Edgar always likes to find out what the consequences are of ignoring advice. He says that helps to troubleshoot problems that his clients run into.

Step-by-Step 7.01

Running the Upgrade Advisor

In this step-by-step, you will run the Upgrade Advisor on your system. To complete this task, you will need the following:

- A PC with Windows XP or older version of Windows
- Internet access (optional)

Step 1

Insert the Windows XP CD. If Autorun is enabled, the Welcome to Microsoft Windows XP screen will appear. If this does not appear, select Start | Run and enter the following and then click OK:

```
d:\SETUP.EXE
[Where d is the drive letter for the CD-ROM drive.]
```

Step 2

At the Welcome to Microsoft Windows XP screen, select Check System Compatibility. On the following page select Check My System Automatically.

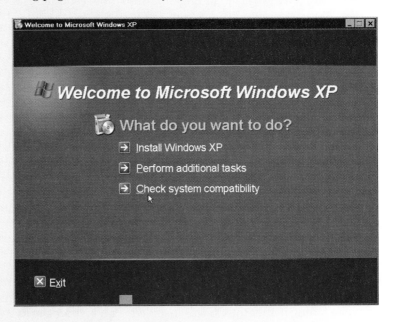

Step 3

The Upgrade Advisor dialog box opens and gives you two choices. If you have an Internet connection, select the first choice, which will download the updated Setup files. If you don't have an Internet connection, select No, Skip This Step and Continue Installing Windows. (Don't worry, you aren't really going to install, yet.) Click Next. The Upgrade Advisor will show the tasks that Dynamic Update is performing, and then it will restart Setup.

Step 4

If you chose to download the updated Setup files in the previous step, perform this step, otherwise, continue to Step 5. After Setup restarts, you'll be back at the same page in the Upgrade Advisor. This time, select No, Skip This Step and Continue Installing Windows, and click Next. The Report System Compatibility page appears next. You can save the information in a file by clicking Save As, and selecting a location. If incompatible items are found, report this to your instructor.

Read the findings that the Upgrade Advisor presents. If a problem was found, click the Details button for instructions. And remember Edgar's experience and follow the instructions. When you have recorded any necessary instructions, click Finish.

Booting into Windows XP Setup

The Windows XP CDs are bootable and Microsoft no longer includes a program to create a set of Setup boot disks. This should not be an issue, because PCs manufactured in the last several years have the ability to boot from CD-ROM. This system BIOS setting, usually described as "boot order," is controlled through a PC's BIOS-based setup program. While we don't recommend that you modify the system settings on your lab computer, if you find that you cannot boot from the Windows XP CD, ask your instructor to help you configure the PC to boot from a CD.

In the unlikely event that your lab computer can't be made to boot from CD, you can create a set of six (Yes!) Windows XP Setup boot disks using a program downloaded from Microsoft's website.

> If you need to create the Setup boot disks, connect to www.support.microsoft.com and search on "Q310994." This article explains how to create the disks and provides links for several versions of the program to create them.

Registration Versus Activation

During setup, you will be prompted to register your product and to activate it. Many people confuse activation with registration. These are two separate operations. Registration is informing Microsoft of the official owner or user of the product, providing contact information such as name, address, company, phone number, e-mail address, and so on. Registration is still entirely optional. Activation is a new method to combat software piracy, meaning that they wish to ensure that each license for Windows XP is used solely on a single computer. It's also more formally called Microsoft Product Activation (MPA). Learn more about activation so that you won't be misinformed.

Mandatory Activation Within 30 Days of Installation   Activation is mandatory, but you may skip this step during installation. You will have 30 days in which to activate the product, during which time it will work normally. If you don't activate it within that time frame, it will be disabled. Don't worry about forgetting, because once it's installed, Windows XP frequently reminds you to activate it with a balloon message over the tray area of the taskbar. The messages even tell you how many days you have left.

Activation Mechanics   Here is how product activation works. When you choose to activate, either during setup or later when XP reminds you to do it, the product ID code that you entered during installation is combined with a 50-digit value that identifies your key hardware components to create an installation ID code. You must send this code to Microsoft, either automatically if you have an Internet connection, or verbally via a phone call to Microsoft. Microsoft then returns a 42-digit product activation code. If you are activating online, you don't have to enter the activation code; it will happen automatically. If you are activating over the phone, you must read the installation ID to a representative and enter the resulting 42-digit activation code into the Activate Windows by Phone dialog box.

No personal information about you is sent as part of the activation process. Figure 7-4 shows the dialog box that will open when you start activation by clicking on the reminder message balloon.

> Learn more about Microsoft Product Activation (MPA) by connecting to www.support .microsoft.com and searching on "activation." You will find articles on activation for Windows XP and other Microsoft products. Notice that there are situations in which you will not be required to do activation.

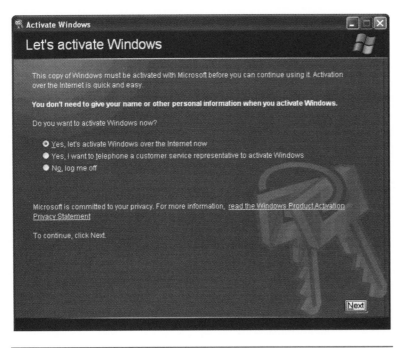

The screenshot shows the "Activate Windows" dialog:

Activate Windows

Let's activate Windows

This copy of Windows must be activated with Microsoft before you can continue using it. Activation over the Internet is quick and easy.

You don't need to give your name or other personal information when you activate Windows.

Do you want to activate Windows now?

○ Yes, let's activate Windows over the Internet now
○ Yes, I want to telephone a customer service representative to activate Windows
○ No, log me off

Microsoft is committed to your privacy. For more information, read the Windows Product Activation Privacy Statement

To continue, click Next.

[Next]

Getting Down to the Business of Installing Windows XP Professional

So you've convinced yourself that it's time to install Windows XP. Any apprehension you may have about the process should be thrown out the window. Installing XP is simple. The wizard will guide you through every step of the process. The onscreen directions are correct and clear. Very few decisions will need to be made. If you are in doubt about a setting, pressing ENTER will likely perform the correct action.

Overall, the installation process takes about an hour. Most of that time will be spent watching the screen. Feel free to walk away as the installation is taking place. If input is needed, the installation program will stop and wait until you click the correct buttons.

● **Figure 7-4.**   Activation will take just seconds with an Internet connection

Step-by-Step 7.02

Installing Windows XP

In this step-by-step, you will do a clean installation of Windows XP. To complete this exercise, you will need the following:

- A Microsoft/Intel standard personal computer (desktop or laptop) compatible with Windows XP Professional, with at least the minimum hardware and configured to boot from CD

- An unpartitioned hard disk (disk 0, the first hard disk)

- The Windows XP Professional CD

- One 3.5-inch diskette to use as an emergency repair disk

- The Product ID code from the envelope of your Windows XP Professional CD

- A 15-character (or less) name for your computer, unique on your network

- The name of the workgroup to be used in the class lab

- A password for the Administrator account on your computer

- The IP address, subnet mask, and other necessary TCP/IP configuration information, or confirmation from your instructor that you should configure Windows XP Professional to get an IP address automatically

Step 1

Insert the Windows XP CD and boot the computer. After inspecting your hardware configuration, XP setup will show the blue character mode setup screen and copy files to your computer. After the files are copied, you will be prompted to remove the CD and reboot the system. Windows setup will start, load system devices, and display the Welcome to Setup screen. Press ENTER to start the installation of XP.

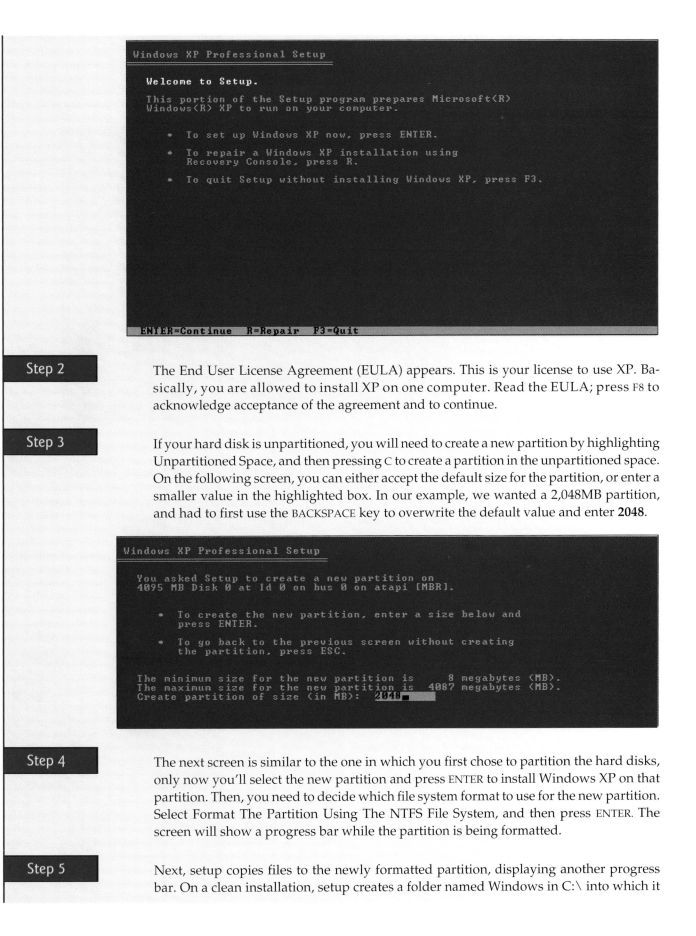

The End User License Agreement (EULA) appears. This is your license to use XP. Basically, you are allowed to install XP on one computer. Read the EULA; press F8 to acknowledge acceptance of the agreement and to continue.

If your hard disk is unpartitioned, you will need to create a new partition by highlighting Unpartitioned Space, and then pressing C to create a partition in the unpartitioned space. On the following screen, you can either accept the default size for the partition, or enter a smaller value in the highlighted box. In our example, we wanted a 2,048MB partition, and had to first use the BACKSPACE key to overwrite the default value and enter **2048**.

The next screen is similar to the one in which you first chose to partition the hard disks, only now you'll select the new partition and press ENTER to install Windows XP on that partition. Then, you need to decide which file system format to use for the new partition. Select Format The Partition Using The NTFS File System, and then press ENTER. The screen will show a progress bar while the partition is being formatted.

Next, setup copies files to the newly formatted partition, displaying another progress bar. On a clean installation, setup creates a folder named Windows in C:\ into which it installs the OS, creating appropriate subfolders below this folder. After it completes copying the base set of files to this location, your computer reboots, and the graphical mode of Windows XP Setup begins. On the left of the screen uncompleted tasks have a white button, completed tasks have a green button, and the current task has a red button.

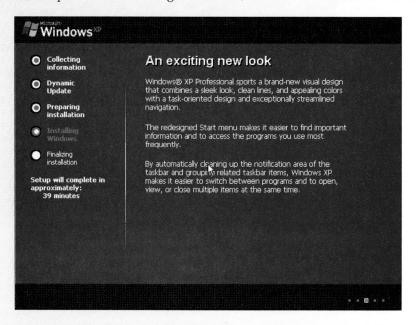

Step 6

On the Regional and Language Options screen, leave the defaults selected and click Next, unless told otherwise by your instructor. On the Personalize Your Software page enter your name and the name of your school or employer. Next, you must enter a valid product key for Windows XP. This can be found on the CD case containing your copy of XP. Be sure to enter it exactly, or you will be unable to continue.

Step 7

Next, you need to name your computer. This identifies your computer on a network. Check with your system administrator for an appropriate name. In addition to a valid name for your computer, you need to create a password for the Administrator user account. This will be the password that allows you to modify and fix the computer. Next set the date, time, and time zone.

Step 8

If a network card was detected, the network components will be installed and you'll have an opportunity to configure the network settings. On the Network Settings page select Typical settings, unless told otherwise by your instructor. Once the networking elements are installed, you need to configure the network. Relax; XP will do most of the work for you. Unless you

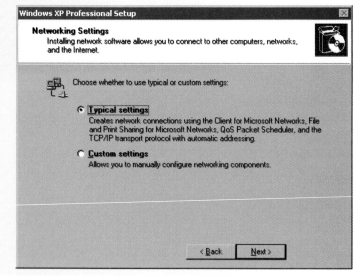

have specific instructions from your network administrator, the default settings are the preferred choices.

Step 9

If your computer participates in a domain-based network, you need to set the domain options. To connect the computer to a domain, you must have administrative rights to the network. The computer shown here will not participate in a domain and is part of the Osborne workgroup. After clicking Next, be prepared to wait for several minutes while XP copies files.

Step 10

After the files required for the final configuration are copied, XP will reboot again. During this reboot, XP determines your screen size and applies the appropriate resolution. This reboot can take several minutes to complete, so be patient. Once the reboot is complete, you must log on as the Administrator. Balloon messages may appear over the tray area of the taskbar. A common message concerns the display resolution. Click the balloon and allow Windows XP to automatically adjust the display settings.

Step 11

Another message reminds you that you have 30 days left for activation. We suggest that when you do a single install, you test it for a few days before activating, in case you need to make any significant changes in the hardware. If you activate and then have to change any of the hardware, you might not be able to reinstall XP because the program will think you are trying to install it on a second computer. If you're not choosing to activate at this time, click the close button of the message balloon. Congratulations! You have completed the Windows XP installation and should have a desktop with the default Bliss background.

Verify Network Access

Once you have completed the installation, if the computer is connected to a network, verify that it can communicate with other computers on the network. Use My Network Places, as you did in Chapter 6, to see any computers on the network besides your own. The only catch is that My Network Places is not where it used to be! You'll find it in My Computer, which is on the Start menu. Once you open My Network Places, click View Workgroup Computers. This will show all the computers in the workgroup or domain

● **Figure 7-5.**   Osborne workgroup with one computer showing

in which your computer resides (recall the workgroup or domain setting from the installation). In Figure 7-5, you can see just one computer, Webster01, in the workgroup Osborne. If you used a workgroup name that was different from that chosen by your fellow students, your computer may also be alone like Webster01 is.

This is the computer on which we installed XP during the step-by-step. To see other workgroups and domains, click Microsoft Windows Network. Figure 7-6 shows three workgroups or computers: Htc, Osborne, and Workgroup. Just seeing other workgroups and domains on the network is confirmation that a network connection is working, because you must be connected and communicating on a network to be aware of the other workgroups, domains, and computers. However, if you are eager to see other computers, open one of these workgroups or domains.

My Network Neighborhood refers to all groupings of computers as workgroups, even though, in Figure 7-6, Htc is a domain, and the others are workgroups.

Install Updates

Now that you have verified network access your next task should be to install updates. This is important, especially if you are on a network and/or the Internet, because many of the updates are to close security holes that are most likely to be exploited over a network. How you actually obtain updates

Updates and service packs were discussed in Chapters 4, 5, and 6.

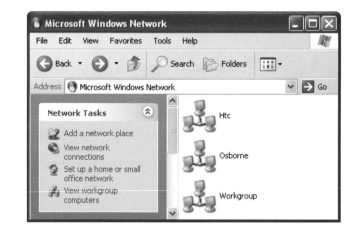

● **Figure 7-6.**   Microsoft Windows Network with three workgroups or domains showing

will depend on the organization (school or business) where you install Windows XP. In some organizations, the IT department may distribute updates intended for new installations on CD so that they can be installed before a computer is even connected to a network. Other organizations may make them available on a shared folder on the network. If you have an Internet connection, you can connect to the Microsoft website and download them for free.

If you're permitted to get the very latest from the Microsoft Update site and you have Internet access to your computer, you can use the Windows Update program from the Control Panel, which is accessed from the Start menu.

Step-by-Step 7.03

Installing Updates

In this step-by-step exercise, you will use Windows Update to connect to the Microsoft Update site; test your computer for installed components, updates and service packs; and install the recommended updates and service packs. To complete this exercise, you will need the following:

- A PC with Windows XP Professional installed as described in Step-by-Step 7.02

- Internet access (confirm that you can access the Internet using Internet Explorer)

Step 1

Log on as Administrator, then select Start | Control Panel. Then click Windows Update. Internet Explorer will connect to the Windows Update web page, and you will see a message asking if you want to install the latest version of Windows Update Control. Click Yes.

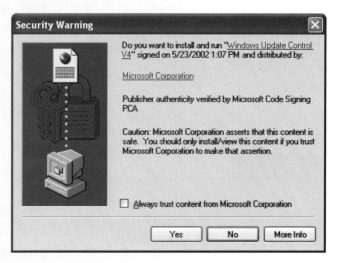

Step 2

After Windows Update Control is installed, the Welcome to Windows Update page will be displayed. Click Scan for Updates, and wait while Windows Update scans your computer. After the scan, click Review and Install Updates. An Internet Explorer message will warn you about sending information to the Internet. Leave the check in the box to not show this message in the future, and click Yes.

Step 3

In the Total Selected Updates page, review the list of updates. You may have to use the scroll bar to view all of the updates. Some can be installed together. Some are described as exclusive and must be installed separately from others. For instance, when we did it for this Step-by-Step, the list included Windows XP Service Pack 1, which had to be installed separately.

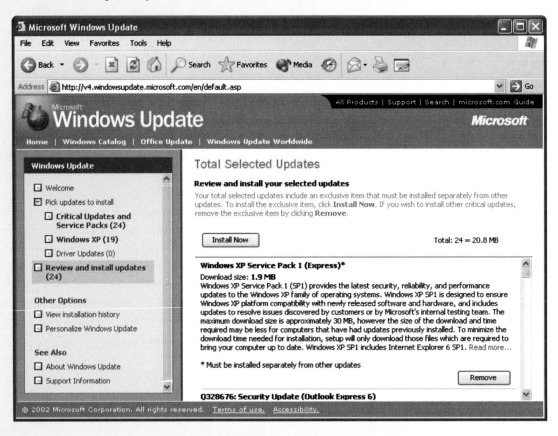

Step 4

Click Remove to remove any updates you don't wish to install at this time. We removed everything but Service Pack 1. Then click Install Now. If a license agreement message appears, read the agreement, and then click Accept. The download will begin and you will see a web page dialog box with progress bars for both the download and installation. As soon as the download is complete, the installation will begin. In the case of a service Pack, the Service Pack Setup wizard will be displayed, and you will have to click Next to continue.

Step 5

If another license agreement page appears, read the agreement, and click I Agree, and then click Next. From this point on, follow the instructions in the wizard. You may also be required to insert the Windows XP CD. Some updates can take several minutes to install and will require a restart.

Windows XP Service Pack 1 Setup Wizard

Updating Your System

Please wait while setup inspects your current configuration, archives your current files and updates your files.

Inspecting your current configuration

Details
Inspecting:

< Back   Finish   Cancel   Help

Step 6

After the restart, if you have not installed all of the recommended updates, restart Windows Update, rescan your computer, and review the remaining updates. Install the other updates. The smaller updates can often be installed together. Repeat until all of the recommended updates have been installed.

Step 7

After you have installed all of the Windows Updates, look for any updates for your applications programs. For instance, if you are using Microsoft Office, you can select Office Update from the Windows Update site and go through a process similar to that for installing the Windows updates. If you have applications from other companies, check out their websites for updates. We realize that you probably have not installed any other software, yet, but include this step for future reference, because you will need to do this on any computer on which you have installed applications.

■ Customizing and Managing Windows XP Professional

Once you have installed Windows XP Professional, configured the OS to work with your network, and installed recommended updates and service packs, it's time to customize the desktop for the user. In the case of a new OS, the first few times you do this, you will need to find familiar tools and perhaps learn how to use new ones.

Like earlier versions of Windows, XP is completely customizable. You can change the desktop, Start button, the way applications work, and hundreds of other settings that you probably have never thought of. Most of this customization is handled through the Control Panel. In this section, we look at some changes to the Control Panel and complete some tasks using Control Panel applets. Then you'll practice other customization tasks, including installing and removing applications.

Compare Control Panels

Flip back to Chapter 3 to see a comparison of the classic Control Panel and the new one in Windows XP. Then open and explore Control Panel in Windows XP on your lab computer. Answer the following questions.

1. Describe the major visual difference between the two, using Windows 2000's Control Panel to represent the Classic view.

   _____

2. Describe how you will work in the new Category view.

   _____

3. Describe what you can do if you absolutely can't bear to work in the new Category view of Control Panel.

   _____

The Windows XP Control Panel

The Windows XP Control Panel has changed greatly in appearance, which you probably noticed when you used the Control Panel in the previous Step-by-Step. Microsoft attempted to make the Control Panel easier for new users to use by grouping the Control Panel applets by functional category, a view they call **Category view**.

The new Control Panel may be easier for the uninitiated to use, but experienced users may be confused at first. To remedy this, Microsoft also provides the **Classic view** of the Control Panel, just as in previous versions of Windows. If you want to use the Classic view, simply click Switch to Classic View. As shown in Figure 7-7, no grouping is present. If you want to go back to the Category view, click Switch to Category View.

A Professional Strategy for Working with Control Panel

Any computer professional who must support desktop users' needs to understand what the user is seeing and experiencing. Therefore, we suggest when you begin to work with a new operating system that you leave as many of the default settings in place as you can tolerate. The Control Panel

• **Figure 7-7.** Control Panel in Classic view

is a good example, because most people will be working with the new Category view. If your work involves phone support, you'd have trouble guiding someone through a Control Panel task if you're unfamiliar with the view they use. Sure, you can instruct them to change to Classic view, complete the task, then switch back, but if you forget to tell them to switch back, then they are left with something that confuses them. Showing a new user too many new things brings them very quickly to the point where they have the "deer in the headlights" look, and you've lost their trust.

Display Settings

Microsoft and most users believe that the user should control how their computer looks. The argument is that if a user has to stare at the screen for eight or more hours a day, then he or she should be able to make the desktop appealing. As in previous versions, Windows XP includes the Display applet for changing the display resolution, background picture, color themes, and the screen saver.

Most organizations don't like users to change their desktops, especially if they can be seen by customers. A standard look on the desktop looks more professional. It also reduces the chance that an employee may offend a customer or co-worker with a poorly chosen desktop.

Adding a Printer to Windows XP

Another customizing task that you will do soon after installing any OS is to add a printer. Actually, you attach the physical printer, and install the correct driver into the OS. Microsoft has made this task nearly transparent, so that in the best of circumstances you are hardly aware that much of anything happened, except that you can print to a new printer.

Because Windows XP is a plug and play OS, most new printers seem to install themselves, especially if the printer uses a USB, IEEE 1394, or infrared port. They are completely plug and play; you simply connect the printer to your computer, and Windows will install the driver and configure the device for you. You should hang around, though, because you may have to insert the Windows XP CD or a disk from the printer manufacturer, if requested.

If you are installing a non–plug and play printer, you will have to use the Add Printer wizard, which you start by selecting Add a Printer from the Printer Tasks list after opening

• Add Printer Wizard

Inside Information

InstallShield

No matter what type of application program you install, if it needs to make changes to Windows, it probably uses a special installation program that runs as a wizard. That program is very often InstallShield, which is from a company of the same name. Software companies purchase the InstallShield products for creating installations for Windows, because InstallShield enables their programmers to create installation programs that work in a standardized fashion. The InstallShield Company specializes in the intricacies of Windows installations, so that programmers in thousands of companies don't have to. Watch for the InstallShield wizard, and/or go to `www.installshield.com` *to learn more about the company and their products.*

Printers and Faxes on the Start menu. In this case, you simply follow the instructions on the screen. Even without a plug and play printer this is pretty painless.

Installing and Working with Applications in Windows XP

For most people, a computer in itself is not important; it's the work (or play) that we can accomplish with the computer that's important. Therefore, Windows XP is no more than a pretty face until you install the applications that will enable the user to do the desired tasks. Installing an application in Windows XP is very much like installing one in Windows 2000 or Windows 98, but you should always practice common tasks in a new OS. In this section, we look briefly at how you install and remove application programs in Windows XP.

Windows XP, like its immediate predecessors, allows you to add programs through a Control Panel applet, now revamped and slightly renamed as Add or Remove Programs. As with its predecessors, you will rarely need to use this option, as setup programs often start as soon as you insert the CD (if autorun is enabled, which it is by default). But if this is not the case, use the Add New Program button in Add or Remove Programs, and it will search for the setup program.

Step-by-Step 7.04

Installing an Application in Windows XP

In this step-by-step, you'll practice installing an application into Windows XP. The application we've chosen is a free 30-day evaluation copy of a popular antivirus program, PC-cillin by Trend Micro, available on the Internet. Since web pages change frequently, the following steps may not exactly match the steps you will need to take when you access the Trend Micro website. You may also choose to install a different application, in which case, the steps will only generally apply.

To complete this step-by-step you will need the following:

■ The computer on which you successfully installed Windows XP Professional in Step-by-Step 7.02

■ Fast Internet access (a 56K modem connection will take hours to download the file)

Step 1

Log on as an Administrator. Use Internet Explorer to connect to `www.trendmicro.com`. Click on Personal, in order to find the antivirus software appropriate for a single user. Click Try Now under the latest version of PC-cillin (PC-cillin 2002 at this time). This will take you to the Download Trial Version page, where you must enter personal information, including a valid e-mail address (that is how you get the activation code to make the software work). After completing the information, click Download.

Step 2

On the next page, click the product file name. Your choices may be between a U.S. version, and an international version. In the File Download dialog box, click Save, and save the file on your desktop. Downloading may take several minutes, depending on the speed of your connection.

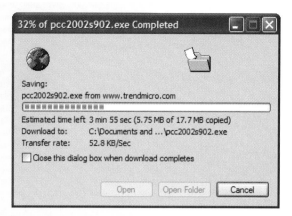

Step 3

When the download is complete, click the Open button to run the installation program. The Location To Save Files page shows where files will be saved. Accept the default location by clicking the Next button. It will take a few minutes to extract the files and save them. Then the InstallShield wizard will appear. Click Next on the Welcome page to begin. Read the License Agreement page, click the radio button to accept the license agreement, and then click Next to continue. This will begin a virus scan of your computer.

Step 4

On the Customer Information page leave the serial key blank (this is only required if you have purchased PC-cillin) and click Next. A Trial Version message will appear to warn you that the trial version does not allow you to use all the functions of the product. Click to place a check in the check box labeled I Wish To Install As Trial Version, then click Next.

Step 5

On the Destination Folder page, click Next to accept the default location for the installation. On the Ready to Install page, click Install. The Installing PC-cillin page will be displayed with a progress bar. When it is done, the final page of the wizard will appear, and you simply click Finish to exit the wizard. After the wizard closes, the desktop appears. The PC-cillin icon appears in the tray area of the taskbar, and you will also find shortcuts for it in Start | All Programs | Trend Micro PC-cillin. Like most antivirus programs PC-cillin runs in the background. The default settings should be fine; you can view and modify the settings by double-clicking the taskbar icon or by selecting PC-cillin from the Trend Micro PC-cillin menu.

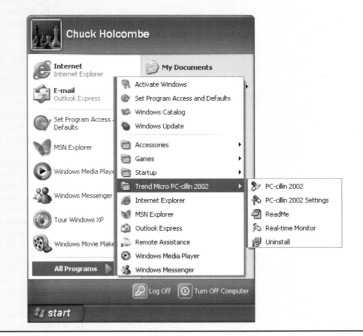

Removing Programs

The longer you have an OS installed, the more housekeeping it requires. One cleanup task is to remove programs that are no longer needed (or never really were). Because Windows XP requires that most software be installed by an administrator, the problem of user-installed harmful or unnecessary programs has almost disappeared, as long as users are not given access to the Administrator account or any other account that is a member of the computer's Administrators group. (Recall the discussion of groups in Chapters 4, 5, and 6.)

Even when only trained IT staff installs programs, it's eventually necessary to remove some of the programs for a variety of reasons. Maybe an application didn't meet expectations, or it outgrew its usefulness. Computers purchased with Windows XP preinstalled often have many programs installed that you'll never use. In Windows XP removing programs is much like in previous versions of Windows. You use the Add or Remove Programs applet in Control Panel. Figure 7-8 shows Add or Remove Programs on a computer with a combination of preinstalled applications and user-installed applications. When

---

Try This!

Use Add or Remove Programs

Although you may not need to remove any programs just yet, familiarize yourself with the new look of the Add or Remove Programs applet and look at the list of currently installed programs. In addition to applications, any updates will be listed here. Try this:

1. Open the Control Panel. Select Add or Remove Programs.

2. Browse through the list of Currently Installed Programs, expanding each one. This list may be empty if you have not updated Windows or installed any programs.

3. If you find a program that should be removed, click the Change/Remove button to begin the uninstall process. Sometimes you must provide the installation CD before the program can be removed!

4. When you have finished exploring, exit from Add or Remove Programs. If you uninstalled an application, you may need to allow the uninstall program to restart the computer.

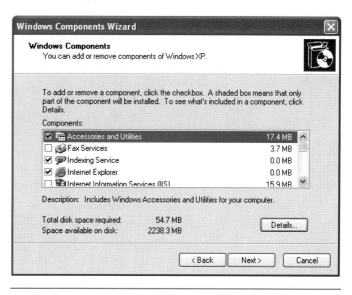

Add or Remove Programs

Currently installed programs: Sort by: Name

Ad-aware 5.83

Adobe Acrobat 5.0   Size   15.97MB

America Online   Size   32.27MB
Used   frequently
Last Used On   4/4/2002
To change this program or remove it from your computer, click Change/Remove.   Change/Remove

Cloudmark SpamNet   Size   0.99MB

DigitalPrint 1.1   Size   2.24MB

DVDExpress   Size   1.82MB

DVgate   Size   1.01MB

Experience VAIO   Size   0.80MB

FullShot V6

ImageStation   Size   0.80MB

ImageStation Demo   Size   0.81MB

InterActual Player   Size   3.40MB

Ipswitch WS_FTP Pro   Size   8.30MB

Media Bar 3.2.12   Size   0.84MB

Microsoft Office XP Professional with FrontPage   Size   244.00MB

Change or Remove Programs | Add New Programs | Add/Remove Windows Components | Set Program Access and Defaults

> Never remove a program by simply deleting it from disk. Even if you succeed in removing all its files, Windows and other programs may still try to start it, and you will be left with error messages and no easy way to stop this from occurring.

● **Figure 7-8.**   Add or Remove Programs

you click a program name, the information expands and often shows you when it was last used and how frequently it's used. In this example, it shows that America Online was frequently used, when in reality we never used it!

Adding or Removing Windows XP Components

When you installed Windows XP, XP tried to guess which built-in components you would need. It installed Notepad, modem support, and games on your computer. These Windows components can be removed from your system if you like. Other components can be added as well. If you are adding components, you'll need a copy of your XP CD, or another location where the Windows XP source files are stored. This is a task that really hasn't changed from previous versions of Windows.

■ Managing User Security in Windows XP

Windows XP is the desktop upgrade to Windows 2000, and as such, it has all the security components of Windows 2000, with some improvements

Windows Components Wizard

Windows Components
You can add or remove components of Windows XP.

To add or remove a component, click the checkbox. A shaded box means that only part of the component will be installed. To see what's included in a component, click Details.

Components:

☑ Accessories and Utilities	17.4 MB
☐ Fax Services	3.7 MB
☑ Indexing Service	0.0 MB
☑ Internet Explorer	0.0 MB
☐ Internet Information Services (IIS)	15.9 MB

Description: Includes Windows Accessories and Utilities for your computer.

Total disk space required: 54.7 MB
Space available on disk: 2238.3 MB   Details...

< Back   Next >   Cancel

● Add or remove components wizard

as well as enhancements to make it easier to manage the security on the desktop. In this section you will practice creating users and creating a password reset disk, which are basic security tasks for a desktop computer.

Users and Groups in Windows XP Professional

Like Windows 2000 Professional, Windows XP Professional has an accounts database, several built-in groups, and two user accounts created during installation—Administrator and Guest—with only the Administrator account enabled by default. In the lab, when you installed Windows XP, you supplied the password for the Administrator account. Since then, this has been the only account you've used to log on to the computer, unless you created a new local account or unless you joined the computer to a domain. We'll assume that your computer doesn't belong to a domain and you'll practice creating local accounts on your Windows XP computer.

Using the Administrator account is just fine when you're doing administrative tasks, such as installing updates, adding printers, adding and removing programs and Windows components, and creating users and groups. However, even on your own computer, you should never log on with such a powerful account when you're doing ordinary tasks, such as writing and printing reports, browsing the Internet, and playing games (Certainly not!). It is the administrator's job to create additional accounts.

Creating Accounts with the User Accounts Applet

Although Windows XP has essentially the same type of accounts database as Windows 2000, the User Accounts Control Panel applet replaces the former Users and Passwords applet and further simplifies user management tasks.

A Simple Tool   In Windows XP, the User Accounts applet hides the complete list of users, using a simple reference to account types that is actually a reference to its group membership. An account that is a member of the local Administrators group is said to be a **Computer Administrator account**, while an account that only belongs to the Local Users group is said to be a Limited account. The users it shows depends on the currently logged-on user. When an Administrator is logged on she will see both types of accounts and the **Guest account**. When a user with a **Limited account** is logged on, she will only see her own account in User Accounts.

> Windows XP allows users to log on from a Welcome screen or from the Log On to Windows dialog box. Switch between these two methods by selecting or deselecting Use the Welcome Screen, a setting found in Control Panel | User Accounts | Change the Way Users Log On or Off.

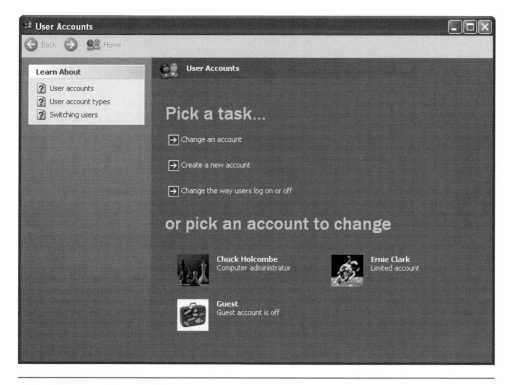

- User Accounts showing a Computer Administrator, a Limited account, and the Guest account

Or a More Complex Tool A knowledgeable administrator can choose to create and manage users through Local Users and Groups in the Computer Management console (right-click My computer and select Manage), which reveals all existing users and groups, but the User Accounts applet is sufficient for managing accounts on a desktop or laptop computer.

More About Windows XP Accounts Creating users is a straightforward process. You need to provide a user name and an initial password. The user can change the password later. You also need to know the type of account to create: Computer Administrator or Limited.

Remember that if a computer is a member of a domain, the users will log on using domain accounts. Therefore, creating local user accounts is mostly done on a stand-alone computer or a networked computer that is only a member of a workgroup. Then you should create one Limited account per user of the computer and an account that is a member of the local Administrators group (in addition to the one created during installation).

The reason for having two Administrator accounts is so that if one administrator is not available, or is not able to log on to the computer, another one can. Simple redundancy. Windows XP actually reminds you to do this; the first time you try to create a local account after installing Windows XP, you'll only be able to create a Computer Administrator account. After that, you'll be allowed to create Limited accounts.

> When creating new user accounts on your own computer, create both a Computer Administrator account and a Limited account for yourself. Use the Administrator account whenever you need to install new software or make changes to the computer. Use the Limited account for your day-to-day work. This protects your computer from mistakes you may make.

If you upgrade from Windows NT or Windows 2000 or from a Windows 9*x* installation in which user profiles were enabled, Setup will migrate the existing accounts to Windows XP.

Password Reset Disk   Windows XP allows the currently logged-on user to create a **password reset disk** that can be used in the case of a forgotten password. This is very important to have, because if you forget your password, and an administrator resets the password using User Accounts or Local Users and Groups, then when you log on using the new password, you'll find that you've lost access to some items, including files that you encrypted when logged on with the forgotten password. When you reset a password with a password reset disk, you can log on using the new password, and still have access to previously encrypted files.

Best of all, with the password reset disk, users have the power to fix their own passwords. Encourage your users to create this disk soon, because you have this power only if you think to create a password reset disk before you forget the password!

If you need to create a password reset disk for a computer on a network (domain), search the help system for Password Reset Disk and follow the instructions for password reset disks for a computer on a domain.

> This is just one of the reasons we warned against using file encryption earlier in the chapter. This is a very advanced feature that should only be used after studying it carefully. It would take more than a chapter just to talk about encryption in depth!

Step-by-Step 7.05

Creating User Accounts, Passwords, and a Password Reset Disk

Like our friend Edgar, you like to practice old skills using the new tools of an operating system. In this step-by-step you will create two new accounts. This is because the first new account you create after installation must be a Computer Administrator, giving you two accounts that are members of the Administrators group. After that, you may create Limited accounts. You will also create passwords for the new accounts, and then you will create a password reset disk for your Administrator account.

To complete this step-by-step you will need the following:

- The computer on which you successfully installed Windows XP Professional in Step-by-Step 7.02
- To be logged on as Administrator
- A blank formatted diskette

Step 1

Open the Control Panel by choosing Start | Control Panel. Then open the User Accounts applet. If you have not created any new accounts since installing Windows XP, there should only be two accounts: Administrator, and Guest. Click Create a New Account. On the Name The New Account page enter a name for the account and click Next.

Step 2

On the Pick an Account Type page the option for Limited is grayed out (unavailable) because this is the first account you have created since installation. This first new account can only be a Computer Administrator. Notice the tasks a Computer Administrator can do then click Create Account.

The account is created, and you're returned to the main page of User Accounts where you should see your new account. *Now* you can create a Limited account. In this case, you'll create one for the intended user of this computer, Luke Redd. Click Create a New Account, enter the name **Luke Redd** on the Name The New Account page, and click Next.

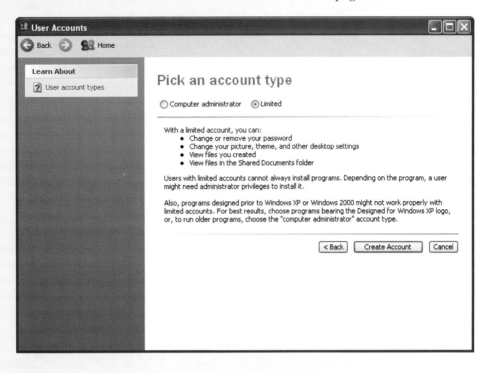

Notice that the Pick an Account Type page now shows both Computer Administrator and Limited as available options. Select Limited, and then click Create Account. Back in the main page Luke Redd will appear as a Limited account.

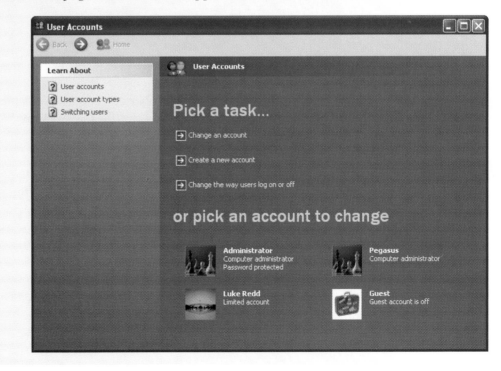

Your two new accounts have blank passwords, which is only tolerable in a very low security environment. As an administrator you need practice assigning passwords for users who will log on with local accounts, because this is a task you should expect to do. Start with the Computer Administrator account you just created. In User Accounts, select Change an Account. On the Pick an Account to Change page, select the new Computer Administrator you just created.

On the following page, select Create a Password. Before creating a password, click on each of the items in the Learn About list to learn how to create a secure password as well as a good password hint, and a message about what to do when you forget your password. Then, use what you learn to fill in the text boxes for the new password and a password hint, and then click Create Password.

Use the Back button to go back to the Pick an Account to Change page, select Luke Redd, and create a password and password hint for that account. When you have done that, use the Back button again to return to the Pick a Task page.

Now you'll create the password reset disk mentioned in the Learn About information you read about in Step 6. On the Pick a Task page, select the account that you are currently logged in as (Administrator). On the next page select Prevent a Forgotten Password from the list of Related Tasks (on the left). Read the Welcome page of the Forgotten Password wizard, and then click Next.

Next insert a blank, formatted disk in drive A: and click Next. On the Create User Account Password page enter the current user account password and click Next. The Creating Password Reset Disk page will show a progress bar while creating the disk. When it is completed, click Next, then click Finish to close the wizard. Make sure the disk is properly labeled, including the account name and computer, then store it in a very safe place.

```
Forgotten Password Wizard                                      [X]

  Creating Password Reset Disk
    Please wait while the wizard creates the disk.


  Progress: 100% complete
  [||||||||||||||||||||||||||||||||||||||||||||||]



                                    < Back    [ Next > ]    Cancel
```

Practicing User Security

The term *hacker* conjures up images of teenagers staying up all night trying to break into corporate computers. Nothing could be further from the truth. Legitimate users of a system perform most hacks. What follows is a true story that points out a significant vulnerability that you can avoid. After that we offer a solution that you may wish to use.

Inviting Trouble

Consider the case of two students, Jeff and Sam, who had a personality conflict. One day, Jeff left school without logging out of the network. Sam, seeing this, sat down at Jeff's seat and proceeded to modify his files for one of his courses. Luckily for Jeff, the instructor in the course knew what Sam had done because several other students witnessed Sam's actions and reported them. Without the other students, Jeff might have failed the course.

This story provides a simple moral: log out of your computer when you're away from your desk. If you fail to log out, you leave your files vulnerable to attack. These files may contain sensitive data crucial to the continued success of the company. A disgruntled employee could destroy these files and hurt the company. Because the damage was done by your account, the blame will fall on your shoulders.

Avoiding Trouble Without Logging Out

There are actually several solutions to the preceding scenario. The one mentioned is to log off before walking away from your computer. The reality is that most people have two objections to this solution: 1) Logging off closes all your open programs, requiring that when you return you log back on and figure out where you left off in your work. 2) People want an automatic solution.

Microsoft has kept these objections in mind while working on this problem with Windows NT, Windows 2000, and Windows XP, gradually achieving better results with each one. The solutions at this point (in addition to simply logging off) are pretty good. Let's look at some options.

Lock Computer   Lock Computer is an option in Windows NT, Windows 2000, and Windows XP. This is preferred to logging off, when you want to leave all your programs running exactly where you left off. It is very simple to do. Before leaving your computer unattended, simply press CTRL-ALT-DELETE to open the Windows Security dialog box and click Lock Computer. That's it. Your desktop will disappear, and the Computer Locked dialog box will appear on the screen. Then when you return, simply press CTRL-ALT-DELETE, enter the password for your account, and you will be back to the desktop exactly as you left it.

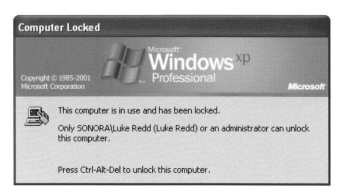

• The Computer Locked dialog box

The Windows XP Screen Saver   Another option that secures your computer when you walk away is a screen saver. The default Windows XP screen saver is already configured when you install Windows XP, so you have probably already noticed this on your lab computer. There are two caveats to using a screen saver.

- A screen saver is not secure unless you configure it to be password protected.

- Even with password protection, the computer is vulnerable during the wait period. A screen saver doesn't turn on until a sustained period of no keyboard or mouse activity. If someone walks up to an unattended computer and uses the mouse or keyboard before the wait period ends, he has as much control of the computer as the logged on account will allow (another reason to not use an administrator account while doing ordinary tasks).

You enable and configure a screen saver in Windows XP just as you did in previous versions of Windows—by using the Screen Saver tab on the Display Properties dialog box.

Switch User can't be used on a computer that is a member of a domain and it will disable Serial Keys, an accessibility feature.

A computer that is going to be shared in this way should have extra memory installed, because each open user session remains in memory until the user logs off.

Switch User   The last walk-away-from-your-computer-with-no-worries option is Fast User Switching, which adds the Switch User option to the Log Off menu. We like Fast User Switching. It's a great feature for a stand-alone computer or one that is on a network as a member of a workgroup. This is a step up from Lock Computer in that more than one user can have their current desktop session remain in memory. This feature allows multiple users to share a computer when their use of the computer overlaps.

Two users, Aretha and Roscoe, work in a small home improvement store's customer service area and share a computer during the same eight-hour shift, using it to schedule flooring product deliveries and installations. No problem—an administrator set up the computer to allow for faster user switching so that neither user has to lose the work they're doing and yet each has an open user session. When Aretha is working on the computer, but must walk away, or allow Roscoe access, she simply selects Start | Log Off | Switch User. Then she can walk away knowing that she can return to her desktop in the exact state she left it. Roscoe can also now log on. When he needs to leave the computer, he also selects Switch User.

Only a Computer Administrator can turn on Switch User. To do this, open User Accounts in Control Panel and select Change the Way Users Log On or Off. Select Fast User Switching, and click Apply Options. You may see a message that Fast User Switching cannot be turned on because Offline Files is currently enabled. If so, click OK to open the Offline Files Settings page of Folder Options, clear the check in the box labeled Enable Offline Files, and click OK. After that detour, you'll be back in the first page of User Accounts and Fast User Switching is turned on. Test it by selecting Start | Log Off. Confirm that the Switch User button is now in the Log Off Windows box.

• The Log Off Windows Box with the Switch User button

Troubleshooting Common Windows XP Problems

If life were perfect, then your computer would work all the time, with no problems. However, no matter how hard you work, your computer will find new ways to annoy you. In this section, we'll review some of the new features for preventing problems and troubleshooting.

Resources for Troubleshooting

When it comes to troubleshooting tools, Windows XP has inherited the best of its predecessors from both Windows families. That is, it has such vintage Windows NT tools as the Last Known Good Configuration startup option for startup failures and the Task Manager for removing errant programs. It has the Recovery Console that was introduced in Windows 2000. The Windows 9x family legacy includes Device Manager and the Safe Mode startup options that improve on those of the Windows 9x family. It also has a completely revamped and improved Windows Help. It has a great tool, System Restore, which was actually introduced in Windows Me, but has been improved in Windows XP. We'll leave the finer details of most of these tools for you to explore through Windows Help and introduce you to...

Device Manager

Device Manager in Windows XP works almost exactly as it did in Windows 2000, except that you can now easily roll back a newly installed device driver to the previously installed driver. This is accessed through the new Rollback Driver button on the Driver tab of the Properties dialog box for devices in Device Manager.

System Restore

Several years ago, Edgar had a bad experience after making several changes to a client's Windows 95 computer. The client was a small engineering company. The chief engineer had made several software and hardware changes and now every time they turned the computer on it entered a self-reboot loop when loading Windows 95. They weren't even able to go into Safe

Mode, and the chief engineer couldn't quite remember all the changes he had made. Edgar finally had to reformat the disk to clean it and reinstall the software and data. If only Edgar had Windows XP and System Restore!

The System Restore tools allow you to restore your computer to its configuration at a previous point in time, called a restore point. Some of these points in time are set automatically. For instance, by default, every time you install new software, XP creates a restore point. Thus, if installation of a program causes your computer to malfunction, simply restore the system to a time point prior to that installation, and the computer should work.

During the restore process, only settings and programs are changed. No data is lost. Your computer will include all programs and settings as of the restore date. This feature is invaluable for overworked administrators and consultants like Edgar. A simple restore will fix many user-generated problems.

To restore to a previous time point, start the **System Restore wizard** by choosing Start | All Programs | Accessories | System Tools | System Restore. Then select the first radio button, Restore My Computer to an Earlier Time, and then click Next.

The second screen shows a calendar with restore points. Any day with a boldface date has a restore point. These points are created after you add or remove software or install Windows updates and during the normal shutdown of your computer. Figure 7-9 shows a restore point when a program was installed. Select a date to restore to and click Next.

The last screen before the system is restored is a warning. It advises you to close all open programs and reminds you that Windows will shut down during the restore process. It also states that the restore operation is completely reversible. Thus, if you go too far back in time, you can restore to a more recent date.

You don't have to count on the automatic creation of restore points. You can open System Restore at any time and simply select Create a Restore Point.

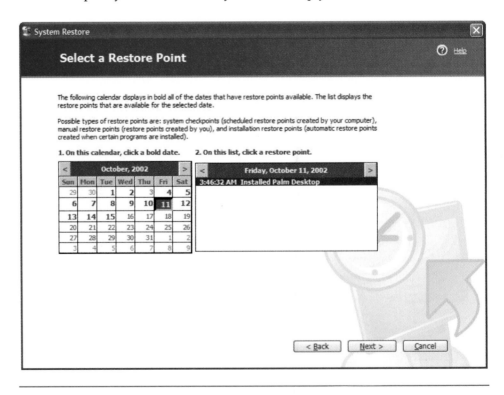

• **Figure 7-9.** Selecting a restore point

This is something to consider doing before making changes that might not trigger an automatic restore point, such as directly editing the registry.

System Restore is turned on by default and uses some of your disk space to save information on restore points. To turn System Restore off or change the disk space usage, open the System Properties applet in Control Panel and select the System Restore tab where you will find these settings.

Troubleshooting Startup Failure with Safe Mode

XP, like earlier versions of Windows, provides several additional ways to boot the system. Safe mode, a boot option available since Windows 95, is a particularly useful boot option. Booting to safe mode allows you to access XP with a minimal set of drivers, which should allow you to run the Control Panel to fix whatever needs fixing.

For example, we connected a very old monitor to an XP computer. XP was running at a screen resolution of 1024×768 which the old monitor did not support. We rebooted, entered safe mode, and changed the resolution to 640×480. Upon rebooting, the computer worked fine.

As you can see in Figure 7-10, safe mode is actually one of several startup options available from the Windows Advanced Options Menu. The first Safe Mode option loads without Network support. If you need network access, you can select the second option. To learn about all the Safe Mode options, search on "safe mode" in the Windows XP Help and Support.

> We have used Safe Mode with Networking as a test of whether or not a startup failure is due to a network component. If you can boot into Safe Mode, but not into Safe Mode with Networking, then reboot to Safe Mode and look at networking components, particularly network adapter drivers.

Creating Startup Disks

Like all other operating systems, Windows XP allows you to create startup disks to use in the event of an emergency. Unlike Windows 2000, XP allows you to create two types of startup disks: a Windows XP startup disk and an MS-DOS startup disk. Both have their uses, and both are handy to have when your computer cannot start.

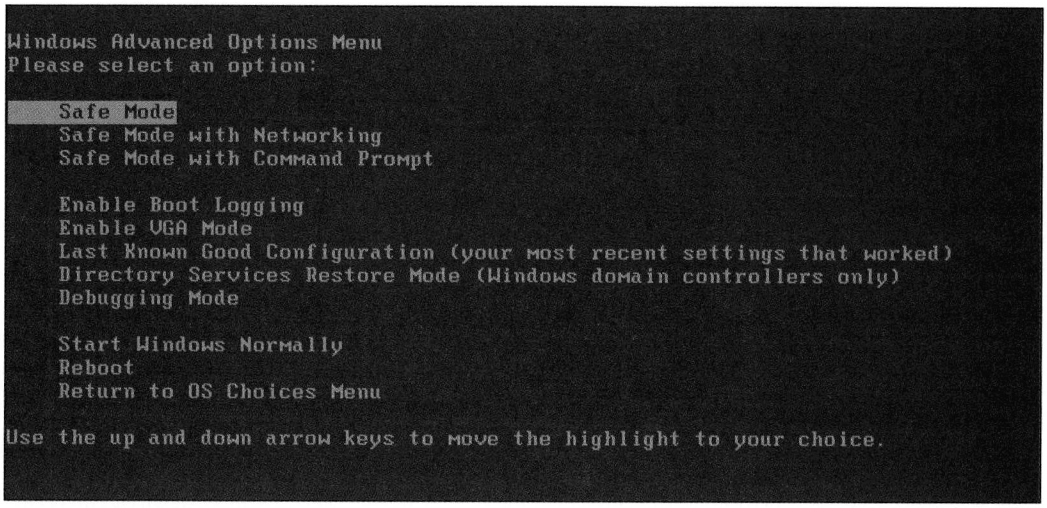

```
Windows Advanced Options Menu
Please select an option:

    Safe Mode
    Safe Mode with Networking
    Safe Mode with Command Prompt

    Enable Boot Logging
    Enable VGA Mode
    Last Known Good Configuration (your most recent settings that worked)
    Directory Services Restore Mode (Windows domain controllers only)
    Debugging Mode

    Start Windows Normally
    Reboot
    Return to OS Choices Menu

Use the up and down arrow keys to move the highlight to your choice.
```

• **Figure 7-10.** Safe Mode is selected from the Windows Advanced Options Menu

Try This!

Windows XP Safe Mode

Don't wait for an emergency before you look at Windows XP safe mode. Start up your computer in safe mode and take a look around. Try This:

1. Boot or reboot the PC. While the graphical initialization screen is visible, press and hold F8. The Windows Advanced Options menu will appear.
2. Select Safe Mode from the available choices. Wait several moments, and safe mode will load.
3. You will be required to log on as administrator. (Notice the poor resolution of the logon screen.) Then you will see a message that Windows is in Safe Mode, and the Safe Mode desktop will appear.
4. Open Control Panel, which in safe mode only appears in Classic view. Open the System applet, select the Hardware tab, and click the Device Manager button. You can work with faulty device drivers here, including disabling or removing them.
5. Select Start | Shutdown | Restart to restart Windows XP.

The Windows XP Startup Disk

The Windows XP startup disk works exactly like a Windows NT startup disk, allowing you to start Windows when one or more of the system files on the root of C: has been damaged or deleted. This will allow you to boot into the GUI.

Consider the following as motivation for having boot disks. Several months ago we had a big problem. Somehow, a computer got infected with a virus. The virus prevented the computer from booting correctly. It overwrote one of the boot files and nothing worked. Luckily, we had a handy-dandy Windows XP startup disk. We copied the correct files to the hard disk and were then able to boot. We were happy that we didn't have to rebuild the computer.

To create a Windows XP startup disk, use the instructions in Chapter 4 in Step-by-Step 4.12. To create an MS-DOS startup disk in Windows XP, open My Computer, right-click the floppy disk drive, and then select Format. In the Format dialog box, select Create an MS-DOS Startup Disk.

MS-DOS Startup Disk

Edgar finds he still needs to keep MS-DOS startup disks on hand. He uses them for tasks such as repartitioning a hard disk, or booting up a new computer, connecting to a network share, and initiating an installation of an OS from the network share. It has been a long time since he actually had an MS-DOS machine around, so he used Windows 95, and then Windows 98 to create startup disks. He was afraid that this capability was lost in Windows XP, and was happily surprised to find it there one day when he was formatting a diskette. Create an MS-DOS Startup Disk is an option when you format a diskette.

An Old Application Will Not Run

You have upgraded your computer to Windows XP. You need to run a program that worked nicely in Windows 95. However, when you start the program in XP, it doesn't perform correctly. To solve this problem, Windows XP allows you to trick the program into thinking that the OS is actually Windows 95 by using compatibility mode.

On the Start menu, locate the shortcut for the offending program. Right-click and select Properties. Select the Compatibility tab. On this tab, place a check in the box under Compatibility mode, then select Windows 95 in the box below, as shown in Figure 7-11. Click OK and test the program. If it still has problems, go back to the Compatibility page and tweak the Display settings and/or turn off advanced text services. If you need help, click the program compatibility link at the bottom of the page.

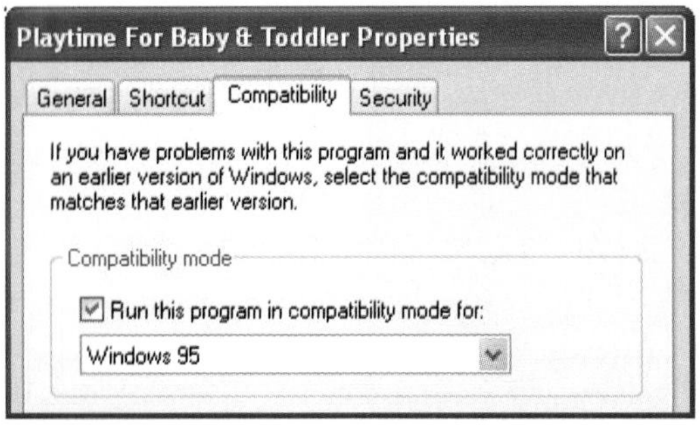

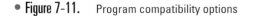

• Figure 7-11. Program compatibility options

Chapter 7 Review

■ Chapter Summary

After reading this chapter and completing the Step-by-Step tutorials and Try This! exercises, you should understand the following facts about Windows XP:

Describe Windows XP Professional Benefits, Features, and Weaknesses

- Windows XP runs software 25 percent faster than Windows 98.

- Windows XP boots faster than Windows 98 or Windows 2000.

- Windows XP uses NTFS for system security and allows you to encrypt files on an NTFS volume.

- Windows XP is stable and compatible with older programs.

- Windows XP automatically updates itself.

- Windows XP has several versions, but only two are appropriate for most desktop and laptop computers: Home and Professional.

Install and Configure Windows XP Professional

- You should run the compatibility checker before installing Windows XP.

- No Setup startup disks are included with Windows XP. If you need to make them you must connect to their website and create them from a program available on the site.

- To combat software piracy, Microsoft requires that you activate Windows XP within 30 days of installation.

- Registration is still optional.

- Soon after installing Windows XP you should verify network access, install new updates, install antivirus software, and create user accounts.

Customize and Manage Windows XP Professional

- Windows XP's default Control Panel is grouped by category.

- Windows XP can be made to look like Windows 2000.

- Windows XP supports both new and old printers.

- Programs can be installed and removed using the Add or Remove Programs applet in the Control Panel.

- Programs should be removed correctly using an uninstall program.

- An administrator can add or remove the optional Windows XP components.

Manage User Security in Windows XP

- Windows XP allows you to set up the system for multiple users.

- Each user on the Windows XP computer has personal customized settings and protected files.

- At least one user must have administrator privileges.

- Each user should create a password reset disk.

- Other users should be of the Limited account type.

- Windows XP allows you to switch users easily.

- For security reasons, you should log out of a computer before walking away from it.

Troubleshoot Common Windows XP Professional Problems

- Windows XP has several boot options.

- One boot option is safe mode, which allows the user to fix Windows XP.

- Windows XP can create two startup disks: an MS-DOS startup and an XP startup disk.

- If an older application does not run well in Windows XP, try the compatibility mode settings.

Key Terms

Category view *(306)*
Classic view *(306)*
compatibility mode *(290)*
Computer Administrator account *(312)*

driver signing *(290)*
encryption *(289)*
Guest account *(312)*
Limited account *(312)*

password reset disk *(314)*
System Restore wizard *(320)*
Windows update *(290)*

Key Term Quiz

Use the Key Terms list to complete the sentences that follow. Not all terms will be used.

1. Each user should create a _____ and keep it handy to avoid being locked out after forgetting a password.

2. The _____ allows you to return your computer to a previous working state.

3. In addition to setting permissions, Windows XP, like Windows 2000 allows you to use _____ to protect files on an NTFS volume.

4. To avoid problems with incompatible drivers, Microsoft uses _____, meaning that they provide a digital signature for device drivers that have gone through Microsoft's device driver certification process.

5. Control Panel has a new default view that is task oriented; this view is called _____.

6. The _____ feature of Windows XP can be automated to keep your Microsoft software up-to-date.

7. If a program written for an older version of Windows does not run under Windows XP, use the _____.

8. After a new installation of Windows XP, you can only log on as Administrator, and the first local account you create must be a/an _____.

9. A local account for an ordinary user should be a/an _____.

10. If you don't like the new Windows XP Control Panel default view, you can switch to _____.

Multiple-Choice Quiz

1. Why does Windows XP use a process called prefetching? Select all that apply.
    a. To speed up OS bootup
    b. To restore system state
    c. To make programs run faster
    d. To activate Windows XP
    e. To authenticate user

2. Which of the following is a benefit of using Windows XP?
    a. Speed
    b. Faster boot times
    c. Automatic virus update
    d. Desktop that reorganizes itself
    e. NTFS version 5

3. Why is NTFS the preferred Windows XP file system over FAT16 or FAT32? Select all that apply.
    a. It enables you to dual boot with older versions of Windows.
    b. It allows you to apply file- and folder-level permissions.
    c. It supports file encryption.
    d. It supports larger hard drive partitions.
    e. It stores files more efficiently.

4. Why does the Windows XP desktop reorganize itself?
    a. To keep your disk defragmented
    b. To update your mailing list
    c. To remind you of to-do tasks

d. To run programs more efficiently

e. To eliminate desktop clutter

5. Which of the following tasks should be performed soon after installing Windows XP?

    a. Check network connectivity

    b. Run Windows update

    c. Create new local users

    d. Create a password reset disk for the Administrator account

    e. Install antivirus software

6. Since Windows XP creates the local Administrator account automatically, why would you need a Limited user account?

    a. To log on to a domain

    b. To install updates

    c. To protect yourself from making mistakes when logged on as a more powerful user

    d. To install software

    e. To play Internet games

7. Why must you activate Windows XP after installation?

    a. This is how you register your product.

    b. It won't start up after installation unless it is activated.

    c. To detect computer viruses.

    d. Microsoft requires it to protect itself against software piracy.

    e. To create limited users.

8. Why should you install updates for Windows XP?

    a. To install new applications

    b. To create a new Computer administrator account

    c. To correct general problems with the program code

    d. To install new games

    e. To correct detected security problems

9. Why would you use the ClearType option in Display Properties | Appearance | Effects?

    a. To make the text on the screen translucent

    b. To smooth the edges of screen fonts

    c. To personalize your desktop

d. To make printed documents more readable

e. To select the Bliss wallpaper

10. Why do software publishers use InstallShield?

    a. It acts as an antivirus program

    b. To create standardized installation programs

    c. To upgrade from Windows Me

    d. To repartition hard disks

    e. To activate Windows XP

11. When you use User Accounts to manage local accounts it shows an account type called Limited account. To which built-in local user group do Limited accounts belong?

    a. Administrators

    b. Users

    c. Guests

    d. Backup Operators

    e. Managers

12. What Windows XP options can you use to protect your computer when you leave your office for lunch?

    a. Fast User Switching

    b. Password-protected screen saver

    c. System Restore

    d. CTRL-ALT-DELETE

    e. Lock Computer

13. What new feature has been added to Windows XP Device Manager that will help you to recover after upgrading your NIC device driver to a new version that doesn't seem to work?

    a. Windows Messenger

    b. Driver Signing

    c. Devices by Type

    d. Device driver rollback

    e. Hidden devices

14. What are the two types of startup disks you can create in Windows XP?

    a. System Restore

    b. Emergency Recovery

    c. Backup

    d. Windows XP startup disk

    e. MS-DOS startup disk

15. Your Windows XP computer will not start up normally, and a driver file that you believe you may need is on a network server. What Advance Options menu item will you select?

    a. Start Windows Normally

    b. Debugging Mode

    c. Enable VGA Mode

    d. Safe Mode With Networking

    e. Enable Boot Logging

■ Essay Quiz

1. Your computer is having trouble booting. You are sure that the cause is a network card or a video card problem. Describe how you would determine the problem.

2. Describe the process for adding a user.

3. Why should you have multiple Computer Administrator accounts?

4. Why should you disable the Guest account?

5. In your opinion, what is the most important feature of XP? Why?

Lab Projects

• Lab Project 7.1

You have joined a new company. You have been given permission to attach your computer, running Windows XP, to the corporate domain. Connect your computer to the domain. You will need to see your instructor for an account with sufficient privileges.

You will need the following:

■ A computer with Windows XP installed

■ An account with permission to join the domain

■ A domain name

Then do the following:

1. Connect your computer to the domain.

2. Log in with your network account.

• Lab Project 7.2

Windows XP is running on an older computer. You want to increase its speed by turning off extraneous animation and features in Windows XP.

You will need the following:

■ A computer running Windows XP

■ The Administrator account for this computer

Then do the following:

1. Use the Advanced tab of System Properties to modify performance.

2. Turn off all video enhancements.

3. Set a dedicated virtual RAM size. A good formula is 1.5 times the size of your RAM.

Macintosh OS 9 and OS X

*"Hey, I know this!
This is UNIX!"*
—FROM THE MOVIE
JURASSIC PARK

We've been talking for seven chapters now about operating systems in general, and we've specifically covered a number of Windows OSs created by Microsoft. Other companies make OSs as well, and now we'll move away from Microsoft products and discuss one of the two most popular non-Microsoft OSs: the Macintosh OSs made by Apple Computer.

In this chapter, we'll explore the Macintosh OS 9 and OS X operating systems, with emphasis on installing the latter because the former is increasingly obsolete and primarily exists as a backward-compatibility layer within OS X. We'll get to know the features of the Mac OS workspace. We'll examine the basic similarities and differences between the two most common Macintosh OSs as well as how they relate to the Windows OSs we've already discussed. We'll look at installing and configuring OS X and managing drives, files, printers, and users, and we'll also take a look at troubleshooting common Mac OS problems.

During the latter stages of editing this chapter, Apple released the 10.2 edition of Mac OS X, also known as Jaguar. OS X discussions in this chapter are still current with a few exceptions, mostly relating to *the addition of options* in preference panels, menus, and installation panes.

In this chapter, you will learn how to:

■ **Describe the history of Apple and the Mac OS**

■ **Use the features of the Mac desktop**

■ **Install and configure Mac OS X**

■ **Get to know the Mac OS X workspace**

■ **Troubleshoot common Mac OS problems**

Introducing Apple and the Macintosh Operating System

Come explore the Mac OS, its history and place in the world of computing, and learn about the main features of Apple's new OS X and its predecessor, OS 9.

• Power Mac G4

A Colorful Contribution to the World of Computing

Apple Computer was founded on April 1, 1976, when high school friends Steven Wozniak and Steven Jobs began marketing the Apple I computer from a garage in Los Altos, California. In those days, personal computing was a hobby industry, and the initial reception to the Apple I was lukewarm. The following year's version, the Apple II, was a different story. Debuting at a local trade show, it was the first personal computer to come in a plastic case and include color graphics, which isn't to say that it had a graphical interface. In 1983, Apple launched the Lisa, the first production computer to use a graphical user interface (GUI). The following year, Apple launched the Macintosh 128k with much fanfare, the first *affordable* personal computer with a GUI.

From these earliest incarnations—credited with popularizing the personal computer beyond the world of techies—to the Smithsonian Institution's awarding of the National Design Award in 2000 to the admittedly not always tasteful but certainly colorful first-generation iMac, Apple computers have without question had a profound impact on the computer industry and have inspired a strong community of proponents.

Macintosh Characteristics

One of the quirks of Apple's history is that, barring one experiment lasting from 1993 to 1997, Apple has never licensed its OS to any other hardware manufacturer, thus irrevocably binding together the OS and the often interesting looking boxes it comes in. This has tended to make the Mac "the sum of more than its parts" in the minds of its dedicated users—and is also noted as one of the key contributing factors to Apple's small overall market share in total units sold.

Courtesy of Apple.

• Two versions of the iMac. Tasteful? Beauty is in the eye of the beholder.

Although Apple currently accounts for just 3.5 percent of the personal computer market in the U.S., with Dell leading the field with 26 percent (IDC, Q1 2002), its strong monitor, sound hardware, and hallmark ease-of-use-OS have helped Apple disproportionately penetrate niche markets, including the commercial publishing industry, the realm of multimedia software development and authoring, and the education sector.

With its latest operating system, OS X (referred to as either OS "ten" or OS "X"), Apple has further refined its user interface while placing it on top of a UNIX system, offering increased stability, networking potential, and security.

There are two distinct Mac operating systems still in widespread use: OS 9 (launched October 1999) and OS X (launched March 2001). As with most personal computers, Macintosh operating systems share common metaphors such as the desktop, files and folders, and the trash can, and hardware falls into certain types. Certain features of the Mac OS and hardware deserve highlighting.

Built-in Multimedia Hardware and Software in the Mac OS

Apple's standard inclusion of what have historically been considered by other hardware manufacturers to be *optional* multimedia elements has tended to make Mac users low maintenance insofar as their technical needs are concerned, when compared with users of other operating systems.

The authors of Mac's operating systems have typically had to consider only one or two hardware platforms, built with basically the same architecture, which makes problems such as component-software conflicts less likely to be issues than with Wintel machines, which require that the operating systems be designed to work on hardware manufactured by a host of other companies.

The standard hardware and software configurations that Macs are distributed with are sufficient to organize a music or photo collection and edit home video. Higher-end configurations additionally allow you to burn CDs and even DVDs. This level of end-user functionality is only now becoming standard on personal computers across the industry.

Ultimately, the computer you choose these days perhaps matters less and less, as companies rush to match and better their competitors, usually within a matter of months. Most computer manufacturers are now beginning to include multimedia hardware and software components as standard features, in line with users' increased expectations.

Macs have contained **sound cards**, the hardware interface that allows your computer to accept and output high-fidelity audio, from surprisingly early in their history. In fact, if you mention the phrase "sound card" to Mac users, many will not understand what you're talking about because a sound card was never presented to them as an option when purchasing their computers, but was included as standard. This is one manifestation of a far harder-to-quantify aspect of the Mac OS: its ease of use.

Ease of Use of the Mac OS

Elijah, age six, is an experienced Mac user, who has used educational software on his mother's Mac since age three, when he apparently picked up the mouse skills just from observing his mother and did as well as his toddler eye-hand coordination would allow. The Mac OS interface is as simple as possible, involving users with as little of the back-end functionality as possible.

In hardware terms, this has meant delivery of a minimum system configuration of computers that contains many extras as standard.

In software terms, the Mac OS has tended to minimize user intervention as much as possible. Elijah's mother knows when she buys new software that all she has to do is insert the disk, and the program will be installed automatically with very little intervention. During software installations, the user is typically asked the fewest questions needed to complete the task. If you compare Windows and Mac installation instructions in software booklets, you'll find that Mac instructions typically are shorter.

Macs—with their single-source hardware, operating system, and software—tend to break only when they're really broken, rather than because someone did something to something while adding a new component or installing some new software. This is an advantage of single-source hardware and software manufacturers.

■ Features of the Mac OS Desktop

Let's take a tour of the Mac OS desktop, beginning with the startup and login processes that quickly get you to the desktop, the overall appearance of the desktop, and the tools you will find there, including the Finder, Apple Menu, Chooser, Control Strip, and Dock. Then we'll concentrate on the specific features you'll find in Mac OS X.

Startup

From the first light of the screen, you'll notice that Macs don't expose users to system-level commands that most users are in no position to assess the importance of. Mac users aren't expected to know any of that "under-the-hood" stuff.

Even as an administrator, your interaction with the computer is simplified, and your capacity to customize the machine is largely limited to system preferences and folder permissions.

There is no AUTOEXEC.BAT file to modify on a Mac. Normal startup has always consisted of the smiley face Mac icon.

Login

Both OS 9 and OS X Macs come with multiple-user capacity. If the computer you are using comes with multiuser capacity that has been implemented, you will need to be assigned a login. When prompted, select your name from the list during the startup process and, as with logins everywhere, enter your password and then click OK.

In both OS 9 and OS X, passwords are encrypted and saved in a database known as the **system keychain**.

• Classic/OS 9 screen with smiley face icon

The Desktop

Once the desktop appears, new visitors from non-Mac operating systems will be relieved to see the same basic metaphors visible: a trash can, a menu reminiscent of the Windows 95 Start menu, and some sort of application launcher. Yes, there are slight differences between the OS 9 and OS X desktops and other non-Mac systems, but this is not entirely unfamiliar territory. Figure 8-1 offers a visual introduction to some of the key GUI elements of the OS 9 and OS X desktops.

The Finder

For the user, the **Finder** is the foundation of the Mac OS. At startup, the OS 9 Finder visibly loads system extensions, which add modular functionality to the operating system. In OS X, such extensions load invisibly. In both OS 9 and OS X, the Finder appears by default after startup; it is the default GUI/desktop view before any application software runs (see Figure 8-1). The Finder is equivalent to Windows Explorer, the Windows file management tool. Functionally, once applications are open in OS 9, the Finder menu, found in the top right corner of the screen functions as an application switcher. Not so in OS X, where this task has been delegated to the Dock.

• OS X startup screen

The five Finder menus in OS 9—File, Edit, View, Special, and Help—offer a variety of file management and power-on/off tools. In OS X, this broadly remains true, although the functions of the Special menu have been moved to a new menu called Finder. A Window menu arranges window views, and a new Go menu offers shortcuts to folders used for storage both on the computer and on the Internet, as in the case of Apple's **iTools** online file storage and file sharing service, now known as **.Mac** (pronounced "dot Mac" and found at mac.com). The .Mac service operates as a virtual hard drive for storing private files and as a website where you can upload files such as photographs and movies for others to view.

The Apple Menu

Found in both OS 9 and OS X on the top left of the desktop, the **Apple Menu** is a pop-up menu located under a tiny Apple logo—rainbow-colored in OS 9 and blue in OS X—unless you are working in Classic, OS X's OS 9 compatibility layer.

In OS 9, the Apple menu allows you to access the following:

- Apple's printer and network port interface (the Chooser)
- System preferences (Control Panels)

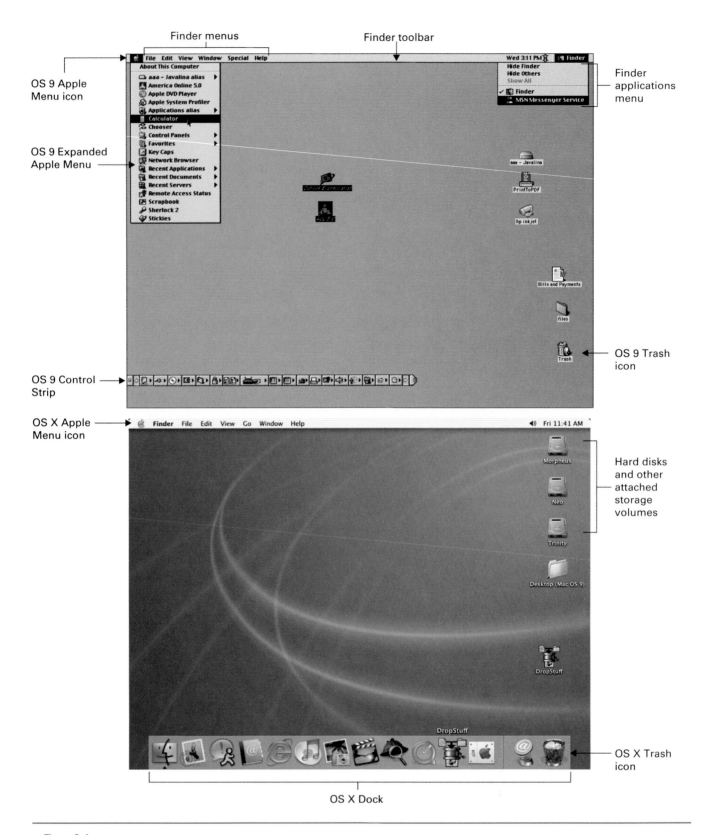

Finder menus

Finder toolbar

OS 9 Apple
Menu icon

Finder
applications
menu

OS 9 Expanded
Apple Menu

OS 9 Trash
icon

OS 9 Control
Strip

OS X Apple
Menu icon

Hard disks
and other
attached
storage
volumes

OS X Trash
icon

OS X Dock

● **Figure 8-1.**   Key features of the Mac OS 9 and OS X desktops

- A system profiling tool that compiles information about your machine to help with technical support inquiries (the Apple System Profiler)

- Folders to access recent applications, documents, and servers

- A modem dialing tool

- And, well, anything you want really. The Apple Menu is highly customizable. You can create aliases for hard disks, network disks, programs, folders, or files and put them in the Apple Menu for easy access. Folders will tree out hierarchically.

In OS X, the Apple Menu is something of a disappointment. It has been reduced to a startup and shutdown menu, with recent items and a shortcut to system preferences. It is not customizable. That functionality has been passed to the Dock.

However, all is not lost for diehard Apple Menu buffs. The System/Disk Utilities section of Apple's OS X Downloads page (found at `apple.com/downloads/macosx/`) has several third-party utilities that will restore functionality to OS X's Apple Menu, including the ability to browse the entire hard disk from this menu.

The Chooser

The **Chooser** was OS 9's printer and network selection tool for Apple's proprietary and now obsolete **AppleTalk** networking protocol. Found on the Apple Menu under OS 9, the Chooser allowed you to specify which printer was active. The active printer is like the default printer in Windows. This is the printer that will be used by all your Mac applications unless you specify another printer. In OS X, when a user chooses the Print command from within an application, the same functionality appears seamlessly within every Print dialog box.

The Control Strip and the Dock

Later versions of Mac OS 9, presumably taking a cue from the popularity of the Microsoft Office toolbar that shipped on Windows computers, saw the institution of a feature known as the Control Strip.

The **Control Strip** is a floating bar on the OS 9 desktop that offers instant tab access to a variety of system preferences, including location, Internet dial-up, and screen resolution. The main failing of the Control Strip was that, while its features could be indeed removed and new ones added, and the strip was theoretically infinitely customizable, it required modules to be specially written for it. Shortcuts to files and folders could not be added by the casual user.

In OS X, the **Dock** is a similar floating bar that replaces the Control Strip. In early versions of OS X, the Dock's default installation state included

Customizing the Apple Menu in OS 9

In this step-by-step exercise, you will customize your Apple menu to allow hierarchical access to any file or folder on your computer. To complete this exercise, you will need the following:

- A Mac computer with any version of OS 9 installed

- A user name and password that will allow you to log on to your computer

Step 1

From inside the Finder, select your hard disk with the mouse and, on the File menu, select Make an Alias (*alias* is Mac's term for a shortcut). If your hard disk is called MyHardDisk, an alias called *MyHardDisk alias* will appear nearby it on the desktop, identifiable as an alias by its italicized title.

Step 2

Open your hard disk. Double-click the folder named System Folder. At the top of the alphabetical listing, you will see Apple Menu Items. Position the window so you can see the alias you created on the desktop.

Step 3

Drag the alias of your hard disk into the Apple Menu Items folder and close the window. If you are in OS 9 or working with a program in the Classic compatibility layer in OS X (the Apple Menu will be rainbow-colored in both instances), you will be able to click the Apple Menu, see your hard disk alias listed, and browse the disk this way.

shortcuts to Mail (Apple's e-mail software), Internet Explorer, iTunes, iMovie, Sherlock, QuickTime, Apple's OS X, System Preferences, and Trash.

Want a file, folder, application, or Internet bookmark in the Dock? Drag it on. Want to remove something that's on there? Drag it off onto the desktop and let go. It will disappear in a puff of smoke, quite literally.

Preferences allow you to choose to have the Dock appear on the right, left, or bottom of the screen; to hide it so that it appears only when the mouse rolls over that area; to size it larger or smaller; and to turn its mouse-over magnification feature on and off. If you plan to have a lot of shortcuts on the Dock and have consequently set its size to be small to fit them all, the magnification feature is useful, enlarging you to see the tiny icons as you roll the mouse over them.

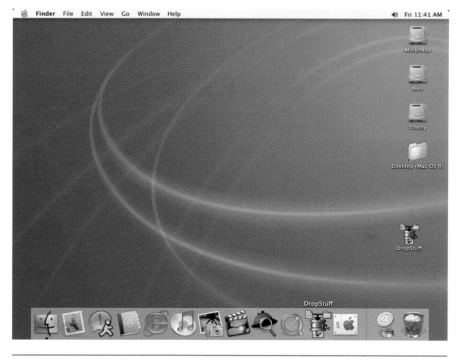

• Adding a shortcut to the Dock for the DropStuff utility

Features of Mac OS X

In OS X, Apple has enhanced the best aspect of the earlier OS 9 and Macs in general—the GUI—and married it with a stable, tried-and-tested UNIX core. Apple has therefore finally responded to the main criticisms of Macs by system administrators who typically work with other platforms, by offering an OS that:

- Is based on a rock solid platform
- Complies with international networking standards
- Adopts tried-and-tested open standard security protocols
- Is better designed to multitask and fulfill a server role
- Allows familiar root-level access to developers and administrators

Whereas before, Apple seemed focused on appealing to creative

Try This!

Adding a Shortcut to the Dock

If you have access to a computer with the OS X desktop, try this:

1. Look around the OS X desktop for something you want to create a shortcut to on the Dock. This can be a hard disk, an application, a file or folder, or a CD. You can choose something from your hard disk if you like.

2. Click the item's icon and drag it onto the Dock. Before letting go of the mouse, move the icon over the Dock to position it between the existing Dock icons where you want it to appear.

3. Release the mouse button. The icon will stay on the Dock and will now function as a shortcut to the item. Want to remove it? Click the item on the Dock and drag it onto the desktop. No, that puff of smoke we were talking about wasn't a figure of speech!

The Hierarchy of Mac Operating Systems

OS 9 made its precursor OS 8 obsolete by the addition of Internet tools that include a hard disk search utility integrated with Internet search engines, multiple-user capacity, Internet file sharing and remote administration, strong file encryption, and a network browser.

Unlike OS 8, OS 9 continues to be distributed by Apple on new machines along with OS X. This dual-OS bundle offers users the option of booting up in either OS 9 or OS X, or running OS 9 as a **compatibility layer** *(also known as Classic) from within OS X, to run older OS 9 software that does not have an OS X equivalent. This allows new users of OS X to upgrade their older software at their own pace, or as is more often the case, at the speed their budget allows.*

However, in the day-to-day reality of working with these two operating systems, anyone with OS X installed will soon find that the OS 9 compatibility layer is relegated from the background to obscurity. There is really no compelling reason, barring simple installation requirements, to continue using OS 9. As a result, in this chapter OS 9 is referred to only where OS X users need to deal with it, and by way of comparison to introduce users familiar with OS 9 to OS X.

professionals at the user end of the purchasing scale, OS X signals Apple's acknowledgment of the people who work as the cogs and wheels that enable our Internet age and the established standards of the software that powers it.

The new OS X GUI—known as **Aqua** because of its blue, fluid appearance—ensures that OS X's interface will feel familiar, although its under-the-hood functionality is clearly aimed at advanced technical users.

While it's always painful to upgrade any computer system, the system performance and usability of OS X when compared to OS 9—to say nothing of the new, free multimedia software that comes bundled with it and is not available for OS 9—makes upgrading worthwhile.

The most recent release of OS X—version 10.2, codenamed **Jaguar**, released in late August 2002—added increased compatibility with Windows servers, more Internet software, and a host of other improvements on the earliest versions of OS X.

At the time of this writing, the list price for OS X is around $129, although many online retailers are offering it for just over $100 after rebate in the U.S.

From the network-ready interface and multidevice connectivity present even in Apple's lower-end hardware to the compatibility and stability advantages brought by OS X's new UNIX core, Apple's latest computers are more functional in a multimedia and multioperating system environment than ever before.

The notable characteristics of Apple computers and the Mac OS discussed in the following paragraphs are not exclusive to Apple or the Mac, but represent discernable traits or major strengths in the OS and hardware.

Built-in Networking Hardware and Software

These days, every Apple computer, from the consumer-level iBooks and iMacs to the prosumer-level and professional-level PowerBooks and G4 desktops, all ship with Ethernet, FireWire (IEEE 1394), and USB ports and are AirPort ready (IEEE 802.11b, a wireless networking standard). This makes Apple computers versatile in terms of the peripherals and networks they can connect with.

In our Internet age, where everyone has a previously unheard of capacity to research products prior to purchase and where home computer advances have brought a hugely increased demand for connectivity with a myriad of digital devices, we have seen the emergence of a new type of consumer who expects consumer-level affordability combined with professional-level features.

Prosumers as they are termed, increasingly drive the digital device and home computer markets, especially in the case of Apple, which has historically prospered in the multimedia sector with features that are now becoming part of mainstream computer functionality.

While earlier versions of the Mac OS have required third-party software, such as Dave (`www.thursby.com/products/dave.html`), for their network connectivity—that is, client software that allowed Macs running OS 8 and 9 to connect to Windows-based networks—OS X's Jaguar incarnation includes a PPTP-based virtual private network (VPN) client to connect to both Windows and other remote networks.

Jaguar's Personal File Services for Windows allows Windows and Mac users to connect and share files without needing any additional software.

Jaguar also allows users to log on to a Microsoft Windows domain, which eases the task of network administrators who need to integrate Macs into Windows networks.

OS X Is Less Vulnerable to Crashes

OS X is built on a core operating system known as Darwin (http://developer.apple.com/darwin/). Its most noticeable feature, when compared to OS 9, is vastly improved system performance.

Darwin is a product of the open-source community. Open source is a development model that evolved naturally on the Internet, in which the nuts and bolts of the code that powers software is made freely available to encourage widespread debugging and modification for the betterment of the entire community. This model has provided the Internet community with an impressive list of software that includes BSD, Linux, Sendmail, Apache, and Perl.

Darwin integrates a number of technologies including a Mach 3.0 kernel, BSD UNIX operating system services, high-performance networking facilities, and support for multiple integrated file systems. This use of Darwin is of particular interest to developers, whose programming efforts on a Mac are now immeasurably more portable to other operating systems.

UNIX is an operating system that was designed to allow multiple users to carry out multiple processes on interconnected computers. As an open-source platform, it has weathered years of public testing on the Internet and has come to be respected as a reliable, efficient, and secure operating system particularly suited to multitasking processes.

Security

The exposure of the Internet and the open-source nature of the UNIX operating system—which has been around for a quarter of a century—have forced commercial UNIX vendors to be open about security issues with their systems. Security holes resulting from a user's turn-

ing on a feature that was switched off by default are not dismissed but rather are considered challenges to the UNIX community, whose users and programmers are so numerous that security fixes are provided swiftly and transparently.

Advanced User System Access

Macs were long criticized for not paying attention to advanced users who have an interest in programming. OS X, unlike OS 9, now offers terminal access to its system. OS X includes the open-source GCC 3.1 compiler, which offers increased code compilation speeds, and standard UNIX math libraries have been optimized to work with Apple's Power PC G4 chip, giving programmers optimal performance without their needing to write Apple-specific code, and increased portability to others' operating systems after development.

Apple's Terminal application (found on the hard disk at Applications | Utilities | Terminal) supports vt100/vt220 emulation and—here's how you

For those interested in the development of the Mac's hardware architecture from the earliest days of the 1977 1-MHz CPU Apple 1 to the dual 1.25-GHz G4 processors of today, `www.apple-history.com` is a professional and comprehensive information resource.

• Mac OS X developer's website

know that it's a piece of Apple software—it can actually be made translucent, so you can see other windows through it.

For detailed technical information, see the Mac OS X Developer Documentation section of Apple's website (`http://developer.apple.com/techpubs/macosx/`).

Strong Multiuser Support

As OS X is a UNIX system, Apple computers now boast very powerful multiuser functionality, including not only customized, password-protected user home directories on the hard disk, but the capacity for administrators to prevent access to core systems and key areas of the hard disk.

For example, when you begin the process of installing any new software in OS X, no matter how small, the system asks you for an administrator password. This is particularly appreciated in situations where the computer is exposed to many people with minimal supervision, as is the case in educational settings, Internet cafés, and households with children.

<table>
<tr><td>✓</td><td>Cross Check</td></tr>
</table>

Compare Windows and Mac OS Features

An OS must provide basic functionality for the user. The following questions ask you to compare some of the features of the Mac OSs with those of Windows 2000 or Windows XP.

1. What term, used in all versions of Windows OSs is the equivalent of the Mac OS term "active printer?"

   _____

   _____

2. Compare the Mac OS X compatibility layer with a feature of the Windows OSs you have studied in this course.

   _____

   _____

3. Using your own observations, list five features of the Mac desktops that are similar to the Windows desktop and make the transition between the two easy. These features can include actions required to do tasks.

   _____

   _____

Choose the Hardware Type for the User Level

Greg owns a professional recording studio that currently offers 24-track analog recording onto 2-inch tape, but he wants to institute a solution whereby he can offer hard disk recording to smaller bands that cannot afford his high-end analog service.

He decides on a Mac G4 desktop system with dual processors, a MOTU 828 FireWire interface with eight inputs, and a copy of ProTools for mixing and mastering—a good beginning for most recording situations that this digital studio will likely deal with. Greg travels a lot and, for the road, has bought a Titanium G4 PowerBook equipped with ProTools so he can take mixing projects with him.

Greg is confident that his chosen solution is adequate, not least because the G4 desktop is expandable to 1.5GB of RAM and has slots for two additional hard disks.

At home, Greg's wife, Kammy, has her own dog-walking business and, as well as simple word processing functionality, needs to run basic client-billing software. They decided a few years ago on an iMac—the Dalmatian model of course—and upgraded to OS X to better control their teenage daughter's use of the computer, as Kammy was worried about her business files being deleted by accident.

Bound inexorably with the software, Apple's hardware is aimed at a variety of user levels. For users wanting the potential to expand their computers to meet new challenges, the G4 desktop and PowerBook laptop allow expansion. For users wanting a robust home or school computer, the sturdily built iMac and iBook are suitable, allowing RAM upgrades but limited internal hardware expansion.

Courtesy of Apple.

- iBook

When Brian bought his 867-MHz G4 desktop, it came with 256MB of RAM and a 60GB hard disk, which was a welcome upgrade from his previous G3 233-MHz PowerBook with 160MB of RAM and a 20GB hard disk. A year later, Brian's web design business has increased his need for basic video editing for clients.

While the G4 system is powerful enough to deal with the processor-intensive rendering that video requires, the hard disk space was pushed to the limit, and multitasking with several different programs necessitated change.

The latter issue was resolved with the addition of RAM to take the system up to just under 1GB. Brian purchased a second 120GB hard disk to handle the massive files that digital video capture produces.

With an iMac, which was certainly a tempting option at the time Brian was thinking about purchasing a new system, this wouldn't have been possible. The iMac allows RAM upgrades but little else. However, this distinction is disappearing somewhat—the G4's speedy backside cache notwithstanding—as excellent FireWire external drives and USB peripherals expand computers virtually infinitely as users' needs grow.

True Plug and Play

Although there are, of course, exceptions to the rule, if you plug a peripheral, such as a printer, into a Mac, it will typically start working immediately. This holds true for installed items even if you plug them in while the computer is already switched on.

Viruses

Because the Mac OS has been a minority operating system, Macs have tended not to be plagued by viruses, unlike Windows systems. OS X's insistence on an administrator password before new software is installed offers an additional barrier of protection. Commercially available virus programs such as Norton AntiVirus (`www.symantec.com/mac/`) are recommended nonetheless.

■ Installing and Configuring Mac OS X

This section details the process of installing and configuring Mac OS X, including the minimum requirements, installation process, and system configuration options following installation. First, let's determine what version of the Mac OS you have installed.

Step-by-Step 8.02

Determining Which Version of the Mac OS Is Installed

In this step-by-step exercise, you will determine which version of the Mac OS is installed. If installing OS X, you will need a minimum of OS 9.1 for OS X to correctly run OS 9 software in the Classic compatibility layer. To complete this exercise, you will need the following:

- A Mac computer with any version of the Mac OS installed

- A user name and password that will allow you to log on to your computer

Step 1

Click an empty area of the desktop.

Step 2

Click the Apple Menu in the top left corner of your desktop and select About This Computer or About This Mac. The screen that pops up shows which version of the Mac OS is installed. Continue to Step 3 if installing OS X.

About This Computer

Mac OS 9.2

Version: Mac OS 9.2.2
Built-in Memory: 160 MB
Virtual Memory: Off
Largest Unused Block: 97 MB   ™ & © Apple Computer, Inc. 1983-2001

Mac OS	46.8 MB	
Outlook Express	11.9 MB	

Although the minimum requirement for OS X is OS 9.1, you can download additional OS 9 updates from Apple's website up to version 9.2.2, the most recent version available at the time of this publication. The OS X 10.1 upgrade package, available from Apple for those with the first release of OS X (which came with OS 9.1), enables you to update Mac OS X to OS X 10.1 and includes the upgrade to take OS 9.1 to OS 9.2.1. For more information see www.apple.com/macosx/upgrade/.

Minimum Requirements

As you will see in the following sections, the official Mac OS X minimum requirements are higher than those typically published by Microsoft for its Windows OSs. This is mostly in response to the Mac's more multimedia-focused basic hardware platform. In addition, since many people with existing Macs will upgrade, we also discuss the minimum OS required to upgrade to OS X.

Hardware Requirements

The minimum hardware requirements for installing Mac OS X are shown in Table 8.1. We view these requirements as realistic for most functions, but you will want to beef up the memory and hard disk space if you regularly plan to undertake image or video editing with your computer.

Software Requirements

To use OS 9 applications from within OS X, you need at least OS 9.1 installed on your computer. If you don't have it installed, a message will appear noting this at the beginning of the OS X installation process, saying that you can upgrade after the installation. You can upgrade your computer from the Mac OS 9.1 CD included with OS X, or you can download the update from Apple's Software Update website.

Before you start the installation of OS X, you may need to update your computer's firmware. Check whether a Firmware Updater is available for your computer on the OS X CD. If you find one, undertake the update process before you install Mac OS X. A good resource for firmware information is Apple's Support site (www.info.apple.com/).

Inside Information

Blast from the Past: System Requirements for OS 9

Compared to OS X, OS 9 has light dietary needs. If you find yourself with very old Macs and only the earliest versions of OS 9 available to install, this list details what you will need at minimum.

- *Mac OS-based Apple computer with a PowerPC processor (PowerPC upgrade cards, 680X0 processors, and OS X Server are not supported)*

- *150 to 250MB of free disk space for an easy installation (the universal installation can be as large as 400MB)*

- *40MB of RAM*

Table 8.1	Minimum Hardware Requirements for OS X
Computer	Power Macintosh G3; PowerBook G3 (except the original PowerBook G3, distinguished by the rainbow-colored Apple logo on its outside case; PowerBook G3s with a white logo are compatible but may require a firmware update); Power Mac G4; PowerBook G4; iMac; iBook.
Hard disk	1.5GB or more disk space available. Installation of Mac OS X on FireWire or USB disks is not fully supported by Apple. In the case of earlier PowerBooks, OS X needs to be installed on a partition that falls within the first 8MB of the hard disk.
RAM	128MB or more.
Video card	Internal monitor support or an Apple-supplied IXMicro, ATI, or NVidia video card.

The Installation

In this step-by-step exercise, you will install Mac OS X and create a configuration necessary for a basic installation. To complete this exercise, you will need the following:

■ A Mac computer with any version of OS 9 installed, 9.1 if you want to complete the

installation with no interruption to update to OS 9.1.

■ A user name and password that will allow you to log on to your computer

■ The OS X installation CD

Step 1

Insert the OS X CD and double-click the Install Mac OS X icon. You will be asked to re-start the computer. Click the Restart button. If the Installer does not open, restart your computer while holding down the C key on your keyboard.

Step 2

OS X and the Installer will load. This may take several minutes, depending on your system. In the Select Language window that appears, click the radio button for the main language you want to use on your computer and then click Continue.

Step 3

In the Welcome to the Mac OS X Installer window, read Important Information about OS X and then click Continue. Read the information in the Software License Agreement window and then click Continue. A dialog box appears, asking if you agree to the terms. Click Agree.

Step 4

The Select Destination window appears asking you to select a destination disk on which to install OS X. Select the disk on which you want to install the OS, making sure it has enough space for the installation.

Step 5

The selected disk shows a green arrow. If you select the Erase Destination and Format As option, all data on the destination disk will be overwritten and lost. Click Continue to proceed. If the version of OS 9 you have is lower than what is required, this is the point when you will find out. You will not be able to select a disk. Frustratingly, in some versions of the OS X installer, you will not be told why!

Step 6

In the Installation Type window, leave Easy Install as it is and click Install. Mac OS X installs. A status bar shows your progress and gives you a rough idea of where you are in the process.

Step 7

When the OS is installed, the computer restarts and moves you to the Mac OS Setup Assistant. If you purchased your computer with OS X installed, you will begin from this point.

Step 8

The Mac OS Setup Assistant now asks you a series of questions beginning with the name of the country you are in. Select the answer and click Continue.

Step 9

The Personalizing Your Settings window appears. Select a keyboard layout and click Continue. You will be taken to the Registration Information window to fill out a form with your personal details. Fill these in and click Continue.

Step 10

You are now asked some marketing questions that have no practical function in the setup process, such as where you use the computer (for example, home or office) and what best describes your type of work. Fill these in and click Continue. This information will be sent to Apple after the Get Internet Ready step, coming right up.

Step 11

Click the Continue buttons until you arrive at the Create Your Account window. This is where you register and set up the administrator account for OS X, an account that has higher access privileges than other users. To administer your computer in the future, you will need to log in as this user. Remember to keep the user name and password in a safe place for future access. Click Continue.

Step 12

In the Get Internet Ready window, you are asked to sign up with a third-party Internet service provider or to choose the I'll Use My Existing Internet Service option. Make a choice and click Continue.

A third option in the Get Internet Ready window is I'm Not Ready to Connect to the Internet. Select this option if you prefer to set up your Internet connection later, or if your service provider requires you to provide your hardware address (MAC address) to connect, common for DSL and cable modem connections. To find your hardware address, launch Network Utility (found in Applications | Utilities | Network Utility) and write down the address that appears at the top of the Interface Information panel.

Step 13

In the How Do You Connect? window, you are asked to choose among Telephone Modem, Local Area Network (LAN), Cable Modem, AirPort Wireless, and DSL (Digital Subscriber Line). Make a choice and click Continue.

Step 14

Enter the connection information you received from your Internet service provider and move on to the next section, which asks you if you want to create an iTools account or enter existing information about your iTools account, which may be called a .Mac account in newer versions of OS X released after this service's title changed. Provide this information or skip to the next section by clicking Continue.

Step 15

If the Now You're Ready to Connect window appears, click Continue to send your registration to Apple via your Internet connection.

Step 16

The Select Time Zone window appears. Choose an option from the pop-up menu and click Continue. The Set Your Date and Time window appears. Enter the correct settings, click Save, and then click Continue. In the final window that appears, click Go.

Getting to Know the Mac OS X Workspace

This section offers an introduction to basic functions and customization options within the Mac OS X workspace, with reference to Mac OS 9 where appropriate. You will learn how to set up system preferences, manage files, print, and create and manage user accounts.

Changing System Preferences

In OS 9, system preferences were changed through the Control Panels folder, accessed through the Apple menu or by browsing the hard disk (/System Folder/Control Panels). In OS X, system preferences can be accessed from the Apple menu or Dock or by browsing the hard disk (Applications | System Preferences). While it is still possible to change preferences in OS 9 from within OS X, note that some Control Panels can no longer be run in Classic mode, the Control Strip being an example.

The following list of system preferences (each preference screen is known as a preference pane) are those found in OS X. Where there is an OS 9 equivalent—which conveniently covers the main functions—the corresponding name of the OS 9 Control Panel is given.

Desktop

The Desktop preference allows you to select a background image or color for your desktop. To select images other than the ones that appear at the bottom, select another option from the Collection pop-up menu. The Appearance Control Panel in OS 9 offered this function.

Dock

The Dock preference allows you to control the size and position of your Dock; toggle the Hide, Magnification, and Minimize effects; and further tweak the latter two settings. There was no Dock in OS 9, but the Control Strip Control Panel performed some of the Dock's functions.

General

The General preference allows you to alter the color of buttons, menus, and windows; select a text and list highlight color; choose the location and behavior of scroll arrows and the scroll bar; and determine the number of applications and documents that appear in the Recent Items submenu of the Apple menu (choose from 5 to 50). These functions were previously available in the Appearance Control Panel in OS 9, with the exception of the number of recent items listed, which was customizable from the Apple menu's Options Control Panel in OS 9.

International

The International preference allows you to choose the language that appears in application menus and dialog boxes and the text behaviors of languages; date, time, and numbering conventions; and the keyboard layout. These functions were offered in four different OS 9 Control Panels: Text, Numbers, Date and Time, and Keyboard.

Login

The Login preference allows you to specify startup applications and login options for OS X's multiuser system. In OS 9, you enabled startup applications by dragging an alias (the Mac's term for a shortcut) of an application into the Startup Items folder (found on the hard disk in /System Folder/Startup Items). User accounts were managed in the Multiple Users Control Panel.

Keep the Dock out of your way! Although the Dock is a useful utility, the magnification option can cause it to get in the way when positioned near application toolbars or open application windows. There is a simple solution. Dock preferences allow you to turn off magnification and reduce the size of the floating launch bar.

Inside Information

ColorSync and Publishing

ColorSync is actually an important preference to be aware of if the computers you are using are to be used for print or multimedia design. ColorSync is an industry-standard color management technology that tries to ensure consistent color throughout an entire production workflow. By correctly configuring ColorSync throughout your workflow, you can minimize the chance of unhappy surprises in the often turbulent world of prepress and publishing.

Apple's website includes some introductory information at `http://www.apple.com/colorsync/`. *In particular, the article "Successful Soft Proofing" by consultant Don Hutcheson is very helpful; you can find it at* `www.apple.com/colorsync/stories/hutcheson/`.

Screen Saver

The Screen Saver preference enables a screen saver and allows its customization. In OS 9, third-party screen savers could be installed, but there was no dedicated Control Panel for them.

Universal Access

The Universal Access preference enables custom keyboard and mouse responsiveness for computer users who require such customization. In OS 9, this functionality required an optional installation from the OS 9 disk.

ColorSync

The ColorSync preference enables users to specify the ColorSync profile for displays and printers for better screen rendering and print output. OS 9 had a ColorSync Control Panel.

Displays

The Displays preference allows users to customize the resolution, number of colors, refresh rate, and display profiles for each supported monitor connected to the computer. In OS 9, the Monitors Control Panel managed these functions.

Energy Saver

The Energy Saver preference offers options for putting your system, display, or hard disk to sleep after a defined period of inactivity and defines situations that will wake the sleeping computer. On laptops, it is possible to select different values for when the laptop is powered from its battery and when it is plugged into a power supply. In OS 9, the corresponding Control Panel was identically titled.

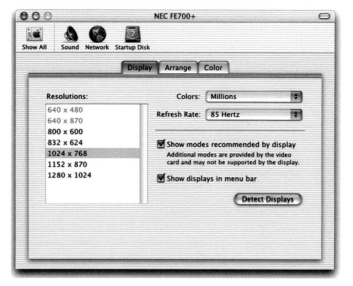

• Displays preference pane

Keyboard

The Keyboard preference allows keyboard behavior customization. An identically titled Control Panel in OS 9 performed the same functions.

Mouse

The Mouse preference lets you customize mouse tracking and double-click speed. In OS 9, the Mouse Control Panel also allowed users to customize cursor width and toggle mouse trails. Mouse trails are not implemented in OS X.

Sound

The Sound preference permits users to select system alert sounds and the alert volume, main volume, and speaker balance and to choose between connected devices for sound input and output. The Sound Control Panel in OS 9 was no different.

If you work with a large number of documents and applications and want a simple way to find them without maintaining a complex set of aliases and Dock items, just increase the number of recent items in the Appearance preference pane in OS 9 and General in OS X. The maximum setting for both is 50. These are then accessible in both versions of the OS from Apple Menu | Recent Items.

Everyone types differently. Some people type faster and therefore require a higher key repeat rate than others, and others are frustrated when their slower key presses result in too many of the same letters. On the Settings tab of the Keyboard preference, try adjusting the Key Repeat Rate and Delay Until Repeat slider bars until you are comfortable with the results.

![Sound preference pane screenshot](Sound preference pane)

• Sound preference pane

Internet

The Internet preference allows users to set up an Apple iTools account, which allows online storage and multimedia file sharing with others. It also allows users to specify the default e-mail and web browser software, home and search pages, news reader and server preferences, and file download destination. Newer versions of Mac OS X reflect Apple's change in the name of this online service; instead of iTools, it is now called .Mac.

OS 9's Internet Control Panel provided the same functionality but included an Advanced tab that specified FTP and other advanced preferences typically specified in web browser preferences. If you change your Internet service provider or switch from dial-up access to DSL, this is one of the two panels you need to access to enter your new information. The other is the Network panel.

Network

The Network preference allows you to manage locations that have a bearing on your network connection, a function more appropriate for laptops, and configure TCP/IP, PPP, proxies, and modem settings. In OS 9, this role was handled by the TCP/IP, Modem, and Remote Access Control Panels.

QuickTime

The QuickTime preference allows customization of QuickTime functionality. Note that QuickTime is not a third-party multimedia company that Apple has partnered with to offer optional services in the same way as it offers Internet accounts via Earthlink. QuickTime is Apple's own multimedia software architecture that has become a multiplatform, industry standard for multimedia content delivery and is used by software developers and hardware manufacturers to offer integrated and coordinated graphics, sounds, video, text, music, virtual reality, and other 3D media.

QuickTime works seamlessly at the system level with OS X and as the earlier OS 9 (which has a corresponding Control Panel, called QuickTime Settings).

Sharing

The Sharing preference enables file sharing with other computers, Apple's Web Sharing, and remote login and management options. In OS 9, the File Sharing and Web Sharing Control Panels handled these functions.

Try This!

Changing the Alert Sounds

Not every sound is pleasing to every ear. For those sounds that need changing, we recommend the following:

1. Go to the Sound preference pane (in OS X) or Control Panel (in OS 9).

2. On the Alerts tab, as shown above, click the name of a new sound other than the one currently highlighted.

3. You will hear the sound. Repeat this process until you find a sound you like; then close the panel.

Classic

The Classic preference enables users to perform a variety of functions relating to the OS 9 **Classic** environment, the compatibility layer that allows users to run OS 9 software from within OS X. The Start/Stop tab of the pane allows you to stop, restart, or forcibly quit Classic mode. The Advanced tab allows you to restart Classic mode with several options and offers an optional Sleep When Inactive setting.

Date and Time

Although the Date and Time preference has seemingly limited functionality, in actual fact it lets you perform a variety of functions. Obviously, it allows you to set the date and time, but the panel also allows you to control the appearance and specifics of the menu bar clock, specify your time zone, and synchronize with one of three global network time servers so that your computer clock is regularly adjusted to the global standard time. OS 9 contained a similar Date and Time Control Panel.

Software Update

Software Update is a fantastic utility that automatically or manually checks for system security and other bug-fix upgrades and new versions of common software programs such as Internet Explorer, downloads them when you agree to installation, and keeps track of what you've downloaded and installed and what you haven't. Software Update existed for Mac OS 9 as well.

In OS X, the utility proves to be more useful. As OS X is a new operating system for Apple, it requires a heightened level of bug fixing and feature tweaking. Software Update is essential during this period, so ensure that the update option is set to Automatic rather than Manual and check for updates regularly.

Speech

Speech is a system preference panel that can enable the use of spoken commands for your computer and offers a place where you can customize the voice with which your computer speaks back. This functionality obviously has great potential in environments where computers are being implemented for people with severe physical disabilities; it has been implemented in Macs for many years. OS 9 had a Speech Control Panel.

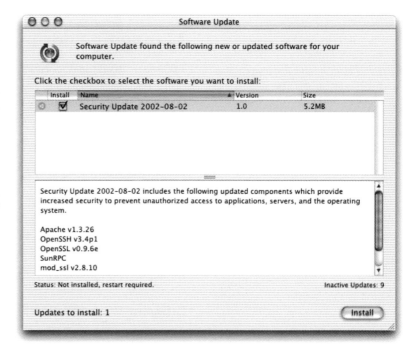

• Sharing preference pane

• Software Update application

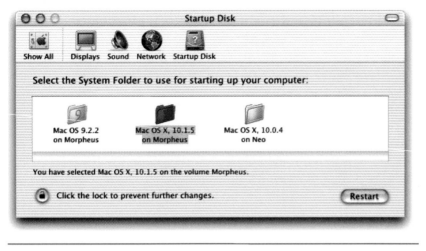

• Startup disk preference pane

Startup Disk

The Startup Disk preference allows you to select which operating system boots up the computer on restart. In OS X, this is typically split between OS 9 and OS X. One reason why you would want to boot from OS 9, for those of you who remember the discussion about the Classic environment, is that OS X offers limited functionality for some OS 9 applications it runs from within the compatibility layer. This is particularly true in the case of third-party peripherals such as scanners, which have either refused to work in OS X or have behaved so badly that booting into OS 9 is the only reasonable option. As more scanner drivers are written for OS X, this will become less of an issue.

Printers and digital camera card readers, on the other hand, when attached to OS X computers, seem to work fine.

Users

The OS X Users preference pane allows you to add, delete, and edit users from your computer. In OS 9, the corresponding Control Panel was Multiple Users.

Managing Files in OS X

The OS X Finder is all you need to know about for file system navigation for daily use of your Macintosh. Unlike Windows, there is no separate Windows Explorer–type interface. On the Mac, the default desktop state *is* "Mac Explorer," if you like. Click the icon for your hard disk, and you've begun to explore.

OS X allows three ways of accessing files: through icon, list, and column views. The Finder saves the preferred view of the first folder or disk opened in a new Finder window. OS 9 offered two of these three ways of viewing folders and files, icon and list, making the transition to the new Mac OS easier for those comfortable with OS 9.

The unifying factor in all three viewing modes in OS X is the ability to navigate the file and folder structure of your disks and to open files and folders by double-clicking them.

Different Ways of Viewing Files and Folders

Here you will be introduced to the different options when viewing files and folders, which you will need to know to work with files. First, you need to know how these different views are selected.

Open your hard disk structure or any folder by double-clicking it. In Mac OS 9 and OS X, you can set view options from the View menu of the Finder. In OS X, you can also set view options from the toolbar of any open folder or disk.

Icon View Icon view is the original Mac approach to viewing folders and files, first implemented in 1984. Not that much has changed. You still select items by clicking them once, and you open them by double-clicking.

The new twist that OS X has brought to this viewing option is that you can set an option so that a folder opens in the same window when you double-click. In OS 9, this action opened the subfolder in a new window. In OS X, this behavior takes place in all three of the view modes. You can turn this option on and off in the Finder preferences.

List View Just as in OS 9, List view displays content in an indented outline format that allows you to see the contents of enclosed folders. This is a powerful means of viewing and organizing your folders and files without having to open new windows for each subfolder, a process that can make your virtual desktop as messy as a real one!

To open a folder, click the triangular icon to the left of the folder icon. To close the folder, simply click the icon again to hide the contents of that folder.

The List view offers a wealth of information about folders and files such as date modified, size, and kind (for example, application or file). If you double-click a folder, that folder opens inside itself, as in the other two view options.

Column View The Column view is new to the Mac OS, appearing in OS X, although its roots originate in the shareware utility Greg's Browser, released in 1989. In Column view, when you select a file by clicking it once, the file's icon or a preview of its contents—text or graphic—is displayed to the right of the selected item.

This view can be very confusing when you first start using it as it resembles an Open dialog box in OS 9 or Windows, but it behaves differently. It is easy to get confused when clicking a folder and having it leap to the left and open something on the right rather than up and down. A sideways scroll bar at the bottom of the dialog box helps you keep track of where you are.

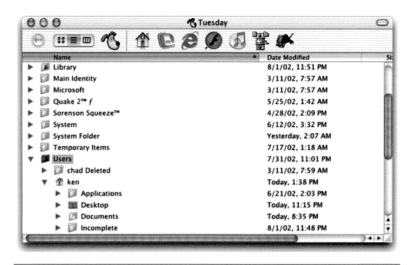

- Finder window in Icon view

- Finder window in List view

- Finder window in Column view

When you open a file from within an application, Column view is the default browsing behavior. UNIX geeks and webmasters will appreciate the following shortcut: If you type a forward slash (/) in the Go To box and press RETURN, you will find yourself browsing at the root of your current hard disk. If you're lost, this is your down-and-dirty compass to get to the root of the matter.

When a window is in Column view, you can change the size of columns by dragging the bottom of the column divider.

Button View Button view is an OS 9-only view option that initially appears similar to the Icon view, except that icons appear bordered by a square button, and a single click, not two, opens them.

The Toolbar In OS X, you use the toolbar to select which one of the three view types you want, and the toolbar also offers plenty of space to place often-used folder, file, and application aliases. To add items to the toolbar, all you need to do is drag the original item into the bar and release, similar to the action of the Dock. This makes an alias of the item that can be accessed from any open window. You can toggle the visibility of the toolbar by clicking the thin lozenge-shaped button located in the upper right corner or the top of the open window.

Introduction to Searching with Sherlock

Sherlock is Apple's combination hard disk and Internet search utility. You can use Sherlock to find files on your hard disk or a variety of information on the Internet. Sherlock can perform as complicated or simple a search as you like through the application of a series of attribute filters to narrow down the search criteria. Although OS X Sherlock has a new look, it performs most of the same functions as the most recent OS 9 version, Sherlock 2.

There are two quick ways to open Sherlock.

From an Alias You can access Sherlock from the Applications folder or put an alias of Sherlock in any Finder toolbar (which would be available any time you open a new window) or on the desktop or in the Dock.

To create an alias—which you can do for any type of application, file, or folder—just select the item and select Make Alias from the File menu, and then drag the alias to wherever you'd like it.

If you'll be dragging the alias to the Dock or Finder window toolbar, you don't have to even create the alias; just select the item and drag it into either location, and an alias will automatically be created.

Finder Shortcuts When you're working in the Finder, you open Sherlock by choosing File and then selecting Find or by using a simple keyboard shortcut: COMMAND-F.

Detailed Searching with Sherlock

The Sherlock window, looking from the top to the bottom, has four basic areas: Channels, Search Box, Sources/Results, and Details.

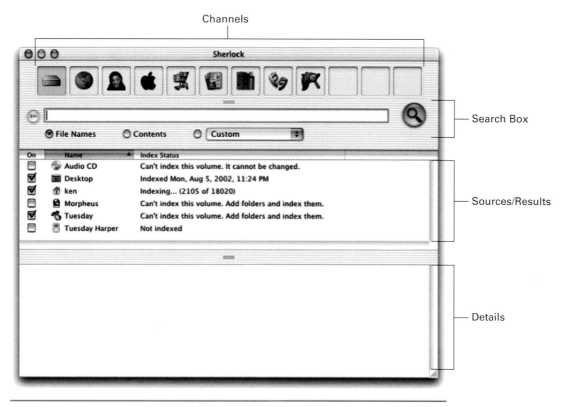

Channels

Search Box

Sources/Results

Details

• Sherlock window showing searchable local volumes

Channels   At the top of the Sherlock window are several smaller windows containing icons, called channels. Each icon represents a different group of searches, beginning, at the left, with the standard search for folders and files on your hard disks and a general Internet search. Moving on to the right, other channels offer Internet searches for websites, products, news, and people. In reality, most give you access to groups of Internet sites and perform a commercial, more than a useful, function. For example, the channel identified by a shopping cart will simultaneously search 1-800-FLOWERS, Amazon.com, Barnes and Noble, eBay, and REI. Check boxes allow you to deselect or select installed sites. For a news search, the channel can perform a simultaneous search of CNET, CNN, Motley Fool, Quicken, the New York Times, and TheStreet.com—which will just not be enough for the average news junkie.

Search Box   The search box area is where you enter what you want to search for and whether you want to search file names or contents or to use a custom option.

Sources/Results   The sources/results area is the large window in the center of Sherlock that shows the sources you can select to search for any particular channel as well as the results of that search after it's performed. To view details of a file or Internet search, click one of the results. The information will be displayed in the details window below.

Details   The details area is where the meat is. Here you will find information about the selected search results, and with a simple double-click you will be taken to its location, be it a web page, file, or folder.

Creating Folders in the Finder

With folders, you can organize your documents and applications. There are two ways to create a new folder:

- Choose New Folder from the File menu in the Finder.
- Use the keyboard shortcut COMMAND-SHIFT-N.

Copying, Pasting, and Deleting Files and Folders

You can copy and paste files and folders into the same or a different document or folder.

- To copy, select the item and choose Copy from the Edit menu (or press COMMAND-C).
- To cut, select the item and choose Cut from the Edit menu (or press COMMAND-X)
- To paste, first either copy or cut a file or folder. Then open the destination folder and select Paste Item from the Edit menu (or press COMMAND-P).
- To delete, choose Delete from the Edit menu (or press COMMAND-DELETE). This moves the file or folder into the trash. To empty the trash, select Empty Trash from the Finder menu of the Finder (or press COMMAND-SHIFT-DELETE).

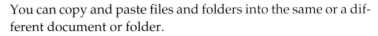

• Copying a folder

Moving and Renaming Files

Moving files and folders is as simple as selecting the item with your mouse, dragging it into the new desired location, and letting go. You also have the option of selecting an item and using the cut and paste options described in the preceding section. To copy a file, hold down the OPTION key as you let go of the file or folder.

There are two ways to rename a file:

- Find the desired item to rename and click—*but* with a short pause in between the two clicks. The name of the item will be highlighted, and you will be able to edit the file name. Click off the item or press RETURN to save the new name.

- Select the item, and in the Finder choose File and then File Info (or press COMMAND-I). This will bring up the information window. In the pop-up menu that displays General Information by default, select Name and Extension. In the box, add whatever new name you want and then close the window.

• Info window

Creating a New Folder to Organize Files

In this exercise, you will create a folder within an existing folder, rename it, and move some files into it. To complete this exercise, you will need the following:

- A Mac computer with any version of the Mac OS installed

- A user name and password that will allow you to log on to your computer

- Files in at least one of the folders of your home directory

Step 1

Open your hard drive by double-clicking its icon. From within the Finder window that opens, click any folder you know has subfolders inside. You will see a list of folders. Double-click on a folder that contains some files.

Step 2

Let's create a new folder. To create a new folder, press COMMAND-SHIFT-NEW or select New Folder from the Finder's File menu. A new folder will appear at the bottom of the list of files, called "untitled folder."

Step 3

Begin typing a new name for the folder; or click the folder once, pause and then click it a second time to highlight its name, and then type a new name.

Step 4

Select a file or folder that you want to place into this folder by clicking it once. If you want to select multiple files or folders to drag into the folder, hold down the SHIFT key while clicking them.

Step 5

When you are finished selecting items you want to put into the new folder you have created, select any one of the highlighted items, drag it over the new folder you created until the folder is highlighted, and then let go. The files will be moved into the new folder. Double-click this folder to check that everything moved as you wanted.

Printing

No matter what type of printer you have, almost every OS X application manages the printing process in the same way, including giving you the ability to create an Adobe PDF document from any Print menu.

The Print command, accessed from the File menu of OS X applications, is your one-stop shop for all printing needs. As in OS 9, printer names appear when printer drivers have been installed. These print drivers prepare page descriptions for printing and talk with the printer. OS X comes with a large set of common USB printer drivers from Epson, Canon, and Hewlett-Packard as well as several for Ethernet-connected printers.

If you have one of the included USB printers, OS X will automatically set that printer as the default printer when it is plugged in. If your printer happens to not use one of the many common printer drivers supplied, you can add drivers to Library | Printers and activate them through the Print menu, which we will discuss later.

In OS 9, you would choose your printer through the Chooser, but in OS X the Chooser represents a now obsolete step; therefore, most of your printer interaction takes place within the Print dialog box within applications. During printing, the Print Center icon appears in the Dock, allowing you to view, hold, or delete jobs.

Step-by-Step 8.05

Adding a Printer

This step-by-step exercise will take you through the process of installing a new printer. To complete this step-by-step exercise, you will need the following:

- A Mac computer with any version of OS X installed

- A user name and password that will allow you to log on to your computer

- A printer to connect to the computer or a connection to a network printer

Step 1

If you are not going to connect to a computer via a network and have a local printer to connect, connect the printer cable to your computer and make sure that the printer is turned on.

Step 2

From the File menu of any application, select Print. If the attached printer does not show up automatically, choose Edit Printer List from the Printer pop-up menu. This brings up the Printer List window of the Print Center utility. Click Add Printer; you will see a list of available printers.

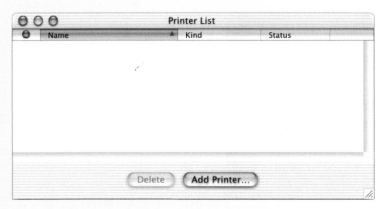

Step 3

Select the appropriate connection type from the Directory Services pop-up menu: USB, LPR (for using TCP/IP protocols to connect to a printer on an intranet or through a domain name server, or DNS), or AppleTalk (for a printer on a local Ethernet network). Click Add to add the printer to your available printer options.

Printing Options

Of course, there are many issues involved in printing. This section covers the most common.

Setting Printer Options

After choosing Print from an application's File menu, you have access to a variety of configurable options from a pop-up menu in the Print dialog box. Additional options may be offered depending on the unique features of your printer and the specific application you are printing from:

- Copies and Pages
- Layout
- Output Options
- Paper Type/Quality
- Color

• Selecting printer options to modify

Copies and Pages　In the Copies and Pages window, you can select the number of copies and whether you want to collate them. You can also specify that an entire document be printed or just specific pages.

Layout　The Layout option lets you select the number of pages you want printed per sheet of paper, specify the layout of the document, and indicate whether you want the pages delineated with a border.

Output Options　The powerful Output Options feature allows you to save your document as Portable Document Format (PDF) or PostScript file. This feature can be very useful for sending preformatted documents to others and for submitting documents to graphic design output bureaus.

Paper Type/Quality　On the Paper Type/Quality tab, you can select the paper type and quality of paper, depending on your printer's features and the type of print media you want to print on.

Color　The Color option lets you vary the color output of the printed material in three areas:

- Saturation (richness of colors)
- Brightness (density of print)
- Color tone (warm to cool tones)

Where to Find the Print Queue

Apple's OS X name for the print queue is the Print Center (/Applications/Utilities/Print Center). The Print Center also automatically launches whenever you print and can be found in the Dock after using a Print command. In OS 9, printers were saved on the desktop, where you could double-click them to access the print queue.

• Print Center window

Where to Find Page Setup

As in other operating systems, Page Setup is found on the File menu of most applications. Here, you will find options for paper size, orientation, and scaling. Depending on your printer driver, you may be offered additional options.

Printing from Applications Running in Classic Mode

Classic application printing completely relies on OS 9 print drivers and does not offer the ability to print to PDF (unless you have installed the shareware utiliy Print To PDF available at `jwwalker.com`). If you add drivers to your OS 9 system, they must be placed in the system's Extensions folder (/System Folder/Extensions). To activate the drivers, you'll have to use the OS 9 Chooser, which is located on the OS 9 Apple menu.

Apart from these few differences, printing in OS 9 is similar to printing in OS X.

Working with User Accounts and Privileges

One of the powerful features introduced in Mac OS 9 that was vastly improved in the new Mac OS X is the ability for any number of people to use a single Mac.

Once granted a login account, individual users can select their own custom settings, such as desktop views and bookmarks, and access their own private storage space: the Home folder, located in the Users folder in the hard disk root directory.

For example, one user might choose a right vertical Dock, but this will not affect the next logged-in user's settings, which may be completely different. Other users may have limited access to your Home folder and vice versa; however, all users have access to a shared folder.

The first-created user account on your computer is automatically designated an administrator. If you happen to forget or lose the administrator password, you can reset it by using the OS X installation CD. To do this, insert the CD and choose Reset Password from the Installer menu. You should keep the CD in a safe place, because anyone with the OS X CD can gain complete access to your system.

Types of Users and Privileges

There are three types of user accounts. Two, Administrator and Ordinary, are self-explanatory. The third, Super User, is an account type that offers UNIX root access to your computer and file system that you should implement only if you know what you are doing. Changing things on your computer in this account mode can result in serious system dysfunction and lost data. Do not implement it unless you are familiar with UNIX.

The main functionality of the three account types is described here.

Administrator Account   This account type is for advanced users or for the person who will administer this computer, add more users, install software, and the like. This level allows you to:

- Change all system preference settings and install software in the main application and library folders
- Create, modify, and delete user accounts

Ordinary Account   This account type is for standard users who you typically need to save from themselves on a regular basis. This account level will minimize those desperate tech support calls! This level allows you to:

- Limit access to only the user's Home folder and the shared folder (/Users/Shared/)

- Prevent access to higher-level system preferences, such as network settings, sharing, software update settings, user setup, and date and time settings

Super User Account This account type is for people familiar with the inner workings of UNIX only. It is not for normal software installation or use. This level of account:

- Gives you complete control over all folders and files on the Mac

- Is seldom needed for normal use

You will seldom need the amount of control over OS X system files that the Super User account allows. OS X is specifically organized to limit the need to change the system files and folders. The files that most users will want to change are located in the main Library folder (administrator access required) or in the user's private Library folder (/Users/YourUsername/Library/), where the Ordinary user has access.

Advanced users may enable this option via the NetInfo Manager (Applications | Utilities | NetInfo Manager).

• Adding a user account

Creating User Accounts

The first user account is set up when you first install OS X. This account is automatically set up with administrator access. After the installation process is complete, you can create additional user accounts.

Step-by-Step 8.06

Adding a New User

In this exercise, you will add a new user to your computer. To complete this exercise, you will need the following:

- A Mac computer with any version of OS X installed

- An administrator account and password that will allow you to log on to your computer

Step 1

Begin the process of creating a new user by choosing System Preferences from the Apple Menu, clicking the Users preference pane, and clicking the New User button.

Step 2

On the Identity tab, type a long and a short name in the corresponding boxes. Both are case sensitive, and the short name is limited to a maximum of eight characters with no spaces. OS X uses the short name for the user's home folder as well as to recognize the user during login processes. The full name and password can be changed later, but the short name is permanent. The user can log in as either.

Step 3

On the Password tab, assign the user password and check the Allow User to Administer This Computer box, if applicable. A password can be anything, even blank for any user not needing administrator access. For higher security, the password should contain, at minimum, one number or symbol: for example, 5$muffins.

Step 4

Click OK to save the user account or Cancel to start again. At this point, you may be prompted to turn off automatic login if it is already enabled. Automatic login bypasses the login window during startup and logs into the default user account when the computer is powered on. With Automatic Login turned off, users are prompted when the computer boots up to choose their individual accounts and passwords. On the Login panel of System Preferences, you can choose which user account is logged into by default.

New User:Tuesday Harper

Identity | Password

Password: •••••••
Must be at least 4 characters

Verify: •••••••
Retype password

Password Hint: funky normal
(optional)

Your hint should not easily reveal your password to others.

☐ Allow user to administer this computer

Cancel | Save

■ Troubleshooting Common Mac OS Problems

This section tells you where to find basic help and offers a guide to the system utilities and keyboard shortcuts to help get you out of trouble. It also discusses how to handle the larger files that you'll encounter in today's computing environment.

Where to Find Help

This section tells you how to find general help in Mac OS 9 and OS X or from within an application.

Help with the OS

If you have questions about how the Mac OS works, the first port of call is the help facility built into the Mac OS. From the Finder, go to the Help menu and select Mac Help. If the system help does not answer your questions and solve your problem, connect to the Internet and visit Apple's support center at www.info.apple.com/. Information is

• OS X Mac Help window (version 10.2)

well organized, and Apple's Knowledge Base, manuals, and related discussion groups are all fully searchable.

Help within Applications

If you are having difficulties with specific software you are using, click the Help menu at the top of the application window and select the option you need. In many cases, there will be a local help file and an option to find online help for the application.

Help
Search Word Help
Word Help Contents
Additional Help Resources
✓ Use the Office Assistant
Downloads and Updates
Visit the Mactopia Web Site
Send Feedback on Word

• Help menu in MS Word

Useful System Utilities

The utilities described here for OS 9 and OS X are useful for basic troubleshooting. As with any situation, if you find yourself in deep water, seek expert advice.

OS X

OS X system utilities offer the same basic functionality as their OS 9 predecessors. A main difference is that some OS X utilities collect some of the disparate functions of several OS 9 utilities and combine them in a single application. Here is a quick guide to OS X's hard disk and network software utilities.

Disk Utility   Found in the OS X Utilities folder (Applications/Utilities/ Disk Utility), Disk Utility offers a summary and usage statistics for all volumes attached to the computer. The utility also includes Disk First Aid, which enables you to verify or repair Mac OS Standard, Mac OS Extended, and UFS formatted disks, including hard disks and CD-ROMs. The software also works as a one-stop shop for erasing and partitioning volumes.

Network Utility   Also found in the OS X Utilities folder (Applications/ Utilities/Network Utility), Network Utility identifies your hardware and IP address, gives you transfer and other network statistics, and performs a variety of other network and Internet scans, lookups, and directory searches, including ping, lookup, traceroute, whois, finger, and port scan.

If your system is crashing a lot, one of the reasons may be damage to the hard disk. Running a diagnostic test with Disk Utility in OS X or Disk First Aid in OS 9 may help you identify and resolve the problem.

• Network Utility window

OS 9

Here is a quick reference to the comparable OS 9 system utilities for installing and partitioning drives, checking and fixing hard disk errors, and exploring the network neighborhood.

Drive Setup   Drive Setup is OS 9's disk erasing, formatting, and partitioning tool and is found in Applications/Utilities/Drive Setup. OS X's install process renames the existing Mac OS 9 Application folder as Applications (Mac OS OS9). With the advent of OS X's Disk Utility, there is no reason to use this tool.

Disk First Aid   Like its OS X cousin, this utility, found in the same folder as Drive Setup, verifies the directory structure of Mac-formatted volumes and repairs problems it finds. Again, use the OS X version if you have access to it.

Network Browser   Network Browser, found on OS 9's Apple menu, shows connected computers and servers. From local tests, OS 9 and OS X are easy to set up for file sharing among several computers over a local Ethernet network. The fall 2002 release of Mac OS X's Jaguar build promises similar simple connectivity with Windows and other servers.

• Network Browser window showing servers kebab and tuesday

Keyboard Shortcuts for Troubleshooting

Keyboard shortcuts can help you get out of application or system freezes. Table 8.2 lists common keyboard shortcuts for OS 9 and OS X.

Table 8.2	Useful Keyboard Shortcuts for OS 9 and OS X
Shortcut Function	**OS 9/OS X Shortcut**
Turn computer on/off	Power key
Stop a process/cancel an operation in progress	COMMAND -. (period)
Force an application to quit	COMMAND-OPTION-ESC
Start computer from CD	Press C during startup

In OS 9, forcing an application to quit sometimes also forced the user to restart the computer, as the freeze would transfer to the Finder. In OS X, forced quits of applications rarely affect the performance of the rest of the computer's functions.

• Freeze recovery information in OS X Mac Help

Issues Caused by Large Files

John's work as a web designer involved a lot of traveling in 1998, so he purchased an Apple PowerBook. As he didn't have a whole lot of money at that point, John bought a 233-MHz version, which shipped at the time with a 6GB hard disk and 32MB of RAM.

Because the graphic design aspect of web design is aimed at a screen destination rather than print, most of the Photoshop work John did involved small files with a screen resolution of 72 dpi, and therefore 32MB of RAM felt sufficient. While it's nice to have maxed out RAM on your computer to enable optimum software speed, the system operated at an acceptable level for the workload John had.

• PowerBook

As time went on and the number of files John created in the course of his work steadily increased, John became aware that he needed to institute some backup for the data. Literally the week before he purchased an external CD-RW drive to accomplish this, disaster struck. Before John's PowerBook reached its first birthday, his computer's hard disk crashed and refused to reboot. Third-party utilities that he rushed to use couldn't help.

John took the computer to an authorized Apple repair shop that specialized in data recovery. After $800 in data rescue fees, he had an answer as to why his system had crashed. Although Photoshop and the other graphic and multimedia software John used were functioning fine for his purposes, something else was going on behind the scenes.

The temporary files that Photoshop creates for its processor-intensive graphical functions are large. When a computer doesn't have much RAM, these files are not held in RAM but are written and rewritten to the hard disk's free space over and over and over. In the case of John's system, this caused massive fragmentation of the hard disk, to the point where the massive database that keeps track of such things became corrupted beyond the system's capacity to recover it.

These days—especially with Apple's promotion of the Mac as "the hub of your digital lifestyle" and its inclusion of music burning, movie editing, photo processing, and DVD creation software on its consumer-level computers—normal users who don't necessarily use their computer as much as John does are increasingly dealing with massive files on a regular basis.

Users who fit the pattern described here should take the following steps to ensure that they don't fall into the same, costly trap that John did:

- Get enough RAM. Remember: There's no such thing as too much RAM. As the price of RAM tends to fluctuate more than the Dow Jones, wait for a low point and get as much as you can for your system. Applications will run faster and more smoothly, and your hard disk is less likely to misbehave regularly.

- Purchase some form of backup solution. CD-RW drives offer an affordable means, and each CD-R has a capacity of 750 to 800MB.

- Make regular backups of all your data. It is up to you to determine which data you have that is most valuable. This data should be backed up regularly. Some software can automate this process: for example, Retrospect Express Backup software by Dantz (distributed as part of Norton's SystemWorks for Macintosh) copies files to a huge variety of removable disks or cartridges, including CD-R, CD-R/RW, Zip, Jaz, SuperDisk, magneto-optical, and DVD devices.

- Once every six months or so, either run third-party optimization software such as Norton Speed Disk (part of the SystemWorks package), which defragments and organizes files on your hard disk, or reformat your computer's hard disk from scratch and reinstall everything. This will ensure that your hard disk is not fragmented, even in the case of excessive use.

Other Backup Options

Other backup options include the following:

- If you have an Apple computer with a SuperDrive that burns DVDs, each DVD-R can be used to hold 4.7GB of data. Data backup onto DVD-R is available only for OS X.

- Purchase an external FireWire drive or a second internal hard disk (for desktop systems only).

- Back up your files to a workplace LAN (speak to your system administrator).

- If you don't have access to a LAN, you can make use of various online storage solutions such as Apple's iDisk (www.mac.com/). These typically are limited to a few hundred megabytes of storage.

Useful System Diagnostic/Repair and Backup Utilities

The following sites offer access to useful software utilities for system diagnosis and repair (SystemWorks, Drive 10, TechTool Pro, and Hard Disk Toolkit) and data backup (Synchronize! Pro X and Backup Toolkit):

- SystemWorks (www.norton.com/)

- Drive 10 and TechTool Pro (www.micromat.com/)

- Synchronize! Pro X (www.Qdea.com/)

- Hard Disk Toolkit and Backup Toolkit (www.fwb.com/)

Chapter 8 Review

Chapter Summary

After reading this chapter and completing the Step-by-Step tutorials and Try This! exercises, you should understand the following facts about Apple computers and the Mac OS:

Describe the History of Apple and the Mac OS

- Apple sold the first affordable personal computer with a graphical user interface.

- Apple has never licensed its operating system (except briefly and experimentally) to any other company, meaning that the hardware and software of the Mac is a proprietary combination.

- Apple accounts for 3.5 percent of personal computer sales in the U.S. Dell leads with 26 percent.

- Macs have traditionally been popular with creative professionals, particularly those needing strong graphical and multimedia performance, and the publishing industry.

- Apple computers are well known for ease of use and an attractive graphical user interface.

- There are two distinct Mac operating systems in wide use: Mac OS 9 and Mac OS X. The GUIs are basically comparable and will not be entirely unfamiliar to Windows users.

- Loaded Apple computers these days ship with the software and hardware that allows you to perform a variety of multimedia tasks, including video editing and DVD burning.

- Mac OS 8, the incarnation before key Internet tools were added, is now obsolete.

- OS 9 software can run on OS X from within a compatibility layer known as Classic.

- OS X is based on a UNIX core and so enjoys greater stability, complies with networking and security standards, and appeals more to system administrators and developers.

- OS X's graphical user interface is known as Aqua.

- All Macs these days ship with Ethernet, FireWire, and USB ports and are AirPort ready.

- Jaguar, the codename for OS X's 10.2 build, has vastly improved connectivity support for Windows and other non-Apple servers.

- Apple's UNIX core is known as Darwin and is a product of the open-source development community, with all the advantages that brings.

- OS X offers strong multiuser support.

- OS X comes ready for many common peripherals such as Canon, Epson, and Hewlett-Packard printers.

- Macs tend to be less likely to be affected by computer viruses than Windows computers.

Use the Features of the Mac Desktop

- The Mac typically hides back-end operations from its users that they do not need to know.

- The Finder is the default state and file management interface of the Mac OS.

- The Apple menu and Chooser are key functional components of OS 9.

- The Dock is a key component of OS X.

- Sherlock is the native local file and Internet content search utility of the Mac.

- The Print menus of applications in OS X contain most printing functionality, and the print queue is called the Print Center.

Install and Configure Mac OS X

- You will need to determine which version of the Mac OS is currently installed. OS 9.1 is the minimum required for an installation of OS X. You may need to upgrade your software.

- Even though Apple's software runs on Apple's proprietary hardware, some hardware configurations will not be sufficient to run OS 9 or OS X. Check to see that your hardware meets the minimum requirements. You may need to upgrade your firmware.

- Have your Internet configuration ready before setup. If your Internet connection is a DSL connection, you will need to get your hardware address registered with your Internet service provider. Do this before installation to avoid an interruption in the process.

Get to Know the Mac OS X Workspace

- In OS X, what were called Control Panels in OS 9 are now described as System Preferences.

- Many OS X System Preferences correspond to the earlier OS 9 Control Panels. Some OS X System Preferences incorporate functionality previously found in more than one Control Panel.

- ColorSync is an important preference to configure for those in the design and publishing industries, as it manages color consistently throughout a multifunction workflow process.

- The Software Update preference is very important as it notifies you when Apple has released important security and functionality updates to your operating system.

- Files and folders may be viewed in three different modes in OS X: Icon view, List view, and Column view. OS 9 has the Icon and List views, does not have Column view, but offers an additional Button view.

- The Sherlock search utility can search local hard disks, the Internet, and even content channels such as news or shopping.

- Adding printers is typically a simple process in the Mac OS, more so in OS X.

- Multiple user accounts for Apple computers are a strong feature of the Mac OS, and are simple to manage.

Troubleshoot Common Mac OS Problems

- Pressing COMMAND-OPTION-ESC forces an application to quit in both versions of the Mac OS. OS X handles this extreme measure very well.

- Use of software that creates large temporary and other files on a computer with limited RAM causes excessive fragmentation of the hard disk. Solutions are to increase RAM and optimize your hard drive a couple of times a year.

■ Key Terms

.Mac *(331)*	**Control Strip** *(333)*	**Mac** *(329)*
Apple Menu *(331)*	**Darwin** *(337)*	**prosumer** *(336)*
AppleTalk *(333)*	**Dock** *(333)*	**Sherlock** *(350)*
Aqua *(336)*	**Finder** *(331)*	**sound card** *(329)*
Chooser *(333)*	**hot swappable** *(337)*	**system keychain** *(330)*
Classic *(347)*	**iTools** *(331)*	**UNIX** *(337)*
compatibility layer *(336)*	**Jaguar** *(336)*	

■ Key Term Quiz

Use the Key Terms list to complete the sentences that follow. Not all terms will be used.

1. Apple is the company, and _____ is the nickname for the computer.

2. To search for files, the utility you need is called _____.

3. Many Mac users do not know what a _____ is.

4. At the core of OS X is a powerful _____ system.

5. The 10.2 version of OS X is nicknamed _____.

6. _____ is the name of Apple's new OS X GUI.

7. There is no _____ in OS X.

8. In OS X, the Dock could be said to have replaced the _____.

9. _____ is Apple's fast peripheral interface, adopted as an industry standard.

10. The _____ sounds like something you might be given in a vegetarian restaurant.

■ Multiple-Choice Quiz

1. Which of the following is the name of Apple's OS X compatibility layer in which older programs can be run?

   a. Jaguar

   b. Sherlock

   c. Finder

   d. Classic

   e. Darwin

2. What is the minimum version of OS 9 that is needed to run older programs from within OS X?

   a. 8.0

   b. 9.0

   c. 9.1

   d. 9.2

   e. 9.3

3. Which of the following is *not* a requirement for installing OS X on a Mac?

   a. 128MB of RAM

   b. A video card or Apple internal monitor support

   c. A DOS partition

   d. The installation disk

   e. A Mac

4. Find the odd one out. Apple computers are well known for:

   a. Ease of use

   b. Design flair

   c. Being waterproof

   d. Multimedia support

   e. Foreign language support

5. The ___ key is a handy shortcut when browsing in an Open menu to return to the root of the hard disk you currently are working in:

   a. *

   b. $

   c. #

   d. /

   e. DELETE

6. There are three file and folder views available when browsing Finder windows. Which of the following five options is *not* one of them:

   a. Date

   b. Icon

   c. List

   d. Column

   e. Aqua

7. Apple's consumer-level laptop is known as the:

   a. iMac

   b. iTop

   c. iLap

   d. iBook

   e. iCarry

8. Apple's Date and Time Control Panel/system preference helps keep the correct time by regularly comparing your system time with:

   a. GMT

   b. The BBC

   c. A network time server

   d. Your watch

   e. The DOS clock

9. The following is *not* one of the multimedia functions made possible by the free software included with a loaded Apple computer these days:

   a. CD burning

   b. DVD burning

   c. DJ mixing

   d. Digital photo organizing

   e. MP3 creation

10. The following is *not* an advantage typical of open-source software development:

    a. Widely available pool of programmers

    b. Fast bug fixing

    c. Free software

    d. Wide distribution

    e. Faster Internet speeds

11. Find the odd one out. Apple's search utility Sherlock can be used to search by:

    a. File name

    b. Contents

    c. File size

    d. Modification date

    e. Usage

12. When you first start an Apple iBook laptop, you see:

    a. Zero scary-looking code

    b. A smiley face icon

    c. Not a lot else happening, thankfully

    d. All of the above

13. Which of the following is the name of the telnet-type program in OS X that allows you to access core systems from a command prompt:

    a. DOS Editor

    b. ResEdit

    c. Terminal

    d. EndUser

    e. iMonkey

14. The following option is not customizable in the OS X Dock:

    a. Size

    b. Position on the screen

    c. Magnification turned on or off

    d. Color

    e. Icons that appear on the Dock

15. You can change the time zone using the following Control Panel/preference pane:

    a. Time Zone

    b. Date and Time

    c. World Time

    d. Latitude

    e. Longitude

■ Essay Quiz

1. Write a few sentences explaining why OS X is a superior operating system to OS 9.

2. You are the network administrator at a school. You need to purchase at least five computers for a new classroom extension that has been added. These computers will need to offer basic multimedia services and support multiple users. Your purchase order allows you to buy either G4 desktop computers or iMacs, which cost half the price. Which do you buy and why?

3. Your copy of Microsoft Word suddenly freezes in mid sentence. Describe the best way to regain control of your Mac.

4. For whom is a good computer operating system designed?

5. Complete this sentence and add a few more supporting your premise: If I could change something about how computers relate to people, it would be….

Lab Projects

• Lab Project 8.1

One of the users of your network, Helen Bandora, married a long-time friend, Jon Moz, and changed her name to Helen Moz.

While it is simple enough to log into OS X as an administrator and alter her long user name to reflect her name change, changing her short name is not possible in OS X because it was used to create the Home directory *hbandora*. Her Home directory is not particularly full, with some Microsoft Word files in the Documents folder and some MP3s in her Music folder.

You decide that it would be only polite to change both login names. What do you do to get her set up with a correctly named account?

You will need a computer with OS X installed on which you have administrator rights.

You will need to do the following:

1. Determine the solution for setting up Mrs. Moz with a correctly named account.

2. Find Helen's Home directory on the hard drive.

3. Implement your solution on the lab computer.

• Lab Project 8.2

The manager of your department has asked you to set up a Mac with two USB printers attached and to teach a user how to print something on each of the two printers.

You will need a computer with OS X installed on which you have administrator rights, plus two USB printers. To make this lab true to life, it would be useful if one printer were a black-and-white laser printer and the other a color inkjet, so there's a good reason someone might switch between the two.

You will need to do the following:

1. Install and check that both printers are working on your lab computer.

2. Find a willing volunteer.

3. Show the volunteers how to use the Print menu from any application to switch between printers.

• Lab Project 8.3

If you ever find yourself the administrator of a large network, you would want to minimize your network's electricity consumption by instituting good energy practices.

You will need a computer with OS X installed. You will need to do the following:

1. Go into the Energy Saver Control Panel and assess the various options you have for controlling the display and hard disk sleep features. Your goal is to reduce the display and hard disk sleep times to the minimum possible without causing the display to dim or the hard disk to spin down intrusively for users.

2. This is a chance to be creative and aware of the types of users of your network and how they interact with the lab environment. Are computers used constantly, requiring a generous display or hard disk sleep time? Is the amount of RAM sufficient for working with files in memory or does the hard disk need to be accessed constantly? What kinds of software do your users use: processor and hard drive-intensive programs such as image manipulation and multimedia programs, or e-mail and word processing software?

Linux

"Would you buy a car with the hood welded shut?"

—PHIL HUGHES
LINUX JOURNAL MAGAZINE

The UNIX operating system has been around for a long time. In the early 1970s, Ken Thompson, a developer working at Bell Labs, was criticized for playing a computer game on company equipment. Ken's response to the criticism was to find an unused computer and write an operating system that would run his game. This operating system was the foundation of UNIX, which has gone on to power the computers of most of the universities, corporations, and governments of the world. UNIX is known as a powerful, stable, and fast system.

In 1991, Linus Torvalds developed an open-source version of UNIX called Linux. Today, Linux has many flavors and can be found on computers ranging from workstations to corporate servers. Linux is a very powerful and popular alternative to Microsoft operating systems.

In this chapter, we explore Red Hat Linux, one of the many available flavors of Linux. Linux is far too broad a topic to give a detailed exploration here, but you will learn why Linux is so popular and when Linux can be a viable choice for use in an organization. You will learn how to work in a Linux environment and how to customize Linux.

In this chapter, you will learn how to:

- Describe Linux features, benefits, and limitations
- Log in, Log off, and use Linux commands
- Manage files and folders
- Use the Gnome desktop
- Configure Linux
- Troubleshoot common Linux problems

▪ Linux Overview

Linux may be new to you, but it has been a hot topic in the computer industry since the mid 1990s. At that time, traditional SCO Group or Berkeley UNIX installations cost thousands of dollars. Services like programming languages or the TCP/IP protocol were an additional charge. Since TCP/IP is the language of the Internet and most UNIX networks, many people felt that charging more for this crucial service made UNIX too expensive.

Linux, a free version of UNIX, had the potential to save corporations millions of dollars. But corporate managers and accountants, while liking the premise of a free OS, didn't know anything about the software, so Linux experts were hired or trained to provide the answers that corporations needed.

To grasp how important this free operating system could be, compare Linux to the engine in your car. An engine costs thousands of dollars, but if a company started making and distributing free engines, the cost of your new car would drop dramatically.

We'll now explain important facts about Linux, including how it was developed, its benefits, drawbacks, and when to use it.

The Development of Linux

The **GNU** organization was created in 1984 for the purpose of developing a free version of a UNIX-like operating system. GNU, a recursive acronym for GNU's Not UNIX, has developed thousands of applications that run on UNIX platforms. Most of these are distributed with versions of Linux.

Learn more about GNU at www.gnu.org.

In 1991, Linus Torvalds started a new hobby. Other people might try inline skating, but Linus wanted to write a better, open-source version of MINIX, one of the flavors of UNIX. Open-source software is software that is distributed with all of its source code, which allows the purchaser to customize the software as necessary. In 1994, Torvalds released the 1.0 kernel of Linux to the world.

Since the software was open source, several companies modified the kernel. Two of the versions available in 1994 were the Slackware and Red Hat kernels. Both included the C++ language, TCP/IP functionality, and primitive web servers. Of course, the code for the kernels was available as well. To obtain a copy, you simply went to an Internet site and selected the products to download.

The **kernel** is the core of the operating system. It contains all of the programs needed to allow the user to interact with the computer. The Linux kernel's code is freely available to any who wish to download it.

Linux's popularity is growing. Cobalt, IBM, and Sun manufacture inexpensive web servers running FreeBSD and the Apache web server. These products help make high-quality, inexpensive web hosting available to the public. Dell offers its customers the option of having Red Hat installed on new server purchases. This reduces the cost of new server equipment by thousands of dollars. CompTIA offers a Linux+ certification. The independent research group IDC has stated that Linux is the fastest growing operating system in the world. There are several reasons that Linux is gaining popularity.

Benefits of Linux

Initially, Linux was popular with the "geek" crowd simply because it was new. It was a badge of honor to run Linux on your home computer *and* be productive. The geeks soon found out that Linux was capable of being cool on its own. They demonstrated that there are several benefits to having Linux on your computer.

Linux Is Inexpensive

The first benefit of Linux is cost. All versions of Linux may be freely downloaded from the Web. If you don't want to download, prepackaged versions of Linux may be purchased online or in computer stores for a modest cost. In addition, the software may be legally shared with your friends. The savings for a company can be incredible. Imagine an IT manager who needs to roll out 1,000 workstations. Rolling out 1,000 Linux stations could cost the company nothing for the operating system software but rolling out 1,000 Windows XP workstations, at $71 per station, could cost the company over $71,000. In addition, when the time comes to upgrade the operating system, the Linux upgrade would still be free, whereas there would be a significant upgrade cost for the Windows solution. All together, the Windows solution would cost an organization a lot more money than the Linux solution.

Linux Can Run on Old Equipment

In addition to being inexpensive, Linux can run on old equipment. Slackware states that its products can run on i386-class machines, which were popular in the late 1980s. A nonprofit organization could provide computers for its employees with donated or very inexpensive equipment. And consider this: we have been using a six-year-old Pentium 166 with 32MB of RAM as a file and web server for over four years. The server has never slowed down, despite increased use.

Linux Is Fast

Linux runs respectably well on old computers, and it is even faster on newer, more powerful computers. This is because Linux programs are very efficient and lean. They use as few resources as possible, and unlike Windows, Linux programs use little, if any, graphics. Graphics can slow a system's response time, making it seem slower than it truly is. Linux may not be pretty, but it sure is fast.

Linux Is Stable

Linux code is well written. This both increases the speed at which Linux runs and improves the stability of the operating system. Linux is next to impossible to crash. If an application crashes, you can simply remove the program from memory and restart your computer. In older versions of Windows, a crashing program had the potential to take down the entire computer. This is one of the reasons why Linux is used on many web servers where stability is crucial. With Linux, web hosting providers can guarantee 99.9 percent uptime.

Finally, Linux is open-source software. This means that **users** can read the source code and modify it as needed. This probably means little to the average user of the final version of a Linux kernel. However, during development, "beta" releases of the kernel are available to developers who will download the code and test it thoroughly. When possible, they will find any

---

Inside Information

Current Linux Vendors

Today, there are several Linux vendors to choose from. All use the most recent Linux kernel in their products. Here are five vendors:

- *FreeBSD (www.freebsd.com)*
- *Mandrake (www.mandrake.com)*
- *Red Hat (www.RedHat.com)*
- *Slackware (www.slackware.com)*
- *SuSE (www.suse.com)*

problems and correct the code. This process helps to ensure that the final release of the kernel is as well written as possible.

Once the final version is released, developers can adjust the kernel as needed. We know a developer who modified his kernel to be more usable for vision impaired users. He added better support for large print output and a command-line narrator that reads the information on the command line. Open source allowed the developer to modify the code to suit his needs.

Drawbacks of Linux

Even though UNIX and Linux operating systems are widely used on corporate servers, web sites, and large-scale networking environments, you still won't find many people using it on their desktop computers or workstations at home. There are several reasons for this.

Security

Because code is distributed with the Linux software, programmers are free to explore how the system works—for good or ill. Although most system vulnerabilities are detected before the product is released, clever programmers can still discover new ones. For example, a technical school student found the algorithm that encrypted the passwords in the school's Red Hat installation. He then cracked all of the passwords for the Linux server and started playing around. Although his intrusions were benign, the implications were clear. If the school's Linux system had been a bank system, its customers could have started bouncing checks!

Lack of Support

No system is 100 percent secure. Even Microsoft products have security vulnerabilities. However, Microsoft products do have extensive documentation and support. Microsoft releases service packs and updates frequently to fix discovered vulnerabilities. Support and documentation for Linux can be spotty at best. A customer who downloads Linux from a server may receive only an electronic manual and access to online help pages.

Limited Software Selection

People purchase computers to run software. Users of Windows computers have many software titles to choose from. Linux users have software in every category but are often limited in their choices. For example, consider Internet browsers. The two most popular browsers are Netscape Navigator and Microsoft Internet Explorer. Both are available for

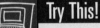

Try This!

Using the Linux Electronic Manual

If you have access to a Linux server or workstation, you can view the electronic manual. Try this:

1. Log in to Linux and enter:

   man ls.

2. The man command opens the documentation, and man ls displays the help screen for the ls command, which is analogous to the dir command in DOS.

3. Scan through the options available for the ls command, then press the spacebar to move to the next page.

4. Count the number of times you must press the spacebar until you reach the end.

5. Press Q to exit. ls is a very simple command, yet it has extensive help.

Linux, but only Netscape has created a Linux version of its latest browser, version 6.32. Internet Explorer's most recent Linux version is 5, despite the fact that Windows XP ships with Internet Explorer version 6.

You are also limited in your choice of word processors. The most popular word processor is Microsoft Word. Chances are good that every computer in your school uses Word. But Word is not available for Linux. Your best choice is **StarOffice**, a suite of applications that contains a word processor. However, StarOffice, although a very nice product, is not Word. A proficient Word user would have to learn some new skills to use StarOffice.

Limited Hardware Support

Just as not all popular software runs on Linux, not all hardware products work with Linux. Red Hat and the other Linux vendors work very hard to support the more common devices. They provide drivers for hardware devices. A driver is a small program that allows the operating system to communicate with the device. Having the correct driver is crucial. If you have a new or unusual device, you may be out of luck. For instance, we have a brand new Hewlett-Packard printer that was detected automatically by Windows XP, yet Red Hat refused to recognize it. Hewlett-Packard has not written a Linux-compatible driver for this new printer yet.

Complexity

The final block in the wall between Linux and greater success is Linux's difficulty of use, or high geek-factor, meaning that only a limited subset of users care to invest the time and effort to learn its intricacies. Linux, like its predecessor UNIX, assumes that you know what you are doing, and it assumes that you know the consequences of every command you type. In contrast, Windows XP asks you to verify everything, and then shows you a pretty animation to confirm the action.

For a beginning user, Linux can be frightening to use; entering the wrong command can have serious consequences. It doesn't help that Linux is also case sensitive, so you must enter the commands in lowercase, and be careful to use the correct case for each subcommand you use with a command. Upper- and lowercase are often different actions. Don't let this frighten you, however. By now, you have spent sufficient time working with operating systems so that you know the basic theory. You'll do fine in Linux.

When to Use Linux

While Linux does have drawbacks, it is useful in several situations. Cost is usually a primary factor when deciding to go with Linux. Here are a few examples of situations in which a Linux solution was a viable option.

Education: Small Budget Combined with Skilled Staff

Pittsburgh Computer School needed to teach its students UNIX. Being a private school with limited funds, the administration opted to install Slackware Linux. Slackware does an excellent job of emulating UNIX at a fraction of the cost. The savings allowed the school to purchase other necessary equipment without increasing student tuition.

Several browsers for Linux are available; however, few are complete browsers. If your browser does not support JavaScript, then you will not be able to see animation, because JavaScript powers much of the animation on the Web. For more information about Linux browsers, see www.netspace.net.au/ ~gcross/browsers.html.

We solved the printer problem by using an older driver for another, similar HP printer. Not all its features are available, but we can print successfully.

Inexpensive Web Servers

Martinez Lawn Service needed a web presence but did not want to pay a lot of money. The company found a hosting solution that uses FreeBSD. The hosting company is able to charge a low fee in part because the OS fee was zero.

Web Development

Amanda is a freelance web developer. For testing purposes, she needs an environment that supports PHP, Perl, and XML, all programming languages for the Web. Amanda installed Red Hat Linux Server along with the Apache web server. Apache and other web servers deliver web pages to a person's computer. A web server powers every page you visit on the web. Apache is one of the most popular servers due to its stability, security, and cost. By having Apache installed at home, Amanda can test her web pages in a realistic setting. If the page works on her computer, it will likely work on the Web. She writes the web pages on her Windows computer and uploads them to her Linux installation for testing.

Preparing for Your Future

John is applying to a bank for a position in the trust department. The software that controls the trust accounts is based on a UNIX database and the employees are expected to know UNIX. John installed Linux on his computer to gain familiarity with UNIX commands.

Why Learn Linux?

By now, you might be thinking that Linux is not worth learning. Nothing could be further from the truth. Linux is very important—in fact, learning Linux can be very beneficial to your future career, regardless of your field of study.

Qualifying for a Job

The first reason to learn Linux is to help you get a job. Linux and UNIX have long been regarded as the "difficult" operating systems. If you learn Linux and place this fact on your resume, you are advertising your intelligence and computer ability. An organization reviewing your resume would see Linux as a big plus. Their reasoning is simple. If you can learn Linux, then you should pick up their internal computer systems very quickly.

For instance, as an undergraduate majoring in mathematics, Cameron landed a job as a debt collector with a small law firm. The firm had problems in the past with employees being unable to work with its debtor system. The system was based on UNIX and was hard to work with. The company rightly figured that Cameron's experience with Linux would allow him to learn their system quickly.

Linux is in use in several industries. Major banks, investment houses, retail establishments, and scientific organizations use Linux to run employee computers. If you want to work in these organizations, Linux knowledge is a must.

Freedom to Choose Your Operating System

Another reason to learn Linux is to give you the freedom and knowledge to choose your operating system. To date, you probably have had experience only with Windows and Apple products. Both make excellent operating

Linux can be used as a desktop OS. However, it is not as easy to use as Windows. If you implement Linux as your desktop OS, be prepared to spend a lot of time configuring Linux and training other users who might need to use your computer.

systems, but if you know only Windows and Mac OS, you are likely to pick only Windows or Mac OS. Understanding Linux allows you to choose Linux if desired.

Improving Your Skills

A final reason to learn Linux is to improve your computer skills. Linux, unlike Windows and Mac OSs, is very unforgiving. It forces you to be very precise when entering commands. Acquiring the habit of being precise now will help you succeed in future computer work.

■ Basic Linux Skills

There are some basic Linux skills and concepts that everyone working with Linux should know. In this section you will practice these skills including logging in and out, working with Linux commands at the Linux prompt, and shutting down the computer.

Getting Access to Linux

Linux has security components that require authentication of each user with a login using a Linux account. When you start a Linux computer it will display the login prompt. Just as in other OSs, you must provide a valid user name and password.

 In Windows we talked about the logon box, in Linux we talk about the login box. The act of authentication in Windows is called logging on, while in Linux it is called logging in.

Inside Information

Root Account

*The **root account** is the most powerful account on a Linux/ UNIX computer. It is capable of doing anything. Be very careful with your use of root. Log in as root only when you need to perform system maintenance tasks.*

*In your encounters with Linux, you may see the term Superuser. The Superuser is not a guy in tights; Superuser is simply another name for **root**, the administrator's log in. This name still appears in UNIX help pages and chat rooms, and if you're going to be cruising these Internet spots, you need to be savvy about the vocabulary.*

Step-by-Step 9.01

Logging In and Out

In this Step-by-Step, you will log in to your computer. To complete this exercise, you need the following:

- A computer with Linux installed
- A user name and password that will allow you to log in to your computer

Step 1

To log in to the Linux computer, type the user name and press ENTER. You will be prompted for a password. Type your password and press ENTER. You will not see the password as you type. If all is correct, you will see the Linux prompt. The prompt typically includes your user name, followed by a @*machine name*. The second instance of your user name indicates the current folder. Finally, the $ sign is the traditional end of a Red Hat Linux prompt. It is often called the $ **prompt**.

```
Red Hat Linux release 7.3 (Valhalla)
Kernel 2.4.18-3 on an i686

localhost login: cottrell
Password:
Last login: Sat Jul 13 21:04:35 on tty1
[cottrell@localhost cottrell]$
```

Step 2

When you are done working in Linux, you will normally log out so that someone else can use the computer. Typing **exit** or pressing CTRL-D logs you out of Linux, which is similar to the Logout option in Windows. Type the command **exit**. You will again see the login screen.

Working with Linux Commands

All right! You can now log in and out of Linux. You should feel pretty pleased. You would like to start using Linux on a daily basis but you realize that you have a lot to learn before you can be productive. Your experience with DOS will be very helpful in your initial explorations of Linux because of the many similarities between them.

The Command Syntax

The Linux command syntax is pretty basic. All lines start with a Linux command. Then, separated by spaces, are optional parameters and switches. Order is usually of little importance, but the space between the commands, parameters, and switches is crucial. However, if you want to use multiple switches for a command, you can combine them into one long switch. For example, consider the Linux command ls, which lists files in a folder. The ls command has several switches, two of which are a and l. To use ls with the a switch, enter **ls -a**. To use both switches, enter either **ls -al** or **ls -la**—either will work. If you want to use a switch and list the /etc folder, you can enter **ls -a /etc**. *In all cases, spaces separate the portions of the command line.*

A switch changes the way that a command works. Parameters are data that the command works on. In general, the command syntax in Linux follows this format:
command -switch parameter

Differences Between DOS and Linux

There are five primary differences between working with DOS and working with Linux.

Case Sensitivity

The first difference is case sensitivity. An operating system that is case sensitive treats *A* differently then *a*. DOS is case insensitive. Thus, DIR is the same command as dir. Linux is case sensitive. The command exit is much different than EXIT (which is not a command).

Designation of Switches

The second difference is the way switches are designated. A switch changes the way that a command runs. For example, in DOS, dir /w displays the files in a folder in a column layout. The / indicates the switch. Linux switches start with a hyphen (-) character. For example, the shutdown -h now command uses the -h switch.

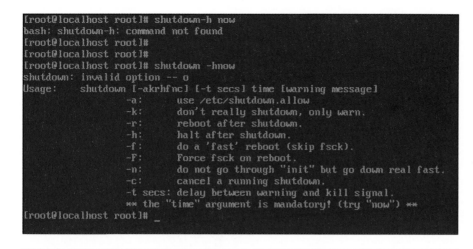

```
[root@localhost root]# shutdown-h now
bash: shutdown-h: command not found
[root@localhost root]#
[root@localhost root]#
[root@localhost root]# shutdown -hnow
shutdown: invalid option -- o
Usage:     shutdown [-akrhfnc] [-t secs] time [warning message]
                        -a:     use /etc/shutdown.allow
                        -k:     don't really shutdown, only warn.
                        -r:     reboot after shutdown.
                        -h:     halt after shutdown.
                        -f:     do a 'fast' reboot (skip fsck).
                        -F:     Force fsck on reboot.
                        -n:     do not go through "init" but go down real fast.
                        -c:     cancel a running shutdown.
                        -t secs: delay between warning and kill signal.
                        ** the "time" argument is mandatory! (try "now") **
[root@localhost root]# _
```

The developers of Linux were also users of DOS, and they included several DOS commands in Linux. In particular, the dir command works in Linux—that is, you can use dir instead of ls. However, dir in Linux supports the same switches as ls rather than the DOS switches you may be more familiar with.

● **Figure 9-1.** Example of a bash error

Use of Spaces

The third difference between DOS and Linux syntax is the use of spaces. DOS allows you to forget a space. For example, dir /ad works with or without a space before the /. In Linux, all parts of the command line must be separated by a space. For example, neither of these commands will work in Linux:

```
shutdown-h now
shutdown -hnow
```

Figure 9-1 shows the error messages each command will generate.

Paths

The fourth difference is the way the paths are built. In DOS and Windows, a path to a folder is built using the backslash (\) character. Thus, a valid path is C:\Winnt\System32. In Linux, you use the forward slash (/) character to indicate a folder. A valid path is /etc/gtk.

Linux Feedback

The fifth difference between DOS and Linux commands is that Linux communicates with you only if there is a problem. In Linux, commands entered will not report that they are successful, though you're warned if the command is incorrect. Figure 9-2 illustrates this trait of Linux. The first command successfully renames a file. Notice that no message is returned to the user. The second command returns an error message. Linux talks back only if you enter a command incorrectly.

In addition to providing little feedback, Linux provides only the bare minimum output. For example, ls is the Linux equivalent of the DOS dir command. Whereas dir returns considerable information about the files it finds, ls returns only the file names. If you want more information, you need to enter a switch. Figure 9-3 shows the results of two different ls options. The first command, ls, simply lists the files. The second command returns a long listing that includes the file attributes. You'll learn more about the ls command later.

Inside Information

The Bash Shell

Bash is the name of the Linux shell, which allows you to interact with Linux by processing commands. Bash is an acronym for Bourne Again Shell. This is an example of Linux humor. The original shell was the Bourne shell. The Bourne developers added several features to improve the shell. Thus, the Bourne shell was "born again." Don't worry if you're not laughing. It takes a true Linux geek to appreciate much of Linux humor. However, if you're going to spend any time with geeks, you should probably talk their language.

```
[cottrell@localhost cottrell]$ mv a.out hello.exe
[cottrell@localhost cottrell]$
[cottrell@localhost cottrell]$
[cottrell@localhost cottrell]$ mv a.out hello.exe
mv: cannot stat `a.out': No such file or directory
[cottrell@localhost cottrell]$ _
```

● **Figure 9-2.** Linux messages

```
[cottrell@localhost cottrell]$ ls
hello.exe   lee.cpp    nsmail     page.html   pay.pl    pool.cpp    tile.cpp
hello.pl    letter     ntp.conf   passwd      perl      stick.png
[cottrell@localhost cottrell]$ ls -l
total 68
-rwxrwxr-x    1 cottrell cottrell   14541 Jul 17 22:26 hello.exe
-rw-rw-r--    1 cottrell cottrell      48 Jul 16 22:38 hello.pl
-rw-rw-r--    1 cottrell cottrell     147 Jul 17 22:25 lee.cpp
-rw-rw-r--    1 cottrell cottrell     186 Aug 17 00:38 letter
drwx------    2 cottrell cottrell    4096 Jul 16 22:43 nsmail
-rw-r--r--    1 cottrell cottrell    2794 Jul 13 22:29 ntp.conf
-rw-rw-r--    1 cottrell cottrell     172 Jul 13 22:10 page.html
-rw-rw-r--    1 cottrell cottrell    1322 Jul 16 22:07 passwd
-rw-r--r--    1 cottrell cottrell     238 Jul 13 23:12 pay.pl
drwxr-xr-x    2 cottrell cottrell    4096 Jul 16 22:39 perl
-rw-rw-r--    1 cottrell cottrell     257 Jul 19 21:51 pool.cpp
-rw-rw-r--    1 cottrell cottrell    7064 Jul 14 00:47 stick.png
-rw-rw-r--    1 cottrell cottrell     256 Jul 13 23:31 tile.cpp
[cottrell@localhost cottrell]$
```

● **Figure 9-3.**   Output from the ls and ls -l command

 man is the command for bringing up the syntax and help files.

Shutting Down a Linux Computer

If you want to turn off your computer, you should shut down Linux correctly. To do this, you need to log in as root. Shutting down Linux is an important task and so it is a task for root. The command to shut down the computer is:

```
shutdown -h now
```

This command tells Linux to shut down immediately and to halt after shutting down. The process will take a few minutes. The shutdown command has several other switches that can be used in place of the -h and now options. One option is the -r switch. This will reboot the system after the shutdown. For a complete list of switches, type **man shutdown** at a Linux prompt.

■ Managing Files and Folders

File management is one of the most important tasks to learn for any operating system. Nearly every chapter in this book has discussed how to copy, name, and view files. In Linux, everything is treated as a file. Web pages and games are files. Folders are files. Even the keyboard

Survey of Operating Systems

Table 9.1	Basic File Management Commands
Command	Description
cd	Changes to another folder.
chmod	Changes the mode or file permissions.
cp	Copies a file.
head	Displays the first 10 lines of a file.
ls	Lists contents of a folder.
mkdir	Makes a folder.
more	Displays a text file, one line at a time.
pico	Creates a text file.
pwd	Prints the working folder.
rm	Deletes a file.

and monitor are treated as files. Learning how to create, manipulate, and use files is crucial to your Linux development. In this section, you will learn the basics of a Linux command. Then you will create a file using pico and you will then copy, move, and delete this file. Finally, you will learn how to create a folder and protect the contents of that folder.

To learn the commands, you must enter them at a Linux prompt. Sit at a Linux computer while reading the following sections. The sections that follow will walk you through the basics of each command. The only goal right now is to learn the commands. Once you have used all of the commands, you will perform an exercise similar to those you may perform on the job. Note that your screen may not look exactly like the ones shown in this book. This is okay. Table 9.1 lists commands for your reference.

Listing the Contents of a Folder

The ls command is the Linux equivalent of the DOS command DIR. The ls command lists the contents of a folder. By default, ls provides only the names of visible files in the current folder. Using switches changes the way that the command runs. Table 9.2 lists the commonly used switches for ls. For a complete list of switches, enter the following: **man ls**.

If you enter the command **ls**, you will get a list of all files in the current folder. Figure 9-4 shows the contents of the /etc folder. Different colors have

Table 9.2	Commonly Used Switches for the ls Command
ls Switch	Description
-a	Lists all files in the folder, including the hidden files. Files are hidden in Linux by making the first character a period, like this: **.bash_profile**.
-l	Displays a long listing of the folder. All file attributes are listed.
-F	Classifies the listing of the folder. In particular, folder names have a / character after the name.
-S	Sorts the output by size.
-t	Sorts the output by time.

```
gnome-vfs-mime-magic    nscd.conf           ssh
gpm-root.conf           nsswitch.conf       sudoers
group                   ntp                 sysconfig
group-                  ntp.conf            sysctl.conf
grub.conf               oaf                 syslog.conf
gshadow                 openldap            termcap
gshadow-                opt                 updatedb.conf
gtk                     pam.d               updfstab.conf
gtk-2.0                 pam_smb.conf        updfstab.conf.default
host.conf               pango               vfontcap
hosts                   paper.config        vfs
hosts.allow             passwd              warnquota.conf
hosts.deny              passwd-             wgetrc
hotplug                 passwd.OLD          wine.reg
identd.conf             pbm2ppa.conf        wine.systemreg
im_palette.pal          php.ini             wine.userreg
im_palette-small.pal    pine.conf           X11
im_palette-tiny.pal     pine.conf.fixed     xinetd.conf
imrc                    pinforc             xinetd.d
info-dir                pluggerrc           xml
init.d                  pnm2ppa.conf        xpdfrc
initlog.conf            ppp                 yp.conf
inittab                 printcap
inputrc                 printcap.local
[cottrell@localhost etc]$
```

● **Figure 9-4.** File listing of the /etc folder

different meanings. White files are simple files. Dark blue files are folders. Green files are programs that you can run at the command prompt or binary files like jpgs. Light blue files are like Windows shortcuts; they are links to files in a different folder.

You might notice that details like date of creation and length were omitted from the output. You must tell ls that you want these details. This requires a switch. Enter the command **ls -l** to see output as shown in Figure 9-5. The first column lists the permissions on the file. The permissions indicate who can read, write, or execute the file. The next column indicates the type of file. The number 1 indicates a normal file, and 2 indicates a folder. Higher numbers indicate that the file is either a link, which is like a shortcut in Windows or a special system file. The next two columns list the owner and last modifier of the file, respectively. The next number indicates the size of the file. The date and time columns indicate when the file was created. Last, the name of the file is shown. If a file is a link (in light blue), the link location is listed; the file after the arrow is the original file, and the light blue file name in this folder is a shortcut to the original file.

Creating a File with pico

You want to write a letter to your instructor. You need to use a text

---

Try This!

Using Wildcards

Linux supports wildcards, which are characters that enable you to list a range of related files. At a Linux command prompt, try this:

1. Enter the command **ls e***. You'll see all files that begin with the letter *e*.

2. Linux supports more wildcards than DOS. You can enter a range of characters as a wildcard. Enter **ls [a-e]***. You see all files that begin with the letters *a* through *e*. The [ ] are part of a Linux feature called regular expressions.

```
-rwxr-xr-x   1 root     root       10888 Mar 24 20:23 rmdir
-rwxr-xr-x   1 rpm      rpm      1735412 Apr 18 17:35 rpm
lrwxrwxrwx   1 root     root           2 Jul  5 12:38 rvi -> vi
lrwxrwxrwx   1 root     root           2 Jul  5 12:38 rview -> vi
-rwxr-xr-x   1 root     root       54949 Apr  5 04:26 sed
-rwxr-xr-x   1 root     root       16700 Sep 17  2001 setserial
-rwxr-xr-x   1 root     root       46780 Jun 25  2001 sfxload
lrwxrwxrwx   1 root     root           4 Jul  5 12:28 sh -> bash
-rwxr-xr-x   1 root     root       11240 Apr  8 12:02 sleep
-rwxr-xr-x   1 root     root       55532 Mar 22 18:02 sort
-rwxr-xr-x   1 root     root       32552 Apr  8 12:02 stty
-rwsr-xr-x   1 root     root       19116 Apr  8 12:02 su
-rwxr-xr-x   1 root     root        9704 Mar 24 20:23 sync
-rwxr-xr-x   1 root     root      155240 Apr  9 13:39 tar
-rwxr-xr-x   1 root     root      288604 Jun 24  2001 tcsh
-rwxr-xr-x   1 root     root       24040 Mar 24 20:23 touch
-rwxr-xr-x   1 root     root        9704 Apr  8 12:02 true
-rwsr-xr-x   1 root     root       30664 Apr  1 18:26 umount
-rwxr-xr-x   1 root     root       10312 Apr  8 12:02 uname
-rwxr-xr-x   1 root     root       24590 Apr 19 12:35 usleep
-rwxr-xr-x   1 root     root      386120 Mar 27 18:20 vi
lrwxrwxrwx   1 root     root           2 Jul  5 12:38 view -> vi
lrwxrwxrwx   1 root     root           8 Jul  5 12:26 ypdomainname -> hostname
-rwxr-xr-x   3 root     root       63555 Mar 13 18:55 zcat
[cottrell@localhost bin]$ _
```

● **Figure 9-5.** File listing details

editor to write the file. Several text editors exist for Linux, but pico is the easiest editor to use. It provides a series of commands at the bottom of the screen and allows you to use the keyboard as expected—BACKSPACE and DELETE work as usual—and the screen will wrap when necessary. This is not true of all Linux editors. Table 9.3 lists handy pico commands.

Now you'll practice using pico to type a simple note to a teacher. You can type paragraphs and sentences just as in Word. Lines wrap properly in pico. Everything works as you expect it to.

Start by entering the command: **pico letter**. Typically, you start pico with the name of the file you want to open. Once pico has opened, type a simple letter. Figure 9-6 shows a letter to an instructor. (Saying nice things to an instructor will rarely hurt your grade!) While you are typing, look at the bottom of the screen. Some common commands are listed for your convenience. The ^ is short for the CTRL key on your keyboard. Thus, CTRL-O will save the

Table 9.3	Common pico Commands
pico Command	**Description**
CTRL-O	Saves the current file. If it is unnamed, you will be prompted to name the file.
CTRL-R	Opens another text file. You will need to enter the name of the file you want to open.
CTRL-T	Spell checks the current document.
CTRL-X	Exits pico. If the current file is unsaved, you will be prompted to save the file.

Inside Information

Using Other Linux Editors

The pico editor is an easy Linux editor to use. Several other editors exist. One of the oldest editors around is vi, which is a line editor. You essentially edit one line at a time. The vi editor has three modes: text, colon, and graphical. To use vi, you must master all three modes.

Another popular Linux editor is Emacs. Emacs is especially popular with developers because it has several programming features. One of these features is called the Emacs dance. When you close a pair of quotation marks or parentheses, the cursor jumps back to the item that you are closing. This feature helps developers with complex code. A downside to Emacs is that the BACKSPACE key does not always work as expected. In a default installation, the BACKSPACE key opens help after the third use. This can be changed by root.

You should learn how to use both editors. Your future career opportunities depend on it.

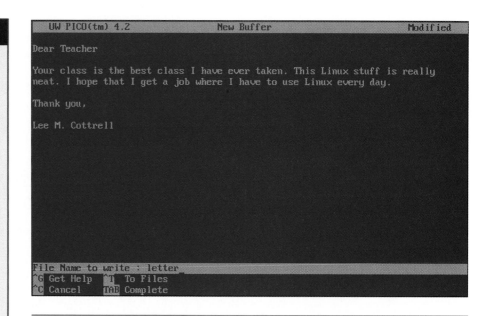

• **Figure 9-6.** Saving a pico file

file to disk. Press CTRL-O to save the file. You will be prompted for a name. Since you want to keep the file as is, you will simply press ENTER.

If you need help with spelling, you are in luck because pico includes a spell checker. Press CTRL-T to spell-check the document. You will quickly notice that the checker is not quite as nice as the spell checker in Microsoft Word.

To exit, press CTRL-X. If you have not saved the file, you will be prompted to enter a file name. If the file name shown is correct, simply press ENTER. Type **ls** at the $ prompt, and you will see the file you created.

Step-by-Step 9.02

Displaying the Contents of Files

A typical Linux folder contains many files. You often need to know what is in the files. Linux has several commands that allow you to see the contents of a file. In this exercise, you practice using two commands to list the contents of files: the more command and the head command.

To complete this step-by-step, you need the following:

- A Linux computer.
- A file called letter. The letter you wrote to your instructor will work nicely.

Step 1

Enter this command: **more letter**. This command displays the contents of the file one page at a time. Since the letter document is small, the entire file is displayed at one time.

| Step 2 | Now enter this: **more /etc/ntp.conf**. You will see a screen like the one shown here. To move through the file, use the spacebar to jump one page at a time. |

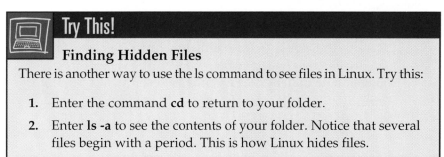

```
[cottrell@localhost cottrell]$ more /etc/ntp.conf
# Prohibit general access to this service.
restrict default ignore

# Permit all access over the loopback interface.  This could
# be tightened as well, but to do so would effect some of
# the administrative functions.
restrict 127.0.0.1


# -- CLIENT NETWORK -------
# Permit systems on this network to synchronize with this
# time service.  Do not permit those systems to modify the
# configuration of this service.  Also, do not use those
# systems as peers for synchronization.
# restrict 192.168.1.0 mask 255.255.255.0 notrust nomodify notrap


# --- OUR TIMESERVERS -----
# or remove the default restrict line
# Permit time synchronization with our time source, but do not
# permit the source to query or modify the service on this system.

# restrict mytrustedtimeserverip mask 255.255.255.255 nomodify notrap noquery
--More--(29%)
```

| Step 3 | Try this command: **head /etc/ntp.conf**. Notice that only the first 10 lines are shown. The head command displays just the first 10 lines of a file, which is helpful in occasions when you don't want to see the entire file. Often, the first few lines suffice. |

Note that the more and head commands are not the only commands that display a file. The commands less, tail, and cat also display files. The less command is nearly equivalent to the more command. The difference is that the less command allows you to move forward and backward in the file, whereas the more command allows you to only move forward. Thus, the less command has more features than the more command. (This is more Linux humor.) The tail command displays the last 10 lines of a file. The cat command displays the entire contents of a file. Be careful with the cat command because "Catting" a large file can take some time.

> **Try This!**
>
> **Finding Hidden Files**
>
> There is another way to use the ls command to see files in Linux. Try this:
>
> 1. Enter the command **cd** to return to your folder.
>
> 2. Enter **ls -a** to see the contents of your folder. Notice that several files begin with a period. This is how Linux hides files.
>
> 3. Practice using the more and head commands to display these files.

Copying Files in Linux

Like DOS and Windows, Linux allows you to copy files. The command to copy a file in Linux is cp. If you are wise, you will make a copy of a file before you change it. This allows you to go back and recover from any changes you make.

> A file you may want to copy is your .bash_profile file. This file is run when you log into Linux. A mistake in this file can cause Linux to not work. By creating a copy of the file, you can recover if you make a mistake when changing this file.

● **Figure 9-7.** Copying the ntp.conf file

You may not have the perl folder shown in this figure.

The cp command requires two parameters. The first is the source file, which can be a file in the current folder or a file in another folder. The second parameter is the location to copy to, which again can be the current folder or a different folder.

As you can see in Figure 9-7, the file ntp.conf has been copied to the current folder. The period at the end represents the current folder. The file ntp.conf resides in the /etc folder. Notice that Linux does not report that it copied a file. You can use the ls command to verify that the file exists.

Deleting Files in Linux

Often you will find you no longer need a file. Deleting unnecessary files frees disk space. The command to delete a file is rm. The rm command requires at least one parameter: the name of the file to delete. If you include more than one file name each file will be erased.

Try This!

Deleting Files

Practice deleting files. Try this:

1. Enter this command: **cp letter oldletter**. Enter **ls** to list your files to verify that the copy operation worked. Then enter this command: **rm oldletter**. Again enter **ls** to verify the operation.

2. To delete the files you copied earlier, enter this command: **rm ntp.conf.** You can delete several files at a time just by listing them with a space between them.

Renaming or Moving Files in Linux

The cp command allows you to have two versions of a file. There are times when you want to rename a file. The net result is one copy of the file. Copying the file and then deleting the original file can accomplish this. However, Linux also provides the mv command. The mv command can rename a file in the current folder or move the file from the current folder to a different folder.

The mv command requires two parameters: the name of the original file and the new name or location of the file. If the original file does not exist, then you will get an error message. If you cannot delete or change the original file, then mv will generate an error message.

Working with Folders in Linux

Linux relies heavily on a folder structure. The structure is similar to that used by Windows XP, which has several predefined folders that are needed by the system. Some hold important system files, and others hold user data. Linux is very similar. It has several folders for system files and an organized series of home folders for each legitimate user.

If you want to work with Linux, you will have to understand the Linux folder structure. The folders can be categorized into two types. The first type consists of folders that you are allowed to change. These are called home folders. Your home folder is the one place in Linux where you have full control over files. By default the other folder category consists of folders that you cannot change. These are often system folders, such as /etc and /bin, or other user's home folders.

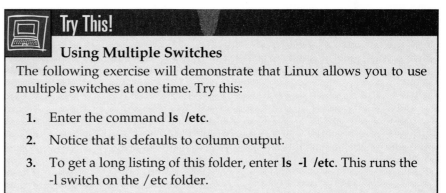

Try This!

Renaming a File

Practice renaming a file. Try this:

1. Log in as a regular user, not root. Use mv to rename your letter. Enter the command **mv letter teacher_letter**. Then list your files. What happened to the letter file?

2. Intentionally generate an error message with mv. You are trying to move the termcap file to your home folder.

3. Enter the command **mv /etc/termcap ~/termcap**. What happens?

When you log in to Linux, you are automatically placed in your **home directory**. This is the place in the Linux computer where you can save your files. Every user has a home folder. Unless you take special steps, your home folder is readable by everyone else on the system. If you installed Linux with the defaults, your home directory path is /home/username. A shortcut for this is ~.

The default installation includes several other folders. The /bin folder contains many of the Linux commands. To see the contents of this folder, enter the command **ls /bin**. Notice that the ls, cp, and more commands are stored in this folder.

The /etc folder contains settings and configuration data for your Linux computer. Do not change anything in this folder unless you know what you are doing. To see the contents of this folder, enter the command **ls /etc**.

The /etc and /bin folders are not the only folders included with a Linux installation. Spend some time exploring your Linux computer to see others. Some have pretty strange names.

> The terms *folder* and *directory* are synonymous in Linux.

Changing to a Folder

As in DOS, the command to change a directory in Linux is cd. The cd command requires just one parameter to run: the name of the folder. If the folder is a child of the current folder, then only the name is needed to change to this folder. For example, suppose that in your home folder you have a child folder called private. To change to this folder, you enter **cd private**. If the folder is not a child of the current folder, you will need to enter the path to the folder. Typically, the path will start with / (the root folder). Each folder in the path is listed after the / and separated by another /. For example, to change to the sbin folder under the /usr folder, you would enter **cd /usr/sbin**.

Try This!

Using Multiple Switches

The following exercise will demonstrate that Linux allows you to use multiple switches at one time. Try this:

1. Enter the command **ls /etc**.

2. Notice that ls defaults to column output.

3. To get a long listing of this folder, enter **ls -l /etc**. This runs the -l switch on the /etc folder.

4. Now enter **ls -la /etc**. This provides a long listing for all files in the /etc folder.

```
[cottrell@localhost cottrell]$ cd /usr/sbin
[cottrell@localhost sbin]$
```

● Figure 9-8. Changing directories

When you correctly use cd to change to a different folder, you are rewarded with a change in your prompt. In Figure 9-8 the user started in the cottrell folder and changed to the sbin folder. The prompt changed to reflect the new folder.

Unfortunately, unless you adjust your settings, Linux does not provide the entire path, unlike DOS. If you are unsure what path you are in, use the command pwd. The pwd command stands for print working directory. When entered, the pwd command simply prints the path to the current folder.

Try This!

Using Relative Path Statements

This exercise will provide practice in using the relative path symbols in Linux. Enter the following cd commands and record what happens. In particular, record the change in your prompt and use pwd to record the full path. Try this:

1. cd /etc

2. cd ..

3. cd

4. cd ../../etc

5. cd ~

6. cd .

To remember the order of the groups, think of the name Ugo. Ugo stands for User, Group, Other.

Creating Folders

Creating a folder in Linux is simple. The command to do so is mkdir. The mkdir command requires at least one parameter: the name of the folder to create. For example, to create a folder called junk, enter the command **mkdir junk**. Because Linux gives you no feedback after you create a folder, use ls to verify that the folder was built.

If more than one parameter is listed, then a folder will be created for each. Therefore, to create several folders at once, enter the command **mkdir perl html bin data**. Again use ls to verify that the folders were built.

Changing File Permissions

One of the benefits of Linux is the great security. However, unless you implement the security features, anyone can access anyone else's folders and files on the Linux computer. To secure your files, you need to decide which files you want to secure.

To implement security for a file, you must change the mode of the file. At the $ prompt, enter **ls -l**, and you'll see something similar to Figure 9-9. Compare the first columns. Notice that pool.cpp has a different set of letters than tile.cpp. These letters are the permissions on the files. The permissions are as follows:

```
[cottrell@localhost cottrell]$ ls -l *.cpp
-rwxrwxrwx    1 cottrell cottrell      257 Jul 19 21:51 pool.cpp
-rwx------    1 cottrell cottrell      256 Jul 13 23:31 tile.cpp
[cottrell@localhost cottrell]$
```

r = read
w = write
x = execute

● Figure 9-9. Comparing file permissions

Survey of Operating Systems

Table 9.4	The chmod Permissions
Permission	Value
Read	4
Write	2
Execute	1

Pool.cpp has the same permissions repeated three times. Linux is not repeating itself; it is listing permissions for three different groups of people. The first three permissions apply to the owner of the file. Normally, if you create a file, then you are the owner. Pool.cpp and tile.cpp allow the owner to read, write, and execute this file. The second set of permissions applies to the group the user belongs to. Groups are used in the working world as a way to organize users. For example, a school may group all faculty members into a single group. This will allow teachers to create files that other instructors can read, but that students cannot read. Pool.cpp can be read by the group Cottrell belongs to, but tile.cpp cannot be read by anyone in that group. The third set of permissions is applied to other people in the world. Again, pool.cpp is readable by the world, but tile.cpp cannot be read by the world. In this example, tile.cpp is extremely secure.

The command to change a file's modes is chmod. The chmod command requires two parameters. The first parameter is the access mode number. The second parameter is the file to change.

The hard part about chmod is determining the access mode number. In Figure 9-9, pool.cpp has access mode number 777, and tile.cpp has access mode number 700. The number can be calculated using the values in Table 9.4. Determine the permission for each setting by adding the values together. Thus, if the owner needs to read, write, and execute a file, the first number is 4 + 2 + 1 = 7. If the group is to also read, write, and execute the file, the second number is also 7. If a user has permission only to read and execute a file, the value is 4 + 1 = 5.

Inside Information

Web Pages and UNIX/Linux

In the early days of the Web, most webmasters had little knowledge of how UNIX worked. They simply knew that they could post their pages on a UNIX computer, and the world could read them. Unfortunately, many did not pay close attention to the modes of the files. Typically, the webmaster set the permissions as 777. This, of course, allowed anyone to change the files.

Several famous web pages were hacked because of this lack of care. Two that stand out as gutsy moves on the part of the hacker were the FBI's web page and the Pentagon's. Both were hacked in a very visible manner. If you start writing web pages on a Linux or UNIX computer, be sure to set permissions for your pages to 755. This lets the world read and execute the page, but the world cannot change the files.

Step-by-Step 9.03

Working with Folders

Imagine that you have been hired by a marketing firm that uses Linux as its primary OS. You will work with a group of users. You will need to create a series of folders that the group can see as well as a private folder that no one else but you can see. Be sure that you are logged in as a regular user. The following steps will allow you to create folders and set permissions on the folders.

You will need the following:

- A Linux computer
- An account on this computer
- Read access to the /etc folder

Step 1	First create the folders needed to work. Use mkdir to create two folders, called wineProject and private, entering this command: **mkdir wineProject private**.

Step 2

Set the permissions on the folders. The private folder needs to be accessed by only you, and the wineProject folder needs to be read and written to by users in your group. Set the permissions appropriately. Enter these two commands: **chmod 700 private** and **chmod 760 wineProject**.

Step 3

You will start populating the wineProject folder with files. A file called wine.reg has been provided for you to start working with. You will need to copy this file to your wineProject folder. Change to the wineProject folder by entering the command **cd wineProject**. Then copy the wine.reg file. For the purposes of this assignment, you can copy the file from the /etc folder. Enter the command **cp /etc/wine.reg**.

Step 4

You have been asked by your boss to keep a daily journal. Naturally, this is private information and will be stored in the private folder. You need to change to this folder. One method is to enter this command: **cd ~/private**. Then enter **pico journal** to start your journal. Make an entry for today and then save it by pressing CTRL-O.

■ Using the Gnome Desktop

You are showing Linux to your client Laurie one day. Laurie likes computers but does not want to type everything at a prompt. She complains that Linux should be as easy to use as Windows.

Laurie is not alone. Most users at some point complain about the command prompt. Visual interfaces are much easier to use, but at a cost. It typically takes longer to perform a task in a **graphical user interface (GUI)** than it does to perform the same task at a command prompt. However, some actions are better performed in a GUI.

The Gnome Desktop

Linux includes a GUI. Recall that during the installation process, we selected the **Gnome** desktop. This is a version of **X Windows**, which is similar to Microsoft Windows. There is a start button and a trash can, and you can use a mouse. To start the Gnome, type **startx** at a command prompt. After a delay, you will see a screen like Figure 9-10.

If you have worked with computers for any time, you may have noticed that you open applications in certain groupings. For example, when you write, you may have Word and a music program open. When you are programming, you may have Access, Word, Visual Studio, a music program, and Internet Explorer open. In Windows, you need to open each program independently. The Gnome, through the Gnome Window Manager, lets you have the applications open and easily accessible, but not always visible. The manager allows you to keep several sets of applications open. To switch between sets, you simply need to switch to different screens.

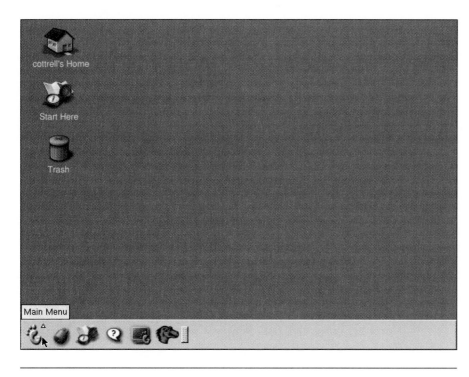

The start button is referred to as the panel. Once you start Gnome, you will log off using the Panel. Shutdown can be accomplished as well, without logging in as root.

● **Figure 9-10.** The Gnome desktop

To understand the manager, think of the traditional Windows desktop. All open applications are accessible through the desktop. The Gnome Window Manager provides you with four desktops. Each desktop can have applications open. To switch to a different application set, you simply need to switch desktops.

The Gnome Window Manager is located in the lower right corner of your screen. By default, the upper left box is selected. The other boxes can be used to hold application sets.

Step-by-Step 9.04

Managing Windows in the Gnome

The following step-by-step exercise will set up two different screens with applications.

You will need the following:

■ A computer with Linux installed

■ The Gnome installed

Step 1 If you have not already started the Gnome, run **startx**. After a few minutes, the Gnome desktop will be loaded on your screen. Leave the default desktop as is; you will create desktops for the bottom two squares.

Step 2

Click the square in the lower left of the square group. You will be rewarded with basically the same screen you had, but with the square pushed in. You will run gedit in this desktop. Choose Panel | Games | Applications | gedit.

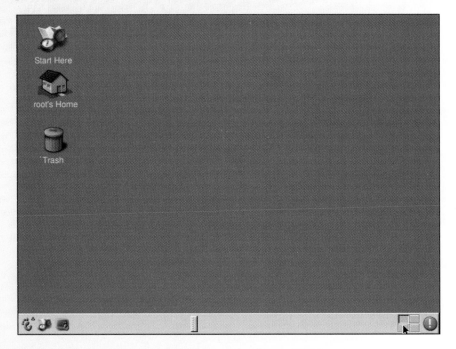

Step 3

You will now set up the lower right desktop to run freecell. Click the lower right square. Gedit will disappear, and the square with gedit will have changed. The lower left square now has an additional square, indicating a running application. Start freecell by choosing Panel | Programs | Games | Freecell.

Step 4

Click back and forth between gedit and freecell. Any changes made to either desktop will reappear when that desktop is activated.

Step 5

Save your changes and exit. Click the Save Current Setup check box to keep your desktops active. The next time you start the Gnome, these applications will open for you. Unfortunately, the Gnome will not place them in separate desktops.

■ Configuring Linux

> Be careful when logged in as root. You have the ability to do anything you want to the system. Remember that Linux does not warn you when you are deleting files. This behavior is especially dangerous when you are logged in as root.

One of the most important tasks you can learn is how to configure an operating system. Rarely will an operating system work for a user without some adjustments. You usually need to add printers or software or change settings. Linux allows most of these changes to be made by the Superuser, root. If you have not already done so, log in as root.

While logged in as a regular user, you can log in as root without logging out. Enter the command **su root** and then enter the root password. You will have root permissions. The su command stands for substitute user. It allows you to substitute the current user with any other user. If no user name is specified, then root is loaded by default.

Managing Users

Linux, like Windows 2000 and Windows XP, allows several users to use one computer. Each user should have a unique user name. This allows the user to save files in an individual folder that can be protected using chmod to hide files from other users.

Try This!

Creating New Users

If you become a system administrator, you will eventually have to create new users. So why not start now? In this quick exercise, you'll create four users: brenda, chris, laurie, and lizzie. Try this:

1. Log in to the system as root. Start by creating one user, brenda.

2. Enter the command **useradd brenda**.

3. Test that the account was added by entering the command **finger brenda**. The finger command searches the user database for any part of a user name or real name. User brenda should have been added.

4. Now add the remaining three names.

To manage users, you will need to learn how to create users, delete users, and change user passwords. For speed, we will create users at the command prompt. We find it faster and more convenient to add and change users at the prompt than to do so using the Gnome. Table 9.5 lists some useful commands for managing users.

Creating Users

Use the useradd command to create a user. This command requires at least one parameter, the user name to be added. Several users can be added at one time. The syntax is as follows:

```
useradd username1, username2, username3
```

Changing User Passwords

Setting up a user without a password is a bad idea. The **password** proves that it is truly user brenda who is logging in. Changing a user's password involves the command passwd. Entering **passwd** without any additional parameters will let you change your password. Enter the original password and then add a user name after the command to change the password. For example, entering **passwd brenda** will change the password for the brenda account. If you are not logged in as root, you cannot change another person's password.

Table 9.5	Common User Commands
Command	**Description**
useradd	Adds a user to the system.
userdel	Removes a user from the system.
passwd	Changes a user's password.
rm	Removes files.
rmdir	Removes an empty directory.
finger	Finds a user name.

Note that selecting passwords can be difficult. Linux will force the password to be complex. No password based on a word or popular character from fiction will work. We like to use the names of bands and albums. For example, Pink Floyd's Dark Side of the Moon is a nice basis for a password. Use the first letters of each word and capitalize one word to get pfDsotm. This password is very hard to guess, and if you pick an album you like, you are unlikely to forget it.

Deleting Users

In any organization, employees leave. For security reasons, these accounts should be removed from the system shortly after the employee leaves. The command userdel allows you to remove a user from a Linux account.

The syntax for userdel is similar to that for passwd and useradd. You use this format:

```
userdel username
```

For example, you can remove the brenda account with the command **userdel brenda**.

Recall that every user gets a home folder to store his or her files. This folder is not removed when the user is deleted—you must remove these files manually. Linux does not provide a good command that handles this. You will need to delete the files in the home folder first. Then delete the folder.

> Linux does provide several switches with the rm command that should remove directories. In theory, the command **rm -fdr foldername** should remove the folder without any prompting or error. In practice, this often results in a "Directory cannot be unlinked" error message.

Step-by-Step 9.05

Deleting an Account

In this step-by-step, you will delete the account brenda.

To perform this exercise, you will need the following:

- An account on the system named brenda
- The root password

Step 1

Log in to the Linux system as root. Delete the user by entering this command: **userdel brenda**. Wait for a moment while the command executes.

Step 2

You will need to change to user brenda's folder. In a default installation of Linux, the home folder for the brenda account will be /home/brenda. Change to this folder with the command **cd /home/brenda**. Enter **pwd** to verify that you have successfully changed to user brenda's folder.

Step 3

List all of user brenda's files. Be sure to include the hidden files. Enter the command **ls -a** to see all files.

Step 4	Delete all of brenda's files. The rm command deletes files. You need to enter **rm *.*** to delete all files. Recall that * is a wildcard that stands for any character or word. Thus, *.* means "any word.any word," or any possible file in the folder. Reenter **ls -a** to verify that all files are gone. The directories . and .. should remain visible.

If the brenda folder had subfolders, you would need to change into these folders and delete all files in them as well. Once the files were deleted, you would need to delete each folder with the rmdir command. The syntax for rmdir is as follows:

```
rmdir foldername
```

In our case, the brenda folder had no subfolders, so you can move on to the last step.

Step 5	You now need to remove the home folder for brenda. To do so, you need to get to the parent folder of brenda, which is /home. Enter the command **cd /home**. List your files and verify that the brenda folder exists. To remove the folder, enter the command **rmdir brenda**. Again list your files and verify that the brenda folder is gone. Change back to your home folder by entering the command **cd**.

Configuring a Printer

The users you added to the Linux computer will need some way to print. Linux supports most modern printers. Configuring printers requires the use of a program called Printtool. Like the Add Printer wizard in Windows, Printtool allows you to select the printer and the port to which the printer is attached. *Port* is a fancy name for the plug on the back of your computer to which the printer attaches. The port for most printers is LPT1, which in Linux is represented by /dev/lp0.

Printtool is best run in the GUI. Printtool is a command-line program that starts a GUI configuration program for your printer. Before you can run Printtool, you need to open a **terminal window** in Gnome. This will allow you to enter command-line Linux commands within the GUI.

Printtool provides a wizard to help you create the printer. It asks you to describe how the printer is connected to the computer and to give the printer a name. Names are typically descriptive of the type of printer. For example, you might name your printer hp842c if you have a Hewlett-Packard 842c printer. You then pick the driver for the printer. Linux will suggest what it thinks will work. Unless you know differently, you should use the driver suggested by Linux. When the wizard finishes, you should print a test page. This verifies that your printer truly works.

Notice the path reference for LPT1. Everything in Linux is a file. Even hardware devices are treated as files.

Step-by-Step 9.06	

Adding a Printer

In this step-by-step, you will add a Hewlett-Packard 842c printer to a Linux computer. Feel free to substitute your own printer.

To complete this exercise, you will need the following:

- A Linux computer
- The root password
- A printer attached to the computer

Step 1

Log in as root and start the GUI. After the desktop loads, you will need to create the terminal window. Right-click the desktop and select New Terminal. At the prompt within the terminal window, enter the command **printtool**. After a short pause, Printtool will open. No printers have been added to this system. Click the New button at the top left of the screen to open the configuration section of Printtool. Click Next to start the configuration.

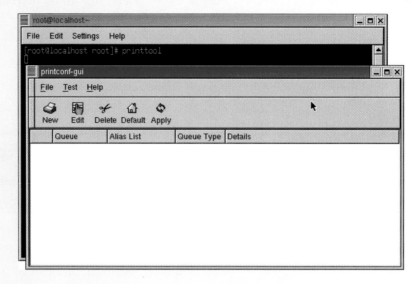

Step 2

You need to pick the type of printer. Your selection depends on the way that your printer is connected to your computer. For a printer that is directly connected to your computer, select Local. The remaining options support various networked printers. You also need to name the computer or printer to which you want to print. Unless your teacher provides different instructions, name your printer hp842c (or something similarly descriptive), select Local, and click Next.

Step 3

Linux will look on the local ports for a printer. In this example, Linux found a printer in the 840 family. In most cases, if the number reported is similar to that of the actual printer, Linux can print to the printer. Click Next to continue. If no printer is listed, then either the printer is not connected to your computer or Linux does not support it. In the second case, check the printer manufacturer's website for an update.

Step 4

After finding the printer, you need to select the print driver, which is the software that allows Linux to talk to the printer. The option preselected by Linux will most likely work. Other drivers may provide additional functionality. Keep the default selection and click Next. The last screen in the configuration step is simply a summary. Click Finish to build the printer. The green check mark means that the printer is the default printer.

Step 5

It is a good idea to test the printer to see if Linux has correctly configured it. Select the printer and choose Test | ASCII Test Page. This sends a small text document to the printer. If all is well, your printer will print. If you have a newer printer, you should also test the US Letter PostScript Testpage. This will send colors and a picture to the printer. It will also test your page borders. If either test fails, remove the printer and start again, selecting a different driver. Eventually, one will work correctly.

Installing Software

Linux, like most modern operating systems, comes loaded with several excellent applications. However, you will need to add software over time. Linux makes installing software easy. If you have installed software on a Windows computer, then you can install software on a Linux computer.

You are going to install StarOffice. StarOffice is similar to Microsoft Office and works pretty well. It includes a full-featured word processor, a spreadsheet program, a presentation program, a drawing program, and a simple database program. Best of all, it is free! StarOffice is included with the Red Hat 7.3 Personal boxed set.

As with most modern software, StarOffice is pretty simple to install. You need to select the language, decide which features to install, and then wait while the software is installed.

> Information and updates to StarOffice can be found at `www.staroffice.com` and `wwws.sun.com/software/star/staroffice`.

Step-by-Step 9.07

Installing StarOffice

The following steps will install StarOffice on your Linux computer.

To complete this exercise, you will need the following:

- A Linux computer
- The StarOffice installation CDs

Step 1

Log in as an ordinary user and start the GUI. Insert the CD and wait a moment. The CD will launch automatically, showing folders containing language choices. Select the desired language by right-clicking and opening the folder. An Adobe Acrobat PDF file describing the installation will be the first item you see. Open this file if desired and read the installation tips. Installation begins on page 9. Single-user installation is covered in Chapter 6 of the guide.

Step 2

To start the installation process, right-click the first .bin file and choose Open. After a few seconds, the installation wizard will start. Several screens will appear. Be sure to read the user license. Click Next until you get to the screen for entering your user data. Fill in the information and then click Next.

Step 3

The next screen asks you to select an installation type. If you are installing StarOffice for your own personal use and are the only user on the computer, select Single User. If you are installing from a network or from another folder on this computer, select User Install. If you are installing to a network, or if other users will use StarOffice on this computer, select Network Install. For this installation, select Single User; then click Next.

Step 4

You are prompted for the location to install the program. Since you logged in as an ordinary user, the files, by default, will be installed in a folder under your home folder. This should be okay, so click Next to continue. If you want the program installed elsewhere, browse to select the appropriate location. Linux will warn you that a folder does not exist. Click Yes to create the folder.

Step 5

StarOffice is now ready to be installed. Click Continue to start the installation. StarOffice is written in the programming language Java. Java support is nice, but not required. The No Java Support option can be chosen for StarOffice. No Java support is better for older computers. This will help the older computers run the software faster.

Step 6

Sit back and wait for several minutes while StarOffice is installed. Read the installation screens. As when you are installing Red Hat, these provide good information about the product. After StarOffice is installed, open the home icon on the desktop. Browse to office52/program. Run the program Soffice.

■ Troubleshooting Common Linux Problems

This section describes some typical problems you may encounter when using Linux and some possible solutions.

The Gnome Will Not Start

Sometimes, the Gnome will not start. Typically, the problem is an improperly selected video card or monitor. It also may not start after a new video card or monitor is added. The solution is to run the Xconfigurator program. This program will walk you through the steps to select the video card and monitor.

Fixing the Gnome

The following step-by-step will fix the video card settings on your Linux computer. You will need the following:

- A computer with Linux installed
- The Gnome installed

Step 1

Log in as root. Run the command **Xconfigurator**. You should see a screen like the one shown here. Your mouse will not work here. Use the TAB key to move around the screen. Tab to the OK button and press ENTER to move on.

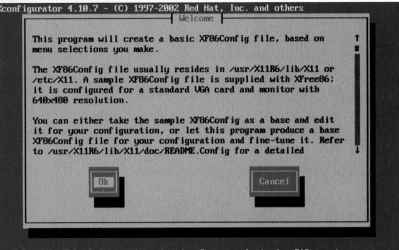

Step 2

The second screen describes what Linux found when probing your hardware. Hardware probing is similar to the process used to detect devices using plug and play in Windows. Typically, the probed settings are correct. When in doubt, go with the default. Select the video card you want to use, tab to the OK button, and press ENTER to move on.

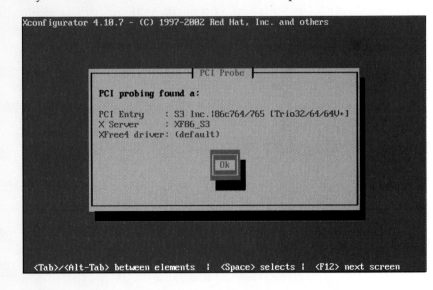

Step 3

You next need to pick the monitor type. The list is quite extensive. Pressing the first letter of your monitor type will take you to the names that begin with that letter in the alphabetical list. Select your monitor and tab to OK. Press ENTER to move to the next screen. Now choose the amount of RAM your video card has. Select the appropriate amount, tab to OK, and press ENTER.

Step 4

The last screen allows you to pick the desired resolution. Higher bit levels result in a nicer-looking screen, but slow the computer. Select what is appropriate for your computer. Then select OK and press ENTER. Xconfigurator will now test the settings. If you see the screen shown, all is well. Select Yes. If this test screen does not appear, you will see an error stating that X Windows cannot run. You will need to rerun Xconfigurator with a different set of values.

> Testing graphic mode 640x480 pixels with 16 bits per pixel
>
> Can you see this message?
>
> Automatic timeout in: 9 seconds
>
> [Yes] [No]

Step 5

When Xconfigurator finishes, you will see the following message. Select Yes to boot in graphical mode. The Gnome should now start. If you need more help, go to www.redhat.com and follow the support and document links.

> Xconfigurator can set up your computer to automatically start X upon booting. Would you like X to start when you reboot?
>
> [Yes] [No]

The Gnome Won't Start at Login

When you installed Linux, you chose to start the command line. After working with the Gnome desktop for some time, you've decided that you want to use the Gnome as the primary shell. To do so, you need to make a simple change to the /etc/inittab file.

Log in as root. Change to the /etc folder with the command **cd /etc**. Make a backup of the inittab file with the command **cp inittab oldinittab**. Now edit the file with the command **pico inittab**.

Scroll down until you find this line:

```
id:3:initdefault:
```

Replace the 3 with a 5. This forces X11 (the name for all Linux GUIs) to run at bootup. Save the file and exit pico. Restart the machine using the command **shutdown -r now**. You will now see a screen like Figure 9-11 when you log in.

I Cannot Save My File

You may sometimes see the error screen shown in Figure 9-12. Typically, this appears after you have been moving around the directory structure in Linux looking for a file. You can use pico to edit the file and then try to save it. If you are not logged in as root, then you cannot save the file anywhere but in your home folder. The solution is to use pico to change the folder.

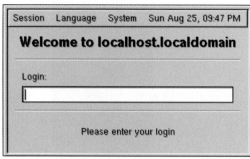

Session Language System   Sun Aug 25, 09:47 PM

Welcome to localhost.localdomain

Login:

Please enter your login

• **Figure 9-11.**   Linux login screen using the Gnome

UW PICO(tm) 4.2   File: passwd

```
root:x:0:0:root:/root:/bin/bash
bin:x:1:1:bin:/bin:/sbin/nologin
daemon:x:2:2:daemon:/sbin:/sbin/nologin
adm:x:3:4:adm:/var/adm:/sbin/nologin
lp:x:4:7:lp:/var/spool/lpd:/sbin/nologin
sync:x:5:0:sync:/sbin:/bin/sync
shutdown:x:6:0:shutdown:/sbin:/sbin/shutdown
halt:x:7:0:halt:/sbin:/sbin/halt
mail:x:8:12:mail:/var/spool/mail:/sbin/nologin
news:x:9:13:news:/var/spool/news:
uucp:x:10:14:uucp:/var/spool/uucp:/sbin/nologin
operator:x:11:0:operator:/root:/sbin/nologin
games:x:12:100:games:/usr/games:/sbin/nologin
gopher:x:13:30:gopher:/var/gopher:/sbin/nologin
ftp:x:14:50:FTP User:/var/ftp:/sbin/nologin
nobody:x:99:99:Nobody:/:/sbin/nologin
vcsa:x:69:69:virtual console memory owner:/dev:/sbin/nologin
mailnull:x:47:47::/var/spool/mqueue:/dev/null
rpm:x:37:37::/var/lib/rpm:/bin/bash
ntp:x:38:38::/etc/ntp:/sbin/nologin
          [ Cannot open file for writing: Permission denied ]
^G Get Help    ^O WriteOut    ^R Read File   ^Y Prev Pg    ^K Cut Text    ^C Cur Pos
^X Exit        ^J Justify     ^W Where is    ^V Next Pg    ^U UnCut Text  ^T To Spell
```

- **Figure 9-12.**   Error screen indicating trouble saving a file

Press CTRL-O as usual to save the file. When the file name appears, press HOME to jump to the beginning of the line. Enter the path to your home folder:

`/home/cottrell/passwd`

My Screen Displays Gibberish

Does your screen display gibberish? This error usually occurs when you head or cat a file that is not text. Figure 9-13 shows the results of entering a head command for the file a.out.

- **Figure 9-13.**   Results of entering a head command for a.out

This is not an error—it is simply the result of trying to view executable code. The code is written in a language that your CPU can understand—but you can't.

Often, after a gibberish display, your prompt and input will be messed up. Linux is now confused and displays the wrong characters. The last line of Figure 9-13 is an attempt to type **ls** at the $ prompt. The easiest way to fix this problem is to log out.

A.out is written in machine language. This is actually binary code. The reason you see characters is that some of the binary instructions in the file happen to match ASCII values.

How Do I Get Help?

Help in Linux is likely different than any help you have ever seen. The help screens provide more information than you could ever want. The motivation behind Linux help is to provide you with an answer to any possible question. You just have to have some working knowledge of the man command.

Consider the ls command. Recall that this is the Linux equivalent of the DOS dir command. The ls command has several switches that modify how it works. To get a comprehensive list, you can use the man command. Enter the command **man ls** to see a screen like Figure 9-14. Use the spacebar to move from screen to screen.

```
LS(1)                        FSF                        LS(1)

NAME
       ls - list directory contents

SYNOPSIS
       ls [OPTION]... [FILE]...

DESCRIPTION
       List information about the FILEs (the current directory by
       default).  Sort entries alphabetically if none of -cftuSUX
       nor --sort.

       -a, --all
              do not hide entries starting with .

       -A, --almost-all
              do not list implied . and ..

       -b, --escape
              print octal escapes for nongraphic characters

       --block-size=SIZE
              use SIZE-byte blocks
:
```

● **Figure 9-14.** The man page for the ls command

■ Chapter Summary

After reading this chapter and completing the Step-by-Step tutorials and Try This! exercises, you should understand the following facts about Linux:

Describe Linux Features, Benefits, and Limitations

- Linux, originally created by Linus Torvalds, is free, open-source software.
- Linux is like UNIX in stability and function.
- Many versions of Linux exist.
- Linux powers inexpensive web servers.
- Support for Linux can be spotty.
- There are fewer software packages for Linux than for Windows.

Work with Linux Commands

- The command to log out of Linux is exit.
- Linux listings provide little detail by default.
- Linux switches start with a -.
- Spaces separate every portion of a Linux command line.
- Linux is case sensitive.
- The command to shut down Linux is shutdown -h now.
- Only root can run the shutdown command.

Manage Files and Folders

- File management is crucial, particularly since everything in Linux is a file.
- pico allows you to create a text file and lets you use CTRL key combinations to perform tasks.
- The more command displays a file one screen at a time.

- The head command displays the first 10 lines of a file.
- The cp command copies files.
- The rm command deletes a file.
- Your home folder is the only place you can save files.
- The mkdir command creates folders.

Use the Gnome Desktop

- The Gnome is a version of X Windows.
- To run the Gnome, enter the command startx.

Configure Linux

- Most configurations are handled by root.
- The adduser command creates a user at the command prompt.
- The passwd command changes user passwords.
- The userdel command deletes a user, but it does not delete the associated home folder.
- The finger command displays information about a user.
- The LPT1 port is represented by the file /dev/lp0.
- Installing software in the Gnome is similar to installing software in Windows.

Troubleshoot Common Linux Problems

- Video problems are solved using the Xconfigurator.
- man is one command for help.
- Displaying a binary file results in garbage on the screen.
- You must have permission to save a file in a folder.

■ Key Terms

$ prompt *(375)*
Gnome *(388)*
GNU *(370)*
graphical user interface (GUI) *(388)*
home directory *(385)*
kernel *(370)*

Linux *(369)*
man *(378)*
password *(391)*
Red Hat Linux *(369)*
root *(375)*
root account *(375)*

StarOffice *(373)*
terminal window *(393)*
user *(371)*
X Windows *(388)*

Key Term Quiz

Use the Key Terms list to complete the sentences that follow. Not all terms will be used.

1. To access the command line in Gnome, you start a _____.

2. Gnome and KDE are examples of _____.

3. When you are logged on as a user, you enter commands at the _____.

4. When a user is created in Linux, the OS creates a _____ on disk for that user.

5. In order to log in to Linux, you need a _____ account.

6. The startx command will start the _____ GUI, provided it is installed in Linux.

7. The _____ organization was created for the purpose of developing a free UNIX-like operating system.

8. The version of Linux used in this chapter is distributed by _____.

9. The _____ will verify a user login.

10. The most powerful account in Linux is named _____.

Multiple-Choice Quiz

1. Linux is based on which operating system?
   a. Windows
   b. UNIX
   c. NT
   d. VMS
   e. CP/M

2. Which of the following are features of Linux?
   a. Fast code
   b. Very stable
   c. Runs on old computers
   d. Inexpensive
   e. All of the above

3. Who was the initial developer responsible for Linux?
   a. Ken Thompson
   b. Linus Torvalds
   c. Steve Jobs
   d. Dennis Ritchie
   e. Fred Cohen

4. Who is the user with the most power and privileges?
   a. Administrator
   b. King
   c. absolute
   d. root
   e. Linus

5. What is the command to leave Linux?
   a. exit
   b. shutdown
   c. bye
   d. log off
   e. quit

6. What is the Linux command to copy a file?
   a. cpy
   b. rm
   c. mv
   d. copy
   e. cp

7. What ls switch displays the file details?
   a. -C
   b. -m
   c. -l
   d. -a
   e. -d

8. What is the command to turn off Linux?
   a. down
   b. shutdown
   c. exit
   d. off
   e. power

9. When you are using pico, what is the key combination to save a file?

   a. CTRL-O

   b. CTRL-S

   c. CTRL-D

   d. CTRL-W

   e. CTRL-V

10. What command displays only the first 10 lines of a file?

   a. more

   b. begin

   c. tail

   d. top

   e. head

11. Ken Thompson originally wrote what became UNIX in order to run what type of application?

   a. Word processor

   b. Spreadsheet

   c. CAD/CAM

   d. Game

   e. Drawing

12. Why is Linux fast? Select all that apply.

   a. It uses few resources.

   b. It only runs on Pentium III or newer.

   c. Linux uses little or no graphics.

   d. It has no security.

   e. All of the above.

13. Which statements are true of Linux command syntax? Select all that apply.

   a. Order of switches and parameters must be strictly followed.

   b. Case is significant.

   c. The space is used as a separator on a Linux command line.

   d. Each line starts with a Linux command.

   e. Case is insignificant.

14. Why would you use the command line rather than the Gnome when you are creating and changing users?

   a. The command line is more intuitive.

   b. Gnome is too cryptic.

   c. The command line is faster.

   d. The command line is more secure.

   e. All of the above.

15. What tool is recommended for installing and configuring a printer in Linux?

   a. Control Panel

   b. Add Printer wizard

   c. Port

   d. LPT1

   e. Printtool

■ Essay Quiz

1. List and explain the reasons that Linux has not taken over the desktop OS market.

2. Discuss how Linux could be used in your school.

3. Discuss how open source can benefit an organization.

4. The Helping Hand, a charitable organization, has asked you to set up its computer systems. The organization has a very limited budget. Describe how Linux can allow users to be productive while costing very little.

5. You try to start the Gnome for the first time on your Linux computer, but it fails. Explain what you learned that may be the most likely problem and how you will resolve it. Be sure to explain how the tool you use works.

Lab Projects

• Lab Project 9.1

Linux and Windows products can share disks. You would like to back up your files to a Windows computer. In particular, you wish to copy the .bash_profile file in your home folder to a Windows computer. Use man to learn the mtools suite. Copy the .bash_profile file to a Windows computer.

• Lab Project 9.2

Use the network configuration tool in Gnome to set up a NIC for use on a LAN. You will need to create a host name, IP address, net mask, and default gateway. Your instructor will supply you with the appropriate information for your lab. If no settings are available, use the following values for a statically set IP address:

Setting	Value
Host name	Your name
Address	192.168.110.30
Net mask	266.255.255.0
Default gateway	192.168.110.29

The program is found by choosing Panel | Programs | System | Network Configuration. You will need to add an Ethernet connection.

Introduction to Network Server Operating Systems

> *"In all large corporations, there is a pervasive fear that someone, somewhere is having fun with a computer on company time. Networks help alleviate that fear."*
>
> —John C. Dvorak

Why connect your PC to a network? As an analogy, consider the Florida Keys, a chain of islands off the tip of Florida. Only a century ago, each key truly was an island, surrounded by ocean. The only way trade could occur between islands, or with the mainland, was by boat. Commerce and the exchange of ideas among people could occur only slowly, and island economies grew very slowly. Then, in the early 1900s, a railway was built connecting many of the islands. People and goods could move much more rapidly between the islands and the mainland. That railway, and today's highway, became the link that made the islands part of a "network." Computer users, too, can vastly improve their effectiveness by understanding and taking advantage of today's networks.

In this chapter, we'll explore the basics of networking, starting with an overview of the hardware and software components and the purposes served by network server operating systems. We'll examine a simple classification of networks based on geography along with some network administration considerations. Then we'll consider the various roles computers play on a network, and we'll see that there are many ways to be "served" on a network. Finally, we'll explore the common roles of network servers, both on private networks and on the Internet; and the server operating systems that support these roles.

In this chapter, you will learn how to:

- Explain the basic concepts of networking
- Describe the dominant server operating systems
- Describe the common roles of network servers
- Protect network resources

■ Basics of Networking

If you connect two or more PCs using communications media, you have a computer network, but why would you want to connect computers? We'll look at the main reasons for creating networks and then examine networks classified by geography and by administrative model. We'll wrap up with a discussion of the components of a network.

Why Network PCs?

Why network PCs? If you think of a stand-alone PC as being like an island without any connection to the rest of the world, you can immediately see how limited it is. You can't reach out through the computer and over the network to access data on other computers, you can't browse the Internet to research your school project, and you can't buy things from far-away places. For these reasons, the vast majority of the world's PCs have the ability to join and become part of a computer network. The reasons for connecting computers are to share resources, to communicate, and to manage network resources. We discuss all three in turn.

Sharing Resources

We asked our friend Avtar if he knew what computers actually share over a network, and he gave a very common answer: data. To an extent, that's true, but the broader answer, and what makes today's computer networks so powerful, is that networks allow individual computers to share network resources. A **network resource** is anything that can be shared over a network.

It's the ability for a user at one computer to access a resource on another computer that makes today's computing so powerful. A resource is not simply, or only, data. Resources include objects such as files and folders, of course, but resources also include physical entities, such as modems, printers, CD and DVD player/recorders, and backup devices. Resources also include services, such as e-mail and fax. You can even sit in front of one PC and take over and control the function of another PC on the network.

The most important word here is *share*. A user at a networked PC can share a file folder, printer, or other resource with other computers and access the resources of other network computers as well. When a PC's resources are shared, it is offering a service to other computers on the network. At that moment, it is a **server**. When a user at a PC accesses a share on other networked computers, that user's computer is a **client** to the service offered by the other computer. So a PC can be both server and client at the same time. Without a network, each PC is just an island, something that is not generally desirable in computing today.

> Remember that the word *share* is both a verb and a noun. This has been a source of confusion for one of the authors. Computers *share* resources. A *share* is the point at which one computer can access the resources of another. Don't confuse these two uses of the term!

Communicating

People can communicate over a network using a variety of methods on both privately owned networks and the Internet. These include electronic mail (e-mail), list servers, newsgroups, and chat rooms. All of these methods allow electronic messages to pass between people. Some allow you the immediacy of a real-time conversation (similar to a phone conversation), and others send messages to you or post them in a place where you can read them. You can even communicate in real time and face to face using video conferencing. Here are some of the more common communication methods.

E-mail   The most common network communication method by far is electronic mail. E-mail works much like ordinary mail. You create a message and address it to the intended recipient. Then, however, rather than depositing it in a mail box, you send it through your computer to a special server that acts like your local post office, directing the mail to the recipient or to the correct address of another post office that can deliver the message to the recipient user. To send and receive e-mail, you need e-mail client software and an account with an e-mail service, which gives you an address, such as *yourname@domainname.ext*, where *yourname* is your unique identifier in that mail service. Your e-mail service may be at your school, your Internet service provider (ISP), or your place of work.

E-Mail Discussion Lists (List Servers)   You may have visited a website on a topic that interests you. Perhaps it is a site for collectors of nineteenth-century high-top shoes, and you happen to be an avid collector of these treasures. You decide you'd like to join the site's **discussion list**, so you sign up and give the site your e-mail address. Now you receive e-mail containing discussions of high-top shoes. If you respond to a discussion, the list server broadcasts your response to the entire discussion list. To participate in a discussion list through an Internet-based list server, you need only Internet access and e-mail. Because they are e-mail based, the discussions are not in real time.

> List server is the generic name for a server that manages e-mail discussion lists. Sometimes people incorrectly use the term *listserv* when referring generically to list servers. Listserv, by L-Soft International, is the name of a commercial product that is used on many list servers. A popular freeware list server is Majordomo.

Newsgroups   A **newsgroup** is an online discussion group. It differs from an e-mail discussion list in that it stores discussion messages on a server so that participants can view the messages online and choose to participate. This discussion can take place in real time or nearly real time, when participants are online and connected to the server. Participants can also choose to connect when they want to catch up on the discussions and add their comments. A discussion in a newsgroup consisting of an initial message and the subsequent responses is called a **thread**.

A newsgroup is a step up from a list server, requiring more administration on the news server, which is the server side of a newsgroup. Traditionally, newsgroup participation has required special software on the client side called a news reader, but many news servers now offer the option of using your Internet browser to participate. This allows you to connect to

---

Try This!

Learn More About List Servers

Connect to an online technical encyclopedia, such as Webopedia, and read more about list servers. Then find list servers on two of your favorite topics. You will need a computer with Internet access. Try this:

1. Use your Internet browser to connect to www.webopedia.com or another online encyclopedia. Find the Search option and search on **List Server** and read the definition.

2. Research the definition of a mailing list, either by clicking a link to Mailing List on the page in the previous step or by searching on **Mailing List**. Notice the distinction between a mailing list on a list server and one you might use from your e-mail client, such as Outlook, Outlook Express, or Eudora.

3. Find a list server on a topic of interest to you. To do this, use an Internet search engine such as Google (www.google.com) and search on **List Server** *Topic*. For instance, we searched on List Server Vanagon to find a list server for Volkswagen Vanagon owners. Notice the directions for joining the list and always check for instructions on leaving a list.

---

the newsgroup from any computer that has an Internet browser, but it does not give you all of the features that may come with news reader client software, such as the ability to store messages. Outlook Express has a news reader. There are literally millions of special interest newsgroups on the Internet. A search of `www.google.com` on **Newsgroup** produced 2.5 million results.

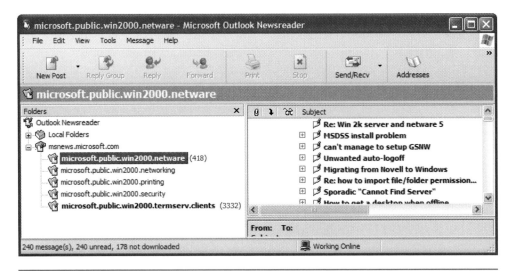

• Microsoft Outlook Newsreader showing one news server and several newsgroups.

Chat Rooms   Unlike a newsgroup, a **chat room** is a virtual room on the Internet where communication sessions called chats do take place in real time, much as in a face-to-face conversation. A search on `www.google.com` using the term **Chat Room** resulted in 2.6 million results.

Client-Server Networks

In a client-server network, the resources are stored on one or more servers. Users at PCs use client software that requests services from appropriate server software on the servers. The client software running on the PCs performs all tasks necessary to request the resources and work with them locally. The server side performs all of the necessary processing on the server to provide the requested services. In this way, processing is distributed.

Centralized Management of Network Resources

Placing resources on networks has led to the need for centralized management of those resources. Network resource management can involve many different tasks. These tasks include making a resource, such as a file folder, available on the network. On a Microsoft Windows network, this is called creating a **share**. A related task is applying the necessary security to network resources. Additional tasks include centralizing data backup and performing myriad other tasks for managing data and physical resources on a network.

Security for One Server In the beginning, network security existed only on the individual server computers on the LAN. Each server had a database of accounts used by its security components to grant access to users wanting to connect to the server. In a server-based security database, an account was (and still is) a listing of information about a user or group or users. You had to have an **account** on that server to connect and to prove that you were the owner of the account for which you provided the user name and password. If what you provided matched the user name and password of an account on that server, you were allowed access. This process of proving who you are is called **authentication**, and it is fundamental to computer security.

Further, each resource you accessed contained a permissions list, and once you were authenticated, your account had to be checked against the list for that resource. If your account was included in this permissions list, you were granted access, but only at the level defined in the permissions list for that resource. This process of confirming what permissions you have for a resource is called **authorization**, and it is also fundamental to computer security.

Share permissions are available in all versions of Windows studied in this book. Share permissions apply only to users accessing a folder as a share via the network. Share permissions can be Full Control, Change, or Read.

File and folder permissions are available only on NTFS volumes and, therefore, only in versions of Windows that support NTFS. File and folder permissions affect both the local, interactive user and those who access the files or folders through a share via the network. These permissions are more complicated than share permissions. File and folder permissions each include a set of standard permissions. The standard permissions are, in turn, composed of combinations of special permissions.

This security model is still used. Figure 10-1 shows the permissions for a network resource, a shared folder called sales, on a Windows 2000 Server. The server is named NAPAVALLEY. The users, Juanita Estevez and Sarah Brown, have accounts in the server's security accounts database, and they have been granted permissions for this share. As the figure shows, Sarah has only Read permission.

Security for Many Servers The biggest problem with the single or autonomous server model was that it didn't scale well for a large multiple-server scenario. What worked in a network with a single server didn't work well in a network with hundreds of servers because you (the user) had to have an account on each server you wanted to access. Even if you used the same user name and password in each account, you still had to go through an authentication process. Today, server security has grown beyond the single-server security model to more centralized models that allow users a single logon to access all network resources.

> Online discussion groups are also called forums. This term covers newsgroups and other online discussion groups that don't require a news reader to participate. See a list of discussion groups on Google by clicking the Groups link on the Google home page.

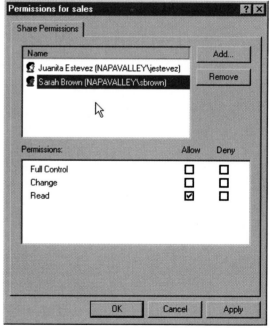

● **Figure 10-1.** Windows folder sharing

Cross Check

NTFS Folder and File Permissions

Review the NTFS folder and file permissions in Chapter 6. Then answer the following questions:

1. List the standard NTFS file permissions in Windows 2000.

   _____

2. How do the standard NTFS folder permissions differ from the standard NTFS file permissions?

   _____

3. You need to assign the modify folder permissions to an account. When you do this in Windows 2000 what other standard permissions are also selected?

   _____

Inside Information

A SAM by Any Other Name...

The local security accounts database on an individual Windows server is called the SAM—short for Security Accounts Manager (go figure!). This is also the name of the component that manages this database. In addition, Microsoft desktop OSs in the Windows NT family also have a local SAM. These OSs include Windows NT Workstation (all versions), Windows 2000 Professional, Windows XP Professional, and Windows XP Home. A SAM database and service was also used in Windows NT domain controllers. Windows 2000 domain controllers use a much more sophisticated system for an Active Directory domain.

Novell and Microsoft started working on separate solutions to this problem in the late 1980s. Microsoft's first solution was the Windows NT domain, which used the same SAM accounts database and is now used only on single servers and desktops. In a Windows NT domain, you see only a logon dialog box when you log on to the domain. Then, when you attempt to connect to a server that is a member of the domain, a service on your computer presents your user name and password to the member server, which passes this information through to a domain controller to authenticate you. You won't even know that this pass-through authentication is happening unless it fails and you receive an error message.

The Windows NT model had some problems, one being that the SAM accounts database had a practical size limit of 40MB, and therefore a single domain could not contain all the accounts required for a very large organization. Many network professionals agreed that what was needed for a large networking environment was a **directory service**, which is a network service that can manage all types of network resources.

In 1994, while Microsoft was still offering the NT Windows model as the answer to multiserver networks, Novell introduced NetWare 4.0 with its NetWare Directory Services (NDS), a true directory service based on the X.500 standard. Novell has continued to improve and upgrade NDS in its NetWare products.

In 2000, Microsoft introduced its first true directory service product: Active Directory (AD). When a Windows 2000 Server is converted to the role of domain controller, it becomes an AD domain controller, which can contain millions of objects in its hierarchical database. Microsoft has continued to improve its directory service in Windows .Net Server 2003 and with additional services and applications that work with Active Directory.

Any server participating in one of these services uses the central accounts database for authentication before allowing users to access its resources, and it also uses these central accounts to assign permissions for the local resources to users and groups. This was true of the Windows NT domain model as well as the directory service models. The biggest difference is AD's ability to manage larger numbers of objects and more types of objects.

Data Backup Networks were not always an easy sell to managers. Some just didn't see the need to spend the money to connect PCs for the sake of sharing data. However, even these holdouts were eventually convinced to approve a LAN installation by being told about the benefits of centralized backups. With a network, all users can save their data to a server. Then, at the end of the day, the data files on the server can be backed up to tape.

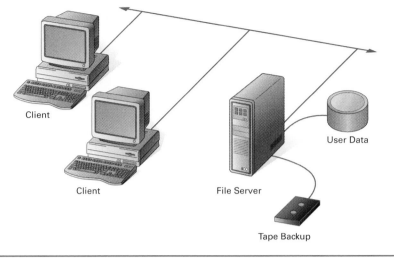

Client

Client

File Server

User Data

Tape Backup

- Centralized backup is superior to the methods used before networks.

Networks, Small to Large

Today, network boundaries seem blurred, especially to the casual user. However, networks can still be classified by size and geography. These traditional classifications include local-area networks (LANs), metropolitan-area networks (MANs), and wide-area networks (WANs).

LANs

A LAN is geographically the smallest type of computer network. It is two or more computers connected by communications media in a small geographical area. That could be a room, a floor of a building, an entire building, or a business or academic campus all connected with a common network technology, and usually at the fastest speeds. We talk about LAN speeds in terms of millions of bits per second or even billions of bits per second, as in 10 Mbps, 100 Mbps, and 1 Gbps. These translate to 10 megabits, 100 megabits, and 1 gigabit (billion bits) per second.

MANs

A MAN is a network that covers a metropolitan area, usually using high-speed fiber-optic cable (operating in the gigabits-per-second range). Although people tend to be less aware of MANs, they exist nonetheless. In fact, a MAN may well be somewhere between you and the Internet. A MAN allows a community of LANs to connect to each other and to the Internet.

Theoretically, all of an organization's data (e-mail, customer lists, inventory, and so on) can be stored in a directory service database. All that is needed is software that knows how to store, manage, and retrieve data from the directory service. This is why Microsoft and Novell each want its particular directory service solution to become the central network service for organizations.

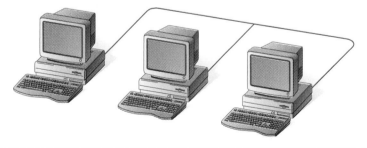

- Local-area network (LAN)

The speed of your communications on any network is a function of the speed of the slowest pathway between you and the servers you are accessing. The weakest link determines your speed.

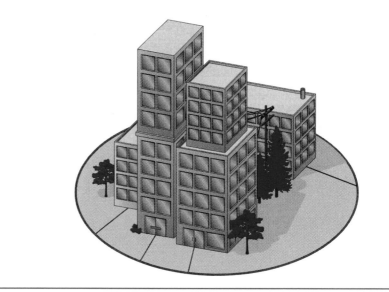

• Metropolitan-area network (MAN)

WANs

A WAN is the largest type of network. It is defined as two or more networks connected over long distances using phone lines or satellite communications. The generic term for such connected networks is an **internetwork**. The most famous and largest of these is the Internet.

WAN speeds range from thousands of bits per second up into the low millions of bits per second range. At the low end today are 56-Kbps modems (56,000 bits per second). At the high end of WAN speeds are parts of the Internet backbone, the connecting infrastructure of the Internet, which runs in the hundreds of millions of bits per second, and may be even faster at this point.

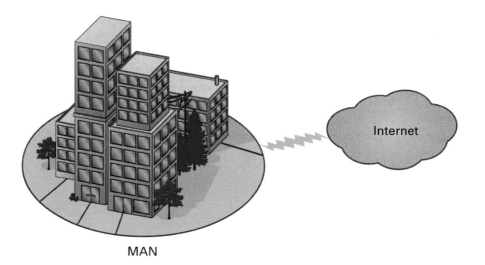

• Wide-area network (WAN)

Logical Network Organization

How the computers on a network are organized for administration, where data is stored, and where the programs you are using actually run are functions of the logical organization of your network. There are two ways to organize a network: using peer-to-peer and server-based arrangements.

Peer-to-Peer Networks

In a peer-to-peer logical network organization, data and other resources are distributed around the network among the PCs that are connected to the network—the same computers that sit on the users' desktops. More important, there is no central authority responsible for security. Our accountant, Tom, has a peer-to-peer network in his office. There are five PCs sitting on the desktops of the two accountants and the three staff members. The most important files are in a share on Tom's computer. Another set of files are in a share on Carrie's computer. Two shared printers are connected to two other computers on the network.

At each PC hosting a resource, an administrator must make that individual resource available as a share, and that computer is considered an equal, or peer, of all others. In addition to taking steps to allow a folder or printer to be shared on the network, the administrator has to consider security needs and take whatever steps are necessary and possible to give access to a file or printer only to those who should have access. In Microsoft networks, a solely peer-to-peer network is called a **workgroup**. Microsoft does not recommend a workgroup of more than 10 computers because of the administrative headaches involved in managing the accounts, shares, and permissions on more than 10 systems.

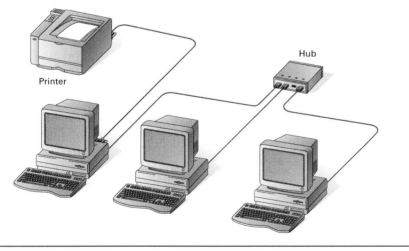

* Peer-to-peer network

Server-Based Networks

The most common administrative organization for PC networks is a server-based arrangement, where each PC on a network interacts with one or more servers. The servers provide a central place for keeping and controlling the resources. The servers are dedicated to providing network services

Inside Information

Did Someone Say 10 Gigabit?
Ten-gigabit networks have been in the works for several years, with test networks installed by various organizations in LAN, MAN, and WAN implementations. In the summer of 2002, the IEEE ratified a new standard for 10-gigabit Ethernet, 802.3ae. Now that there is a new standard, if you browse the websites of network vendors such as Cisco and 3COM, you'll start to see more 10-gigabit network products. Cisco had products listed before the ratification of the new standard. However, in small LANs 10 Mbps and 100 Mbps are still adequate. Learn more at the 10 Gigabit Ethernet Alliance website, at www.10gea.org. *Warning! The whitepapers at this site are very technical—not exactly light Saturday afternoon reading.*

and are not used as desktop computers. Computers that connect to a server must have appropriate software to access the resources of the server. This software is called client software. A Microsoft server-based network with central administration is called a domain.

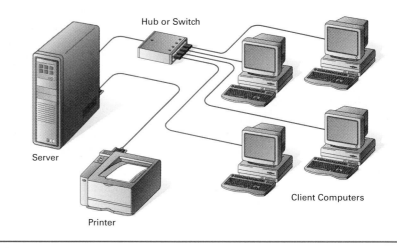

• Server-based network

Hybrid Networks

But wait—because any given network can include a combination of all of the things we've talked about, dividing the network world into peer-to-peer and server-based networks really isn't accurate either. Any given network can have various combinations of peer-to-peer and server-based arrangements and thus be a hybrid. For instance, all current Microsoft desktop operating systems already include the service that allows each computer to share its files and printers. This service can be enabled, even if you are in a server-based network, and your desktop computers can share resources much as they would in a strictly peer-to-peer network. In a Microsoft Windows domain (either type), an administrator of one of these desktop "servers" can assign permissions for local network resources to accounts in the domain database.

Step-by-Step 10.01

Peer-to-Peer or Server-Based Network?

In this step-by-step exercise, you will use the OS to determine whether your class lab is on a network, and you'll look for clues that tell you whether it is peer-to-peer, server-based, or both. Yes, we do know that you could just walk around and look at the back of each computer for physical proof that it is or isn't

on a network, but let's see if you can determine that status through your OS.

To complete this step-by-step exercise, you will need a lab computer running Windows or Linux (the illustrations show Windows XP).

Step 1

As you log on to your computer, take a close look at the Log On to Windows dialog box. If the Log On To pull-down menu gives you a domain on which to log on, then you have access to a network. If the only choice is to log on to your computer, rather than to a domain, your computer may be part of a peer-to-peer network.

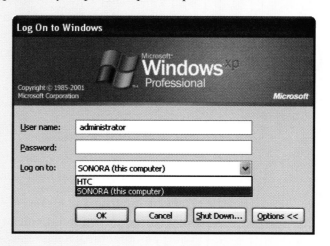

Step 2

If you couldn't determine if your computer was on a network in the previous step, open My Network Places. If you are able to see file and print servers on your network, then you know you're on a network. Remember that this service is turned on by default in the current versions of Windows.

Step 3

Now determine if you're connected to a server-based network. Open My Network Places and look for a computer that you know to be a dedicated server. In the illustration below, we can see a computer, HTC1, which we know is a dedicated server. The computer SONORA is running Windows Professional and doesn't qualify as a dedicated server.

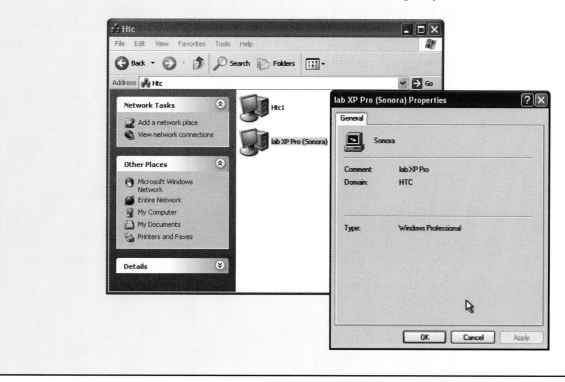

Network Pieces and Parts

So what are the pieces and parts that make up a network? Obviously, there are PCs, but there are many other components as well. Some components are physical, like the hardware used inside a PC that connects it to the network, the media (wires, or broadcast and receiving antennas in the case of wireless) that make the connections work, and the connection points the communications media connects to—the nodes. Yet other components include the software that makes everything work together—the drivers, network operating systems (NOSs), and services—and the protocols. Let's build your understanding of basic network theory by examining these pieces.

Physical Components

There are several types of hardware components that connect your computer to the network and that connect networks to other networks.

Network Interface and Media   Let's start with the computer in front of you, called a **node** when it is connected to a network. To connect to a network, your computer must have a network interface, which is a device that sends and receives signals over the network media. The network interface to connect to a LAN is an integrated circuit card installed in your computer called a network interface card (NIC). The network interface device for a dial-up connection to a network is a modem (*mo*dulator/*dem*odulator). Whatever the device, it must be able to work with the specific media of your network. A wireless device must have a NIC with antennas for sending and receiving radio frequency (RF) signals.

The media carries the signals between devices on the network. In the beginning, of course, network media was metal wire (think telephone cable), and the vast majority of it in developed countries still is. But other media work well for specific needs and are gaining ground rapidly. Optical signals are fed through fiber-optic cables, which, though still cable, is made of glass instead of metal. Fiber-optic media can transmit data much faster than wire-based media. The media that is getting a lot of attention lately are the radio or infrared signals transmitted to receivers. This wireless media makes physical connection unnecessary. These different media all do essentially the same thing: they carry data bits from one place to another.

Other Network Connection Devices   So what else is needed to make a network work, in addition to the network connection devices in each computer and the media? A number of other network devices are required to move data between computers and between connected networks. They include the following:

- Network **hubs** and **switches** that the media from each node connects to.
- Network devices called routers that carry traffic from network to network.
- Network security devices, especially firewalls. A firewall is a hardware component that is usually placed at the point where a private network (or group of networks) connects to a public, untrusted, network, the Internet. A firewall works to prevent unauthorized access to computers and data on a network.

Software Components

The software components that make it possible to use a computer network include drivers, network operating systems, and services.

Drivers You need a software driver to allow your OS to control the network interface device (NIC or modem). Most NICs or modems come with software drivers for several different OSs. If your interface device does not have a driver for your OS, you should check the manufacturer's website or the Microsoft website.

Network Operating Systems (NOSs) A network operating system (NOS) contains the basic program code that allows your computer to communicate on a network. Other software components are installed in the NOS to provide network access. The term *NOS* had more meaning when the OS and NOS were separate programs, or were even from different vendors. In the 1980s, a desktop computer usually ran DOS, and you added a NOS to connect to a network. In all Microsoft OSs since Windows for Workgroups, the OS and the NOS are combined. This is also true of the Mac OSs and the many flavors of UNIX. You can use the term NOS to refer to OSs that are designed primarily to function as network servers.

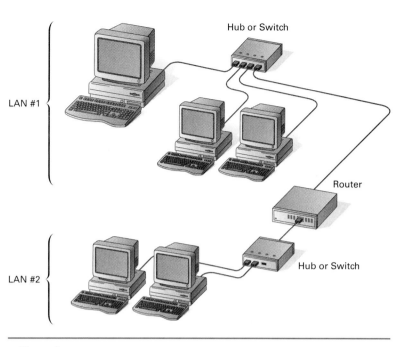

• Network components

Services Services are individual programs that provide a certain function or set of functions and are usually active behind the scenes. Each Windows OS has many services that provide both network and non-network functions. Figure 10-2 shows a partial list of services on a Windows XP computer. The workstation service enables your computer to access the network shares as a client, and the server service allows a computer to provide basic server services such as file and print sharing. Another service, Netlogon, sends your authentication request from your PC to a server, when you log on to a Windows domain.

• **Figure 10-2.** Windows XP services

Try This!

Learn More About Network Devices

Research network devices on the Internet. Try this:

1. Download and watch a superb movie at `www.warriorsofthe.net` that shows dramatically how a network operates. It requires broadband access and a multimedia PC. The full movie is 12.6 minutes long and requires downloading a 78MB, 118MB, or 148MB file, depending on the quality you want to see. There is also a 55-second trailer available in 5MB and 10MB versions
2. Use a technical dictionary or encyclopedia to find the following definitions. If you don't have one handy, check out these Internet sites: `www.webopedia.com` and `www.techweb.com/encyclopedia`.

    a. Router

    ____

    b. Hub

    ____

    c. Firewall

    ____

    d. Switch

    ____

Protocols

Because there are so many kinds of media, and so many kinds of network devices, and so many ways of arranging nodes in a network, some agreed-upon rules are needed that each component has to follow for the network to function correctly. These rules are called **protocols**. There are many, many different protocols and different kinds, or levels, of protocols. Some apply directly to the way that data is placed on the hardware; these are often called transport protocols. Other protocols, called communications protocols, work at a level above the hardware. Communications protocols depend on the hardware, but are not concerned with how the hardware works.

Of course, someone has to pay attention to the hardware protocols, at least to ensure that your network hardware devices can connect your computer to the network and can communicate with the other devices on the network. For instance, there are certain wireless network devices that comply with different standards and cannot communicate with each other.

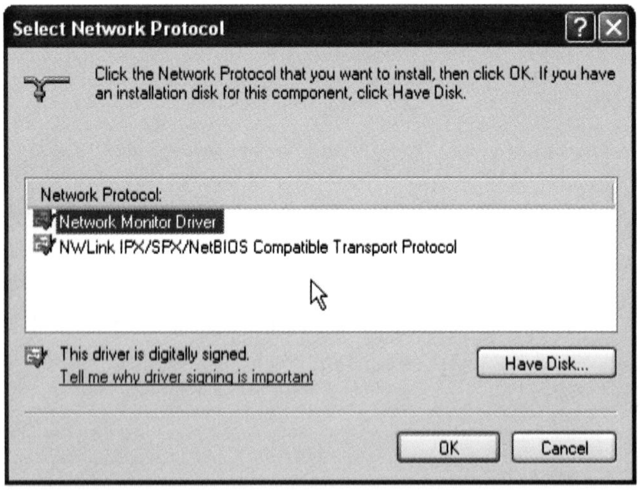

• **Figure 10-3.** Select Network Protocol dialog box

Common Protocol Suites Communication protocols are usually combined into suites that work together. The most common protocol suite on networks today is TCP/IP, but other network protocol suites are still in use in small- to medium-sized departmental LANs. These include Microsoft's NetBEUI (very rarely used today), Apple's AppleTalk (replaced in newer versions of the Mac OS by TCP/IP), and Novell's IPX/SPX, which still has a greater presence than the other two, but is also being replaced with TCP/IP. Windows 2000 and Windows XP install TCP/IP by default, but there are other protocols that you can optionally install, as shown in Figure 10-3. To see this dialog box in Windows XP, click Install on the General page of the Local Area Connection Properties dialog box, and then select Protocol, and click Add.

Protocols for Network Printers In Windows 2000 and earlier versions of Windows, you may also see DLC, a very old network protocol used for PC-to-mainframe connections and also used by Hewlett-Packard for its printers that connected directly to a network. Most network printers today use TCP/IP.

An Apple Among Oranges Although Network Monitor Driver is listed in the protocol list, it is simply a driver that enables your computer to monitor network traffic. You would install it on your desktop computer only if your network administrator needs it to collect information about your network using a program called Network Monitor that runs on Windows servers.

NWLink IPX/SPX/NetBIOS Compatible Transport Protocol is Microsoft's version of Novell's IPX/SPX protocol.

■ Dominant Network Server Operating Systems

A network operating system (NOS) is an operating system that provides basic network services. Most network servers in use today—on both private and public networks—have modular software components. The server administrators select the services needed and install them in the NOS. The services may or may not be from the same vendor as the NOS. The underlying NOS will be a server product from Microsoft or Novell or will be a variant of UNIX. In the following sections, we explore basic server concepts and the NOSs available today.

Basic Server Concepts

A server is a computer on a network that provides a service to other computers. A client is a software component on a computer that accesses the service of a server. The first service provided in early LANs, and still in use even today, is the service that allows a server to provide access to its local files to users over the network.

One problem with understanding networking is the somewhat ambiguous nature of the terminology. Let's go back to the concept of resource sharing. When we discuss sharing, we have to ask who does the sharing, and who just accesses the resource. To make the answer a little less ambiguous, we use the terms *server* and *client*.

Any system that wants to share its resources must run a program or service that does the sharing. At that instant, the system is a server. Any system that wants to access resources must run a program that does the accessing. At that instant, the system is a client. In a peer-to-peer network, each system must have both client and server software available. All current versions of Windows desktop OSs are capable of playing both roles simultaneously. Thus, the role of server is not limited to powerful computer systems with vast resources, although that is the common perception. In fact, any computer connected to a network may play many roles at once.

This leads us to the topic of the complexity of network servers. Network servers offer many, many services, but most of these services run on top of one of a handful of network operating systems from Microsoft, Novell, or any of several UNIX vendors.

Windows NT/2000/.Net Server Operating Systems

Microsoft has several server operating system products under each of their major Windows versions. The major server versions in use today include Windows NT 4.0 and Windows 2000. Windows .Net Server 2003 is the latest version, with a 2003 release date.

Windows NT 4.0

Although not truly a current product, Windows NT 4.0 is still running on many servers. Its server products include the Server and Enterprise editions. The first is a general-purpose server used for file and print services and as a domain controller in small- to medium-sized organizations; the second is designed for larger network servers and came only as an OEM product preinstalled on servers.

Windows 2000

There are three Windows 2000 Server products: Windows 2000 Server, Windows 2000 Advanced Server, and Windows 2000 Datacenter Server. In capability, these translate to medium, large, and jumbo. Windows 2000 Server is the base server operating system for network file, print, intranet, and application servers. Windows 2000 Advanced Server is targeted at line-of-business applications, e-commerce, and web servers. It can use more processors (up to eight) and more memory (up to 8GB) than its smaller sibling, which can use only half of these resources. Both of these are available as separate retail products, even though Advanced Server is effectively an upgrade to Windows NT 4.0 Enterprise Edition, and the third Windows 2000 Server product, Windows 2000 Datacenter Server, is available only in OEM versions on very high-end servers with up to 32 processors and up to 64GB of memory. This version is targeted at very large data warehousing, econometric analysis, science and engineering applications, and very large websites.

UNIX/Linux Server Operating Systems

The many versions of UNIX are growing in popularity within organizations. UNIX has long been the server OS of choice for hosting certain network infrastructure services, such as DNS and DHCP services on the Internet and within many organizations. UNIX-based systems also are used most often to run Apache Server software, developed by the Apache Software Foundation (www.apache.org). Apache Server software is reported to be on as much as 60 percent of all web servers. Running these various services gives UNIX a huge presence on the Internet.

Windows .Net Server 2003 includes four products: Standard Server, Enterprise Server, Datacenter Server, and Web Server.

Novell Server Operating Systems

Novell's NetWare server OS dominated the LAN server market in the 1980s but declined in the 1990s. Novell introduced Novell Directory Services in its NetWare 4.0 product in 1984, years ahead of Microsoft's introduction of competing directory services in Windows 2000. Novell still is an important server OS vendor, bringing out new versions of NetWare and developing and improving the services that run on its server OSs. At this writing, Novell's latest version is NetWare 6.0, but there are still organizations running 10-year-old NetWare 3.12 servers.

Common Roles of Network Servers

Think of all of the reasons for using a network, and you'll find that there's a server role for each reason. Early LAN networking, in the 1980s, focused on file and printer sharing because hard drives and printers were expensive, and it was worth connecting computers to share. Today there are many additional server roles, on both private intranets and on the Internet. One physical server computer may be dedicated to a single role, or it may play a combination of roles. These roles sometimes come in the form of elaborate services, such as e-mail, that can be added to a network operating system, in which case, the service is an extra-cost option not built into the server OS. The source of an added service may be the same vendor as the OS or a third-party vendor. In the following sections, we look at just a few of the many roles that servers play in today's networks.

File and Print Servers

When you're using a computer at school or work, do you save the word processing, spreadsheet, graphics, and other data files to a network server? A computer that allows you to connect to it to store files is a file server. Do you access a printer connected to the network? A server that gives you access to a network printer is a print server. These two roles are often combined and performed by the same server. In Microsoft networking, this combined service is called File and Printer Sharing for Microsoft Networks. The client side is called Client for Microsoft Networks.

- File and Printer Sharing for Microsoft Networks

Mail Servers

In the early days of PC networks, the basic information sharing need was satisfied by file and printer sharing. The electronic delivery and management of messages within most large private and governmental organizations was already the turf of the mainframe systems. However, as LAN networks proliferated and became more reliable and more interconnected, communication of messages within organizations was gradually moved from the larger systems to servers on these networks. A server that transmits, receives, and stores e-mail is called a mail server. The messages transmitted electronically are called e-mail.

Today, in addition to the mail servers within organizations, there are many Internet-based mail servers. Most people can communicate via e-mail seamlessly both within organizations and over the Internet. In fact, for many individuals, e-mail is the most compelling reason to have Internet access from home. In the 1980s, we subscribed to an Internet messaging service (CompuServe), but found that we received only infrequent messages from a few other technical people. Today, we conduct most of our business by Internet e-mail and stay in touch with many family members connected to the Internet in addition to our technical and business associates.

In a Microsoft network, the e-mail server is Exchange; in a NetWare environment, it is GroupWise. Both of these products do much more than simply manage e-mail.

Data Backup Servers

Centralized data backup has long been an important network service. For real data safety, the data is frequently put on removable media (tape, disk, and so on) and stored somewhere safely away from the computer. In the simplest scenario, users save all of their data to one or more network servers.

Each server is then backed up nightly. This moves the backup task from the desktop to the server room. A small organization may have a tape backup system on each server, but things can become messy as the number of servers grows. There are several vendors who sell centralized backup systems that use a dedicated backup server, large tape archiving systems, and specialized client software that runs on each computer that has its data backed up to the central backup server. Just a few of these vendors are Novastor, Syncsort, and Computer Associates. Most major vendors have backup services that run on Windows (various versions), Novell, and UNIX OSs.

There are also a large number of Internet-based backup services that allow subscribers to back up data over the Internet to their servers. Some of the vendors who sell backup software have added Internet backup services to their list of products. Just a few of these vendors are CapSure, Connected, Xdrive, Clunk Click, and 1stForData.

Try This!

Find a Backup Service

You are looking for an Internet-based backup service to back up the 15 desktop computers in a small office. Look for a service that will allow you to back up 5GB of data from each computer nightly. Try this:

1. Use your web browser to connect to www.connected.com. Search the site for a product that will work for your office. Find the cost of subscribing for 15 computers. Look for a free trial version of the product you want to try.

   _____

2. Repeat Step 1 using the www.xdrive.com website.

   _____

3. Repeat Step 1 using the www.novastor.com website.

   _____

4. Repeat Step 1 using the www.1stfordata.com website.

   _____

Application Servers

An application server is a program that acts as an intermediary between users running client software and a large back-end business application or database. The client-side component can be a simple web browser on a minimally configured network computer called a **thin client** that may not even have a hard disk. This model is replacing the client-server application, in which a more robust, or "fat," client was required to connect to and interact with the server application. Another Internet-based service now is provided by application service providers (ASPs), which manage application servers for many customers from a central location.

Web Servers

Web servers are found on the Internet, hosting millions of web pages. They are also found on private networks, replacing file servers in some cases. Some content that was previously made available to employees and students on file servers, or even on physical bulletin boards and in-house publications, is now published on the company intranet. An intranet is a private internal network using Internet technologies, such as web servers.

For many years, users connecting to the Internet could see only text content. There were no graphical pages such as we now see on the Web. The Internet existed, but not the Web. People often think that the Internet and the Web are simply different names for the same thing. They are not. The Web uses the Internet, but it uses its own protocols.

The Web came about thanks to the efforts of Tim Berners-Lee, a communications and text-handling expert who worked in the CERN physics laboratory in Geneva, Switzerland. He sought to help physicists from around the world as they collaborated on projects. He is credited with designing the hypertext markup language (HTML), the "killer technology" that made the World Wide Web possible. This is the language of the World Wide Web. The pages you view on the Web with your browser are written in this language, which your browser transfers to your computer using the Hypertext Transfer Protocol (HTTP) and then interprets the text commands on the page into the graphical elements you see on your screen. A URL for a web page includes "http" to show the browser the protocol required to connect to the page to which the URL points. In this book, we usually omit the protocol prefix, because your browser will attempt to use the HTTP protocol by default.

■ Sharing and Protecting Resources

Effective sharing and protection of network resources is always carefully planned. In a medium- to large-sized organization, this plan is developed taking into consideration the work processes, company goals, user needs, and a host of other issues. The person who implements this plan is the administrator. In this section, we look at some of the tasks of the administrator who must implement the plan for sharing and protecting network resources. Our perspective is that of a Windows Active Directory domain administrator who depends on Windows 2000 servers. The server-side tasks include adding a computer to a domain, creating user accounts and groups, and creating file and print shares. The client-side tasks include connecting to resources and testing the network security.

Adding Computers to a Microsoft Domain

A Windows Active Directory domain has several types of security accounts. A security account is one to which permissions and rights can be assigned. There are security accounts for computers, users, and groups. A computer account actually has a password it provides when it logs on to the domain (yes, computers log on, too), and when it connects to another computer.

Some Computers Can Join a Domain

An administrator has two tasks to perform before a computer can log on to a domain. First, the administrator must create an account for the computer in the domain, and then the administrator must have the computer join the domain. It takes a special right in the domain to create an account, and only someone with special rights to a computer can make it join a domain.

If you want to log on to a Windows domain from a Windows NT, Windows 2000, or Windows XP Professional computer, the computer must be a member of the domain. Once a computer joins a domain, it has a computer account in the domain. This is how even desktop computers become resources of a domain.

Some Computers Cannot Join a Domain

Not all computers that can connect to Windows domain networks have security accounts. In particular, a Windows 9x computer cannot join a domain and have a security account in the domain. What it can do is enjoy some of the benefits of membership. The first one is that a user can log on to a domain from Windows 9x computers if it is configured for a user domain logon. Then, once logged on to the domain, a user can assign permissions to access local shares to users and groups in the domain. With Windows NT, Windows 2000, and Windows XP Professional computers, each computer must have an account in a domain and be logged on to a domain before a user sitting at that computer can log on to a domain.

Joining a computer to a domain is important even if you never intend to share a folder or printer on that computer, because there are other benefits of membership. These include centralized management of the desktop computer by administrators in the domain and your ability to log on to that computer using a domain user account. These things are possible because when the computer joins the domain, certain group accounts in the domain become members of local groups, which gives the domain administrators administrative rights on the local computer and allows domain users to log on to the local computer.

One of the differences between the Windows XP Home and Windows XP Professional products is that a Windows XP Home computer cannot join a Windows NT or Active Directory domain.

Step-by-Step 10.02

Adding a Computer to a Domain

In this exercise, you will add a Windows computer to a domain. To complete this exercise, you'll need the following:

- A computer with Windows 2000 Professional or Windows XP Professional (Windows XP Home cannot join a domain) that is a member of a workgroup

- A user name and password of an account with local administrator rights

- A user name and password of a user account in the domain

- The name of a Windows domain on your network

- A user name and password of an account in the domain with permission to join a computer to the domain (you will need an Administrator account for a Windows NT domain, but an ordinary user account for an Active Directory domain)

Step 1

Log on to the local machine with an account that is a member of the Administrators group. Right-click My Computer and then select Properties. In the System Properties dialog box, select Computer Name (Windows XP) or Network Identification (Windows 2000).

Step 2

In Windows XP, click Network ID to run the Network Identification wizard (for Windows 2000, skip to Step 4). Provide the answers for a computer on a business network with a domain and be sure to enter the domain name in the Domain box on the User Account and Domain Information page, as well as the user name and password for an account in the domain. The Network Identification wizard will add this domain user to your local computer, which means that it will create the local user profile.

Step 3

You then need to determine the level of access to grant to the user. Then, unless an administrator has already created a computer account in the domain, provide a user name and password for an account that can join a computer to a domain (a member of the Domain Administrators group works in both types of Microsoft domains). Click OK twice and then click Yes to reboot. Skip to Step 5.

Step 4

In Windows 2000, click Properties and complete the Identification Changes dialog box, selecting Domain and entering the name of the domain you want to join. Click OK. Enter the name and password of a user with permission to join the domain and click OK twice and then click Yes to reboot.

Step 5

After the reboot, log on to the domain using a domain user account. Be sure to select the domain by clicking Options to make the Log On To box visible.

Creating User and Group Accounts

Using worksheets created from the network administration plan, an administrator creates the domain user and group accounts. Organizing users into groups that have common resource access needs allows an administrator to avoid the many steps involved in assigning unique permissions to each user in the organization. That would be too much like administering a workgroup!

Now you'll learn about the types of groups in a Windows domain, the account policies, and the permissions that can be assigned to users and groups.

Users and Group Membership

In a Windows domain, the administrator can create several types of groups. These group types are similar, but they vary in scope and membership between Windows NT domains and Active Directory domains.

Domain Users   Each user who logs on to a domain must have a domain user account. Domain user accounts contain identifying information about each user. At minimum, each user must have a user name and password to log on. This name can be up to 20 characters, and most organizations establish a standard for creating the user name from the user's full name.

Windows NT Domain Groups   An NT domain (one in which all the domain controllers are Windows NT Server systems) has two types of groups: local and global. A local group is used to assign permissions to resources on those same domain controllers and can contain only user and group accounts from that domain. A global group is used to assign permissions to resources on other computers in the domain, and to resources in a domain that trusts the domain in which the global group resides. A global group can contain only users from the local domain.

Here is how an administrator works with these group types. Consider an NT domain named SchoolDom. The domain includes several shared folders and printers that should be accessed only by the managers and clerks in the school registration office. The group membership plan recognizes that the managers and clerks will have different access needs to various resources; therefore, they will be placed into two separate global groups, named Regmgrs and Regclerks. The registration printers should be available to all registration employees, but not to other employees; therefore, a local group, Regprint, will be used for the registration printers.

Are you still with us? Good! Note that there are certain data files that only managers need to access, so another local group, Regdata1, is created for giving access to these folders. Yet another set of data files must be available to all of the users in the Registration department; therefore, another local group, Regdata2, is created. Table 10.1 shows a sample group membership planning

A Windows NT domain accepts passwords of up to 14 characters, and an Active Directory domain accepts passwords of up to 104 characters. In a mixed environment, to maintain compatibility across the board, keep password length to 14 or fewer characters.

Inside Information

Get Server Software Free (Almost)

Server OSs are very expensive, but both Microsoft and Novell have in the past made evaluation copies of their OSs available. Evaluation copies stop working after a specified period of time. They are intended for people who want to learn about the software before buying it. Presently, Microsoft sells a 120-day evaluation version of Windows 2000 Advanced Server for $7.95. To get it, connect to `http://microsoft.order-2.com/trialstore/`. *Select .Net Enterprise Servers and then scroll down until you find Windows 2000 Advanced Server 120-Day Eval. After the release of .Net Server 2003, the Windows 2000 choice may be replaced by .Net Server 2003. Choose one of these server OSs. Then check out, at which time you must fill out a form and provide a method of paying for the purchase. Don't be put off if the site states that it will take many weeks to deliver the CD. In our experience, CDs have been delivered from Microsoft in about half the time predicted.*

Table 10.1	Group Member Planning Sheet— Windows NT Domain	
Group Name	**Group Type**	**Group Membership**
Regprint	Local	Regmgrs Regclerks
Regdata1	Local	Regmgrs
Regdata2	Local	Regclerks
Regmgrs	Global	Mai Ling (mling) Juan Martinez (jmartinez)
Regclerks	Global	Sarah Webster (swebster) Allison Romain (aromain) Tom Harrah (tharrah) Walter Brown (wbrown)

sheet for a Windows NT domain, with the user name shown in parentheses next to each user's full name. User names are created using the first initial and the last name. A naming policy should also define what is to be done to avoid duplicate names, such as for John Brown and James Brown. In that case, the policy may allow the use of the middle initial or a number in the name.

Active Directory Domain Groups   Active Directory domains are those with Windows 2000 or newer domain controllers. The group story here is much more complicated than that of Windows NT domains, and we will tell only a part of it here, because the finer details will help you only if you are close to becoming an Active Directory administrator.

An Active Directory domain also has local and global groups, but the local groups are called domain local groups, and although they work much like the local groups of Windows NT domains, they have greater scope. Whereas the local groups for a Windows NT domain can be used only to assign permissions to resources on the actual domain controllers, in a Windows 2000 domain, the domain local groups can be used to assign permissions to resources on any computer with an account in the domain. Domain local groups can contain user accounts from the same domain, global groups from the same domain or a trusted domain, and other domain local groups. This last is a practice called nesting, and it should be used with caution, because it adds a level of real complexity to your administration.

Table 10.2 shows the scenario from Table 10.1 using Active Directory groups. There is also an additional global group for night clerks, Regnight, in the registration office. They produce reports on a special printer for which a new domain local group has been created, Regprint2. They also must print to the same printers as the Regprint domain local group; therefore, these groups are nested. Now, if this all seems like too much trouble considering the number of users involved, you're correct. However, when there are dozens or hundreds of users in each global group, this scheme actually saves work.

Table 10.2	Group Member Planning Sheet—Active Directory Domain	
Group Name	**Group Type**	**Group Membership**
Regprint	Domain local	Regmgrs Regclerks Regprint2
Regdata1	Domain local	Regmgrs
Regdata2	Domain local	Regclerks
Regmgrs	Global	Mai Ling (mling) Juan Martinez (jmartinez)
Regclerks	Global	Sarah Webster (swebster) Allison Romain (aromain) Tom Harrah (tharrah) Walter Brown (wbrown)
Regnight	Global	Marisa Tortelli (mtortelli) Glen Olson (golson)
Regprint2	Domain local	Regnight

Creating User Accounts

You need to practice working with domain groups. If your classroom lab has a Windows NT or Windows Active Directory domain, your instructor will have created the appropriate accounts from Table 10.1 or Table 10.2. In the lab, you will create the local group accounts on your computer, even though you would not have to do this in a Windows Active Directory domain, and you would have to do this in an NT domain only if the resource to be shared were on your local computers. We have you do this because you are not likely to have Domain Admin membership, and also so that each person in the classroom can work independently.

To complete this step-by-step exercise, you will need the following:

- A computer with Windows 2000 Professional or Windows XP Professional that is a member of a domain

- A domain account that is a member of your computer's Power Users or Administrators group

Step 1

Log on to the domain with an account that is a member of the local computer's Power Users or Administrators group. Right-click My Computer and then select Manage. (Note: My Computer is on the desktop in Windows 2000 and on the Start menu in Windows XP Professional.) In the Computer Management window, expand Local Users and Groups and then Groups. You will see the default groups created on your local computer. Right-click in an empty area in the right window pane and select New Group.

Step 2

Complete the New Group form for Regprint by first entering the group name then clicking the Add button. Then, in the Select Users or Groups dialog box add the members from the domain, as shown in Table 10.1. Remember that you need to add groups from the domain to this group. If you need help in completing the form, search the Help (or Help and Support) program.

Step 3 Repeat Step 2, creating the local groups Regdata1 and Regdata2. You will use these groups in the next Step-by-Step exercise.

Passwords

Although Windows (all versions) allows you to use a blank password by default, you should always use a password on a computer that is on a network. This can be enforced by local password policies in Windows NT and the versions of Windows that have evolved from Windows NT. A domain-level password policy affects all users who log on to the domain. There are administrative tasks required to set either local- or domain-level password policies.

In your class lab, you may not be concerned about security, and you may choose a password that is easy to remember. Your instructor will advise you on the password policies in the computer lab. Any time you are concerned about computer security, we recommend that you use all security features available to you and create the strongest password possible. For instance, Windows NT, Windows XP, and Windows 2000 all allow you to have mixed case in a password, as well as a mix of alphabetic characters, numeric characters, and other symbols. We recommend that you create strong passwords that have more than eight characters and a mix of uppercase and lowercase characters, numeric characters, and symbols. Creating such a password is easy—the hard part is remembering the password after you create it. Do not use your name or any common words, because an intruder can discover such a password simply by knowing a little about you and guessing or by using password-cracking software that uses a dictionary of common names and words. You should also change your password frequently. Oh yeah—don't write your password on your office calendar, on Post-it notes, or on a whiteboard!

> Domain-level password policies override local-level password policies when users are logging on to a domain.

> Windows *is not* case sensitive in regard to user names, computer names, domains, workgroups, or file names. But it *is* case sensitive when it comes to passwords, so be sure you carefully enter your password and remember the exact password, including uppercase and lowercase and special symbols.

Creating Shares

Once users and groups are created, you can assign permissions to them for the resources they need to access. Creating shares after you know who needs to access a resource enables you to assign the appropriate permissions immediately, but you can create shares at any time. If the shares are to be on an NTFS volume, you need to perform a preparation step before actually creating shares: setting NTFS file and folder permissions. We highly recommend the use of NTFS on any Windows computer that supports NTFS and that has multiple users accessing the file system, either interactively at the computer or over the network. After you have set permissions, create the share and set share-level permissions.

Setting File-Level Permissions

The file permissions on an NTFS volume are the last defense against unauthorized users coming over the network. Set permissions at the most restrictive level that will allow the right users to accomplish their work. Table 10.3 shows our NTFS permissions worksheet.

Creating a Share and Setting Share-Level Permissions

Your local files and folders are not visible over the network until one or more shares are created. Remember: A file share is the point at which a user, using client software, can access your file system. This is called *file sharing*, but a share point must point to a *folder*. Once a share is created, permissions can be set. This is important because the default permissions give the group Everyone full control. The Everyone group is every user connected to the network—even those who have not been authenticated. This means that if the share is created without first setting NTFS permissions (when available) on the folders and files under the share, anyone coming over the network can access these shares.

![Permissions for Registration dialog box showing Share Permissions tab with Everyone group selected and Full Control, Change, Read all allowed]

• Share Permissions page

The most important step is to remove the Everyone group from the share permissions. Beyond that, you must assign permissions that are not more restrictive than the NTFS permissions you have assigned to the underlying folders and files. Combining share permissions and NTFS permissions is like sending the network user through two doors. Imagine that as the user approaches the share door, he is carrying a backpack full of permissions that

Table 10.3	NTFS Permissions Worksheet	
Folder	**Users/Groups**	**Permissions**
Registration	Regdata1	Everything but Full Control and Take Ownership
Registration	Regdata2	Read, Write, and Execute
Registration	Administrators (local computer)	Full Control
	SYSTEM	Full Control
	CREATOR OWNER	Full Control
Registration\database	Regdata1	Everything but Full Control and Take Ownership
	Regdata2	Read, Write, and Execute
	Administrators (local computer)	Full Control
	SYSTEM	Full Control
	CREATOR OWNER	Full Control
Registration\forms	Regdata1	Everything but Full Control and Take Ownership
	Regdata2	Read, Write, and Execute
	Administrators (local computer)	Full Control
	SYSTEM	Full Control
	CREATOR OWNER	Full Control

add up to full control. At the share door, the security system acts as an electronic customs agent, confiscating the permissions not granted to this user's individual or group accounts. Now his backpack is lighter as he approaches the NTFS door to the folder or file he is accessing. At that door, another agent looks at the NTFS permissions for him and for all of the groups he belongs to, combines them, and declares that although he is allowed NTFS Full Control permissions, because he left some permissions at the share door, he cannot be allowed to have full control.

Step-by-Step 10.04

Setting Permissions and Sharing Folders

In this step-by-step exercise, you will implement the folder sharing plan for the registration office. Rather than do this on a server, you'll perform these steps on your lab computer, using the local groups you created in Step-by-Step 10.03. You'll first create the folder hierarchy and NTFS permissions required for the registration office employees, using the NTFS permission worksheet in Table 10.3. Then you'll create the share. Finally, you'll set permissions on

the share. To complete this step-by-step exercise, you will need the following:

- A computer with Windows 2000 Professional or Windows XP Professional that is a member of a domain

- A domain account that is a member of your computer's Power Users or Administrators group

Step 1

Log on to the domain using an account that is a member of your computer's Power Users or Administrators group. Open Windows Explorer or My Computer and expand drive C:. Create the folders shown on the NTFS permissions worksheet (Table 10.3).

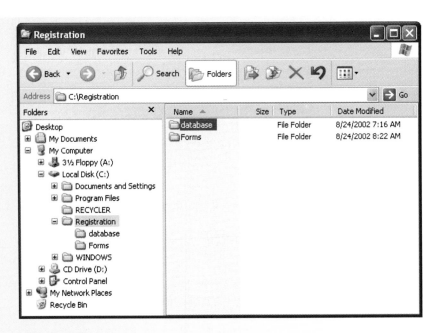

Step 2

After creating the folders, you need to block inheritance on the Registration folder so that it will not inherit the permissions of the parent folder. This will enable you to remove some of the permissions. To block inheritance, right-click the Registration folder and then select Properties | Security. On the Security tab, click Advanced. In the Advanced Security Settings dialog box, clear the Inherit from Parent the Permission Entries That Apply to Child Objects check box. In the Security box, select Copy.

Step 3

On the Permissions page, remove permissions for users and groups that are not included on the NTFS permission worksheet. Add the permissions for the Regdata1 and Regdata2 groups. If you need help in assigning permissions, check out Help (Help and Support).

Advanced Security Settings for Registration

Permissions | Auditing | Owner | Effective Permissions

To view more information about Special permissions, select a permission entry, and then click Edit.

Permission entries:

Type	Name	Permission	Inherited From	Apply To
Allow	Administrators (HOST...	Full Control	<not inherited>	This folde
Allow	CREATOR OWNER	Full Control	<not inherited>	Subfolder:
Allow	RegData1 (HOSTA\...	Special	<not inherited>	This folde
Allow	RegData2 (HOSTA\...	Read, Write & Execute	<not inherited>	This folde
Allow	SYSTEM	Full Control	<not inherited>	This folde

Add... | Edit... | Remove

☐ Inherit from parent the permission entries that apply to child objects. Include these with entries explicitly defined here.

☐ Replace permission entries on all child objects with entries shown here that apply to child objects

OK | Cancel | Apply

Step 4

In Step 2, you blocked inheritance of permissions from the parent of the Registration folder and copied the parent's permissions. Then in Step 3 you removed any accounts that were not in your planning sheet for the Registration folder. You do not need to block inheritance on the folders below Registration because the permissions you set for Registration are identical to what you need for the folders below, and these permissions will be inherited by those folders. You still need to remove any accounts not included on your NTFS permissions worksheet, as you did in Step 3. Do that now.

Step 5

Create a share pointing to the Registration folder and then set permissions. Right-click the Registration folder and select Sharing and Security. This opens the Sharing tab of the Properties dialog box. Select Share This Folder. The default share name is the same as that of the underlying folder, but you can change this name if you wish. Sometimes it is necessary to change the name to a shorter name for DOS and Windows 3.1 clients that cannot access shares with names longer than 11 characters. Leave the share name as Registration and click Permissions. Add the Regdata1 and Regdata2 groups.

Permissions for Registration

Share Permissions

Group or user names:

- Everyone
- RegData1 (HOSTA\RegData1)
- RegData2 (HOSTA\RegData2)

Add... | Remove

Permissions for RegData2	Allow	Deny
Full Control	☐	☐
Change	☐	☐
Read	☑	☐

OK | Cancel | Apply

Step 6

Now that you have added groups, remove the Everyone group. Give the

---

Regdata1 and Regdata2 group Full Control permissions. The registration share is now open for business!

Connecting Clients to Shares

Once shares have been created, network clients can connect to the shares from their computers. For a frequently accessed share, map a drive letter to the share and select to have it reconnect at logon. **Mapping** assigns one of your local, unused drive letters to a share out on the network. This provides a logical connection to the share from your computer.

Step-by-Step 10.05

Mapping to a Share

Administrators often need to map drives from a desktop computer to network shares. As with many operations, there are several ways to do this. Using the accounts and the shares you created in the earlier step-by-step exercises, you will create a share. To complete this step-by-step exercise, you will need the following:

- A computer with Windows 2000 Professional or Windows XP Professional that is a member of a domain

- The domain user and group accounts from Table 10.1 created by the instructor in a domain

Step 1

If you are still logged on from the previous step-by-step exercise, log off and log back on to the domain as Sarah Webster (swebster). Right-click My Computer and select Map Network Drive. In the Folder text box within the Map Network Drive dialog box, type *computername***registration**, where *computername* is the name of another lab computer on which Step-by-Step 10.04 was completed. You can select a different drive letter if you wish. Then confirm that the Reconnect at Logon check box is selected and click Finish.

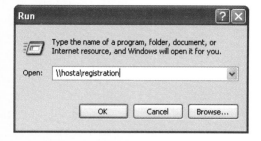

Test the connection. Open My Computer and locate the new mapped drive. Notice that you can also see the folder below that drive. Open the database folder and create a text file and name it **SARAH.TXT**.

Step 3

Log off as Sarah Webster and log back on as Allison Romain (aromain). Open My Computer or Windows Explorer. Allison does not have the drive mapping that you created for Sarah. Create a drive mapping for Allison, using a different method. Choose Start | Run. In the Open text box, type ***computername*\registration**. Click OK.

Step 4

Back in My Computer, open the new database folder and attempt to delete the file SARAH.TXT. At first, it appears that you will be permitted to delete the file, but if the permissions are set correctly, you will not be able to delete it. Click OK to close the error message.

Step 5

Create a text file and name it **ALLISON.TXT**.

Step 6

Log off as Allison and log back on as Mai Ling (mling). Open My Computer and notice that Mai Ling does not have a drive mapping to the Registration share. Use yet another method to map a drive. Open a command prompt and type **net use * *computername*\registration**.

Step 7

Return to My Computer and open the new database folder and delete the files SARAH.TXT. and ALLISON.TXT.

Chapter 10 Review

Chapter Summary

After reading this chapter and completing the Step-by-Step tutorials and Try This! exercises, you should understand the following facts about networking:

Explain the Basic Concepts of Networking

- A computer network consists of two or more computers connected by communications media in order to share resources, communicate, and centralize management of resources.

- A LAN is limited geographically to a room, a floor of a building, an entire building, or a campus that is all connected with a common network technology, usually at the fastest speeds (10 Mbps, 100 Mbps, or 1 Gbps).

- A MAN is a network that covers a metropolitan area, usually connected by a high-speed fiber-optic cable, and that runs at speeds measured in gigabits per second.

- A WAN is two or more networks connected over long distances using phone lines or satellite communications with speeds normally ranging from thousands of bits per second to millions of bits per second.

- A peer-to-peer network has no central authority responsible for security, and the management of resources becomes more difficult as the number of PCs increases.

- A server-based network provides a central place for keeping and controlling resources.

- A client is the software that requests services from server software.

- A Microsoft server-based network with central administration is called a domain.

- You may find peer-to-peer and dedicated server-based networks combined in a sort of hybrid network.

- Network hardware components include network interface, media, hubs, switches, routers, and firewalls.

- Network software components include network operating systems, device drivers, services, and protocols.

Describe the Dominant Server Operating Systems

- A server is a computer on a network that provides a service to other computers.

- A client is a computer on a network that accesses the service of a server.

- Microsoft's major server versions in use today include Windows NT 4.0 and Windows 2000.

- Windows .Net Server 2003 is the latest version (2003 release date).

- Windows NT 4.0 is still running on many servers today. Its server products include the Server and Enterprise editions.

- Windows 2000 Server products include Windows 2000 Server, Windows 2000 Advanced Server, and Windows 2000 Datacenter Server.

- Linux and the many other versions of UNIX are growing in popularity within organizations. UNIX is popular for hosting DNS and DHCP services.

- UNIX is on a large percentage of Internet web servers.

- Novell's NetWare server OS dominated the LAN server market in the 1980s but declined in the 1990s, although Novell introduced Novell Directory Services in 1984, years ahead of Microsoft's competing Active Directory.

Describe the Common Roles of Network Servers

- File and printer sharing was the earliest role for servers. It's still a huge function of servers.

- A server that transmits, receives, and stores e-mail is called a mail server.

- In a Microsoft network, the e-mail server is called Exchange. In a NetWare environment, the e-mail server is GroupWise. Both of these products do much more than simply manage e-mail.

- Centralized data backup has long been an important network service, and several vendors sell centralized backup systems that use a dedicated backup server, large tape archiving systems, and specialized client software.

- There are a large number of Internet-based backup services that allow subscribers to back up data over the Internet to their servers.

- An application server is a program that acts as an intermediary between users running client software and a large back-end business application or database.

- Web servers are found on the Internet, hosting millions of web pages, and they are also found on private networks, replacing file servers in some cases.

Protect Network Resources

- Effective sharing and protection of network resources requires careful planning.

- The network administrator implements the plan for sharing and protecting network resources.

- An administrator's server-side tasks include adding a computer to a domain, creating user accounts and groups, and creating file and print shares.

- An administrator's client-side tasks include connecting to resources and testing network security.

- A security account is one to which permissions and rights can be assigned

- A Windows Active Directory domain has several types of security accounts.

- Administrators save time and effort by organizing users into groups that have common resource needs.

- Groups in Windows NT domains and Active Directory domains are similar but vary in scope and membership.

- Planning for effective use of user accounts and group accounts is complex but worthwhile.

- After users and groups have been created, create shares to give users access to the resources they need. If a share is on an NTFS volume, set NTFS permissions on the underlying files and folders before creating the share.

- When you create a new share, immediately set the permissions on the share. You will usually remove the Everyone group from the permissions list.

- Once shares have been created, network clients can connect to the shares from their computers.

- Mapping assigns one of your local, unused drive letters to a share out on the network. For a frequently accessed share, map a drive letter to the share and have it reconnect at logon.

Key Terms

account *(409)*	**hub** *(416)*	**server** *(406)*
authentication *(409)*	**internetwork** *(412)*	**share** *(409)*
authorization *(409)*	**mapping** *(436)*	**switch** *(416)*
chat room *(408)*	**network resource** *(406)*	**thin client** *(423)*
client *(406)*	**newsgroup** *(407)*	**thread** *(407)*
directory service *(410)*	**node** *(416)*	**workgroup** *(413)*
discussion list *(407)*	**protocol** *(418)*	

Key Term Quiz

Use the Key Terms list to complete the sentences that follow. Not all terms will be used.

1. A user may addess network services using a minimally configured network computer called a/an _____.

2. When a computer on a Microsoft network is solely part of a peer-to-peer network, it belongs to a/an _____.

3. The rules by which network services operate are called _____.

4. When you do _____, you assign one of your local, unused drive letters to a share out on the network.

5. The chain of linked messages in a newsgroup is called a/an _____.

6. When a computer or other device is connected to a network, it is called a/an _____.

7. A group of connected computers is a/an _____.

8. PCs on a network share much more than data; they share _____(s).

9. Making a resource, such as a file or folder, available to other computers on a Microsoft network is called creating a/an _____.

10. A/an _____ is a virtual space on the Internet where communication can take place in real time.

Multiple-Choice Quiz

1. Why are computers networked? (Select all that apply.)
   a. To share resources
   b. To permit communication
   c. To save money
   d. To facilitate data backup
   e. To facilitate resource management

2. Really Good Stuff is a specialty mail-order company with 25 computer users who need to access central inventory and customer databases on a network server. Which administrative network structure would you expect to find in the company's office?
   a. Peer-to-peer
   b. Quality circles
   c. Maple leaf
   d. Server-based
   e. Dialog box

3. What communication methods are sometimes called forums?
   a. Dial-up
   b. Cell phone
   c. Newsgroup
   d. E-mail discussion list
   e. Chat room

4. Which of the following are common network server roles? (Select all that apply.)
   a. File and print
   b. Mail
   c. Web
   d. Data backup
   e. Application

5. Which network operating system is on more web servers than the others?
   a. Windows .Net
   b. Linux
   c. Windows 2000
   d. Apache Server
   e. Novell NetWare 6

6. In 1994, which company introduced a directory service product based on the x.500 standards?
   a. IBM
   b. Microsoft
   c. Apple
   d. Bell Labs
   e. Novell

7. Which of the following are considered network media? Select all that apply.
   a. CD-ROM
   b. Radio or infrared
   c. Wire
   d. Glass fiber
   e. Walls

8. Why would an administrator want a trust relationship between two Windows domains?
   a. To allow the accounts from one domain to use the resources of another
   b. To allow the resources of one domain to exist in another domain
   c. To create groups in two domains at a time
   d. To create user accounts in two domains at a time
   e. To allow users to access the Internet

9. Why are users placed into group accounts?

   a. To simplify administration.

   b. To confuse you.

   c. It is the only way to assign permissions to users.

   d. To classify users by student or employee ID number.

   e. To enable users to log on.

10. Why create a share?

    a. To give users an e-mail account

    b. To allow users to log on to a domain

    c. To provide a point of access to a file system

    d. To give users access to an entire domain

    e. To keep unauthorized users out of your computer

11. Why would you remove the Everyone group from a permissions list and add users and groups?

    a. It includes all users.

    b. It does not include administrators.

    c. It exists only in a domain.

    d. It exists only in a workgroup.

    e. It exists only in Windows XP Home.

12. Which of the following may be true of a network server? Select all that apply.

    a. It must be dedicated to one role.

    b. It may be both a client and server.

    c. It may perform several server roles.

    d. It may be on a private network or on the Internet.

    e. All of the above.

13. Which network service is now the most compelling reason for placing users on a network?

    a. Web services

    b. Applications services

    c. File and print sharing

    d. E-mail

    e. List service

14. When preparing to create a share on an NTFS volume, why should you set NTFS file and folder permissions before creating the share?

    a. Users will not be able to access the files until NTFS permissions are set.

    b. NTFS will not allow a share to be created until NTFS permissions are created.

    c. The default permissions on a new share give the Everyone group full control.

    d. The question is wrong; there is no reason for setting NTFS permissions first.

    e. None of the above.

15. Which of the following are true after a computer joins a Microsoft domain? Select all that apply.

    a. The computer now has an account in the domain.

    b. Users can only log on to the domain.

    c. Users can log on to the domain or to the local computer.

    d. Some domain groups become members of the computer's local groups.

    e. Administrators may centrally manage the computer.

■ Essay Quiz

1. Write a few sentences describing why managers should want backup systems on their networks. Feel free to draw on your own experience and include your own assumptions and conclusions.

2. Although not stated in this chapter, there is one network communication method that may, by itself, be the most compelling reason for many people to be on a network or on the Internet.

   Come to your own conclusion about which method this is and support your answer with an explanation. You can use your own experience and opinion or do a little research to answer this question.

3. Why is it important to set permissions at the NTFS level before creating a share?

Lab Projects

• Lab Project 10.1

Conduct a survey. Gather information about the networks of six organizations (businesses or schools) in your area. Try to vary the size of the organization you approach for this information, so that you have a variety of results. You may find that some organizations have both peer-to-peer and dedicated servers on their networks. Use Table 10.4 to organize your information.

After you gather the information, attempt to determine whether these organizations match the model for keeping a strictly peer-to-peer network to less than 10 users. If your results vary from this model, try to determine whether there was justification for going beyond 10 users on a peer-to-peer network.

• Lab Project 10.2

You work for a company that provides desktop support services to small business clients. Today you have been asked to go to the site of a potential new client company and gather information about its computers and network. This is the information your company will use to determine the level of service the customer will require and the monthly fee scale for a one-year contract. You have decided that some of the information you need to gather is that which is included in the network survey form in Table 10.4.

Describe other information that you believe your boss needs to know.

Gather information about the current network computers, hardware, and software. Determine the information you will need and create two or more forms that will help you gather the information. To give you a head start, you can use the form provided in Lab Project 10.1 as one form or part of one form, but more information is required. Create at least one more form with additional information you will gather.

Table 10.4	Network Survey			
Company Name	Number of Employees	Number of Employees Who Use Computers	Peer-to-Peer (Y/N) / Number of Computers	Number of Dedicated Servers / Number of Clients

About A+ Certification

This book is designed to introduce you to microcomputer operating systems and help you build the skills you'll need to enjoy a successful career in the field of information technology. As you gain valuable experience and load up on a treasure trove of skills, you'll find that many doors will open. But as you're starting out on your new career, one way that you can show potential employers you have the skills to do the job is to earn an industry certification.

■ What's Certification?

A certification is a license that documents a certain level of skill and knowledge in a particular area of expertise. To attain a certification, you usually have to pass an exam. A lot of professions use certifications as a way to demonstrate skills and show potential employers or clients they are qualified to do the job. For example, if you want a job in accounting, you need to get a *Certified Public Accountant* (CPA) certification. If you want to be an auto mechanic, you should get an *Automotive Service Excellence* (ASE) certification. These certifications are recognized by everyone in the industry as proof of a certain level of competence and ability.

Certifications in the field of computer technology are particularly important because changes in technology happen so quickly. Even after you graduate from school, you'll need to keep up with changes in technology in order to advance your career. This doesn't mean you need to keep going back to school every few months, but it does mean you should keep up with the latest changes. Certifications are one way you can show that you're up to date on the latest technologies that matter to your profession.

There are many ways to study for a certification. You can buy a self-study guide at a bookstore, take a course at your local college or university, or find information online. There are also many vendor certifications that will verify you have the skills and knowledge in a particular company's product. You can find information about vendor-specific certifications at the company's website. For example, Microsoft (www.microsoft.com) offers several different certifications for its software. The *Microsoft Certified Systems Administrator* (MCSA) and *Microsoft Certified Systems Engineer* (MCSE) are two popular certifications that experienced network administrators use to demonstrate their ability to use and manage Microsoft Windows networking technologies.

■ A+ Certification

Most PC technicians and other computer specialists start with the A+ Certification exam, which is an industry-supported, vendor-neutral certification designed to demonstrate basic knowledge and skills in supporting microcomputers. For this reason, the A+ Certification is widely recognized by thousands of companies around the world, including IBM, Epson, Hewlett-Packard, Minolta, AT&T, Novell, Panasonic, Microsoft, and Sun Microsystems, to name just a few. A+ Certification is composed of two exams: Hardware Technologies and Operating System Technologies. By passing both these exams, you demonstrate the skills of a PC technician with at least six months of experience.

A+ Certification is part of a program developed by the *Computing Technology Industry Association* (CompTIA), which is a nonprofit trade organization with a membership of over 8,000 computer resellers, distributors, manufacturers, and training companies. In addition to A+ Certification, CompTIA offers additional certifications that cover other areas of the computer industry.

Preparing for the A+ Certification Exam

As of the publication date of this book, the A+ Operating System Technology exam only tests skills associated with DOS, Windows 9x, Windows NT, and Windows 2000. It's likely that Windows XP will be tested when CompTIA updates the exam.

While *Survey of Operating Systems* is not designed to be an A+ Certification study guide, it does provide a good foundation for learning how to use, configure, and troubleshoot PC operating systems as well as Macintosh and Linux operating systems, which are not covered on the A+ exam. Most of the topics covered in the A+ Operating System Technologies Exam are covered in this book. A listing of exam objectives and the chapters in which they are taught are listed in tables below. To prepare fully for the exam, we suggest you read *Mike Meyers' A+ Certification All-in-One Exam Guide* (McGraw-Hill/Osborne), which provides friendly, yet thorough coverage of all the A+ Certification topics.

1.0 Operating System Fundamentals

Objectives	Chapters
1.1 Identify the operating system's functions, structure, and major system files to navigate the operating system and get to needed technical information.	1, 2, 3, 4, 5, 6
1.2 Identify basic concepts and procedures for creating, viewing and managing files, directories and disks. This includes procedures for changing file attributes and the ramifications of those changes.	1, 2, 3, 4, 5, 6

2.0 Installation, Configuration, and Upgrading

Objectives	Chapters
2.1 Identify the procedures for installing Windows 9x, and Windows 2000, and for bringing the software to a basic operational level.	5, 6
2.2 Identify steps to perform an operating system upgrade.	5, 6
2.3 Identify the basic system boot sequences and boot methods, including the steps to create an emergency boot disk with utilities installed for Windows 9x, Windows NT, and Windows 2000.	4, 5, 6
2.4 Identify procedures for loading/adding and configuring application device drivers, and the necessary software for certain devices.	2, 3, 4, 5, 6

3.0 Diagnosing and Troubleshooting

Objectives	Chapters
3.1 Recognize and interpret the meaning of common error codes and startup messages from the boot sequence, and identify steps to correct the problems.	2, 3, 4, 5, 6
3.2 Recognize common problems and determine how to resolve them.	2, 3, 4, 5, 6

4.0 Networks

Objectives	Chapters
4.1 Identify the networking capabilities of Windows including procedures for connecting to the network.	3, 4, 5, 6

$ prompt (Pronounced "dollar" prompt) The Linux prompt at which you enter commands. (9)

.Mac (Pronounced "dot Mac.") Apple's online file storage and file sharing service, available at `mac.com`. The .Mac service offers a virtual hard drive where you can store private files and a website where you can upload files such as photographs and movies for others to view. (8)

286 protected mode An operating mode of the Intel processors that first appeared in the 80286 processor. In this mode, only 16MB of RAM is available, and there is no support for virtual DOS machines. (1)

386 protected mode An operating mode of the Intel processors that first appeared in the 80386 processor. In this mode, up to 4GB of RAM can be used, and there is support for 32-bit code and virtual DOS machines. (1)

8.3 alias In Windows versions beginning with NT, an 8.3 FAT file system–compliant name given to a file with a long file name (LFN) in addition to the LFN. (5)

account In a security accounts database, an account is a listing of information about a user (user account) or group (group account). A user account is used for authentication, and both user and group accounts are used for authorization with assigned permissions. (10)

Active Channel website A website that delivers updated information to a subscriber's computer on a regular schedule. (5)

Active Desktop A feature introduced in Windows 98 that lets you put web content directly on your Windows desktop. In web view objects on the desktop behave like links in a web page that you can open with a single-click. (3)

Active Directory domain A Microsoft domain in which some or all of the servers maintaining the domain database are running a Windows 2000 Professional Server OS or higher. Active Directory is a directory service. (6)

allocation unit The minimum space that a file system can give to a file, also known as a cluster. Even if the file contains only 14 bytes, if the allocations unit/cluster size is 32,768 bytes, then 32,768 bytes will be used. (4)

Apple Menu A pop-up menu located at the top left of the Mac OS desktop. It looks like a tiny Apple icon, which is rainbow-colored in OS 9 and blue in OS X. (8)

applet Applets are mini-application programs such as those in Control Panel that allow you (or an administrator) to configure your software and hardware. (3)

AppleTalk Apple's proprietary and now obsolete networking protocol. (8)

application An application is software that allows you to perform useful functions, such as writing a report or calculating a budget. (2)

Aqua Apple's new OS X GUI, code-named Aqua because of its blue, fluid appearance. (8)

authentication Validation of the user account and password. Before giving the user access to the computer, the operating system will verify that the user name and password is valid. (1)

automated installation An installation of Windows that uses scripts prepared ahead of time. An automated installation can run either unattended or with very little input from a user. (5)

authorization The process of confirming the permissions you have for a resource. (10)

Autorun A feature that enables Windows to automatically find and run the program needed to open and run a CD or other application. (6)

binary digit Also called "bit," the smallest unit of storage (on disk or in memory). A single bit is like a light switch: either on or off. On represents 1, and off represents 0. (1)

binding A linked relationship between network components that establishes the order in which each network component handles network communications. (10)

bit *See* binary digit. (1)

Blue Screen of Death (BSOD) Widely used term for the blue character-mode screen that displays a Stop or Fatal Error message, indicating that Windows has become unstable and has stopped. (4)

boot disk The disk containing the programs that are used to start an OS. In the case of DOS, the complete OS can fit on a single diskette or on a hard disk. Windows NT, Windows 2000, and Windows XP are all too big to fit on a diskette, and normally boot from a hard disk. It is possible to create a boot or startup disk for these OSs containing only the initial boot files from the root directory of the system partition. (2)

boot files   Files used to start up (boot) an OS. (4)

boot loader   The program in Linux that loads programs into the boot disk. (9)

boot partition   The name for the partition that contains the system files in Windows NT or greater. (4)

bootstrap loader   A small ROM-BIOS program that searches for a boot sector on disk. Once it finds one, it loads it into memory. The boot sector program then looks on the disk from which it was loaded for system files, which it will, in turn, load into memory. (2)

byte   A group of 8 bits. A single byte can represent a character, like the letter A, or a very simple command, like move down one line. (1)

Category view   A Windows XP Control Panel view where the applets are arranged in task categories, rather than being arranged alphabetically. (7)

CD key   A code printed on the package of an installation disk that must be entered into the system during installation to enable the software to be installed on the computer. (6)

central processing unit (CPU)   An integrated circuit (chip) that performs the calculations, or processing, for a computer. (1)

chat room   A virtual room on the Internet where communication sessions called chats take place in real time, much as in a face-to-face conversation. (10)

Chooser   The OS 9 printer and network selection tool for Apple's proprietary and now obsolete AppleTalk networking protocol. (8)

Classic   The compatibility layer that allows users to run OS 9 software from within OS X. (8)

Classic view   A Windows XP Control Panel view where the applets are arranged alphabetically, rather than being arranged in categories. (7)

clean installation   Installation of an OS onto a hard disk from which all data has been removed, or that never contained any data. (4)

client   A software component on a computer that accesses services of a network server. (1 & 10)

cluster   *See* allocation unit. (2)

cold boot   A method of starting up a computer by turning on the power switch. (2)

command prompt   In DOS, the normal character mode user interface. In Windows, a text-based environment that resembles an MS-DOS prompt, from which you can launch any program that can be run in Windows. (3)

compatibility layer   A way to run older OS 9 software that does not have an OS X equivalent from within OS X. (8)

compatibility mode   A Windows XP feature that emulates an older Windows operating system. This is used with legacy programs that will not run in Windows XP. (7)

Computer Administrator account   In Windows XP, a simplified reference to an account that is a member of the local Administrators group. This term is used in the User Accounts applet. (7)

Control Panel   A post-Windows 3.1 feature containing numerous applets that you can use to adjust the configuration of several aspects of the OS. (6)

Control Strip   A floating bar on the OS 9 desktop that offers instant tab access to a variety of System Preferences, including location, Internet dial-up, and screen resolution. (8)

conventional memory   In real mode, the architecture of the PC allows only the first 640KB of RAM to be used as the workspace for the operating system, application programs, and data. This memory is referred to as conventional memory. (2)

copy   An operation that creates duplicate data in a new location, leaving the original data in place. (3)

critical update   Updates that solve security problems or problems that can potentially cause major failures. (5)

current window   The active window that receives input from the keyboard when the user types. (1)

cursor   A graphical pointer that can be moved around a GUI by manipulating a pointing device. (1)

Darwin   The core operating system of OS X. Darwin integrates a number of technologies including a Mach 3.0 kernel, BSD UNIX operating system services, high-performance networking facilities, and support for multiple integrated file systems. (8)

defragmentation   When files are accessed and modified they become fragmented, with pieces of the files scattered in various places on the disk. A defragmentation program rearranges the files into contiguous pieces. (4)

device driver   A device driver is software that is added to an OS to control a device. You need a component-specific device driver for each unique hardware component that will interact with the OS. (1)

device management   The device management function controls hardware devices through the use of device drivers. (1)

directory   An older term for a type of file that can contain other directories as well as files. The newer term is folder. (1)

directory service   A network service that can manage all types of network resources. (10)

discussion list   A list of people with a common interest maintained by a service called a list server. Each list member receives e-mails containing discussions of interest, and each member can also participate in the discussions by sending e-mails to the list. (10)

disk drive   A drive that stores data and programs by writing them onto the surface of small spinning platters using either magnetic or optical technology. (1)

display screen   A display screen shows visual output from the computer. Traditionally, a display screen was built around a cathode-ray tube (CRT), like a TV set. Flat-panel displays (FPDs), are replacing CRTs on the desktop. (1)

Dock   The Dock is a floating bar in OS X that replaced OS 9's Control Strip. (8)

domain   A Microsoft domain is a collection of accounts representing network computers, users, and groups of users, all maintained in a central security accounts database for ease of administration. (3)

domain name   On the Internet, a name that is part of the Domain Name Service (DNS). An example of a domain name is mcgraw-hill.com. (10)

DOS prompt   The user interface of DOS, also called a command prompt. A text-mode screen showing, at minimum, the current drive letter followed by a blinking cursor, indicating that the command interpreter is ready for input. (2)

driver   *See* device driver (2)

driver signing   Verification that Microsoft has certified a device driver. Signing also verifies that the driver is actually from the vendor, and not a potential computer virus. (7)

encryption   Translating a file into code that is unintelligible to anyone who doesn't have the key to decode it. (7)

external command   A command program stored on disk instead of within DOS. DOS looks for an external command program on disk if it cannot find a command program internally. (2)

FAT16 file system   The FAT file system used on hard disks. (2)

FAT32 file system   The FAT file system available with Windows since Windows 95 OSR2 (OEM Service Release 2) in the fall of 1996. (2)

file allocation table (FAT)   The file allocation table (FAT) is the component of the FAT file system that an OS uses to remember where your files reside on disk. (2)

file attribute   A component of files or directory entries that determines how an operating system handles the file. In the FAT file system, the attributes are: read-only, archive, system, hidden, volume label, and directory. (2)

file management   An operating system function that allows the operating system to read, write, and modify data. (1)

file system   The means an operating system uses to organize information on disks. (6)

Finder   The default GUI/desktop view in both OS 9 and OS X before any application software runs. (8)

firewall   A network security device that prevents unauthorized access to computers and data on a network. Firewalls are usually placed at the point where a private network (or group of networks) connects to a public, untrusted, network, like the Internet. (10)

focus   Where the system's attention is at any given moment. A user can switch between tasks by giving the focus to the application the user brings to the foreground in the current window. (1)

folder   A type of file that can contain other folders as well as files. Often also called directory. (1)

gigabyte   1,073,741,824 bytes, or 2^{30} bytes. Giga means billion. (1)

Gnome   The name of a Linux GUI environment. (9)

GNU   The GNU Project launched in 1984 to develop a complete, free UNIX-like operating system. (GNU, a recursive acronym for "GNU's Not Unix," is pronounced "guh-NEW"). (9)

graphical user interface (GUI)   A user interface that takes advantage of a computer's graphics capabilities to make it easier to use. (1, 3, & 9)

group   A collection of users. The system administrator can assign rights and permissions to a group, rather than setting those rights and permissions individually. (6)

Guest account   A built-in account in Windows NT, Windows 2000, and Windows XP that is disabled by default. If enabled, users without accounts can access a computer, but only have the rights and permissions of the guest account. (7)

GUI The acronym for graphical user interface. (9)

Hardware Compatibility List (HCL) A list of hardware supported by the OS. Some versions of Windows come with an HCL. (6)

home directory The place in a Linux system where you can save your files. When you log in to Linux, you are automatically placed in your home directory. Every user has one. (9)

hot-swappable A plug and play peripheral device that can be plugged into a computer while it is running, and the computer does not need to be restarted while connecting or disconnecting the device. (8)

hub A network device to which media from each node connects. A hub repeats any signal to every port. (10)

hyperlink A link to a different location or document. That location can be elsewhere in the same document, or in another document, or it can be a universal resource locator (URL) that points to a web page, FTP site, or other resource on the Internet. (5)

hypertext markup language (HTML) The language of the World Wide Web. The pages you view on the Web with your browser are written in this language, which your browser interprets in order to display the pages on the screen. (5)

image An exact duplicate of the entire hard drive contents, including the OS and all installed software, that is used to install copies of an OS and associated applications on multiple computers. (4)

Indexing Service A service that speeds up hard drive searches by maintaining indexes of the files (both properties and contents) on your hard drive. (6)

input Sending something into the computer is called input. Examples are entering information via the keyboard or having your word processing program read a file from disk. (1)

input/output (I/O) Anything sent into a computer (input); anything coming out of a computer (output). Every keystroke you enter, files read in, and even voice commands are input. Output can include a printed page, what you see on the screen, and even sounds. (1)

internal command A command program that DOS stores within COMMAND.COM. Internal commmands are always in memory with the OS. (2)

internetwork Two or more networks connected over long distances. An internetwork usually includes LANs connected via WAN. (10)

ISP Internet service provider; an access point to the Internet. (10)

iTools Former name for Apple's online file storage and file sharing service, now known as .Mac. (8)

Jaguar Codename of Mac OS X, Version 10.2, released in late August 2002. (8)

job management An operating system function that controls the order and time in which programs are run. For example, a print program can manage and prioritize multiple print jobs. (1)

kernel The core of the operating system. It contains all of the programs needed to allow the user to interact with the computer. (9)

kilobyte 1,024 bytes, or 2^{10} bytes. Kilo means thousand. (1)

Knowledge Base A database of articles on problems and solutions created by Microsoft Support Services. (5)

launch by association A method of launching an application in Windows in which opening a data file opens the associated program. (3)

Limited account In Windows XP, a general reference to an account that is a member of the local Users group. This term is used in the User Accounts applet. With this account type, users can access the computer, but they cannot make any changes to the computer. (7)

Linux An open-source version of UNIX developed by Linus Torvalds in 1991. (9)

logical drive A portion of a physical hard drive that appears to be a drive with a letter assigned to it. (2)

long file name (LFN) A file name that breaks the 8.3 file naming rules by allowing up to 255 characters (including spaces). LFNs are supported by the VFAT driver on all implementations of FAT in 32-bit Windows. (5)

Mac The nickname for Apple's computers which comes from its 1984 model: the Macintosh. (8)

man A Linux command that accesses an electronic manual. It is used in conjunction with other commands to provide command usage information and syntax. (9)

manual installation A method of installing an OS that requires interaction from the user throughout the entire process. The installer must provide information and respond to messages. (5)

mapping The assignment of a local, unused drive letter to a share out on a network, providing a logical connection to the share. (10)

megabyte   1,048,576 bytes, or 2^{20} bytes. Mega means million. (1)

memory   The physical chips that store programs and data. There are two basic types: random-access memory (RAM) and read-only memory (ROM). (1)

memory management   An operating system function that manages and tracks the placement of programs and data in memory. Advanced operating systems, such as Windows NT, Windows 2000, and Windows XP use a scheme for making optimal use of memory. (1)

menu   A menu is a list of choices. Menus are found in both character-based and GUI OSs. (3)

microcomputer   A computer built around a microprocessor. (1)

microprocessor   An integrated circuit (chip) which performs the calculations, or processing, for a computer. (1)

monitor   A video display using CRT (cathode-ray tube) technology. (1)

motherboard   The central circuit board of a computer. All other devices connect to it in one way or another. (1)

mouse   An input device connected to the computer. Mouse movement is translated into movement of the cursor on the display screen. (1)

move   An operation that picks up data from one location and moves it to another. (3)

MS-DOS compatibility mode   A mode that allows Windows 9*x* to use MS-DOS device drivers for older equipment. Running in MS-DOS compatibility mode enables use of both 16-bit and 32-bit programs, but such use slows down the OS and makes it more prone to failure. (5)

MS-DOS mode   A mode that allows Windows 9*x* to run DOS. In MS-DOS mode, Windows 9*x* loads a real-mode copy of MS-DOS. (5)

multitasking   Two or more programs (tasks) running simultaneously on a computer. (1)

network operating system (NOS)   Software that enhances a basic OS by adding networking features. NOSs allow you to connect to a network. (1)

network resource   Anything that can be accessed over a network. (10)

newsgroup   An online discussion group. It differs from an e-mail discussion list in that it stores discussion messages on a server. Users can view the messages online and participate anytime. (10)

node   The term used for a computer connected to a network. (10)

NTFS   NTFS is short for NT file system. It has features to improve reliability over the FAT file system, such as transaction logs to help recover from disk failures. It also allows controlled file access by setting permissions for directories and/or individual files. (4)

NTLDR   The NT operating system Loader on a Windows NT, Windows 2000, and Windows XP computer. NTLDR begins the process of bringing all the many OS components into memory. (4)

octet   A group of eight binary digits, such as 10011011. Four octets make up an IP address. (10)

open source   A certification standard issued by the Open Source Initiative (OSI) that requires that the source code of a computer program be made available free of charge to the general public. (9)

operating system (OS)   An operating system is a collection of programs that provides a computer with critical functionality, such as the user interface, management of hardware and software, and ways of creating, managing, and using files. (1)

output   What comes out of a computer, such as text and graphics on a screen display or a printed page. Output also includes sounds that emanate from the computer's speaker. (1)

packet   One of the pieces into which data is broken for network communications. (10)

partition   An area of a physical hard disk that defines space that will be used for logical drives. (2)

password   A code entered by a user to validate their right to use the system. (9)

password reset disk   A disk that you can create in Windows XP by running the Forgotten Password wizard. This diskette lets you reset your password, and it allows you to recover your user account and personalized computer settings. (7)

patches   Software fixes to problems with software. (4)

PC   *See* personal computer. (1)

peer-to-peer networking   A type of networking where desktop computers act as file and print servers to their peers. (1)

peripheral device   A very broad term most often used to refer to nonessential add-on computer devices such as digital cameras, printers, scanners, pointing devices, and external modems and disk drives. (1)

permission   Used in the protection of files, folders, and other objects. Permissions define what a user or group can do with an object. (4)

personal computer (PC)   A microcomputer that complies with the Microsoft/Intel set of standards. (1)

pico   The name of a Linux text editor. (9)

plug and play   The ability of a computer to automatically detect and configure a hardware device. To work, the computer, the device, and the OS must all comply with the same plug and play standard. (5)

pointing device   An input device that is used to move a cursor around on a graphical user interface (GUI). The most common pointing device is a mouse, but other kinds include track balls, joysticks, and light pens. (1)

primary directory entry   On a FAT file system, the directory entry 32-bit Windows uses to store the standard directory information, including an 8.3 file name. In the case of a long file name, additional (secondary) directory entries are needed to store the long file name itself. (5)

processor   *See* microprocessor. (1)

prosumer   A new type of consumer who expects consumer-level affordability combined with professional-level features. Prosumers increasingly drive the digital device and home computer markets. (8)

protected memory space   Refers to the Windows NT, Windows 2000, and Windows XP method of isolating running applications. If a poorly written application program crashes, other running applications or the OS itself will not be affected. (6)

protocol   A set of rules. Network protocols govern many aspects of network communications. (10)

Quick Launch toolbar   A special toolbar located on the taskbar, from which applications can be launched by a single click. (3)

RAM   *See* random-access memory. (1)

random-access memory (RAM)   Volatile memory. The random-access memory in a computer stores active programs and data while the computer is operating. (1)

read-only memory (ROM)   Non-volatile memory that is used to store programs permanently. When the computer is turned off, the contents of ROM remain intact. (1)

ROM BIOS   *See* read-only memory basic input-output system. (1)

read-only memory basic input-output system (ROM BIOS)   A set of program instructions for starting the computer, as well as for controlling communication between the processor and other components (input and output). (1)

real mode   The mode in which an Intel processor starts up when the computer is turned on. It is very limited, offers the operating system just a small amount of memory to work with, and does not allow for multitasking, protection of the hardware from other software, or support for virtual machines. (1)

Red Hat Linux   One of several vendors of prepackaged Linux operating systems. (9)

refresh rate   The refresh rate defines how often the computer display is refreshed to keep the image flicker free. In every case, this setting must be above 60 Hertz to reduce eyestrain. (6)

rights   Privileges to perform system-wide functions, such as accessing the computer from the network, backing up files, changing the system time, or loading and unloading device drivers. Rights exist in the local accounts database of Windows NT, Windows 2000, and Windows XP computers, as well as in Windows domains. (4)

root   The administrator of a Linux system. Also known as the Superuser, root has the power to do all administrative tasks on a Linux system, such as adding, changing, and deleting users and files. (9)

root account   The most powerful account on a Linux/UNIX computer. It is capable of doing anything. (9)

root directory   A directory with special features: it is at the top level, and it is the only one that the FORMAT command creates. (2)

router   The network device that directs traffic to destinations beyond the local network. (10)

safe mode   A startup mode in which Windows 9*x*, Windows 2000, and Windows XP start without using all of the drivers and components that would normally be loaded. Use safe mode when your computer will not start normally. (5)

secondary directory entry   In 32-bit Windows OSs, a long file name is stored in as many secondary directory entries as are necessary to hold the entire LFN. *See also* primary directory entry. (5)

security   The function of an operating system that provides password-protected authentication of the user before allowing access to the local computer. Security features may restrict what a user can do on a computer. (1)

security account   An entity that exists in a security accounts database. Security accounts are used for authentication and authorization. (4)

server   A computer that plays one or more of several important roles in a network. In all of these roles, it provides services to other computers (clients). (1 & 10)

service pack   A bundle of patches or software updates released periodically by Microsoft. (4)

share   v. To make a resource, such as a file folder or printer, available on the network. n. The shared resource. (10)

Sherlock   Apple's combination hard disk and Internet search utility. (8)

Show Desktop button   In Windows 98 and newer versions, this feature minimizes all open windows so that you can see the desktop. The button is included by default on the Quick Launch toolbar. (5)

single-tasking   The inability to run more than one task at a time. (2)

small office/home office (SOHO)   Refers to a business with one or very few employees based in a private home or very small office. (5)

sound card   The hardware interface that allows your computer to output high fidelity audio. (8)

special folder   Disk folders that Windows treats differently than others. Special folders include the Start Menu, Recycle Bin, Favorites, Printers, and so on. (3)

StarOffice   A suite of programs for the Linux OS similar to Microsoft Office that includes a full-featured word processor, a spreadsheet program, a presentation program, a drawing program, and a simple database program. It is included with the Red Hat Linux 7.3 Personal boxed set. (9)

startup disk   *See* boot disk. (2)

switch   A network device to which media from each node connects. A switch repeats a signal only to the destination port. (10)

syntax   A set of rules for correctly entering a specific command at the command line. The rules include the command name and the parameters that act as instructions to the command. (2)

system files   Important components of the OS, including the operating system kernel, the files containing the OS settings from the registry, and various driver files. (4)

system keychain   A database in both OS 9 and OS X that contains encrypted passwords. (8)

system partition   The active partition on which the boot files reside in Windows NT and higher. This is usually referred to as drive C:. (4)

System Restore wizard   Allows a user to choose to restore the computer to a previous restore point. Restore points are created after adding or removing software, after installing Windows updates, and during the normal shutdown of your computer. (7)

task management   An operating system function in multitasking OSs that controls the focus. The user can switch between tasks by giving the focus to the application the user brings to the foreground. (1)

taskbar   A GUI object, usually on the bottom of the Windows desktop, containing the Start menu, the system tray, and buttons for any currently opened windows. You can switch between windows using these buttons. Programs can be launched from the Start menu, and from an optional Quick Launch toolbar. (3)

TCP/IP   Acronym for Transmission Control Protocol/Internet Protocol, which is the name of a suite of network protocols. These two protocols, and the others that make up the suite, allow computers to access the Internet. (1)

terabyte   1,099,511,627,776 bytes, or 2^{40} bytes. Tera means trillion. (1)

terminal window   A window where the user can enter command-line Linux commands within the GUI. (9)

thin client   A minimally configured network computer that may not even have a hard disk. (10)

thread   A discussion in a newsgroup consisting of an initial message and the subsequent responses. (10)

UNIX   An operating system designed to allow multiple users to carry out multiple processes on interconnected computers. Found on a range of computers from mainframe on down to workstations. The ancestor of today's Linux. (8)

upgrade installation   An upgrade installation installs a new OS into the same directory as the previous OS. An upgrade can only be done with a successor OS to the currently installed OS, and it must be capable of taking on the settings of the previous OS. Upgrades are possible between most adjacent versions of Windows and between Mac OS versions, but never from Windows to Mac OS or visa versa. (5)

user   The person who uses the operating system to make use of the computer. (9 & 10)

user account   The most basic element of Windows NT, Windows 2000, and Windows XP security. Each user must present a valid user name and password of a local or domain user account to log on to a Windows NT, Windows 2000, or Windows XP computer. (6)

user interface   The software layer, sometimes called the shell, through which the user communicates with the OS, which, in turn, communicates with the computer. (1)

user profile   In Windows, a set of folders and desktop settings that are unique for each user. (5)

utility   A program that allows you to perform useful tasks, usually computer management functions or diagnostics, such as upgrading the program in your computer's ROM BIOS or looking for errors on your disk. (2)

VFAT   *See* virtual file allocation table. (4)

VFAT file system driver   A driver that the protected mode versions of Windows use as the interface between applications and file systems. (5)

virtual device driver (VxD)   A device driver that allows more than one program to use a device. A Windows 9*x* virtual device driver usually has a file name suffix of V*x*D, where *x* refers to the type of display (*D* for display). (6)

virtual file allocation table (VFAT)   An implementation of FAT (introduced in Windows 95) that supports long file names. (4)

virtual machine   A virtual machine is a computer program that emulates a PC in memory. Virtual machine programs are used with DOS and Windows 3.*x* applications so that they can run in multitasking OSs. (2)

virtual memory   Virtual memory allows more code and data to be stored in memory than the actual physical system memory can hold by swapping information that is not immediately necessary between RAM and disk. (1)

virtual memory manager   An operating system component that moves code and data, as necessary, to the virtual memory portion of the disk. Thus this disk space is used as if it were memory, not just disk storage space. This transfer is performed for code and data that is part of any program that is open but inactive. (1)

volume   On a disk, each area that is defined as a drive. A primary partition has a single volume, and an extended partition can contain one or more volumes. (4)

warm boot   Restarting a computer without a power-down and power-up cycle, using CTRL-ALT-DELETE or a Reset button. (2)

window   A window is a bordered area of the desktop used by a single program. (3)

Windows NT domain   A domain in which all servers maintaining the domain database are running a Windows NT Server OS. (6)

Windows update   A program used to connect to the Microsoft Windows Update site and download software updates. (7)

WINVER   A program that displays the Windows version information. (4)

wizard   In Windows, GUI programs that lead you through the steps to perform tasks, such as installing a printer (Add Printer wizard) or connecting to a network (Network Connection wizard). (4)

workgroup   In a Microsoft network, a group of computers on a network that share printers and folders. (3 & 10)

X Windows   A Linux GUI similar to Microsoft's Windows. (9)

INTERNATIONAL CONTACT INFORMATION

AUSTRALIA
McGraw-Hill Book Company Australia Pty. Ltd.
TEL +61-2-9900-1800
FAX +61-2-9878-8881
http://www.mcgraw-hill.com.au
books-it_sydney@mcgraw-hill.com

CANADA
McGraw-Hill Ryerson Ltd.
TEL +905-430-5000
FAX +905-430-5020
http://www.mcgraw-hill.ca

**GREECE, MIDDLE EAST, & AFRICA
(Excluding South Africa)**
McGraw-Hill Hellas
TEL +30-210-6560-990
TEL +30-210-6560-993
TEL +30-210-6560-994
FAX +30-210-6545-525

MEXICO (Also serving Latin America)
McGraw-Hill Interamericana Editores S.A. de C.V.
TEL +525-117-1583
FAX +525-117-1589
http://www.mcgraw-hill.com.mx
fernando_castellanos@mcgraw-hill.com

SINGAPORE (Serving Asia)
McGraw-Hill Book Company
TEL +65-6863-1580
FAX +65-6862-3354
http://www.mcgraw-hill.com.sg
mghasia@mcgraw-hill.com

SOUTH AFRICA
McGraw-Hill South Africa
TEL +27-11-622-7512
FAX +27-11-622-9045
robyn_swanepoel@mcgraw-hill.com

SPAIN
McGraw-Hill/Interamericana de España, S.A.U.
TEL +34-91-180-3000
FAX +34-91-372-8513
http://www.mcgraw-hill.es
professional@mcgraw-hill.es

**UNITED KINGDOM, NORTHERN,
EASTERN, & CENTRAL EUROPE**
McGraw-Hill Education Europe
TEL +44-1-628-502500
FAX +44-1-628-770224
http://www.mcgraw-hill.co.uk
computing_europe@mcgraw-hill.com

ALL OTHER INQUIRIES Contact:
McGraw-Hill/Osborne
TEL +1-510-596-6600
FAX +1-510-596-7600
http://www.osborne.com
omg_international@mcgraw-hill.com